Praise for

WILLIAM TECUMSEH

SHERMAN

by James Lee McDonough

"Superbly researched and richly detailed, James McDonough's *William Tecumseh Sherman* judiciously guides the reader through the epic life of the man who might be history's most complicated soldier. For Sherman fans it is a must-read, and for others, a worthwhile endeavor."
— Robert L. O'Connell, best-selling author of *Fierce Patriot: The Tangled Lives of William Tecumseh Sherman*

"James McDonough's *William Tecumseh Sherman* is the first major biography of this complex, challenging figure in almost a quarter century, and it is deeply researched and thoughtfully presented. Engagingly written, it brings new perspective to Sherman's prewar years and the benefit of a lifetime of study to his Civil War career. Perhaps no one will ever completely capture Sherman, but McDonough's wide net snares more than enough of the new with the old to make this a life well worth reading."
— William C. Davis, author of *Crucible of Command: Ulysses S. Grant and Robert E. Lee—The War They Fought, the Peace They Forged*

"Masterly . . . the product of a historian's lifelong study. . . . [A] full-blooded narrative."
— Carl Rollyson, *The Wall Street Journal*

"[McDonough] tells this story well."
— Thomas E. Ricks, *The New York Times Book Review*

D1292242

WILLIAM TECUMSEH
SHERMAN

In the Service of My Country
A LIFE

JAMES LEE McDONOUGH

W. W. NORTON & COMPANY
Independent Publishers Since 1923
New York • London

For information about permission to reproduce selections from this book,
write to Permissions, W. W. Norton & Company, Inc.,
500 Fifth Avenue, New York, NY 10110

For information about special discounts for bulk purchases, please contact
W. W. Norton Special Sales at specialsales@wwnorton.com or 800-233-4830

Manufacturing by Quad Graphics Fairfield
Book design by Chris Welch Design
Production manager: Julia Druskin

ISBN 978-0-393-35420-1 pbk.

W. W. Norton & Company, Inc.
500 Fifth Avenue, New York, N.Y. 10110
www.wwnorton.com

W. W. Norton & Company Ltd.
15 Carlisle Street, London W1D 3BS

1 2 3 4 5 6 7 8 9 0

To my former students at Lipscomb University,
Pepperdine University and Auburn University,
who understood and appreciated
the significance of history

CONTENTS

PREFACE

William Tecumseh Sherman is remembered today as a major American historical figure, one whose Civil War career was both highly significant and controversial. This biography presents and analyzes Sherman's generalship. His battles, campaigns and marches are recounted, often in greater detail, and sometimes with different interpretations, than previous biographies. For example, I am convinced, after taking another look at the Battle of Shiloh, that Sherman deserves more credit for that Union triumph than earlier biographers have assigned him; indeed, more credit than I gave him in my book about Shiloh, which I researched and wrote between 1971 and 1973.

This is certainly not to say that I have neglected the rest of Sherman's life. Far from it. The man was forty-one years old when the Civil War began, and the prewar years are arresting and crucial if one hopes to understand the General who developed into one of the nation's great military leaders. Following the war, Sherman was the general-in-chief of the U.S. Army for fifteen years, from 1868 to 1883.

From the early days of the U.S. Military Academy, the Seminole Wars in Florida, the antebellum Charleston aristocratic culture, the mad California Gold Rush, the early and wild years of San Francisco, the adventurous and dangerous water journeys between the East and West Coasts before the railroads and the Panama Canal, the wars against the Plains Indians, the building of the transcontinental railroad, the settlement of the great West and more—Sherman saw them all.

After the Civil War, wherever he lived and traveled, Sherman occupied the social limelight. With some his relationship was close and personal. He could be a lively, witty and substantive dinner companion. He always held strong opinions. However, unlike many outspoken people, he was not merely opinionated, but possessed an impressive store of knowledge to support his point of view.

Sherman's interests were wide-ranging, and his talents considerable. He liked to ride horses and enjoyed hunting. He admired painting and artistic endeavors and was an amateur artist himself. He appreciated good writing and he knew how to turn a memorable phrase. He was a capable and honest businessman. He liked a circus. He loved to dance. He found much pleasure in attending the theater. He relished every opportunity to travel. He was a complex, engaging, intriguing character, the most fascinating, in my opinion, of all high-ranking Civil War personalities.

I approached this biography with a considerable degree of admiration and respect for Sherman. Upon learning more about the man, I sometimes admired him even more—for example, in his banking days in California, he demonstrated, during trying economic times, an uncommonly high standard of ethical responsibility and concern for his investors. At other times, I found Sherman troubling, even offensive.

Whatever Sherman is saying and doing, one factor is consistent: he is never boring. If I had known him, I sometimes think I would have liked him—and then again, I realize that, upon occasion, he undoubtedly would have irritated me. My somewhat mixed feelings about him, I think, are advantageous—if one strives for understanding and objectivity. While I acknowledge these goals to be unattainable in an absolute sense, that is no justification for not striving to achieve them. Harboring either an excessive fondness, a pitfall of many a biographer, or an intense dislike of one's subject is not conducive to producing a satisfactory assessment.

For more than forty years I have lived, off and on, with Sherman. All of his Civil War career I have studied in depth, writing several books in which Sherman was a major figure. As to his life as a whole, I have brought a perspective to this study, being now older than Sherman was when he died, that would have been impossible years ago. This biography has enabled me to examine not only Sherman but the Civil War as well, from a matured perspective, crafting and refining some changes of analysis relative both to the war and to Sherman, as well as to reflect upon Nineteenth Century America—Sherman's Century. For me, a Sherman biography has long seemed "a natural" project.

Finally, a few explanations are necessary. The general reader will find it helpful to keep in mind that the vast majority of United States soldiers who fought in the Civil War were so-called National Volunteers, rather than regular army. Consequently the rank of a regular army officer like Sherman can be confusing. When Sherman went back into the U.S. Army at the beginning of the war, he became a colonel. After the Battle of Bull Run, he was promoted to brigadier general of volunteers, while remaining a colonel in the regular army. Following the Battle of Shiloh, he was advanced to major general of volunteers. Not until 1863, after Vicksburg, did he become a brigadier general in the regular army. In 1864 he was promoted to major general in the regular army, the rank he held for the remainder of the war.

Sherman was a prolific writer, by any standard of comparison, and I have tried to present his words, phrases and sentences exactly as he penned them, without any effort to correct the occasional grammatical mistakes (which are very few considering how much and how rapidly he wrote), the misspelled words or the terms unacceptable today, most notably the word "nigger." Several peculiarities of his writing will be apparent, such as sometimes capitalizing the first letter of a word when there is no reason to do so (many people of his era did this); sometimes expressing "damned" as "d——d"; or spelling a word more than one way, even the name of his son: "Willie" and "Willy." I decided that the reader should get the full, unvarnished Sherman whenever he is quoted.

Of course, I alone am responsible for all statements of fact, interpretations, analyses and conclusions presented herein.

James Lee McDonough
October 2015

WILLIAM TECUMSEH
SHERMAN

DEATH STARED US ALL
IN THE FACE

Initially the rain came softly, then gradually intensified until torrents of water pounded the bloodstained earth. The downpour, relentless through most of the night, was sometimes driven in sheets by a cold wind that swept the battlefield. Flashes of lightning momentarily illuminated the pronounced blackness, revealing innumerable bodies of dead and wounded strewn across the fields and the rolling timberland. All during the night, at fifteen-minute intervals, the guns of the U.S.S. *Lexington* and the U.S.S. *Tyler* roared from the Tennessee River, sending 8-inch shells arching toward the Confederate lines. Their red fuses briefly lit up the sky, eerily exposing the wasted humanity, before screaming down, exploding and indiscriminately scattering flesh-mutilating iron fragments in every direction. A Southern general thought the majority of the shells actually—and ironically—fell among wounded Union soldiers, a heartrending "friendly fire." Like intermittent presentations from a gigantic kaleidoscope of horrors, incredible scenes again and again assaulted the eyes and the psyche of both armies.[1]

Countless soldiers reported hearing the agonizing groans and cries of the wounded, numbering in the thousands, as they lay between the lines in the water and mud. Many who themselves had escaped injury found it difficult, if not impossible, to escape the awful screams of soldiers that often rent the air as surgeons amputated mangled arms and legs. Some men felt as if the long hours of discomfort, depression, frustration and suffering would never cease. A sixteen-year-old Ohioan remembered listening to a comrade's disconcerting story in which "nearly all his friends and acquaintances figured as corpses." As the rain continued to fall, "a streaming, drenching, semi-tropical downpour," the young soldier thought "there never was a night so long, so hideous, or so utterly uncomfortable."[2]

That fearful night was Sunday, April 6, 1862. The site of the savage clash lay in southern Tennessee, about one hundred miles east of Memphis. Called Pittsburg Landing, the place was a steamboat docking point on the west bank of the Tennessee River, only twenty miles north of the strategically vital railroad junction at Corinth, Mississippi, where the north–south Mobile & Ohio Railroad crossed the east–west Memphis & Charleston line. Soon to be better known as Shiloh, a Biblical term commonly translated as "place of peace," the name identified a Methodist church located two and a half miles southwest of the landing. The Civil War had already raged for nearly a year, but nothing comparable with this monumental engagement along the banks of the Tennessee had yet occurred. Casualties would number nearly five times those of Bull Run, which stood as the biggest fight of 1861. The brutal struggle at Shiloh, fought on April 6 and 7, was an unforgettable fray, without precedent in American history to that time, and truly constituted the first great battle in a conflict unlike any ever waged by Americans before or since.[3]

Lean, red-haired, forty-two-year-old William Tecumseh Sherman, a brigadier general of volunteers, was prominent among those who experienced Shiloh's full fury. He commanded a green division (not even one regiment had previously been under fire) and his encampment lay on both sides of Shiloh Church, composing the army's right front and flank. There, together with Brigadier General Benjamin M. Prentiss's division to the east, which was equally inexperienced, Sherman occupied the most advanced ground when the enemy attacked. Unfortunately for Sherman, Prentiss and the men they led, a wide gap existed between their two divisions. If another Federal division had been stationed between Sherman and Prentiss, thus constituting a three-division, continuous front—as had been envisioned but not implemented—these

Union forces, even though facing combat for the first time, obviously would have presented a more formidable challenge to the advancing Confederates. Instead, the left flank of Sherman's Fifth Division, as his command had been designated, lay open, highly vulnerable to an enveloping movement by the enemy.

Sherman faced still other problems when the Southerners attacked, not the least of which was the ammunition situation in his division. Because weapons in the Union Army had not yet been standardized, Sherman's command utilized six different kinds of shoulder arms, with each type necessitating a different caliber of ammunition. Colonel Jesse Hildebrand's Third Brigade alone employed three types of muskets. When the troops were engaged in the heat of a battle, such diversity in armament presented a serious, time-consuming, logistical disadvantage whenever ammunition required replenishing—and well before noon, Sherman's supply was running low. His division, however, it should be noted, was not the only Union command plagued by a diversity of arms.[4]

Worse, the Rebel attack caught Sherman by surprise. Probably "not a man was bayoneted in or near his tent," as the General afterward assured his younger brother, U.S. Senator John Sherman of Ohio, in a letter denying such sensational newspaper reports then circulating in the North, but Sherman's claim in the same letter that "I was always ready for an attack" simply was not true. He never made provisions for adequate outposting and patrolling that might have detected an advance by the Confederate Army. He also allowed the Fifty-Third Ohio Regiment, of Hildebrand's Third Brigade, to remain in a badly exposed position south and east of his main encampments near Shiloh Church, thereby contributing yet more to the fragility of his division's left flank. Nor were his division batteries brought forward and defensively positioned to help repel an enemy assault if it should come.[5]

Although Sherman himself later admitted that "from about the first of April we were conscious that the Rebel cavalry in our front was getting bolder and more saucy"—action which should have suggested to the General the possibility that the Confederate cavalry was being used to mask an advance by their entire army—the plain truth is that Sherman's mind was closed to any such scenario. He believed the Grayclads intended nothing more along his front than the mounting of periodic annoyances. With each passing day he seemed to grow ever more adamant in that conviction.[6]

Perhaps in part Sherman's dangerous assumption developed as a result of Major General Henry W. Halleck's orders. Recently promoted to the command of all Federal forces west of the Appalachians, with headquarters at St. Louis, Halleck had clearly instructed, more than once, that Major General Ulysses Simpson Grant's army at Pittsburg Landing should do nothing that might provoke a battle with the enemy concentrating at Corinth. Halleck himself, after major reinforcements from Nashville and elsewhere joined Grant's army, planned to assume field command of all the Union forces gathered at Pittsburg and march against the Rebels. (This time Halleck intended to garner glory like Grant had harvested at Forts Henry and Donelson.)[7]

Sherman, in immediate command at Pittsburg, since Grant was headquartered nine miles downstream at Savannah, was well aware of Halleck's instructions not to bring on a general fight. Possibly then, Sherman may have been dissuaded, to a degree, from taking measures required to keep fully abreast of the Confederate Army's location. This of course, if true, does not excuse Sherman's failure. One of the very worst mistakes any general can make is simply to assume that a nearby and powerful enemy force will remain in place, day after day, waiting to be attacked. That, unfortunately, is what Sherman did, while ignoring numerous warning signs of possible, even imminent danger.

Finally, during Saturday afternoon, April 5, only a few precious hours before the Southern assault at dawn the next morning, the General's irritability with those who reported sightings of the enemy close at hand reached a white-hot level. Colonel Jesse Appler of the Fifty-Third Ohio, Sherman's most advanced regiment, sent word that a large force of Rebels was approaching. The message was not the first warning from the jittery, inexperienced colonel; and it must have seemed a bit too much for Sherman's patience to endure at that particular moment. Listening to Appler's communiqué with disgust, Sherman sent an aide to deliver his response, curtly declaring to the colonel that "there is no enemy closer than Corinth," and Appler could "take his damn regiment back to Ohio!"[8]

Certainly Sherman knew from the various picket clashes of recent days that at least some Confederates were closer than Corinth. But the General's strongly held opinion was that the Federal Army faced no immediate threat. Thus, on the same day that Appler claimed the enemy was coming, a supremely confident Sherman wrote U. S. Grant, the army's commander: "I have no doubt that nothing will occur today more than some picket firing. ... I do not apprehend anything like an attack on our position." He believed the Confederate forays of recent days, including a particularly audacious incursion on Friday afternoon, were merely reconnaissances in force. Grant was of the same mind as Sherman. Fearlessness and offense were the watchwords for the two key men of the Union Army. There would be no full-scale engagement, they thought, until the Federals were ready to move against the Rebels at Corinth.[9]

How Sherman could have so completely missed or ignored the signs that should have alerted him to the imminent danger remains a puzzle. Perhaps, besides his preconceived idea that the Rebels would not attack, and the possible influence of General Halleck, he overcompensated, trying to avoid the kind of criticism he had encountered earlier in Kentucky. Sherman had there lost his command, as newspaper accounts focused on his nervous disposition, spreading stories that he feared every little enemy cavalry patrol, convinced that such actions foreshadowed a major Confederate advance. Mockingly, they publicized his estimate that 200,000 men would be necessary to put down the rebellion in the Mississippi Valley alone—a figure that later appeared prophetic, but was then viewed as a wild exaggeration. Rumors of insanity, fueled by the press, began to be associated with Sherman. In his home state, the *Cincinnati Commercial* of December 11, 1861, forthrightly, embarrassingly proclaimed that he was "insane," having gone "stark mad" in Kentucky. In years to come, the General might find amusement in recalling accusations that he was crazy. Not in the spring of 1862 though.

The Kentucky experience remained fresh in his mind. More time would have to pass before Sherman could take delight in reflecting that he had the last laugh on the insanity issue. At Pittsburg Landing, he did not intend to make the Kentucky mistake again. Also, since his West Point days, Sherman, like many graduates of the Point, harbored a disdain for militia officers. If the Fifty-Third Ohio's commander had been an academy graduate, perhaps Sherman might have taken him seriously. But a "might have been" does not count, and the fact is, regardless of the reason, Sherman had laid himself open to a surprise attack.[10]

A Union soldier, writing after the war, memorably summarized the judgment of many when he said there was "one cloud on [Sherman's] horizon; one blot on his escutcheon—he was surprised at Shiloh." Indeed he was. Ironically, the attack warning that at last resonated with Sherman on that fateful Sunday morning came from the jumpy Colonel Appler. Sherman initially was not impressed, reflecting upon the source from which the alert originated. The General replied with a touch of sarcasm, "You must be badly scared over there." However, within a short time, Sherman had second thoughts. Sounds of gunfire increased in volume and drew closer; very possibly indicating more than picket firing. Sherman summoned his staff, mounted up and rode forward to learn for himself what was happening at the camp of the Fifty-Third Ohio.[11]

He soon got an eyeful. Lifting his binoculars, he first opined that a sharp skirmish must be under way. Then, shifting his glasses to the right, in the direction that an officer was pointing, the General suddenly, finally, recognized the truth. "My God, we are attacked!" he reportedly exclaimed, while gazing upon the "glistening bayonets of heavy masses of infantry," as his official report characterized the sight of the advancing Rebels. Almost at the same instant, Thomas D. Holiday, Second Illinois Cavalry, Sherman's orderly, who was riding beside him, was struck and killed by Confederate fire.[12]

ONCE THE BATTLE was joined, this man of high-strung, nervous energy, a man plagued by a chronic asthmatic condition that sometimes increased his irritability, experienced a remarkable transformation. Sherman became cool and proficient as he directed his division in the heat of the intense, murderous struggle at Shiloh. Observers said he seemed to appear where he was needed, armed with a grasp of events taking place all along the line, and often anticipating, as is one of the marks of a good military leader, what would occur before it developed.

The General at once emphasized to Colonel Appler that he *must* hold his position as long as possible, because his regiment occupied a key location for protecting the left flank of the entire division. Supporting units, promised Sherman, would be sent forward immediately to assist his regiment in defending its ground. Also, Sherman dispatched riders galloping to alert division commanders Major General John A. McClernand and Brigadier General Stephen A. Hurlbut, both located to his rear, as well as Prentiss, off to his left. (The latter was already heavily engaged with the enemy.) And the General cautioned Captain A. C. Waterhouse that his Battery E, First Illinois Light Artillery, should hold its fire until the Confederates crossed the ravine in their front and began ascending the slope toward his guns. Sherman then rode off to prepare the rest of his command for the Rebel onslaught.[13]

Thus from the beginning Sherman was in the thickest of the fight, where "the battle raged fiercest," as he later wrote. Something of the impression Shiloh was making on him is movingly conveyed in letters penned for his wife soon after the battle: "The scenes on this field," he declared as he described the wounded, maimed and "the mangled bodies" of dead soldiers "in every conceivable shape," with heads decapitated and limbs blown away, "would have cured anybody of war." Also, he stated in a matter-of-fact style that he did not expect to survive the war. "This gives me little trouble," he added, "but I do feel for the thousands that think another battle will end the war."[14]

Soon covered with dust and grime, his face, hair and grizzled, short-cropped beard darkened with powder, Sherman sat his horse somewhere in the midst of the gory scene on the Union right. Quickly moving from place to place, he ensured that his men, generally facing south-southwest, were correctly deployed to make the best possible defensive

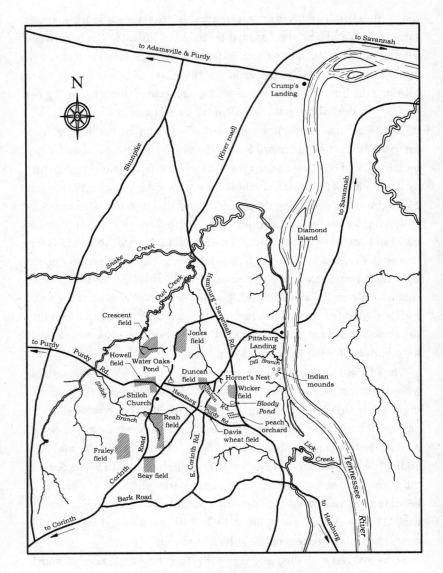

THE SHILOH BATTLEFIELD

*Fought on April 6–7, 1862, the Battle of Shiloh saw 100,000 soldiers engage
in a furious struggle across fields and forests, orchards and ravines, creeks
and swampy areas. Map by Jim Moon Jr.*

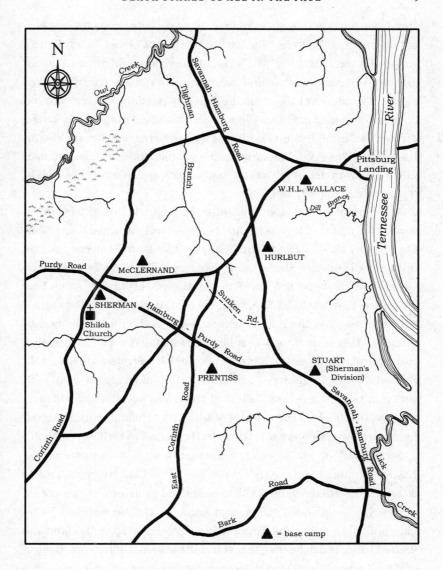

SHILOH—POSITION OF UNION DIVISIONS

When the Confederates attacked the Union Army early on the morning of Sunday, April 6, 1862, they approached from Corinth, Mississippi, about twenty miles southwest of Pittsburg Landing. Map by Jim Moon Jr.

stand. Somehow, although outnumbered by six Rebel brigades converging on his three brigades, and assisted only by Colonel Julius Raith's supporting brigade from McClernand's division, which came up in answer to Sherman's call for aid, he managed to stall the enemy advance along his front. Benefiting from the defensive advantage of high ground both east and west of Shiloh Church, Sherman held his position for the greater part of three hours, while his men inflicted heavy casualties on the enemy. (The Sixth Mississippi, for example, suffered some 300 men killed and wounded out of a total force of 425, and most of those fell in front of Sherman's division.)[15]

At one point on that bloody morning the General's horse, "a beautiful sorrel race mare ... to which I had become much attached," was "shot dead" under him. Captain John T. Taylor, an aide to Sherman, said he dismounted and gave Sherman his own horse. "Well, my boy," said the General, "didn't I promise you all the fighting you could do?" When Taylor's horse also fell under Sherman, the captain recalled, "We caught a battery horse, and the general mounted him and, in less than twenty minutes," that animal too was killed. Sherman noted additionally that two more of his horses, hitched to trees near his tent, were killed as well. Remarkably, Taylor declared that as the battle "filled my very soul with awe, if ... not absolute fear," he thought Sherman's conduct "instilled ... a feeling that it was grand to be there with him." Undoubtedly, Sherman impressed those who saw him in battle. He seemed to thrive in combat.[16]

Soon after the clash began, according to an artilleryman named Edward Bouton, Sherman rode up on the left of his battery and, while watching the effect of the artillery shots and praising the gun crews' accuracy, was wounded in his right hand. As Bouton watched, Sherman pulled a handkerchief from his pocket and wrapped it about the injured hand, which he then thrust inside the breast of his coat. Bouton said the General hardly took his eyes away from the action as he calmly dealt with the injury, and then rode off to check with other portions of his command. A young private who observed Sherman riding nearby declared the General "a splendid soldier, erect in his saddle, his eye bent forward," and thought he appeared "a veritable war eagle."[17]

At some point, while his division fought on the Shiloh Church line, Sherman sent an aide riding to find General Grant, conveying a message that if the army's leader chanced to have any extra men, he certainly could use them. Sherman also assured Grant that he would continue the struggle with the men at hand, whatever the situation. "We are holding them pretty well just now," he reported, "but it's hot as hell."[18]

Sherman might have held even longer at the Shiloh Church line if he could have secured his left flank. But Jesse Appler went to pieces early on. Appler's Fifty-Third Ohio Regiment was strongly defending its position until the jittery colonel completely lost his nerve, shouting "Retreat, and save yourselves!" Many of his regiment followed Appler at once, heading for the rear, although others did not hear his order and continued firing until they saw their comrades falling back. Retreating in disorder, part of the Fifty-Third at last rallied behind Colonel Raith's brigade. Appler, however, could provide no leadership, allegedly alternating between taking refuge behind a tree and staggering about in a daze. Finally he could no longer endure the intense firing and frantic action of the horrendous scene and headed for the rear on the run. What remained of his regiment dissolved, as more and more men followed the example of their commander.[19]

A disgusted Sherman later reported that Appler's regiment had broken after losing no officers and only seven men. Colonel Jesse Hildebrand's brigade continued to disintegrate. The Fifty-Seventh Ohio held slightly longer than the Fifty-Third, but under heavy pressure from the aggressive Rebels, soon began melting away, many of its men disappearing to the rear. According to Sherman the Fifty-Seventh's loss was two officers and seven men. Only the Seventy-Seventh Ohio remained to protect Sherman's left flank, and when ultimately it began crumbling, Sherman's position at Shiloh Church became hopeless. With the enemy pressing all along his front and positioned to turn his left flank, the General had no choice except to retreat.[20]

Sherman has sometimes been criticized for holding his ground at the church when the attack began, rather than immediately dropping back to join up with McClernand's command. Sherman made the right decision. The front of his division was protected by the rugged morass of Shiloh Branch, overgrown with shrubs, saplings, and vines, a swampy area that split the oncoming Confederate line into separate forces, slowing down and disorganizing the attackers. Sherman also enjoyed the defensive advantage of high ground, from which he looked down upon Shiloh Branch and the Rebels, as they began struggling up the rather steep hillside, in the face of the fierce fire from his men, both west and east of Shiloh Church. When the Confederates did mount enough pressure to drive Sherman back, they left a literal pavement of dead and wounded on the hillside. If Sherman had initially fallen back, such a movement might well have shaken the confidence of his inexperienced men to resist the onslaught, and added to the general confusion besetting the Federal Army. Thus Sherman's stand at the church bought sorely needed time for the Union Army, as well as drawing enemy troops to his front—Rebels who could have been used to better advantage on the Confederate right, since their plan was to turn the Federal eastern flank and cut the Yankees off from the landing.[21]

CONDUCTING A WITHDRAWAL under fire is a difficult assignment. But shortly after ten o'clock, Sherman had his Fifth Division—although minus most of Hildebrand's Third Brigade, many of whom, as previously noted, had already fled from the front—occupying a new position near the crossroads of the Hamburg–Purdy Road and the Pittsburg–Corinth Road, approximately a quarter mile north of Shiloh Church. There he linked up with McClernand's First Division, composed of troops who had fought at Fort Donelson, which came up immediately on his left. Sherman was trying to re-form west of the crossroads and a little north of the Hamburg–Purdy Road, which there ran along an east–west line.

It was a hazardous business in which he engaged, for Ralph P. Buckland's Fourth Brigade had become badly disorganized, its green troops forced to stage a fighting retreat against the fierce, hard-driving Rebels. Making matters worse, Sherman lost contact for a time with John A. McDowell's First Brigade, which was cut off from him when the enemy succeeded in occupying a section of the Hamburg–Purdy Road, west of the crossroads. Sherman's Second Brigade, under David Stuart, had been encamped far to the east, beyond Prentiss's division, obviously unable to join up and fight with Sherman.[22]

Not long after Sherman withdrew from the Shiloh Church line, General Grant rode up. Sherman was the only West Point graduate among the six division commanders in Grant's army, and he was the leader in whom Grant placed the greatest confidence. Grant told Sherman that Lew Wallace's Third Division, which had been encamped four or five miles to the north at Crump's Landing, would soon be arriving to support him. Also, Grant assured Sherman that the vanguard of Major General Don Carlos Buell's Army of the Ohio, which had been marching from Nashville, was near at hand, and would be ferried across the Tennessee River, providing substantial reinforcements within a few hours. Sherman responded that his situation was not too bad, but he worried about running out of ammunition. Grant promised his friend that he had already made provision for more ammunition, which could be expected to arrive shortly. Additionally he informed Sherman that the situation did not look as good on the army's left flank. Grant, probably believing that Sherman, with McClernand's division assisting him, could hold his ground, moved eastward toward that portion of the front which most concerned him. He had been pleased with Sherman's performance and later wrote: "I never deemed it important to stay long with Sherman."[23]

Actually, within minutes of Grant's departure, "an assault of gigantic proportion," to quote Stacy Allen, longtime Shiloh National Military Park historian, struck Sherman and McClernand. Between about 10:30 and 11:00, the Confederate commander, Albert Sidney Johnston, who probably and mistakenly thought his primary objective of turning the Union left flank and cutting the Yankees off from the river had been achieved, proceeded to send approximately two-thirds of all his brigades "either directly or in support" (again quoting Allen) in a massive attack on Sherman and McClernand. Also strengthening the Rebel onslaught were reserves that General P. G. T. Beauregard, Johnston's second in command, directed toward the sound of the heaviest firing.[24]

McClernand's division was badly positioned to withstand the assault. Occupying the crest of a slight ridge, and thus basically without protection, McClernand's men lay fully vulnerable to the intense Confederate fire. Within a few brief minutes McClernand suffered crippling casualties and was forced to rapidly give ground. When McClernand's line crumpled, thereby completely exposing Sherman's left flank, Sherman too was compelled to retreat within a short time. The overpowering Rebel assault wreaked havoc among the Federal troops. The two divisions became seriously intermingled as they fell back, sustaining many casualties and losing a number of cannon. Striving desperately to halt the retreat of their men, Sherman and McClernand were able to hold and regroup only after withdrawing northward for nearly a mile.[25]

Fortunately for the Federals, the Confederate attack lost momentum as it traversed such a great distance, thus allowing the Union soldiers a brief respite. Sherman took full advantage of the break in the action. Perhaps sensing that the enemy required time to reorganize, the General worked quickly to seize the initiative from the Rebels. He was back in touch with McDowell's brigade, which was then close at hand, as was Buckland's brigade. Also, a fresh regiment of Missourians from W. H. L. (Will) Wallace's Second Division came up to support him. And John McClernand's hard-hit division had been reinforced by two Iowa regiments, as yet unbloodied, which Grant, probably remembering Sherman's request for more troops, had sent from Pittsburg Landing to strengthen the army's right flank.[26]

This, Sherman perceived, was the instant to strike! The enemy well might be taken aback by the unexpectedness of a bold move. With no minutes to spare, Sherman did not attempt to straighten out his and McClernand's intermingled units; rather he simply divided their forces in half, more or less, with Sherman taking command of the right-hand sector and McClernand the left. The time likely was near noon when the two divisions counterattacked. The rapidly launched, fierce Union assault was not anticipated, at least not by most of the Confederates, who suddenly looked up to see the enemy bearing down upon them, with Sherman's right brigade even extending for a distance beyond the Confederate left flank. The vicious attack drove the Rebels back for nearly a half mile, and cost them many casualties.[27]

When the vigor of the Federal counterattack was spent, Sherman and McClernand pulled back a short distance and re-formed. Then, for well over an hour, both sides engaged in a brutal, close-range combat, as each strove to gain an advantage over the other. It was the Southerners, bringing up a reserve brigade (the last in their army), who ultimately marshaled the strength that forced Sherman and McClernand once more to fall back, retreating to the area from which they had mounted their counterattack. Eventually, after yet more hard fighting, they were compelled to withdraw still farther to the north, while bearing slightly east, and closer to the river landing. Their divisions had been badly mauled, but the Confederates had paid dearly for the ground they gained—both in blood and time.[28]

Off to the southeast, only a few hundred yards distant, along an old wagon trace that later became known as the Sunken Road, the divisions of Will Wallace, Stephen Hurlbut and Benjamin Prentiss had grittily thrown back a number of charges, until the Confederates attacking that site of slaughter said it was like a "Hornets' Nest," and the name stuck. The determined stand of Wallace, Hurlbut and Prentiss (Wallace commanding the greatest number of troops and Prentiss the least), throughout the heat of that April Sunday, undoubtedly helped save the Union Army from destruction.[29]

However, if Sherman had not fought coolly, valiantly and effectively—first on the Shiloh Church line, and then in tandem with John McClernand after falling back to a second position—continually engaging large numbers of Confederates in severe fighting throughout the morning and much of the afternoon, the Southerners likely would have overwhelmed the Hornets' Nest much earlier, enveloping the position on its western flank. Without Sherman and McClernand there was nothing to stop the Rebels from turning that flank. Historian Timothy B. Smith, who spent several years working at Shiloh National Military Park, echoed the insightful, revisionist conclusions of Stacy Allen. Smith wrote that "ten out of sixteen Confederate brigades can be documented as being located on the western third of the battlefield for the majority of the time between 10:00 a.m. and 5:00 p.m."[30]

Furthermore, the huge numbers of dead and wounded in the area defended by Sherman and McClernand, which are established by an 1866 document derived from workers who located and buried bodies on the battlefield, obviously constitutes strong corroborative evidence of the long and savage struggle in which Sherman and McClernand were involved. Thus the most recent Shiloh scholarship clearly elevates the decisive significance of Sherman's role in the battle. It is also support-ive of Grant's striking declaration in his memoirs that the Union Army "buried, by actual count, more of the enemy's dead in front of the divi-sions of McClernand and Sherman alone" than the official total of Con-federate killed (1,728) for their entire army. Sherman and, secondly, McClernand deserve at least as much credit for saving the Union Army from defeat at Shiloh as Prentiss, Hurlbut and Will Wallace. Sherman had made a major contribution to the ultimate Union triumph, and it all began when he chose to fight at Shiloh Church, rather than falling back initially to join up with McClernand. When at last the day's carnage had subsided, and in spite of the sometimes torrential night of rain, Sher-man sought out the army's commander, General U. S. Grant, whom he had last seen in mid-to-late afternoon.[31]

He found Grant standing under a tree, somewhere in the vicinity of Pittsburg Landing. Sherman remembered that Grant was chewing on a cigar and carrying a lantern. The commander's coat collar was pulled up around his ears and his hat drawn down over his face to protect him from the rain. Sherman considered asking him if he was thinking about retreating. After all, the army had been driven from position after posi-tion, taking heavy losses—the remnants of two divisions in the Hor-nets' Nest eventually surrendering—and finally occupying a last line of defense covering Pittsburg Landing, two and a half miles behind its original front. (Confederate General P. G. T. Beauregard actually occu-pied Sherman's tent near Shiloh Church.) At the last instant, just before Sherman spoke, he said that he changed his mind about mentioning any possibility of a withdrawal. As Sherman himself expressed the matter, he was "moved by some wise and sudden instinct" not to broach any thought of retreat.[32]

"Well Grant," said Sherman, "we've had the devil's own day, haven't we?" "Yes," replied Grant; "lick 'em tomorrow, though." Grant's laconic response conveyed more than empty bravado. Occupying formidable defensive ground covering the landing, with infantry and artillery concentrated along a line much shorter than the army's initial front, Grant knew he held a stronger position than when the battle began. Lew Wallace, later to become internationally renowned as the author of *Ben Hur*, had finally come up on the army's right flank after marching and countermarching his 7,000-man division from its camp several miles north of Pittsburg Landing. Also, thousands of troops from Major General Don Carlos Buell's Army of the Ohio were being ferried across the Tennessee, taking position on the left flank and, together with Wallace, totaling more than 20,000 additional soldiers.[33]

Soon after sunrise on April 7, the Union Army advanced, Sherman's division still on the right. Driving straight ahead, the Union force overpowered the disorganized Confederates, who had received no reinforcements. The Federals gained a hard-fought, strategic triumph—one of the greatest U.S. victories of the war. The fighting on Shiloh's second day did not equal Sunday's sustained bloodletting, but at times the conflict's savagery did rise to an unforgettable intensity. Sherman later declared in his memoirs that the din of musketry near the Hamburg–Purdy Road on that Monday was the severest that he ever heard. Regardless of how the two days compared, the significant factor was that the Rebels had lost a battle they desperately needed to win, and were now condemned to continue waging the war from a critically weakened position.[34]

For Sherman, like many soldiers on both sides, Shiloh proved the bloodiest battle he ever saw. More important, Shiloh became the turning point of his military career. While West Point, an exhilarating personal experience of earlier years, had sparked within the young man great expectations for the future, Sherman found his subsequent time in the army somewhat boring and disappointing. Then came the war with Mexico, initially reviving his dormant hopes of significant martial achievement, only to have such dreams utterly destroyed—the nadir of all his army service to that point—when he never even saw combat. On the other hand, many of Sherman's peers emerged from the conflict with enviable military laurels, a factor that only deepened his sense of frustration. Nor had the Civil War started well for Sherman, the lowest point experienced in the fall of 1861 when, suffering a period of mental distress, some newspapers, as earlier noted, pronounced him "crazy."

All of this changed with Shiloh. General Grant praised Sherman's display of "great judgment and skill" and correctly stated, as recent scholarship has confirmed, that the battle's "hardest fighting was in front of [Sherman's and McClernand's] divisions." Grant wrote, "McClernand told me on that day . . . that he profited much by having so able a commander [as Sherman] supporting him." When Henry W. Halleck, supreme Federal commander in the western theater of war, arrived at Pittsburg Landing soon after the battle, he wasted no time in commending Sherman to the secretary of war. "It is the unanimous opinion here that Brigadier General W. T. Sherman saved the fortune of the day on the 6th instance," he informed the secretary, and then credited Sherman further with having "contributed largely to the glorious victory on the 7th. He was in the thickest of the fight on both days." Halleck concluded with a recommendation that Sherman be promoted to major general of volunteers.

Also, Brigadier General William "Bull" Nelson, a blustery Kentuckian whose division was the first unit of Buell's reinforcing army to reach the battlefield, praised Sherman's leadership as decisive. Allowing for bias and exaggeration—for Nelson liked to think his division arrived in the nick of time to save Grant's army—his commendation of Sherman is still striking. "During eight hours the fate of the army depended on the life of one man," proclaimed Nelson. If General Sherman had fallen, Nelson declared that "the army would have been captured or destroyed." Possibly Sherman may have been, once the battle was joined, the indispensable Union general (assuming such a creature did exist) at Shiloh on April 6.[35]

Others of less consequence than Grant, Halleck and Nelson likewise offered their praise, and many soldiers cheered Sherman. To the Northern public he became a hero. Sherman himself, after Shiloh, believed in himself in a way that he had not previously. Following that fiery trial, "when we were enveloped and death stared us all in the face," Sherman *knew* that he could command men successfully in the heat of the fiercest battle. For the first time he himself believed, because he could conceive of no greater challenge than Shiloh, that he was actually as good in battle—"my seniors in rank leaned on me"—as he had hoped and thought he could be.

"For instance," he wrote to his father-in-law, Thomas Ewing, "McClernand's division was a mere squad at 5 p.m. Sunday, and he gave it up as a gone day, when I assured him we could and would hold our ground till night, and night promised strong reinforcements." Declaring that he was "not in search of Glory or Fame," Sherman confidently asserted, "I know I can take what position I choose among my peers." Writing in the same vein only a few days afterward, Sherman told his brother: "I find ... that in times of danger and trouble all lean on me. During Sunday afternoon April 6, McClernand leaned on me all the time, but since the Battle he has ignored the fact. Everyone of my staff heard him despair and despond, and I actually gave orders to his troops."

Shiloh had been dreadful, yet magnificently inspiring. Wonderfully buoyed up by the experience, Sherman henceforth exhibited both confidence and total, all-consuming, physical and emotional commitment to the war, even if he never expected to survive it. Shiloh marked the irreversible resurgence of Sherman as a soldier. Looking back years later, with the wisdom of historical perspective, Sherman pronounced Shiloh "one of the most important [victories] which has ever occurred on this continent." He also considered it "the turning point," that made possible "all our western campaigns." His judgment of Shiloh's significance—viewed in the context of the great winter–spring campaign of 1862, a Union offensive in which Shiloh was the bloodiest battle—constituted little if any exaggeration. And what Sherman declared of Shiloh's importance in the war, he might well have said of Shiloh's impact on his own career, as a general in the U.S. Army.[36]

Chapter One

MY FATHER NAMED ME
WILLIAM *TECUMSEH*

Tecumseh, who was a Shawnee warrior, became the most famous Indian leader of his age, widely known among both white settlers west of the Appalachians and Native Americans. Some said his name meant "Shooting Star"; others translated it as "Crouching Panther." The son of a Shawnee father and a Creek mother whose parents once had lived in the region known as Tennessee, Tecumseh traveled south from the Ohio area in the early 1790s, at the urging of his older brother Cheeseekau. Bringing a band of Shawnee warriors to reinforce the group led by Cheeseekau, and in tandem with Chickamauga Indians, Tecumseh engaged in raiding the Cumberland River Valley settlements in the general vicinity of the fledgling, decade-old town of Nashville. When Cheeseekau was killed, Tecumseh, then only about twenty-four years old, was selected as the new leader. For several months he and his Shawnees continued raiding Tennessee settlements, before returning to the Ohio country upon learning that a United States Army, led by Revolutionary War hero General "Mad Anthony" Wayne, was advancing into that area.[1]

Tecumseh was greatly disturbed by the ever growing encroachment of white settlers. He sought to devise a plan that would protect all Indian peoples. Convinced that Native Americans could not live alongside whites without sacrificing their way of life, the chief envisioned a vast intertribal confederacy, encompassing Indians everywhere and dedicated to arresting the United States takeover of Indian lands. Indians, he believed, must renounce all white practices and possessions, and return to their old ways—the ways sanctioned by antiquity. Traveling extensively throughout the South—from Missouri and Kentucky to Mississippi, Florida and North Carolina—he urged Native Americans everywhere to make common cause with the Shawnees and their northern allies, in a great war of survival against the expanding whites. If not stopped, these whites, with their corrupting whiskey and gold, would seize all the land, and also enslave or exterminate the Indians.[2]

Wherever he spoke, the tall Tecumseh made converts as "his eyes burned with supernatural luster," remarked a witness, "and his whole frame trembled with emotion," and his "voice resounded over the multitude." What Tecumseh apparently hoped to achieve was a kind of Indian holy war, in alliance with the king of England, to overthrow the new American nation. Presumably he foresaw a restoration of British colonial status as the fate of the Americans once they were defeated. But not all Indians responded, and probably their numbers would not have been sufficient for the task if the converts had reached 100 percent.[3]

Then the War of 1812 began and the Shawnee chief viewed the conflict as a great opportunity to achieve his vision of a vast, inviolate Indian territory. As an ally of the British, he commanded about 2,000 warriors, and contributed significantly to British successes early in the war. Ultimately however, he ran afoul of British Colonel Henry Proctor, who possessed neither the abilities nor the humane instincts of the Shawnee leader. Above all, the Englishman did not share the goals of his Indian ally. A discouraged Tecumseh attempted to persuade Proctor not to withdraw into Canada, but his arguments failed to convince the colonel.[4]

The end came in October 1813, when Tecumseh perished a short distance north of Lake Erie, at the Battle of the Thames. As the Shawnee chief and his warriors fought to cover the British retreat to eastern Ontario, Tecumseh reportedly was shot again and again while encouraging his men to stand and fight. Stories circulated that after the battle depraved whites, in quest of "souvenirs," cut strips of skin from Tecumseh's thighs. Another report alleged that a group of Kentuckians skinned the corpse of an Indian they thought to be Tecumseh. Others said the Indians hid his body to prevent just such a desecration. Several men claimed to have killed the great Shawnee, most notably Richard Johnson of Kentucky, who in later years became vice president of the United States under Martin Van Buren. Tecumseh's death was an awful blow to the spirit of the eastern Indians, particularly the Shawnee, many of whom thought the charismatic leader possessed supernatural abilities.[5]

A little over six years after Tecumseh's death, on February 8, 1820, a white woman in Ohio named Mary Sherman, gave birth to her sixth child, a son whom Charles Robert Sherman, husband of Mary, christened Tecumseh. Considering that many Americans despised Indians, one might suspect that Charles Sherman had played a cruel joke on his infant when he pinned "Tecumseh" on him. Charles Sherman had no such perverted goal in mind. He called his son Tecumseh because, however unlikely for a white man of that era, Charles Sherman deeply admired the Shawnee warrior. Years afterward the son would write, "I think my father . . . caught a fancy for the great chief."[6]

Tecumseh was not only an inspiring leader of his people. In a war often characterized by torture, mutilation, scalping and burning—sometimes involving the wounded and prisoners, sometimes even women and children—he had been known to show mercy. He reportedly denounced both Indians and his British allies for inhumane practices. Legends grew of his personal intervention to stop massacres. Charles Sherman was not the only white man who believed the reports of Tecumseh's magnanimity. Those who did believe, a distinct minority to be sure, nevertheless constituted refreshing evidence that at least some white men were capable of being fair-minded about racial and cultural issues.[7]

For Charles Sherman, Tecumseh likely represented both a noble and a romanticized character. After the Shawnee chieftain's death, Charles Sherman decided to name his next son after the legendary Indian leader. However, Charles's wife, Mary, insisted that their new son, born in 1814, be named for her brother James. Already an earlier son had been named for her other brother, Charles. Their first girl had been named for the mother (but Mary Elizabeth Sherman was known as Elizabeth), and two more girls followed the birth of James. Thus the father had to wait a long time to realize his wish, but at last, in 1820 (Mary having no more brothers) Charles honored the admirable Shawnee by naming his new child, appropriately a red-haired boy, after Tecumseh. When someone thought the name unusual, even unbecoming for a white infant, the father responded, "Tecumseh was a great warrior."[8]

That name, in view of the boy's eventual role in Native American relations, proved to be packed with irony. Soon after graduation from West Point, young Tecumseh experienced his initial contact with Indians, and from the start was plagued by a conflicted attitude toward them. The stoic resignation of a band of Seminole captives in Florida impressed him, perhaps because he himself could be stoically inclined at times. "I wish you could see the group in its savage state," he wrote his brother John. "Although many have lost their husbands and fathers and wives and children, yet they show no grief." Several were badly wounded. "One little girl, with a ball through the back and coming out in the cheek scarce utters a murmur," while a grown woman, suffering from buckshot "through and through, bears it with the fortitude of a veteran soldier."[9]

About three years later, writing from near Marietta, Georgia, the young soldier spoke movingly of the Cherokees, "who used to live here but a few years ago. They had good homes, fields and orchards, and had made rapid advances to civilization, but a Christian people wanted their lands and must have them." In disgust, Sherman vented his anger at the manner in which Americans had mistreated those Native Americans. "If ever a curse could fall upon a people or nation for pure and unalloyed villainy towards a part of God's creatures," he raged, "we deserve it for not protecting the Cherokees that lately lived and hunted in peace and plenty through the hills and in the valleys that stretch from the base of Kennesaw Mountain."[10]

Yet, even as early as his sojourn in Florida, and despite a degree of sympathy both then and later for the plight of the Indians, Sherman generally viewed Native Americans as inferior beings. Talking with the Seminoles was a waste of time, he thought, for they "will break their word when it is to their interest," and he concluded that the only way to smash their determined, unorthodox and unceasing resistance was "a war of extermination." Years later, when dealing with the Plains Indians, he would come back to this brutal strategy.[11]   ·

Occasionally, to be sure, Sherman would manifest a sympathy for those "poor devils, more to be pitied than dreaded," as he wrote General Grant in August 1866. In essence, though, he continued to view Indians as tragic figures: a people doomed because they would not, perhaps could not, transform their way of life into that of the white man. From time to time, Sherman might speak harsh words against the despicable and lawless acts of Americans greedy for Indian land. In fact, he undoubtedly despised the whole dirty business, involving the U.S. Army, which he loved, with the clashes between Native Americans and frontiersmen. But in the final reckoning, he believed that the outnumbered red tribes, burdened by, as he viewed them, a more primitive way of life, would not survive the onrush of a superior people.[12]

"We must act with vindictive earnestness against the Sioux," he told Grant, following the killing of a number of soldiers at the hands of those famous Indians, "even to their extermination, men, women and children." When the Cheyennes and Arapahos took to the war path, Sherman wrote his wife, "Probably in the end it will be better to kill them all." To brother John, he said, "We must not let up this time, . . . till they are killed or humbled." Still again he wrote, "The more we can kill this year, the less will have to be killed the next war, for the more I see of these Indians, the more convinced I am that they will all have to be killed or be maintained as a species of pauper." Despite eventually implementing such ruthless strategy against the Indians, and becoming virtually a symbol of America's destructive policy against the Plains tribes, there is no evidence that Sherman disliked his Indian name—or ever desired, for any reason, to change it.[13]

CHARLES SHERMAN was descended from a Judge Samuel Sherman who had emigrated from England in the first half of the seventeenth century. Charles represented the fifth generation of his line in America. His father, grandfather and great-grandfather, like Samuel, were all judges. Also, all lived in Connecticut, where Charles was born in Norwalk in 1788. Charles attended Dartmouth College, then studied law and gained admission to the bar, apparently prepared to follow in the footsteps of his Connecticut ancestors. Instead, the young lawyer, recently wed to Mary Hoyt, a graduate of Poughkeepsie, New York's prestigious Female Seminary, succumbed to the lure of the West.[14]

Charles and Mary, with their firstborn child, also christened Charles, bravely embarked upon a horseback ride for hundreds of miles through the wilderness, generally heading southwest, until they reached Lancaster in southeastern Ohio. Charles had previously scouted the little frontier town, situated on the Hocking River, and county seat of Fairfield County, where he opened a law office. Enamored by a sense of adventure, as well as perceptions of economic success, Charles convinced Mary that their future lay in Lancaster. The center of Lancaster rested on a hill, and the Shermans built a two-story, solid if unspectacular frame house on Main Street. Charles proved likable, hardworking, and was quickly recognized as a leading citizen. No other couple could match Charles and Mary for quality of education and their home became a social and cultural center in that small outpost of civilization. In 1823 Charles was named a judge of the Ohio Supreme Court, additional evidence of his steadily increasing prominence.[15]

Only a few years after the Shermans arrived, Lancaster had welcomed another talented newcomer, Thomas Ewing, who would quickly make his mark as one of Ohio's most wealthy, influential and powerful men. A lawyer by profession, Ewing was a formidable character, both physically and intellectually. He and his wife, Maria Boyle, whom he married in 1820, built a fine home on Main Street. Atop Lancaster's hill, the Ewing residence lay only a couple of houses up from the Shermans, with whom they soon became good friends. Sherman and Ewing grew especially close as the years passed, their legal work around the state often conducive to traveling together. The Sherman and Ewing children, increasing in numbers virtually every year, became friends too and played together much of the time.[16]

By 1829 there were eleven Sherman children, six boys and five girls. Charles Sherman's mother, Betsy Stoddard Sherman, had also come to live with him after the death of his father, Taylor. Providing life's necessities for such a large family proved a demanding task. Sherman worked long hours, often away from home, riding the circuit from 1817 to 1823 as a lawyer, and thereafter on the Ohio Supreme Court. Life must have seemed good for the Sherman family, prominent citizens of a growing town that some believed would likely become the state capital.[17]

However, as any thinking person knows, appearances are often deceptive. Charles still struggled to pay the debts from his unfortunate stint, soon after arriving in Lancaster, as tax collector for the Third District of Ohio—debts resulting from no fault of his own, and which, if his sense of ethical responsibility had not been keen, he could have avoided by declaring bankruptcy. Instead, he admirably chose to accept the debt, which, while further enhancing his enviable reputation as an honorable and trustworthy lawyer, saddled him with economic obligations for the rest of his life. Coupled with the demands of his ever growing family, Charles Sherman had the majority of his earnings committed before the money ever reached his hands. Perhaps—*if* life were fair—all would have been fine in the long view. But in June 1829 tragedy struck.[18]

Mary Sherman, shocked upon receiving news that her husband lay seriously ill one hundred miles away in Lebanon, Ohio, started at once for his bedside. But Charles passed before she could reach him. He was forty-one years old. Years later General Sherman declared typhoid was the likely cause of his father's death. Mary was left with the house and furniture, a small amount of stock, eleven children (one an infant girl) and her strong-willed mother-in-law. Relatives and friends were sorely needed to step forward and help bear her burdens. To their credit, they did.[19]

The mental impact on nine-year-old Tecumseh (by then known as "Cump," because his younger siblings found Tecumseh too difficult to pronounce) was far-reaching. A man might be impressive and competent, successful at his profession, and still die poor, leaving his family in desperate circumstances, dependent upon others for help. If it happened to his father, the same could be Cump's fate as well. All his life, once he himself became a father, he would worry about debt and death, fearful of dying and leaving his family poverty-stricken.

Actually, as the children found foster homes, Cump fared well. In some ways, better than any of his siblings. His father's friend Thomas Ewing was the man who assumed responsibility for Cump. Reportedly, Ewing had one request. He preferred the smartest of the Sherman boys, to which Cump's oldest sister, Elizabeth, is said to have replied: "Take Cump; he's the brightest." Whether or not Elizabeth's advice proved decisive, Cump was the one Ewing selected. "I took him home," said Ewing of the redhead, "and he became, thereafter, my boy."[20]

The evidence supports the claim. Cump was fully integrated into the Ewing household, where seven other children lived, at least so far as Thomas Ewing could control the matter. He did not adopt Cump, perhaps respecting the wishes of the boy's mother. In addition to Thomas and Maria's four children, they were also raising a nephew and two nieces. Among the boys was Philemon Ewing, known as Phil, only slightly younger than Cump, and probably Cump's best friend. Cump already knew all the children of course; most notable among them in the years to come was five-year-old Ellen Ewing, the girl he would marry.[21]

Thomas Ewing had gained fame as a criminal lawyer and become a very wealthy man; he was also a well-read man, whose excellent memory and understanding made him one of the best-informed persons of his era. In 1831 he was chosen by the state legislature for the United States Senate. Obviously the wealth, knowledge, power and influence of Thomas Ewing might open some doors of opportunity for young Tecumseh, which Charles Sherman, despite all of his good qualities, could never have done.[22]

That is, if Cump desired that such doors be opened. Actually, the nine-year-old's development revealed an independent-minded lad, one strongly inclined to achieve on his own merit whatever he might, or might not, accomplish in life. Some men prove readily receptive to the influence and connections of relatives and friends who—for whatever reasons, and varied those motivations certainly may be—assure for them economic comfort, even great wealth; men who, after the fact, often somehow convince themselves they are rugged individualists, self-made persons, forever praising their maker. Cump would be too independent, and realistic, for any such delusions of grandeur. He would have considered it nonsense.

This is not to say that Thomas Ewing had little impact on Cump's life. Quite the contrary. The young Sherman respected his foster father. He admired Ewing's intellect, once calling him "an intellectual giant," and respected his financial accomplishments. And he deeply desired the approval of Thomas Ewing. Being a part of the Ewing household ensured, too, that he would hear the English language spoken with grammatical correctness—and sometimes with enviable style. From time to time prominent people were guests in the Ewing home, another of those benefits, impossible to measure precisely, but unquestionably of advantage. Later in life, Sherman became an excellent public speaker as well as an engaging conversationalist. The associations of his childhood and teen years surely nurtured those talents.[23]

Sherman's political views, virtually down the line, came to be those of Thomas Ewing. He generally favored the Whigs, who were supportive of protective tariffs and internal improvements at government expense— in essence, Henry Clay's "American System." (He did, however, develop serious misgivings about a national bank.) The Constitution of the United States, in Sherman's view, stood as one of the most admirable documents of Western civilization and was to be defended without qualification. A staunch nationalist, he thought nearly anything con- tributing to the nation's growth, strength, stability and general prog- ress desirable and justified. While slavery did concern him, he believed the institution should be supported, fearing dire consequences for the nation if Northerners turned against the South's "peculiar institution." Abolitionists potentially posed a greater problem for the nation than did slave owners. How much of this came from Ewing, and how much Sherman embraced on his own, are questions impossible to answer. At the least, his respect for "Mr. Ewing," as he called him (the Ewings were not "father" and "mother," only "Mr." and "Mrs."), particularly Ewing's intellect, would have paved a comfortable path, conducive to the acceptance of Ewing's Whiggery.[24]

There was another significant way in which Tecumseh's life would be changed by his new relationship with the Ewing family—although only the passage of time could reveal the full impact of that transformation. It involved religion. Cump's mother adhered to the Presbyterian faith, while his father had been a Congregationalist. Charles Sherman's Masonic associations, however, seemed to be of greater importance to him than Congregationalism. Thomas Ewing, born into a Presbyterian family, did not appear to consider religion significant, but apparently to humor his wife, Maria, a staunch Catholic, and perhaps because he was a good family man, he occasionally attended Catholic services with the family. Thus Maria Ewing, devout Irish Catholic to the core, determined the family's religious observances. She decided that Cump must be baptized a Catholic if he were going to be a part of the Ewing family.[25]

Cump's mother gave her permission for the baptism but failed to attend the ceremony even though she was close at hand. When the priest, a Father Dominic Young who was visiting from a nearby monastery (according to Ellen Sherman's 1880 recollection), agreed to perform the sacrament, he inquired about the boy's name. Taken by surprise, he was probably appalled. Tecumseh would not do. The "pagan" name must, at the least, be balanced by one more suitable, he said: "a Scriptural or Saint's name must be used in the ceremony." The month was June, near the day, if not actually the day of the feast of Saint William. Hence Tecumseh was christened "William"—neither for a relative nor for a friend of the family, but after a saint! The red-haired boy, whether he then indicated the fact or not, did not like what had occurred. Decades later he would write: "My father named me William *Tecumseh*."

Possibly he was right. John Sherman, his younger brother, claimed all the Sherman children had been baptized as Presbyterians by the Reverend John Wright. Ellen Sherman had heard the story of Cump's Presbyterian baptism, and also that the Presbyterian parson gave him the name William. If the reverend did apply the name William, it seems highly unlikely that he would have done so without the approval of the infant's father. Thus, in a real sense, Tecumseh's father truly would have named him William Tecumseh. Ellen did not believe the story of the alleged Presbyterian baptism, both because she remembered as a five-year-old watching Father Young baptize Cump and also because, intensely Catholic like her mother, she wanted to believe her husband's baptism had been Catholic. Whatever the facts about the Presbyterian baptism and the origin of the name William, Sherman was clearly baptized by a priest when he was nine or ten years old. But he would accept neither Catholic dogma nor ritual. "I am not a Catholic," he wrote John in 1875, "and could not be because they exact a blind obedience and subordination that is entirely foreign to my nature."[26]

In his early twenties, in a letter to Ellen written from Florida, Sherman declared that in the years since leaving the Ewing home for West Point he had adhered to "no particular creed." The purity of Christian morals he did acknowledge but, beyond that, he considered inconsequential the importance usually attached to "minor points of doctrine or form." While believing "in good works rather than faith," not only "as revealed in scripture," but also, he noted, as "taught by the experience of all ages and common sense," nevertheless the Catholic creed was not for him. As a grown man he would have little time for any organized religion.[27]

That fact would present an ongoing problem with his wife, a dedicated Catholic, "working like a beaver to spread the faith," as he remarked. Although Sherman was remarkably tolerant about her religion and influence on their children's religion, her never-ceasing efforts to persuade him to practice the Catholic faith became tiresome, occasionally quite annoying. Once, in the midst of a row about religion, she reminded him, "You knew when you married me that I was a Catholic," to which he rejoined: "Of course I did, but I didn't know that you would get worse every year." When his son Tom decided to become a Catholic priest, Sherman was beside himself, becoming more anti-Catholic than ever before. "Not only am I not a Catholic," he raged, "but an enemy so bitter that written words can convey no meaning."[28]

Late in life, when an old army associate from Civil War days was visiting with him, Sherman warned the man "not to talk religion with [his wife]." As to himself, Sherman said, "It makes no difference. Why, I guess I don't believe in anything, so in this room talk as you please." And as Sherman was dying, his Catholic children (their mother already deceased), knowing that their father would never accept the last rites of the Catholic Church, brought in a priest for that purpose while the General lay unconscious. Thus for Sherman, "William," in its own peculiar manner, proved a name as permeated with irony as was "Tecumseh."[29]

Chapter Two

I WAS NOTIFIED TO
PREPARE FOR WEST POINT

When sixteen-year-old William Tecumseh Sherman set off for the United States Military Academy, forty miles above New York City on the west bank of the Hudson River, the chances are, except for two or three trips into Pennsylvania with Maria Ewing when she visited relatives, he had never been outside the state of Ohio. He had accompanied Mary Sherman once or twice a year—driving his mother by the time he became a teenager—on a journey to visit his paternal grandmother, Betsy Stoddard Sherman, in Mansfield (she had moved there to live with a daughter, Mrs. Betsy Parker, after Cump's father died). But that seventy-five-mile trip to northern Ohio, obviously, did not take the young boy very far from Lancaster. It was an era when travel was difficult and most people never ventured far from home. Mostly he spent his time in Lancaster, where an endless round of work, play and schooling demanded attention and energy.[1]

As for his maternal grandmother, Mary Raymond Hoyt, Sherman apparently never mentioned her, and perhaps never saw her. Historian Stanley P. Hirshson discovered that she lived into her seventies, at which time young Sherman was well into his ninth year. Hirshson has built a convincing case that Mary Raymond Hoyt suffered from mental illness. This may explain why Sherman, who usually seemed abreast of family connections, chose not to speak of her. Quite likely her malady proved hereditary, notably in the later life of both her youngest son, Charles, a successful merchant in New York City, and also William Tecumseh's younger brother John, who excelled for years as a lawyer and a powerful, well-known, national politician.[2]

Like all the Ewing children, Sherman had actively participated in such chores as cutting and stacking firewood, starting and tending fires, working in the garden, milking the cow and helping prepare the house for company upon special occasions. He liked baseball, fishing and swimming and, with some other youngsters in town, organized a society to put on plays—apparently the beginning of a lifelong passion for the theater. The young lad possessed a mischievous streak, too, and in his later years admitted that he enjoyed the company of "the worst young rascal in town," a fellow named Bill King. He also confessed to pestering one of Lancaster's preachers by stealing his kindling on Saturday nights, hoping thereby to make life tougher for the pastor on Sunday mornings. Several stories of Sherman's boyish, errant ways have survived through the years. One can only speculate as to how many are true.[3]

One of the amusing tales, which might well have been more serious than it was, involved a number of friends with whom Cump played a primitive form of baseball, using homemade yarn balls. From time to time the balls were hit into a garden adjoining the playing field, whose owner became irate at his garden being trampled by young boys retrieving balls. When the man began confiscating the balls and throwing them into his stove, Sherman and his buddies sought revenge. They filled a ball with gunpowder. Soon the unsuspecting garden owner seized the devilishly prepared thing and cast it into the stove; a fiery explosion rocked the house, leaving the man suffering with burns and damage to his home. The boys, naturally, had waited close by to observe the result of their scheme. Suddenly the angry man burst forth from his house, intent upon chasing down the culprits. He managed to catch the slowest of the boys as they ran and, so the story goes, whipped him severely. Sherman and the others, being more fleet of foot, escaped unscathed.[4]

A highlight of the Lancaster summer months came when the Ewing children, including Sherman of course, visited the farm of Thomas Ewing's sister, Sarah Clark, for several days. At least once, Sherman and Philemon Ewing, less than a year apart in age, and who had become good buddies, spent the entire summer at Aunt Sarah's farm. There they enjoyed roaming the woods and hunting for rabbit and squirrel.

They also armed themselves, whenever venturing into the forest, with sturdy clubs for protection against the legendary hoop snake. Possibly the boys learned of that dreaded reptile from their aunt, although any number of relatives, or family friends, might have been the first to apprise them of the creature. Tales then circulated widely of how the terrifying snake would form itself into a big circle, like a hoop standing upright and, as if it were a wheel, come rolling after its prey, young boys being its most desirable victims.

Sherman and Philemon planned, if accosted by the horrifying reptile, to race toward a tree, then jump aside at the last instant, hoping that the striking snake would embed its horn-tail in the tree trunk, thereby trapping itself and eventually dying, because it would be unable to extricate its tail. Or, if they chose, the boys could readily bash the ensnared creature to death with their clubs. The tree would perish too, according to the conventional wisdom, its leaves falling off within minutes as a result of the snake's incredibly potent venom.[5]

There is no evidence indicating that Cump, as a preteenager, ever gave any thought to a military career. No doubt he would have been aware of the local militia activities, for militias were always prominent on the frontier. Many years later, Sherman would observe in his memoirs that "nearly every man had to be somewhat of a soldier," because the Indians still occupied extensive territory in the Old Northwest. However, this is not to say that the militia impressed him. Militia drill days often seemed occasions, basically, to party, featuring barbecue, watermelons and alcohol, mixed with foot races, wrestling matches and occasional fistfights.[6]

As to the serious business involved in soldiering, militia arms had not been standardized. Neither had uniforms, the variety of which sometimes appeared absurd. Officers seemed, at best, only minimally familiar with military drill, and the parade ground often looked comical. John Sherman, who was three years Cump's junior, considered his older brother a somewhat nonaggressive, even passive figure. Later, John wrote that Cump "was a steady student, quiet in his manner and easily moved by sympathy or affection. I was regarded as a wild, reckless lad, eager in controversy and ready to fight." John thought that no one could have anticipated that his brother "was to be a great warrior and I a plodding lawyer and politician."[7]

William Tecumseh would become the man his father evidently envisioned when he christened the infant Tecumseh. As Senator Ewing stated in an 1835 letter to Secretary of War Lewis Cass, in which he sought an appointment for Sherman to West Point, the boy's father "often expressed before his death" a wish that his son "should receive an education which would fit him for the public service in the army or navy." According to Ewing, Sherman's mother preferred West Point over Annapolis. The senator did not give Mrs. Sherman's reasons. Ewing praised Cump to Secretary Cass as a strong athlete, and "a good Latin, Greek, and French scholar." He further described him as "very good" in mathematics.[8]

As to his general education, Sherman praised his teachers, saying he went to "as good a school as any in Ohio." His father, in tandem with Thomas Ewing, had been a driving force in creating the first school in Lancaster, which provided well for the boy's earliest education. Then came Sam and John Howe, brothers who implemented the Lancaster Academy's growing reputation, turning it into a first-rate institution. Sherman did excellent work in all subjects, becoming proficient in arithmetic, and learning Latin and French. Ewing probably stretched the truth a bit in applying the term "scholar" to Sherman's knowledge of Greek.

While the youngster preferred to play rather than spend his time sitting at school, nevertheless he did not fail to master his subjects. Clearly he liked to read, and was blessed with a good memory. Then came a message from his foster father, notifying the boy "to prepare for West Point." Learning that Senator Ewing probably would succeed in getting him appointed to the military academy, beginning in June 1836, Sherman said that through the fall of 1835 and the spring of 1836, "I devoted

myself . . . to mathematics and French, . . . known to be the chief requirements for admission to West Point."[9]

Some children go through a period of being disturbed by one or more
of their physical characteristics: perhaps warts on their hands, moles
on their face, large feet, etc. Sherman experienced a problem with his
red hair, which for years he disliked. Occasionally taunted by a foster
brother calling him a "red-haired woodpecker," he even tried to dye it
a different color, only to see it turn to a sickening green. Eventually he
adjusted to the supposed malady and accepted the red hair, particularly after he came to believe that Native Americans sought especially
to scalp redheads. He considered his hair a challenging symbol against
Indians.[10]

As long as William Tecumseh remained a part of the Ewing household, religious observances claimed a regular and substantial quantity
of his time. When visiting Thomas Ewing's sister Sarah Clark, who was
Protestant, Sherman or one of the Ewing boys was required on Sunday
mornings to read a chapter from the Bible. This, however, must have
seemed a minor irritant when compared with Catholic religious observances under the tutelage of Maria Ewing. One Sunday a month a priest
came to Lancaster, which meant that mass must be attended, followed
by religious indoctrination conducted by the priest at the Ewing house.
Attendance by the children was mandatory. On all other Sunday mornings, Maria herself directed Christian rituals in her dining room. These
sessions also were mandatory. There she read prayers, Bible verses and
other religious literature, recited the rosary and queried the children
from the catechism.

Probably worst of all for Sherman, entailing what otherwise might
have been a pleasant, twenty-mile ride into the countryside, were the
occasional Sunday trips to the Dominican monastery in the town of
Somerset. Unfortunately, from the young lad's perspective, the journey
had to be made before dawn, even in summer when the sun rose earlier
than during other seasons of the year, in order to arrive in time for mass.
Following mass came visits with priests and nuns, resulting in an all-
day religious affair; the family usually returned home to Lancaster only

after dark. Never again, when Sherman left the Ewing home for West Point, would he spend entire Sundays in religious rituals.[11]

Not that Sundays at the Point provided the cadet with freedom of religious expression. Like most colleges throughout the country in those days, West Point required the student body to attend chapel on the first day of the week. This had not been the academy's practice in the early days. But during the superintendency of Sylvanus Thayer, who significantly shaped the institution's development in the 1820s, West Point began holding high-church Episcopalian services. That aristocratic faith, esteemed as the ideal religion for "an officer and a gentleman," symbolized the dignity and patrician manners which Thayer hoped would characterize the West Point graduate. The Episcopalian services typically lasted about two hours and constituted a continuing plague on Sherman, who said that he found the minister "a great bore."[12]

Sherman certainly was not alone in that judgment. Cadet George W. Cullum declared that before his West Point experience he looked forward to church, where he would visit with friends, especially "my female acquaintances." But at the academy he was forced to "sit . . . on a backless bench," squeezed among his "fellow sufferers," all the while enduring "a dry discourse." It should be noted that some West Point cadets were deeply moved by exposure to the faith, and became Episcopalian clergymen, fueling a degree of sarcastic criticism occasionally leveled at the military academy as "a great place to make preachers." That charge was unfair. Relatively few pursued a ministerial career, while the majority of the young men seem not to have taken religion very seriously. For young Sherman, four years of exposure to the Episcopal faith would have no more impact than had nearly seven years of Roman Catholicism.[13]

If Sherman reflected upon the United States Constitution and its wisely mandated separation of church and state, he might have been a bit troubled that a school created and supported by the federal government demanded attendance at Episcopal church services. The religious practices of other colleges, institutions privately funded and without any relation to the U.S. government, obviously established no precedent for West Point. Only the naval academy and the Point operated at federal expense and with federal oversight. But since Sherman placed no meaningful significance in any organized religion—much like Thomas Ewing—the chances are that he viewed the matter as merely an unwelcome requirement of a program that he well knew, before arriving at the military academy, would be "very strict."[14]

There were, not surprisingly, occasional disturbances during the chapel services. Some cadets made groaning noises, chewed tobacco and messed up the floor with tobacco juice. One would suppose, too, that the religious issue was among the subjects of nighttime discussions in the barracks. Whatever Sherman's thoughts may have been on this matter, and if he ever expressed an opinion to anyone—other than his remark about the minister's sermons being "boring"—the evidence thereof is yet to be discovered. Sherman probably realized that the required chapel attendance was not going to be changed anytime soon, if ever.[15]

Perhaps he had heard about the fate of the three officer-instructors who protested to Thayer in the late 1820s that compulsory chapel attendance violated their rights under the U.S. Constitution. Thayer sent their plea to Washington, and they got a response from the secretary of war, saying that the government had no desire "to interfere ... with their conscientious scruples, and would, therefore, send them where attendance upon Divine service would not be necessary." They were reassigned to the frontier. This solution undoubtedly served as a lesson to all who might become disgruntled with chapel services in the future.[16]

IN THE SPRING of 1836 Sherman received his official appointment to the United States Military Academy. He welcomed the opportunity, as he wrote Thomas Ewing, "with great satisfaction." Having obtained his mother's consent to accept the appointment "as a cadet in the service of the U. S.," he embarked upon the longest trip of his first sixteen years—the first time, too, that he traveled alone. Thomas Ewing wanted him to spend a few days in the nation's capital, to refresh the boy after the opening leg of the trek. Visits with relatives in Philadelphia and New

York would also break up the tiring, sometimes monotonous journey to West Point.

Leaving Lancaster in a stagecoach for Zanesville, Sherman there transferred to the Great National Road, which was the best west-to-east route of the time. He said that the stages "generally traveled in gangs" of up to six coaches, "each drawn by four good horses, carrying nine passengers inside and three or four outside." The trip to Washington entailed three days, traveling day and night, and the weather was often overcast, rainy and dreary. Arriving in Frederick, Maryland, the young man faced a decision. He could opt for the recently completed Baltimore & Ohio Railroad into Washington via Baltimore, or take, as he expressed it, "a two-horse hack ready to start for Washington direct." He chose the hack, "not having full faith in the novel and dangerous railroad." (Herein lies an irony, for a quarter of a century later, during history's "first railroad war," Sherman would demonstrate, to a degree unmatched by any commander on either side, the strategic value of the railroad in war.)[17]

The next morning Sherman contacted Senator Ewing, who boarded with a number of his peers at the corner of Third and C Streets, and trunk in tow, the boy moved in with the senator. Sherman spent a week in Washington, visiting with Ewing and seeing the sights of the nation's capital. Years later Sherman declared: "I saw more of the place in that time than I ever have since in the many years of residence there." The president of the United States was Andrew Jackson and "Old Hickory" then, as Cump said, "was at the zenith of his fame." Young Sherman found the hero of the Battle of New Orleans a fascinating figure—despite the facts that Jackson was a Democrat and Sherman's sympathies were aligned with the Whigs, and that even then his foster father was preparing to stand against Jackson's banking policy.

"I recall looking at him a full hour one morning, through the wood railing on Pennsylvania Avenue," Sherman reminisced, watching as the President "paced up and down the gravel walk on the north front of the White House." He said that Jackson appeared "smaller than I had expected." The President always had been a tall, slender figure, never burdened with excess weight; but his wounds from duels and war, plus the hardships of military campaigning—not to mention the ravages of time—had taken a heavy toll on his physique, and in later years Jackson became quite thin and gaunt. During the week Sherman spent in the capital, he saw a number of the nation's political celebrities, notably Vice President Martin Van Buren, whom Jackson preferred as his successor. Among other memorable personages, he recalled seeing John C. Calhoun, Daniel Webster, Henry Clay and Lewis Cass.[18]

At the appointed time, Sherman departed on the next leg of his journey, accompanied by two other newly appointed cadets with whom he became acquainted in Washington. This time he decided to risk the Iron Horse, taking the railroad part of the way to Philadelphia. Did the influence of the two other cadets persuade him to make his initial trip on a train? Alternating between rail and water transport, Sherman journeyed first to Baltimore by train, then took a boat to Havre de Grace, followed by another train ride into Wilmington, Delaware, and finally a boat to Philadelphia. After a visit with his older sister, Mary Elizabeth, who had married the son of a successful Philadelphia merchant, he resumed the northward bound series of boat and rail rides, arriving at last for his first taste of New York City.

The experience proved positive—very much so. New York had surpassed Philadelphia as the largest city in the nation, and was certainly the most cosmopolitan. Sherman stayed a week there, visiting his mother's relatives, particularly remembering her brother Charles Hoyt "at his beautiful place on Brooklyn Heights." He also passed some time with his uncle James Hoyt, who, like Charles, was a well-heeled merchant.[19]

Probably, however, the highlight of his initial New York adventure was the theater. The New York stage made a deep impression, as the young man witnessed his first professional performance. Throughout his life, Sherman would remain a devotee of theatrical productions, seemingly enjoying the stage more than any other form of entertainment. (Somewhat fittingly, in this regard, the last few years of Sherman's life would be spent in New York.)[20]

Then came the day of departure for the final leg of the young man's trip to West Point, quite possibly the hour arriving sooner than he would have preferred. On the other hand, the rising anticipation of a new and challenging way of life undoubtedly generated excitement. From the deck of the *Cornelius Vanderbilt*, his eyes took in the river sights as the steamer plied the Hudson northward, transporting him to his home for the next four years. Compared with today's expansive campus, the West Point of Sherman's day was small and austere. Yet then, as now, the academy's stunning geographical location could not fail to impress, whether in the fullness of summer's foliage or the glistening magnificence of a winter snowfall.[21]

For visitors approaching from the river, the site of West Point looms majestically on the horizon. The high bluff of the stream's west bank rises precipitously nearly 200 feet up from the water. At the top, the academy's stone buildings rest upon a high shelf of land known as the Plain, which grandly overlooks the Hudson. This broad, generally level, forty-acre riverine setting is eloquently complemented by lofty, forested heights ascending to the west, creating an inspirational natural backdrop for the school. From locations on the Plain, like Trophy Point, and sites on the steep hills west of the Plain, there are sublime vistas in every direction.[22]

The magnificence of West Point's setting is appropriately matched by the significance of its historic role during the American Revolution. The Point's military importance stemmed from a combination of cannon placed high on the cliffs above the Hudson and the river's abrupt changes of direction within a short distance. Streaming southward from its Adirondack headwaters, the Hudson River suddenly is forced by the granite barrier of "the West Point" into a 90 degree sweep to the east. Then, in a third of a mile, having flanked the Point, the river turns sharply to the south once more, resuming its generally direct flow to the ocean.

The Hudson's two tight and difficult turns, first left and then right, forced warships and transports, in the days before steam power, to reduce speed dramatically while navigating the river's two right angles. The task was especially difficult, of course, if a ship were approaching against the current. During the Revolutionary War, the Americans stretched a great iron chain across the river. This daunting obstacle was strung from the west bank to Constitution Island, placing the barrier in the middle of the Hudson's abrupt turns. Thus any British ship attempting to run past the guns of the West Point fortress, which was the largest in America, faced a formidable challenge. West Point stymied the British strategic plan to control the Hudson River, and thereby sever New England from the rest of the colonies. George Washington described West Point as "the key to America."[23]

After the war, when West Point and the surrounding land were purchased by the United States government in 1790, the site became an obvious possibility for a national military academy. Washington strongly favored the establishment of such an institution. He believed that the struggle against Great Britain had proven the necessity of training competent military leaders for the future. So too did Henry Knox, Washington's chief of artillery during the Revolution and the first secretary of war. Knox was distressed that no American possessed the engineering skills required to build a fortress. Alexander Hamilton, always a staunch supporter of the military and the nation's first secretary of the treasury, also thought that the army needed an academy. Other influential men endorsed it as well. Officially established in 1802 with the support of President Thomas Jefferson, who favored both a national university and an emphasis on the training of engineers to develop the nation's infrastructure, the institution would endure a long period of struggle, with its very survival sometimes in doubt.

Those who feared a standing army, and they were numerous, claimed the academy nurtured an elitist military aristocracy, at national expense, which someday likely would threaten the freedom of the young country. Accordingly, they sought to destroy the school, arguing that a regular army was unnecessary for the nation's defense anyway. The militias, they claimed, could do the job—this in the face of much evidence to the contrary, especially in the War of 1812, when the militias sometimes turned and ran when they confronted the enemy. The academy's own shortcomings did not help its cause. For example, when Alden Partridge became superintendent of the school, his peculiar and perplexing mixture of competence and ineptness, combined with an alarming dash of quirkiness, kept the academy in almost constant turmoil. Fortunately, the man following Partridge, Sylvanus Thayer, who had been educated at Dartmouth and West Point, provided capable, enlightened leadership—so much so that he came to be known as the "Father of the Military Academy."[24]

Serving as superintendent from 1817 to 1833, Major Thayer shaped the institution for years to come. Without him, or someone of equal stature, West Point probably would have perished. Thirty-two years old when President James Monroe chose him for the job, Thayer traced his military tastes to his boyhood. Fascinated by the American Revolution, and aware of the major role France played as an ally of the United States, the young man developed into an ardent admirer of Napoleon Bonaparte— and apparently all French military achievements. He jumped at the chance, in 1816, to tour Europe for the U.S. Army. There he studied the military schools of France, rightly considered the best in the world, and took in French coastal fortifications. He also sent back French books on military science and engineering for the library at West Point.

Thayer knew his role as superintendent would be a serious challenge. Not only was the school in "a mess and a subject of constant political contention," but also a number of cadets were hostile to any change of leadership, five faculty members were under arrest and the revenge-seeking, ex-superintendent Partridge hoped to undermine Thayer's authority and reputation. Indeed, Partridge proved more than once that he was nothing if not a jealous, petty little man whose only true interest was himself. In spite of myriad problems, Thayer succeeded.[25]

"Thayer's greatest contribution to the Academy," observed historian Stephen Ambrose, "was the system he created, but he was able to introduce that system only through the strength of his own character." Standing staunchly against incompetence and political favoritism, Thayer's academic and disciplinary policies soon became standard practice at the academy. His regime was demanding, as fifteen-hour days were packed with class work, drill and study. The academy's most important courses, in Thayer's judgment, were French, because the truly significant military works had been published in that language, and mathematics, which was indispensable for engineering.

Living conditions were spartan. Cadets slept "on mattresses thrown on the bare floors," with only small fireplaces providing heat. They usually studied while wrapped in blankets. Summer vacations became a luxury of past regimes. Thayer's cadets camped on the Plain during the summer and "learned to be soldiers." Their only visit home, during the entire four years, came after the sophomore year. Quite possibly, "all of the hardships of West Point life," as Ambrose claimed, "paled beside the food." The monotonous fare consisted of boiled potatoes, boiled beef, boiled fish, boiled pudding, stale bread, and black coffee—"uniformly ghastly," according to one cadet.[26]

Despite the demanding, tough existence, the fame of the school increased and applications for admittance grew. The school's critics, however, refused to give up, their voices rising dramatically when Andrew Jackson's Democratic Party won the presidency in 1828. Ambitious, unscrupulous politicians and advocates for the common man cried out against the establishment of a military "aristocracy" for the sons of the wealthy. It was an era when "aristocrat" became regularly employed by Democrats as a political smear, much the same as today's right-wing politicians have demonized the word "liberal." Worse, Jackson himself, who once praised West Point as "the best school in the world," turned against the academy. For reasons not entirely rational, the President came to despise Thayer. For example, Thayer's friendship with John C. Calhoun irritated "Old Hickory," who disliked Calhoun intensely. Ironically, given Jackson's own wielding of arbitrary power, the President once bellowed that "Sylvanus Thayer is a tyrant! The autocrat of all the Russias couldn't exercise more power."[27]

Thayer loved West Point and he enjoyed being the academy's superintendent. He came to realize, though, that with Andrew Jackson, you were either his friend or his enemy, that in the mind of Old Hickory differences often became personal feuds. Fearing his clash with the President might ultimately destroy West Point, Thayer resigned his superintendency in 1833, after Jackson had been elected to a second term. Never again would he return to the academy grounds, not even for a day. But every professor at the school had been appointed by him, and most would remain in their positions for many years, even decades. Sylvanus Thayer was gone, but the system he instituted would endure.[28]

Sherman, like all who matriculated the Point with him, would be the product of a military academy envisioned and implemented by Thayer. Thayer had laid the foundation for a "hallowed venue," as many cadets would come to think of West Point—an institution, eventually, of "legendary figures and legendary deeds."[29] Robert E. Lee had graduated with the class of 1829, finishing second among his mates, but destined to become the first of the school's great military talents.[30] And when the sixteen-year-old Sherman landed on the wharf at West Point in June 1836, the academy gained another cadet whose career one day would elevate him to the front rank of its legendary figures.

Chapter Three

In the Service
of My Country

Stepping off the gangway at West Point, Sherman first saw "a soldier with his dress & sword and slate in his hand." That man recorded the name of every new cadet coming off the *Cornelius Vanderbilt*, afterward instructing the men (for no longer would they be considered "boys") to take "the winding road that mounts to the plain." There Sherman met the adjutant of the military academy, Lieutenant Charles F. Smith. His office was located on the second floor of "a magnificent stone building," observed Sherman, where the young man presented his credentials.[1]

He thought Smith an impressive soldier, an opinion that he never found reason to change. In the decades to come—following thirteen years at West Point, distinguished service in the Mexican War and a stint as commander of the Department of Utah—not a few regular officers came to consider the crusty, square-shouldered Smith the all-around best soldier in the army. As a major general in the Civil War, he would play a leading role at Fort Donelson, commanding a division, and for a while afterward replaced Grant as the army commander. But prior to the Battle of Shiloh, Smith experienced a freakish rowboat accident, and soon succumbed to an infection that today probably could have been easily cured.[2]

From the office of the adjutant, Sherman was directed to the treasurer's office for the purpose of depositing "his *spare cash*"—as the young cadet expressed the mandatory separation from his money. Thenceforth he would receive sixteen dollars per month from the U.S. government, plus an additional twelve dollars per month for rations. All the academy's charges were expected to commence their military schooling on an equal financial footing. Then he was "shown to the Barracks," and along with six other newcomers, "thrust...into a room," not half large enough, and "without a blanket or anything else whereon to lay [one's] head."[3]

Next came an inaugural meeting with the academy superintendent, Colonel Rene E. De Russy, whom Sherman characterized as "Emperor in [these] dominions." Along with several faculty members, Colonel De Russy conducted a preliminary examination, designed to ensure that every young man possessed a fundamental knowledge of reading and arithmetic. Having successfully navigated his prelim, which presented no problem whatsoever, Sherman was then issued "the sum total of a *Plebes* estate," one lamp, one bucket, one broom and two blankets.[4]

Yet another important event of the first day occurred when Sherman, as he later wrote in his memoirs, "became installed as the 'plebe' of my fellow-townsman," William "Bill" Irwin, then entering his third year at the academy. The duty of a plebe, or first-year man, was to serve his upper-class man: to run errands for him, clean his gun and other equipment and generally make himself useful.[5]

"Upper classmen, it seems," observed historians James Lynch and Ronald Bailey, "could not resist ... having a little fun at the expense of the bewildered neophytes. ... Still, there was nothing approaching the ... improper and debasing behavior ... that in later years came to plague the Academy." Cadets of all classes freely associated with one another if they so chose, and since the cadet corps numbered far less than today, many of the men came to know one another well, regardless of their class. This situation contributed to building a tightly knit cadet camaraderie, which most of the men would honor for the remainder of their lives.[6]

After depositing the simple articles of his self-defined *"Plebes* estate" in his assigned room, Sherman experienced a few free moments. Soon, however, he was aroused by "a rattling drum" and a commanding, no-nonsense voice that carried strongly through the barracks: "Turn out

New Cadets!" Rushing down the stairway, Sherman gathered for the first time at the Point with "his comrades for life," as he memorably characterized them, men "from Maine to Louisiana and from Iowa to Florida." They were being summoned to view the evening parade, which Sherman thought an inspiring spectacle. He could "feel the beauty of Military parade and Show—the fine music—the *old* cadets marching by companies, stepping as one man—all forming in line—[hearing] the echo of commands, . . . the roar of the evening gun & seeing the flag fall and the parade dismissed." What followed was not so magnificent. The cadets were "marched to Supper, fared badly," and afterward were "ordered to rise and marched back [to the barracks] to be again incarcerated." His first day at West Point had come to a close.[7]

Although Sherman was only sixteen years old, the minimum age required for admission to West Point (the maximum age being twenty-one), he was physically strong, able to hold his own with the older cadets. He was also a fun-loving young man who found that the school's rules and regulations hampered his style. For years the academy had tolerated an unlimited number of black marks, or demerits for misbehavior. But the system had been altered, and 200 demerits in any year resulted in a cadet's being expelled. In Sherman's eyes the demerit program was a nuisance, involving only minor misconduct; therefore, the accumulation of demerits was of relatively little importance.

In a letter to Senator Ewing, Sherman listed the number of demerits exacted for certain offenses: 1 demerit for soiled clothing (occasionally Sherman would have a grease spot on his trousers from clandestine, nighttime, hash-making in his room), 3 demerits for missing roll call and 8 demerits for absence from drill or parade. Demerits resulted also from such misdemeanors as talking in the ranks, visiting the rooms of other cadets at forbidden times and failing to have one's shoes properly shined. Years later, Sherman declared that his "average demerits, per annum, were about 150." Actually they were not that high, averaging a little under 100 per year. His final year he received 148, which ran up his average. He never came close to the 200 that would have resulted in dismissal. He thought most cadets were "fine fellows up to any kind of devilment or fun which must occasionally be resorted to as the only relief after our arduous duties and studies."[8]

While Sherman relished having a good time, he also demonstrated considerable maturity. Among his classmates, he established a close rapport with Stewart Van Vliet of Vermont and George H. Thomas, a Virginian, ultimately regarded as one of the top Union generals of the Civil War. "That the Vermonter at twenty-one years of age and the Virginian at twenty," observed Sherman's astute biographer Lloyd Lewis, "should have taken the sixteen-year-old Ohio youth as their intimate was evidence that Sherman had matured early." Years later, after the death of Thomas, Sherman spoke of the Virginian as "high-toned" and of "extraordinary courage."[9]

From the beginning, Sherman took to the academic life at West Point, probably the strongest evidence of his early maturity. In one of the first letters he wrote home after arriving at the academy, he expressed a straightforward confidence in his ability to compete scholastically: "From what I have seen of my classmates I have no doubt that I might be among the first." This early self-assurance in both his intellectual potential and his work ethic was no mere braggadocio. Of the 119 young men who entered the Point in Sherman's class, only 42 would survive the four-year ordeal. He would finish sixth in the class of 1840 and, except for demerits reducing his standing, would have ranked fourth. He thus would have qualified as a graduate of honor (meaning one of the first five cadets in his class) and been eligible for the army's elite branch, the Corps of Engineers, had he taken the accumulation of demerits a little more seriously.[10]

When Sherman entered West Point, "the routine of military training and instruction," as he later wrote, was "fully established, and has remained almost the same ever since." The schedule was demanding. The day began at 5:30, as reveille aroused the cadets from their slumber. Quickly they dressed in uncomfortable gray and white uniforms, pulling on trousers that buttoned along the side. (Not until he graduated were the buttons changed to a more practical front position, despite the protests of ladies who thought the new design immodest.)[11]

Breakfast was followed by study, both in and out of class, until broken by lunch at 1:00 p.m. Then came more study, plus drill, followed by a brief respite before supper at six o'clock. After supper, it was back to the books until 10:00 p.m., when taps sounded and lights were to be extinguished. Roll call, inspections and guard duty also got worked into the typical hard day of a cadet, who sometimes felt compelled to study after hours, using a candle for light. Of course he had to somehow hide the light in order to escape detection.[12]

During his days at West Point a few changes did occur, which the cadets generally welcomed. Superintendent De Russy initiated a ball to conclude the summer encampment, a step that Sherman considered quite appropriate. De Russy also took a genuine interest in the academy band and succeeded in improving its quality. Then, when Major Richard Delafield became superintendent in 1838, he allowed the men to sleep on beds instead of on the floor. This, predictably, constituted a very popular adjustment of cadet life. Delafield also replaced candles with oil lamps, another change meeting with widespread approval.[13]

The principal professors while Sherman was at West Point were Dennis Hart Mahan, the legendary engineering instructor; William H. C. Bartlett, professor of natural philosophy (physics), recognized as a national authority on astronomy; J. W. Bailey in chemistry; Albert E. Church in mathematics; Claudius Berard in French; and Sherman's personal favorite, the drawing professor, Robert Walter Weir, who became one of the nation's leading painters.[14]

Weir was a gifted artist who had honed his skills by studying in Florence and Rome. For more than forty years he served as West Point's drawing master, establishing a deserved reputation as one of the most unique and memorable faculty members ever to be associated with the academy. Under Weir's tutelage, Sherman discovered that he had a previously unknown talent for drawing. During his second year, he ranked first in drawing, achieving a perfect score. "I flourish as usual with regard to my studies, especially in drawing," he wrote Phil Ewing, "which is an entirely new thing." Most of his drawings at West Point were of either Greek and Roman warriors or landscapes. His interests in art would broaden. A little over two years after graduation, while stationed at Fort Moultrie, South Carolina, he wrote to Ellen Ewing, who had become his most frequent correspondent during the West Point days, that he had "taken a notion into my head that I could paint."[15]

He described how he went into Charleston and acquired "a full set of artist's equipments, prepared my studio, and without any instructions whatever, have finished a couple of landscapes and faces which they tell me are very good." Declaring that he had developed "a great love for painting," Sherman claimed a near obsessive "fascination" was overwhelming him, which "sometimes . . . amounts to pain to lay down the brush." He wondered if perhaps he should stop painting, "discarding it altogether," before the onset of artistic flair "swallows all of [my] attention, to the neglect of my duties."[16]

While Sherman did well in every subject he studied at West Point, he did find chemistry particularly vexing. Once he wrote Phil Ewing that "I have been cursing for the last month . . . all Chemists that ever did exist." Immediately reconsidering the breadth of such a chastisement, he stated: "I ought not to have included all Chemists for our professor is a perfect Gentleman [who] renders Chemistry as interesting as *possible*." Although the subject may not have been to his liking, he studied diligently and when that school year ended, he ranked sixth in his class in chemistry. "In studies I always held a respectable reputation with the professors," he declared in his memoirs, "and generally ranked among the best, especially in drawing, chemistry, mathematics, and natural philosophy." He well might have included French in his list of achievements. In the final examinations prior to graduation, he scored 96 out of a possible 100 points in both French and drawing.[17]

Sherman recognized his intellectual prowess early on, and took every opportunity to broaden his knowledge. While he clearly came to view himself as a competent military man and engineer, he also took pride in developing a wide-ranging, general fund of information. Whether science, art and law, or dancing, riding and the theater, Sherman's keen mind and abilities ranged across a far-reaching cerebral and physical horizon. Although he did not like the regimen of the Point, speaking of "a monotonous life" in which "we drill and recite all day [and] bone . . . all night," and while he seemingly flaunted the rules more than ever during his senior year, he nevertheless developed a warm feeling for West Point, and for graduates of the academy. In the profession of arms he was experiencing a sense of place, belonging and loyalty. The biographer Basil H. Liddell Hart strikingly and accurately expressed the essence of his character evolution when he wrote: "The germ of soldiering is now in his blood, and never will it loose its hold. All that is spiritual in the West Point tradition has been absorbed into his soul, as into his mind all that is profitable in the West Point education."[18]

Sherman already acknowledged a particular mystique associated with the academy when he wrote to Ellen Ewing in May 1839, conveying his delight in the possibility that she might visit the Point during the coming summer. "Will you ever have a better opportunity? Is not West Point worth visiting? Is not the scenery of the finest order in the world in its vicinity? Are there not incidents in its history that render it dear to us all? I might ask a hundred such questions which any individual who has ever been here would be compelled to answer in the affirmative." A few sentences afterward, he closed with yet more encouragement: "Let me once more advise you to come this summer if you can." Ellen's trip did not materialize, much to Sherman's disappointment. In fact, although her father and her brother Phil went to see him during the final examination week in 1840, Ellen never got to West Point while he was a cadet.[19]

Even more revealing of his strong, positive attitude about the military, and the U.S. Army, was his disapproval of Bill Irwin's plan to quit the army as soon as possible and become a lawyer. Writing to Ellen and speaking "plainly and candidly," Sherman declared: "I would rather be a blacksmith. Indeed, the nearer we come to . . . graduation day, the higher opinion I conceive of the duties and life of an officer of the United States Army, and the more confirmed in the wish of spending my life in the service of my country. Think of that!"[20]

Upon learning, during his final year at West Point, that his younger brother John had decided to study the law, Sherman reacted negatively, almost disdainfully, writing "for my part, it would be my last choice.

Everybody studies law nowadays, and to be a lawyer without being exceedingly eminent—which it is to be hoped you will be some day—is not a sufficient equivalent for their risks and immense study and labor." Sherman proceeded to elaborate upon the satisfaction and security of the military profession. "As soon as I graduate I am entitled by law to a commission in the army, and from my standing in the class to a choice of corps. To be stationed in the east or west, to be in the artillery, infantry, or dragoons, depends entirely on my choice. . . . Whether I remain in the army for life or not . . . one thing is certain—that I will never study another profession." Unquestionably, he had become comfortable with the life of a soldier, in spite of the regimentation at the Point. He firmly believed that he was going to like real soldiering even more, wherever he might be stationed.[21]

In his memoirs, Sherman wrote: "At the Academy, I was not considered a good soldier, for at no time was I selected for any office, but remained a private throughout the whole four years." That statement conveys an element of truth, particularly regarding the impact of demerits, but is basically misleading about how he was regarded by both faculty and cadets. Professor Mahan's summary description of young Sherman is far more satisfactory. He called Sherman "eager, impetuous, restless." He said that if Cadet Sherman was not at work, "he was into mischief. If while explaining something . . . at the blackboard, I heard any . . . disturbance, denoting some fun, I was seldom wrong in turning . . . to Mr. Sherman." But, Mahan continued, "one was more than repaid for any slight annoyance . . . by his irrepressible good nature, and by the clear thought and energy he threw into his work."[22]

Cadets liked Sherman, too. William Starke Rosecrans penned an interesting appraisal of him: "Sherman was two classes above me," wrote Rosecrans, declaring that he was "one of the most popular and brightest fellows in the academy." He remembered him as "a red-headed fellow, who was always prepared for a lark of any kind." Rosecrans praised the "clandestine midnight feasts, at which Sherman usually made the hash. He was considered the best hash-maker at West Point, and this, in our day, was a great honor."

Remarking that the food given the cadets "was cheap and poor," Rose-crans then stated: "I sometimes think that the only meals we relished were our midnight hash lunches." He related how "Old Cump" would mash the potatoes, "mixing them with pepper, salt, and butter in such a way as to make the most appetizing dish. This he would cook in a stew-pan over the fire—we had grates in those days—and when it was done we would eat it sizzling hot on our bread, which we had toasted." Occa-sionally a cadet might manage to appropriate a particular delicacy as his contribution to the stew, with perhaps nothing being prized so much as oysters. As the cadets relished their late-night repast, Rosecrans said, "we would tell stories and have a jolly good time; and Sherman was one of the best story tellers of the lot." Also, noted Rosecrans, he "was one of those fellows who used to go down to Benny Havens's of the dark night at the risk of expulsion to eat oysters and have a good time."[23]

Back in 1824, a genial Irishman named Benny Havens had opened a tavern on the bank of the Hudson River, in Buttermilk Falls, which lay about a mile and a half south of West Point. Described in a bicentennial history of the U.S. Military Academy as "an instant success," the estab-lishment specialized "in buckwheat cakes and flips, and serving a wide variety of spirituous liquors. It was, of course, off limits to cadets, who formed nonetheless a large percentage of its customers." Indeed, from 1826 onward, by decree of then Superintendent Thayer, cadets were for-bidden all liquor at all times.

From the moment of Thayer's order, which constituted a bowing to the era's powerful temperance advocates, many a cadet's thirst for illegal liquid mounted remarkably. Simultaneously, Benny Havens's tavern prospered. Enticing the Point's young men like an enchanting Greek siren, the Havens public house would be in operation long after the Civil War. Benny and his wife occasionally even ran liquor to cadets at the academy. When their actions were discovered by the authorities, the Havenses thenceforth enjoyed "a unique honor of being the only two American citizens forbidden to set foot on the post of West Point."[24]

When Sherman arrived at the academy, the Havens tavern was already an institution of renown, well on its way to becoming, as one writer expressed it, "the most famous establishment in all West Point history, honored by song, story and hundreds of cadet visitors." One reason for Sherman's great reputation as a hash-maker was that he occasionally acquired food from Benny's, smuggled it back to his room and mixed it into his stew. Benny himself proved easy to deal with, willing to barter for a blanket, a candle or some other item if a cadet did not have cash available. Despite his friend Bill Irwin's being caught at Benny's and court-martialed, Sherman would not be deterred, continuing to seek the good food and drink of the legendary establishment. Irwin was soon reinstated, a not unusual occurrence—unless West Point sought to expel a young man for reasons other than visiting Benny's.[25]

During Sherman's academy years, he crossed paths with a number of cadets who became famous during the Civil War. Among his own classmates, none would become more prominent, with the exception of Sherman himself, than George H. Thomas, the general deservedly remembered as "the Rock of Chickamauga." Stewart Van Vliet would serve throughout the Civil War, although never approaching the stature of Sherman or Thomas. Sherman enjoyed a lifelong friendship with Van Vliet. Graduating first in Sherman's class was Paul O. Hebert, from Louisiana, who worked for a time as assistant professor of engineering at West Point. He fought in the war with Mexico, being breveted a colonel for "Gallant and Meritorious Conduct in the Battle of Molino Del Rey." Afterward, he became the governor of Louisiana.[26]

When the Civil War erupted, Hebert joined the Confederacy. In fact, several of Sherman's classmates became prominent in the Confederate Army, including Richard S. Ewell, Bushrod R. Johnson, Thomas Jordan and John P. McCown. Another classmate Sherman recalled vividly was a fellow Ohioan, Job R. H. Lancaster, six feet five inches tall "in his stockings," according to Sherman, with shoulders that measured "a yard across." Lancaster weighed a solid 260 pounds and was said never to have been exposed to a math book before arriving at the Point. Nevertheless, he graduated seventh in the class, only to die the next year while serving in the Seminole Wars, struck by lightning near Crystal River, Florida.[27]

Among those completing their final year at the Point while Sherman experienced his first were Joseph Hooker, whom Sherman never liked (and the feeling seemed to be mutual), John Sedgwick, Jubal Early, John C. Pemberton and the most notable future Confederate general in the class—the enigmatic Braxton Bragg of North Carolina. Other notable cadets in the classes ahead of Cump included Union generals-to-be Henry W. Halleck, Edward O. C. Ord and Irvin McDowell. Casting their fortunes with the Confederacy would be William J. Hardee, as well as the Creole with the grand and delightful name Pierre Gustav Toutant Beauregard.

Matriculating in the classes behind Sherman were such future Union officers as Don Carlos Buell, Nathaniel Lyon, John Pope, John F. Reynolds, William S. Rosecrans and Julius P. Garesche. Garesche would serve as assistant adjutant general (chief of staff) to Rosecrans at the Battle of Stones River, having long believed that he would be killed in his first battle. In a gory episode, he was decapitated by a cannonball that narrowly missed Rosecrans. Stephen D. Carpenter, a member of Sherman's class, would also be killed at Stones River.

In Sherman's final year at the Point, among the plebes was a young fellow named Ulysses S. Grant, who was called "Sam." There was nothing about Grant's appearance that caused the average person to remember him. He said very little to anybody, and Sherman later acknowledged that he hardly noticed Grant. Regardless of his unlikely appearance and demeanor, Grant, like Sherman, would rise to the top of West Point's legendary graduates.[28]

During the summer of 1837, Sherman enjoyed a brief furlough. Since the time was too short for a trip to Ohio, he headed for New York, once again visiting Charles Hoyt, his mother's brother. Exploring the intriguing city proved a wonderful break after the restrictive atmosphere of West Point. The museums, the gardens, the parks, the navy yards, vied for his attention. Above all, in the mind of young Sherman, towered the theater. As for New York City itself, he unabashedly declared that he was "in love with the place."[29]

Returning to the Point for the commencement of his second year,

Sherman soon got off an interesting letter to thirteen-year-old Ellen Ewing, whom he once described as "my best Lancaster correspondent" during his cadet years. She had sent him some candy which "was so very good" that he invited some of his friends "to come and taste it." Alas, they so relished the taste that "they put it beyond my power (although very desirous to do so) to reserve some for the next day." Then he gave Ellen a glowing description of the newly instituted military ball.

"A great many ladies [were] in attendance," he wrote, and the room "was decorated in true military style; the walls were literally covered with burnished sabres and bayonets, as well as with wreaths and flags." The ball was certainly a grand affair, but what most accorded with Sherman's taste was the all-male, "royal 'stag dance.' . . . I think I never saw the encampment so enlivening. There were about 150 cadets dancing before a double row of candles and a great many ladies and gentlemen looking on." He delighted in energetic dancing and singing with the other cadets—some males leading, while others danced the woman's role. The ritual embodied camaraderie, and it would last well into the twentieth century. Sherman always liked to dance, and increasingly enjoyed the company of women who loved dancing.

He closed the letter to his foster sister with a reference to the demanding studies that lay ahead of him "until next June, when I expect to have the extreme pleasure of visiting Lancaster." Sherman's second year at the academy went well. Academically he continued to perform admirably, improving his scores in French, mathematics, and drawing (ranking number one in drawing, as previously noted), while raising his overall class rank from ninth to sixth, and keeping his demerits under fifty. The latter constituted a notable achievement. A week into December, he penned a letter to his brother John, revealing his Christmas plans.[30]

"Preparation for the Christmas spree is now all the go. I have joined in with about a dozen others and laid the foundation for a very good dinner costing about three dollars apiece." Yet he realized the meal would lack some prized ingredients. "I wish we could get ahold of some of our western turkeys, chickens, and the like, which cannot be obtained here except at an enormous price, and as money is something to us like

teeth, we are obliged to go without." He also noted the unusually warm
weather. "Winter seems to be very reluctant about setting in," he wrote.
"This time last winter, the river was closed [frozen over], and we had fine
skating, but no doubt it will soon set in with a vengeance, giving us our
full share of north winds." Obviously the cadets were hard-pressed to
find recreational activities to counter the dull routine of their academic
life and unappetizing food. Even horsemanship—which one might suppose a natural course at a military academy in Sherman's day, when officers rode horses and cavalry played an important role in battle—would
not be introduced until 1839.[31]

By early spring of 1838, Sherman and his classmates were, as he
phrased it, "feeding on the anticipations of a fine furlough." They looked
forward, he wrote Phil Ewing, to the "good dinners they shall enjoy
... the balls, dances, parties, etc. ...—in a word they expect all kinds of
pleasures and not one of pain." Parties, food and girls were much on
Sherman's mind. Perhaps, after two years of essentially austere living,
Sherman expected too much of his "fine furlough." The two-month
break from study and drill, and the opportunities to enjoy good food
were surely welcome, but all in all, the Ohio visit proved less rewarding
than anticipated.[32]

Dividing time between the Shermans and the Ewings, Sherman traversed the state during his vacation. In addition to Lancaster, he spent
time in Cincinnati, Dayton, Columbus, Oxford, Mansfield and San-
dusky. For the first time, he met his father's brother, Daniel Sherman, "a
very fine old man, but," he afterward told his younger brother John, "I
do not think he resembles father (if you recollect him)." In Columbus, he
visited Thomas Ewing, who was again practicing law, after the state legislature did not reelect him to the U.S. Senate. Ellen Ewing, then fourteen, who had not seen Sherman in two years, seemed quite impressed
by his appearance, struck by how Cump's "training at West Point had
developed him physically; how straight and strong he was, how clear
and bright-eyed, and what ... pride ... in his bearing." He looked "very
grand" in his uniform.[33]

Before returning to West Point, Sherman stopped at Buffalo to visit

Niagara Falls, which he said "far surpassed anything my imagination had pictured from its description." He relished another visit, although briefly, to New York City. While enjoying again the time spent with his mother's relatives, and the charms of the city, he seemed to be a bit taken aback when he chanced to run into a former resident of Lancaster, who having deserted his family, had "a great big whore (I expect) on his arm." Sherman reported to Phil Ewing, "I left him as soon as common politeness would admit." Arriving back at West Point, Sherman was becoming, for his age and day, a well-traveled young man. All his life he would seek opportunities to visit new places.[34]

During 1839 a tense situation developed between the United States and Great Britain over the boundary line separating Maine and New Brunswick. Many Americans, harking back to the Revolutionary War and the War of 1812, looked upon Great Britain as their young nation's hereditary enemy. Trouble had flared in 1837, when hundreds of Americans supported a short-lived Canadian insurrection against Britain. Then, two years later, lumberjacks from Maine and Canada disputed the national ownership of the timber-rich valley of the Aroostook River. Their clash also involved a British plan to build a road, for strategic purposes in the event of war, from Halifax to Quebec; a road projected to pass through the territory in question. The so-called Aroostook War just might widen into a full-scale conflict. Sherman kept abreast of the issues, reading the *National Gazette*, as well as newspapers sent to him from Lancaster.[35]

In a letter dated March 10, 1839, he wrote Ellen, "All the talk in this part of the world now is about war with England. Every person seems anxious for it and none more so than the very persons who would most suffer by it, the officers of the army and the corps of cadets." Should war break out, "we would be commissioned and sent into the 'field'—at all times preferable to studying mathematics or philosophy, and it would undoubtedly prove a better school for the soldier than this." But Sherman did not believe the conflict likely. "I cannot think that England," he wrote, "will take the same stand in this controversy that her colony has done. If, however, she does, war will be inevitable." A month later, in a letter to John Sherman, he again addressed the border issue. "I presume you have heard of these Maine difficulties before now. . . . For my part, there is no nation that I would prefer being at variance with than the British, in this case more especially as our cause is plainly right and just." In another letter, apparently with a dash at military humor, he said that "books are thrown in the corner, and broadswords and foils supply their place. Such lunging, cutting and slashing—enough to dispose of at least a thousand British a day."[36]

Certainly the passions of some Americans had been deeply aroused against Great Britain and once again, as in the War of 1812, eager expansionists dreamed of annexing the vast Canadian territory. But Sherman was right in thinking that Britain would not fight a third war with the United States in order merely to support the prideful stance of her colony. Eventually then, the Maine–New Brunswick boundary question and a few other disputed matters between the United States and the United Kingdom were peacefully and satisfactorily settled through the amicable negotiations of Daniel Webster and Lord Alexander Ashburton.[37]

WHEN SHERMAN ENTERED his senior year at West Point, and could see the goal of all his efforts drawing near, his attitude toward a military career seemed ever more positive. In camp, he delighted in having a plebe at his call, "whom I made, of course, tend to a plebe's duty, . . . bringing water, policing the tent, cleaning my gun, and accouterments, and the like." He repaid the plebe with "the usual and cheap coin—advice." As for his studies, Sherman seemed very comfortable during his last year at the Point, and his grades again were high. The fact that he accumulated more demerits than in any previous year indicates, perhaps, an impatience to get on with "real" soldiering, and the development of a superior attitude. There is no doubt that Sherman believed he had gained a prized education and was about to take his place among a very special, prestigious group of men, as an officer of the United States Army.[38]

His letters reveal that he was giving a lot of thought to where he would first serve after graduation. To his mother he wrote that his number one choice, barring an outbreak of war with England, would be the Fifth Infantry Regiment, "because it is stationed on the north-west frontier, a country which I have always felt a strong inclination to see." Furthermore, Sherman thought it likely that "the Indians will break out again, in which case I should have an opportunity of seeing some active service." However, if war with Great Britain should erupt, he preferred service with the artillery, because "it is stationed east of the mountains, which would be the seat of war." Obviously he hoped for a taste of combat, as the path to military promotion. He also nurtured a young man's enchantment with the alleged glory and fame of warfare.[39]

As the day of graduation from West Point approached, Sherman must have found the attitude of the Ewings disconcerting. They advised him to resign from the army after graduation and take up the law, engineering or some other profession. Apparently, as they saw the matter, his West Point education should be nothing more than a stepping-stone to a civilian career. He was being asked to turn his back upon the army, the institution that had given him significant direction, an establishment that would provide a regular salary, enabling him to support both himself and his mother and never again have to call upon anyone for financial assistance. Little wonder that in revealing to Ellen Ewing his hope of service with the infantry, he wrote that it was in order to be assigned "in the Far West, out of the reach of what is termed *civilization*."[40]

Sherman graduated from West Point in June 1840. With justifiable pride in his excellent record, a satisfying camaraderie as a USMA alumnus and the anticipation of a significant career "in the service of my country," the day must have been a happy occasion. Yet, at the same time, he likely experienced a degree of disappointment and even frustration, knowing that Thomas Ewing, whose influence had placed him at the Point, really wanted him now to reject the army. Although both Ewing and his son Phil were present at West Point for Cump's great day, he knew they were engaged in a campaign tour on behalf of William Henry Harrison, the Whig candidate for the presidency. Perhaps he wondered if they otherwise would have made the long trip to West Point. Probably most disappointing, Ellen Ewing, Sherman's faithful and constant correspondent, was not at hand for his triumphal celebration, thus never visiting him during the four years that had become the most important period in shaping his life.

As Sherman and his classmates anticipated the future, the Civil War lay twenty-one years ahead of them. Beyond doubt, those two decades proved disappointing for several of the men. In fact, fourteen of the class, fully one-third of those who graduated in 1840, would already be dead when the Civil War began. Two were killed fighting in the Mexican War, and another died in Mexico during that conflict. Four members of the class died in accidents, and still others from natural causes. One man, William Torrey, simply disappeared, last heard from in 1845 in Venice, on his way to Constantinople to seek military service under the sultan.[41]

Sherman himself would find those twenty-one years after West Point increasingly hard and, for the most part, unrewarding. Ultimately, of course, the Civil War would change all that, as if the stars of destiny had fallen upon him at long last. He would rise to become the most successful and famous of his academy classmates—indeed, one of the great soldiers in American military history.

Chapter Four

SAND AND SUN, SEMINOLES AND SPANIARDS

When Sherman graduated from the United States Military Academy in the summer of 1840, the nation was passionately engaged in a shameful presidential campaign—arguably the most asinine election in American history. The Whig Party, meeting at Harrisburg, Pennsylvania, in December 1839, had gotten an early start on their mission of unseating the incumbent president, New Yorker Martin Van Buren. Perennial candidate Henry Clay of Kentucky fully expected to be the party's standard-bearer and did lead the field of candidates on the first ballot. But the raucous Whigs, taking a cue from the recent success of the Jacksonian Democrats, turned instead to a military hero. William Henry Harrison, who had claimed victory against a force of attacking Indians at the Battle of Tippecanoe, in 1811, gained the nomination.

The Whigs published no platform, content merely to pummel Van Buren and the Democrats, blaming them for the economic depression that had plagued the country during the past four years. When John Tyler of Virginia was nominated for vice president, someone devised the catchy slogan "Tippecanoe and Tyler too." Silly elaboration quickly followed:

Tippecanoe and Tyler too, Tippecanoe and Tyler too,
   And with them we'll beat little Van, Van, Van,
Oh, Van is a used-up man.

Thus began an increasingly embarrassing contest for the nation's highest political office. All who valued sensible government surely must have cringed as the level of campaigning went rapidly downhill once the *Baltimore Republican*, a Democratic newspaper, unwittingly presented the Whigs with a rousing election theme. The paper declared that General Harrison, "upon condition of . . . receiving a pension of $2,000 and a barrel of cider," would doubtless withdraw "all pretensions" to the presidency "and spend his days in a log cabin on the banks of the Ohio."

At once seizing the initiative, the Whigs rambunctiously propagandized, deviously extolling their hero-general as a man of the people. It was not the "spin" that the paper's editor had in mind. Absurdities escalated and lies abounded as the Whigs vigorously rode the "log cabin and hard cider" theme. Never mind that Harrison came from one of the first families of Virginia, resided in a spacious home bearing no resemblance to a log cabin and never showed any preference for hard cider—or that President Van Buren actually rose from humble origins.[1]

Facts became irrelevant as the gurus of presidential hoopla demonstrated their genius for the ridiculous, perhaps matched only by their disdain for the truth. Little log cabins were placed on wheels and rolled through the streets at rallies where cider flowed freely to quench the thirst of the common man. Even Thomas Ewing, stump speaking for General Harrison, addressed several thousand Whigs in New York City, as his son Phil reported, "at the dedication of a *log cabin* in the heart of the city." Oratorical demagoguery smeared Van Buren as a despicable aristocrat living in incredible luxury at the White House "Palace," while rhymesters continued their unscrupulous, goofy work:

> *Let Van from his coolers of silver drink wine,*
> *And lounge on his cushioned settee;*
> *Our man on his buckeye bench can recline,*
> *Content with hard cider is he!*[2]

Democratic Vice President Richard Johnson of Kentucky attempted to offset the propagandistic prowess of General Harrison as an Indian fighter. He claimed, as earlier noted, to have killed the legendary Tecumseh at the Battle of the Thames in 1813. Johnson delighted in relating his version of Tecumseh's fate and proudly exhibited a bloodstained shirt, said to have been stripped from the chieftain's dead body. This story inspired perhaps the most irrelevant and idiotic ditty of the entire campaign:

Rumpsy dumpsy, Rumpsy dumpsy,
Colonel Johnson killed Tecumseh.[3]

The bustling, crude election, won by the hero of Tippecanoe, clearly proved that mass political parties were firmly entrenched upon the American scene. Nearly seven times as many voters turned out in 1840 as in 1824. Some observers declared the development a positive good for the country. This was, they proclaimed, electioneering at its best in a vigorous young country.[4]

But such fiery political conflict did not set well with Sherman. While he knew that he could not change what was happening, he did not have to like it—and he didn't. As Lloyd Lewis pertinently observed, he "shrank from the shambles." Already disenchanted with politics, the 1840 election served as confirmation of the twenty-year-old's serious concerns for the future of the nation's government. The "log cabin and hard cider" campaign, again quoting Lewis's memorable words, "completed the aristocratic work of West Point." Sherman's distrust of the American political landscape hardened in the following months and years.[5]

To Ellen he declared that "the people are fickle in the extreme, varying from one party to the other without rhyme or reason." The squabbling of the parties themselves reminded him of a struggle "between two greedy pelicans quarreling over a dead fish." When John Tyler succeeded to the presidency upon the sudden death of Harrison, and twice vetoed congressional bills to reestablish a second Bank of the United States, he became a traitor, in the eyes of many Whigs, to the party's principles. Four members of the cabinet resigned in protest, including Secretary of the Treasury Thomas Ewing, and some Whig supporters burned the President in effigy. To Sherman such action was reprehensible—"a disgrace to Washington that the President should be insulted in his own house and burned in effigy in the face of the whole city." Fervently he declared his hope that the perpetrators would be "held up to the contempt of the world."[6]

Politics was fundamentally an unsavory business, as Sherman viewed the matter, and he wanted no part of it. Typically he spoke of the political scene only with a pronounced disdain. "What the devil are you doing?" he blurted, demanding an explanation of his younger brother John in 1844, when he learned that John had been speaking on behalf of Henry Clay's presidential campaign against the Tennessee Democrat James K. Polk. "Stump speaking?" he inquired incredulously. "I really thought you were too decent for that." He continued that he thought John "at least" possessed "sufficient pride not to humble and cringe to beg for party or popular favor." John was not to be dissuaded from pursuing a political career, just as Sherman had no intention of turning away from his life in the U.S. Army. Sherman's negative, scornful attitude toward politics was firmly established by the time that the rambunctious mendacity of the 1840 campaign ground to a conclusion—if not before. He would never change. Not even decades later, when he knew that he probably could be the nation's president if he so desired.[7]

A CUSTOMARY THREE-MONTH furlough followed Sherman's graduation from West Point. After calling on fifteen-year-old Ellen, who for the last two years had been a student at the Convent of the Visitation in Washington, he headed to Ohio. There he visited with family and friends while awaiting his assignment in the regular army. Most of the time in Lancaster was spent at his mother's house. Up the street at the Ewing household, visitors were coming and going that summer, many of them politicians working on William Henry Harrison's presidential campaign. Harrison himself visited the Ewing home at least once and, as earlier noted, Thomas Ewing would be tapped as the triumphant Harrison's secretary of the treasury.[8]

Spending the majority of his furlough in either Lancaster or Mansfield, Sherman "in due season," as he quaintly expressed it, was appointed and commissioned second lieutenant of Third Artillery, Company A. He would be serving in Florida and was ordered to report at Fort Columbus, on Governors Island in New York harbor, at the end of September. Sherman seemed fully ready to get on with his military career. He wrote of having "a natural curiosity to see strange places and peoples, both of which exist in Florida." The prospect of soon being involved in the U.S. Army's long, frustrating war against the Seminole Indians did not disturb him. But first, leaving Ohio a little earlier than otherwise necessary, Sherman journeyed to western New York and again took in the spectacular sight of Niagara Falls, before returning to West Point.[9]

The trip to West Point, from which he had been away less than three months, is significant. He had found the camaraderie of the academy deeply satisfying, and becoming an officer of the U.S. Army proved equally fulfilling. While he never liked the academy's regimentation, and was happy to be removed from that aspect of the experience, he was proud to be a graduate of West Point. For as long as he lived, he made periodic journeys, almost like pilgrimages, back to the Point. For Sherman, it was as if West Point had become a hallowed place.

Perhaps not surprisingly, and in a sense fittingly, he violated an academy regulation during his brief visit. He spent a half hour or more talking with some of his friends in the barracks during their study time, which constituted a breach of the rules. He thought—or at least he professed—that his new status as a second lieutenant exempted him from the regulation. Upon the academy's discovery that he had visited cadets during study hours, he was ordered to Fort Columbus under recommendation that he be court-martialed.

He managed to write his way out of the problem, apologizing to Superintendent Delafield. "I can only say that I had no intention of openly setting the regulations at defiance," he stated. "In fact," claimed Sherman, "I do not think I thought of rules at all, but acted in accordance with my feelings, which prompted me to do a . . . friendly act, bid my friends a farewell upon parting with them, some perhaps forever." He had struck the right note with Delafield. (Or possibly Delafield feared Thomas Ewing might intervene on Sherman's behalf if he pursued the matter.) The superintendent recommended that Sherman be restored to duty and Secretary of War Joel R. Poinsett dropped the charges against the newly commissioned second lieutenant.[10]

Thus, in early October 1840, Sherman sailed first for Savannah, Georgia, where "we transferred to a small steamer and proceeded by the inland route to St. Augustine, Florida." The "we" of which he spoke, in addition to a company of army recruits, included a dog, "a most beautiful black pointer" that he had taken along for companionship. Soon he boarded a steamer called the *William Gaston*, which took him still farther down the east coast of Florida, finally arriving off the bar of the Indian River, where the little vessel anchored.[11]

Transferring to a whaleboat with a crew of four, "steered by a character of some note, known as the Pilot Ashlock," Sherman recalled that they were "carried through the surf over the bar, into the mouth of Indian River Inlet." Darkness was upon them, as they changed to a still smaller boat, which Ashlock guided through a channel in the midst of mangrove islands. It was the roosting place of thousands of pelicans, which "rose in clouds and circled above our heads." The scene was vividly memorable, for "the water below was alive with fish, whose course through it could be seen by the phosphoric wake." Emerging into a broad lagoon, the lights of Fort Pierce came into view as Ashlock steered the vessel to a small wharf.[12]

Sherman had arrived at his first army post. The twenty-year-old had never seen anything like Florida. The entire peninsula was "one mass of sand," he told his brother. "It is cut up by innumerable rivers, streams, and rivulets, which, watering the soil, nourish a rank growth of weeds and grass." These were continually decomposing, and producing a very rich soil, resulting over time in "a heavy growth of live oak, palmetto, and scrub of every kind." This widespread, thick growth composed "the dreaded hummocks, the stronghold of the Indians."

Sherman explained that in the hummocks the Seminole built his hut, and grew his corn and pumpkins, while the numerous streams provided an abundance of fish and alligators, and the palmetto its cabbage. Thus the Indian, he declared, "conceals his little fire and hut, secures his escape, [is enabled] to creep within a few yards of the deer or turkey feeding on the border, and drive his copper-headed, barbed arrow through the vital part. In a word," he concluded, "the deep streams, bordered by the dense hummock, have enabled the Indians thus far to elude the pursuit of our army." His succinct summation of the army's problems with the Florida Indians would be difficult to surpass.[13]

After several months of service in Florida, Sherman thought that the Seminole warfare was the kind of fight "which every young officer should be thoroughly acquainted with, as the Indian is most likely to be our chief enemy in times to come." Obviously the young lieutenant could not then foresee the coming of the Civil War, nor even the much nearer at hand clash with Mexico. He was right, however, in concluding that in the future the U.S. Army would experience a long struggle against Native Americans, although he likely had little concept of the major role he himself would play in those engagements.[14]

As Sherman observed the stealthy, guerrilla-like Seminole warriors, he realized the tactics required to defeat them. They would never fight in Napoleonic style, and they were difficult to kill or capture. But if the army struck at their spirit and broke down their morale, Sherman believed they eventually would be overcome. The winning strategy—and Sherman was impressed by Colonel William J. Worth's policy at the time—required raiding Seminole villages, burning their huts and destroying their corn. If the army attacked the Indian ruthlessly, smashing his supplies, undermining his very way of life—and year round, even during the stifling summer—Sherman believed they could not endure. His concept of fighting Native Americans resurfaced with a vengeance, during the Civil War, at the expense of the Confederacy.[15]

Much later, less than a decade before his death, Sherman made a very interesting comment about the Indians and Florida. "Indeed Florida was the Indian's paradise," he wrote. He observed that the territory "was of little value to us, and it was a great pity to remove the Seminoles at all, for we could have collected there all the Choctaws, Creeks, Cherokees, and Chickasaws, in addition to the Seminoles." He believed that the Indians "would have thrived in the Peninsula, whereas they now occupy lands that are very valuable, . . . coveted by their white neighbors on all sides." As for Florida's worth to the whites, he thought there was little to recommend the place.[16]

When Sherman arrived at Fort Pierce, the small-scale but awful guerrilla war against the Seminoles had been dragging on for years. Officially lasting six years, the conflict "in ugly incidents" continued even longer. "At that time . . . the war consisted in hunting up and securing the small fragments [of the scattered Indians]," Sherman wrote. The captives were then "sent to join . . . their tribe of Seminoles already established in the Indian Territory west of Arkansas." Known as the Second Seminole War—the first involved Andrew Jackson's 1818 foray, when he captured Spanish Pensacola and claimed West Florida for the United States—this struggle had begun before Sherman ever entered West Point. Most of the military victories in the war (and many encounters proved indecisive) were gained by the Seminoles with hit-and-run tactics. When the Indians lost their great leader Osceola, captured through trickery at a supposed peace council in 1837, other chiefs rose to the challenge, continuing a bitter resistance against being shipped westward to the Indian Territory. The U.S. Army sent more and more troops against them, and the Seminoles retreated deeper and deeper into the Florida jungles and swamps. Ultimately about three thousand Indians were forced westward, but the war grew ever more costly. Soldiers died of disease, as well as at the hands of the defiant Indian marauding parties and ambushes.[17]

The conflict entailed an intermittent type of struggle that sometimes involved lengthy periods of relative inactivity. During the stifling heat and heavy humidity of the long summer, the army customarily did not campaign. When Sherman began his tour of duty, he encountered a pronounced lull in army activities, providing an opportunity at once to acquaint himself with new and nonmilitary pursuits. Sherman adapted readily to his novel surroundings, particularly becoming friendly with "the Pilot Ashlock," whom he praised as "the best fisherman I ever saw." Soon Ashlock initiated him "into the mysteries of shark-spearing, trolling for red fish, and taking the sheep's-head and mullet." There were also nets for catching green turtles, of which he said that "an ample supply" was always on hand. Sherman relished seafood and took full advantage of Florida's offerings. "I do not recall in my whole experience," he later declared, "a spot on earth where fish, oysters, and green turtles so abound as at Fort Pierce, Florida."[18]

He seemed to thrive on living "in a most primitive style," as he described his Florida existence. The sun was hot, but often there was a breeze. He enjoyed good health, managing to escape malaria and other ailments which often afflicted the men in that tropical climate. Although he tended to dislike most of Florida's white settlers, as well as the militia, he was fascinated that they "boast of the largest rattlesnakes, alligators, sharks ... cranes and pelicans on the coast." He himself decorated his cabin with seashells, feathers and wings of birds, the head and teeth of a shark and the skin of a rattlesnake. He also enjoyed having various animals around. In addition to a fawn that slept in his bedroom, he wrote: "I've got more pets now than any bachelor in the country—innumerable chickens, tame pigeons, white rabbits and a full-blood Indian pony— rather small matters for a man to deal with ... but it is far better to spend time in trifles such as these than drinking and gambling." A young officer who met Sherman for the first time during those Florida days depicted him as "thin and spare, but ... cheerful, loquacious, active and communicative to an extraordinary degree." Sherman was cheered by the early arrival of Stewart Van Vliet, his former classmate and good friend from West Point, who came with a detachment of troops to strengthen the post. Eventually George H. Thomas would also serve with Sherman in Florida, as well as Edward O. C. Ord.[19]

Although Sherman actually had little confidence in the strength of Fort Pierce to withstand a major assault by the Seminoles, he professed not to be worried. "If the Indians were to take a notion on a very dark night to pounce upon us we might get the worst of it," he confided to Phil Ewing, "but we rely upon their cowardice." Even after the initial charms of his Florida service wore thin, Sherman had no patience with soldiers who failed to adjust as well as he, and wanted to leave. Speaking of those who "have demanded to be relieved from duty in Florida," he declared that "an absurdity." Stating that he himself had made up his mind "to stay here until the end of the war," he also acknowledged that "when that will be God only knows." In truth, he wondered whether the war with the Seminoles would ever be over, but he believed he could soldier with any man, and he took his duty as an officer quite seriously.[20]

Sherman could be tough, both on himself and those under his command. Unfortunately, he made a grievous error of judgment soon after arriving in Florida, one that resulted in a soldier's death. He agreed to shoulder the responsibilities of the post doctor while the doctor took a short leave. At morning sick call, Sherman thought a soldier merely faked illness and ordered the regimental sergeant to run the alleged pretender around the fort. The man collapsed and died. In his memoirs, Sherman made no mention of the man's death.[21]

He did relate the striking circumstances of another soldier's murder. The man was a sergeant and a formidable Indian fighter. On an expedition searching for Indians, during which a clash occurred with nearly fifty Seminoles, according to Sherman's account, the sergeant "was said to have dispatched three warriors." Taking the scalp of one of his victims, the triumphant soldier brought it back as a trophy. Sherman said the man "was so elated that . . . he had to celebrate his victory by a big drunk." Perhaps he celebrated in another manner as well.

The wife of one of the post soldiers, who cooked for the garrison, "was somewhat of a flirt," declared Sherman, "and rather fond of admiration." The sergeant, unfortunately for his well-being, had become attracted to the woman. As Sherman described the affair, he "hung around the mess-house more than the husband fancied." The husband, "a poor weakly soldier," in Sherman's estimate, reported the circumstances to the post commander, who reprimanded the sergeant for his behavior. Evidently the officer's words proved of little consequence.

Within a few days the woman's husband again approached the sergeant's commanding officer, once more appealing for his assistance. With a flurry of ill-advised words, and demonstrating a deplorable lack of judgment (although in fairness he probably never anticipated what followed), the officer snapped, as Sherman remembered, "Haven't you got a musket? Can't you defend your own family?" The man walked out and within a very short interval the report of a gun was heard near the mess-house, the irate husband having wasted no time in seizing a musket and inflicting a mortal wound upon his wife's admirer.

The law and army regulations specified that the accused murderer be turned over to the nearest civil court, which convened in St. Augustine. Among the witnesses summoned to St. Augustine for the murder trial was Sherman's fishing tutor, the Pilot Ashlock. Some weeks later, having given his testimony at the trial, Ashlock returned to Indian River in memorable fashion, accompanied by "a very handsome woman," in Sherman's judgment. He thought she "was probably eighteen or twenty years old." Ashlock had "availed himself of the chance to take a wife to share with him the solitude of his desolate hut on the beach at the Indian River."

Also with Ashlock and his new bride was the woman's younger sister, "a very pretty little Minorcan girl of about fourteen years of age." First bringing ashore his wife, her sister, their chests of clothes and possessions, and the mail for the fort, Ashlock then left them on the beach near his hut, while he returned to the steamer that had transported them from St. Augustine. Waiting on board the vessel were several soldiers whom Ashlock needed to carry ashore in his whaleboat. All of this Sherman observed because, as acting quartermaster, and informed by the sentinel on the roof of the fort that the smoke of a steamer could be seen approaching, he had headed to the beach to get the incoming mail—an event always eagerly anticipated. It was the last time he saw Ashlock alive, disaster striking as the pilot and eight or ten soldiers tried to make their way over the bar of the Indian River. Sherman explained that "a heavy breaker upset the boat" while the vessel was crossing the bar, "and all were lost except the boy who pulled the boat-oar." The lad, assisted by a rope, somehow managed to hold on to the boat, drifting with it outside the breakers, "and was finally beached near a mile down the coast."

Ashlock's new bride, having watched in helpless horror as her husband and the others apparently "perished amid the sharks and the waves," nevertheless clung to a slim hope that somehow Ashlock might have survived. "Strange to say," recalled Sherman, the pilot "could not swim, although he had been employed on the water all his life." The distraught young woman sat slumped on her chest of clothes, weeping, while her sister continued crying out, appealing for "a miracle" (Sherman's words). "All I could do," he declared, was "take the two disconsolate females up to the fort, and give them the use of my own quarters."

The next morning Sherman returned to the beach, accompanied by Ord, where they found two bodies washed ashore, "torn all to pieces by the sharks, which literally swarmed the inlet at every new tide." When at last the weather somewhat moderated, Sherman said he took a crew of soldiers in a whaleboat and ventured over "that terrible bar," and boarded the steamer, which lay anchored about a mile offshore. There he learned definitively that Ashlock, and all with him excepting the one young boy, had perished. In fact, when the captain of the steamer had dispatched three men in one of his own boats, attempting to rescue Ashlock and the others, the deadly surf had claimed two more lives. Likewise upset in the heavy breakers, only one of the men managed to escape the sharks and successfully battle his way to safety beyond the churning water.

"This sad and fatal catastrophe made us all *afraid* of that bar"—a statement with which, presumably, no reasonable person would quibble. In returning to the shore after his visit with the steamer's captain, Sherman decided against recrossing the treacherous barrier, "adopting the more prudent course of beaching the boat below the inlet, which insured us a good ducking," but clearly entailed less risk to their lives. Afterward he somberly bore to the young widow "the absolute truth, that her husband was lost forever."

The two women soon journeyed back to St. Augustine, "carrying all of Ashlock's worldly goods and effects," which according to Sherman did not amount to much. Also, Mrs. Ashlock received some three hundred dollars owed to the pilot for his services to the U.S. Army. In the final analysis, as Sherman viewed "the calamity," he thought the sisters had been saved from "a long life of banishment on the beach of Indian River." Later he saw the two in St. Augustine, and the younger woman again a few years afterward in Charleston. For Sherman, just living in Florida, totally apart from contact with Native Americans, was proving an adventure in itself.[22]

SHERMAN'S PRIMARY MISSION in Florida—although obviously relegated to the background at times—involved the elusive Seminole. Because the Indians were broadly scattered, the soldiers at Fort Pierce launched several wide-ranging expeditions during the winter of 1841. Sometimes Sherman participated; at other times, seemingly more often, he remained behind with responsibilities at the fort. "Our expeditions were mostly made in boats in the lagoons extending from . . . near two hundred miles above the fort, down to Jupiter Inlet, about fifty miles below," he wrote, "and in the many streams which emptied therein." Results were mixed, as occasionally the raiding parties never even sighted an Indian. At other times, he said, "we succeeded in picking up small parties of men, women and children." His memoirs, except for hints, refrain from mentioning examples of the brutality involved. Reporting to Phil Ewing about one of the raids, in a letter written at the time, Sherman said the soldiers struck at dawn, taking the Indians unaware, and "captured 23 and killed 6 women and a baby and a child." Afterward the soldiers burned the village. Such killing expeditions are well documented.[23]

This certainly is not to say that the Seminoles, for their part, typically treated prisoners kindly. One of Sherman's most vividly memorable Florida experiences involved the noted Seminole chief Coacoochee, or Wild Cat. Sherman described him as "a very handsome young Indian warrior, not more than twenty-five years old." Conversing with the chief through a black translator after Coacoochee became a prisoner, Sherman wrote Phil Ewing that the boastful Seminole described the capture of six white men and a black man after their ship had wrecked off the coast. The warrior told how he and his party subsequently beat out the brains of their captives. Sherman seemed fascinated that Wild Cat seized the occasion "to initiate his son," as Sherman expressed it, urging the Indian boy to kill a white youth, "as a free lesson in manhood."[24]

Sherman first encountered Chief Coacoochee in rather dramatic fashion. One day in the spring of 1841, the sentinel stationed on the roof at Fort Pierce loudly sounded the dreadful alarm "Indians! Indians!" Sherman said everyone instantly sprang to his weapon, and the men quickly formed up on the parade ground, as four Indians on horseback approached the post from the rear. Signaling their peaceful intentions, the Seminoles rode straight up to the gateway, dismounted and came in. They communicated through an English-speaking black man named Joe—probably a fugitive slave, as many such made their way to Florida and took up with the Native Americans. When conducted to Fort Pierce's commanding officer, Major Thomas Childs, Joe explained that the warriors came on behalf of Chief Coacoochee, one of the most noted Seminole chiefs. Joe proceeded to unwrap a piece of paper sent by the Indian chief, which Joe said was intended for the scrutiny of the big chief of the fort.

It was a safe-conduct pass entitling Coacoochee to come into Fort Pierce and receive provisions and assistance while gathering his people to lead them out of Florida and to the Indian Territory. The paper was signed by Colonel William Worth, commanding all U.S. forces in Florida, with headquarters near Tampa Bay—an officer whom Sherman, in a letter to Ellen a few months later, amusingly referred to as "his Mightiness on the Big Cypress." Joe explained that he had been sent to see if the paper would be honored. Major Childs replied that the paper was "all right" (Sherman's words) and inquired "Where is Coacoochee?" Told that he was near at hand, Childs replied that the chief ought to come on into the fort. Joe offered to go get him. But Major Childs, no doubt wanting to make sure that Coacoochee did not elude him, ordered Sherman to take eight or ten mounted men and escort the chief into the fort.

Detailing ten men to saddle up, Sherman also took one of the Indians and Joe of course, for guidance and communication. After riding five or six miles, Sherman said that he "began to suspect treachery, of which I had heard so much ... [from] the older officers." When Sherman inquired how much farther they had to go, Joe's responses were not reassuring. Sherman said he "always answered, 'Only a little way.'"

Finally they approached one of the hummocks, "standing like an island in the interminable pine-forest," where Sherman saw "a few loitering Indians, which Joe pointed out as *the place.*" Apprehensive of a trap, Sherman halted the guard, ordering the sergeant to watch him closely, and proceeded alone with his guides. Near the hummock, about a dozen warriors arose and surrounded him.

"When in their midst, I inquired for the chief Coacoochee," said Sherman, whereupon a striking-looking young warrior approached, "slapping his breast" and declaring "Me Coacoochee." Sherman explained that he had been sent by his "chief" to escort Coacoochee to the fort. The Indian leader wanted Sherman to get down from his horse and "talk." Sherman said that he "had no 'talk' in me, but that, on his reaching the post, he could talk as much as he pleased with the 'big chief,' Major Childs." Sherman later recounted how the Indians around him "all seemed to be ... in no hurry; and I noticed that all of their guns were leaning against a tree." Perhaps he sensed impending danger. Whatever his thoughts, he demonstrated the coolness and decisiveness that would often characterize his actions at critical moments.

Sherman signaled to the sergeant, who rapidly advanced with the escort. Sherman immediately ordered him to "secure the rifles," which he quickly proceeded to do. Coacoochee appeared to be enraged, but Sherman said he "explained" to the chief that the Indian warriors were tired, while the soldiers were not. Thus the soldiers would carry the guns for the Indians, while Sherman would provide a horse for the Seminole chief to ride. Whatever Coacoochee may have thought of Sherman's "explanation," Sherman's men controlled all the firearms.

Sherman preferred to leave for the fort at once, but Coacoochee insisted that before they departed, he must bathe and dress appropriately for his meeting with Major Childs. Sherman relented, no doubt fascinated by the chief's preparations, which he later described in detail. Stripping off his clothes, Wild Cat washed himself in a nearby pond and then "began to dress in all his Indian finery, which consisted of buckskin leggins, moccasins, and several shirts." The chief "put on vests, one after another, and one of them had the marks of a bullet, just above the pocket, with the stain of blood." From the pocket, Coacoochee pulled out a one-dollar bank note, "and the rascal had the impudence," wrote Sherman, "to ask me to give him silver coin for that dollar." He surmised that the chief had killed the wearer, and was disappointed because he found a paper note instead of a silver dollar. At last the chief was prepared, climaxing the colorful dressing ritual when he donned a turban enhanced with ostrich feathers. Then mounting the horse provided, the splendidly arrayed Coacoochee rode with Sherman back to Fort Pierce.

The chief told Major Childs that he "was tired of war" and ready to lead his people out of Florida. Because they were widely scattered, he said that he needed a month to gather them up, as well as more rations to sustain him. Childs readily agreed both to the month's time and the provisions, whereupon Sherman said the "talk" ceased, and "Coacoochee and his envoys proceeded to get . . . drunk, which was easily done by the agency of commissary whiskey." They stayed at Fort Pierce through the night, and the next day departed. The major had no faith in Wild Cat's sincerity, and seemingly neither did Sherman. When the chief showed up at the fort a month later, he brought with him only twenty warriors and no women and children.

Major Childs had already determined, in such an event, to immediately seize Coacoochee and whoever accompanied him. He arranged for Lieutenant George Taylor to lure the chief and his uncle, who was also an important leader, into the lieutenant's room on pretense of providing "some good brandy, instead of the common commissary whiskey." While the first sergeant and another soldier, together with the assistance of Taylor, seized the apparently unsuspecting chief and his uncle, Sherman and Van Vliet, each leading a section of soldiers, simultaneously secured the larger party of warriors. Sherman came upon them from the front, while Van Vliet's men blocked the open windows in the rear of the building.

That very evening reinforcements from St. Augustine arrived at Fort Pierce. Upon the orders of Major Childs, Sherman then led a band of soldiers who marched during the night and the next day, continuing southward for "some fifty miles, to Lake Okeechobee, in hopes to capture the balance of the tribe." The chase was to no avail. The Seminoles had "taken the alarm and escaped." Coacoochee and his warriors were soon put aboard a schooner bound for New Orleans, from where they expected to be dispatched to the Indian Territory. Colonel Worth intervened, however, recalling the group to Tampa Bay. He had decided to give Wild Cat one more chance to bring in his people. That time the chief returned, accompanied by a number of the women and children, all of whom were then shipped westward.

Thus Sherman had been involved in one of the army's successes, which he characterized as "a heavy loss to the Seminoles." But the young lieutenant was a realist, and acknowledged that "there still remained in the Peninsula a few hundred warriors with their families scattered ... who were concealed in the most inaccessible hummocks and swamps. They had no difficulty in finding plenty of food anywhere and everywhere." These Seminoles were never to be conquered, as the U.S. Army eventually gave up the long, difficult and costly effort to force them from their homes. But the end would not occur until after Sherman had left Florida, and apparently he grew ever more frustrated with the struggle against the Seminoles. Several times during 1841, he expressed an impatience with both the nature and the length of the struggle.[25]

ALTHOUGH FORT PIERCE entailed an isolated existence far down Florida's east coast, Sherman did his best to stay abreast of news from the nation's capital. Reading newspapers whenever he could acquire them, and gleaning information about current events from his brother John and other correspondents, he freely and often strongly expressed his thoughts and convictions about major issues of the day. While he generally favored the Whig Party and Henry Clay, he became incensed that the Whigs were attempting to reestablish the Bank of the United States, destroyed in the mid-1830s by Andrew Jackson. Obviously Sherman thought Jackson, even if a Democrat, did a good thing when he dispatched that "hydra of corruption"—one of the choice phrases Old Hickory employed with relish whenever he spoke of the bank.

Even though Sherman's foster father, as secretary of the treasury, had sponsored the Whig's bank bill in the Senate, Sherman did not restrain his opinion on the subject. In fact, he could mount a tirade against banks of which Jackson himself would have been proud. Voicing disgust with "bankers, brokers & hangers on," he denounced them universally. If a banker had "ever assisted an honest poor man, without exaction and usury, I would like to hear of it," he thundered.[26]

By early September of 1841, Sherman continued to find Florida appealing. "Although Florida is losing many of the charms that novelty inspires, still I cannot say that I am very tired of staying here," he wrote Ellen, adding that he possessed "many of the comforts of life, and what is the greatest of all blessings, good health." He thought there was just enough action "to give experience to the mind, and strength to the constitution." Also, he hoped "that a very long period shall not elapse before I shall have the pleasure of hearing from you again," and made it clear that he looked forward not merely to Ellen's letters, but to the time, however distant, when he might see her once more. Telling her of the Indian pony which he had acquired, he spoke of the importance "to all persons to ride well." He declared that whenever he got home again "the first thing I will expect of you will be to mount the wildest horse and charge over the hills and plains. Next to drawing, it is the most ladylike accomplishment in my mind."[27]

Was he playfully seeking to amuse Ellen with such a mental image, one that he himself actually considered absurd, and thought that she would too? Or did the thought of a good-looking woman riding a wild horse stir within him some erotic fantasy? Yet again, perhaps he had in mind the pure practicality of a woman, as well as a man, needing to ride well in those days of primitive transportation and merely indulged, as he so often did, his penchant and ability for easily turning an attention-grabbing phrase. Whatever crossed Sherman's mind as he wrote, the association of a woman's artistic talent with her charging over hills and plains on a wild horse, which he characterized as "ladylike," is memorable.

Throughout the tour of duty in Florida, Sherman engaged in extensive correspondence, establishing a pattern he would follow all his life. The majority of letters were addressed to Ellen, Phil Ewing and his brother John. One person to whom he seldom wrote, at any time of his life, was Thomas Ewing, which makes a request addressed to his future father-in-law of more than passing interest. (When he once needed five dollars while a cadet at the Point, for instance, he turned to his mother for assistance, despite knowing that her resources were meager indeed when compared with the wealth of Ewing.) But becoming concerned while at Fort Pierce that the Third Artillery might be moved somewhere in the north or east of the country, "and stationed in the vicinity of some city, from which God spare me," he wrote to the well-connected Ewing, wondering if his foster father might facilitate a transfer to the western Plains. He was enamored of a life close to nature, a life that entailed keeping his wants few and simple. Obviously, his was a complex and sometimes contradictory mind. For a man who loved the theater, a desire to continue a military exile from civilization is a bit of an enigma.[28]

Although service on the Great Plains did not materialize, Sherman was promoted to first lieutenant on November 30, 1841. Achieving that rank typically entailed half a dozen years or more. To reach the grade approximately a year and a half after graduation from West Point was highly unusual. "I have been exceedingly fortunate," he informed his brother. Maybe the rapid promotion reflected a combination of good luck and the army's recognition of a young man's potential. One also wonders if the influence of Thomas Ewing might have played a part.[29]

Sherman's promotion meant a transfer from Company A to Company G, taking him from Fort Pierce to St. Augustine. Years later, writing his memoirs, he grew somewhat nostalgic about the time he spent at Fort Pierce. Speaking of "the fragrance of the air, the abundance of game and fish, and just enough of adventure," he declared that the combination "gave to life a relish." Nevertheless, he quickly adjusted to the charms of St. Augustine, where he found "many pleasant families" and came to "remember the old place with pleasure." He arrived in St. Augustine shortly before Christmas, and found himself assigned to command a detachment of twenty soldiers at Picolata, on the St. Johns River, about eighteen miles from the city.[30]

He was pleased that a good and safe road connected Picolata with St. Augustine. He acknowledged in a letter to Ellen that many murders had been committed along the road in the past, "but none since we took Coacoochee, whose party had formerly infested the road. Now there is considered no danger and persons pass ... constantly in parties of two and three." To both John and Ellen, he spoke glowingly of his situation at Picolata. "It is a very beautiful spot indeed," he told Ellen. "Magnificent live oak trees shade the yard, enclosing my splendid quarters, and the St. John's, a noble sheet of water, about one and a half miles broad, adds beauty to the whole." Sherman was not exaggerating the breadth of the St. Johns River, and the wild, exotic setting clearly delighted him.[31]

"In fact I would much prefer being here to St. Augustine," he explained to Ellen, "for 'tis like being in the country with all the advantages of both town and country, for with a good horse I can ride over [to St. Augustine] at any time in a couple of hours, get books, see the ladies, etc." The ladies seem to have been very much on Sherman's mind. While he assured his brother that St. Augustine's old English families, which were not numerous, and "the few Americans whom the delightful climate has enticed," constituted "the best society," he was enamored of the Spaniards. He meant the women, whom he depicted as "very ignorant" and possessing "no desire to travel beyond their own circle." Nevertheless, he told Ellen that they were "very pretty, with beautiful hair and eyes which have ... allured many officers." More than a dozen, he said, had succumbed to marriage. Sherman did not intend to fall into that trap, but he readily admitted a deep admiration for the beauty of the women, and especially their grace in dancing.[32]

Penning a letter to his brother on February 15, 1842, Sherman enthused about the preservation of the "ceremonies and festivities of old Spain." He said that "Balls, masquerades, etc., are celebrated during the gay season of the Carnival (just over)," and although he clearly found the activities fascinating, he did not fail to note the contrast between public and private religious conduct among St. Augustine's Catholics. "The most religious observance of Lent" characterized their public lives, he wrote, "whilst in private they cannot refrain from dancing and making merry." Sherman, not surprisingly, had no problem whatsoever with their merriment.

"Indeed, I never saw anything like it—dancing, dancing, and nothing but dancing, but not such as you see in the north. Such ease and grace I never before beheld," he told John. "A lady will waltz all the evening without fatigue, because it is done slowly, with grace; but it is in the Spanish dance they more especially excel, enchanting all who behold or participate." While he made no mention to Ellen of the contrast between public and private actions during Lent, he was equally straightforward, as with his brother, in admitting his admiration for the Spanish dance, "most beautiful, graceful and enchanting," he told her—"much more the beauty of the ladies themselves." In the coming months, declared the young soldier, "I must certainly make an attempt to learn the Spanish dance."[33]

It was not to be. His posting in the St. Augustine area proved brief. Within only a few weeks of settling in at Picolata, in February 1842, Sherman was ordered to Fort Morgan, Mobile Point. "The roving life in Florida," as he characterized the experience, had come to an end. Actually, he had been anticipating the transfer, just not expecting it so soon. But as usual, Sherman would adapt easily to the change. In aptitude, discipline and personality, he was proving well suited for life in the army.[34]

Chapter Five

Military Camaraderie, Southern Aristocracy, Prospective Matrimony

"Why don't I leave the Army? You ask. Why should I?" Thus responded Sherman from Fort Morgan, Mobile Point, as he addressed Ellen's query in early April 1842. "It is the profession for which my education alone fits me." Probably thinking of the possibility of war with Great Britain over the control of Oregon territory, a clash with Mexico about Texas, or further conflict with Native Americans, he declared that "all appearances indicate the rapid approach of a time when the soldier will be required to do his proper labor, when a splendid field will be spread before him." There was "every reason" to remain a soldier. "Moreover, I am content and happy," professed the young lieutenant, "and it would be foolish to spring into the world barehanded and unprepared." Sherman's closing words on the subject cited the experience of officers who had gone before, men who, for whatever reason, had left the army only later to characterize their decision as "the most foolish act of their life."[1]

He then turned to religion, which Ellen had again recommended to him. Indeed, he said she spoke "so liberally and feelingly upon the subject" that he felt compelled to reply. His answer, as he surely was aware, could not have been to her liking. Straightforwardly he responded, as noted earlier, that for the past six years since first leaving Ohio for West Point, he had neither practiced nor professed any religious creed. Believing "in good works rather than faith" as the basis of "all true religion," Sherman saluted Christianity and Catholicism, yet simultaneously refused to elevate the wisdom "revealed in Scripture" above the principles "taught by the experience of all the ages and common sense."[2]

Quickly moving away from religion, Sherman proceeded to describe his life at Mobile in detail. Fort Morgan lay on the east side of the entrance to Mobile Bay, situated near the end of a narrow, east–west peninsula. It was well positioned to guard the waterway into the port city, located about forty miles to the north. However, as Sherman recalled in his memoirs, the fort had not been occupied for several years, was filthy, and "little or no stores" were to be found. As quartermaster and commissary, he proceeded at once to rectify the latter situation.[3]

Journeying to Mobile on a schooner, Sherman quickly "procured all essentials for the troops, and returned to the post." Within a short time he and his peers had put the fort "in as good order as possible; and had regular guard-mounting and parades." As on the Atlantic coast of Florida, he discovered that Gulf coast seafood was very fine. "We found magnificent fishing with the seine on the outer beach, and sometimes in a single haul we would take ten or fifteen barrels of the best kind of fish, . . . pompinos, red-fish, snappers, etc." Still, army life at Fort Morgan proved dreary and boring, "a desolate state," he lamented, "of . . . woebegone bachelors."

Then "the young ladies of Mobile" staged a surprise invasion. Having prevailed upon some male friends to provide water transportation, a large number of women, Sherman said, "landed at our wharf, marched boldly into the very heart of the citadel and carried the fort by storm." He was pleased. After conducting a tour of the fort for the women—the guns, embrasures, casemates, etc.—the soldiers were invited on board the ladies' ship, where a band provided music, and wine and refreshments were available. Continuing with his military analogy, Sherman declared the women "played their batteries so well that they prevailed upon five out of the seven officers to go up to the city with them, myself among the number." While three men returned to the fort after only a day, Sherman spent six days there, as did one other.

"A more delightful time you could not imagine," he enthused to Ellen. "It would take a volume to name the ladies," and record their "kindness . . .

their beauties and accomplishments." He claimed that "we were invited everywhere and the bright button [a reference to his army uniform and its eye-catching buttons] was a passport at all times to the houses of the best [people]." In addition to young women, who seemingly constituted the chief attraction, Sherman found the city generally pleasing, as he enjoyed hot-air balloon ascensions, theatrical performances and painting exhibits, along with parties and balls. He thought "the beautiful streets of hotels, stores, shops, etc. . . . as gorgeously ornamented as New York." That was a notable compliment, when one remembers the high esteem in which he held that city.[4]

Sherman's posting at Fort Morgan lasted a mere three months, but as often as possible he journeyed into Mobile, even if prices there were so expensive that "only millionaires can flourish." Sherman possessed a great advantage, however, because of the presence of Cornelia Bull, a cousin on his mother's side of the family. She was married to a wealthy merchant, living in a fine house "about two miles out in the country," and Sherman considered her "a most charming woman with a family of three lovely children." Cornelia and her husband "insisted upon my making it my home," he wrote, "whenever I should visit Mobile." He described to Ellen the pleasures that he experienced there: "roses of every hue and shape, and size and color" adorning the latticed portico, the arbor of shade trees, the "delightful" horseback rides, "the strawberries and cream"—all composing "an air of quiet and home" that was "a perfect paradise to me." But most of Sherman's time was spent, not in "the most beautiful suburbs and country seats" of Mobile, but rather in the desolate fortress at the entrance to the bay.[5]

Surely he welcomed orders taking his regiment to Fort Moultrie at Charleston harbor. Most military personnel considered it a choice posting. Nevertheless, Sherman knew he would miss his cousin and his friends in Mobile. Sailing first to Pensacola in early June, and from there embarking for Charleston, he declared that "the weather was hot, the winds light, and we made a long passage; but at last reached Charleston harbor . . . and took post in Fort Moultrie" on Sullivan's Island. There he would be stationed for four years, a period when he acquired a store of valuable information about the South—particularly the Deep South. The knowledge proved quite helpful some twenty years later, during the Civil War. He once blurted, "I knew more of Georgia than the rebels did." That boastful statement, although doubtless angering many Confederate sympathizers when they learned of it, was hardly an exaggeration.[6]

THERE WAS NO BLINKING at the fact that the famous and cosmopolitan port of Charleston proved enticing to many army men. Since it was easily accessible by steamboat, which ran the short distance to and from Fort Moultrie four times a day, military personnel could often be found in the beautiful heart of the city. Also, the village of Moultrieville lay close by the fort; this small town served as a summer resort for wealthy Charlestonians. During Sherman's time there, Charleston was a proud, aristocratic city of 30,000 inhabitants. Located in the southeastern portion of South Carolina, at the confluence of the Ashley, Cooper and Wando Rivers, the city exercised leadership in the public opinion of the South that was, in Sherman's words, "far out of proportion to her population, wealth, or commerce."[7]

From the first Sherman, who all his adult life held to an unwavering nationalism, found the politics of Charleston repugnant. The picturesque city had developed into the hotbed of "Southern rights." Previously, he observed in reference to the "nullification" crisis during Jackson's presidency, "the inhabitants had almost inaugurated civil war." The doctrine of nullification of a United States law by a single, disgruntled state, and the veneration of John C. Calhoun's ideas, were deeply disturbing to him. With pronounced disdain he viewed the young men of Carolina as snobbish indolents, "worthless sons of . . . proud . . . families," boasting of "their state, their aristocracy, . . . their patriarchal chivalry and glory." He pronounced it "all trash."[8]

As for military duties, Sherman found a mostly simple and easy life. Four companies of the Third Artillery, totaling about 250 men, made up the garrison. Since the Third Artillery was headquartered at Fort Moultrie, the regimental commander, Colonel William Gates, resided there, as well as the regimental band of about fifteen instruments. Other companies of the Third Artillery were spread up and down the Atlantic coast. Sherman's Company G was commanded by Captain Robert Anderson from Kentucky, later to become well-known at the beginning of the Civil War when he commanded Fort Sumter. (Sumter was under construction in the early 1840s.) The daily routine started with reveille and drill at sunrise. Breakfast followed at seven, then dress parade at eight, and a change of guard thirty minutes later. By nine o'clock, as a general rule, the men had "nothing [left] to do but amuse ourselves." Sunday was a marginal exception, in that "we have an extra quantity of music, parade, and inspection."[9]

Sherman said that to pass the time "some read, some write, some loaf and some go to the city." He and the other officers occasionally engaged in lively discussions—military tactics, strategy and history, politics, the social scene, and more. Several of the men then stationed at Fort Moultrie possessed remarkable military potential. In addition to Sherman, George H. Thomas, John F. Reynolds, Thomas W. Sherman (no relation) and Erasmus D. Keyes would rise to high rank in the Federal Army. The hot-tempered Braxton Bragg, choosing to stand with his native North Carolina, would one day command a major Confederate army.

This small group of talented young officers at Fort Moultrie ultimately proved, in convincing fashion, that they knew how to wage war. They were not pleased when news arrived in August that, because the war against the Seminoles was over, Congress had voted to reduce the size of the army, already small, and reduce the pay of officers. Sherman groused "that every year [the army is] threatened with either disbandment or . . . a reduction in pay." Such a policy, he believed, was likely to drive away "every reasonable and good officer."[10]

He deeply resented having his pay cut by forty dollars a year, particularly when Thomas, Maria and Ellen Ewing all wanted him to turn to a civil career anyway. He believed that his salary was fully earned—and all the more considering the unofficial duties expected of a young officer. Charleston nourished a major social season and her proud, wealthy citizens expected the presence of army officers for all the events. Sherman wrote his brother that such invitations "must be accepted or give offence." Some occasions were highly formal, demanding that he be dressed in full uniform, perhaps for a ball, the opera, or the theater. Parties varied greatly, quoting Sherman's description, "from the highly aristocratic and fashionable, with sword and epaulettes," to such outings as "horse-racing, picnicking, boating, fishing, swimming, and God knows what not."[11]

Probably the balls were the worst events. The young lieutenant felt put upon, knowing as he did that his presence was merely to add glitter and pageantry to the evening. He found dancing at the balls an irritant. "They dance only the same old set of French quadrilles," lacking in both variety and beauty. With a critical eye, he realized that much of the dancing was too fast, thus eliminating the possibility of smooth, graceful and enchanting movement. The dancing of the Charleston women, when compared with the ease and allure emanating from the beautiful Spanish dancers of St. Augustine, he considered markedly unattractive. He even characterized the Charleston dancing as "painful" to watch. He also thought most of the conversations he experienced were empty and forced. "A life of this kind does well enough for a while," he wrote, perhaps striving to demonstrate a degree of tolerance, "but soon surfeits with its flippancy." Still again he remarked that "pride and vanity, hypocrisy and flippance reign triumphant."[12]

Little wonder that Sherman and the other Fort Moultrie officers devised a rotating duty roster for the obligations placed upon them by Charleston society. Alternating their increasingly boring duty, only two or possibly three men attended any particular party—unless the occasion appeared grandly unique or demanding. Nevertheless, Sherman's social life was not found totally lacking in rewarding moments. He somehow managed to identify more than one young woman whose company seems to have been tolerable. Adamantly, however, he disavowed all desire for any binding relationship. Early on in his Charleston days, prior to a full acquaintance with the local customs regarding courtship, he took a buggy ride with a young lady. Only afterward (or so he claimed), did he learn to his dismay that such "familiarity" was viewed

as the equivalent of an engagement to be married. Staunchly he proclaimed that as an officer of the army, he would "never" marry!

Whatever his true views about marriage, Sherman undoubtedly possessed a keen eye for attractive women—even if they were Southern and
Charleston lassies. Years later he readily recalled the names of several:
"Mary Johnson, the pretty Miss North, and others of the Charleston
girls." Most of all he remembered "my old attachment to Mary Lamb,"
whom he had escorted to many events, and saw "frequently." In fact,
Sherman said so much about her in his letters that Ellen asked if he
intended to bring her to Ohio when he got a furlough. "I thank the Lord,"
he rejoined, "that I am not so far gone as to commit so foolish an act."[13]

The women of his acquaintance certainly add a bit of spice to his
legend. While he frequently mentions various attractive women with
whom he came in contact through the years, and readily acknowl-
edges their charms, he never writes to anyone of anything more. If he
became intimate with some—and Sherman did not marry until he was
thirty years old—he gives no indication of such in his letters. He did discuss many subjects in writing and conversation, and sometimes freely
employed profanity, particularly when in the company of army officers;
but to his credit, he never wrote, and apparently never spoke, about
sexual matters with anyone—although he obviously was enamored of
the fairer sex.

While stationed at Fort Moultrie, Sherman found, besides the pretty
women, several other outlets for his wide-ranging interests and abundant energy. He liked to ride, and frequently took long jaunts on horseback. Sometimes the trips involved military duties; for example, once
riding to Augusta to serve as "a sort of peace-maker," as he characterized the assignment in his memoirs, when a problem arose among the
officers of the Third Artillery's Company B. He stayed in Georgia for
several months, the difficulty finally resolved with the transfer of a few
officers to other posts. He served on several court-martial boards, more
than once requiring travel beyond the borders of South Carolina. One
assignment, investigating an officer's alleged misconduct, took him all
the way to Key West. Upon other occasions he would ride thirty, forty,

even fifty miles to hunt and socialize. He might journey several miles to view the countryside, examine a plantation or simply to enjoy wandering and exploring alone. He also took up painting.[14]

In fact, Sherman seems to have become rather obsessed with painting. At West Point, drawing had been his favorite class and he had talent. He could represent the human body, male and female, in perfect proportions and various stances. While in South Carolina, many satisfying hours were devoted to improving and broadening his artistic skills. Frequently he visited the home of his company commander, Captain Robert Anderson. The captain and his wife had acquired numerous books of elegant engravings and paintings that Sherman sometimes studied. (Occasionally too, he escorted Mrs. Anderson when she shopped in Charleston.) To Ellen, he confided that his "great love for painting" worried him.

He feared the passion was becoming an addiction that potentially might consume him. If Ellen shared his thoughts about painting with her father, Thomas Ewing could not have been pleased. The life of a painter, unless one were extremely talented and blessed with originality and associations with well-connected people, and also a bit of luck, generally promised to be no more rewarding monetarily than that of a soldier. Very likely not as rewarding. The well-heeled Ewing, now both a former U.S. senator and secretary of the treasury, really hoped young Sherman would take up some lucrative civil pursuit. Certainly painting would not have been among Ewing's choices for him. But painting, as it turned out, constituted nothing more than a phase of Sherman's life and seems largely to have passed by the time he left South Carolina. Occasionally in later life he might pick up a brush or make a sketch. Always he would appreciate artistic talent and enjoy viewing paintings. However, the great passion for doing it himself had ceased.[15]

The young lieutenant continued his prolific letter writing too, penning numerous interesting and often long messages to friends and relatives. In this regard, the pattern of his life would never change. For a time, he also engaged in the serious pursuit of legal knowledge, probably in part to be conversant with the profession of his younger brother John.

"Look out," he once playfully warned John, "that I don't turn out a pet-tifogging lawyer, and rival you in fame at some cross-roads in the Far West." Sherman knew that Thomas Ewing would approve. "After cast-ing about me, and some reflection," he once wrote Ellen, "I have seized upon a book that young lawyers groan over—Blackstone." Proclaiming that he had "with avidity swallowed its contents," and vowing to "con-tinue to study and read hard," he confessed that "somehow or other I do not feel as though I would make a good lawyer." The feeling had nothing to do, he quickly added, with understanding legal matters, because he met "with little difficulty in mastering the necessary book knowledge." The problem was that his education had been "such as to give me almost a contempt for the bombast and stuff that form the chief constituents of Modern Oratory." Fortunately, Sherman realized that while he pos-sessed the necessary intellect, he really did not have the interest or the temperament to become a successful lawyer.[16]

In the late summer of 1843, Sherman received a most welcome fur-lough, enabling him to visit Ohio for the first time in three years. The Buckeye State, although lacking the "bright and delightful" weather to which he had grown accustomed in the Deep South, nevertheless was home to "all whom I love and regard as friends." Soon he was spending time in Columbus, Lancaster and Mansfield. Thomas Ewing was once more practicing law in Lancaster, as well as in the nation's capital. His daughter Ellen had celebrated her nineteenth birthday, and Sherman made the pleasant discovery that the little girl whom he had been writ-ing since he first left for West Point had become a charming young lady.

Ellen Ewing was not a classic beauty, but her mature demeanor and general appearance, accentuated by black hair and blue eyes, caused Sherman to see his foster sister in a way that he never had before. For her part, Ellen had been impressed earlier with the young, red-haired lieutenant, keenly aware of his sharp intellect and his wiry rugged-ness. When he left her that fall, the two seemingly had an understand-ing that they would one day marry. That understanding was formalized when Sherman later wrote Thomas Ewing, requesting his permission to marry Ellen. If Ewing harbored any misgivings about the match—and

he did, basically due to Sherman's military career—they were not sufficient to prevent him from giving his consent to the union.

When Ellen later accepted in writing Sherman's marriage proposal,
she also conveyed a strong desire that he would become a Catholic and
leave the army. He replied that he would do neither. He did promise to
keep an open mind and "a wish to believe, if possible," in her faith. Sherman would never believe, and the more he read of Christian writers,
some recommended by Ellen, the stronger became his non-belief. She
would never relent in her determined campaign to make him a Catholic and, predictably, their clash over religion caused considerable frustration in the years to come. As to his army career, Sherman thought
Thomas Ewing "had long since relinquished . . . his opposition," only to
learn that his prospective father-in-law, like his fiancée, still hoped he
would resign his army commission in favor of "Civil Life." Thus two tormenting issues loomed ominously upon the future horizon of the young
lieutenant.[17]

Although he might have prolonged his Ohio visit, Sherman always had
a wanderlust. He determined, before returning to Fort Moultrie, to see
more of the country he served as an army officer. An account of the journey back to South Carolina was penned in a letter to his brother John
soon after he returned to duty. "It was about the middle of November,"
he wrote, when "I deposited my bones in the Chilicothe stage." Traveling
first to Portsmouth, Ohio, and from there down the Ohio River to Cincinnati, he visited "in our queen city" with his brothers Lampson and
Hoyt, who were then employed by the *Cincinnati Gazette*. While spending time with his siblings, he met several people whom he considered
interesting, some of them artists, and as he later recalled, "especially
Miss Sallie Carneal, then quite a belle, and noted for her fine voice."[18]

Departing for St. Louis on a steamboat called *Manhattan*, Sherman
found the vessel left much to be desired, "loaded with every species of
animal from men to Durham cattle. There were more than 200 souls
on board a second-class boat, from which circumstance you can readily infer that the bodily comforts were not well cared for." Yet the young
lieutenant was "much pleased" to stop at Louisville, "a beautiful place,"

for several hours. "In fact," he enthused, "the whole river realized my wildest conceptions."[19]

On November 23, Sherman reached the broad Ohio's confluence with the powerful, magnificent Mississippi. The impact—visually, mentally, even spiritually—proved indelible. A lifelong enchantment with the "Father of Waters" had begun. Again and again through the years Sherman seemed to draw personal strength from the rivers, above all the Mississippi, that he came to regard as the great geographical guarantor of an indestructible national unity. He said, as Southern secession loomed closer, as well as after Civil War became a reality, that whoever controls the Missouri, the Ohio and the Mississippi Rivers controls the continent. And after the war, fittingly, Sherman derived pleasure in visiting with Mark Twain—obviously, a man whose life and work were profoundly influenced by the grand river—at his Connecticut home.[20]

The next day Sherman arrived at St. Louis, a bustling young city of some 30,000 to 40,000 inhabitants—a place he would come to love, and eventually call home for a number of years. He spent ten days perusing the river city, admiring its strategic location at the meeting of the Missouri and the Mississippi. He counted "thirty-six good steamboats receiving and discharging cargo at the levee." Naturally he took in the art gallery and paid a visit to the Catholic cathedral—perhaps thinking of Ellen. He visited Colonel Stephen W. Kearny, who was in command of the arsenal at Jefferson Barracks. He also spent some time with Pacificus Ord, the brother of his close friend Edward O. C. Ord. Soon after, he told John that St. Louis possessed "great merits and beauty." While initially much impressed with the city's bright future, he hesitated to pronounce it the equal of Cincinnati. But it would not be long before he changed his mind—in fact coming to think of this future metropolis as the great city of inland America.[21]

Four days into December Sherman resumed his odyssey. With first impressions of St. Louis fresh in his mind, he watched the city slowly shrink in the distance as he headed south on "a new and very fine boat, called the *John Aull*," doubtless a welcome change from the cramped *Manhattan*. Once more he anticipated new vistas, while rolling on the Great

River, bound for the exotic and already legendary port of New Orleans. Snow was falling when the ship steamed past Cairo, Illinois—"a heavy snowstorm" according to Sherman—while the landscape, "wintery and devoid of verdure," quickly became "clothed in a ghost-like garb." Gradually, however, the snow was left behind, and "the grass and trees showed the change of latitude, and when . . . we reached New Orleans, the roses were in full bloom . . . and a tropical air" permeated the city.[22]

Sherman lingered for the better part of a week, immersed in the enthralling and unique ambience of the cosmopolitan port. He took in the theaters, attended a masquerade ball and sampled a number of restaurants, dining on such offerings as shrimp, crab, oysters, gumbo and more. Of course, as everywhere he journeyed, Sherman did not neglect the military, calling on the officers of the Seventh Infantry, before embarking by steamer for Mobile.[23]

After a couple of pleasant days visiting friends in the Alabama port city, Sherman entered upon the last sweep of his roundabout return to Fort Moultrie. Evidently the last miles were the worst—particularly the trip from "a town called Montgomery." His description for his brother John says it all. "There, on a vehicle called a car, on what was denominated a railroad, [I journeyed] to a town called Franklin, from which place I staged it over roads such as you have about Mansfield, except the clay is slipperier, the hills shorter and steeper, and the drivers such as can be had nowhere else. Thus I went 120 miles to a town in Georgia called Griffin. Here I waited twenty-four hours for the cars, which had as usual run off the track." When eventually the train got under way to Macon, twelve hours were consumed in traversing a distance of only sixty miles. "At last," concluded Sherman, "on the 27th of December, after an absence of five months and two days, I stood once more in my old quarters at Fort Moultrie."[24]

He was pleased again to experience the warm weather, bright flowers and cheerful sunlight. While an abundance of leisure time at Fort Moultrie could be boring, Sherman increasingly found that the army was keeping him busy. Three weeks into January he had a new assignment. Colonel Sylvester Churchill, inspector general of the army, had chosen Sherman to assist him in investigating the claims of Georgia militia seeking reimbursement for alleged losses, particularly of their horses, while serving in Florida during the Seminole Wars.

Telling Ellen of his new orders in a letter dated February 8, 1844, Sherman revealingly admitted: "I might have declined joining Colonel Churchill's staff, but it will serve to advance my future and I hope secure for me the good opinion of one of the most influential men in our Army." This is not the sentiment of an officer who seriously contemplates abandoning his military career. The letter is equally enlightening about his attitude toward Ellen's religious wishes for him. While he breezily proclaims, "I snatch at the opportunity" to examine the doctrines of "your church," he strikingly observes, in the same sentence, that "the Fates are arraigned against me." He is "ordered into Georgia and Alabama where religion, except of the rudest species, is never found." Also remarkable was his postscript to the letter. Observing that all his Charleston friends were "the same," he noted only one person specifically: "Mary Lamb is well and *sympathizes* with me that I am sent into Barbarous Georgia during the races the last of February and the consequent Balls. That I may avoid them is one motive for going."

Within a week Sherman was in "Barbarous Georgia." Traveling by rail to Madison, the twenty-four-year-old first lieutenant there boarded the mail coach for the remainder of his trip. When the coach stopped in the small north Georgia town of Marthasville, Sherman got out of his cramped quarters and stretched. That moment, considered in historical retrospect, is rather eerie. There is no reason to think that he sensed anything out of the ordinary, such as a future premonition, when he gazed upon the village and waited to resume his trek. But unlikely as it might seem, he stood at a place with which, in time to come, his name would be forever associated. Two decades later he would return as a major general of the U.S. Army, commanding a hundred thousand soldiers, when little Marthasville had become Atlanta, a city then second to none as a Confederate war-production center and rail crossroads, and a symbol of defiant resistance. Sherman and Atlanta. Strange indeed are the twists of fate.

Soon boarding again, he rode the short distance to Marietta and reported for duty to Colonel Churchill on February 17. The colonel, assisted by a lieutenant named R. P. Hammond, was already at work. Sherman, Hammond and the colonel and his family all lived in a tavern, with the three officers working out of a nearby office. Their investigation revealed fraud on an alarming scale and served to reinforce Sherman's already negative view of "citizen-soldiers." He thought "they were about the d——dest rascals that could be found in the United States." Most reported that they had lost one or more horses while serving in Florida, but many of the horses were discovered to be alive and healthy. Others had been killed sure enough—although at the hands of their owners, who valued the prospect of financial reimbursement more than the life of their animals. Also, virtually every owner overstated the value of the loss supposedly suffered. "I have unfolded some pretty pieces of rascality," Sherman sarcastically commented, "for an honest and religious people." Later, back at Fort Moultrie, he would speak of having been "away among the Barbarians and heathens, robbing them of their ... dreams of Gold and Silver."[25]

Remaining in Marietta approximately six weeks, while he labored to expose the militia wrongdoers, Sherman sometimes took a break and rode to the top of a nearby mountain known as Kennesaw. From its towering height he could gaze southward toward Marthasville, while off to the north, some fifteen miles away, lay Allatoona. Once he rode to Allatoona, turning aside to visit the large Indian mounds on the bank of the Etowah River, and spending a couple of days with a Colonel Lewis Tumlin, who owned a plantation on which the mounds were erected. "Thus by a mere accident," Sherman wrote in his memoirs, "I was enabled to traverse on horseback the very ground where in after-years I had to conduct vast armies." Significantly, he even made topographical sketches of the terrain over which he passed.[26]

Then Colonel Churchill moved the investigation to northeast Alabama, and Sherman took in still more of the South. Riding to Rome, Georgia, he turned west and north, crossed Sand Mountain and arrived at Bellefonte, Alabama, on the banks of the Tennessee River. Sherman made note in his diary about the young women in the area, several of whom he thought pretty and intelligent. Some he considered "strapping girls," apparently a complimentary description. Ellen was always rather frail, so perhaps the contrast drew his attention. He was also impressed by the region's natural beauty. The mountains, ridges and a major river made a memorable impact.[27]

His favorable sense of northeast Alabama grew strong and vivid, so impelling that months later he suggested to Ellen the possibility of living there. He remained keenly aware that both she and her father opposed his army career. Thus he proposed to take a long leave of absence from the army, "go to the northern part of Alabama, select some pretty place and then see what may be done as a surveyor or draughtsman, in each of which I am fully competent—should I meet with partial success then I can complete what I have done at the Law which I can master sufficiently by one winter's study in a Law office." He implored Ellen to "think well of . . . the resolution I have made of never living in Ohio, or accepting ought from any one there."

Ellen's response was likely disconcerting. It surely should have raised a red flag in the mind of a man who took little interest in religion. She said that she would prefer to live in Memphis. The reason, even more of a surprise, involved the Dominican prior of Somerset, Bishop Richard P. Miles, who had recently moved to that city on the bluffs of the Mississippi River. Sherman replied that he did not think she would like Memphis. In any case, it would not, he said, "be politic to select [Memphis] to enjoy the presence of a favorite bishop—he may be there one year or fifty—at most the prospect of his proximity would be so much a matter of chance as not to enter into serious calculation." Wherever they might go, Sherman assured her that "we will find kind and good men. . . . I still have my eye on North Alabama but will not make a definite final choice for some time." Thus he strove not to sound overly harsh, although compelled to reject her idea of selecting a place to live based on the presence of a clergyman. Doubtless he hoped that Ellen somehow would come to accept his life in the U.S. Army.[28]

By late spring of 1844 Sherman was once more at his Fort Moultrie post. During the following months, army duties continued to be occasionally leavened by socializing, hunting, fishing and various explorations. Of course he continually carried on a correspondence with Ellen that centered around their plans. In January 1845 he went hunting at a plantation on the east branch of the Cooper River, about fifty miles from Fort Moultrie. The outing was planned solely as a pleasure jaunt, but it quickly came to an unwelcome conclusion.

Accompanied by Lieutenant John F. Reynolds and James Poyas, son of the plantation owner, Sherman had little more than taken his stand when a deer emerged from a swamp near Poyas, who fired and wounded the animal in the leg. Crazed by shock and pain, the deer plunged back into the swamp, only to appear again near Sherman, who immediately mounted his horse and gave chase. Galloping across a wooded area filled with pine trees, the horse failed to clear a fallen log, snagging a forefoot and smashing hard to the ground. Sherman's heavy, double-barreled gun caught his right arm at an awkward angle as he fell, dislocating the arm at the shoulder when he slammed against the earth.

Reynolds came rushing to his aid as Sherman struggled to his feet. Fortunately the horse had not been seriously injured and Sherman's initial pain was relatively mild. But soon the discomfort increased, and he remembered that the arm ached "so that it was almost unendurable." After riding about three miles, he said "we came to a negro hut, where I got off and rested." Reynolds rode away in search of help. When the lieutenant returned, Sherman's arm was "so swollen and painful that I could not ride." He described how "they rigged up an old gig belonging to the negro, in which I was carried" for several miles to the plantation house.

A doctor was summoned, who tried "the usual methods of setting the arm, but without success," declared Sherman. "At last," he related, the doctor "got a set of double pulleys and cords, with which he succeeded in extending the muscles and getting the bone into place." The healing process obviously would require some time. Disabled and still in considerable pain, Sherman applied for a leave and headed north late in January.[29]

This was not the first time that the young man had been injured while riding a horse. When a boy of only seven years, and astride his father's mount, known as "Old Dick," who was "somewhat in a hurry," according to Sherman's recollection, he had been thrown among a pile of stones from which the young lad was "picked up apparently a dead boy." Of course he did recover ("My time was not yet"), although the scars incurred remained with him for life. More than likely the latest injury added a few more indelible mementos.[30]

Chapter Six

AND THEN THERE
WAS A WAR ON

When Sherman returned to Fort Moultrie on March 9, 1845, having fully recovered from his injury, the nation had a new president. Only five days earlier, James Knox Polk, an avowed expansionist from Tennessee, had been inaugurated as the eleventh president of the United States. While Sherman had favored Henry Clay, he was not surprised by Polk's triumph. Back in September he had predicted that the Kentuckian would not win.[1]

Clay had come close to victory: closer than in 1824, when the "Cock of Kentucky" placed a distant third behind Andrew Jackson and John Quincy Adams; also closer than in Jackson's solid triumph over him eight years later. If the Great Compromiser, as Clay increasingly came to be known, had carried New York in 1844, which he very nearly did, the legendary Kentuckian would have secured the nation's highest office by a margin of seven electoral votes.[2]

Ironically, in view of Clay's early political posturing, the issue of manifest destiny seems to have cost him the presidency. Clay, in truth, had been a manifest destiny man long before the phrase was coined. In the run-up to the War of 1812, soon after the young, slim and volatile politician had taken his seat in Congress as a "war hawk," he delivered a powerful oration. The speech was never to be forgotten by Clay's supporters, and helped establish him as a national figure. While he did not utter the words "manifest destiny" (a phrase that did not appear until the mid-1840s), that concept was the essence of his stance in his early career.

"I am not, sir, in favor of cherishing the passion of conquest," he stated. "But I must . . . declare my hope to see, ere long, the *new* United States (if you will allow me the expression) embracing not only the old thirteen States, but the entire country east of the Mississippi, including East Florida, and . . . territories to the north . . . also." Hailed as "the Western Star"—eloquent, gifted, defiant, charismatic—the fighting cock from Kentucky then seemed the virile epitome of the American expansionist spirit.[3]

By the 1840s, however, the aging bluegrass leader had become the embodiment of prudence—at least when he analyzed the emotionally packed issue of Texas. Annexing Texas involved the westward expansion of slavery, increased power for the slave states in the U.S. Congress, the growing sectional divisiveness between free states and slave states— and a likely war with Mexico. Clay wanted no part of it, deeming Texas annexation "dangerous to the integrity of the Union." The Whigs agreed, unanimously nominating the Kentuckian for president at their convention, while making no mention of Texas in their platform.[4]

At times in American political history the major parties have evidenced no substantial differences on key issues, but 1844 was no such election. The Democrats, convening in Baltimore soon after the Whigs adjourned there, repudiated former president Martin Van Buren's quest for another term, selecting instead Polk, the first "dark horse" candidate to garner the nomination of a major party. They took an uncompromising stand in favor of territorial expansion, arrogantly advocating "the reoccupation of Oregon and the reannexation of Texas."

With the Tennessean Polk as their candidate, the Democrats knew they were backing a man dedicated to expansion; they just didn't grasp the full degree of his passion. Although California was hardly mentioned during the campaign, and Texas and Oregon dominated the fervid political rhetoric, the future Golden State was very much in the mind of the candidate. For Polk, that great stretch of Pacific coast, with its magnificent harbors, represented a defining goal, an indispensable acquisition should he become president. Never mind that the United States had no legitimate claim to California—not even, as in the case of Texas, a flood of American emigration. Regardless, Polk coveted that immense, strategic territory and was determined to acquire it. Probably there was no more ardent expansionist in the entire nation than the man some Tennesseans called Young Hickory. In his unwavering drive to possess California Young Hickory would prove to be just as tough as Old Hickory, Andrew Jackson.[5]

When Henry Clay began at last to recognize the extent of expansionist fever gripping the nation, he tried to modify his position on Texas. Clay stated that he had "no personal objection" to annexing Texas if the territory could be acquired "without dishonor, without war, with the common consent of the Union, and upon just and fair terms." His declaration was no match for impassioned, spread-eagle oratory. Expansionist politicians, unscrupulously working to manipulate nationalist emotions, cried out for Texas and Oregon whatever the cost. Apparently some of the reckless souls were ready to accept war with either Mexico or Great Britain, or even both at the same time. And there was not any way to separate Texas from the fiery issue of slavery, since slaves were already in Texas.[6]

The slavery question, like an ever widening cancerous growth, seriously weakened the Whig Party. Antislavery Whigs, believing the movement for Texas annexation stemmed from a slave-state conspiracy to increase slave territory, turned away from the Kentuckian in significant numbers. Many sought a new political home with the recently formed Liberty Party, whose name conveyed its stance on slavery. Having garnered a mere 7,000 votes in 1840, the Liberty Party polled more than 62,000 votes in 1844. In western New York, Liberty presidential candidate James G. Birney drew enough votes away from Clay to enable Polk to carry the state, and with it the presidency. Although Polk won easily in the electoral college, 170 to 105, across the nation the contest was much closer. He eked out a narrow plurality of only 38,000 popular votes, and notably did not carry his own state.

The signs for the coming years were ominous. The power of slaveholding Southern Democrats disturbed antislavery Northerners who saw their influence in the party's councils dwindling. Some began turning away from the Democrats, convinced that the party was destined for domination by Southern slaveholders. Their worst fears soon seemed confirmed, for the annexation of Texas was accomplished even before Polk's inauguration as president.

President John Tyler of Virginia, apparently taking Polk's election as a mandate for expansion, called upon Congress to annex Texas, a former Mexican colony that had fought for its independence, by a joint resolution of both houses. Of the twenty-six states then making up the Union, half condoned slavery and half were free. Following a tense, spirited debate over slavery, the House voted for the measure by a count of 120 to 98, while the vote in the Senate was still closer, 27 to 25. Tyler signed the resolution three days before Polk became president. There was a controversial provision that Texas, with its own consent, might be divided into as many as five states. This gave rise to yet more, and often bitter controversy about the expansion of the "peculiar institution," and the potential for ever greater slave state representation, power and influence in the halls of Congress.[7]

"As to Texas being annexed for the sole purpose of extending slavery," Sherman wrote his brother John, "I do not believe it." He acknowledged that "some politicians" might think so, and "abolitionists may act upon [that concept]," but Sherman could accept no such interpretation. His views of the issue must be tempered by the realization that, while sometimes highly critical of the Southern aristocracy, he never seemed to be troubled by the existence of slavery. Again writing John, he said, "I have never seen the least sign of disaffection on the part of the negroes, and have seen them in the cotton fields and rice ditches, met them hunting at all hours of day and on the road at night, without anything but 'How d'ye, Massa? Please give me some bac.'" He did not think there was any possibility of a revolt, not "even such danger in case of war." Writing a striking postscript in a letter to Ellen, he instructed: "Tell Bub [foster brother Hugh Ewing] I got the abolition pamphlet written by that crazy fool Bob Leverig today and shall I think turn it over to some of our negro

servants [slaves] for their amusement." When the Civil War came, however, Sherman, unlike some Southerners both then and today, was never
blind to the reality of what had caused the conflict. Writing years afterward, he declared that since the Civil War "has come and gone, we can
rest secure in the knowledge that as the chief cause, slavery, has been
eradicated forever, it is not likely to come again."[8]

WHATEVER THE CONSEQUENCES of Texas annexation relative to the
expansion of slavery, war with Mexico seemed a distinct possibility in
March 1845. Two days after James K. Polk became president, Juan N.
Almonte, the Mexican ambassador to the United States, broke off relations and headed for home, as he had been instructed to do if the United
States moved to acquire Texas. Almonte characterized the U.S. acquisition of Texas "an act of aggression," and proclaimed that the measure
was "the most unjust which can be found recorded in the annals of
modern history."[9]

Naturally Sherman and his peers at Fort Moultrie pondered the likelihood of a Mexican conflict. Only a few months earlier he had commented to Ellen about rumors that Britain was arming Mexico so that
she could recover the Texas republic: "I do not believe there is a shadow
of a chance for so fortunate a war." ("Fortunate" because it would present the possibility of combat experience other than the Seminole Wars,
and well might lead to an advancement in his rank.) After the triumph of
Polk, and the passage of a resolution to annex Texas, the situation obviously had changed. "We all [then] expected war as a matter of course,"
Sherman later declared. Yet by June 1845, he once more thought war
unlikely. "No doubt the Mexicans feel hostile towards us," and might
resort to war, but he thought such a decision would be unreasonable.
Mexico "is unable to carry on war," Sherman wrote, declaring that "her
government is hardly secure, their provinces are rebelling, and it would
require all her force and influence to maintain their own dependents."[10]

Meanwhile, life at Fort Moultrie followed its normal pattern of
"monotonous drill and duty," social obligations and an occasional oppor-

tunity "to ramble among the green and noble live oaks—the most magnificent evergreen in our forest." That spring he wrote John that he had
been "to Wilmington [North Carolina] to stand by a young friend who
exchanged the independence of the bachelor for the charms of Governor Dudley's daughter. We had a brilliant wedding—dinner parties and
balls for three days." Then duty called once more. "I am going to return
to Charleston tonight by sea," he told John, "and expect to be turned
wrong side out, as the wind is blowing a half gale." Sherman's circle of
contacts among the wealthy citizens continued to expand and on January 4, 1846, he told John, "I am pretty well acquainted with all the rich
people round about, and have from them enough invitations for the balance of the winter."[11]

Clearly, when all the pros and cons are weighed, Sherman felt at
home in the army, much as he had at West Point. Promotion might be
disconcertingly slow, and a lieutenant's pay inadequate to support a
wife and children except in absolutely minimal fashion, but the military camaraderie continued to suit Sherman. The army also gave him a
coveted status. He was welcome in the homes of the wealthiest people.
He mingled with the prominent Southern men (even if he did consider
many of them snobs) and delighted in the company of young ladies. After
he and Ellen planned to marry, he hoped for her "to spend one year at
Fort Moultrie . . . that you might . . . become familiar with Garrison life."
Touting the elitism that he considered inherently characteristic of army
life, he testified, "I have known ladies to form a most singular attachment to [army] life which I could only account for by the fact that in the
Army one is sure of being thrown in contact with *Ladies* and Gentlemen
only."[12]

Sherman's dedication to the army and fond memories of West Point
were again displayed when Hugh Boyle Ewing entered the military
academy. After Sherman's furlough following his shoulder injury in
early 1845, he returned to Fort Moultrie via New York and West Point.
The justification for sailing up the Hudson to the academy was to see
how Hugh was getting along. He forwarded a positive report to Thomas
Ewing, who had been less than enthusiastic about his son's decision

to pursue a military education. Hugh was "in good health and spirits," wrote Sherman. He was "well set up, square shoulders, full in the chest and withal a fine looking soldierly fellow—in manner and conversation much more manly than when at home." Sherman claimed that Hugh daily became "more attached to his books and duties."[13]

Hugh Ewing struggled at the academy for four years, his consistently low academic standing preventing him from ever graduating. Although Sherman had warned the youngster of the difficult work he would encounter at West Point, Thomas Ewing, to some degree, held Sherman responsible for Hugh's decision to go there. Sherman did encourage him to apply, perhaps because he sensed that Hugh's mind was already set. Whatever, precisely, Sherman's role may have been in bringing about Hugh's West Point years, he decided to write a letter to Thomas Ewing describing the impact that the military academy has upon a young man. Sherman wrote as if his thoughts were generic. Actually, he could hardly have penned a better appraisal of how the West Point experience molded him. One suspects that is exactly what he intended.

Observing that the young men are "almost entirely excluded from the world during the four most important years of their life," he asserted that as a result they are "easily convinced of the superiority of them-selves over everybody else, acquire a sort of *contempt for civil pursuits* [emphasis added], and live in the hope of one day acquiring the glorious fame of a military hero." Such feelings, he concluded, leave "an impres-sion upon the mind long after their better reason and judgment have convinced them of their fallacy."

Sherman remained keenly aware that both Ellen and her father strongly favored some brand of a "civil pursuit" for his career. Yet he made it clear, always trying to choose his words and expressions care-fully, that he did not wish to give up the military. He hoped to marry his foster sister, and he held Thomas Ewing in high esteem; but neither they nor anyone else would ever undermine his fondness for West Point and the United States Army. Years later, after the fall of Vicksburg, Sherman told the officers and men of his command that the U.S. Army is "in fact, the most perfect machine which the wisdom of man has ever devised."[14]

As 1845 progressed, Sherman's thoughts often were with Ellen. "All of my comrades are away at a small party at the other end of the island," he wrote to her on June 9, "whilst I alone sit here in dead silence." Then he declared, "Where my thoughts are you can tell," and expressed the wish that "for a few short hours you could enjoy [the night], sitting on our piazza by the faint light of the new moon, listening to the rustling surf of the sea, and cooled by the fresh breeze that comes over the ocean." With romantic, near poetic words, he attested: "It is truly a lovely night, when one may sit for hours and enjoy undisturbed that gentle quiet and repose that resembles a life of dreams rather than actual existence in this rascally world."[15]

Indeed Ellen's and Sherman's actual relationship evidenced a bit of the "rascally world," certainly more so than "a life of dreams." Their face-to-face meeting early in the year—when at last they laid aside "deceitful pen and ink," to quote Sherman, and communicated their thoughts in person—did not lead to the resolution of issues for which he had hoped. In addition to disagreements about his army career and Catholicism, the young couple also faced a problem about where to live once they were married. Ellen wanted to remain close to her family, which likely would be impossible if Sherman stayed in the military. Even if he left the army, he did not want to live in Ohio, for fear he would somehow eventually slip into dependence upon Thomas Ewing. Also, in a letter to Hugh, Sherman once declared, "I do not know positively whether I shall all my life keep to the Army, but should I leave I should not return to Ohio ... as I must confess I do not like the people in it as well as some other states; besides young men always seem to get along better away from their homes." His last phrase just might be interpreted as an underlying, perhaps even subconscious reference to Thomas Ewing—a concern that the powerful man's close proximity would threaten Sherman's ability to control his own destiny, as well as that of his family.[16]

Even some of Sherman's expressions of concern about Ellen's health are coupled with the possibility of leaving Ohio in favor of a warmer climate. "I fear your health is too delicate for exposure to your rude weather," he once wrote. "Whenever this crosses my mind I fear I violate one of the Holy Commandments in coveting the wealth so foolishly lavished by those who do not deserve it." His use for such riches would not be selfish, he asserted, "but that I might share it with you, and bring you to this mild and delightful climate [Charleston] . . . a scene so . . . different from the storms and gales of the North with its bitter cold and snow." This is not to say that Sherman was insincere in writing about what locale might be best for his fiancée's health. Nevertheless, as also in speaking about possibly living in Alabama, such warmer climates as he suggested obviously would eliminate the prospect of living close to the Ewing family.[17]

Many of Sherman's letters—whether addressed to Ellen, his brother John, Thomas Ewing or someone else—clearly convey a pronounced reluctance to leave the army. Yet he does occasionally discuss that issue as a possibility, whereas accepting Catholicism or living in Ohio is never seriously entertained. Regarding the army, one senses that he would be greatly relieved if a war erupted and swept him into action. He could stay in the army, at least for the duration of the conflict, after which no one could predict what might occur. Meanwhile, in the winter of 1845–1846, Sherman experienced a busy social calendar, which was hardly unusual.

"I had to go to North Carolina on a wedding tour at Christmas time," he told John. Noting that "the planters have plenty to eat and drink, and can, without seeming inconvenience, entertain any number of straggling acquaintances," he added that the army officers, "when we expect any assemblage large enough to dance . . . take along four or five musicians . . . which makes us doubly welcome during the Christmas holidays." A few weeks later he told Ellen, "The coming month [February] is the grand time of festivity in Charleston. It is the time fixed by custom for the planters to throng the city for . . . public balls and the races." He had "already received an invitation to a wedding party . . . and a public ball a few days after."[18]

Sherman apparently remained convinced that a war was unlikely, despite persistent rumors. All apprehension of war with England had subsided, he told Ellen on January 31, 1846, "and no occupation is left for us but the proposed invasion of Mexico, which holds out but a slim prospect to a military aspirant." He thought that "Mexico may threaten again . . . but her threats are likely to end in the same words and inactivity as heretofore." He would not be surprised, nor would anyone else, he asserted, if the new Mexican leader recognized "the absolute necessity of making some definite arrangement with [the United States] which would remove the last warlike bone of contention that we have. So," he concluded, "the prospect of a peaceful year is strong, and it therefore becomes me to make all possible preparation to leave the service." The tone of his war thoughts to John strike a different chord, particularly notable regarding his future in the army. "If war takes place," he wrote, "I shall do all I can to better my future and rank, but if it slides by, as other rumors have, I must remain contented with my present commission."[19]

AND THEN the war came. "Mr. Polk's War," some Americans would call it, especially in New England where opposition was strong. Antislavery men believed that the President, seeking the expansion of slavery, had provoked Mexico into war. Actually Polk had little concern whether Texas would be slave or free, and he never wanted war, preferring to consummate his plans for expansion through the expenditure of money rather than blood. He was ready, however, to risk the blood, all the while firmly convinced that diplomatic pressure would achieve his goals. "There will be no war with Mexico," he had assured his brother.[20]

To negotiate with Mexico on behalf of the United States, Polk selected John Mason Slidell, whom he made envoy extraordinary and minister plenipoteniary. Slidell was a native New Yorker who had been practicing law in New Orleans since 1819 and was comfortable with the Spanish language. He arrived in Mexico in November 1845, with instructions to seek "a permanent boundary between Mexico and the United States," including California and the territory to the east (New Mexico), for which he was authorized to offer up to $25 million. (If necessary the President was willing to go as high as $40 million.) From the Mexican point of view, the major cause of disagreement with the United States was the American annexation of Texas, but Slidell had no authorization to even discuss that subject. For Polk, it was a false issue, because Texas had functioned as a republic, independent of Mexico, for nine years before its recent U.S. annexation. Simply expressed, Polk considered Mexico to be in a highly unstable condition, which was true, as well as unprepared to make war, and consequently he believed her government would readily settle for the money offered.[21]

If the effort to buy California and New Mexico should fail, Polk was pursuing another plan to acquire that vast territory; namely, fomenting a rebellion in California against Mexican rule. In mid-October 1845, the President informed Thomas O. Larkin, the American consul in Monterey, that while he would make no attempt to entice California to join the United States, if her people wished "to unite their destiny with ours, they would be received as bretheren." Polk's thinly veiled desires were obvious to Larkin, who was himself an advocate of U.S. expansion. Accordingly, he began marshaling Americans who could be counted on to support a revolution.[22]

Meanwhile, Polk ordered General Zachary Taylor, who had been stationed in Texas, to advance with his command to the Rio Grande, the line Texans claimed as their border with Mexico. Polk's purpose was a show of force, designed to further pressure the Mexican government to settle the boundary issues on the terms proposed by the United States. The movement only made relations worse. Mexico viewed the action as an aggressive one, because it placed American troops in territory "doubly disputed": that is, Mexico accepted neither the U.S. annexation of Texas nor the Rio Grande boundary. To Mexico, the southwest boundary of Texas was the Nueces River. That Taylor was instructed, once positioned at the river, to take no action that might result in a fight was unknown to the Mexicans. Besides, in Mexico's eyes, the very advance to the Rio Grande clearly constituted provocative behavior. Mexico "blustered and threatened" in response to the American move, but her soldiers remained south of the Rio Grande. Consequently, Polk believed all the more that his tactics were working. His vigorous show of strength at the Rio Grande, coupled with a bold diplomatic initiative and an enticing offer of American dollars, would both gain the magnificent coastal strip of California, as well as New Mexico, and also avoid war. Unfortunately, Polk had misinterpreted the situation.[23]

John Slidell could not make any diplomatic progress. No Mexican officials wanted to negotiate with the American, fearing a patriotic backlash from Mexicans who despised the gringos—of whom there were many. Simultaneous with the Mexican crisis, the Polk administration faced a long-festering problem with Great Britain. Polk apparently believed, sincerely, that the American claim to all of the Oregon territory was "clear and unquestionable." His rhetoric egged on Americans who demanded that the decades-old British-American joint occupation of Oregon be terminated, even if it meant yet another war with John Bull. The issue was exacerbated by wild (and false) rumors of British plans to move southward into California. Polk was so angry and frustrated at one point that he wanted Congress to terminate the joint Oregon occupation with Great Britain unilaterally, and take full control of the area.[24]

While the Oregon issue still hung in the fire, Polk decided the time had come to deal decisively with Mexico. As the President talked with his secretary of state, he dismissed any connection of the Mexican and British issues. "We should do our duty," he declared to James Buchanan, "towards both Mexico and Great Britain." The United States should firmly maintain its rights, "and leave the rest to God and the country." These are the righteous words of a man who evaluates issues in either black or white, unmindful or even disdainful of nuances in gray. On May 9, 1846, the President told his cabinet that he had determined to move against Mexico. He would ask Congress to declare war, on the basis of, first, the unpaid $3.5 million owed in damages to American citizens and their property and, second, the Mexican refusal to negotiate with Slidell. A couple of cabinet members possessed the wisdom and courage to advise Polk that he needed more solid grounds for such a momentous step.[25]

As fate would have it, that very evening news of bloodshed arrived. In late April, Mexican troops had crossed the Rio Grande and attacked General Taylor's force. A number of Americans had been killed and wounded. This was the event for which, in recent weeks, Polk had hoped.

Thus, despite "all our efforts" to avoid bloodshed, the President assured Congress that war exists by the act of Mexico herself. American blood, he asserted, had been shed "on American soil." Congress quickly passed a war resolution. The vote in the House was overwhelming, 174–14, and even more one-sided in the Senate, 40–2. On May 13, Polk signed the declaration of war.[26]

Fortunately for the nation and for Polk, the British proved, in the long run, less bellicose about Oregon than the President and some of his supporters. Having earlier rejected a United States proposal to divide the Oregon territory along the 49th parallel, the British eventually reconsidered. During the early months of 1846, they decided the matter was not worth fighting over. The British themselves renewed the proposal to divide Oregon along the 49th parallel. The touchy Polk, still irritated by the previous British rebuff, offered no recommendation, simply turning the matter over to the Senate for whatever decision that body might deem appropriate.

Since the nation was already at war with Mexico, the majority of senators had the good sense to accept a reasonable compromise rather than risk any possibility of a simultaneous conflict with Great Britain. Many northern expansionists were not pleased with the Oregon Compromise, convinced that the Southern President Polk, after the nation got all of Texas, had betrayed their interests in refusing to stand up for all of Oregon. Clearly, however, by any objective standard, the compromise was both reasonable and achieved without bloodshed. Those people who seem always ready to fight somebody, somewhere, about something—as were a number of both Americans and Mexicans—already had their war under way.[27]

Sherman was elated when he learned there was a war on. For a professional army officer, war could mean glory, promotion and increased salary. The possibility of more money, for a soldier who hoped to marry, certainly made war welcome. His only fear was that somehow he might be left out of the action. Even before war was declared, he had applied for a transfer to the likely war zone. Instead he found himself assigned to recruiting duty, and ordered northward. Keenly disappointed, the young lieutenant precipitately tried to take matters into his own hands, only to receive a stinging rebuke from a superior officer who ordered Sherman back to his post. Then in June 1846 he finally experienced a bit of luck, receiving a letter from the adjutant general's office directing him to New York City. There he must report to Captain Christopher Tompkins, commander of Company F, Third Artillery. The company was about to ship out for California, and Captain Tompkins had specifically requested that Lieutenant Sherman join him.[28]

"Ordered to California by Sea round Cape Horn!" he exclaimed in a hurriedly composed June 30 letter to Ellen. "Is not this enough to rouse the most placid? Indeed it is so great an event that I can not realize it in its full force." Soon Sherman would be sailing for the scene of active military operations against Mexico on the Pacific coast. Exactly where he might serve seemed of little consequence. He just wanted to get in on the action. When the California orders came through, he was working at his recruiting post in Pittsburgh. At once he feared that he might not be able to reach New York before the ship departed, in which case, he wrote, "I shall be ruined." All through the night he labored to finalize his reports at the recruiting office in order to leave the next morning. Then, throwing "a few things in my valise," he left the rest of his possessions "in confusion, to be packed up and sent to [Ohio]." Traveling by boat, stagecoach and railroad, he made the trip to New York "in a great hurry," and arrived on July 2—there learning, thankfully, that his ship would not be sailing for nearly two weeks.[29]

Although eager to get under way, Sherman was disturbed because he had not seen his mother before leaving. "What will she think of me?" he inquired of Ellen. "What will the family think?" he continued. "Can't you do something to allay the feeling of grief she must feel?" As for Ellen, he declared that "the hardest part . . . is that we can no longer communicate by letter." Obviously he knew they could still write to each other, but many months likely would pass before the letters could be delivered. The reality was that they would be completely cut off from each other for long periods of time. Additionally, he lamented that he was setting forth upon "a wild and long expedition" without possessing any token from his betrothed, except "a small lock of hair." This one remembrance, however, he hastened to assure her, had always "been guarded when all else was neglected."[30]

Nevertheless, despite such sorrow of parting—"You will think of me will you not?"—he keenly relished the exciting adventure which he anticipated was about to unfold. Sherman and his comrades were to be "pioneers . . . in a far off world." Once this Mexican War became history, Sherman thought he then would be too old to embark upon another career. The passage of so much time would "cut off from me all hope of afterward abandoning this my profession for any other," thus compelling him to "do the best I can under the circumstances." The army, thanks to the war with Mexico, now controlled his irrevocable destiny, as he saw it, for better or worse. Doubtless he hoped this scenario would impress Ellen and persuade her to accept his life in the military.[31]

On July 14, 1846, Sherman finally set sail, aboard a U.S. storeship known as the *Lexington*. She was an old warship, originally rated as a sloop of war and carrying twenty guns. During trial runs the *Lexington* had proved too slow for war purposes. Thus she was converted into a storeship for transporting supplies of all kinds to the Pacific. Sherman noted that six guns still remained for her defense, all located on the upper, or spar, deck. "Our cargo is very heavy," he wrote to Ellen, "as we carry out so many heavy guns for California service, and the magazine of the ship could not contain half our powder which amounts to about eight hundred barrels."[32]

Sherman was pleased with his quarters which were located in "a good state-room in company with my old friend [Edward] Ord." Lieutenant Ord served as the senior first lieutenant under Captain Tompkins, while Sherman was the junior first lieutenant. There were two second lieutenants. Altogether, Company F of the Third Artillery consisted of one hundred and thirteen enlisted men and five officers. Lieutenant Henry Wager Halleck of the engineers, a West Point contemporary of Sherman, was also on board, as well as Dr. James L. Ord, another brother of Edward, who accompanied the expedition as a surgeon. The naval officer in charge of the vessel was Lieutenant-Commander Theodorus

Bailey, with a crew of about fifty. Sherman recorded that four women sailed with them, the wives of soldiers; along with two children, "to whom the sailors are fast teaching all the oaths in their calendar." Sherman observed additionally that a coop full of chickens, half a dozen pigs and a cat were on board.[33]

Nearly three weeks out of New York, Sherman seemed in good spirits, noting that "the day is beautiful and our ... ship is pitching along at a good rate." He felt fortunate that he had been to sea often and thus was accustomed to various restrictions, particularly on the use of water, which some of the men found troublesome. Nor, he assured Ellen, "have I been in the least sea-sick." He declared that he had given up cigars. "The reason was, it hurt my breast and I gave it up before leaving Pittsburgh and already experience relief." Confidently he predicted: "The habit shall never be resumed," only to claim, in the same sentence, that "nowhere is the temptation so great as on ship-board where one has so much time hanging heavily upon his hands."[34]

Although Sherman had been to sea a number of times, living with the hardships of ocean travel and passing through some rough weather, nothing in his previous experience came close to comparing with the voyage around the Horn. The journey consumed more than half of a year, becoming a trying tutorial in patience, as one long day of discomfort and boredom succeeded another, only to be broken by occasional periods of sheer terror. When the taxing ordeal had passed at last, Sherman's war in California would bear little resemblance to anything that he might possibly have imagined.

Because the ship's crew was shorthanded and soldiers need to be kept busy anyway, the company was divided into four squads, under the four lieutenants, and arrangements made with the naval officers for the army to help the sailors. While the soldiers worked on the deck, the sailors worked aloft with the rigging. Sherman said that "on fair days we drilled our men at the manual, and generally kept them employed as much as possible, giving great attention to the police and cleanliness of their dress and bunks." When not occupied with such duties, he composed lengthy letters to friends and relatives; above all to Ellen, although there was no chance to mail them until the *Lexington* reached Rio de Janeiro. Some of the officers had brought along books, which Sherman was allowed to borrow. He was interested in reading anything he could find about California. "All authors seem to agree that the part of California we are going to is a perfect paradise," he told Ellen, "and should belong to the United States."[35]

The time that Sherman passed in reading books apparently increased as the length of the voyage increased. Henry Halleck, already nick-named "Old Brains" because he recently wrote a book called *Elements of Military Art and Science*, was probably the most studious officer aboard the *Lexington*. He made quite an impression on Sherman. Years later, during the Civil War, in a letter to Thomas Ewing, he extolled Halleck as a grand strategist. He recalled that "in our voyage around Cape Horn many a time when others were struggling to kill time, he was using it in hard study." Even when, according to Sherman, "the Sea was high, & the ship rolling, the Sky darkening so that daylight did not reach his state-room, he stood on a stool, his book & candle on the upper berth, and a bed strap round his middle secured to the frame to support him in the wild tossing of the ship."[36]

The voyage from New York to Rio passed without incident, and with few noteworthy occurrences. Sherman did tell Ellen about crossing the equator on August 28, and the consequent customary ritual in honor of Poseidon—or Neptune, since the sailors employed the Roman terminol-ogy. "Old Neptune usually mounts the bow of the ship," wrote Cump, dripping with "brine and accompanied by his beautiful wife. They then proceed to initiate the novices." The traditional initiation consisted of shaving "with a large razor" all those who never before had crossed south of the equator, and so it was done to the greenhorn sailors. But the soldiers, who far outnumbered the entire naval crew, proved less than enthusiastic about endorsing that time-honored custom of the sea. Thus Neptune was not to have his way with the Third Artillery. As for Sher-man, he did allow the vessel's commander to sprinkle him with seawa-ter, and administer an oath, whereby he swore that he would comport himself always like "a true son of Neptune."[37]

In the same letter Sherman told Ellen that "forty-six days have now passed since our departure, and looking back upon them nothing is seen that will leave an impression save the monotonous flight of time." Decades later, he still remembered vividly the humdrum of the lengthy voyage. "At last," he wrote, "after sixty days of absolute monotony," the *Lexington* arrived at Rio, and slowly moved into the harbor. "Words will not describe the beauty of this perfect harbor," he declared, "nor the delightful feeling after a long voyage of its fragrant airs, and the entire contrast between all things there and what we had left in New York."[38]

As quickly as possible, Sherman was off the ship, accompanied by the Ord brothers, Halleck and some other officers. The *Lexington* had anchored at a wharf near the famous French Hotel Pharoux, which featured a gourmet restaurant. Sherman named beefsteak, omelets, potatoes, bread and butter, oranges, bananas, ice cream, iced liquors and coffee among the delights that contributed to a most welcome repast. "I need hardly add," he told Ellen, that "after fifty-nine days' abstinence from such luxuries, ample justice was done."[39]

Sherman said the group also visited the Rua da Ouvador, which was Rio's main street, where most of the stores and shops of the city were located. There he found displayed "every article of use and luxury that man or woman could desire: ladies' bonnets, artificial flowers made of shells, silk and feathers, all made by girls who sit in rows at their task looking their prettiest." Strolling along the paved street for nearly a mile, Sherman admitted in his memoirs that he did so "as much to see the pretty girls as the flowers which they so skillfully made." And not surprisingly, he went to the theater his first night in Rio, noting that the Emperor Dom Pedro and his empress, the daughter of the king of Sicily, were also in attendance. He spent about a week in the city and paid at least one more visit to the theater. "Upon Sundays and all festivals the Theater is thronged," he informed Ellen, remarking that he "heard the opera of *Beatrice di Tenda*," pronouncing it "better than any opera in New Orleans. The Theater too is larger than that of the St. Charles, the largest in the United States."[40]

Sherman thoroughly enjoyed the time he spent in Rio, exploring the city to the fullest extent possible during his brief sojourn. His tastes were eclectic and insatiable. He visited the churches, admiring the architecture, statues, altars and paintings. His concerns were essentially aesthetic, cultural and generally academic, rather than spiritual. "I stood in the Sanctum Sanctorum of the Conventa do Pradus, or Santo Bento," he told Ellen. "It was beautiful, for it is the chapel of the richest monastery and convent of the Brazilian Empire." Then he proceeded to describe it for her in detail—perhaps more specifics than she ever wanted to know. He also studied the red-tiled Portuguese and Spanish houses, and made sketches of some. The harbor of the port city, with its numerous fleet of war vessels and merchant ships, impressed him too. "Really it far surpasses New York Bay in every respect—in the facility for entrance, the depth of water and bold outlines of scenery," he wrote Ellen. He drew a map of the harbor in ink on the last page of his September 16 letter, pronouncing his effort "tolerably good, except it is a little too narrow." He visited the Emperor's Palace, the Botanic Gardens and the aqueduct that supplied water for the city. The aqueduct clearly fascinated him and he examined it in detail, impressed with its durability and efficiency.[41]

"The thing I best recall," Sherman later wrote about Rio, "is a visit Halleck and I made to Corcovado," a high mountain "which overtops all others and stands like a king among the many peaks that are in sight." From this height a beautiful mountain stream, locally known as the "Mother of Waters," supplied the city of a quarter of a million via the aqueduct. The trek up the Corcovado proved "steep and long; the path was winding round and round the hill, so that it was half past two before we stood upon the summit." He declared that "the scene was magnificent." He and Halleck had walked ten miles to reach the peak, "and the same distance lay between us and dinner." Consequently, the sun was setting when they finally enjoyed "a hearty, substantial dinner, to which ample justice was done, for we were hungry, wet and cold."[42]

While Sherman obviously was impressed by the natural beauty of Rio's setting, appreciated the architecture and grandeur of its churches, admired the engineering of the city's aqueduct and enjoyed the opera and theater, and more, he spoke disparagingly of "the lazy Portuguese."

He wrote Ellen that "the people generally are well dressed, but form a curious medley of all colors," with "blacks being able to attain all ranks in society." He viewed Rio's culture as a peculiar paradox, noting that although blacks might rise to a high position, at the same time "slavery in its worst form is practiced openly, even the importation of slaves by the thousands from Africa." Such a scene made him uncomfortable.[43]

The status of blacks in Rio was a minor concern to Sherman, however, when compared with the war against Mexico. Observing that "the war excites much speculation here," he informed Ellen that everyone seemed to think "the people of the United States are determined to possess North Mexico, regardless of the principles involved." His own opinion was that "such is pretty near the truth, but we will hear all about it when we get to California." By the time the *Lexington* put to sea once more, resuming her southward course, Sherman was ready to depart.[44]

"We sailed from Rio on the evening of the 21st of September," he wrote his sister Elizabeth, "and ran down the coast of South America with nothing to disturb the usual monotony" for more than three weeks. Then, a few miles north and east of Cape Horn, the *Lexington* plowed into, as Sherman characterized it, "the sea so much dreaded by sailors." The weather had become quite cold, but he reported that "a bright sun made us for the day think the dangers ... more imaginary than real." Never had he been more wrong. Late that afternoon Sherman watched as a heavy mass of clouds arose to the southwest, "boiling up and up till it gave way to a howling wind ... charged with snow squalls that swallowed up everything."[45]

Then "began the scuffle, and for twelve whole days and nights," he told Ellen, "clouds of snow with gales followed each other in quick succession." The ship was driven farther and farther to the east as the powerful winds, heavy with snow and sleet, swept her far off course. Sherman found himself enveloped by "waves such as I had never seen before" as the sea "ran very high and made many breaches over us." Given his zest for experiencing life to the fullest, and since there was no escaping Neptune's fury, he sought satiation; fearlessly attempting to perceive, to the greatest degree possible, the unmitigated wrath of the sea god. "Amidst the heaviest of the storm," he wrote, "I had to go on deck ... impelled by curiosity to see the gale, to watch the big wave coming on as though it would engulf all, and the old *Lexington* rise slowly to its very summit and majestically sink into the next valley, ready to rise upon the next height."[46]

Sherman also confided to Ellen that he sometimes lay in his berth for hours, "listening to the creaking of the timbers," and wondering how man "with his limited strength," could build a ship strong enough to withstand such constant pounding from the weight of the gigantic waves. He wondered "how long this particular [vessel] can stand it," and whether in case of disaster he should "try his chances with a floating spar, or like the monkey, clap my hands to my head and go down without a struggle." Everything, sooner or later, has an end. The storms subsided, the *Lexington* survived, and with winds to her advantage, Cape Horn eventually came into view.[47]

Passing close by the jagged, snow-clad height, Sherman imagined that the worst was over, and that for the first time the ship would be heading northward to California. Again he was mistaken. Another powerful storm arose, which he declared "served us more rudely than its predecessor." More than once he thought that "the ship must be swamped." He wrote Elizabeth that the *Lexington*'s captain, who had rounded the Horn a dozen times, as well as another naval officer whose life at sea had been even more extensive, told him that they had "never encountered so heavy a sea or such persevering head gales."[48]

Continuing with the account for his sister, Sherman recorded that "often our decks were covered with ice and snow, the rigging dangling with icicles, whilst the wind moaned and whistled." He would not attempt, he said, to give an idea of "the height or force of the waves." Words were inadequate—the thing had to be experienced before anyone could possibly understand the dreadful scenes. He reported to Ellen that after ten more days of storm, they were "still south of Cape Horn, the crew worn out and all dispirited. ... The wind still continues from the north-west and God only knows when it will cease." The rounding of Cape Horn must have seemed like a voyage from hell. The superstitious among the sailors, recorded Sherman, claimed that like Jonah's fate in the Old Testament, heaven was punishing them "for being the instruments in an iniquitous cause." (Did this mean the war with Mexico? Sherman did not say.)[49]

After such a time-consuming, violent and terrifying passage around the Horn, Sherman understandably had no wish to repeat the voyage in the other direction. His instructions to Elizabeth, while a tad tongue-in-cheek, are memorable: "If you hear about a subscription opening to dig a canal across the Isthmus of Panama, you may put me down any amount, for really I do not fancy a voyage of twenty-four thousand miles to accomplish a distance of less than two thousand." When he did return east, he hoped to pass through Mexico. However, he told Elizabeth that he did not "dream of a return to the United States for five or six years." He was still "anxious to hear the state of the war," and get to the area where fighting was taking place.[50]

When at last the *Lexington* made the harbor at Valparaíso, she was sixty-four days out from Rio. Sherman did not think the Chilean port compared with Rio, but there were both British and American vessels in the harbor, and some of them carried news from California. It was not what he had hoped to hear. All California's coastal towns were reported already in possession of the American fleet. Thus, Sherman concluded, the Third Artillery probably would have "little to do other than land and fortify either San Francisco or Monterey—no fighting." That, he thought, was "too bad," especially after coming so far. Actually, he still had a long way to go before reaching California, and it was late in January 1847 when the *Lexington* finally arrived off the coast, near Monterey.[51]

Chapter Seven

DEPRIVED OF
MILITARY GLORY

Landing in California, like much of the long and tedious voyage from New York, was anything but routine. Due to a navigational miscalculation—"one of those accidents so provoking," lamented Sherman—the *Lexington* sailed approximately forty miles north of Monterey before her master navigator finally discerned the ship's true location. Little would the error have mattered if the Pacific had lived up to its name; but before the *Lexington* could retrace her course, a storm boiled up. "We then began to beat south against a head wind," reported Sherman, "which gradually increased into a gale." The ship was buffeted about for several days. He wrote Ellen that one night "we lay into a gale which would have done credit to Cape Horn." Sherman knew, "while cursing that unfortunate observation on the north star," that otherwise the ship would have been "snugly anchored [at Monterey Bay] before the storm arose."[1]

When the mighty winds at last abated, the *Lexington* headed into the bay, much to the relief of everyone on board. Coming out to meet her in a smaller vessel was Lieutenant Henry Wise, master of the U.S. frigate *Independence*, whose assignment was to guide the *Lexington* to her anchorage. Once aboard, Wise quickly briefed all the men who cared to listen. Wise's version of the state of affairs in California proved rather alarming. He reported that the Californians were in rebellion; that General Stephen W. Kearny, after marching from Santa Fe, had fought a battle at San Pasqual in which he lost several officers and men; that fighting was going on at Los Angeles; that the whole country harbored guerrillas who opposed the Americans; and that the naval fleet under Commodore Robert F. Stockton was far down the coast at San Diego— much too far away to render any assistance.[2]

"We imagined that we should have to debark and begin fighting at once," remembered Sherman. "Swords were brought out, guns oiled and made ready, and everything was in a bustle when the old *Lexington* dropped her anchor ... after a voyage of one hundred and ninety-eight days from New York." As quartermaster and commissary, Sherman anticipated that he would be very busy. Supplying the troops and supervising the disbursement of money constituted major responsibilities. He also significantly observed that "nothing could [have been] more peaceful in its looks than Monterey" when the *Lexington* reached her anchorage.[3]

Sherman's assessment was correct. The appearance of Monterey proved not in the least deceptive. The town looked peaceful because it was peaceful, and the *Lexington*'s landing was totally unopposed. Henry Wise's report had greatly exaggerated the extent of guerrilla activity and the number of Californians in rebellion. Fighting in Los Angeles posed no immediate concern because of its great distance from Monterey, and naval forces at San Diego were of no need or value at Monterey anyway. The earlier news garnered in Valparaíso, that the war in California had passed them by, seemed to be confirmed. Sherman would write: "I fear that I leaped the mark in search of [military] glory by coming to California, but such is the cast of fortune, and all must abide by its decrees." Beyond doubt some soldiers, unlike Sherman, rejoiced to know that apparently fortune's decrees had exempted them from the fighting. As fate decreed, Company F would be the Third Artillery's only unit never to see action in the war.[4]

Sherman found that fact hard to take. Never once engaged in combat, while his West Point peers were winning military laurels in Mexico, proved keenly disappointing and even embarrassing to a man of Sherman's abilities, ambition and dedication to the armed services of his country. Convinced that the Mexican conflict was the only chance for military achievement in his day, Sherman didn't get beyond his disillusionment over failing to get into that action until more than a decade later, when the Civil War presented an unexpected and even greater military opportunity. Several of his letters, penned during the California years, clearly convey how deeply he felt his loss and how difficult it was for him to cope with that reality.

He learned of exciting campaigns being waged hundreds of miles to the south. He heard of Zachary Taylor's battle at Buena Vista, of Winfield Scott's capture of Veracruz, the battle of Cerro Gordo and the advance of Scott's army as far as Puebla. "These brilliant scenes nearly kill us," he grieved, "who are . . . deprived of such precious pieces of military glory." Probably his disappointment in missing the war colored his general attitude toward California. He told Ellen, "I do not like California as a country. It is dry and barren notwithstanding some of the glowing accounts." California's "garden spots," were only "beautiful and fertile in contrast to the dry parched-up hills that envelope them." Some officers were purchasing property, but Sherman "wouldn't give two counties of Ohio, Kentucky or Tennessee for the whole of California."[5]

Months later he seemed still dominated by a pessimistic mind-set, mourning his loss of any chance for military fulfillment. "I am so completely banished that I feel I am losing all hope, all elasticity of spirit," he wrote. Asserting that he felt ten years older than when he sailed for California, he told Ellen that he no longer experienced a desire for exercise as he did in former days. Then he got to the crux of the matter: "To hear of the war in Mexico and the brilliant deeds of the army, of my own regiment, and my own old associates, everyone of whom has gained honors, and I out here in California, banished from fame, from everything that is dear and no more prospect of ever getting back than one of the old adobe houses that mark a California ranch!" In late August of 1848, Sherman confided to Ellen, "I have felt tempted to send my resignation to Washington and I really feel ashamed to wear epaulettes after having passed through a war without smelling gunpowder, but God knows I couldn't help it."[6]

Sherman was compelled to conclude that his career as a soldier had reached a dead end. Such an outcome proved truly bitter, especially when contrasted with the grand euphoria he had experienced upon learning that at last there was a war on. He had embarked for California with youthful spirit and anticipation, eager to know "the glorious thing called war," and dreaming of military laurels. But upon reaching California, the life that enveloped and even in a sense ensnared him bore little resemblance to his cherished hopes and expectations, and soon proved barren of any meaningful opportunities for advancement in his chosen profession.

Despite his disillusionment, Sherman demonstrated a remarkable resilience, strongly sustained by a capacity for long hours of work, a high-energy level and a lifestyle of near incessant activity. Limited opportunities for military accomplishment did not stop Sherman from making the most of his time in California. And what a time it was! He participated in the origins of a magnificent state—one characterized by myriad variations of geography, climate, resources and people, the whole creating an immeasurable potential for wealth and power. Above all, Sherman was present when gold was discovered, witnessing the far-reaching impact of that precious metal as the word went forth across the North American continent and around the globe. The experience taught him fundamental lessons about life itself, as he viewed deplorable changes wrought in the lives and values of men and women, many of whom quickly succumbed to raw, irrational, even barbaric impulses of greed. He beheld a society dramatically transformed, in an amazingly short period of time. It was not a pretty sight.

SOON AFTER SHERMAN arrived in the future Golden State, he began venturing forth to examine his surroundings. Years later he wrote that "Ord and I, impatient to look inland, got permission and started for the mission of San Juan Bautista." Mounted on horses and with their carbines handy, Sherman and his friend traveled some thirty-five miles from Monterey and made the acquaintance of several people. Being at the mission on a Sunday, he said that Ord, "who was somewhat of a Catholic," entered the church, attracting the attention of all, with his clanking spurs and American uniform.[7]

Then in late April, Sherman got an opportunity to see much more of the country. General Kearny decided to make a trip to Los Angeles and take Sherman along as his aide. Sherman was quite pleased. Although Kearny had received two lance wounds in the fight at San Pasqual, when Sherman saw the general soon afterward, he wrote Ellen that "nevertheless his face wore that smile so characteristic of him. He has always been a favorite model of mine and I was peculiarly glad to see him." In the highly publicized controversy between Kearny and John C. Frémont, the so-called Pathfinder of the West, about who exercised supreme power in California, Sherman favored Kearny, as might have been expected. Sherman thought, like most of the army officers, that "if anyone else had put on such airs" as the Pathfinder, defying Kearny and claiming to be the rightful governor of California even though the general outranked him, he would have been dealt with harshly. Sherman attributed Frémont's stature to the influence of his powerful father-in-law, Senator Thomas Hart Benton of Missouri. Also Frémont commanded volunteers rather than regular soldiers, a factor predictably stirring Sherman's ire. Frémont's volunteers, Sherman stated, caused much disorder across the countryside, having "committed many excesses." There is evidence that Sherman also did not like Frémont personally. Neither did he care for Robert Stockton, the naval officer who initially positioned himself with Fremont against Kearny. He wrote Ellen, speaking of Stockton, that "the Grandioso . . . is a great blatherscythe [who] talks too much and does too little," as well as engaging in various "California acts of foolishness." He did not cite any examples of this "foolishness."

Sherman was excited about the trip to Los Angeles. It would enable him "to see all the country [between Monterey and Los Angeles] and be thrown in contact with men who are to influence this new country." As usual, he was seizing the chance to meet important people. The one drawback was the mode of transportation to Los Angeles: traveling by sea on the old *Lexington*. Returning to Monterey, however, would likely be on horseback, an adventure eagerly anticipated, when he could explore a great deal of territory that he had never visited before.[8]

Sailing down the coast with a welcome fair wind, the *Lexington* soon anchored at Los Angeles. Sherman recalled that General Kearny held to his arm as they ascended a steep path up the bluff from the landing, where horses awaited them. Once more at home on horseback, Sherman enjoyed the twenty-mile ride across the plain from the sea to Los Angeles, a trip of about three hours. While the general and Sherman rode, the accompanying infantry followed on foot. "We spent several days very pleasantly at Los Angeles," he later wrote, "then, as now, the chief *pueblo* of the south, famous for its grapes, fruits, and wines." One day he rode up a high ridge, seeking a vantage point from which to examine the entire valley. The view was impressive and he estimated that the space of ground cultivated in vineyards probably stretched about five miles in length, by a mile in width, a portion of which encompassed the town itself. "The climate was so moderate," he observed, "that oranges, figs, pomegranates, etc., were generally to be found in every yard or inclosure."[9]

Although he savored the time spent in Los Angeles, Sherman was not unhappy when his departure date arrived. As General Kearny sailed for Monterey, Sherman set out by land, with about forty troops, some mounted on mules and others on horses. Averaging approximately thirty miles per day, he relished "the best kind of opportunity for seeing the country." At night everyone slept on the ground in the open air. He marveled at how "sparsely populated indeed" was the region, as he encountered only a few families living at the various missions.[10]

Throughout the years in California Sherman seized every chance to explore the countryside, certainly in part because of his wide-ranging interests and curiosity, but probably also simply to keep his mind occupied. One of his passions was hunting. Writing Ellen that he kept about forty horses grazing some seven miles from Monterey, in the Carmel Valley, under a guard, he said he rode out frequently, spent the night and then hunted alone in the morning. Again he told her: "I have my horse and gun and am in the hills all the time when not on duty. . . . I want to kill a grizzly bear, the terror of the land." For a time, Sherman's quest to bring down a grizzly apparently became a near obsession. "I was out all the day before yesterday tramping over the mountains to get a shot at a grizzly," he wrote in another letter. He said he finally spotted one, "but the fellow made tracks and I pursued till I was exhausted and sick. . . . My poor horse no doubt hopes I will continue so till he can recover his spirits in the wild oats pasture that he enjoys during my confinement." The chances are that Sherman never felled "the terror of the land." If he did, he failed to mention the kill in any of his many surviving letters to Ellen, and it seems highly unlikely that he would have kept silent about a triumph sought with such gusto.[11]

Sherman's social calendar also kept him occupied. Not long after arriving in Monterey he attended a play that made a very favorable impression. He wrote several paragraphs telling Ellen about *The Temptation and Fall of Man*, commenting about the actors and actresses, particularly noting Dolores Gomez, who "played the part [of Eve] to perfection." He thought the sets were well conceived, especially the Garden of Eden, which was "executed with great taste. . . . The whole [production] struck me forcibly, especially the good taste that marked the stage, the dresses and the performance." Years later, when he had attended a great many productions, some in the most impressive theaters of America and Europe, he still remembered that Monterey presentation.[12]

And Sherman seems seldom to have missed a chance to attend a party in California. Clearly he became familiar with the fandango occasions, where he delighted in observing the fairer sex. "The women are like all other Spanish women, the prouder the more Castilian blood they can boast of." He observed that "some are pretty, and all dance and waltz well," although he claimed they "scorn the vulgar accomplishments of reading and writing." Two months after arriving in California, he informed Ellen that he had attended several lively Spanish-American dances. He seemed fascinated by the popular custom of breaking a *cascarone* over the head of a preferred member of the opposite sex. He said that they were "eggshells filled with essences, a gold leaf and spangles mixed with [clips of] colored papers, which they break over the heads of favorites." Sherman experienced a number of fandangos, "beginning before sundown and ending after daylight." By midnight "every head was bespangled and besmeared with cologne."[13]

Nearly a year later Sherman was still enjoying the fandango circuit, and telling Ellen more about the etiquette of the merrymaking. "It is polite to avoid a Cascarone, but when a gentleman gets a Cascarone on his head he is bound to return it, which is sometimes quite difficult when the ladies are skilled in dodging." At a recent gathering, he declared, "there were upwards of four hundred Cascarones broken among a party of not over twenty-five persons." Then, revealing a culturally open-minded attitude, he concluded that "the customs of Monterey are as sensible as the customs of other places, and must be respected."[14]

Among other local customs of particular interest, Sherman observed the funeral of a little girl, about nine years of age. He stood on the piazza of the Government House while the funeral procession slowly passed. He wrote that several women carried the neat and delicately decorated bier on which the small and beautiful child lay. Behind the bier followed a crowd, "not silently two by two, but gaily . . . and with a band of music." He noted that "guns were fired from the houses which they passed, and upon inquiry, finding that such was the custom . . . , we got out several pistols and fired a perfect salvo, of rejoicing that the child had gone to heaven. Such is custom." Observing that in some communities there would be a year of mourning, Sherman stated, "I like this custom best, and want no one to weep my exit or to let it detain them one minute from any occupation or pleasure."[15]

Sherman's appreciation of selected local customs should not be interpreted to mean that he respected the Californians generally. Far from it. His primary description of the Mexican Californians was "lazy," the same word he chose for the Portuguese in Rio and the Chileans in Valparaíso. Though acknowledging that some Californians were "famous horsemen," he also wrote Ellen that the "lazy devils" do not like "our ways, our institutions, our restlessness." He charged that "our internal taxes, our labors all are too complicated for their lazy brains, and lazy hands." He declared they were so lacking in ambition that all they want is "a good horse, a lasso, a glazed hat and tassels, a flashy serapa, slashed pantaloons tipped with velvet and corded with bright silk ties, and a pair of spurs as big as a plate." Thus provisioned, the typical male happily consumed "his greasy platter of beans and mutton." Having been accustomed, for example, to living with no fireplaces in warmer country to the south, he said they still thought they needed none when they moved farther north. "If you were to transplant a Mexican from his native city to Canada," Sherman alleged that the man "would not think of warming his house by artificial heat. Many a night have I shivered in a big cold adobe house," he wrote. Mexicans in California "are bad enough, but in Mexico," he concluded, "they are far worse."[16]

Sherman's attitude toward the California women was much more favorable than his opinion of the men. He told Ellen that "the women are better, kinder, and more industrious." He admired their work ethic. "They . . . wash all the clothes, grind all the corn on a stone by rubbing another over it, plant . . . patches of onions and red peppers, and do all the cooking." He found their appearance pleasing, remarking that "some of them are quite pretty, amiable, and have good minds which, if cultivated, would make them above the average."[17]

Perhaps Sherman's appreciation of the California females stemmed from a basic preference for the company of women. Earlier he held the Spanish women of St. Augustine in higher esteem than the men. The belles of Mobile and Charleston generally received higher marks than had the males. Even the young women of the backcountry in northeast Alabama merited an approving nod from Sherman. This pattern involves more than a young man's sexual libido. That is a part of it, to be sure. But years after the Civil War when Sherman was older, in his mid-fifties and sixties, he still sought the company of women whenever he got the chance.

Was Sherman sexually intimate with any women other than his wife? The milieu of his relationships with women—established over the years via his letters, as well as through various social activities, such as parties, dinners, dances, weddings and the theater—strongly suggests that he simply liked and preferred associations with the opposite sex. This, of course, is not to deny that one or more relationships might have developed beyond the platonic. The foregoing does not mean that he experienced any difficulties in relating to men. From his first years at West Point, where he certainly proved popular with other cadets, as well as throughout his life, he readily connected with men of both military and civil standing. This was true of peers, as well as of officers of superior rank, businessmen and politicians with greater authority than he and those who served under him. Following the Civil War, no general on either side was held in higher esteem by the men whom he had commanded. There is no question that Sherman got on quite well with men, but always he liked associating with women.

During the summer of 1848, Sherman enjoyed the most pleasant accommodations of his years in California. "I have been living very comfortably in the family of Doña Augustias," he wrote Ellen in late August. Sherman characterized her as "the very first lady of Monterey and in fact of California." She was "very kind and intelligent." Also he remarked that "her pretty little daughter Manuelita makes a good sister." As for Doña Augustias's husband, Don Manuel Jimeno, Sherman reported that the man "passes most of his time on his ranch about forty miles away, so that I am a species of guardian to the family." Sherman thought his fortunate circumstances were too good to last long. It is hardly surprising that rumors eventually surfaced alleging that Sherman had become involved in a romantic attachment with Doña Augustias.[18]

In the winter of 1849, Ellen wrote Cump suggesting he should seek a more robust young woman for his wife. If he were to marry a California lady, Ellen promised that she would welcome her genuinely and warmly to the family in Ohio. Expressing serious concern about her seemingly chronic poor health, Ellen said she doubted she herself possessed the necessary strength to make Sherman a good wife.

The psychology motivating Ellen's message is thought provoking. Did she really believe that she should remain single because of her troublesome physical condition, which during this period kept her confined at times almost as if she were an invalid? Or was she responding, as best she knew how when they were so far apart, to Sherman's rather frequent observations and laudatory remarks about the women with whom he came in contact? Whatever prompted her suggestion that he marry someone else, Sherman forthrightly discounted such a possibility, assuring her that he had no interest in any other woman. "My love for you," he affirmed, "has never abated, and never wavered." If Sherman ever considered turning to another during his long separation from Ellen, he wisely kept his thoughts to himself.[19]

FOR THE GREATER PART of his California tour, Sherman was under the command of Colonel Richard B. Mason, General Kearny having headed back east in the late spring of 1847. Mason was the most powerful man in California, serving as the military governor, and he made Sherman his assistant adjutant general. Sherman prepared the official reports that Mason sent to Washington, and whatever orders he issued for the Tenth Military District; he also served as the Colonel's trusted advisor. Henry Halleck too became an important player during Mason's tenure, acting as his foremost advisor for civil affairs. However, while Sherman's new position entailed more influence, power and prestige, the duties constituted, as historian Basil Liddell Hart astutely observed, "perhaps less valuable experience ... than when, on first landing [in California], he had acted as quartermaster and commissary of the force and thereby acquired a grounding in emergency supply problems."[20]

Sherman was well pleased with his new commander. "Colonel Mason is an excellent man," he told Ellen in an October 1847 letter. With the passage of time, Sherman's positive appraisal grew ever more favorable. He considered Mason a man "of stern character, deemed by some harsh and severe, but in all my intercourse with him he was kind and agreeable. He had a large fund of good sense, and, during our long period of service together, I enjoyed his unlimited confidence." Sherman characterized the colonel as "honest to a fault, [and] the very embodiment of the principle of fidelity to the interests of the General Government." In his private as well as public expenditures, Mason was "extremely economical, but not penurious." Of such a commanding officer, he predictably would approve, for the very same appraisal fit Lieutenant Sherman.[21]

Sherman's respect for Mason was all the greater because he fully realized that California presented a very difficult challenge for any governor. "A bold, enterprising, and speculative set of men," wrote Sherman, "who were engaged in every sort of game to make money," populated the territory. He knew firsthand that the colonel was pressured by the numerous greedy and unscrupulous to use his position to gain wealth for himself, through supporting their untoward schemes in quest of a fortune. Colonel Mason resisted such temptation and, although making some bitter enemies, he faithfully discharged his duties. "He is entitled to all praise," concluded Sherman, for having wisely controlled California, and prepared the way for the eventual establishment of a civil government.[22]

Mason clearly governed California with a strong military hand, which Sherman thoroughly approved. Sherman's lack of patience with democratic-republican government, an attitude nascent in his late teens and early twenties, emerged full blown during the California years. Democratic-republican government, in Sherman's judgment, too often proved excruciatingly slow in the formulation and implementation of law, and also frequently suffered from the ambitions and machinations of corrupt politicians. Sherman had been in California territory a little over a year when he wrote his brother John, "Military law is supreme here." He declared that "we ride down" the few lawyers who appear, and have no laws "save the Articles of War and the Regulations of Police, and yet a more quiet community could not exist."[23]

Sherman seemed to be needling John about the legal profession, which he delighted in doing from time to time. However, his comments also evidenced a pronounced respect for a hard-nosed military government that could act quickly and effectively. Regarding courts of law, Sherman assured John that the military governor would not establish any such institutions, "because the coming of lawyers to California is a bad omen." Already, in his opinion, "the few lawyers" who had ventured to take up residence on the West Coast were more than enough.[24]

While U.S. military law reigned supreme in California as long as the war with Mexico endured, government on the local level functioned under the *alcaldes* (mayors), much as it had in the days of the Mexican regime. Generally the system worked, with Colonel Mason serving basically as a vigilant overseer, ensuring that government by the *alcaldes* ran competently, fair-mindedly and nonabusively. Usually the *alcaldes* did operate acceptably, despite periodic rumors to the contrary. One notable instance of trouble occurred, however, and Sherman readily became involved in resolving the problem. In the little community of Sonoma, an *alcalde* by the name of John H. Nash, referred to as "an old man" by Sherman, refused to obey an order, issued by General Kearny just before he left California, that Nash must surrender his office. Because Nash's election had come during the Frémont-Stockton era, Kearney deemed it invalid. In July 1847, after Nash had defied the order for weeks, Colonel Mason decided to enforce his predecessor's decision. If California were truly under military law, then the *alcalde* had no right to defy an order of the military governor, whether Kearny or Mason. Sherman certainly wanted Nash removed, as an example that no one could trifle with military law. "I suggested to the Colonel," Sherman wrote, "that the case being a test one, he had better send me up to Sonoma, and I would settle it quick enough." With Mason's consent, Sherman eagerly proceeded against the "rebellious" fellow, telling Ellen that Nash would profit from "a little military law."[25]

Sherman laid careful plans, stealthily cooperating with the navy, which provided both round-trip sea transportation from Monterey and the necessary manpower. With the support of naval officer Louis McLane and eight sailors, Sherman led the clandestine force into Sonoma, intending to take Nash by surprise. Such a sizable contingent, merely for the purpose of apprehending "an old man," might seem like overkill. However, Sherman's intelligence, which at best was rather sketchy, indicated that Sonoma was a dangerous little village where most of the American residents sympathized with Nash. Sherman might need every man he had with him.[26]

Learning that Nash, who was a bachelor, was having dinner at the home of a lawyer friend, in the company of two women, Sherman quickly proceeded to take advantage of the man's vulnerable situation. "Post-ing an armed sailor on each side of the house," Sherman reported that "we knocked at the door and walked in." He and McLane were armed with pistols and, just as they hoped, found the two couples seated at the dinner table. Sherman inquired if Nash were present, and one of the women pointed him out. Sherman informed the man that he was under arrest. Nash's host vociferously objected "in theatrical style," according to Sherman's description, "and with loud words," until Sherman told him to shut up or he would take him prisoner also. Heading back to the ship with Nash, Sherman was gone by the next morning.[27]

Nash experienced a rough trip to Monterey. "Poor old Mr. Nash," remembered Sherman, "was half dead from sea-sickness and fear." He said Nash worried that Colonel Mason "would treat him with extreme military rigor." Nothing of the kind happened. The colonel dealt with him kindly, and Nash promised to surrender his office immediately and cause no more trouble. He proved true to his word. Sherman was pleased, viewing the successful operation, small though it had been, as a notable triumph for military law in California.[28]

AND THEN CAME the Gold Rush. "California is fast settling into its origi-nal and deserved obscurity," Sherman ironically declared to his brother in a letter penned shortly before he learned about the discovery of the precious metal. His judgment about California's "obscurity," in retro-spect, is amusing and obviously dead wrong. Later Sherman would write that the discovery of gold in California "revolutionized the whole coun-try, and actually moved the whole civilized world." In that appraisal he did not exaggerate.[29]

On a fateful Sunday morning in January 1848, a man by the name of James Marshall, employed by John Augustus Sutter on a sawmill project along the American River, found traces of gold in the foothills of the Sierra Nevada. Sutter was a highly successful Swiss entrepre-neur. He had built a substantial personal empire at the confluence of the Sacramento and American Rivers (eventually the site of the city of

Sacramento), which he named New Helvetia. Americans simply called it Sutter's Fort.

Sherman, in the course of performing his duties, came to know Sutter, who recounted to him how Marshall, "a half-crazy man at best," walked in looking "strangely wild." Inquiring if anyone was within hearing distance, Marshall even looked under a bed before he would say anything more. Finally he divulged the news to Sutter that he had discovered gold. Sutter said Marshall then laid before him "the pellicles of gold he had picked up in a ditch." Sutter attempted to keep the discovery secret, fearful lest a gold rush overwhelm his business.

He instructed Marshall to go back to work at the mill and say nothing about his find to anyone. But Marshall, as Sherman phrased it, "could not keep out of his wonderful ditch," and the news of what he had discovered leaked out. When other Sutter employees wanted to garner a share of the gold, Marshall threatened to shoot them if they tried. Rather than confront the man, they began "prospecting" farther downstream. From that point on, no one could suppress the scintillating news of gold in California.[30]

Sherman first learned about the gold in the spring of 1848, when two messengers from Sutter arrived at Colonel Mason's office in Monterey. They told Sherman that they wanted to see the colonel, and he ushered them into Mason's office. Within a short time Mason came to the door and summoned Sherman. The colonel then pointed to some mineral pieces the men had laid on his desk, and asked "What is this?" Sherman said he examined a couple of the larger objects and responded, "Is it gold?" Mason wanted to know if he had ever seen gold in its native state. He had, in north Georgia, and only a few years ago. Taking a piece in his teeth, Sherman thought "the metallic lustre was perfect." He procured an axe and a hatchet and proceeded to beat the largest piece of the ore flat. He concluded, "beyond doubt," that it was gold.[31]

What Sutter sought from Mason was a preemption to the land where the precious metal had been discovered. Of course the colonel had no authority to grant Sutter's request. Claims to the land, which Sutter had acquired from the Indians and cited as evidence of ownership, were of no consequence because the United States did not recognize any Indian rights to the land. California was still a Mexican province anyway, simply held by the United States military forces as a conquered territory. U.S. law would not apply until the war ended, a treaty was signed and public surveys conducted. Mason instructed Sherman to prepare a letter, explaining to Sutter that the colonel, acting as the military governor of California, possessed no power to promise him a title to the land. The letter concluded with an assurance that since there were no settlements within forty miles of where Marshall had found gold, Sutter "was not likely to be disturbed by trespassers." The colonel had no inkling of the "Gold Fever" about to sweep California.[32]

So rapidly did the rush develop that by late spring stories of fabulous gold discoveries were spreading throughout California. People left their jobs and poured into the gold country. New arrivals from the east joined them. Some soldiers deserted, despite the threat of the death penalty for desertion during wartime, and headed toward the mining area. The reports of gold came faster and faster, and the price of everything useful for mining, from mules and horses to tin pans and staples, began to rise. "Everybody was talking of Gold! Gold!" remembered Sherman, "until it assumed the character of a fever." He wrote at the time that "the aged have called for their crutches," noted that even children were infected by the addictive quest, and sarcastically remarked that "the lazy Californians are actually working"—for gold that is.[33]

Sherman admitted that he himself was also caught in the grip of gold, eager to see the mines with his own eyes. "I . . . at last convinced Colonel Mason," he said, "that it was our duty" to examine the gold mine sites and "report the truth to our government." He had a compelling point. Acting on the colonel's orders, Sherman made the necessary preparations for the trip, selecting "four good soldiers" to accompany them, along with "a good outfit of horses and pack-mules." The colonel's black servant, Aaron, made the journey, too. On June 17, 1848, the party headed north. Arriving in San Francisco they found that most of the male inhabitants had left for the mines. Quickly pressing on, the group soon arrived at New Helvetia, where John A. Sutter "was monarch of all he surveyed," exercising authority to punish "even unto death," declared Sherman, "a power he did not fail to use."[34]

There they stayed for the remainder of June and into July, making excursions to various mining sites. Sherman "began to see the full effect of the gold," he wrote Captain Henry S. Turner, with whom he had become friends soon after arriving in California. Horses recently worth $15 or $20 were selling for $75 or $100. He gave several examples of the dramatically escalating prices. He also described Sutter and the lavish dinner the wealthy, influential Swiss hosted on July 4, in honor of the American presence. About fifty people, mostly Americans, together with a few foreigners and Californians, sat at large tables and Sutter presided. Colonel Mason sat on Sutter's right and Sherman on his left. "The usual toasts, songs, speeches, etc., passed off," wrote Sherman, "and a liberal quantity of liquor [was] disposed of, champagne, Madeira, Sherry, etc.; upon the whole a dinner that would have done credit in any frontier town."

Sherman clearly relished the occasion and estimated that the affair must have cost fifteen hundred or two thousand dollars. He thought the balding, five-foot-six-inch Sutter had a "striking" personal appearance. Sherman credited the Swiss with fluency in several languages, including Indian tongues, and declared that he exercised "more control over the tribes of the Sacramento than any man living." Sutter had "played a conspicuous part in the history of this country" since 1838, Sherman wrote, "and is likely to continue his onward career."[35]

When Mason and Sherman returned to Monterey they knew they were facing a serious problem. "The sudden development of so much wealth has played the devil with the country," Sherman declared. "Everybody has gone [to the mines], save women and officers. Our soldiers are deserting and we can't stop it," he lamented. "A tailor won't work a day, nor a shoemaker, nor any other tradesman,—all have gone to the mines. The sailors desert their ships as fast as they come." Colonel Mason had been attempting to send reports to Washington, but no ship captain had succeeded in getting a crew together to sail. Sherman had carefully prepared a letter and map that Mason, after making a few modifications, finally got off to Washington, along with gold samples, as reliable evidence for the government that gold had indeed been discovered. As Sherman wrote his brother: "This is not fiction; it is truth."[36]

Then, further complicating the army's difficulties in California, came news that the Treaty of Guadalupe Hidalgo had concluded the war with Mexico. Although the treaty had been signed by the State Department's chief clerk, Nicholas P. Trist, on February 2, 1848, ratified by the U.S. Senate on March 10 and officially accepted by Mexico in May, word did not reach Colonel Mason's office until late summer, arriving by overland courier from Baja California. The United States would pay Mexico $15 million and assume the damage claims of American citizens against Mexico, which totaled $3.25 million. For her part, Mexico agreed to recognize the Rio Grande as the boundary of Texas from the Gulf of Mexico to El Paso, and cede to the United States the vast territory of New Mexico and Upper California. This area encompassed almost a million square miles, or approximately one-half of Mexico. It comprised all of the future state of California, and large portions of the states of New Mexico, Arizona, Utah and Nevada.[37]

Sherman viewed Guadalupe Hidalgo with disgust. "Great Jehovah, what a treaty!" he exclaimed. "A conquering army, in the country of an enemy, making such terms! No wonder we could not impress the Mexicans with respect for us. . . . If we were at war," he raged, "we should never have made apologies for it by paying fifteen millions." There were other provisions of which he disapproved. "Every article of the treaty," he indignantly exaggerated to Captain Turner, "is just such . . . as Mexico would have imposed on us had she been the conqueror."

Unimpressed that the United States was acquiring an enormous chunk of Mexican territory, Sherman complained because Mexico had not relinquished Baja California, a region where her government had exercised nothing more than "a shadow of an authority" for many years. He thought peace could not last long, since "the feeling of the Mexican people toward the Yankees is of such a hostile character." The Mexicans, he declared, "deserve richly a better whipping than they got, and they will have to receive it before they are content." Acknowledging Ellen's sensitivities, which he characterized as "horrified at ... war," Sherman assured her that "you cannot imagine ... the obstinate pride, egotism and nonsense [of the Mexicans.]"[38]

Regardless of Sherman's disapproval of the peace treaty, and whether or not one sympathizes with his negative assessment of that document, he was certainly correct when he observed that "peace increases our difficulties." The end of the war meant that the army's volunteers had to be discharged. Hardly a hundred regular soldiers then remained in California, and they were making only seven dollars per month. "Of course they are deserting [to the gold country] as fast as they can," Sherman reported, "and in a very short time there will not be a dozen left; and we officers will be alone ... with heavy magazines and valuable stores unguarded." (At one point a soldier who cooked for the officers deserted, carrying off Sherman's prized double-barreled shotgun.) Peace also made California an American territory "in which the military officers can exercise no constitutional authority." Thus, Sherman concluded in his August letter to Turner, "at a critical moment, all force, civil and military, is withdrawn, and the country filled with the hardest kind of a population of deserters and foreigners."[39]

Actually, the "foreigners" were just beginning to appear in August 1848, relatively speaking. By 1849 people were coming to California from all over the world, as well as the eastern United States. During that year, according to the best estimates, more than 80,000 gold seekers, most having thrown caution to the wind, reached California. Only about half of them were Americans. A host of people came from Europe, some refugees from the failed revolutions that erupted across various European cities in 1848. A few were remarkable personages, like Lola Montez, lover of Duke Louis of Bavaria, who fled to California during the 1848 revolution in that country. The Gold Rush also attracted some of the first Chinese migrants to the U.S. Pacific coast. People came from South America and even from the far reaches of Australia.[40]

At the time gold was discovered, the population of California, excluding Native Americans, numbered about 14,000. Within four years, the count exploded to more than 220,000. San Francisco, an inconsequential village initially called Yerba Buena, leaped from a population of fewer than 500 to more than 20,000 inhabitants within a few months. Sherman poked a bit of fun at himself in his memoirs, recalling that an army acquaintance once advised him to invest in the little town of Yerba Buena. Sherman wrote: "I felt actually insulted that he should think me such a fool as to pay money for property in such a horrid place as Yerba Buena." The population at the time, he said, "was estimated at about 400, of whom Kanakas (natives of the Sandwich Islands) formed the bulk."[41]

Ninety-five percent of all the gold seekers were male. With an almost total absence of women (except for prostitutes), children and families, the society created by the men was unusually volatile and generally unsavory. Only a few of the adventurers became wealthy. Most of the "forty-niners" never struck it rich. Eventually they either returned home or, more often, stayed in California eking out a meager existence. There was also a class of men who made good money "prospecting" on the prospectors—that is, selling the gold seekers whatever they needed (or thought they needed), at greatly inflated prices. Sherman spoke the truth when he described the California atmosphere of the Gold Rush days as one of crazed excitement, greed and violence.[42]

While prices of just about everything skyrocketed, an army officer's pay remained the same, and rapidly became inadequate. Not until 1850 did Congress increase the wage, and then by a mere two dollars per month. The situation was so distressing that Sherman formed a partnership with William Warner, a fellow officer, and Norman Bestor, a civilian, to run a store in Coloma. Each man invested five hundred dollars, according to Sherman, with Bestor in charge of the store. Sherman realized a profit of about 300 percent, which, along with trimming his expenses as much as possible, helped him to survive. His army pay was seventy dollars a month, and he declared that "no one would even try to hire a servant under three hundred dollars. Had it not been for the fifteen hundred dollars I had made in the store at Coloma, I could not have lived through the winter."

Sherman also engaged in surveying, helping to organize a party to study the Sierra Nevada, in search of a possible railroad route through the massive barrier. William Warner was granted a leave of absence from the army in order to pick up extra money surveying. One of his clients was John Sutter, with whom he contracted to lay out the town of Sacramento. While working on the Sierra Nevada project, however, Warner was killed by Indians. Sherman wanted the guilty men punished, but the task proved impossible, particularly with the onset of a hard winter.[43]

While Sherman's feelings about his friend are certainly understandable, many Native Americans in California suffered gravely as a result of the Gold Rush. It led, according to historian Alan Brinkley, "to an overt exploitation of Indians that resembled slavery in all but name." Native Americans were apprehended for "loitering" and assigned to a term of "indentured" labor, and white vigilantes, calling themselves "Indian hunters," sometimes killed them. "Conflicts over gold intersected with racial and ethnic tensions," continued Brinkley, "to make the [California] territory an unusually turbulent place."[44]

Although Sherman and his peers clearly found life more difficult as the gold seekers arrived by the tens of thousands, they did find time for occasional merrymaking. "The season [the winter of 1848–49] was unusually rainy and severe," Sherman observed, "but we passed the time with the usual round of dances and parties." Particularly notable was the commemoration of George Washington's birthday. As was customary, Sherman said the army officers "celebrated the 22nd of February with a grand ball, given in the new stone school-house [in Monterey], which Alcalde Walter Colton had built. It was the largest and best hall then in California." Sherman rated the ball "a really handsome affair, and we kept it up nearly all night."[45]

But the periodic partying provided only limited relief from dull army duties, distasteful problems and disappointments. The winter of 1849 brought a change of command. In February Colonel Mason received orders to return to Washington. Sherman was very sorry to see him leave (Mason would die of cholera in St. Louis in the summer of 1850). Just before the colonel departed from California, he approved Sherman's application for an extended leave, and he did it with a strongly worded endorsement. Perhaps Mason praised his lieutenant too highly.

The new commander, Brigadier General Persifer F. Smith, declined to grant the leave. No doubt thinking that he could use such an able officer's help in taking over his new command, he made Sherman his adjutant. Later, Smith did give Sherman a shorter leave.

Smith also decided to set up headquarters in San Francisco, which brought still more change for Sherman. He did not like leaving his friends in Monterey, but as he wrote Ellen, "it was to my interest" to go with Smith. Nor did he adjust well to San Francisco, where "the rains were heavy and the mud fearful. I have seen mules stumble in the street, and drown in the liquid mud!" he claimed. He stated in his memoirs that "gambling was the chief occupation of the people," and said that "preachers ... forgot their creeds and took ... to keeping gambling-houses." He told Ellen, "This country is worse than ever. A house can not be rented for any price and men will not hire for twenty times the wages of any other country on earth. I really don't see how our officers can stand it much longer." Declaring "my hopes in life are all destroyed," he said that when the Second Infantry Regiment arrived, scheduled for May, he would make "a great effort" to get away, and go to the gold mines himself.[46]

Interestingly, Sherman recalled observing General Smith in San Francisco, more than once, "take off his hat when meeting a negro, and on being asked the reason of his politeness, would answer that they were the only real gentlemen in California." Sherman stated in his memoirs that "the fidelity of Colonel Mason's boy 'Aaron,' and of General Smith's boy 'Isaac,' at a time when every white man laughed at promises as something made to be broken, has given me a kindly feeling of respect for the negroes." This statement is striking in view of Sherman's racism, and calls to mind his actions during the Civil War, when he often shook hands and talked with blacks who appeared in his path, especially during the marches through Georgia and Carolina. Might he have been remembering Smith's attitude toward blacks in California?

Unfortunately, when the Second Infantry Regiment arrived, it presented a serious problem: the prospect of mass desertion to the gold fields. Twenty-eight men boldly and defiantly deserted for the gold mines. If these soldiers were not apprehended, quite possibly the whole regiment might follow. At the time, Sherman happened to be in Monterey with General Smith, who was staying at the house of former consul Thomas Larkin, while Sherman occupied "my old rooms" at the home of Doña Augustias. Learning of the deserters, and armed with a musket, Sherman led a group of seven volunteers, all officers since the soldiers could not be trusted, in pursuit. About six miles out from town, he and three other officers who had forged ahead easily captured six of the men, who neither expected to be pursued nor heard the sound of approaching horses until Sherman and the others were right on them.

Ordering one of the officers to march the prisoners back to Monterey, Sherman and the rest continued the pursuit through the night. By dawn, then riding at a gallop, Sherman was closing in on most of the other deserters, who had stopped at an old adobe house. "I had the best horse, and was considerably ahead [of the other pursuers]," he remembered. Upon looking back, he could see some more officers coming up fast. Thus he did not hesitate, galloping toward the house, brandishing his musket. Rapidly dismounting, he captured two men outside the adobe dwelling and, gesturing with his cocked weapon, ordered them into the house, which was filled with deserters. "They naturally supposed that I had a strong party with me," he wrote, and "when I ordered them to 'fall in' they obeyed." The other officers arrived to find Sherman disarming his captives. As in Florida when confronting the Seminoles, Sherman demonstrated aggressive leadership, bravery, good military instincts and quick thinking. While it was a small affair, Sherman relished the challenge and excitement, and certainly acquitted himself well.[47]

But such a brief little triumph could not offset the bad news that continued to plague him. He was quite upset when he heard that Colonel Mason had been promoted to brigadier general in recognition of his service in California. While pleased for Mason, Sherman felt embarrassed that he himself, after his loyal service, had not been promoted, an action that the army often took in recognition of an able lieutenant working with a colonel who had been elevated to brigadier. Never seeing combat during the Mexican conflict had been deeply disappointing, and struggling to survive economically made things worse. For the army to overlook him when his colonel had been promoted seemed too much. Self-respect, he said, compelled him to resign. He did write a resignation letter, but General Smith refused to accept it.

Instead, the general spoke encouragingly. Assuring Sherman that a promotion had to come in the near future, Smith also promised that "on the first good opportunity" he would send Sherman east as a bearer of dispatches for Winfield Scott, the army's commanding general. In the meantime, Sherman and the other officers were urged by Smith, who was very aware of their financial hardship, to use their spare time wisely, and "go into any business that would enable [them] to make money." Sherman sought more work surveying, sometimes paid partly in money and partly in land. From selling lots, and his surveying fees, he made a few thousand dollars. Always a keen observer, he noted that "the mass of people were busy at gold and mammoth speculation," while simultaneously "a set of busy politicians were at work to secure the prizes of civil government." Among those named in the latter category was John C. Frémont.[48]

Finally, at the end of 1849, General Smith prepared the promised dispatches and ordered Sherman to deliver them in person to General Scott in New York City. Sherman also agreed to escort two sons of Doña Augustias, aged eleven and thirteen, to Georgetown College in Washington to pursue their education. "The Doña gave me a bag of gold-dust," said Sherman, "to pay for their passage and to deposit at the college." Traveling by the steamship *Oregon*, he left California on January 2, 1850. Instead of going around the Horn, he journeyed across Central America by mule, boat and steamer, resuming the water trek in the western Gulf of Mexico, again on a steamship. "We reached New York about the close of January," he wrote, "after a safe and pleasant trip." What a marked and welcome contrast with his journey to California on the old sailing vessel *Lexington*. It was almost exactly three years since he had arrived in California. After "cleaning up somewhat," Sherman said he delivered his dispatches to General Scott's office, "and was *ordered* to dine with him the next day."[49]

Sherman remembered that "the general questioned me pretty closely in regard to things on the Pacific coast, especially the politics," when he dined with Scott, his wife, daughter and son-in-law the following evening. No doubt the general, who hoped to become president, besides recognizing Sherman as a bright young officer, was aware, too, that Sherman had grown up in the household of the influential Thomas Ewing. Scott proved to be a pleasant host. He also told Sherman several stories about his "old army comrades" in the recent battles around Mexico City. As Sherman listened, he said "I felt deeply the fact that . . . my comrades had fought great battles, and yet I had not heard a hostile shot." But in view of future developments, General Scott's most remarkable statement of the evening came, as Sherman remembered, "when he startled me with the assertion that our 'country was on the eve of a terrible civil war.'"[50]

Chapter Eight

California Again—
A Brand-New Game

On Wednesday, May 1, 1850, thirty-year-old William Tecumseh Sherman finally married Ellen Boyle Ewing. Their long engagement had failed to resolve any of the basic differences haunting the relationship. Cump was no nearer to accepting Ellen's Catholicism—or any organized religion for that matter—than when the two first discussed the nagging issue. Nor, despite the financial difficulties of military life in Gold Rush California, was Sherman inclined to leave the army—particularly if resignation might mean living in Ohio and working for Thomas Ewing. Furthermore, since returning from California, he had lost significant weight, suffering from what one doctor diagnosed as "Mexican Dysentery." Yet he reflected that "I never for one moment was troubled by it" in California. Asthma, too, periodically bothered him since returning from the West Coast, as did the thought of supporting a wife on the meager salary of a first lieutenant. While he hoped, and with good reason, for a promotion to captain, there were no guarantees of advancement; the financial gain of a captaincy would be minimal.[1]

Nevertheless, Sherman had written Ellen in late March, assuring her that the time for their marriage was at hand. The army had granted him a six-month leave of absence, and he pledged "to gormandize" in order to "fill up the volume of a man" before considering himself worthy of "publicly assuming the high trust of your guardian and master." Flaring poetic, he declared that he "always rejoiced to see the flowers bloom, and

nature put off her gray, morose garment for the brighter one of Spring."
He thought May 1 "peculiarly appropriate, for we can unite our day of joy
with all nature, and will have all her beauties to cheer us."[2]

Because of Thomas Ewing's long prominence in the nation's capital, the wedding took place in Washington, D.C., and was a major social
event. "A large and distinguished company," to borrow Sherman's
phrase, attended the ceremony. Henry Clay and Daniel Webster were
among the guests. So too were General Zachary Taylor, "Old Rough
and Ready," the hero of the Mexican War who was now president of the
United States, as well as all the members of his cabinet. Three days after
the wedding, Ellen wrote her mother: "Did you know that I actually
kissed the President? I did not know what I was doing until I had kissed
him." Ellen's impulsive behavior testifies persuasively to her happiness
upon the grand occasion, even if Sherman's lack of faith had denied her a
cherished Roman Catholic wedding.[3]

Sherman had told Ellen he would be married in "a plain suit of dress
clothes . . . as any plain citizen." Admitting that he preferred "the jingle
and style military," he knew his bride did not and claimed that he had
decided it was "best to doff it." Yet on their wedding day he appeared
splendidly arrayed in full military uniform, including saber and spurs.
Did his fondness for military regalia overwhelm his initial intention?
Or was he possibly making a statement to both Ellen and his foster
parents/in-laws, that he was not going to be pressured into resigning his
commission?[4]

The newlyweds embarked upon an extended honeymoon, joined by
Ellen's younger brother Tom, a not uncommon practice in those days. In
Philadelphia they visited Cump's sister Elizabeth, about whom he was
deeply distressed, because her alcoholic husband's lack of stability and
business sense had reduced his family to near poverty. Recently Sherman had sent Elizabeth fifteen hundred dollars, but her husband wasted
the money on another fruitless scheme. The next stop was New York,
where Ellen wrote that they toured a "Man of War," bristling with "can-
nons enough . . . to frighten the ladies."[5]

The highlight of the New York visit, without a doubt, was dinner with

General and Mrs. Winfield Scott, and members of the Scott family, at the general's residence. "The dinner was very nice," Ellen told her mother. She thought both the general and his wife were "exceedingly friendly and kind." Their daughters were friendly also, though Ellen found them "not very pretty." The general "spoke frequently of his friend 'the honorable Thomas Ewing,'" which surely pleased Ellen, who adored her father. Thomas Ewing was a good man to have on your side if you were a Whig, like General Scott, with ambitions to become president.[6]

Next on the agenda was the U.S. Military Academy. On Friday morning, May 10, at seven o'clock, they took a boat up the Hudson to West Point.[7] Sherman had to be happy, not only to return again to the academy, which always lifted his spirits, but to do so with Ellen at his side. Perhaps he hoped that the atmosphere of the Point might cast some magical spell over his new bride, or that she might acquire at least a measure of open-minded understanding and toleration, if not appreciation, of his military commitment. If such thoughts crossed his mind, they were in vain. There is no evidence that the aura of West Point had any positive impact upon Ellen.

They next traveled across New York state to view the splendor of Niagara Falls. Then it was on to Ohio to see family and friends, before returning to Washington. Ellen frequently corresponded with her mother throughout the honeymoon trip. Writing on May 9, "Ascension Day," Maria Ewing teasingly chided Ellen about her dinner with "the great . . . General Scott"; fearful that such a "flattering" experience would make Ellen "so vain" that her friends in Ohio would not recognize her. Mother Ewing noted that Henry Clay, who had given Ellen a silver bouquet holder as a wedding present, "told your father at Sir Henry's [British Minister to the United States Sir Henry Bulwer] that he had intended to call on you each day since the wedding, but had been quite unwell." Clay had not known that Ellen and Sherman left town immediately after the nuptials. The legendary Kentuckian promised to call soon after Ellen's return. Obviously Sherman's new bride was well connected among the most powerful people.[8]

Mrs. Ewing found much satisfaction in her daughter's grand wedding, contrasting it with another that she declared "rather a slim affair; at all events would not compare with ours." She also wrote Ellen that one of the ladies who assisted with the Ewing-Sherman event "congratulates herself quite much on the occasion of [the recent wedding's] failing to come up to yours." One wonders what Sherman thought—if Ellen shared that letter with him—of this amusing touch of competitive snobbery on the part of his new mother-in-law. Whatever his musings about Mrs. Ewing's pride in their illustrious wedding, if he saw Maria's remarks in a letter dated June 8, he would not have appreciated them. Acknowledging Ellen's "frequent and affectionate letters," Mrs. Ewing told her that "your dear Father . . . has determined you will be back with us this summer, to remain, we all hope, for the coming winter at least. Your Father is very anxious, I assure you, for you to return to remain." These were ominous words indeed relative to the future of the marriage, indicative of the strong-willed Ewing's potential interference and control over the lives of his daughter and son-in-law. Marrying into the financially comfortable and politically prominent Ewing family surely held promise for Sherman's well-being—but there would be a price to pay.[9]

The newlyweds were back in the nation's capital on a very hot July 4, when an elaborate celebration was staged at the base of the Washington Monument, which was under construction. President Taylor attended the huge rally, listening to several speeches extolling the grandness of the Union. He ate too much, became overheated and soon was seriously ill. Suffering from cholera morbus, a gastrointestinal illness (according to historians George Tindall and David Shi), Taylor's condition rapidly worsened. Five days later he was dead.[10]

"General Taylor's sudden death," remembered Sherman, "created great alarm." The raging sectional quarrel over the issue of slavery, particularly the expansion of that "peculiar institution," had reached crisis proportions and everyone in Washington seemed on edge. Sherman was in the Senate gallery when Vice President Millard Fillmore, a New York lawyer, took the oath of office as the thirteenth president of the United States. Sherman later wrote of Fillmore's "splendid physical proportions and commanding appearance."[11]

Sherman took part in the funeral of President Taylor as a mounted aide. "Hardly was General Taylor decently buried in the Congressional Cemetery," he recalled, "when the political struggle recommenced." He seized the occasion to again advise brother John against the life of a politician, writing in July: "I hope the political history of the past year will make a strong impression on your mind not to seek honors or distinction through that channel." His perspective is understandable. The history of the past year had been tense, emotional and raucous. Hot-tempered representatives sometimes expressed themselves in unacceptable language, and fistfights actually broke out on the floor of Congress. Both senators from Mississippi engaged spectacularly in unbecoming behavior. Henry S. Foote brandished a loaded revolver during a passionate debate in the Senate, while Jefferson Davis "invited" Congressman William Bissell of Illinois to meet him somewhere outside the District of Columbia to settle a dispute—clearly a challenge to a duel (which was illegal). Cooler heads finally managed to avert that confrontation.[12]

THE GREAT ISSUE of 1850 was slavery in the territories, particularly the vast territory acquired from Mexico. Triggered by the discovery of gold in California, the long-simmering problems associated with the "peculiar institution," in all their ramifications, had come to a boiling point. From the nation's beginning, the tormenting political, economic, sectional and racial issues of slavery were never far removed from fierce debate. By 1850 many members of Congress believed that the United States stood on the verge of disunion.

It is a striking fact that the term "slavery" never appeared in the Constitution of the United States—until the Thirteenth Amendment, in December 1865, abolished the institution. Nevertheless, slavery presented a serious problem at the Constitutional Convention in 1787, leading to a contentious struggle between delegates from Northern and Southern states. Ultimately a compromise resolved the immediate issue, establishing the so-called federal ratio, whereby a slave was counted as three-fifths of a person for both representation in the U.S. Congress and taxation. The framers of the Constitution nimbly side-stepped employing the word "slavery" in their document, speaking of an enumeration of "free persons," followed by the consideration of "all other persons."[13]

Over the next several decades slavery periodically reared its ugly head, claiming national attention in different ways and in varying degrees. When the foreign slave trade was abolished by Congress in 1808, some viewed the event as a move toward the eventual extinction of slavery itself. On the contrary, outlawing the African slave trade only increased the value of slaves already in the country, and sometimes encouraged the breeding of slaves in parts of the soil-exhausted Upper South. A dramatic expansion of the "cotton belt" created a thriving domestic market in the Lower South. New plantations demanded huge numbers of slaves. By 1860 about 300,000 Africans had been smuggled into the slave states—in spite of such activity being a crime punishable by death—thus contributing greatly to the natural increase. The total slave population had grown from slightly less than 700,000 in 1790 to more than 3,200,000 by 1850.[14]

A major sectional controversy erupted over slavery in 1819; a far-reaching quarrel which impacted the nation up until 1850. The issue was the admission of Missouri as a slave state—Thomas Jefferson's "fire bell in the night," as he famously characterized the alarming arguments between free states and slave states concerning the expansion of slavery. Most of the arguments over slavery would reverberate for decades to come. When all the fiery congressional rhetoric at last subsided and the votes were counted, Maine had been admitted to the Union as a free state, balanced against the slave state of Missouri, making a total of eleven free states and eleven slave states. During the three decades following the acceptance of the Missouri Compromise, the balance of free states and slave states was faithfully maintained, reaching a total of fifteen each by 1850, thus continuing to ensure slave state parity in the U.S. Senate, despite being outnumbered significantly in the House. Also, a dividing line separating free territory from slave territory, the 36° 30' parallel—the southern border of Missouri—was honored throughout those years, establishing a strong precedent for containing slavery within a specified region.

Nevertheless, the free states and slave states gradually grew further apart. The contributing factors were many. Diverging economies were inseparably linked with diverging cultures. Industrial and urban development of the free states, along with their rapidly growing population, increasingly differentiated them from the agrarian and rural life of the less populous slave states. The abolitionist movement developing in the North was viewed with alarm in the slave states, where it was thought to be stronger than it actually was. Southern slave interests considered the abolitionists a potential threat to their possession of human "property." All the more so because these staunch opponents of slavery, some of them preachers, branded the institution as both an affront to the natural rights of mankind and a moral wrong: a "sin" that would damn one's immortal soul. The two largest Protestant denominations, Baptist and Methodist, each split into two groups along sectional lines, with slavery the most pronounced issue. The slave states were further disturbed by both slave insurrections and rumors of insurrections, which some Southerners readily attributed to the incitement of abolitionists. Even the South Carolina nullification issue of President Jackson's day, which concerned tariff policy, was fraught with strong implications for the future of slavery. All this and more, despite the Missouri Compromise, contributed to an incessant underlying friction between the sections.

Then came a tidal wave. The destructive force was loosed early in the Mexican War, a conflict that proved to be among the most significant in which the United States had ever engaged. The war was less than three months old when President Polk, whose greatest single concern as chief executive was geographical expansion—above all the acquisition of California—requested a $2 million appropriation from Congress to facilitate negotiations with Mexico. Polk hoped the money would lead to an early peace treaty and expedite an American takeover of New Mexico and California territories.

It was then that David Wilmot, a first-term Democratic congressman from Pennsylvania, introduced his never-to-be-forgotten proviso. Like many who feared that "Mr. Polk's War" had little or nothing to do with manifest destiny, and everything to do with acquiring more slave territory, Wilmot explained that he did not oppose national territorial expansion. But in any additional land that might be acquired from Mexico, Wilmot proposed, quoting from the Northwest Ordinance of 1787, that "neither slavery nor involuntary servitude shall ever exist in any part of said territory." The United States had twice banned slavery in federal territory, first in the Old Northwest and later in the Louisiana Purchase north of 36°30', except for Missouri. Furthermore, Mexico already prohibited slavery. Thus the United States, in forbidding slavery in any land acquired from Mexico, would be doing nothing more than recognizing the status quo. Wilmot's Proviso readily passed the U.S. House of Representatives, but was rejected by the Senate.

In the months to follow, the proviso, in somewhat varying form, was reintroduced time and again, but never accepted by both houses. The proposal set off a passionate, ongoing debate, forcing politicians, regardless of their time-honored, pronounced reluctance, to declare where they stood on the issue of slavery expansion.

Then in 1848 the presidential election powerfully dramatized, for all the nation to see, that the issue of slavery expansion could be neither ignored nor sidestepped. Both Democrats and Whigs tried to avoid a firm position on the slavery question. Both then watched as a sizable faction of dissidents bolted each party. "Conscience Whigs" and "Barnburner Democrats" joined the earlier Liberty Party to create the Free Soil Party, dedicated first and foremost to arresting the spread of slavery. It became the prototype of the Republicans, soon to replace the Whigs as one of the nation's two major political parties.

Maybe, just maybe, the issue of slavery in the Mexican cession might somehow have been successfully compromised for the long term—if time had not suddenly and unpredictably become a major factor. The discovery of gold in California early in 1848, simultaneous with the Treaty of Guadalupe Hidalgo, which awarded California to the United States, introduced a new dimension into the vexing question of slavery in the territories. California's stable, responsible, decent citizens found themselves overwhelmed by the disreputable "gold fever" crowd. They needed and demanded a strong government that could protect them and control an increasingly dangerous criminal element.[15]

President Taylor did not hesitate to step up. Born in Virginia and raised in Kentucky, he maintained a home in Louisiana and owned a slave plantation in Mississippi. As a Southerner, Taylor favored upholding slavery where it existed, but as a military man of national principles, he viewed the issue of slavery in the territories as a great irritant. He "had no more use for [John C.] Calhoun's proslavery abstractions than Jackson had for his nullification doctrine," wrote historians Tindall and Shi—particularly since Taylor doubted slavery could profitably exist in California anyway.[16]

In his annual message to Congress on December 4, 1849, the President endorsed immediate statehood for California as a free state, attempting to avoid the divisive issue of slavery during a territorial stage of government. For New Mexico he recommended the same solution. As for those Southern congressmen who were voicing threats of secession, Taylor vowed to meet "whatever dangers may threaten [the Union]." He promised to "maintain [the Union] in its integrity." Those who threatened a disruption of the Union deserved no concessions whatsoever. He believed that they would back down in the face of strength.[17]

While the President's stance stunned the South and surprised many in the North, actually his proposal was not new. In the previous Congress, Stephen A. Douglas of Illinois had advocated bringing the Mexican cession directly to statehood, thereby avoiding the Wilmot issue of slavery in the territories. Zachary Taylor's secretary of the navy, William B. Preston of Virginia, had also supported such a proposal in that Congress. Furthermore California, privately encouraged by the President, had already drafted a state constitution that excluded slavery. But Taylor's simple solution never had much, if any, chance of being accepted. The admission of California as a free state would destroy, probably for all time, the precarious equilibrium of fifteen free states and fifteen slave states.

New Mexico and Utah were already shaping up as additional free states. Not a single slave territory waited to become a state. Senator John Bell of Tennessee strongly favored dividing Texas to make more slave states, an idea originally advanced, as earlier noted, when Texas was annexed. But proud Texas expansionists, seeking to acquire a large portion of New Mexico, were not in the least interested. The slaveholding South was steadily declining into a minority status, out of step with the nation—and out of step with all of Western civilization. The sectional dispute had grown ever more heated, taking on increasingly serious dimensions. The Mexican cession presented other issues in addition to the expansion of slavery, and slavery presented other problems throughout the nation. To say that the United States was facing catastrophe in the year of 1850 is not an exaggeration.[18]

SHERMAN CLOSELY FOLLOWED the momentous events, perhaps with even keener interest after hearing General Scott's assertion that the nation was on the eve of a terrible civil war. Sherman's greatest concern, assuming that war could be averted, was the fate of California. Near the end of his three adventurous years there, which were highlighted by the great Gold Rush, he also had been present at its constitutional convention as an observer for his commanding officer. The exclusion of slavery had generated very little debate at the convention. California's free-state constitution was adopted by a large majority, even though many of the men who participated in framing it came from Southern states.[19]

Because of Sherman's six-month leave of absence from the army, which began in February 1850, he often found time, both before and after his marriage, to attend the congressional debates in Washington, especially in the Senate, where he listened to Clay, Webster, Benton, Foote, William L. Dayton and others—"the many real orators of the day," he said. Most of all he was impressed by Henry Clay, the longtime Whig leader, and one of the few politicians whom Sherman genuinely respected. It was Clay who, in January 1850, introduced a series of proposals designed to address the most serious issues troubling the Union, above all the contention involving slavery, and provide a comprehensive settlement acceptable to the nation.

In early February, for the better part of two days, Clay spoke in support of the policies he advocated. The speech was a detailed discussion of eight resolutions, interwoven with an emotional portrayal of the vulnerability of the Union, and an earnest plea for a spirit of compromise, to avoid a civil war. In Clay's mind, disunion inevitably meant civil war. As the following tumultuous weeks turned into months, the seventy-two-year-old Kentuckian rose time and again, in all seventy times, to passionately defend the proposals that eventually became the Compromise of 1850. Clay was "an embodiment of grace, wit and eloquence."[20]

The Kentuckian advocated that California be admitted to the Union as a free state while the remainder of the Mexican cession would be organized into New Mexico and Utah Territories, without "any restriction or condition on the subject of slavery," thus rejecting the Wilmot Proviso. Presumably, because the Mexican cession was widely deemed geographically unsuitable for slavery, both territories were destined to become free states. Clay also proposed that a complex boundary dispute between Texas and New Mexico be settled in favor of the latter. In return the United States would assume the Texas public debt of some $10 million. Within the nation's capital, Clay contended that the interstate slave trade should be abolished, but the existence of slavery itself would be reaffirmed in the District of Columbia. Finally, Clay called for a stronger fugitive slave law, requiring state and local assistance for federal marshals, anywhere in the United States, as they attempted to recover and return runaway slaves to their owners.[21]

Such were the proposals with which Clay launched a legendary senatorial effort to address the crisis of 1850. During the next six months an intense Congress debated Clay's resolutions, as the nation faced the possibility of breaking up. Elder statesmen Clay and Webster served as the preeminent spokesmen for the Union. They were countered by John C. Calhoun, long regarded as a formidable champion of Southern sectionalism. Appearing "pale and feeble in the extreme," according to Sherman's observation when he saw Calhoun seated in the Senate, the fabled South Carolinian died that spring. The mantle of Southern leadership then passed to Jefferson Davis, who, like Calhoun, deplored the compromise as representing an aggressive Northern triumph that would lead to disunion and war. Many others joined in the enthralling forensic clashes—William H. Seward, Stephen A. Douglas, Lewis Cass, James M. Mason, John Bell, Salmon P. Chase and Thomas Hart Benton among them.[22]

When Sherman learned that Daniel Webster would be making one last speech on July 17, before leaving the Senate to become President Fillmore's secretary of state, he went to the Capitol much earlier than usual, determined to hear the great orator's final address. He found that the galleries already were overflowing, and a dense crowd clogged the entranceway. Somehow he managed to find a seat, near General Scott as it turned out, and listened to Webster's entire speech. He was disappointed and "tired long before [the address] was finished." He declared too that the speech possessed "none of the fire of oratory, or intensity of feeling, that marked all of Mr. Clay's efforts."[23]

Despite Henry Clay's marvelous ability and near heroic endeavors, his sweeping compromise went down to defeat on July 31. Deeply disappointed and near exhaustion, Clay left Washington to recuperate. At that point Senator Stephen A. Douglas took the lead in a continuing and determined pursuit of the compromise measures. He employed a different strategy from that of Clay. Douglas sagely realized that a minority of senators, who favored all the compromise proposals, constituted a bloc of votes holding the key to success.

Proceeding to consider each measure separately, Douglas augmented that staunch compromise bloc with sectional votes—sometimes Northern and sometimes Southern—until he built a majority vote for each of the five different proposals into which he had restructured Clay's eight resolutions. Approved by the Senate over a period of several days in September, the proposals composed, when taken together, the Compromise of 1850. Nor had Douglas been unmindful of the House of Representatives. Since late winter he had been formulating plans with House leaders to gain support for Clay's proposals. More than any other person,

Stephen Douglas deserved the credit for engineering the passage of the famous compromise.[24]

The achievement did engender an initial, widespread sense of relief, in both the North and South. Once the deciding votes had been recorded, effervescent crowds celebrated on the streets of Washington, perhaps symbolic of the mood all across the nation. Undoubtedly many American citizens, throughout the land, honestly intended to honor the compromise. Millard Fillmore, whose ascension to the presidency had removed the near certainty of a veto by Zachary Taylor, declared the compromise "a final and irrevocable settlement" of the slavery issue.[25]

Viewed realistically, it was only a temporary reprieve, and it soon began to disintegrate. The immediate and single most troubling provision was the fugitive slave law, which proved increasingly disruptive in Northern towns and cities, often impossible to enforce and leading to violence. It raised once again the emotional issues of a sectional nature. From the start, an ominous undercurrent of anger and foreboding lay just below the national surface. William H. Seward of New York never changed his mind about the compromise being "inherently vicious and wrong." Salmon P. Chase correctly observed that "the question of slavery in the territories has been avoided. It has not been settled." From a Southern perspective, John Bell said, "The crisis is not past; nor can ... harmony be restored to the country until the North shall cease to vex the South upon the subject of slavery." Jefferson Davis regarded 1850 as a critical watershed: "For the first time we are about permanently to destroy the balance of power between the sections." From a historical perspective, David Potter described it as "the Armistice of 1850."[26]

BEFORE THE COMPROMISE became law, Sherman's six-month leave of absence expired and he returned to duty with the army, pleased to be stationed in St. Louis, the strategically located, fast-growing river port on the Mississippi that had impressed him favorably years earlier. "Beyond doubt," he wrote as he trumpeted the city's destiny for Ellen's consideration, "in time it will be one of the greatest places on the continent." Arriving by steamboat from Cincinnati around mid-September, he reported at Jefferson Barracks to Captain Braxton Bragg, a friend since West Point days, who then commanded (Light) Company C, Third Artillery.[27]

Ellen did not accompany her husband to St. Louis, "detained by a cause common to married women," as he referenced Ellen's pregnancy in a letter to her brother Hugh. Sherman had wanted her to go with him, but Ellen's parents contended that she should remain in Lancaster until the baby's birth. Thus the matter was decided, although Sherman was not pleased about it. At least there was good news from the army concerning his long awaited promotion. As General Scott had assured Thomas Ewing, Sherman did receive one of the four new captaincies in the Subsistence Department, his commission bearing the date of September 27, 1850. The promotion necessitated that he live not at Jefferson Barracks but actually in St. Louis, near the businesses that provided the army supplies for the region. Consequently he took a room at the Planters' House, then and for many years to come recognized as the finest hotel in the city.[28]

Sherman's promotion, "one of the best appointments in the army," he assured Ellen, reinforced his conviction to stay "in the service of my country," as he had proudly stated when he was an academy cadet. To turn away from his army career after the promotion would be foolish indeed. For her part, Ellen shared neither his enthusiasm for the military life, which was nothing new of course, nor his fondness for St. Louis, which she had never visited. "I can't bear to think of going away out to St. Louis," she confided to her mother soon after she married. "It is so very very distant and the journey is by water—a mode of travel I do not like." Then, in the fall of 1850, Ellen got a letter from Sherman that presented a truly distressing possibility. He wrote that he might be sent to Oregon. Suddenly a journey to St. Louis, in comparison, must have seemed like a pleasant little excursion down the Ohio. Ellen had no intention of going to Oregon. The Oregon post never materialized, but the red flags were flying. There would be rough water ahead for the Sherman marriage.[29]

Growing lonely and apparently rather irritated, Sherman straightforwardly told Ellen that she ought to be with him. He would be forced, in an effort to occupy his time in St. Louis, to seek company at the hotels, theaters and concerts. Whatever, precisely, such a statement meant, he left to her imagination. At Christmastime he made a brief trip to Ohio, visiting with Ellen and making plans for her to join him once the baby arrived. In January his mood continued gloomy. The winter was "bitter cold," and the river closed because of ice, which kept him from receiving the New York daily paper to which he subscribed. Brother John must inform him, he instructed, about the political news in Washington. "Again let me advise you," he concluded, "to shun politics like poison, except it advance you in the profession of law." On January 28, 1851, the first Sherman child was born, a girl named Maria in honor of Ellen's mother, although she soon became known as Minnie. Sherman wanted his wife and child to join him in St. Louis as quickly as Ellen regained sufficient strength. When she showed little inclination to leave her parents, Sherman went to Ohio in March and, following a discussion with Thomas Ewing, returned to St. Louis accompanied by Ellen and Minnie.[30]

The Planters' accommodations proved to be cramped and Sherman bought a house on Choteau Avenue. He had always lived frugally during his bachelor days, saving sufficient money to help support his mother and occasionally make loans to friends and family members. Such generosity became a thing of the past. Worse, within a few months he confided to John that he was forced to tap his savings to keep abreast of monthly expenses. In addition to Ellen and the baby, there was a nurse for Minnie, and two servants for Ellen. He had to deny Ellen's request for new furniture, and he experienced frustrating difficulties in trying to collect a major portion of the money owed him from the sale of a California property.

Stewart Van Vliet, Sherman's friend from cadet days, and his wife moved in to live with the Shermans and shouldered a portion of the household expenses. Sherman also acquired an interest in some land. The land acquisition actually evolved from the legal work of Thomas Ewing and Henry Stoddard, a cousin of Sherman's father who resided in Dayton, Ohio. Ewing and Stoddard represented the estate of Major

Amos Stoddard, who had been killed in the War of 1812 and whose descendants claimed the officer owned a St. Louis farm. When Ewing finally succeeded in establishing the title of the heirs, he profited substantially. Buying a sizable piece of the property for himself, Ewing authorized Sherman to manage the investment for him. Ewing also bought a block of land for Ellen. As a result of acting as agent and manager for his father-in-law's interests, Sherman broadened his knowledge of real estate and business—good experience, as fate dictated, for the future. Nevertheless, Sherman's overall financial situation continued to darken. The pay of an army captain provided little hope of ever turning the problem around.[31]

Perhaps the most important happening during Sherman's two years in St. Louis, taking the long view, was the rekindling of a warm friendship established in California with Major Henry S. Turner. Sherman liked Turner, who had left the army for a career as a banker. The two men became lifelong friends, with Sherman coming to think of Turner as his closest friend. He once wrote Ellen's brother, "Major Turner is every inch a man and you cannot know a better." The association with Turner would soon have a great impact on Sherman's life.

Meanwhile, Ellen's mother regularly urged her daughter to return to Lancaster. Only three months after Ellen had accompanied Cump to St. Louis, Mrs. Ewing instructed, "Let me know as soon as possible whether we may expect you to return with your father." Thomas Ewing was then in St. Louis working on the Stoddard case. "I hope you will certainly come, for I should suffer great anxiety . . . were you to remain longer in [St. Louis] than June." Perhaps she was referring to the possibility of a cholera epidemic. (Sherman's posting to St. Louis the previous year had been delayed a few days because of a cholera outbreak in the late summer.)

Seven days later, Mother Ewing wrote again of her hope that Ellen soon would be traveling back to Ohio with her father. She feared Ellen had been lax in trying to convince Sherman to leave the army. "I hope," she wrote, "that you have not given up all idea of persuading your husband to resign his post in the Army. . . . It is an established fact," she

claimed, "that the longer an officer remains in the Army, the more reluctance he has to leave it ... [becoming] more attached to his profession
every day." Since Thomas Ewing was still working in St. Louis, Maria
instructed Ellen to enlist his help.[32]

Despite Maria's hopes for her daughter's early return to Lancaster,
Ellen endured her homesickness and remained in St. Louis for a year.
She made some friends, mostly Catholics, and found comfort in the
regular exercise of her religion and in the care of Minnie. By the spring
of 1852, she was again pregnant and the Sherman finances had continued to deteriorate. Partly to economize, and partly because Ellen never
cared for St. Louis and wanted to be with her parents until the baby's
birth, Sherman consented that she and Minnie should return to Ohio.
He then sold their house, while making plans to auction his remaining
California property. Regardless of the economic pressures, he resisted
any thought of assistance from his father-in-law. On May 30, 1852, he
implored Ellen to "always tell me" if she needed anything, and ordered
her, "on no account receive anything from your father. He has enough
dependent upon him."[33]

Sherman was not a happy man. He loved Ellen and looked forward to
the birth of their second child. But Ellen's strong attachment to her parents and Lancaster, which fostered an easy readiness to be away from her
husband for long periods of time, plus her obsession with Catholicism
(better that Minnie die, she thought, than ever turn away from the faith),
became constant and pronounced irritants. He and Ellen had been separated far too much since their marriage, and Sherman declared that "the
effect has been serious upon us." Furthermore, in August he received a
letter from Mr. Ewing, expressing his desire that Ellen remain in Ohio
for the winter, even though the new baby was expected by the middle of
November. The obvious fact that Sherman needed more money weighed
heavily upon his mind as well. Probably some of the asthma attacks that
he was experiencing in St. Louis were triggered in part by the stress
he was under. He also craved a more interesting military assignment.
"There is absolutely nothing stirring in this city," he wrote, "except beg-
gars who are becoming more numerous every day."[34]

While Sherman had blown hot and cold about California during his military service there, after Ellen went back to Ohio, the memories of West Coast life seemed to flood in upon him. "I can not shake off [California's] effect on me," he confided to Hugh Boyle Ewing. He reminisced about the "wild roving life on mule back, sleeping on the ground and bivouacking with wild gold seekers." He wrote of a fondness for "Monterey and the valley and hills of Carmel . . . and the wild scenes of the Gold Mountains." California fever coursed through his veins. His attachment "to civilization and refinement" had been permanently weakened, he thought, and "the quiet life" in St. Louis "stripped of all interest and charm." He looked forward to a new army posting, which he believed likely to be in Oregon, or possibly at Fort Leavenworth, the latter "a most beautiful spot," he said, although "in the midst of wild Indian country."[35]

The new assignment came even sooner than anticipated. The location proved something of a surprise—in spite of rumors he had heard. He would be journeying down the Mississippi, with duty at the great port of New Orleans. Shortly before he left St. Louis, however, he received "the sad tidings" of his "poor mother's death, so sudden and unexpected." More than two decades had passed since the death of Sherman's father had left his mother dependent upon others to care for their children. "Poor mother," he grieved in a letter to Ellen. "She has had hard times and nothing but the kindest, most affectionate and simple heart, could have borne her up" under such difficult circumstances. Mourning her death, and missing the company of Ellen and Minnie, Sherman boarded a steamboat for New Orleans.[36]

His new mission, fortunately for his mental well-being, compelled him to focus on working for the army. He had been ordered to clean up corruption and nepotism in the New Orleans commissary operations. General George Gibson, head of the Subsistence Department of the U.S. Army in Washington, had chosen his man well. Sherman took a room at the St. Louis Hotel and proceeded to completely overhaul the army's operation. Seeking good quality and just prices for all manner of foodstuffs, he soon became well-known in New Orleans as an officer who was scrupulously honest. He also became, as he wrote his brother John, "somewhat of an item here," invited to "elegant banquets" and various social gatherings.[37]

On November 17, 1852, Ellen gave birth to another girl. Named Mary Elizabeth, after Cump's mother and one of his sisters, she soon came to be called Lizzie. Sherman regularly wrote Ellen about the good weather in New Orleans, and other virtues of the city, while deploring "the cold miserable climate of Ohio." Whether because of his efforts in praise of the Crescent City or otherwise, Ellen decided not to spend the winter in Lancaster. Sherman was pleased when she arrived in New Orleans in late December, along with Minnie, Lizzie, a nursemaid and his sister Fanny. He rented a house on Magazine Street, convenient to Canal Street and the French Quarter, as well as the wharves at the river, where he conducted much of the army business. The house was superior to the one in St. Louis. Sherman was happy to be living again with his family, and he continued to enjoy the camaraderie of the army officers stationed in the city. But like St. Louis, New Orleans was too expensive for a captain's pay—more so in fact than St. Louis. It was at this point that Sherman got a career-changing, finance-altering and probably unexpected opportunity: Henry S. Turner approached him about managing a bank in California.[38]

AFTER MAJOR TURNER left the army, he had become a banker with the St. Louis firm of Lucas & Simonds. A competing St. Louis banking house, Page, Bacon & Company, had opened a branch in San Francisco in 1850, which within two years appeared to be a success. Consequently, James H. Lucas, the senior partner of Lucas & Simonds, decided that his firm should move into California, also locating in San Francisco. Lucas wanted Turner to manage the new branch. However, Turner did not want to leave St. Louis, where his wife and children were content. He was willing to work on the West Coast for a few months, until the business could be firmly established, but not indefinitely. Besides, he assured Lucas, he knew just the man for the job.[39]

Sherman, of course, was the person Turner had in mind. He knew

Sherman as a man of high intelligence and common sense, hardworking and trustworthy. He had a good knowledge of California, especially the Monterey–San Francisco region. He possessed administrative and managerial skills, of which Turner was well aware from observing his quartermaster and commissary endeavors in Monterey, St. Louis and New Orleans. His management of Ewing's St. Louis property enhanced his business résumé. Turner was correct in assessing Sherman, even though he had no banking experience, as possessing "an extraordinary business capacity."[40]

Consequently, Turner visited Sherman in New Orleans, explaining fully what would be expected of him as a banker in California. Already Turner was prepared to embark for San Francisco to inaugurate the bank. If Sherman followed soon, he could assist with the venture. Once the operation was running smoothly, Turner would return to St. Louis. Shortly after Turner departed, James Lucas arrived in New Orleans. He wanted to talk face-to-face with Sherman, whom he knew only through Turner's assessment. Lucas was pleased with what he saw and continued the pitch that banking in California would be a wise career move. Sherman wondered about establishing a branch bank in New Orleans, but Lucas was interested only in California.

Lucas impressed Sherman favorably. He was a wealthy man, with extensive real estate holdings in St. Louis, who made a solid appearance and seemed to possess a firm grasp of the banking business. He and Turner made a persuasive team, and Sherman found their proposition very tempting. Although he did not want to leave the army, the salary of a captain—or even a major or colonel, if ever he should be so fortunate in rank—could not support a growing family in a satisfactory manner. Certainly not in the lifestyle to which Ellen was accustomed and desired. The San Francisco banking position would more than double his salary immediately. It would also award him an interest in the firm.[41]

There were other advantages. The continuing pressure from Ellen and her parents to leave the army would be relieved. The challenges of a new profession promised to add a touch of zest to life. Furthermore, there was excitement about returning to California, where admittedly his "fancy" of late had been drifting. He could also take a six-month leave of absence from the army, as Turner suggested, while he evaluated the prospective new direction of his life. If the responsibilities of a banker proved not to his liking, he could return to the military. Also, resigning from the army would not be so painful in 1853 as it would have been earlier. Like most army men, Sherman viewed the Mexican War as the great military epoch of his generation. The war, however, had passed him by, in terms of experiencing combat, leaving scant hope that he would ever see action, or be able to earn rapid advancement during wartime.[42]

After mulling over the decision, and discussing the matter with Ellen, Sherman applied for a six-month leave of absence from the army. By late winter of 1853, he was on his way back to California, ready to assume the responsibilities of a new career as a banker. Ellen and the children headed upriver for Ohio, traveling aboard a steamboat named *Tecumseh*. On February 27, 1853, Maria Ewing penned a letter to her daughter, saying that she regretted not being able to see "Cumpy" before he embarked for the West Coast. She prayed that God would "grant him a safe and speedy voyage to California, and that he may return in safety at the termination of the year to see his family." As for Ellen possibly going to California to join him at some future date, Maria instructed: "Do not my dear Ellen think of ever going there. I should never consent to it, nor do I think your Father ever would."[43]

SHERMAN LEFT NEW ORLEANS on March 6, bound for Nicaragua on a small steamer. From Greytown he transferred to a riverboat to go up the San Juan River, and then "across beautiful Lake Nicaragua, studded with volcanic islands," before completing the trip to the Pacific coast by mule. From San Juan del Sur, he headed north for San Francisco on a slow, wooden steamship called the S.S. *Lewis*. Having secured a berth in one of the best staterooms on the deck of the *Lewis*, Sherman said that he gave it up to a lady from New Orleans and her friend, who sought his help because their quarters were "unendurable." Their names were then recorded with Sherman's, as "Captain Sherman and ladies." At every meal thereafter, Sherman said the steward inquired, "Captain Sherman, will you bring your ladies to the table?" The New Orleans woman sometimes entertained the passengers by singing, which Sherman complimented, and he also noted that the two were modest and well behaved. Only after reaching San Francisco did he learn from a friend that the New Orleans lady "was a woman of the town." Concluding the story, he remarked that "society in California was then decidedly mixed."[44]

All went well until the last night of the voyage when, around 4:00 a.m., Sherman was awakened by a heavy jolt and an alarming, grating noise. Then the ship struck again, even harder, and the engine stopped. The vessel was snared on a reef. It was pitch-dark and a heavy fog enshrouded the stricken ship, as she rose and fell with the swell of the ocean. Fortunately the water was relatively calm, although the strain on the hull from the bumping and quivering foretold the vessel's eventual breakup. The S.S. *Lewis* would go to pieces the following night and Sherman later reflected that "had there been an average sea during the night of our shipwreck, none of us probably would have escaped."[45]

As it was, many passengers feared the ship would sink at once, and great confusion prevailed. One passenger attempted to lower a lifeboat, only to be stopped in his tracks by the captain of the *Lewis*, who loudly threatened, "Let go that falls or, damn you, I'll blow your head off!" Sherman appreciated the captain's instant response. He knew the frightened crowd must be kept in check. Guards were quickly posted at the lifeboats; the officers and crew remained "perfectly cool and self-possessed," thought Sherman, and succeeded in calming the passengers. When the fog at last lifted, the shoreline was revealed to be only a mile or so away.[46]

Using the small boats, the crew began ferrying the nearly 400 passengers to the beach. Sherman was among the last to depart, remaining beside the captain who, with map and compass, was trying to determine their location. After all the women and children, and "the worst-scared men," had gone ashore, Sherman took "a can of crackers and some sardines" and followed. The ship had wrecked near Bolinas Bay, eighteen miles north of the Golden Gate. Upon reaching the shore, and still unaware of their location, Sherman and a young man struck out to find help.[47]

After walking about two miles, they came upon a small schooner in a creek, loaded with lumber for shipment to San Francisco. The schooner captain, informing Sherman of their location, agreed to take him to the city. Sherman sent a message back to the *Lewis* captain, telling him of their location, and promising to send help when he arrived in the city. As the schooner glided rapidly southward, Sherman relaxed a bit, reclining on the pile of lumber and enjoying the view of the coastline. Nearing their destination, the force of the wind suddenly combined with a strong ebb tide flowing out of the bay, seized the schooner, drove her bow under water, and the craft went over on her side. Sherman found himself in the water. He crawled up on the keel, satisfied the vessel would not sink because of her cargo.[48]

The schooner captain and his assistants were all safe, but the ship was drifting steadily out to sea. They began signaling another vessel, and were gratified to see it "tack and stand toward us." They had been spotted also by a man in a smaller boat who soon rowed alongside. The larger vessel arrived afterward, its captain willing to assist the schooner, while Sherman and his young companion were then rowed to the shore in the little boat, landing at Fort Point.

"Once there, I was at home," Sherman said, "and we footed it up to the Presidio." He quickly obtained horses, rode into the city, contacted the Nicaragua Steamship Company and arranged for the rescue of the *Lewis* passengers at dawn the next morning. All survived the ordeal. The arduous day had been long, dangerous and unforgettable. Was it a bad omen for the soldier turning to banking? That thought did cross Sherman's mind. Later he wrote that "two shipwrecks in one day [was] not a good beginning for a new peaceful career."[49]

Sherman next proceeded to hunt up Major Turner—often he referred to Turner by the rank his friend held when he left the army. Turner was boarding at a house on Clay Street. Naturally Sherman decided to do the same. During the following weeks he and Turner frequently ate together, often at Martin's, a French restaurant located at the corner of

Montgomery and California Streets. Usually Brigadier General Ethan Allen Hitchcock, commanding the Department of California, "messed with us," recalled Sherman, as did a captain and a lieutenant. Sherman always sought out army men, with whom he felt at ease.[50]

Turner had already established the bank, renting a property for $600 a month on the east side of Montgomery Street, between California and Sacramento Streets. Known as Lucas, Turner & Company, the enterprise was located across the street from Page, Bacon & Company of St. Louis, then the leading banking firm among the score of institutions operating in San Francisco. Sherman described Page, Bacon as "going full blast" in a new granite building. Other banks seemed to be doing a prosperous business—although half would fail within a year or so. "San Francisco was on the top wave of speculation and prosperity," Sherman later wrote. He thought that "everybody seemed to be making money fast." The city was basking in the clutches of boundless optimism. Major Turner, basically a conservative man who chose his words carefully, trumpeted San Francisco's "final destiny as one of the great commercial cities of the world."[51]

Sherman was amazed by the city's transformation in the few years since he last saw it, calling San Francisco "the most extraordinary place on earth." Formerly a tiny settlement he once described in a letter to his brother John as "a poor contemptible village," it had grown to 50,000 people. Sherman plunged into studying business conditions in San Francisco—"this new and untried scheme of banking"—with the same energy and diligence that had characterized his career in the army. He concluded that Turner had not been thinking big enough. The bank had $100,000 in capital. Sherman thought $300,000 a more realistic figure. He also wanted a branch in Sacramento and believed that the bank should own the building in which it operated. He favored a multistory structure, with banking operations conducted on the first floor, while the upper floors were let out for rent.[52]

Turner thought that opening a branch would be overreaching. The two friends discussed the capitalization issue at length, coming to a compromise figure of $200,000, and a line of credit in New York for $50,000.

Obviously Lucas, the bank principal in St. Louis, needed to approve. Sherman agreed to make a trip to St. Louis and confer with him. Sherman wrote John that with adequate capital, business prospects looked good, "the best going," he declared, "provided we have plenty of money." Otherwise, he would "stick to Uncle Sam."[53]

In mid-July, Sherman embarked for New York, by way of Nicaragua, leaving Turner to manage the bank until he returned, assisted by Benjamin R. Nisbet and James Reilly. From New York, Sherman traveled to St. Louis, making a brief stop in Ohio to see his family. If Lucas agreed to the money proposed, Sherman intended to take Ellen and the children to California. Arriving in St. Louis, he found Lucas strongly supportive. Lucas even consented to put up $50,000 for construction of the new office building that Sherman advocated. The decision was made. Sherman would resign from the army, and remain with the California bank until at least 1860.[54]

The family situation, however, defied a smooth resolution. The Ewings clearly were depressed at the thought of their daughter and young granddaughters, one of whom was less than a year old, departing for far-off California. They insisted that one child remain with them. Ellen presented their case to her husband, and although taken aback and displeased, Sherman reluctantly agreed. The older girl, Minnie, would stay in Ohio at the home of the Ewings.

On September 3, 1853, Sherman wrote his letter of resignation from the army. More than seventeen years had passed since he began a military career as a cadet on the banks of the Hudson. The decision to abandon that career had been agonizing. "I sometimes think that I am an out and out fool," he lamented only a short time earlier, when worrying about leaving the army for a speculative banking job on the West Coast. The army had been like a family and the trying time he had just been through probably brought home that fact. He likely felt a touch of sadness and a sense of loss on the day he resigned. He had taken the big step, though, and would have to live with the decision, whatever the consequences.[55]

Chapter Nine

Golden State Banker

$\triangleright$herman's decision to become a banker, the profession he pursued for half a decade during the 1850s, is imbued with irony. Both before and after those adventurous, tumultuous California years, he penned sweeping and virile denunciations of bankers and banking. Typically, he declared to brother John in the 1840s that all bankers were "selfish scoundrels," while he viewed banking and gambling, he told John in the late 1850s, as "synonymous terms." "No wonder," he once wrote Ellen, that bankers are "debarred all chances of heaven."[1]

Why then, after the long, agonizing decision to leave the army, did Sherman choose to try his hand at banking? Ellen's view, according to Sherman, was that Henry Turner had "roped" him into the decision. Her explanation was oversimplified, probably stemming from a pronounced bias against living in California, as well as homesickness for life in Ohio. Sherman eventually concluded, as he wrote Ellen's brother, that she was incapable of "appreciating the advantages that I have here." He told Turner, "Mrs. Sherman has a very poor opinion of California generally." Ellen, in fact, had written her mother about California in December 1853: "I fear nothing will ever reconcile me to this place." She was right: nothing ever did.[2]

This is not to deny that Turner's influence played a part in Sherman's decision to take up banking, but other factors were involved. The influence and backing of James Lucas, one of the most financially successful men in St. Louis, clearly became significant in Sherman's thinking. Perhaps of even greater importance, Lucas, Turner and Sherman were all three possessed by "California fever," a malaise afflicting a great many people. San Francisco, they believed, presented an unprecedented opportunity for accumulating big-time wealth. Yet another consideration might have crossed Sherman's mind. Unless men of integrity and character, like Sherman, became bankers, then the business for sure would be dominated by the "scoundrels" he so rightly despised.

Thomas Ewing's impressive financial achievements, together with Ellen's manifest respect and love for her father (she would keep his picture centered over her mantel in California), inevitably constituted a high standard of comparison, which Sherman found impossible to ignore. If he could succeed as the manager of a major West Coast bank, he would prove to his own satisfaction that he was truly worthy of association with the Ewing family. Plus he would have escaped living in Ohio, the very thought of which he detested. Finally, banking took him back to California, a place for which he had developed a genuine fondness.

Whatever the complexities explaining Sherman's choice of banking, he pursued the new career with characteristic assurance and determination, despite deteriorating health from frequent and sometimes severe asthma attacks. Fortunately, Sherman had an enormous capacity for work, even when plagued by poor health, because his banking years became, as Dwight L. Clarke, a California banker who wrote a valuable account of Sherman's tenure in the profession, concluded, "the most hectic and crisis-laden of his life up to 1861."[3]

Banking in California presented a distinct challenge. Not only did Sherman have no banking experience whatsoever, California banking was unlike banking anywhere else in the nation. Throughout the United States, paper bank notes circulated in great quantity, while gold and silver were in comparative short supply. In California, however, gold circulated in abundance. Saloons and general stores had a set of scales for weighing gold dust, which became the most prevalent circulating medium, at a price of $16 an ounce. In fact, many a business, whatever its nature, possessed a set of scales, since gold dust seemed to be ubiquitous. When California became a state in 1850, for example, the production of gold in that year was valued at $80 million, approximately double the U.S. government's total budget.[4]

As Sherman analyzed the California banking scene, he proved to be, as goes the popular expression, "a quick study." He mastered the realities—the strengths, weaknesses and peculiarities—of banking in San Francisco. Banking then was a laissez-faire activity, totally unrestricted and unregulated, except for one major provision: an absolute ban on paper money. Many California pioneers, having come from the east, retained an elephantine memory of the Panic of 1837, which had been triggered in great part by state banks issuing huge amounts of paper money that became worthless if the issuing bank succumbed to a financial crisis.[5]

When the California constitutional convention had met in the fall of 1849 (as Sherman well knew, because he was in attendance), impassioned speakers denounced banks as institutions of inherent evil. The delegates then incorporated in the California state constitution a provision that stated: "The legislature of this state shall prohibit by law any person or persons, association, company or corporation from . . . creating paper to circulate as money." With paper money banned, some bartering continued, just as before the discovery of gold; obviously land, in the form of ranches, farms and speculative investment, was of value, as were improvements to the land, such as houses, barns, etc. Real estate was taxed, however, and worse, titles to land were often in dispute. The upshot was that everything possessed limited value when compared with gold.[6]

Significantly, the constitutional convention also prohibited the state of California from chartering any bank. It was as if the delegates thought they had only to fear paper money and state-chartered banks. Consequently, any individual or association could open an office, provide a safe and encourage the public to entrust that establishment with its financial business. "Bankers," many of them with little or no previous experience in the profession, quickly appeared in considerable numbers, and plunged into an unregulated, wide-open arena. The result, as Dwight

Clarke concludes, was that "for nearly three decades, banking in California was to offer a perfect example of unrestricted laissez-faire."[7]

Sherman's approach to banking was basically conservative. Despite a
great demand for credit and a going interest rate of 3 percent per month,
he took care not to overextend the funds he let out at interest. Also, once
Henry Turner went back to St. Louis, in November 1853, he managed the
affairs of Lucas, Turner & Company very closely, much as he supervised
commissary responsibilities when he was in the army, where all financial disbursements were handled directly by him. Recalling his time as
a banker, Sherman wrote, "I signed all bills of exchange, and insisted on
[chief clerk Benjamin] Nisbet consulting me on all loans and discounts."
Sherman was keenly aware of the turbulent California economy in
which he operated. He was equally aware of his responsibilities to Lucas
and Turner, as well as the people who entrusted to him the safekeeping and investment of their funds. He put in long days at the bank, often
when he really was not well. "There must be but one head," he declared,
"and that head must know everything."[8]

Indeed Sherman strove diligently to master everything required
for a successful banking operation, including getting to know well the
city's political and business leaders, especially the merchants and the
shipping interests. He also made it a point to keep fully abreast of his
banking competition. By early 1854, Lucas, Turner & Company was
clearly in good condition. The bank showed increasing deposits, and
enjoyed a lively business in making loans and selling bills of exchange.
That March 15, the bank's total deposits were over $250,000, with cash
on hand of more than $550,000—very respectable amounts for that
time and place.

Sherman believed that in another year the firm's numbers would
exceed $1 million. San Francisco, he wrote Turner, "is beyond question
the great seaport of Western America," and potentially the great commercial center of "the Northwest coast as well as that of Mexico, the
Sandwich Islands, etc." The financial opportunities, he thought, were
virtually unlimited. "Neither Mr. Lucas nor yourself," he told Turner,

"desire to be small bankers and I assure you that I am ambitious of making our name famous among the nations of the earth."[9]

A particular point of satisfaction for Sherman was the fact that army officers had been investing with Lucas, Turner & Company. The great bulk of his trust accounts came from these men. In mid-April, he wrote Turner that the firm was then carrying all the deposits of army officers stationed in California. Many of those officers knew Sherman personally. Others soon learned about the former soldier turned banker, and felt comfortable entrusting their funds with him. Newly arriving officers were often directed to Sherman by those already using his firm. This was remarkable testimony to the high regard in which his army peers continued to hold him. Disassociating himself from a military career, particularly his army "family," was proving difficult for Sherman.[10]

Among her husband's army friends, Ellen clearly welcomed the frequent presence of one particular officer. The commander of the Department of California, Brigadier General Ethan Hitchcock, liked to play the flute. Ellen enjoyed playing piano and soon after she arrived in San Francisco, Sherman surprised her with the gift of a fine instrument. "General Hitchcock," Ellen wrote her mother, "visits us often, and he has brought me some accompaniments to the flute . . . he being a good performer on that instrument and very fond of music."

While Sherman complained that the pieces were all "so disguised by variations that you can only catch the air occasionally," Ellen declared, "I quite fancy them and though I have very little hopes that the General and I will ever be sufficiently practiced to delight the public, yet I am glad to have something to do that will improve my music and make my fingers more nimble." Often in the evenings, when Sherman and Ellen did not have any company, Ellen told her mother that she would play both "before and after dinner . . . all the spirited pieces I ever knew for the amusement of Cump and Lizzie, who generally dance and romp during the whole of my performance." Playing the piano, which Ellen described as "a pretty boudoir," lifted her spirit and eased the stress, for a while, that she experienced in adjusting to her new life.[11]

....

THROUGHOUT THE FIRST HALF of 1854, part of Sherman's time was spent in keeping a watchful eye on the construction of his new bank. For $32,000 he had purchased a lot facing Montgomery Street, "the Wall Street of San Francisco," he said. The site lay at the corner of Montgomery and Jackson Streets, and Sherman considered it an excellent location. "Jackson Street is now a great thoroughfare to the Clipper wharves lying north of Pacific," he wrote Turner. The bank would be near all "the heavy business of the country." Every one of the bank's competitors was situated farther away from the wharves where the clipper ships docked.[12]

"I then thought that all the heavy business would remain toward the foot of Broadway and Jackson Street," Sherman later wrote in his *Memoirs*, "because there were the deepest water and the best wharves, but in this I made a mistake." The city's business concentration drifted in the opposite direction; proving only, as many an investor has learned to his grief, that even a man of high intelligence and perception often is unable to fathom the enigmatic paths of urban development. Sherman really did not make a "mistake." The choice was a fine location for his day, and then appeared to be a good site for the future as well.[13]

The three-story brick building, with a full basement, cost approximately $50,000. The bank's business would be conducted on the first floor, while the second and third floors provided attractive offices for rent to lawyers, insurance agencies, shipping concerns and other enterprises. The structure was strongly built, with ninety-six piles being sunk, at a price of twenty-eight dollars each. Sherman commented in his *Memoirs* that he had seen the building recently, and several earthquakes "had made no impression on it." He would have been pleased to know that it also survived the great earthquake of 1906. Because of his demanding duties in supervising banking operations, he could not be as vigilant in overseeing construction of the new building as he would have liked. So he paid a man just to keep a close eye on the project. He did not intend for his banking house to collapse, either figuratively or literally.[14]

On July 14, 1854, Sherman proudly informed Turner that Lucas, Turner & Company now occupied the new building. The structure, he wrote, was "all we could expect, plenty of light, easy of access, large, roomy and beautiful." He considered it "the handsomest building in this town," and declared, "I enjoy it as much as an artist does a fine picture." Some rooms on the second and third floors were already rented when the building opened, and numerous prospects sought the others. The building was a boost for business. "During the whole of 1854," recalled Sherman, "our business steadily grew, our average deposits going up to half a million, and our sales of exchange and consequent shipment of bullion averaging two hundred thousand dollars per steamer." More trust accounts were opened, not only by army officers but some by customers of Lucas & Simonds in St. Louis, and others by San Francisco friends and customers.[15]

While the banking business grew and prospered, Sherman was simultaneously experiencing the worst asthma attacks, and related bronchial and chest problems, of his life. In midsummer of 1854, soon after the opening of the new bank building, and following an all-night bout with asthma, Sherman confided to Turner: "I have little or no faith in my prolonged existence." The asthma, he wrote, "is so fixed on me and is so serious at times that I care but little how soon it terminates fatally." Turner responded by "pitching into me like a thousand bricks," as Sherman described his friend's reply.

"Why the Devil can't you let an old soldier growl a little?" Sherman, who was thirty-four at the time, queried in a letter to "My Dear Turner." He and Turner always conversed in a straightforward manner. Turner should, Sherman advised, "let my asthma bear its full share of blame." He stated that he had been forced "for nights, weeks and months of nights," to sit up more or less all night "breathing like a broken winded horse, thankful for a couple of hours repose," which he supposed, left one's "nerves and temper somewhat unsettled." Sherman added that while "breathing the smoke of nitre paper" through the night, as he sought to gain a measure of relief, he reflected "that this climate will sooner or later kill me dead as a herring." Nevertheless, he assured Turner "I have never for an instant diverted my thoughts or determination from the business that has been entrusted to me."[16]

Many of Ellen's letters to her mother confirm that Sherman was not exaggerating when he spoke of his health problems, which nearly always related to asthma. Only a few weeks after she arrived in San Francisco, Ellen wrote Maria Ewing that Cump was up nearly every night, and sometimes all night. She said that he took medicine constantly to help him sleep, which she feared would injure him, and declared that he himself did not think that he would live very long. She worried that his miserable health foretold the onset of consumption. A few days later Ellen wrote that he was running a fever, having "no appetite and a continued hard cough. If he does not get better when spring comes I shall despair of his ever being well here, and I see no prospect of getting him away before his six years are passed, should he live so long. . . . Cump himself thinks that he will never be better."[17]

As for Ellen, Sherman's health problems constituted only one of the reasons for her dislike of California. From the time that she stepped off the steamer in October 1853, Ellen seldom had anything positive to say about life in San Francisco or the Golden State. She soon penned a long letter to her mother summarizing many details of her generally unpleasant voyage from New York to California. For several days after leaving New York she had been seasick. After recovering, she found the ship's accommodations (all of the quarters, not just hers) cramped and poorly furnished. Other concerns presented themselves, such as distasteful food and lack of freshwater. Above all, she was deeply saddened by the death of several people during the trip, who were buried at sea. A year later, in a letter to Maria, she said that those deaths had alarmed her "more than anything else in the world."[18]

Arriving in San Francisco, Ellen commented upon the "narrow and crowded" streets, the houses without yards, "front or rear" and the awful mud with which one had to contend. Nearly everything was more expensive than in Ohio or Washington, D.C. She found it difficult to employ a good cook, with four girls proving unsatisfactory within a span of only a few weeks. She thought that anybody coming to California would regret it. "There are *hundreds* here who would go home had they the money to take them." As for the moral climate, she wrote her mother that San Francisco was *"thoroughly* wicked." She had been told that more than half the women were prostitutes. In another letter, she wrote of "the horrible wickedness that prevails ... in this most forlorn place." San Francisco, she asserted, was going the way of the Biblical Sodom. In this connection, Sherman reported to Turner in mid-April 1854 that the city council recently "abolished ... bawdy houses, ... and you do not now see troops of girls displaying themselves on horseback and carriages. ... Such women," he declared, "can not be changed or reformed," but at least, he concluded, "their practices are hidden away."[19]

Ellen spent a lot of time composing letters to her mother, as she frequently had done ever since she married. She eagerly looked forward to all communications that came from home—and "home" is how she continued to think of her mother and father in Lancaster, all the more so with her firstborn in their care.[20] The letters from Maria Ewing typically provided news about Ohio or Washington events. Sometimes they were amusing, but with few exceptions, her letters carried news and comments of a religious nature, always extolling the virtues of Catholicism. For instance, Maria wrote Ellen about a Mrs. Peter, "a charming woman ... full of faith and zeal," who spoke continually of the wonders of the Catholic religion in Italy and France, where, according to her, "it is a common thing ... for a miracle to be performed." Mrs. Peter herself "witnessed two whilst in France." If Mother Ewing filled her whole sheet of paper, it would not be possible to tell of "half the relics that [Mrs. Peter] has in her cabinet." For her part, Ellen's letters kept her mother informed about Catholicism and its leaders in California. One of Ellen's greatest concerns, about which she wrote Maria periodically, was Minnie's religious development. Minnie's aunts and cousins should all know, emphatically, Ellen instructed, that Minnie was to be raised with "no tinge towards protestantism." Maria must never allow the girl to go to Mansfield alone. She was to go only if Maria accompanied her, for fear that she might come under the influence of Sherman's Protestant relatives there. Minnie was to visit them only if "under my restraining influence or yours."[21]

Ellen was very upset by the rise of the anti-Catholic Know-Nothing Party. An enormous influx of Irish and Germans in the 1840s and 1850s, many of whom were Roman Catholic, had enabled that church, by the early 1850s, to emerge from decades as a negligible minority and become the single most numerous religious group in the nation. Longtime Protestant fears of the Church of Rome and "Popish" practices increased markedly, combining with a growing and general antiforeign bias. The result was the formation, in New York, of an American "nativist" party.

Known as the Order of the Star-Spangled Banner (some liked to say the "Supreme" Order of the Star-Spangled Banner, while also giddily styling themselves as "Sons of the Sires of Seventy-Six"), the American Party was secretive, from which came the moniker "Know-Nothings." Membership required a person to be descended from at least two generations of native-born Americans who had never been members of the Catholic Church. The Know-Nothings freely and irresponsibly exploited patriotic emotions, racial bigotry, religious intolerance and sexual fantasies, the last sometimes involving supposed "Popish brothels" (convents). As the group developed into a formidable third party, striving zealously, and for a time seemingly on the brink of achieving major-party status, violent actions sometimes followed in the wake of their deplorable, misguided efforts.[22]

In the fall of 1854, Ellen wrote her mother about the threat from the Know-Nothings. She said there were serious concerns that her own parish church would be destroyed about the time of that November's election. Fortunately it was spared. She declared that most of the prejudice in California was directed against the Irish Catholics. "The stronger their prejudice," she declared, "the more I boast of my descent and thank God for the faith which the Irish have kept inviolate through so many years of suffering and privation." Sherman, of course, attempted to keep abreast of both national and local politics. Henry Turner wrote him about the defeat of Thomas Hart Benton, long a formidable presence in the U.S. Senate. Sherman considered Benton's downfall "highly gratifying and I sincerely rejoice." Although not a Catholic, Sherman had no love for the Know-Nothings. He sarcastically revealed both their ignorance and underhanded actions in a letter he wrote Turner describing their success in electing a new mayor.[23]

But when the politics of 1854 are objectively analyzed, in terms of immediate results and long-term consequences weighed in the historical balances, the year's most important development without a doubt was the Kansas-Nebraska Act. Engineered by Senator Stephen A. Douglas of Illinois, the "Little Giant," Kansas-Nebraska reopened the strife over slavery—strife that "the fearful struggle of 1850,"[24] as Douglas himself characterized the midcentury compromise, had supposedly laid to rest. Kansas-Nebraska thus cast a long, dark shadow, one of immensely greater national significance than the fortunes of the nativist American Party. In rekindling the issue of the expansion of slavery, it set the nation on the road to the Civil War.

Of course Senator Douglas, a dedicated Unionist, never intended any such outcome. Ironically, he had devised the strategy and spearheaded the effort that finally achieved the passage of the Compromise of 1850. Equally ironic, his basic motivations in 1854 had nothing to do with slavery. A fervent expansionist, Douglas intended to organize the territory west of Missouri and Iowa for settlement, hoping to promote the construction of a transcontinental railroad along a northern route, and connect Chicago with the Pacific Ocean. He intended to remove "the barbarian wall" of Indians blocking American westward advance, and "authorize and encourage a continuous line of settlements to the Pacific." The Iron Horse, steaming west from Chicago, would serve as the advance agent of manifest destiny.[25]

It was not to be that simple. Between January, when Senator Douglas introduced the "Nebraska" bill, and late May when "Kansas-Nebraska" passed by a 37–14 vote in the Senate and 113–100 in the House, Douglas's proposal underwent a remarkable transformation. Instead of a railroad bill, amazingly it emerged as a proslavery bill. Nebraska Territory had been divided into two parts: Kansas and Nebraska. The Missouri Compromise ban on slavery north of 36° 30', which had stood for thirty-four years and was almost sacred to the opponents of slavery's expansion, would be repealed.[26]

The issue of slavery in the new territories was to be determined by popular sovereignty. Nebraska, lying west of free-state Iowa, would presumably become a free state, but Kansas, located west of slave-state Missouri, well might choose to enter the Union as a slave state—particularly if zealous slavery advocates seized the opportunity to gain another slave state, which they soon set about to do. Senator Douglas, although acknowledging to a friend that repealing the Missouri Compromise ban "will raise a hell of a storm," woefully underestimated the destructive power that his bill unleashed. More than once, Douglas had declared that he cared not whether slavery was voted up or down. The senator's relative indifference perhaps explains his failure to understand the intensity of feelings, pro and con, about the institution. Besides, if Kansas-Nebraska were going to pass, Douglas needed Southern support, along with some Northern Democratic backing. The Southern votes were ready—but only if Douglas catered to Southern demands that the Missouri Compromise line be repealed. And so he did. Also, if the senator were going to gain the Democratic nomination for president in 1856, an ambition never far removed from his thoughts, Southern support clearly would be imperative.[27]

The deed was done. Results were instant, sweeping and ominous. With an unfailing vision, at least on this issue, Senator Charles Sumner, a Massachusetts abolitionist, foresaw the dire consequences, which he expressed in the pronouncement that Kansas-Nebraska was "at once the worst and the best which Congress ever enacted." It was "the worst bill, inasmuch as it is a present victory for Slavery. . . . It is the best bill . . . for it . . . annuls all past compromises with Slavery, and makes all future compromises impossible. Thus it puts Freedom and Slavery face to face, and bids them grapple. Who can doubt the result?"[28]

Grapple they did. Massive political restructuring erupted all across the Northern states, and to a lesser degree in the Southern. The already weakened Whig Party was destroyed, as large numbers of Northern

Whigs turned to the rapidly organizing Republican Party—a new political institution dedicated, above all, to arresting the spread of slavery. Many Southern Whigs defected to the Democratic Party, whose strength shifted steadily to the slave states. Still other Whigs, north and south, moved into the Know-Nothing camp. Kansas-Nebraska divided the Northern Democrats, many of whom were shocked by the audacious repeal of the Missouri Compromise line, and became, very quickly, candidates for a fresh political allegiance.

The most enduring political legacy of Kansas-Nebraska was the creation of the Republican Party. Totally Northern in composition, the Republicans united former Whigs, Democrats, Free Soilers, Know-Nothings—all of whom opposed the Kansas-Nebraska Act and demanded, for whatever reason, that the expansion of slavery must cease. Friendly to business interests, but pledged first and foremost to oppose the spread of slavery, the purely sectional Republicans virtually exploded on the political scene.

And of course Kansas-Nebraska soon produced an awful situation in Kansas Territory. Because popular sovereignty would determine the slavery question, various Northern and Southern associations quickly developed for the purpose of encouraging their partisans to settle in Kansas. Most famous was the New England Emigrant Aid Society. Other Northern groups followed its lead, while Southern efforts centered in Missouri. Within weeks free-state and slave-state advocates vied for power. Incendiary rhetoric poisoned the air while election fraud became widespread. Missouri border ruffians rode over the line and voted in the Kansas elections, attempting to offset the greater number of free-state advocates moving into the territory. Tension increased and violence mounted. Territorial governors appointed by President Franklin Pierce could not control the situation. Civil war was coming early to the plains of Kansas.[29]

Sherman was following the momentous national developments as best he could from the West Coast, where news always arrived long after events in the east had occurred. In the fall of 1854, John Sherman was elected to the U.S. House of Representatives from Ohio's Thirteenth

District. Obviously Cump's periodic, strongly expressed pleas for his younger brother to stay away from politics had failed to take effect.

Probably feeling that he should, at the least, offer some small measure of congratulations, Sherman wrote to John on November 30. "I have seen by the papers that you are elected to Congress. I suppose you feel entitled to the congratulations of all the family, and I should not have been so late in giving you mine, only I expected that you would announce by letter the fact of your plans." He then declared that being elected "is of course a higher honor than to occupy a seat in the House of Representatives." The House, in his opinion, was merely a training ground "for higher honors," by which he meant the Senate. Should John aspire to a seat there, he would "be proud to learn of your success." Having given his congratulations, while simultaneously revealing that he was not particularly impressed, the older brother, predictably, next offered advice on how to proceed. "As a young member, I hope you will not be too forward, especially on the question of slavery, which it seems is rising more and more . . . into a question of real danger."

Sherman obviously was right about the danger. Reminding John that he had lived for several years in the South, he asserted that, from a practical standpoint, "I think I know . . . more of slavery than you do. . . . There are certain lands in the South that can not be inhabited in the summer by the whites, and yet the negro thrives in it—this I know." Contending that "forced negro labor" was essential for the production of "rice, sugar and certain kinds of cotton," Sherman declared slavery, regardless of what anyone thought, could not be abolished "except by force and the consequent breaking up of our present government." As to the Kansas-Nebraska bill, he stated it "was a mistake on the part of the South, a vital mistake that will do them more harm than all the violent abolitionists in the country." He also believed that Missouri should never have been admitted to the Union as a slave state, but after the passage of three decades, he saw no remedy except in Missouri itself, where he declared that economic self-interest would at some future date dictate its abolishment. "Let slavery extend along the shores of the Gulf of Mexico, but not in the high salubrious prairies of the West."[30]

Sherman continued to offer his brother advice from time to time. The letters to John are valuable in revealing his thinking about vital issues of the era, particularly leading up to the Civil War. Meanwhile, the Sherman family continued to grow. He wrote Turner that the increase was coming "at an awful rate." William Ewing Sherman, "a boy of the reddest kind," who became known as Willie, was born on June 8, 1854. Sherman was pleased to have a son, and Willie seemingly became his favorite child, but the financial responsibilities worried him. If raising the boy "takes as much money in proportion as his birth, with doctors, nurses and church fees," he confided to Turner, "I might as well forego the dream I often conjure up of living in St. Louis with a small and certain income." A fourth child, who would be christened Thomas Ewing Sherman, was also born while he and Ellen resided in California.[31]

The couple was spending considerably more money than Sherman was making, which predictably became a source of tension between husband and wife. According to Ellen, in a letter to her mother on November 24, 1854, *"our expenses this year have been one third more than double [Cump's] salary. . . .* Were we to live any more economically than we do, we would be considered mean. But I drop the subject in deep disgust." Compared with most people, Sherman and Ellen actually were living well, but undoubtedly not within their income.[32]

Ellen expressed part of the reason they were overextended: "We must keep up a certain degree of respectability (I hate that word) and be prepared to entertain company, at least in a social way." Sherman would have agreed that a successful banker should appear comfortable financially, as well as stable and conservative. He believed though that the economic problems were compounded because, as he wrote Turner, "Mrs. Sherman [he always referred to Ellen as Mrs. Sherman when writing Turner] is utterly deaf to all ideas of economy, not extravagant, but not caring for money where the children are concerned. You can see the difference." Insufficient funds would plague the couple through all their California days.[33]

Ellen's desire to return to Ohio for a visit with her parents and Minnie also became a sore point, impacting their financial troubles. She wanted to take the children with her when she made the journey. However, Ellen said that Cump insisted upon Lizzie and Willie's remaining in California. His point of view was that the young children should not be subjected to such a hard and dangerous trip. Willie was not even a year old. Sherman said that Ellen could go to her parents for a long visit, but not with the children—unless she agreed to stay in Ohio with them indefinitely, while he tried to improve the family's financial position. Possibly he hoped to persuade Ellen to remain in California by denying permission for the children to make the trip.

In mid-December 1854, Sherman wrote Ellen's brother, Hugh Boyle Ewing, with whom he enjoyed a close relationship and could speak freely. "Ellen still proposes to go home in April," he told Hugh, "but I think with you that it is positive cruelty to take the children back and forth on so long a voyage and journey." He then claimed that Ellen would be willing to leave them with him in San Francisco while she made the trip, except for the interference of her parents. "Every letter she has from her mother, and your father too," he told Hugh, "advises her to bring them along. I can not yet tell what will be done, but," he cynically declared, "I can have the satisfaction of knowing that in any alternative the blame falls on me."[34]

Two days before Christmas, Sherman penned a very revealing letter to Turner. After summarizing banking business, he turned to personal matters. "I can not confide to Mrs. Sherman the fact that I am not saving money," he wrote. Clearly Mrs. Sherman, judging from that November letter to her mother, knew more about their finances than her husband thought—or was willing to tell Turner. Even with his recent dividend, Sherman said he owed as much money as his house and furniture were worth. Then he stated that he wanted Ellen to take the children to Ohio, and stay there, while he saved some money; "but I can not say a word about economy," he wrote, without Ellen declaring that she would rather see him living on a farm in the east, "barely subsisting my family than [to be in California]."

As for Ellen's trip to Ohio, he told Turner that she planned to go in April, leaving the children with him, and "thus imposing on me the double charges of maintaining a family here, and paying her expenses to and from Ohio." What the result would be, Sherman acknowledged that he could not predict, but asserted "that ladies, when their children or parents are concerned, are as blind to reason as mad bulls." He did admit, in another letter to Turner, that the wreck of the *Yankee Blade* off Santa Barbara in the fall of 1854 had a powerful impact on Ellen, greatly increasing her fear of the sea. More than thirty passengers drowned when the ship crashed on a reef, including some ladies whom Ellen knew. "She now talks of leaving the children with me," wrote Sherman, "so as only to risk her own life."[35]

BY LATE 1854, simultaneous with Sherman's growing personal financial problems and family issues, "the Wall Street of San Francisco" showed disconcerting signs that the bears were massing to challenge the bulls. Several stock companies failed, merchants recorded declining sales and Sherman detected a "steady depreciation of real estate." How soon he realized that he was facing a full-scale recession is impossible to determine. At least by mid-January of 1855 he must have seen the situation rather clearly. He wrote Turner, listing a number of businesses that had failed, some of which owed the bank money. He proclaimed that all the men "who swore . . . that California land produces ten times as much as any other land" had ended up broke. Nothing in California, in Sherman's judgment, was substantial except the gold mines.[36]

Sherman's consistently good instincts, and perceptions of human character, did result in significantly limiting the bank's losses in a sensational scandal, entitled by Sherman "the great Meiggs failure, swindle, forgery and flight." Henry A. (Honest Harry) Meiggs was a lumber merchant and sawmill operator, participating in various speculative undertakings, for which he often borrowed large amounts of money. Benjamin Nisbet, Sherman's chief clerk, had full confidence in the man—according to Sherman. It should be noted that six months later, in a "Confidential" letter replying to a query from Turner, Sherman said that Nisbet had no respect for years, superior education, or anything except money, and was friendly with only prosperous people. Nisbet easily fell under the spell of Meiggs. As for Sherman, "for some reason," which he apparently found vague and difficult to analyze, "I feared or mistrusted [Meiggs] and . . . cautioned Nisbet not to extend his credit." As Sherman reflected upon the fact that Meiggs owed his firm about $80,000, maintained bank accounts in other institutions and was "generally a borrower," he determined to restrict his total loan amount to $25,000.[37]

Shortly after Sherman decided to contract his credit, Meiggs appeared in quest of another $20,000, reportedly for a business of his in Mendocino, which was, Sherman sarcastically noted, "based upon calculations that could not fail." Sherman listened to the man's arguments but renewed his decision to limit Meiggs's credit. How fortunate that he did, successfully demanding that Meiggs make arrangements at once to pay the remainder that he owed. Soon afterward, Meiggs and his family stole away, sailing for South America and leaving debts of well over $800,000. Compared with others, Sherman's loss was minimal. He took possession of Meiggs's house and some other property for which the bank held a mortgage, and reported to Turner that he did not hold any forged paper, of which Meiggs was responsible for nearly half a million. Sherman had come out better than any other banker doing business with "Honest Harry." James Reilly, one of Sherman's tellers, was among the many duped by the swindler, and "lost his all," said Sherman—a sum of about $1,500. Sherman considered the episode a disaster for the city, which began "a series of failures in San Francisco, that extended through the next two years."[38]

As the new year of 1855 came in, despite the deteriorating local economy, Sherman decided to build a new house. He knew that Ellen did not care for the place they had bought soon after their arrival. Probably he thought a new and larger home, in a more desirable section of the city, might help his wife be content in California; and in any case would be a better investment of their money. The cost, for lot and house, came to $10,000. In mid-February, Ellen wrote her mother about the project, conveying a generally positive attitude: "Cump has bought a large lot in a retired, pleasant (comparatively) part of the city, where he is having a large house built." She said they would have a well, a stable and a carriage house; keep a cow, a horse and chickens. There would be flower beds, and a more secure yard in which the children could play. She believed the family would be "more comfortable and have more room indoors and out."[39]

Two days after Ellen penned that letter to Maria Ewing, Sherman's bank faced a major crisis. The financial storm was not totally without warning, although the timing came as a surprise. Years later, Sherman wrote that during the winter of 1854–1855, he received "frequent intimations" in letters from the partners in Missouri "that the [St. Louis] bank of Page, Bacon & Company was in trouble." The difficulties grew out of the bank's relationship to the Ohio & Mississippi Railroad. Having advanced large sums of money to the line's contractors, the bank became seriously overextended. Still, in California, Page, Bacon remained the most prominent banking house in the state, and nobody on the West Coast, remembered Sherman, "doubted their wealth and stability." Then came the shocking news from the east.[40]

On Saturday, February 17, the mail steamer *Oregon* was approaching the San Francisco wharves, when a man on board yelled out to an acquaintance ashore, saying that Page, Bacon & Company of St. Louis had failed! The word spread like wildfire, inaugurating a steady run on the San Francisco branch of the company, which forced it under by the latter part of the following week. One of the Page, Bacon partners, a man named Henry Haight, took to drinking heavily during the crisis, according to Sherman, and proclaimed in the presence of several bankers and investors, including Sherman, that "all the banks [in San Francisco] would break."[41]

Haight's prophecy of doom was bruited about, supplying yet more fuel to the financial fires. Every bank in the city faced high withdrawals. The climax came on February 23, long to be remembered in San Francisco as "Black Friday." The condition of Lucas, Turner & Company was strong, thanks to Sherman's careful, conservative practices. His deposit account was approximately $600,000, "and we had in our vault about five hundred thousand dollars in coin and bullion, besides an equal amount of good bills receivable." According to his calculations, he could meet nearly all of the bank's obligations, and also raise additional money from friends and supporters if worse came to worst—and indeed, as Wellington famously remarked of Waterloo, the crisis did become "a damn near run thing."[42]

When Sherman reached the bank early that Friday morning, he was "thunderstruck to see the crowd and tumult." Bad news reigned. Adams & Company did not open; nor did Wells, Fargo & Company. Robinson & Wright Savings closed soon after opening. Rumors ran rife that every bank in the city would fail. Many of Sherman's depositors were bent on withdrawing their money. He confidently told them that "what others are doing, we know not," but Lucas, Turner & Company would not break, and any customer feeling nervous about his money was welcome to withdraw it. By noon the bank had paid out $337,000 in cash.[43]

The run continued through the afternoon. Sherman worked to reassure customers that the bank was sound, and he was grateful that "several gentlemen of my personal acquaintance merely asked my word of honor that their money was safe, and went away." Others, who had large accounts, were willing to accept gold bars rather than coin, which proved very helpful. Still other customers made modest deposits, and "rather ostentatiously," reported Sherman, actions calculated to engender confidence. Yet he afterward admitted that things looked bad in late afternoon, shortly before closing—thankfully having persevered until the usual closing time.[44]

When Sherman left the bank that evening, he "resolved not to sleep until I had collected from those owing the bank a part of their debts." A few men were immediately able to assist, while others promised to make partial payment on their debt the next morning. The greatest single boost came from Richard P. Hammond, a West Point contemporary of Sherman who had served with distinction in the Mexican War, afterward resigning from the army with the brevet rank of major. Hammond made $40,000 available for the emergency if necessary—far more than Sherman had suggested—with the understanding that Hammond would get the money back no later than March 1. Some other army customers also helped out. The loyalty of army friends in the crisis left a deep impression on Sherman, all the more confirming his faith in the superiority and camaraderie of men who had experienced a West Point education.[45]

When Lucas, Turner & Company opened for business on Saturday morning, February 24, Sherman's apprehensions of a continuing run on the bank thankfully did not materialize. On the contrary, money began to come back on deposit, and by closing time he had seen a considerable increase. Instead of an exciting day, it had been one of absolute calm. At last Sherman could relax. He recalled that for an entire week he had hardly slept, not because of asthma, as he wrote Turner, but from "a rigid distraction of nerve, mind and body."[46]

Sherman had survived a major financial challenge, in which seven of San Francisco's nineteen banks failed. The reputation of Lucas, Turner & Company rose dramatically; it was now considered by many citizens to be the strongest bank in the city. Sherman justifiably took satisfaction in the triumph. Once again, as when he faced hostile Indians in Florida, disaster at sea or deserting troops in California, he remained calm, thought clearly and acted decisively. He also came away from the crisis with little or no respect for some of the city's leading bankers and businessmen. Page, Bacon & Company's Haight had lost his nerve. Sherman already thought Dr. Stephen A. Wright of Robinson & Wright, "an ass to have spent $147,000 for a [banking] house in these days [late 1854]." He said, too, that he would not forget the selfishness of Wells, Fargo & Company, "in leaving us to bear the brunt of a panic in part created by them."[47]

Ellen proudly penned a letter to her father, informing him of the banking crisis and detailing how Sherman's firm withstood the pressure. The popularity of Lucas, Turner & Company "cannot henceforth be questioned," she announced. Writing to her mother, she said Cump was "very much delighted to have so triumphed over many who really wished to see [the business] come down with themselves." The entire community had witnessed the strength of Sherman's bank on a day possessing "all the bustle and excitement of a battle." Sherman himself sometimes spoke of "the Battle of the 23rd of February."[48]

Although Ellen admired her husband's achievement in successfully facing the financial crisis, she actually did confess to him that she would have liked to see the bank fail. Ellen believed if that had happened, he "would have gone home"—obviously meaning Ohio, or at least somewhere back east. To say that Sherman was not pleased by Ellen's attitude is an understatement—all the more as her feelings were revealed while he was still celebrating his hard-won victory.[49]

In early March Sherman hosted a dinner party for all the bank employees, in recognition and appreciation of their extra and demanding work during the crisis. Shortly after, he fell ill. For several days he remained at home "suffering greatly," in Ellen's words, "from a severe attack of his disease [undoubtedly meaning asthma], aggravated by cold and inflamation of the lungs." The doctor applied "a great many remedies," wrote Ellen, "but nothing gave him so much relief as copious cupping on the back." In this procedure the administrator forms the fingers of each hand like a cup and, rapidly alternating, beats on the patient's back to help loosen the buildup of mucus.[50]

Meanwhile, arrangements had been made for friends, Mr. and Mrs. Samuel M. Bowman, to move in with Sherman and the children while Ellen made the long trip to Ohio. In early April the new house was finished, the Shermans occupied it at once, soon joined by the Bowmans, and on April 17, Ellen sailed for New York aboard the steamer *Golden Age*. Shortly before leaving, she had told Maria that the children "will have the care of a mother and Cump will have a comfortable house and so I can remain with you quite a long time if they keep well."[51]

Ellen soon had more reason than ever to fear the sea. Drawing within a day's distance of Panama on a moonlit night and running at full speed, the *Golden Age* struck a sunken reef, ripping out a piece of the hull. At once the ship began to fill with water. Fortunately Commodore J. T. Watkins was on deck and immediately turned the bow of his vessel straight for a nearby island. "The water rose rapidly in the hold," as Sherman described the scene, based upon Ellen's recollections. "The passengers were all assembled, fearful of going down; the fires [were soon smothered] out, . . . and when her bow touched gently on the beach,

... the vessel's stern [quickly slipped below the water]." If the *Golden Age* had sunk in midchannel, most of the thousand passengers aboard probably would have drowned. Having averted disaster, Ellen continued her journey aboard the *John L. Stevens*, reaching New York without further incident.[52]

When Sherman learned of the *Golden Age* wreck, he was greatly relieved by the news that no loss of life had occurred. He and Ellen had some serious issues between them, but each genuinely cared for the other, and during the seven months while they were separated, they wrote frequently. While she was away, Sherman immersed himself in managing the bank, as well as other concerns. Improving transportation in California was becoming a priority, and with Turner's approval Sherman subscribed on behalf of Lucas, Turner & Company to the construction of the Sacramento Valley Railroad. This was a line laying track eastward from Sacramento. It was the first railroad built in California. Sherman became vice president of the company and was offered the presidency, but declined. Twenty-two miles of track were laid, which eventually became part of the Central Pacific Railroad, the first transcontinental line.[53]

Sherman also chaired a committee advocating that Congress should authorize the construction of an overland wagon road to link California with the east. He thought that the time for "the Great National Rail Road has not yet come," but a "good wagon road is very timely." Its cost would be relatively small compared with the benefits. Instructing his congressman brother John, Sherman wrote: "Advocate the Wagon Road with all the force you possess, and you will do a good thing." He declared that California, "independent of gold," was of immense value to the Union because it afforded "so good a harbor and point of commerce from which we can trade with the Pacific Islands, with Mexico and the Asiatic Continent."[54]

In the meantime San Francisco's dull economy continued its decline. Sherman was definitely bearish when he wrote to Hugh Boyle Ewing in late June 1855. San Francisco had "grown too fast. Men got rich too fast, and now are tumbling back into their proper ranks quite as fast." Times were not likely to be "as profitable as before." Sherman gave his foster brother the power of attorney to manage his St. Louis property, which he was instructed to lease, either for a term of years, or from month to month. The only limit, Sherman stated, was a period of six years, for then "if I live, I may want to enter in possession myself." He was not expecting "much revenue" from the property, "but still everything helps," he wrote, because "my expenses here are necessarily so heavy that my idea of fortune dwindles each year . . . [in] this uncertain country."[55]

As for the children, Sherman told Hugh Ewing that "Lizzie & Willie are pictures of health, & good specimens of young America." Later he wrote that "Willy [spelling change by Sherman] & Lizzie are developing fast and will [bring] no discredit on the family either in appearance or intellect." Even if working hard, and often through the night before the departure of a steamer carrying mail east for his parent firm, Sherman was also spending a lot of time with the children. Perhaps he was more motivated to enjoy their company when he thought of Minnie, growing up in Ohio "an utter stranger to me," as he had told Hugh some months earlier.[56]

When Ellen returned to San Francisco late in 1855, although without Minnie of course, Sherman was pleased to see her. He hoped that the long visit in Ohio might engender a more favorable attitude toward remaining in California. That hope was forlorn, and probably predictable. In the weeks following her return from the east, Ellen seemed to become ever more discontent in San Francisco. She "is hostile beyond measure to California and my remaining here," he told Turner. He wrote Ellen's brother that her "persistent hostility to California" forced him to turn his thoughts to the east, "but always with the determination to stay here at the least four years yet." His wife's negativity toward the Golden State, added to the demands of his work at the bank, made Sherman's life unpleasant, and he also thought, affected his health.[57]

Fundamentally, Sherman and Ellen each desired the other to be something that they either did not wish to be, or were simply incapable of being. That impasse always haunted their marriage, but never more persistently than during the California years. As fate would have it, 1856 became the last full year the couple lived in San Francisco, although neither expected it at the beginning. Sherman remained resolved, as the new year came in, to fulfill his "enlistment," as he frequently referenced his banking commitment.

ABOVE ALL 1856 would be remembered in San Francisco, as the year of the Vigilantes. Five years earlier, vigilantes had made their appearance as frightened citizens briefly took the law into their own hands. In the spring of 1856 they came back with a vengeance. San Francisco, without question, was a corrupt, volatile, and dangerous city, in which many men spoke and wrote in fiery, intemperate language. Verbal personal attacks, hair-trigger tempers, bullying tactics and exaggerated notions of honor were all too common. A potentially explosive milieu had been created, and it suddenly erupted in frightening, violent lawlessness.

Two sensational killings in May aroused public emotions to a fever pitch. A man by the name of Charles Cora, considered by Sherman a "scoundrel," killed William H. Richardson, a United States marshal. Sherman said in a letter to John that a lot of people believed Cora was "compelled to kill Richardson, or be killed himself." Even more alarming was the shooting of a man with the memorable name of James King of William, a popular editorial writer for San Francisco's *Daily Evening Bulletin*. A fearless enemy of corrupt politicians and criminals, he was shot on the street with a revolver, at close range, by James P. Casey, editor of the city's *Sunday Times*. King and Casey had been at odds for months. This time Casey became enraged upon reading King's documented assertion that Casey had once served time in New York's Sing Sing Prison. Casey shot King on the same day that the offending piece was published.[58]

Sherman knew both men. He strongly disliked Casey, saying he had "recklessly attacked all the bankers and decent people of this city" at the time of the Black Friday crisis. For a while Casey's printing office had been located in Sherman's bank building. If the editor had not moved, Sherman claimed that he had been ready to chuck him and his press out of the window. Casey's victim did not die immediately, lingering for the better part of a week, while public excitement escalated. The old Vigilance Committee was revived, with followers soon numbering several thousand. Casey had joined Charles Cora in the city jail, where the sheriff and his relatively small posse feared that the Vigilantes would surely storm the place if King died. Sherman did not want to become involved, but everyone knew about his army background, and the governor of California, J. Neely Johnson, had recently persuaded him to accept a commission as major general of the Second Division of Militia, embracing San Francisco—a decision that Sherman made with considerable reluctance and regretted almost immediately.[59]

The San Francisco sheriff and his deputies sought Sherman's advice about defending the jail. He concluded that the jail itself was "utterly indefensible." Only by occupying specific buildings around the jail might one possibly conduct a successful defense. However, it was too late for this move because the Vigilantes had taken control of those sites. The sheriff faced a hopeless situation if the Vigilantes came for the prisoners. And soon they did, not waiting to see whether or not King would recover. Masses of people, Sherman thought "at least ten thousand," moved toward the jail as he and a few other men watched from the roof of a nearby structure. The governor's recent declaration that California had matured beyond resorting to mobs and vigilance committees might as well have never been uttered. Rather than sacrifice himself and his handful of supporters, the sheriff surrendered his prisoners under protest.[60]

Sherman fittingly alluded to the French Revolution as he wrote Turner, declaring that "all the elements of the Paris Committee of [Public] Safety are here and once put in motion, they can not be stopped." The Vigilance Committee's deliberations were in secret and nobody knew what they might do. On May 20, King worsened and breathed his last breath. The committee, claiming to have fairly tried Casey and Cora, then hanged both men. Soon it was obvious that the committee had no intention of surrendering power. Sherman proposed, Ellen informed her mother, that she should go back to Ohio."[61]

Maria and Thomas Ewing fully agreed. Sherman had written a long letter to Mr. Ewing, fully detailing the lawless situation. "It was most shocking," Maria told her daughter, but she "rejoiced in the prospect of your return to your home." She believed that surely, "if such a terrible state of things are to continue to exist, if the city is to be governed by Mob law and Lynching, Mr. Sherman will be willing to give up the Country and return to his home." Maria added that "if your Pa gets home this evening he will write you a long letter in which, he said (before he left for Cincinnati), he will urge you to return home as soon as possible."[62]

But for once Ellen was not interested in returning to Ohio. She felt a strong sense of loyalty to her husband in such a difficult time, and she was incensed by the wanton violence of the Vigilantes. Aware that both Casey and Cora were Catholic, Ellen viewed the Vigilantes, initially at least, as a political movement, motivated "by the Know-Nothing spirit." She had little sympathy for King, claiming that he had dealt in "false and gross personal abuse" of a Catholic priest, and "goaded this poor Casey on to madness and he shot him." Ellen openly condemned Vigilante actions, considered them guilty of treason and was convinced, like Sherman, that their blatant takeover of San Francisco was destroying the prosperity of the city.[63]

The Vigilantes did possess their fair share of Know-Nothings, but they drew heavily from the entire political spectrum. Also, while counting a host of rowdies among their followers, the Vigilantes acquired, deplorably, many of "the best people" in San Francisco. In fact, a substantial number of the prosperous, and allegedly responsible people of the city were among the leaders of the movement. Ellen was appalled, as well she might be, and declared it "disgraceful" that most of the city's preachers supported the Vigilantes. She did note "a few honorable exceptions," particularly mentioning the minister of the largest Presbyterian church in the city, who stood in defiance of "prominent" Vigilantes who were members of his congregation.[64]

Sherman grew more apprehensive by the day, worried about how the bank was being affected. When in early June the governor declared that San Francisco was in a state of insurrection and called upon Sherman to assemble the militia the response was minimal, and the pro-Vigilante press mocked Sherman. When he next learned that Brigadier General

John Wool, whom Sherman believed had promised arms and ammunition for the militia, was not sending them—claiming that he never made such a commitment—Sherman resigned his militia commission. Only with reluctance had he accepted it in the first place, and now the mission appeared hopeless. Sherman continued to suffer criticism at the hands of the press, but at least he could once again devote his energy totally to business.[65]

Throughout June and into July Vigilante rule continued unabated. On July 7, Sherman wrote John, "The Vigilance Committee is in full blast . . . has Judge Terry in their power, and had the man Hopkins died, they would have hung him. . . . Where the matter is to end I cannot imagine." He referred to Judge David S. Terry, a native of Kentucky, former Texas Ranger and lawyer who had been elected to the California Supreme Court. Terry became involved in a brawl with Sterling A. Hopkins, a Know-Nothing member of the Vigilance Committee, who had served as the executioner of Casey and Cora. Terry stabbed Hopkins with a knife, and faced some danger of being immediately hanged. He spent about two months in prison, probably surviving, as Sherman noted, only because Hopkins recovered from his wound. (Terry later participated in California's most famous duel, in which he killed U.S. Senator David C. Broderick, in 1859.)[66]

Sherman told his brother that since resigning his militia commission he had "kept purposely aloof from all parties." Being in a business "where large interests are at stake," he felt that he must act with prudence and discretion. Writing to John again in early August, he indicated that the Vigilantes were still in full control. "For three months we have been governed by a self-constituted committee," he declared, "who have hung four men, banished some twenty others, arrested, imprisoned and ironed many men, and who [still] hold a judge of the Supreme Court in their power." He admitted that the city had previously suffered from "a bad administration of law, and more than a fair share of rowdies," but he thought the Vigilance Committee was no better, "and if we are to be governed by the mere opinion of the Committee and not by officers of our own choice, I would prefer at once to have a dictator."[67]

....

MORE THAN two thousand miles away to the east, the nation experienced another sensational, violent episode, which coincided with the hanging of Casey and Cora. This occurred in Washington, D.C., in the chamber of the United States Senate, the startling and unsettling event garnered far greater national publicity than the actions of the California Vigilantes. On May 20, Senator Charles Sumner, in a virile, abusive, impassioned presentation on the floor of the Senate, inveighed at length against the South, slavery and lawlessness in Kansas, which he scathingly blamed upon those who promoted the expansion of the "peculiar institution." The speech became famously, and many thought infamously, known as "the Crime Against Kansas." Senators generally, Northern as well as Southern, considered the vituperative oration, in the words of historian David Potter, as "almost uniquely offensive."

Its effect upon Congressman Preston Brooks of South Carolina proved maddening. Brooks was angered by Sumner's sneering censure of his aged uncle, Senator Andrew Pickens Butler, also from South Carolina. Sumner, in incredibly bad taste, mocked Butler's "loose expectoration" of speech, while likening the elderly man to Don Quixote and his fixation upon Dulcinea in choosing a "mistress," polluted in the world's eyes, "but chaste in his sight—I mean the harlot Slavery." Brooks determined that he must "avenge" his kinsman. Knowing that Sumner would not accept a challenge to a duel, he attacked Sumner while he worked at his Senate desk, beating the abolitionist over the head with a cane until he lost consciousness. Many who initially disapproved of Sumner's speech tended to be sympathetic after Brooks attacked him. The state of Massachusetts chose not to replace Sumner, but waited for him to recover sufficiently to resume work, thus leaving his Senate seat vacant for the next three years—a constant reminder in the nation's Capitol of a Southern congressman's hotheaded violence and the emotional explosiveness that had become inextricably associated with the issue of slavery.

Two days after the shock of the Sumner-Brooks affair, John Brown, fancying himself an avenging angel of Jehovah with a divine mission to strike a blow against slavery on the plains of Kansas, led an attack upon proslavery settlers at a site called Pottawatomie. Allegedly in revenge for the recent attack on the free-state town of Lawrence, Brown and his followers dragged five men from their houses, killed them and with broadswords mutilated the bodies of their victims—who in fact had nothing to do with the raid on Lawrence. Violence in "Bleeding Kansas" continued to escalate. Free-state advocates soon retaliated. In a small-scale pitched battle, several people died on each side, including one of Brown's sons. By the end of 1856, Kansas had seen about 200 people killed and $2 million in property destroyed.[68]

Sherman read of these momentous events in the newspapers arriving from the east, as well as in letters from Turner and his brother John. (John Sherman was in Westport, Missouri, along with two other congressmen, conducting a fact-finding investigation of conditions in Kansas, at the time of the Pottawatomie massacre.) Writing to John on August 19, 1856, Sherman was strikingly prophetic: "I am sorry the South did not avail herself of the chance to show her independence of the nigger question by voting for the expulsion of Brooks," he declared, "but it seems now that every question is determined not on its merits, but on the nigger question. Unless people both North and South learn more moderation, we will see sights in the way of Civil War." He concluded by observing: "Of course the North have the strength and must prevail, though the . . . South could and would be desperate enough."[69]

Chapter Ten

I WAS FIT FOR THE ARMY
BUT NOTHING ELSE

In the fall of 1856, Sherman voted for James Buchanan, Democrat from Pennsylvania, for president of the United States. It was the only time that he ever cast a ballot in a presidential election. The choice of Buchanan, at a glance, might seem puzzling. Sherman had generally sympathized with the national economic stance of the Whigs, and their legendary leader, Henry Clay of Kentucky. Since Clay's death and the virtual demise of the Whigs following the Kansas-Nebraska Act, the newly organized Republican Party, despite its totally Northern makeup, was closer to traditional Whig economic values than were the Democrats. Also, Sherman's younger brother sat in the U.S. House of Representatives as a Republican.

But Sherman knew John C. Frémont, the Republican candidate for the presidency. He had met Fremont, the Pathfinder of the West, while serving with the army in California. "I have seen Frémont several times since 1847," he wrote John, "and regard him as a small man out of whom to make a president. If he is qualified, anybody may aspire to that office." Some of Frémont's actions in California were "simply ridiculous . . . [and] selfish in the highest degree." Addressing John days later, and assuming his brother would "lend [his] influence to elect Frémont," Sherman reiterated his negative view. Gloomily he concluded, with a tone of resignation, that if Frémont wins, "I will not make myself miserable, as it does seem politicians . . . no longer are able to manage the affairs of our government."[1]

Quite possibly Sherman turned away from the Republicans too because he considered them extremists; their adamant, sectional opposition to the expansion of slavery was highly provocative to the slave states. In Sherman's view, free-state aggressiveness was both unnecessary and unwise. "Time and facts," he wrote John, "are accomplishing all you aim at, viz: the preponderance of the free over the slave states." That very reason, which he termed "so manifest," explained why the people of the South "are tetchy and nervous." Sherman cautioned John not to imitate the inflammatory rhetoric of New York's William H. Seward or Ohio's Joshua Giddings. John should avoid the subject of slavery "as a dirty black one." He believed "no provoking speeches are necessary, but on the contrary defeat the object in view."[2]

Sherman thought Buchanan would probably carry California, which he did. He also carried the slave states and enough free states to win the presidency in a very close contest. A slight change of votes in Pennsylvania and Illinois would have elected Frémont. By the time of Buchanan's election, San Francisco was at last free from the rule of the Vigilance Committee. Through summary hangings, banishments and imprisonments, the Vigilantes claimed to have successfully purged the city of rowdies and roughs. Laying down their arms, they declared victory for law and order, staged a triumphal parade—"a grand jubilee," Sherman told John—and proceeded to write a "history" of the movement, of course extolling the supposed virtues of their cause.[3]

However, the traumatic episode, as Sherman fully realized, bode potential ill for the future. The experience and memory of the Vigilance Committee, he wrote, had been "fixed on this country" like a part of the government. A powerful precedent had been set, and he believed that any grievance, "real or fancied," held the possibility of a vigilante revival. Years later, when penning his memoirs, Sherman again deplored the threat to law posed by such an unconstitutional organization. The Vigilantes gave "great stimulus," he wrote, "to a dangerous principle, that would at any time justify the mob in seizing all the power of government."[4]

While vigilante rule had ended by the fall of 1856, California's economy continued to decline. "All kinds of businesses became unsettled," according to Sherman. Joint-stock companies organized to bring water down from the head of the mountain streams went bankrupt. Foreign capital was withdrawn, or invested in property that could not be sold. A large number of merchants went bankrupt. Agriculture languished. California and San Francisco repudiated part of their public debt, costing Lucas, Turner & Company about $30,000; meanwhile real estate, which Sherman had considered "first-class security" only a year earlier, "became utterly unsalable." Loaning money proved "risky in the extreme," he said. "I labored hard to collect old debts, and strove, in making new loans, to be on the safe side." The general California business climate was unsettling, and the San Francisco community particularly was badly shaken.[5]

Sherman's personal finances showed no improvement either. Ellen sent her mother a revealing letter during the summer of 1856. Noting that "we do not live within our salary," she wrote that Cump was "unwilling to draw more, although they offered in St. Louis to double it. He says it is not honest for a man to accept a salary so large when the profits do not justify it." Ellen declared that she and her husband differed "upon that point." She believed that he "ought to draw salary sufficient to support his family here, as we are *obliged* to live." Sherman was paying "a large interest on the money with which he built [their] house," and Ellen said that to reduce expenses they were "letting the horse and cow go, and dispensing with the services of the [hired] man." For Sherman, all of this culminated "in rather a gloomy view of things."[6]

The bright hopes of 1853 had never been realized. San Francisco's economy unexpectedly had begun turning sour rather early in Sherman's banking tenure. His frequent, detailed reports to the St. Louis partners indicated that no upswing could yet be expected. The big-time profits originally envisioned seemed unlikely ever to materialize. Thus

James Lucas and Henry Turner made the decision to close the San Francisco firm. Sherman received the news from Turner early in 1857, and it took him by surprise. Certainly he recognized that 1856 had been a bad year, but he never expected that the partners would take such a final step without first making an on-site appraisal of the situation.[7]

Nevertheless, the deed was done. Sherman must close the bank in an orderly manner. The task required careful management, so as not to incite a run on the firm. There was some good news—of a kind. The St. Louis partners wanted to open a branch in New York City, with Sherman in charge of the operation. He accepted, because he had to support his family, and he surely considered New York preferable to Ohio. For a time, though, he was haunted by a suspicion that his powerful father-in-law, with important connections in St. Louis, might somehow have exerted influence on the partners to bring Ellen and him back to the eastern part of the country. Apparently that did not happen. Sherman was troubled, too, by the thought that his chronic asthma might have weighed heavily in the decision of Lucas and Turner. Perhaps above all, he just did not want to leave California and his San Francisco firm.

"I think Cump feels great regret at leaving here," Ellen informed her mother, "as he had fully made up his mind to spend his life here, and would rather do that than relinquish his undertaking." Sherman was not ready to give up the banking venture. He still believed, as he wrote Turner, that "in time we could do well out here." Furthermore, in San Francisco he was a person of influence, a leading citizen of the community. And he had come to like California. He memorably asserted that he wished he could remain "all of [his] life, even with asthma, which is worse here," he revealed to Turner, "than in any other spot I have thus far found."[8]

Such a striking statement about asthma, which often made his nights in San Francisco miserable, and sometimes the days as well, demands reflection. Not only does it speak convincingly of his fondness for California; it reminds us as well of the few asthmatic problems during his earlier years. The cold climate at West Point, the service in the often steaming heat of Florida, the continuing, high-humidity years in

Charleston and the first tour in California with the army in and around Monterey—all presented relatively few problems for him.

This is not to deny, as Sherman himself often mentioned, that the Bay City's climate was conducive to asthma. But an additional factor well may have been stress. Although stress is not a cause of asthma, it is capable of triggering it. From the time that Sherman and Ellen married, even while they lived in St. Louis, his asthma attacks came with greater frequency and severity than ever before. Sherman's life in the 1850s grew increasingly and sometimes highly stressful, all the more after he left the army and plunged into banking in San Francisco. Financial problems, of course, can create tremendous stress. That the mounting level and nature of his stress related to the frequency of the asthma attacks appears quite likely.

As Sherman reluctantly contemplated leaving the Golden State, he also experienced apprehensiveness about the demands upon a New York banker. He wasn't sure that he was up to dealing with New York's hardened capitalists and their manipulative, unscrupulous shenanigans. Having been brought up, as he said, believing that it was wrong to lie, cheat and steal, he feared he was "not fit to cope with modern bankers, brokers and land agents." In California "I am somebody," he told Turner, but in New York City he worried that he would be "swallowed up in that vast gulf of mankind." Still, he knew Turner and Lucas had confidence in his abilities. He left California determined to succeed at the new job in the nation's largest city.[9]

For her part, Ellen was near ecstatic to be leaving California, and apparently for all time. "Things wear a glorious aspect," she wrote her mother. Having "always said," Ellen reminded Maria, that she would as soon have "title to lots in the moon as in California," she could feel no sympathy for Cump's disappointment. To have remained in San Francisco "would have been at too great a sacrifice on my part." She happily anticipated staying in Lancaster with the children while her husband proceeded with the business in New York.[10]

Sherman left California harboring a great deal of resentment toward Ellen. He was convinced that she deserved considerable blame for the closing of Lucas, Turner & Company. He certainly blamed himself, too. Ellen's determined refusal to accept California as home; her extravagant spending; the constant, manifest longing for her parents, and their reciprocal desire for her to return "home" to Ohio—all generated a strong sense that his wife had not supported him as a wife should. Sherman would never forget how Ellen despised San Francisco and dragged him down financially, as he interpreted their West Coast experience. While his great military achievements in the Civil War softened the memories of those years, he never put the resentment totally behind him.[11]

THE TIMING of the California banking venture had proven less than ideal. The timing of the New York City project was worse. The bank opened under the same name as in California—Lucas, Turner & Company—at 12 Wall Street on July 21, 1857. Within weeks, a major financial storm descended upon the nation: the Panic of 1857. "Everything went along swimmingly" until some days into August, remembered Sherman, "when all of Wall Street was thrown into a spasm." Triggering the convulsion was the failure of the New York branch of the Ohio Life Insurance and Trust Company, headquartered in Cincinnati. Ohio Life had become one of New York's most respected financial institutions. The New York branch developed into a powerful player on Wall Street, and many New York banks were heavily involved with it. But bad management, poor judgment and fraud brought the company down.

When its president announced that the bank "has suspended payment," he simultaneously assured the public that Ohio Life's capital was "sound and reliable." Actually much of the capital was invested in speculative railroad bonds, the firm's cashier had embezzled a large sum of money and total liabilities numbered between $5 and $7 million, a very large amount for that time. The lie was soon exposed. The New York branch collapsed, and its failure quickly brought ruin to the Ohio parent firm, as well as a number of other New York banks.[12]

"In the very midst of this panic," wrote Sherman, came startling news of disaster to the steamer *Central America*, the same ship Ellen and he had recently sailed on from the Isthmus of Panama to New York. The ship had gone down in a gale near Savannah, carrying several hundred passengers to their death. The sinking also was an economic catastrophe. The *Central America* was transporting a fortune. Many New York bankers counted on its safe arrival in order to survive. Now the treasure lay at the bottom of the Atlantic, while more confusion, fear, and dread plagued Wall Street.[13]

On October 13, Sherman wrote Turner that "all hell has broken loose. . . . There is a run on every bank of the city, many of which have gone in." He saw "no reason why all must not succumb." The money crisis was extending all over the country. The Bank of Pennsylvania in Philadelphia, the state's leading financial institution, with major ties to New York banks, had closed its doors. "The wildest excitement" prevailed in the second largest U.S. city, with serious repercussions in New York, New England and elsewhere. Another round of bank failures followed. The nation's economy was suffering from a variety of ills. Too much gold from California tended to inflate the currency. The end of the Crimean War, which had stimulated agricultural production for export to Europe, left Northern farmers with surplus grain and no market. Manufacturing overproduction also played a part, as did rampant speculation in railroads and land, plus the weaknesses of an unregulated state bank-note system. More than five thousand businesses failed within a year, accompanied by extensive unemployment and food riots in several Northern cities. Historians Thomas Bailey and David Kennedy concluded that "psychologically [the Panic] was probably the worst of the nineteenth century."[14]

Because everything in the 1850s seemed to be sucked into an ever expanding whirlpool of sectionalism and slavery, Northern businessmen, in an oversimplified analysis, generally blamed the panic on the South, particularly the Democratic-sponsored tariff of 1857, which reduced rates to the lowest point in forty-one years. Northern manufacturers began strenuously demanding higher rates, claiming the necessity of protection from foreign competition. A Northern call for free farms of 160 acres to be carved from the federal public domain also gained strength, and it constituted another flash point with the South. Northern economic interests found increasing compatibility with Northern antislavery elements and moved into the Republican Party, attempting to offset the growing power of Southern Democrats.

The rural, agricultural South, for its part, suffered minimal damage from the Panic, as the price of cotton only declined slightly and recovered quickly. The result was an arrogant, and oversimplified notion (like that in the North) among leading Southern politicians that the slave economy had been vindicated and proven superior to the Northern, capitalistic, free-labor system. "King Cotton" was indispensable to the economy of England—indeed, indispensable to the economy of all the Western world. It was "a fatal delusion," wrote Bailey and Kennedy, "which helped drive the overconfident Southerners closer to a shooting showdown."[15]

A potential civil war did not trouble Sherman in the late summer and early fall of 1857. He was working diligently to keep his bank solvent. "We had large cash balances in the Metropolitan Bank and in the Bank of America, all safe," he remembered, "and we held, for the ... St. Louis house, at least two hundred thousand dollars, of St. Louis city and county bonds, and of acceptances falling due right along, none extending beyond ninety days." Sherman was doing a good job, while facing ruinous circumstances in New York, and "did not dream," he said, of any danger in St. Louis. But in mid-September, James Lucas wrote him that he was very worried. Money matters in St. Louis, he declared, "were extremely tight." If Lucas, with all his wealth (several million invested in the best real estate), business savvy and prestige, was deeply concerned, then Sherman concluded that he himself had reason to fear the worst.[16]

Unfortunately, both were correct. Early one October morning, a New York paper announced the closing of the St. Louis company. Sherman at once hurried down to his office where he was officially notified of the closing by telegraph from St. Louis. He was instructed to make proper disposition of the New York banking affairs as soon as possible, and come to St. Louis with whatever assets might be available. Through no fault of his own, Sherman's New York banking venture was closing, doomed by the failure of the St. Louis parent house. "Tell Mr. Lucas I sympathize with him deeply," a disgusted Sherman told Turner. "I hope he will clean out and never again undertake so disreputable a business as banking."[17]

To Ellen he wrote: "I seem to fall on bad times in business, for I am not fairly installed before failures have begun." He was convinced that banking did not "suit" him, and he wished that "I were out of it, at some honest employment, but I am in it and must persevere [through the aftermath of the firm's failure]." He also claimed, the initial phrase of which likely did not set well with Ellen, "I can lose my own money and property without feeling much, but to lose what is confided to me by others I can't stand." Lashing out at his wife, he bitingly charged: "You will no doubt be glad at last to have attained your wish to see me out of the Army and out of employment." Some days later, he told her, "If I were a rich man—of which there is not the remotest chance—I would as soon try the faro table as risk the chances of banking."[18]

After leaving New York, Sherman spent the rest of 1857 in St. Louis, helping Lucas and Turner sort through the closed firm's assets. In San Francisco there were bank holdings that certainly could yield money: property to be sold or leased, and debts to be collected, the latter valued at about $200,000. Sherman did not think that Benjamin Nisbet, who had been left in charge when Sherman went to New York, was up to the task. Nisbet "cannot see things as they are," declared Sherman, and he added that if "big bankers" were headed "right to destruction, he would go along." Sherman knew that he himself possessed "a more intimate knowledge of the [California] property and interests than anyone else." He castigated himself as a "fool" for having left California without having first reclaimed more of the bank's money. When Turner suggested that Sherman might need "to return to California for a while," he seemed to jump at the chance. "I am perfectly willing," he said.[19]

In late November, as Sherman anticipated returning to the West Coast, he declared to Hugh Boyle Ewing: "If I had no family I would stay in California all my life . . . but though I see mighty slim prospects in the future, I will return [to the east] and try something, God knows what." He felt "bound in honor to do all I can for [the St. Louis firm] as long as I can be of service." He had also confided to his brother-in-law, at an earlier date, that "my California adventure was attended with such heavy expenses, and such sacrifice in breaking up at a time of awful depression that it will require . . . absolute economy for a long time, and I must work like the devil." That sentence was penned *before* the Panic of 1857 struck.[20]

Significantly too, shortly after leaving the Golden State, and before the ravages of the panic were upon him, Sherman told Ellen, "Our fate has been cast in a wrong time, and I regret that I ever left the Army." References to the army, often accompanied by nostalgic remarks, would grow more frequent in the months to come, especially after the general collapse of the New York banks and his St. Louis parent firm. Probably he hoped to prepare Ellen for a resumption of his army career, if he should get the opportunity. After leaving New York, he told her, "I ought to have had sense enough to know that I was fit for the Army but nothing else." With a strong rejoinder she implored, "Please do not mention the army to me again unless you have made up your mind that we [she and the children] are not worth working for."[21]

In December 1857, when some officers were speculating about a possible increase in the size of the army, Sherman wrote his congressman brother at least twice, saying that he would like to return "to my old business (the Army), for which I am better qualified than any other." If such an increase did occur, there would be a "great press for the higher appointments of Colonel, Lieutenant-Colonel, and Major." Nevertheless, he told John, "I have many friends among the higher officers, and think . . . I might get one of them." Clearly he hoped for John's assistance in the quest. Sherman also applied to the adjutant general of the army, asking for any field officer commission that might be available. Just before returning to California, he informed Turner of what he had done. Regardless of Ellen's wishes, Sherman was spreading the word among all his friends who might have any influence that he wanted back in the army. But the size of the army was not increased, and the possibility of reinstatement afterward seemed quite remote.[22]

Right after the new year, Sherman was aboard a steamer, sailing back to the Golden State. Ellen and the children remained in Lancaster. He arrived in San Francisco on January 28, transported from Panama by the *Golden Gate*. Benjamin Nisbet and his new wife—a young lady from an "extravagant" family, said Sherman, who disapproved of Nisbet's choice—had already embarked for St. Louis. Nisbet's departure probably facilitated Sherman's work, enabling him to proceed without any encumbrance. Reducing expenses to a minimum, he pursued debtors "with all possible dispatch," although forced "in some instances" to make sacrifices and compromises. "Property continued almost unsalable," he recalled, "and prices were less than a half of what they had been in 1853–54."

In trying to collect debts and rents he received "innumerable promises," but relatively little hard cash. He added that "suicides are very common." Speaking of the downfall of one prominent citizen, who had been feigning insanity, Sherman claimed, in a sarcastically obvious allusion to his own experience, that the fellow "is no more insane than any other man who was fool enough to attempt to live in California with a family." He also put his own house on the market, hoping to get $7,000, but soon decided to ask $6,000 for the place in which he had invested $10,000. Finding no buyer, he leased it, as he did with some of the bank properties.[23]

Sherman was particularly worried about the money he had invested for his army friends, a total of about $130,000. Legally, Lucas, Turner & Company was not obligated to cover their losses, but Sherman felt that he himself was honor-bound to make them good, "to stand some of their loss." It was an attitude reminiscent of his father, Charles, who had strapped himself financially, over a long term, to pay back money that the law did not require, but which he considered ethically binding. Sherman sold a large portion of his own land, acquired in California, Missouri and Illinois in earlier and less encumbered years. Eventually he was able to return the full amount with which his army friends had entrusted him, but his own investments were virtually depleted. His actions were evidence of both an extraordinarily high personal ethical standard and, more, a deep sense of military camaraderie. Even if no longer in the army, he still valued his army connections above all others. Of course he now hoped to return to the military, and he knew that his generous actions would not be forgotten among the officer corps.[24]

By July 1858, Sherman felt that he had done all that was possible in San Francisco, "having collected and remitted every cent that I could raise, and got all the property in the best shape possible." Good news came from St. Louis that business was reviving. Perhaps he might find employment there. He also was growing concerned that Ellen, worried about his health (asthma having afflicted him every night since he returned to San Francisco), would impulsively sail to join him. If she did, he would be out a thousand dollars "useless expense," he told Turner, which would constitute "the last stroke to my financial existence." Sherman said he "put all the papers, with a full letter of instructions, and power of attorney, in the hands of William Blanding, Esq.," and headed back east. There the obvious and unavoidable question at once demanded an answer: How to support his wife and family, "all accustomed," in Sherman's words, "to more than the average comforts of life"?[25]

While Sherman was still cleaning up the banking mess in San Francisco, Thomas Ewing offered him employment at the Hocking Valley salt wells and coal mines in Chauncey, Ohio. Sherman reluctantly responded that he would accept the job. But when he was back in Lancaster, he could not bring himself to face what he had always said he would never do. In his desperation to make a living, and in yet another manifestation of irony, Sherman turned to the law, despite the disparaging remarks he had often uttered about the legal profession. Of his fitness for the law, he told Ellen, "If I turn lawyer, it will be bungle, bungle, from Monday to Sunday, but if it must be, so be it."[26]

The choice did seem to make sense. Two of Thomas Ewing's sons, Hugh Boyle and Thomas Jr., both of whom were lawyers, had opened a practice with their father's help in Leavenworth, Kansas, where they and their father had purchased a great deal of land, some near the town and some out in the country. Mr. Ewing simply turned over his share of the legal firm to Sherman, and the new business of Sherman & Ewing was established. Hugh and Tom Jr. were to manage all business in court, while Sherman would oversee the financial side. Nevertheless, Sherman understandably felt that he ought to have a license to practice law, particularly since "Sherman" headed the name of their firm. Anticipating that copious legal reading would be required, followed by an examination, he was somewhat amazed when a United States judge at once admitted him to the bar "on the ground of general intelligence." His "general intelligence," however, did not prove sufficient the one time that he was forced to handle a case in court when both Tom and Hugh were out of town. Lacking any court experience whatsoever, it is hardly surprising that he lost.[27]

Not long after Sherman first arrived in Kansas, in September 1858, he rode a few miles up the Missouri River to Fort Leavenworth. Stewart Van Vliet, his friend and classmate from West Point, served as the fort's quartermaster. The two were glad to see each other again. Sherman said Van Vliet at once gave him "the most lucrative single case" that he received for some time. He was contracted to superintend repairs to the military road from Fort Leavenworth to Fort Riley, a distance of nearly 140 miles to the west. Van Vliet provided him with a four-mule ambulance and a driver for the work. Upon arrival at Fort Riley, he wasted little time in getting off a letter to Ellen, telling her how he felt "perfectly at home with the sound of bugle and drum, with officers and soldiers, whom I know not of former acquaintance save of one, but because I know their feelings and prejudices." The experience "makes me regret my being out of service thus to meet my old comrades, in the open field, just where I most like to be. But I must banish soldiering from my mind, and look to the bridges and gullies and round holes of the road." Sherman was continuing a campaign to make sure Ellen would have no doubt about his intentions if he should somehow find an opportunity to get back in the service.[28]

Shortly after receiving his account of the sojourn at Fort Riley, Ellen announced that she was no longer willing to live separately from her spouse. Perhaps her motivation sprang solely from a pure and genuine desire to be at the side of her husband. On the other hand, Ellen was a smart woman who would certainly have realized that if she hoped to stop Cump from possibly returning to the military, her chances of success would be greater if she were with him, rather than residing with her parents in Lancaster.[29]

She promised that she would "be more amiable than you have ever known me." She was willing even "to live far from the church" if necessary. Cump "must not leave [her in Lancaster] this winter," for she could not "lead this unnatural life any longer, suffering anxiety on your account as I do." She told him that she was "in bad health and ... unhappy, and I beg you to take me with you somewhere." Ellen's timing proved fortuitous, for already Sherman had decided that she should join him. He also ordered her to "bring *all the children*." Sherman thought Minnie had spent far too much of her life apart from him. Nor did he want one of his other children left at the Ewing home as a substitute for Minnie's leaving.[30]

When Ellen arrived in Leavenworth, however, Minnie was not with her. The young child had lived with her grandparents for so long that she did not want to leave. One strongly suspects that Thomas and Maria encouraged her, at least subtly, to remain in Lancaster. Nevertheless, Sherman was happy to have Ellen and three of the children with him once more. They moved in with Tom Jr., who had a large house. Ellen seemed in a remarkably optimistic mood. She soon wrote her mother, "I have never before felt like calling any place home but Father's house, but fortunately I am favorably impressed with *everything* here and feel that we shall build up a *home* and I trust attract our dear friends to it."[31]

Unfortunately, Ellen's "feel" for building a home in Leavenworth lacked a sound financial basis. The firm of Sherman & Ewing was not finding sufficient work to support three families. This fact Ellen soon realized, when she again wrote to Maria, acknowledging a check for one hundred dollars from "dear Father." She intended to hold the money in reserve until "I really need it." Money had been "running pretty low," she admitted, with nothing coming in. She "might even be obliged to go home again for want of means to live here." Tom and Boyle (as she usually referred to Hugh Boyle) were away, and with Cump "ignorant of the details of the law business, we can get nothing to do all winter." As to property that her father had recently given her in the Leavenworth area, "and which he thinks will support me if everything else fails, a part of it is quite far out of town and part of it in a most *disreputable* neighborhood and will not sell."[32]

At the beginning of 1859 the firm added another partner, young Daniel McCook, who would later serve as a colonel under Sherman in the Civil War. The addition of McCook, however talented he may have been, seems rather strange when the Sherman & Ewing partnership was struggling financially. Perhaps Tom Jr., being frequently away from Leavenworth, had simply felt it necessary to bring in another lawyer. Sherman, however, was obviously skeptical, telling Hugh Boyle that their business "must swell considerably before we have work for us four."[33]

Such an increase in the business was not about to happen, and by late March, with Ellen again pregnant and longing for Lancaster, Sherman sadly watched his wife and children depart. When Maria Ewing learned that Ellen was about to return to Ohio, she penned an ever so slightly veiled "I told you so" message: "We all think you were a little premature in going out, the place being so new, and comfortable houses so scarce, and that you had better stay here until Cumpy builds a comfortable house for you." Within about two weeks after Ellen left Kansas, Sherman wrote, clearly in a depressed frame of mind, telling her that the weather "is so cold that I can hardly hold my pen. San Francisco can't hold a candle to the prairies of Kansas for wind." Then framing a gloomy, often quoted assessment of his future, Sherman said, "I look upon myself as a dead cock in the pit, not worthy of further notice."[34]

During the spring, Sherman's fortunes likely reached an all-time low, in his own estimation anyway, as he constructed a small frame house and a barn, and put up fencing on a tract of land near Leavenworth owned by his father-in-law. "This helped to pass away time," he remembered in his memoirs, but admitted that the work "afforded little profit." He was happy for his brother John, who sailed in April, aboard the steamer *Vanderbilt,* for a tour of Europe. Sherman's eclectic interests, wide-ranging knowledge and keen intellect naturally made him envious of his brother's opportunity—although not in a mean-spirited manner. "I would very much like to be with you and make the trip," he told John, "although my tastes might lead me to traverse fields and places which have no interest to you; but Europe ... the concentrated history and civilization of our time, has in every part interest enough for all men." He urged John to write him about where he went and what he observed.[35]

At the very time of John's tour, war broke out in northern Italy. Emperor Louis Napoleon III of France, having formed an alliance with the forces of Piedmont, fought a short but bloody war against Austria. Defeating the Austrians at the Battle of Magenta, and again at the Battle of Solferino three weeks later, the French and their Piedmont ally appeared poised to drive Austria completely out of Italy. But Napoleon III, fearful of rising clerical opposition and other problems, suddenly, and without consulting his Italian ally, concluded the armistice of Villafranca with the Austrian Emperor Francis Joseph. By the terms of the Treaty of Zurich, Lombardy was annexed to Piedmont, but Venetia remained under Austrian rule. Progress had been made toward a free and unified Italy, but Italian nationalists were bitterly disappointed that France had pulled back when it seemed all of Italy might be freed of foreign powers.[36]

Sherman was excited about the war and tried to learn all he could about the conflict. He wrote to John, relative to the war, "I should like of all things to be in your stead." John's interests, however, were elsewhere. He had become enamored with Paris, "the capital of gaiety." The city was "a striking contrast to any I have ever seen," he enthused. "The streets are alive with people, and bands are playing in the gardens and palaces." He marveled at the groups of singers, the cafés, restaurants and broad promenades filled with delightful men and women. He knew "very well" from his knowledge of history that some of "the gayest spots have been the scenes of frightful cruelties," but no signs of such bloody times were any longer to be seen, and the Parisians, he assured Cump, "surely seem happy now." After seven weeks in Great Britain, John wrote that he was "constantly contrasting the people of Paris with the English: the conclusion is all in favor of the Parisians." He thought the French government was "much more tolerable" than the British. The latter was "a government of the aristocracy ... exclusive, repelling, and narrow." His travels were providing him with a great fund of information and, possibly referring to the expense of the excursion, he said that he would "never regret the trip." Next was Italy, "and the seat of war," where he expected to visit the battlefield of Magenta.[37]

Perhaps thoughts of the war in Italy, and his brother's journey to the scenes of fighting quickened Sherman's efforts to return to the army. Besides, his prospects of success in Leavenworth had reached a dead end. In June 1859 he wrote Major Don Carlos Buell, a friend he had known since West Point. Buell was serving in Washington, D.C., as assistant adjutant general of the army. Sherman inquired whether there was a vacancy among the army paymasters, or any military opening that Buell might know about. The major told him of a new military school being organized in Louisiana, suggesting that Sherman apply for the post of superintendent.[38]

The position would pay $3,500 annually, and Buell thought that Sherman might have a good chance of being selected. The president of the new academy's board of supervisors was George Mason Graham, the half brother of the late Richard B. Mason, who had been Sherman's commanding officer and close friend in California. Incidentally, Buell had married Mason's widow. Such connections were promising, and Sherman certainly possessed good qualifications for the position. He applied at once, for the filing deadline was near at hand.[39]

Initially the board offered the superintendency to a Louisiana native, Pierre Gustave Toutant Beauregard, a man soon to become famous as a Confederate general. However, Beauregard turned down the appointment, and Sherman was then selected, with the title of "superintendent and professor of engineering, architecture, and drawing" at the Louisiana State Seminary of Learning in Alexandria (the forerunner of the Louisiana State University). In the letter of appointment, Sherman was addressed as "Major Sherman," and thus he was known at the school from that time forward. Unquestionably, the influence of George Mason Graham was a prime factor in Sherman's securing the position. Plans were formulated to open the institution on January 1, 1860, for approximately one hundred students.[40]

Remarkably, another business possibility opened up soon after Sherman accepted the superintendency of the military school. It was, of all things, yet another banking job, and would entail managing a firm in London. Hugh Boyle Ewing and Thomas Ewing Jr. were among the entrepreneurs associated with the venture, which was spearheaded by a wealthy citizen of Cincinnati. Sherman was offered a two-year contract, paying more than twice his wages at the Louisiana military academy. He felt compelled to consider the offer seriously because, as he told Graham, Ellen "is . . . strongly in favor of the London project," preferring England to "coming south with our children," and her father "writes me urgently to go."[41]

But Sherman also told Graham, "I mistrust all financial schemes." He recalled that "just seven years ago I was similarly situated in New Orleans, commissary U.S. Army," when he had been persuaded "to go to California as a banker with prospects more brilliant than those now offered me." There, he continued, "without any fault, negligence, or want of ability" on his part, "the losses of others" had dragged him down. Sherman was skeptical, too, about the promised remuneration for the London assignment. Perhaps it would never materialize. He had to know as well, based upon the history of his marriage, that Ellen and the children were in the end not likely to accompany him to England, whereas he hoped to prevail upon her to unite his family in Louisiana. Even if he was not back in the army, he had a job that involved a military way of life, and that fact pleased him. Despite the pressure from Ellen and her parents, he decided that he had spent enough time as a banker.[42]

★ *Chapter Eleven* ★

In a Hell of a Fix

During the late summer and throughout the fall of 1859, Sherman stayed busy planning for the opening of the new military school. He sought pertinent information from West Point, the Virginia Military Institute, the Kentucky Military Institute and George B. McClellan, a West Pointer then serving as president of the Illinois Central Railroad. Some years earlier McClellan had visited several European military schools, and Sherman wanted to make comparisons between American and European practices. George Mason Graham, also a West Point man and veteran of the Mexican War, was helping him in every way that he could. The two seemed to like each other from the first and worked well together. Graham made a fact-finding visit to VMI and Sherman sent him a list of questions he hoped to have answered, concerning all manner of equipment used, procedures followed, as well as prices and wages at the Virginia institution. He tried to think of everything. Concerned about the Louisiana climate, with its heat and humidity, he asked Graham, for example, "Can we not select a dress more becoming, quite as economical, and better adapted to climate than the grey cloth of West Point and Virginia?"[1]

The bulk of equipment and supplies for the new school had to come out of New Orleans; some of them were produced there, although far more were imported. In the course of arranging for the academy's requirements, Sherman spent several days in the Crescent City. His superintendency of a military-oriented institution was an interesting challenge, and a welcome job. However, it was not the army, and his new work keenly reminded him of the life he once led as a soldier. "I am . . . at the City Hotel which is crowded," he wrote Ellen, "and have therefore come to this my old office . . . to do my writing. I wish I were here legitimately, but that is now past, and I must do my best in the sphere in which events have cast me. All things here look familiar, the streets, houses, levees, drays, etc., and many of the old servants are still about the office, who remember me well, and fly around at my bidding as of old."[2]

Sherman was also writing to his brother, advising moderation on the slavery issue, just as he had been doing ever since John first was elected to the U.S. Congress. Sherman had more reason than ever before to be worried about what John might say on the subject. "As you are becoming a man of note and are a Republican," he explained in September, "and as I go south among gentlemen who have always owned slaves, and . . . whose feelings may pervert every public expression of yours . . . I would like to see you take the highest ground consistent with your party creed." A few weeks later, Sherman acknowledged that "a majority in Congress has an absolute right to govern the whole country; but the North, being so strong in every sense . . . can well afford to be generous, even to making reasonable concessions to the weaknesses and prejudices of the South." He thus hoped to see John's position "yet more moderate."[3]

During the latter part of 1859, Sherman had to spend some time winding up his responsibilities with the law firm in Kansas. Family affairs demanded attention as well. For the fifth time he became a father, when Eleanor Mary Sherman, who would become known as Ellie, was born on September 5. Soon after Ellie's delivery in Lancaster, Sherman visited the new military school in Kentucky. Following a brief, fact-finding stay in the Bluegrass State, he left for the Louisiana assignment, by way of St. Louis, where he narrowly, and regrettably, missed seeing Henry Turner but enjoyed a satisfying visit with James Lucas.[4]

Good news had arrived from San Francisco. Sherman's house had finally been sold, bringing $5,600. Moving the property at last, in a depressed economy, brought a sense of relief. He had long before deeded the house to Henry Turner as security for his indebtedness to the firm, contracted because his and Ellen's expenses exceeded their income. James Lucas insisted, however, that the money from the sale—all of it— should go to Sherman for his faithful service, and Turner agreed. Sherman protested, to no avail. The money was an unexpected surprise, and helped ease the increasing financial pressure that had been troubling him, seemingly more than ever before, during recent months.[5]

THEN JOHN BROWN resurfaced—and with results immensely greater than when he first appeared in Kansas. Looking the part of a long-bearded Old Testament patriarch, while thundering against the "wicked curse of slavery" with the fanatical zeal and ringing certainty of an ancient prophet speaking on behalf of Jehovah, he struck the federal arsenal in Harpers Ferry, Virginia, under cover of darkness on October 16, 1859. Leading nineteen men, including five blacks, he succeeded in capturing the federal arsenal and armory, and seizing a few hostages. Brown grandiosely envisioned nothing less than the overthrow of slavery. Apparently he intended to establish a mountain stronghold, take hostages from slave-owning families and arm large numbers of slaves. Slave insurrections would then be initiated across the Southern states.[6]

But Brown had made no provisions to feed the pitifully small group that he led and never informed any slaves that he was initiating an insurrection. Having seized the arsenal, he simply waited—presumably waiting for the slaves to rise. Mentally, Brown was not "a well-adjusted man." Probably any slaves who learned of the projected revolt had sense enough to realize that it could not succeed. Having refused to retreat to the mountains while an escape route still lay open, Brown and his little band soon found themselves cut off and surrounded.[7]

A force of U.S. Marines broke down the barricaded doors and quickly overwhelmed Brown and his followers. Ten of the nineteen were killed (including two of Brown's sons), while Brown himself was beaten unconscious and turned over to the state of Virginia. Charged with treason against the state, conspiracy to foment a slave insurrection and murder, he was brought to trial one week after being captured. With remarkable haste, Brown was convicted on October 31, and hanged on December 2 at Charlestown, Virginia (now West Virginia).[8]

Although of unsound mind, Brown seemed to realize that he would be worth more to the antislavery cause in death than he had ever been in life. Having uttered eloquent words on behalf of freedom for the slaves at his sentencing, he courageously faced the hangman's noose. He became an instant martyr. Moderate men in the North, including many Republicans—among them William H. Seward and Abraham Lincoln— sincerely deplored Brown's actions. But abolitionists, infuriated by his execution, praised his righteous efforts on behalf of freedom. Ralph Waldo Emerson famously declared that Brown had made "the gallows as glorious as the cross." The hallowed memory of the martyred Brown intensified during the following weeks and months, eventually giving birth to the moving and now legendary refrain: "John Brown's body lies a-mould'ring in the grave, but his soul is marching on."[9]

Many Southern minds were enraged at the mere mention of John Brown. They often made no distinction between Brown and the Republican Party, which had become, in their eyes, the party of abolition. Anyone proposing the containment of slavery was advocating its destruction. Throughout the late fall and the winter of 1859–1860, rumors of slave insurrections, often stemming from panic in the wake of Brown's raid, swept the South. All persons from the North came under suspicion. Many were driven out of the region. Brown's raid also strengthened and emboldened Southern politicians who favored secession from the Union.[10]

The tremendous impact of John Brown left Sherman increasingly concerned about the destiny of the nation, as well as his own position in the Deep South. "As long as the abolitionists and the Republicans seem to threaten the safety of slave property, so long will this excitement last," he told Ellen, "and no one can foresee its result." He wrote that "these southern politicians have so long cried out wolf that many believe the wolf has come," and he was afraid that "in some moment of anger they [may] commit an act resulting in Civil War." He also said

that "all here [he was in New Orleans at the time] talk as if a dissolution of the Union were not only a possibility but a probability of easy
execution." He prophesied that if secession is attempted, "we will have
Civil War of the most horrible kind." He wrote Thomas Ewing Jr. that
he used to laugh at talk about disunion, "but I now begin to fear it may
be attempted."[11]

The inflamed Southern passions triggered by John Brown's raid did
not involve Sherman in any specific manner. But unfortunately, a foolish action by his brother had a bearing on his position as he prepared
for the superintendency of the Louisiana military school. John Sherman
had emerged as the leading candidate to take up the gavel as the new
speaker of the House of Representatives. The problem was that John had
recently endorsed an abridgement of Hinton Helper's highly controversial book *The Impending Crisis of the South*. John had not read the book,
or the compendium, merely relying upon assurances from Republican
friends that his name should appear among the supporting signatures.
Very likely, he did not understand the degree of animosity the book had
raised in the South, where it was being burned and banned.[12]

Hinton Helper was a nonaristocratic North Carolinian who despised
slavery. He attempted to prove, with an array of statistics, that the despicable institution effectively impoverished the nonslaveholding white
people—who of course constituted the great majority of the Southern
population. Although he hoped to see slavery destroyed, Helper had
no love for the slaves themselves, whom he considered inferior beings.
Wealthy slave owners had more than one reason to fear Helper's thesis.
Not only was he calling for the destruction of slavery, he was striving
to raise class consciousness. He was preaching class warfare—trying to
arouse the Southern masses against an impoverishing domination by
a wealthy oligarchy based on plantation slavery. The message of class
warfare, whenever and wherever it sounds, naturally alarms the ultra-
wealthy, who strive mightily through whatever means—propaganda,
diversion, intimidation, etc.—to smother the challenge.[13]

The contest for Speaker of the House dragged on for weeks, with
John Sherman always within a few votes of success. At one point in mid-

December, he had garnered 112 of the 114 votes required to elect. But ultimately, John was unable to gain the Southern support necessary for victory. While the issue remained in doubt, Sherman wrote Ellen about John's chances of success, and the impact he anticipated, win or lose, upon his own position. "I regret he ever signed that Helper book.... Had it not been for that, I think he might be elected, but as it is, I do not see how he can expect any southern votes, and without them it seems that his election is impossible." His brother's extreme stance would harm Sherman, "not among the [board of] supervisors, but in the legislature where the friends of the Seminary must look for help." Southern news-papers were alluding to "the impropriety" of Northern teachers coming south. If John, in the heat of debate, should take "extreme ground," Sherman was sure people would then learn "that I am his brother from Ohio ... universally esteemed as an abolition state."[14]

Sherman worried, too, that misfortune might be stalking him again. "I have had such bad luck," he wrote Ellen, "in California and New York, that I fear I shall be overtaken here by a similar catastrophe." Some key Louisiana men, like Graham, Braxton Bragg and Cump's West Point classmate Paul Hebert, who had recently been governor of the state, knew that he was not an abolitionist. But Sherman realized that many others would be biased against him, even though he himself was neither a Republican nor an abolitionist. In a letter to Thomas Ewing Jr., writ-ten two days before Christmas, he declared, "You can readily imagine the delicate position I now hold at the head of a seminary ... to open January 1, for the instruction and training of young men to science and arms, at the same time that John Sherman's name is bandied about as the representative of all that is held here murderous and detestable."[15]

He then proceeded, briefly and straightforwardly, to tell Tom Ewing how he viewed slavery, the Negro and the threat to the Union: "I would not if I could abolish or modify slavery. I don't know that I would mate-rially change the actual political relation of master and slave." He said that "Negroes in the great numbers that exist here must of necessity be slaves. Theoretical notions of humanity and religion cannot shake the commercial fact that their labor is of great value and cannot be dispensed with." He did wish that slavery had never existed, because of the volatile emotions from which the institution had become inseparable.

The "dread of revolt, sedition, or external interference" with slavery, he observed, "makes men [who are] ordinarily calm almost mad." Sherman felt, "moderate as my views are," that he was under suspicion, "and if I do not actually join in the praises of slavery, I may be denounced as an abolitionist." He knew that "respectable men" were talking about secession from the Union, and if that happened, there was no question about the result. "Disunion and Civil War are synonymous terms," he declared. The reason, fundamentally, was the great Mississippi, with its major tributaries, the Ohio and the Missouri. "The Mississippi, source and mouth, must be controlled by one government. . . . Louisiana occupies the mouth of a river whose heads go far north, and does not admit of a 'cut off.' Therefore, a peaceable disunion, which men here think possible, is absurd." But if secession occurs, Sherman "of course" would stand by the Union.[16]

As long as the struggle for Speaker of the House remained an issue, keeping John Sherman's name prominently in the news, Cump worried about the effect on his own future. "What I apprehend," he wrote Ellen, "is that . . . I will first be watched and suspected, then maybe addressed officially to know my opinion, and lastly some fool in the legislature will denounce me as an abolitionist spy." He believed that his views on slavery "are good enough for this country [the South]," but because of John being "so marked a Republican," he feared that his own name might become "so suspected" that it could "damage the prospects of the Seminary." He breathed a little easier when the House finally turned to William Pennington of New Jersey, an old-line Whig who supported the fugitive slave act and had lined up with the Republicans, as its speaker.[17]

THE NEW SCHOOL opened as scheduled on Monday, January 2, 1860, located near the little village of Alexandria. The institution occupied a single large structure of more than thirty rooms, standing on a hill surrounded by 400 acres of land. The building was three lofty stories tall, accented by five towers, each of which extended an additional story. Sherman described the venue as "a gorgeous palace, altogether too good for its purpose." Five professors, including Sherman, were on hand at the beginning, all well qualified. The number of cadets was less than expected. By January 12, forty young men were present, and by January 24, the number had increased to fifty-one. However, the total count for the opening session never came close to the early projection of one hundred, eventually reaching a maximum in the midsixties.[18]

Sherman's attitude was upbeat when he wrote Ellen on January 12. "Everything moves along satisfactorily," he said, and "all seem pleased, and gentlemen have been here from New Orleans and other distant points who are much pleased." More cadets were coming, and "nobody has said boo about John." He asserted that "the supervisors can't spare me. I manage their affairs to their perfect satisfaction." Some days later he remarked about visiting ladies, parting from their sons, and observed that "the most vicious boys come recommended with all the virtues of saints." He added, "Of course, I promised to be a father to them all."[19]

From the start Sherman placed the cadets on a strict schedule, emphasizing mathematics, foreign language and military drill. After breakfast at seven, they studied math for three hours, followed by two hours of instruction in French, before eating lunch. Then came two hours of Latin, with physical exercise afterward, consisting of an hour of intense drill, before dinner in the evening. Sherman was stern about discipline while also building a reputation for being fair. He considered the cadets generally well behaved, as he wrote Ellen's father in late January.

When two young men got in a fight, one of them producing a knife, Sherman at once expelled the cadet with the knife. Upon a full investigation, from which he learned that the other cadet was equally to blame for starting the fight, he kicked that boy out also. Sherman was demonstrating that he would not tolerate unruly behavior. Five more cadets were expelled before the term ended. He characterized some of the youngsters as "ill bred and utterly without discipline." Perhaps the worst boys came from the wealthiest families. "I will see whether I am to govern here, or be governed by the cast off boys of rich planters." He told Ellen's brother Tom that "the boys are wilful and govern their parents despotically."[20]

In mid-February, Sherman made a trip to Baton Rouge, and spent a few days lobbying the legislature. He had dinner with the governor, Thomas O. Moore, a strong backer of the school, and impressively fielded questions from his guests. He dined another evening with the state attorney general. The legislature was very supportive, promising to build a house for Sherman's family and provide the new seminary with a sizable endowment. The legislature soon appropriated money to build two faculty houses, begin a library, and raise Sherman's annual salary to four thousand dollars. He wrote Tom Jr., conveying an optimistic enthusiasm: "I am down here at the legislature, log rolling for a bill to the interest of our institution. I have no doubt of success." Then he mused, "I can not but laugh in my sleeve at the seeming influence I possess, dining with the governor, hobnobbing with the leading men of Louisiana, whilst John is universally blackguarded as an awful abolitionist." Tom Jr., like John Sherman, was strongly associated with the Republicans, leading Cump to jokingly remark, "If they find me advising with you and John, two desperate Blacks, they will suspect me of treason and hang me."[21]

Within a few days Sherman was back at Alexandria, overseeing the academy and once more dealing with "my share of petty troubles and annoyances," but also feeling pressure from Ellen and her parents, who continued urging him to take the banking job in London. In mid-March he made a brief trip to Ohio, visiting with his family and conferring in Cincinnati with David Gibson, one of the officers of the London venture. Despite the wishes of his wife and the Ewings, Sherman stood his ground. He was not going to give up "a certainty for an uncertainty." As he wrote Ellen shortly before taking the train to Ohio, he knew that if he went to London, she would not go with him; and he keenly felt that turning away from the Louisiana school, particularly after the manner in which Graham and others had championed him, would not be an ethical action. There was also the fact that Sherman liked his new military-type association.[22]

"I never did fancy the London scheme," he wrote Hugh Boyle Ewing after arriving back in Louisiana, having "always doubted its success." The letter to Hugh, whom he seemed to trust with his innermost thoughts, as noted previously, expressed an intriguing longing. Was the revelation merely a nostalgic musing, or an absolute desire? "To tell the truth," Sherman said, "I would rather be in California with an old mule, traveling from place to place and fetching up occasionally at Doña Augustias, but I must consider my family."[23]

While Sherman had traveled most of the way to Ohio by rail, he came back on the river, aboard "the swiftest boat going down [the Ohio and the Mississippi]." The reason for taking the boat, he informed Graham, was "I have with me a valuable horse that I do not think should or could be safely conveyed without my being along." The horse was named Clay, and its presence perhaps symbolized Sherman's commitment to stay with the new job in the Bayou State. After he was back at the academy, and enjoying riding his horse, he wrote Ellen that Clay had arrived in Alexandria "in fine condition, well pleased with his trip," having experienced "no dread of steamboats." In fact, he claimed Clay "had a fine opportunity to study the steam engine, and is now familiar with all its parts." Sherman also noted that "the cadets seemed glad to see me." Their new uniforms had arrived and they "looked finely" in them. He told Ellen that "everything has worked well in my absence, and now I can begin to provide for the future."[24]

Sherman clearly was worried about the future, relative especially to whenever Ellen and the children arrived. He feared that four thousand dollars a year would be inadequate. He had no doubt, he told Tom Jr., that "one of our first troubles will be that Ellen's servants will all quit, after we have gone into debt to get them here, and then she will have to wait on herself or buy a nigger. What will you think of that—our buying niggers?" He well knew that Ellen was strongly opposed to owning slaves. "But it is inevitable," he claimed. "Everybody owns their own servants." The servants Ellen would bring from Ohio would shortly "get married to some roving Texas trader ... with a few hundred dollars in pocket," leaving the Shermans "compelled to do without or buy." With a touch of sardonic humor, he warned Tom, "I have made this point to Ellen, and you must be careful in your Black Republican speeches not to be down on us too hard, for your own sister may be forced by necessity to traffic in human flesh."[25]

But all of this would be months in the future, because their house probably would not be ready before sometime in November, and Ellen would come only when the place was finished. Meanwhile, Sherman seemed quite satisfied with his work in general at the school. Clearly he was not getting wealthy, even if, as he hoped, his salary should be increased to five thousand yearly. Nevertheless, he held a position respected by many of Louisiana's leading men. He was engaged in work that made him reasonably content, and for which he felt thoroughly competent.

Living in the Deep South, however, Sherman was constantly reminded of the highly emotional issues that troubled the country. As the spring of 1860 progressed, the dark clouds of sectionalism continued their steady, threatening accumulation, lying low and heavy upon the national horizon, and menacingly packed with the destructive winds of slavery. Back in winter, Sherman had written John that he "did not like the looks of the times." The slave states, particularly in the Deep South, were sending commissions from state to state, exploring possible Southern actions if a Republican should be elected president. The political turmoil was great, and there was "universal belief in the South that disunion is not only possible but certain."[26]

The political situation worsened in April, when the Democratic Party held its national convention in Charleston, South Carolina, a hotbed of Southern extremism, unmatched in that respect by any other slave state. The convention could not nominate a presidential candidate, breaking up over the Southern demand for a federal slave code in all U.S. territory. When that measure was defeated, Alabama's delegates walked out of the convention, followed by many other Southern delegates, most of them from the Deep South. The remaining delegates then adjourned, after agreeing to reassemble in Baltimore in mid-June. The cooling-off period did not work, and the Democrats finally split, with the Northern delegates nominating Senator Stephen A. Douglas for president, while the Southerners named John C. Breckinridge of Kentucky, then the vice president. The Southern Democratic platform did call for enacting the federal slave code in the territories.[27]

After the Democrats broke up in Charleston, Sherman became yet more apprehensive about the nation's future, and wrote John that "this year's presidential election will be a dangerous one; may actually result in civil war, though I still can not believe the South would actually secede in the event of the election of a Republican." He continued preaching moderation, telling John that "so certain and inevitable is it that the physical and political power of this nation must pass into the hands of the free states, that I think you all can afford to take things easy, [and] bear the buffets of a sinking dynasty." In another message to John he declared, "The worst feature of things now is the familiarity with which the subject of dissolution is talked about. But I can not believe anyone, even . . . [Jefferson] Davis, would be rash enough to take the first step." Having learned that Ellen's father "also is out for Lincoln," Sherman thought it "probable that I will be even more 'suspect' than last year." He was sure that "all the reasoning and truth in the world would not convince a Southern man that the Republicans are not abolitionists." Ominously he concluded, "You may rest assured that the tone of feeling [in the South] is such that civil war and anarchy are very possible."[28]

Obviously Sherman, having made a total commitment to working with the Louisiana academy, wanted to believe that the nation's critical issues would be resolved peacefully. He thought that the slavery question should never have taken on such magnitude. It was a false issue, in his judgment, veiling the deeper problem of sectional power. He assured Ellen that "northern men don't care any more about the rights and humanity of the negroes than the southerners." He did not believe that "the present excitement in politics is anything more than the signs of the passage of power from southern politicians to northern and western politicians." But once more contemplating the power of emotion, he admitted to Ellen, "Of course no one can guess what the wild unbridled passions of men may do."[29]

....

THE INITIAL TERM at the Louisiana academy concluded at the end of July. Following examinations, an elaborate ball was held in celebration of the occasion, "with as much publicity as possible," wrote Sherman, in order "to attract general notice." Afterward, the cadets were free until the first of November, when school would resume. In the meantime, Sherman traveled north, first visiting the family in Lancaster, and then proceeding to Washington, D.C., where he conferred with Major Buell and Secretary of War John B. Floyd, hoping to procure muskets for the cadets by the beginning of the new school year. "Surprised to meet with such easy success," he remarked that he got "a prompt promise" of two hundred cadet muskets, as well as other equipment, and all did arrive in Louisiana as scheduled, before November.[30]

Then Sherman left for New York, where he met with Professor F. W. Smith. The two gathered various supplies and equipment for the school, purchasing uniforms, textbooks and hundreds of works of history and fiction to stock the new library. Returning to Lancaster, Sherman spent several weeks with his family before heading back to Louisiana. He was anxious to learn how construction progressed on his new house. The structure was nearing completion, and he said he "pushed forward" the building of fences and gates and all other work. In early November, about the same time that the school year began, he moved into the house, although it was not completely finished. But he did not send for Ellen and the children to join him.[31]

"Political excitement was at its very height," according to Sherman, with the presidential election dominating most conversations, "and it was constantly asserted that Mr. Lincoln's election would imperil the Union." Some friends advised him to vote for John Bell of Tennessee, on the Constitutional Union ticket, apparently so no one would think that he favored Lincoln. The Illinois rail-splitter was not even on the ballot in Louisiana, as in most slave states. Sherman refused to vote, however; not because he favored Lincoln (actually he preferred Bell), but because he was disgusted with the political scene. In the aftermath of Lincoln's election, Sherman wrote Ellen that "many gentlemen who were heretofore moderate . . . now begin to . . . go with the foolish mad crowd that seems bent on the dissolution of [the Union]." He said people had "ceased to reason or think of consequences."

He told Southern friends that war would be folly:

> You people speak so lightly of war. You don't know what you are talking about. . . . You mistake . . . the people of the North. They . . . are not going to let this country be destroyed without a mighty effort to save it. . . . The North can make a steam-engine, locomotive or railway car; hardly a yard of cloth or shoes can you [the South] make. You are rushing into war with one of the most powerful, ingeniously mechanical and determined people on earth—right at your doors. . . . Only in your spirit and determination are you prepared for war. In all else you are totally unprepared, with a bad cause to start with . . . in the end you will surely fail.

It was a striking summary of Northern strength.[32]

Sherman decided that bringing his family to Alexandria would be premature. Indeed it would have been. Soon after the presidential election, South Carolina's leaders proceeded with the action they long had threatened. In Charleston on December 20, a specially elected convention voted unanimously to secede from the Union, and called upon the South to form "a great Slaveholding Confederacy." By February 1, 1861, six more states had declared their separation from the United States of America, Louisiana among them. On February 4, representatives of the seven states breaking away from the Union met in Montgomery, Alabama, to form a new government. Within less than a week, they adopted a provisional constitution for the Confederate States of America and named Jefferson Davis as their president. Once Louisiana voted for secession on January 26, Sherman's position became untenable. He would have to resign from the academy and go north. There was no alternative. The existence of slavery had presented no problem for him, but the dissolution of the Union, as he had openly stated, and without any qualification, was an action he could never support. With disgust, Sherman informed Ellen that "everybody is striving for the honor of pouring out the deepest insult to Uncle Sam."[33]

Actually, Sherman had realized, several weeks prior to the secession of Louisiana, that he no longer had a future in the South. He just found it hard to face the fact. In mid-December, he wrote his daughter Minnie that "the dream and hope . . . that we could all be together . . . in a house of our own . . . is, I fear, about to vanish." On January 1, he correctly predicted to Ellen, "Louisiana will surely secede this month." Also, his situation at the new school had become increasingly difficult. Discipline problems seemed to be mounting. He told Ellen on January 8 that it is "all I can do" to suppress disorder and irregularity. A cadet had recently threatened him "with a loaded pistol" when he discovered a whiskey jug in the young man's room.[34]

January 10 brought really bad news for Sherman. Governor Moore of Louisiana, alarmed by a message from the state's U.S. senators, saying the U.S. military might reinforce two forts near the mouth of the Mississippi River, proceeded to seize those installations, as well as a fort on Lake Pontchartrain and the federal arsenal at Baton Rouge. The action directly impacted Sherman, because his Alexandria military academy had been designated a state arsenal (Sherman being paid an additional five hundred dollars yearly as its director), and the governor at once sent a large number of the confiscated arms, as well as munitions, to the school for storage.[35]

"I remember well," wrote Sherman in his memoirs, "that I was strongly and bitterly impressed by the seizure of the arsenal." At the time, he wrote Graham that he had been "waiting as patiently as a Redheaded person could" for Louisiana's decision about secession. Then came tidings of the governor's actions, which he regarded, he told both Graham and John Sherman, as "acts of war." Above all, he thought the capture of the Baton Rouge arsenal, because U.S. troops were stationed there at the request of Louisiana authorities, "a breach of common decency," as well as an act of war. Not only had Sherman been made the receiver of stolen goods, he was particularly embarrassed because "these goods [were] the property of the United States." He wrote, in what was probably an understatement, "This grated hard on my feelings as an ex-army-officer." The familiar "U.S." insignia had been "simply scratched off" the boxes.[36]

Before Sherman could leave Louisiana, he believed that he had a responsibility to see that all school records were in proper form, and all property and money accounted for. The institution must not be damaged by his withdrawal from the superintendency. Also, he needed to collect the money owed him, which had to be approved by the legislature. It was three weeks into February before everything was in order. He then stopped briefly in New Orleans, staying at the St. Louis Hotel, while delivering the necessary documents to make "the final settlement" at the bank that handled funds for the school. He was there on Washington's birthday, February 22, which was observed in a manner different from any previous Washington day commemoration that Sherman had ever experienced. New Orleans held a grand military parade celebrating, according to Sherman, "their emancipation from the despotism of the United States Government." That evening he wrote in his diary: "Glorious rejoicing at the downfall of our country."[37]

Arriving in Lancaster on March 2, he enjoyed a brief reunion with his family, before journeying on to the nation's capital at the urging of his brother. John thought Washington might offer some attractive possibilities. John's star was continuing to rise. He had just been appointed U.S. senator from Ohio, replacing Salmon P. Chase, then entering President Lincoln's cabinet as secretary of the treasury. John wanted his brother to meet Lincoln, inaugurated less than a week, the sixteenth president of the United States. John introduced him as his brother who had just arrived from Louisiana. Lincoln immediately inquired "how are they getting along down there?" Sherman replied with one of his favorite expressions: "They think they are getting along swimmingly—they are preparing for war." Lincoln responded with, as Sherman recalled, "Oh, well! I guess we will manage to keep house." Taken aback, Sherman wrote: "I was silenced; said no more to him."[38]

Initial impressions of people, whether positive or negative, are obviously based upon inadequate evidence, and frequently they are wrong.

Sherman "was sadly disappointed" with Lincoln. He was also disturbed by what he observed in the capital. "Even in the War Department," he heard "open, unconcealed talk, amounting to high-treason." When he and John were out of Lincoln's presence, he turned upon John, damning politicians. "You [politicians] have got things in a hell of a fix, and you may get them out as best you can." As for Sherman, he "would have no more to do with it." In retrospect, his declaration is amusingly ironic. For no military figure, except for Grant, would have as much to do with winning the war for the Union as Sherman.[39]

Chapter Twelve

No Man Can Foresee
the End

"And the War came"—to quote Lincoln's masterly prose in his hauntingly memorable second inaugural address. "Neither party," declared the President only a few weeks before he was assassinated, "expected for the war the magnitude or the duration which it has ... attained." Each side "looked for an easier triumph," and anticipated results "less fundamental and astounding." But a hellish dynamic was generated by "this mighty scourge of war." The awful conflict evolved into a consuming force that few had envisioned and none could control.[1]

When the incredible thing began, as always in times of change and crisis, and seemingly all the more when war is the issue, gifted souls in the North and South proclaimed the future with impassioned tones and remarkable certainty. Some were sure there would be no war at all. Others predicted that one clash, or at the most two or three, would conclude the fray. Sherman remembered hearing Southern orators state that a lady's thimble was sufficient to hold all the blood that might be shed. They took for granted that the slave states had the right to secede from the union, and once the Confederacy had been established, regarded secession as a fait accompli. If somehow the war did come, they thought it assuredly would be short and glorious.[2]

Sherman had a better idea than most of how the war would develop. He believed it was to be "a long war—very long—much longer than any politician thinks." He predicted horrendous casualties and declared that "it will take vast power to win so extensive a country [as the slave states]." He had no doubt that the Southerners would fight. Sherman's knowledge of the South, acquired while living in various slave states, together with his recent quasi-military position in Louisiana, gave him a more accurate sense than Americans generally possessed of the immense consequences likely to be involved in a civil conflict.[3]

At times he actually overestimated the war's duration and bloodshed. Striking, alarming projections—like the 300,000 casualties per year that he predicted after Shiloh—stemmed to some degree from a pessimistic tendency that was a part of his personality. Also, he sometimes found satisfaction in the use of hyperbole. Perhaps his most astute assessment came in a letter to his father-in-law, whom he always wrote in a realistic and serious vein. "I doubt," he addressed the "Honorable Thomas Ewing" in early 1861, "if any living man foresees the End."[4]

Indeed. The American Civil War became a momentous turning point and proved to be the single greatest determining experience of the nation's history. The war preserved the Union against the advocates of a Southern Confederacy who sought to maintain a way of life based upon slave labor—a way of life out of step with Western civilization. The conflict led to the destruction of slavery. It also resulted in Northern political and economic domination of the nation for decades to come, thereby fundamentally defining how the United States would develop. In addition to bitter, long-enduring sectional animosities, more pronounced in the defeated South than in the victorious North, the Civil War bequeathed a major racial problem. Although the slaves were freed, they were widely resented and exploited, in both the North and South. Civil rights were withheld, and little progress was made toward improvement until World War II.

The terrible clash was totally unlike any war the nation had previously endured. According to the century-old, most frequently cited estimate of the war's death toll, 620,000 soldiers lost their lives, either killed in battle or dead from disease. Approximately 360,000 were Union troops, with 260,000 Confederates. This is equivalent, in terms of war deaths as a percentage of the U.S. population, of some 6 million dead in 2015. The losses fell disproportionately upon the Confederacy, which had a much smaller manpower pool than the Union. Another perspective, often cited but nevertheless provocative and instructive, is that the loss of American life in the Civil War was as great as in all other U.S. conflicts combined through Vietnam.

While such losses, in a country with a population of only 31 million, are obviously enormous, they probably constitute a significant under-count. Historian J. David Hacker wrote an article in *Civil War History*, presenting a persuasive argument "that approximately 750,000 men lost their lives in the conflict" and that the undercount of Confederate deaths has been considerably more than the Federal undercount. The upper bounds of Hacker's data point possibly to more than 800,000 deaths—an equivalent of between 7.5 to 8 million American deaths if such a war were waged today. And of course, as usual in war, more soldiers suffered wounds than were killed in combat. Often the wounded were maimed, physically, mentally or both—psychologically impaired for the remain-der of their lives. About 15 percent of the wounded ultimately succumbed to their injuries. Adding still further to the human cost of the conflict are the estimated 50,000 Southern civilians who died.[5]

A single word, in the context of this immense loss and suffering, comes repeatedly to mind: tragedy. The words of Alexander Stephens, vice president of the Confederacy, were remarkably straightforward: "Our new government is founded upon . . . the great truth that the negro is not equal to the white man; that slavery . . . is his natural and normal condition."[6] Whatever may be written about the causes of the vast American struggle, and whether or not Americans think the preserva-tion of the Union and the freeing of the slaves were worth the enormous cost in human life and misery, the Confederacy and slavery are insepa-rably linked for all time—or at least for as long as humans seek truth in rendering the past.

When the war began, the United States Army was totally unprepared for the immense task it would face. Its entire strength, officers and men, numbered only 16,000. About one-third of the force soon journeyed south to support the Confederacy. Most of the officers, regardless of which side they chose, had never commanded any unit larger than a regiment. Even Winfield Scott, who had led his "gallant little army" in a magnificent campaign from Veracruz to Mexico City, which became the most notable military endeavor of the Mexican conflict, never at any time commanded more than approximately 11,000 soldiers. By 1861 Scott was of no value in the field anyway, being in his midseventies, monstrously overweight and unable to mount a horse—or as Sherman expressed his condition, "very old, very heavy, and very unwieldy."[7]

In a war where armies numbering 40,000, 50,000 and more became typical—for example, Sherman would command 100,000 soldiers when he began moving toward Atlanta in the spring of 1864—military leaders faced a challenge far beyond anything they had previously experienced, or for which they had been prepared. Generals who successfully led a force of 10,000 may be utter failures when given the responsibility for four or five times that many troops. Of this fact Sherman seemed well aware. He spoke positively of George B. McClellan and George H. Thomas, but did not think much of numerous men who were gaining positions of command, noting "an old saying that one campaign in Washington is worth more than five in the field."[8]

With such generals, he wrote his father-in-law, "as [Nathaniel P.] Banks, [Andrew H.] Reeder, [John C.] Frémont, & [Newton] Schleich, nothing but good luck, or the mere force of numbers will extricate us from Calamitous results." A few days later he added John Pope to his growing list of the unqualified, as he told Tom Ewing Jr. that the aforementioned incompetents "will afford to Bragg & Davis & Beauregard the liveliest pleasure." He considered it "a pity," when the North enjoyed a winning manpower bulge, "to balance the chances by a choice of such leaders." In other correspondence he named still more officers whom he considered inadequate—notably, Irvin McDowell, who soon would lead the Union Army at the First Battle of Bull Run. With few exceptions, Sherman's judgments proved true.[9]

This is not to say that Sherman considered himself qualified for high command. He did not, deploring his lack of any combat experience leading soldiers in Mexico. He had missed the chance of a "schooling with ... troops in the field" when he had been compelled to spend the war in California. Sherman told his brother John, who was urging him to get back in the army, where John predicted that he would surely gain "a high position for life," that he feared "you all [meaning brothers John and Charles, Thomas Ewing and others] overrate my powers and abilities and [would] place me in a position above my merits, a worse step than below." Sherman anticipated that many men would be "swept away by succeeding tides"; only in time would the truly able be identified and rise to lead. "Once real war begins," he told Tom Ewing Jr., "new men, heretofore unheard of, will emerge from obscurity, equal to any occasion." His prophecy would prove accurate and Sherman himself would be one of those men. As for the present, if he should participate, whatever his rank and assignments, he certainly intended to avoid being numbered among the incompetents, of which he fully expected a lengthy list.[10]

In addition to massive armies and immense casualties, the Civil War proved unprecedented in other significant aspects. Weaponry, which had undergone little change for several centuries, took a quantum leap between the war with Mexico and the Civil War. The armies in Mexico fought with muzzle-loading, single-shot, smoothbore muskets, whose effective range was approximately one hundred yards. Thus infantry assaults, ideally coupled with artillery support, stood a good chance of succeeding against defenders armed with smoothbore pieces, who needed nearly half a minute to reload their weapon. By the Civil War, however, the rifled musket, featuring a range of about five hundred yards, had become a practicable weapon. It could be loaded a little faster—possibly three times per minute—than a smoothbore. American-made .58 caliber Springfields and British-made .577 caliber Enfields (the latter able to use the same bullet as the Springfield) were soon highly prized on Civil War battlefields.

Defenders armed with rifled muskets were thought to enjoy a pronounced advantage against most assaulting forces. However, recent scholarship suggests that the weapon's effect has been somewhat exaggerated. At short range, the smoothbore was about as accurate as a rifled weapon, and most combat in the Civil War took place within the range of a smoothbore. Furthermore, fire from rifled muskets, unlike bullets from the smoothbore, followed a parabolic trajectory. At midrange rifled-musket fire passed above the enemy, thereby creating two killing zones, one at short range and the other at long range. Troops between the two zones advanced unharmed.

Also, many Civil War battlefields were filled with thickets, woods, hills and ravines, which often made detection of targets at three, four or five hundred yards impossible. The rifled musket thus represented a remarkable but nevertheless, when analyzed from a tactical perspective, relatively incremental advancement in weaponry. At the same time, the psychological impact on an attacking force, who knew the vastly superior range of the rifled musket, should not be underestimated. Furthermore, by the latter part of the war, some Federal units were equipped with repeating weapons, obviously adding still more strength, whether assaulting or defending. Rifled artillery, featuring greater range and striking power, became more common.

Warfare was also transformed by the railroad, markedly increasing the ease and speed at which large numbers of soldiers and equipment could be transported over hundreds of miles. The invention of the telegraph made instant communication possible in the Civil War, and the development of armored ships changed the face of naval warfare. There would even be experimentation with hot-air balloons for air reconnaissance, and primitive submarines. Sometimes called the first modern war, the Civil War was fundamentally different from anything the nation had ever experienced or anticipated. The conflict demanded army commanders with greater and more varied abilities than in earlier American wars—above all, men who thought in terms of grand strategy, and possessed the large-scale logistical talents necessary for waging such a war. Sherman was endowed potentially with the leadership qualities required by the Civil War, but for several months he staunchly resisted having any part of the unfolding tragedy.[11]

....

SHERMAN HAD LEFT Louisiana in a gloomy, depressed and rather disgusted frame of mind. "Our situation," he told Ellen, "is too bad to think of. I have got pretty near to the end of my rope—I have neither health, strength or purpose to start out life anew." In another letter he warned Ellen to "be prepared for the hardest kind of times," and added, "It does seem that the whole world conspires against us." Continuing the same theme in a later message, he again deplored having "to make a new start in life," and noted that "as soon as I get established anywhere some convulsion obliges me to change." He had even lost "poor Clay," the horse he affectionately spoke of in letters to various correspondents, and for several weeks tried to save from glanders, but finally had to have shot after a last-resort tracheotomy was unsuccessful.[12]

Sherman also vented his frustrations in correspondence with John. "I must settle up my affairs [in Louisiana] and start again, the fourth time in four years," he lamented to his brother. "Each time," he claimed, had resulted "from Calamity—California, New York, Leavenworth, & now Louisiana." He was compelled to "cast loose again with nothing." Grasping for something positive in all his struggles, Sherman assured John that he was "more and more content" not to be connected "with Banking & Credit," which he now regarded, seemingly indulging once more in hyperbole, as "the most disastrous of all vocations." Financially, as usual, Ellen was a source of worry. He confided to John, "however willing Ellen may be in theory [to lead a simple life], yet in practice she must have an array of servants and other comforts that money alone can give." Shortly before leaving Louisiana, Sherman again warned his wife of their dire financial plight: "I'm going to be as stingy as a miser till I see my way out of the woods, when you may go it again with a looseness— Affectionately, W. T. Sherman."[13]

Getting "out of the woods" financially appeared anything but easy. Of course with war looking more and more likely, the path was open at last for Sherman to return to the army. His brothers, his father-in-law and his brothers-in-law all encouraged him to do so. He learned that friends in the military, including General Scott, the U.S. Army's top-ranking officer, hoped to see him back in the service. Even Ellen suddenly seemed in favor of the army. "You will never be happy in this world," she wrote shortly before he left Louisiana, "unless you go into the army again." She requested John to find Cump an acceptable appointment, "convinced that he will never be happy out of the Army." That Ellen would finally relent after her longtime opposition to her husband's army career comes as a bit of a surprise.

Possibly she truly, at last, was convinced that Cump would never be content unless he got back in the military. Perhaps she might have been motivated by more than her husband's happiness. She did not possess a tolerance for slavery, and consequently did not have any warm feeling for the slave states. In fact, she was enraged by the attitude of Southern secessionists, and had been angered by James Buchanan's dealing with South Carolina, considering the President weak and sympathetic to the South. The government would have stood firm "if [Andrew] Jackson had been in [Buchanan's] place," she declared. Ellen even railed against Henry Turner's Southern sympathies, decrying him for turning his back upon the government that educated him for the military and supported him for years. Nor did she like the idea of resuming life in St. Louis, a city for which she never cared, located in a slave state, and the site that seemed to be Sherman's preference for making a new start. If he went back to the army, however, their relationship probably would be more amiable, and she could feel confident about continuing to reside in Lancaster for the foreseeable future.[14]

But much as Sherman had hoped in recent years for a chance to return to the military, the prospect of fighting in a civil war did not attract him in the least. Over the years he had made many friends in the South, "kind, good friends," he told his daughter Minnie, as he attempted to explain to her how "people are deceived and drawn on step by step, till war, death and destruction are upon them." The Southern people were in the grip of a delusion, and "when people believe a delusion they believe it harder than a real fact." During the past year Sherman had made more friends in the South, particularly G. Mason Graham, Professor David F. Boyd and Dr. S. A. Smith, with whom he worked effectively on behalf of the Louisiana military academy. Even his closest friend, Henry Turner, sympathized with the South, as did James Lucas. The idea of going to war against these people, as well as Southern friends from earlier years, was deeply troubling. Years afterward, David Boyd wrote Sherman: "I remember well how it grieved you to leave us, and how sorry were we to see you go."[15]

Sherman was also disgusted by the way the war came about. "On the negro question," he wrote David Boyd in April 1861, "I am satisfied there is and was no cause for a severance of the old Union." Later in that month, he told his brother John, "On the necessity of maintaining a government, and that government the old constitutional one, I have never wavered, but I do recoil from a war when the negro is the only question." He believed the war could and should have been avoided, the issues compromised. He blamed the Northern abolitionists and the Southern so-called Fire Eaters. Most of all he laid the ultimate responsibility for the war at the feet of politicians, north and south, who pandered to the prejudices and ignorance of their constituents and placed the interests of self and party above the well-being of the nation. He labeled "the petty machinery of party ... disgusting." Thus the issues, especially slavery, had become so sectionalized and emotionally packed that men no longer thought or acted rationally. Having ceased to reason, as Sherman viewed the incredible tragedy, the nation blundered into war.[16]

Furthermore, like his wife, Sherman believed that President Buchanan had erred miserably in dealing with South Carolina. "I regard the failure of Buchanan to strengthen Major [Robert] Anderson" at Charleston harbor, he wrote Ellen, "as absolutely fatal." He told John that Anderson—"my old captain"—should have been "promptly reinforced," and the U.S. Navy strengthened to control the sea. If these actions had been taken, Sherman believed that the secessionists would have known at once that the United States was firmly committed to defend its rights and territory. A few days later, again writing John, he declared that if Buchanan had made Fort Sumter "impregnable with an adequate force backed by a couple of first class Steam Frigates—he would have checkmated this [secessionist] movement, and allowed time for adjusting the differences." He continued to sound this theme in several letters. Also, he did "not care about rejoining an army subject to the order and control of Politicians who have not the sense to Govern, and the Spirit to stand by their officers who . . . act with vigor and sense." He implored his brother to "kick all platforms . . . to the Devil, and look the Questions that now threaten our national existence square in the face— and generally aim to be a U.S. Statesman instead of a mere Republican, a mere partizan." Sherman believed that the nation faced an unprecedented crisis—a crisis demanding pure statesmanship if the nation were to be saved from destruction.[17]

When Sherman first met Lincoln he was not impressed, as mentioned earlier. While he began to think more favorably of the new president in the following weeks—acknowledging that Lincoln faced "an awful task" and would merit "the admiration of the world" if he could deal with the rebellion successfully—he simply was not convinced that the new administration was "yet up to the magnitude of the occasion." When the Confederates fired on Fort Sumter and Lincoln called for 75,000 volunteers for three months' service, Sherman famously remarked that "you might as well attempt to put out the flames of a burning house with a squirt gun." He thought the President's call should have been for 300,000—and for a much longer time. If the nation were totally committed to saving the Union, Sherman had no doubt of an ultimate, inevitable triumph. He feared, however, that the country was not going to effectively employ its potential, massive superiority in industrial war production and manpower.[18]

Meanwhile, as the national crisis escalated, Sherman accepted the presidency of the St. Louis Rail Road Company, still hoping to avoid the gathering clouds of war. The appointment came through Henry Turner and James Lucas, the latter being the main stockholder in the horse-drawn streetcar company. In late March, Sherman again took up residence in his favorite city, this time accompanied by all five of his children and Ellen. Two servants also made the journey with them from Ohio. The family moved into a large house at 226 Locust Street, which Sherman rented from Lucas. John Hunter and Ellen's brother Charles, who had formed a law partnership, agreed to board with them.

Sherman's starting salary of two thousand dollars a year, with the hope of a raise in the near future, was not nearly adequate to support his large family and necessitated the sale of some of Ellen's property, which had been a gift from her father. Even worse was the fact that the new job presented no challenge to a man of Sherman's talents. He was totally unsuited for the boring work of a streetcar executive—particularly when "the whole air was full of wars and rumors of wars" and armies were marshaling, while he remained isolated from them.[19]

The call of the army grew stronger. In early April, Sherman was offered the chief clerkship of the War Department, with the promise of an appointment as assistant secretary of war when the U.S. Congress met. His brother John and others urged him to accept, believing it would be a step toward a high rank in the army. Maria Ewing wrote Ellen approvingly, as if Sherman's acceptance were a foregone conclusion, saying that "fortunately for Cumpy (as he is perfectly unhappy if he is not constantly employed) . . . so honorable and for these times so lucrative a position has been offered him, [which is] quite a compliment." However, Sherman considered the position beneath his merits, and rebelled at the thought of a desk job. If he should return to the army, he intended to lead soldiers in battle. John straightforwardly told his older brother that because of his army background he could not avoid taking part in the conflict. "You are regarded with favor [in the War Department]," John assured him. "It will be your own fault if you do not gain a very high position in the Army." Tom Ewing Jr., who like John had good political connections, inquired exactly what position Sherman wanted, promising to work with General Scott in an attempt to secure it for him. He thought that his brother-in-law had better offer his services soon, or his opportunities well might be gone.[20]

There was yet another consideration. Rumors had begun to circulate that perhaps Sherman did not return to the army because he was a Southern sympathizer. The decision to take up residence in St. Louis only fueled the fire of such allegations. Of course there was never any chance whatsoever, as Sherman made abundantly clear in letters to various people in the North and South, that he could have supported secession. From at least as far back as his West Point days, he had been an ardent nationalist. He ordered John not to represent him to people in Washington "as a Republican—but as an American," and back on January 18, he unequivocally instructed Governor Moore of Louisiana to "relieve me as superintendent [of the military academy] the moment the State determines to secede, for on no earthly account will I do any act, or think any thought hostile to or in defiance of the old Government of the United States."[21]

Simply put, as he told Tom Ewing Jr., "Secession is Treason." He wrote Professor Boyd, "I am *ultra*—I believe in *coercion* and cannot comprehend how any Government can exist unless it defend its integrity." The idea that "any part of a people may carry off a part of the Common Territory without consent or purchase, I cannot understand." Sherman lashed out bitterly as the Confederacy was being formed in Montgomery, telling Tom Jr. to instruct his longtime friend Stewart Van Vliet that he should "seize Fort Leavenworth—hoist the Bear Flag [the Californian symbol of conquest], and declare himself independent of all Creation. Sell the mules, horses, wagons, etc., of the late Uncle Sam, and depart for Paris & spend the proceeds like a Gentleman—That is modern doctrine."[22]

Interestingly, there were friends in the South who would have welcomed Sherman's support of the Confederacy, and who tried to persuade him accordingly. Dr. S. A. Smith wrote him on April 24, 1861. Acknowledging the receipt of a recent letter from Sherman revealing his decision to settle in St. Louis, Smith said, "How much I hope that you will be able to come to the conclusion that your adopted state is right in opposing herself to the mad career of the Union Splitter and his fanatical crew. How delighted we all should be," he continued, "to hear that in the coming contest we might boast of the possession of your fine talents and high military qualities." If Sherman replied to this letter, his response has not been found.[23]

....

SECESSION BREATHED HOT in Missouri in 1861. Sherman's decision to reside in St. Louis is intriguing, particularly in view of his disdain for those who would break up the Union. The state had a new governor, Claiborne Fox Jackson, who was an ardent secessionist. He stated that if the United States applied force against any seceded state, such action would lead Missouri to join the Confederacy. The secessionists received a setback, however, when the convention elected to consider the issue proved strongly pro-Union and voted to stand with the United States. Then came Fort Sumter. When Lincoln, in its aftermath, called upon Missouri for troops to put down the rebellion, Governor Jackson's bitterly defiant reply, framed in language verging on the demented, characterized the President's request as "illegal, unconstitutional, revolutionary, inhuman, diabolical, and can not be complied with." Jackson had a lot of support. Missouri's lieutenant governor, the speaker of the house and many members of the state legislature were in favor of secession and laid plans to tear Missouri from the Union. They strengthened the pro-Confederate state militia, requested artillery from Jefferson Davis and focused their attention upon capturing the 60,000 muskets and other military equipment stored in the United States arsenal in St. Louis—the largest arsenal in any slave state. Already they had taken the small government arsenal at Liberty.[24]

Sherman observed that "all the leading [Missouri] politicians were for the South in case of a war." He said manifestations of Confederate sympathizers abounded throughout St. Louis. He remembered that a house on "the northwest corner of Fifth and Pine was the rebel headquarters, where the rebel flag was hung publicly, and the crowds about the Planters' House were all more or less rebel." Also, he said there was "a [military] camp in Lindell's Grove, at the end of Olive Street [Camp Jackson, it was called]," that was nominally "a state camp of instruction, but beyond doubt, was in the interest of the Southern cause." All the while, according to Sherman, "the newspapers fanned the public excitement to the highest pitch," and advocates of each side threatened the other with violence.[25]

Jackson and the secessionists well might have succeeded in capturing the St. Louis arsenal, had it not been for Captain Nathaniel Lyon, who commanded the U.S. troops stationed at the arsenal, and Congressman Francis P. Blair Jr., the brother of Postmaster General Montgomery Blair. Fortunately for the United States, Lyon and Blair managed to keep abreast of Governor Jackson's plans, aided immensely by Union spies. In dire need of more soldiers, Lyon recruited several regiments from among the German-American population, which was strongly antislave and pro-Union—in fact, the very backbone of Unionism in St. Louis. Then, employing a diversion, Lyon and Blair arranged for more than 20,000 of the best weapons in the arsenal to be secretly transferred across the Mississippi for safekeeping in Illinois.[26]

Captain Lyon next decided to move against Camp Jackson. Posing in a dress and shawl as Frank Blair's mother-in-law, Lyon, who was a small, wiry man, made a personal reconnaissance of the site in a carriage. He then struck the next day, May 10, with two companies of regular army soldiers and four regiments of his new German-American forces, surrounding and compelling the surrender of about 700 men and their arms. The pro-Southern militia, taken totally by surprise, surrendered without firing a shot. As Lyon marched his prisoners through the city, leading them to the arsenal for incarceration, a growing crowd of spectators became increasingly raucous. When someone, thought to have been drunk, fired and shot an officer in the leg, the troops opened fire on the crowd, killing between twenty and thirty people.[27]

Sherman himself witnessed the melee. Thinking the danger had passed, he took his young son Willy to watch the prisoners being marched from Camp Jackson to the U.S. arsenal. When the shooting erupted, Charley Ewing, who was standing close to Willy, shielded the lad with his body, as all immediately went to the ground. Once the firing slackened, Sherman jerked up Willy and dashed for cover, later blaming himself for foolishly exposing his child to danger. During the night some German-Americans were murdered, and the following day another clash took place in which several more people were killed. Perhaps the volatile climate in Missouri, climaxed by the bloody events in the streets of St. Louis, had a determining impact on Sherman's thinking. On May 11, he wrote Tom Ewing Jr., "If we are to have a long and desperate Civil Struggle, I suppose I must take part, and if so I prefer service with Regulars." He knew that in Washington the lobbying on his behalf by friends and relatives was continuing.[28]

When Sherman left Louisiana he had no good choices about where to live or how to support his family. He seemed as strongly opposed to Ohio as ever, still disturbed by the thought of becoming dependent upon his father-in-law. Nor was California a possibility. Ellen certainly would not have accompanied him to the West Coast again, and there was no promise of work there anyway. While St. Louis was not a panacea, he had friends and family connections there. Most important, he knew he had a job—even if the salary was inadequate for his needs. Maybe his pay would be increased. Maybe other opportunities would be presented. St. Louis, in Sherman's view, would have seemed the least objectionable of his options.

After residing there for a few weeks, however, the financial obligations well may have weighed even more heavily than anticipated, especially with all of his family present, and servants to support. Relatives and friends continued advising him, strongly, to get back in the army. President Lincoln was working to increase the size of the U.S. military, both the regular army and the volunteers, the latter to be enlisted for three years' service. At last, in Sherman's words, "the Government was trying to rise to a level with the occasion." If so, then returning to the army might make more sense than any other course.[29]

Within less than a month after the bloody St. Louis imbroglio, Sherman received a dispatch from his brother Charles in Washington, informing him that he had been appointed a colonel of the Thirteenth Regular Infantry, a new outfit that was being formed. He was wanted at the capital immediately. Sherman wrote in his memoirs, "I could no longer defer action." He arrived in Washington in early June, and General Scott placed him on his staff. He was assigned to inspection duty, which entailed reporting on military units and installations all around the capital. He wrote John that his job would be "to keep well advised of the character and kind of men who are in Military service . . . near Washington, and . . . report to General Scott in person."

After more than seven and one half years' absence, Sherman had returned to the U.S. Army. He would not leave again until he retired. In St. Louis, Ellen packed up the children and headed back to Ohio. She was pregnant once more. Another daughter, who would be named Rachel, arrived on July 5. Sherman had thought he would be returning to St. Louis to raise his regiment, and thus could help Ellen prepare for the move to Lancaster. General Scott, however, named someone else to raise the Thirteenth Regulars and ordered Sherman to go to work for him at once. While Sherman's name officially remained on the roster as Colonel of the Thirteenth Regular Infantry for a long time, he would never command the regiment. In fact, he remained on duty with Scott only until the end of June, when he was given command of a brigade in the army under General Irvin McDowell—the army being marshaled for a general advance against the Confederate forces who were positioned less than thirty miles west-southwest of Washington. When he assumed command on June 30, Sherman's task was to prepare four regiments of inexperienced volunteers for combat, as quickly as possible. He was virtually certain there would not be enough time to train his troops properly. He was right. The first big battle of the war was only three weeks away.[30]

Chapter Thirteen

Action at Bull Run

Sunday morning, July 21, 1861, dawned clear and the sun rose big and red. The day promised to be hot, in more ways than one, because the first major battle of the Civil War was at hand. There was nothing to compare with what was about to happen. Recent, small-scale clashes in western Virginia, and at Big Bethel on the peninsula between the James and York Rivers, would pale into relative insignificance when compared with the bloodletting at Bull Run. The river that gave the battle its name was a fairly formidable forty-foot-wide stream, "with ugly ragged banks" according to Sherman, which flowed in a generally northwest-to-southeast direction as it meandered across the area where the opposing armies were marshaling.[1]

Brigadier General Irvin McDowell's hastily formed Army of the Potomac, numbering about 34,000, was drawn up a short distance from the northeast banks of the stream; while Brigadier General P. G. T. Beauregard, who had been a classmate of McDowell at West Point, commanded approximately 20,000 Confederates, spread along an eight- or nine-mile front on the opposite side of the winding river. Beauregard, viewed in the South as a dashing hero after Fort Sumter, was being substantially reinforced. Joseph E. Johnston, leading 12,000 troops, had slipped away from Robert Patterson's Federal force in the Shenandoah Valley. Most of Johnston's men had already arrived, and the rest were drawing near. Beauregard was positioned to defend Manassas Junc-

tion, where the Manassas Gap Railroad intersected the vital Orange
& Alexandria, with its connections to the new Confederate capital at
Richmond.[2]

Events had developed rapidly since Virginia seceded from the Union.
After Richmond became the capital of the Confederacy in late May, the
United States capital in Washington lay within approximately a hundred
miles, and many people, north and south, anticipated that a major battle
would soon occur somewhere between the two cities. Aggressive Southern expansionists were dreaming of adding the slave state of Maryland
to their confederacy, and by force of military invasion if necessary. With
Washington, D.C., totally encompassed by Virginia and Maryland, the
U.S. capital would be compelled to capitulate—or so ran the theorizing
among some "Southrons," as they delighted in styling themselves.[3]

Americans in Washington were thinking in equally aggressive terms.
Many officials in the nation's capital strongly favored a grand offensive.
"We should bring on the battle," demanded one impatient member of the
U.S. Congress, doubtless speaking for a host of other representatives.
Senator Lyman Trumbull of Illinois called for an "immediate movement
of the troops," with the objective of taking Richmond before the Confederate Congress could meet in late July. Northern newspaper editors
were of like mind. "On to Richmond" became the masthead slogan of
Horace Greeley's widely influential *New York Tribune*, and other papers
at once backed his cry for action. The time had come to crush the rebellion. One battle, and the deed would be done. President Lincoln stood
with those demanding action.[4]

However, General Winfield Scott demonstrated no enthusiasm for an
immediate offensive. He believed that going to war with the army he had
made no sense. The troops were simply too raw, and he did not like the
idea of a campaign in Virginia anyway. Scott advocated that no forward
movement should be made before the fall. Then, advised the nation's
most experienced soldier, the line of advance should be down the great
Mississippi, dividing the Confederacy and seizing New Orleans with a
simultaneous, amphibious advance from the Gulf of Mexico, while placing a strong blockade around the Southern coastline. Scott's "anaconda"

plan, as some called it, would thereby isolate the Confederacy and slowly squeeze it to death.[5]

Also General McDowell, even if he had never commanded troops in battle, knew that his green army was not ready for offensive operations; and other officers of military training agreed. Certainly Sherman understood there was great risk in attacking with an inadequately prepared army. Admittedly, Sherman continued to nourish his deep disdain for volunteer soldiers, but that bias did not alter the fact, plainly evident to any one with open eyes, that the mass of the Union Army consisted of ill-trained and ill-disciplined units. He wrote Ellen that "the volunteers do pretty much as they please." He observed that "on the Slightest provocation," they fire their weapons, and reported that the day before "there was an ugly stampede of 800 Massachusetts men." He also penned a letter to his brother John, stating "the volunteers test my patience by their irregularities." He accused them of "robbing, shooting in direct opposition to orders, and like conduct showing a great want of Discipline—Twill take time to make soldiers of them."[6]

But President Lincoln determined that the army must take the offensive immediately. When General McDowell protested that the soldiers needed more time for training, Lincoln replied with his oft quoted assessment that both sides were "all green together," as if that nullified McDowell's argument.[7]

Perhaps, given the circumstances, the President had no other choice. A Confederate army positioned within a short distance of the capital could not be ignored. Both the public and the politicians demanded that the Rebels be driven away. Enlistment time for the ninety-day men who volunteered after Fort Sumter would soon be up. Many congressmen believed those troops should not go home before being engaged in a campaign. Sherman said that the volunteers had also taken up the cry "On to Richmond."[8]

While Lincoln liked General Scott's concept of how the war should be fought—and in the long term the aging general's plans certainly did help win the conflict—the President realized that a great host of people demanded immediate battle with an enemy embarrassingly positioned at the doorstep of the nation's capital. "The temper of Congress and the people," remembered Sherman, "would not permit the slow and methodical preparation desired by General Scott." Without action soon, the President feared that Northern morale, both of the army and the general public, would suffer severe damage—not to mention harm to America's image abroad. The U.S. forces, Lincoln concluded, must move against the Rebels at once. And so he ordered.[9]

General McDowell reluctantly began his advance on July 16. From the start, all manner of problems plagued the movement. McDowell was leading an army fully three times the size of Scott's force in Mexico, and neither he nor his division and brigade commanders knew much about how to do it. As for the ninety-day men, they had not been impressive on the parade ground; now, on the march, they proved physically unfit. Carrying full equipment on a hot day, the army covered only six miles and that distance exhausted a large number of men. Five days would be consumed before the marching, bringing up supplies, reconnoitering and organizing for an attack were at last completed.[10]

Discipline was woefully lacking among the volunteers. Sherman's criticisms were not exaggerated. They broke ranks in search of water, picked blackberries, discharged firearms and looted. Houses were plundered, animals shot and some structures were set on fire. When the volunteers' equipment became heavy, it was dropped by the wayside; sometimes they even dispensed with ammunition. The day before the battle, two regiments of ninety-day men, announcing that their enlistment was expired, headed back to Washington. All in all, their conduct seemed to be confirming Sherman's worst nightmares about the unreliability of volunteer soldiers.[11]

The Union Army heading for Manassas Junction consisted of four divisions, each with a strength of about 8,000 men. Brigadier General Daniel Tyler's First Division led the advance, and Sherman's Third Brigade, numbering 3,400, marched in Tyler's division. General McDowell established his headquarters in Centreville and came up with a well-conceived attack plan. Sherman wrote that Bull Run "was one of the best-planned battles of the war." Learning that Beauregard's forces occupied good defensive ground behind the river, McDowell discarded any thought of a frontal assault. Hoping to take the Confederates by surprise, he determined to feign a head-on attack while moving to strike their left flank with half of his army.[12]

Tyler's lead division would conduct the feint, moving out from its camps at two o'clock on the morning of July 21. Tramping west-southwest along the Warrenton Turnpike, as the road from Washington was known in that vicinity, Tyler was to advance to the Stone Bridge over Bull Run. There, on the opposite side of the river, Nathan G. Evans's small Confederate brigade of two regiments and a handful of cavalry formed the weak left flank of the Rebel army—although the Federals did not know how few Confederates defended the bridge. Tyler was to make a strong demonstration against the enemy, capturing the bridge if possible, convincing the Confederates that this was the focal point of the Union attack. To further aid in screening the main assault, one brigade from the Fourth Division would feint an attack at Blackburn's Ford, some three miles south of the Stone Bridge.[13]

Meanwhile, the Second and Third Divisions would be marching to launch the real attack against the Confederate left flank. Brigadier General David Hunter's Second Division would follow in the wake of Tyler's First, until he crossed Cub Run, a stream roughly paralleling Bull Run about two miles back of the Stone Bridge. There Hunter's command would turn to the right, make a sweeping advance of several miles to the north and west and cross Bull Run at Sudley Springs Ford. Brigadier General Samuel Heintzelman's Third Division would follow Hunter's troops. Once across Bull Run, the two divisions would strike southward in battle array. If all went well, the Rebels would be under great pressure, enabling the First Division to drive across the river at or near the Stone Bridge and significantly strengthen the Federal attack.[14]

As the Union forces prepared for their early move that Sunday morning, General Beauregard, with approval from the recently arrived Joe Johnston, also planned to take the offensive. He even issued the orders. Curiously, Beauregard's intention, like McDowell's, was to attack the left flank of his enemy. However, Beauregard's orders never reached some of the brigade commanders. Nevertheless, two Rebel brigades did actually cross Bull Run as the Southern army began lurching into position for an attack. Before the Confederates could assemble and strike, Beauregard learned that McDowell had already brought on the battle.[15]

The Union commander's carefully designed plan of attack may have seemed nearly flawless on paper, but the implementation went askew from the beginning. Not that anyone should have been surprised, considering that all the previous marching had been halting and time-consuming. Worse than the advance from Washington, the Union Army had to move into attack position in the dark. Tyler's division, leading off to launch the big diversion at the Stone Bridge, was slow getting under way. Troops became confused about their place in line, and the road on which they were to march. Thus the First Division took excessive time moving beyond the crossroads at Cub Run, where the flanking divisions marching behind Tyler were to swing off to the right.[16]

Once the Second and Third Divisions finally turned northward, heading toward Sudley Springs Ford, the going was very slow. Men groped along in the dark, and frequently blundered into one another. Accordion action in the marching units ("hurry up and stop") contributed to the slowness of the advance. They had been awake since shortly after midnight. They were tired, many were hungry and grousing, when at last the head of the column reached Sudley Springs Ford at 9:30 a.m.—2½ hours later than intended. Another thirty minutes to an hour passed before Hunter and Heintzelman got their troops across Bull Run and advanced to attack.[17]

Meanwhile, Daniel Tyler's First Division had arrived at the Stone Bridge at about 5:30, opening the battle with an artillery shot across the river. Several more artillery pieces soon went into action, but they fired slowly, and only one of Tyler's brigades provided support with rifled-musket fire. The demonstration was not at all convincing. The Confederates soon concluded that the Stone Bridge would not be the main point of attack. Sherman's brigade lay on the north side of the road, behind the infantry who were conducting the demonstration. As usual, Sherman was restless. He rode to the river, examining the ground and seeking a place to ford the stream.[18]

Confederate horsemen showed him what he was looking for, although that was never their intention. Sherman described what happened in a letter to Ellen: "About 9 o'clock I was well down to the River—with some skirmishers and observed two men on horseback ride along a hill, descend, cross the stream and ride out toward us." One Rebel waved his gun over his head, making himself conspicuous, and loudly shouted: "You D——d black abolitionists, come on." Sherman permitted his men to fire on the man, but none of them hit the brazen fellow, who eventually rode back across the river. If a Rebel could cross Bull Run at that point, obviously the Union troops could, too. The site was approximately a half mile north of the Stone Bridge.[19]

At about the same time, a Confederate signal officer, located on a high observation point, spotted through his spyglass the reflection of the sun's rays as they struck metal—bayonets, field pieces, rifled muskets— in the vicinity of Sudley Springs Ford. Sending word immediately to Beauregard's command post, the officer also signaled Colonel Evans at the Stone Bridge: "Look out for your left; you are turned." Evans, who conducted his command well that day, reacted at once. Leaving four companies and two artillery pieces to continue bluffing the Union troops at the Stone Bridge, which he had been effectively achieving for some time, Evans took approximately 1,100 men and moved rapidly to meet the enemy on his flank. He positioned his men in a strip of woods along Matthews Hill, facing toward Sudley Springs Ford, which was less than a mile distant. The Confederates enjoyed a clear field of fire to their front, and here they opened with artillery (two pieces) and infantry fire, when the Federals drew within a range of approximately 600 yards. The time was near 10:30.[20]

Soon hard-pressed by the advancing Federals, who significantly outnumbered him, Evans called for help. He was reinforced by two Southern brigades, moving up to the fight and close at hand, which brought the total Confederate strength at Matthews Hill to approximately 4,500. Then, as the second Union division in the flanking force came up, deployed and

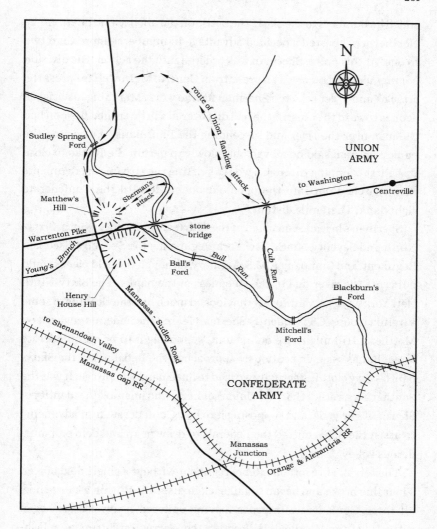

BULL RUN BATTLEFIELD

On Sunday, July 21, 1861, Sherman saw action at Bull Run (Manassas), the first significant battle of the Civil War. Map by Jim Moon Jr.

added its numbers to the clash, the battle on the hill became intense. The Northerners boasted a decided advantage in numbers—more than two to one. At this point, Sherman was ordered into the action. His division commander had received an order from General McDowell to "press the attack," and Tyler selected Sherman for the work. Marching his brigade at once toward the crossing he had discovered a little earlier, he soon had the men over the river and "ascending the Bluff Bank." Once atop the bank, Sherman said he moved out "slowly to permit the Ranks to close up." First tramping through a woods skirting the stream, the regiments then marched out into the open, advancing toward the Confederate right flank, a half mile distant.[21]

Sherman's brigade consisted of the Thirteenth, Twenty-Ninth, Sixty-Ninth and Seventy-Ninth New York Regiments; the Second Wisconsin Regiment; and Company E, U.S. Artillery, although the field pieces could not cross the river due to the steepness of the banks. The Sixty-Ninth New York wore gray uniforms that looked much like the clothing of some Virginia troops. Consequently Sherman feared the Federals engaged on Matthews Hill might fire on his unit, supposing it to be a Confederate force. But as his men cautiously approached the Rebel flank, the Sixty-Ninth's gray clothing actually worked to Sherman's advantage. It was the Southerners, rather than the Union soldiers, who mistook the identity of Sherman's brigade, and supposing it to be a Confederate unit advancing to assist them, permitted the Federals to draw near, and deliver a murderous volley.[22]

The terrible fire left one Rebel regiment without a single field officer. Their line broke and began to fall back in disorder. Within a short time, all three Confederate brigades, having suffered heavy losses, began retreating from Matthews Hill, across the Warrenton Turnpike, splashing through a little creek called Young's Branch, and afterward struggling up the rise of Henry Hill, where they finally rallied. Sherman's Civil War combat debut, effectively striking the enemy in flank, was auspicious; and the additional strength of his brigade, attacking where it did and when it did, may have been decisive in driving the Rebels from Matthews Hill. "Indeed," wrote one historian of the battle, "if Sherman's crossing had come just half an hour sooner, all three Confederate brigades would have been nearly surrounded and possibly destroyed." Another historian praised Sherman in the following words: "In his first major battle General Sherman was giving clear evidence of his ability as a tactician." In reality, the fog of war had worked a bit of magic on his behalf. Chance determined the advantageous angle at which his brigade approached the enemy flank. Chance accounted for his command being misidentified by the Rebels, and thus permitted to advance within very close range, where they delivered devastating fire.[23]

The battle, to this point, could hardly have gone better for the Union Army. In fact, General McDowell rode along the line uttering shouts of "Victory," and exclaiming, "The day is ours." Telegraph messages to Washington conveyed strong assurances that the Rebel lines were broken, and "a glorious victory" was at hand. The dispatches were so positive that President Lincoln, after going to church that morning, decided to take his usual Sunday afternoon carriage ride. But as the Federal forces eagerly pursued the Confederates to Henry Hill in the early afternoon, they found the enemy rallying, and strengthened by fresh troops. The battle was far from over. The fiercest stage of the clash was just beginning.[24]

The fight quickly became a confused melee. Some Federals wore gray while some Confederates wore blue. Both sides presented a number of men in fancy-dress, multicolored uniforms. The New York Zouaves accented their striking outfits with red baggy pants, and the Louisiana Zouaves were also decked out in baggy trousers, except that theirs featured blue and white stripes. Other men simply went to war wearing the same clothes they donned for a day of work on the farm. The Confederate flag was similar to the U.S. flag, and when hanging limply with no breeze affecting it, as often was the case, one could not tell if the banner was Union or Rebel. Mix in a widespread pall of black powder smoke generally obscuring the battle area and, understandably, both Federals and Confederates at times fired on their own troops, or failed to fire on an approaching foe—as when Sherman's brigade had advanced to the battle.

The elated Union troops scrambling up Henry Hill may have thought "the day is ours," as their commander zealously proclaimed, but there they soon discovered a well-positioned and significantly strengthened enemy. Thomas Jonathan Jackson's five-regiment Rebel brigade had established a defensive line slightly behind the crest of Henry Hill, one that the U.S. forces could not see until they topped the rise. Jackson's troops anchored the Confederate stand, and Bernard Bee, trying to rally his shaken brigade, famously called out, only minutes before he was mortally wounded: "There stands Jackson like a stone wall! Rally behind the Virginians!" Rally they did, and more Southern reinforcements came up from the rear. "Once the resistance had hardened," remarks Basil Liddell Hart, "it was a calculable probability ... that the ... Confederates on the hill would be able to repulse superior numbers in an attack which had now become purely frontal."[25]

Worse for the Federals, only four of the eight brigades that were close enough to have reached Henry Hill in time for the clash were actually brought into the action. And these were fed into the battle piecemeal. Sherman's brigade advanced on the left side of the Union forces. When he received an order to attack, Sherman sent in his regiments one at a time—a common mistake of commanders, both at Bull Run and on many a future field of battle. Only when his Second Wisconsin, first into the fray, was falling back, did Sherman send in the Seventy-Ninth New York. As the latter faltered, he ordered the Sixty-Ninth New York to attack. Twice they charged; afterward the Sixty-Ninth troops blamed their failure, at least in part, upon the Seventy-Ninth regiment as it stumbled back through their ranks in demoralized disarray.

Sherman's troops took heavy losses. For the entire battle, he said 111 of his men were killed, 205 wounded, and 293 missing, a total of 609. Most of the killed and wounded came in the fight for Henry Hill. Up to that point, Sherman thought the volunteers "had done well," and added, "I do think it was impossible to stand long in that fire." Perhaps he was right about the severity of the enemy fire, but his brigade's chances of success would have been greater if he had attacked with more than one regiment at a time. Of course the ultimate responsibility for the piecemeal effort lay with the army's commander, who did nothing to halt such attacks by Sherman and other brigade leaders. For the record, McDowell himself ordered some individual regiments to attack in turn, even when several regiments were available to go into action simultaneously. Also, looking at the big picture of the battle, nearly half of McDowell's army never got into the fight.[26]

From about 2:00 to 4:00 p.m. the battle raged, with charges and countercharges on the plateau of Henry Hill. The momentum of the clash finally turned in favor of the Confederates. The decisive attack came when the last of Joe Johnston's army, two brigades arriving by rail from the Shenandoah, detrained and marched rapidly toward the sound of the guns. Their angle of advance chanced to strike McDowell's right flank, forcing the Federals to give ground. Beauregard sensed the moment, raised a cheer and attacked all along the line. Confederate pressure on the Union Army became too great, and the men began falling back toward Bull Run. McDowell and other officers tried to bring them to a halt, but to no avail. More and more Federals were breaking away and heading to the rear. Initially there was some order to the retreat, but things rapidly went from bad to worse.[27]

Sherman was among the officers trying to restore order. He and Colonel Michael Corcoran, commanding the predominantly Irish Sixty-Ninth New York, managed briefly to halt the troops and form the brigade into a ragged, irregular square, only to see their work "fall to pieces," in Sherman's words, in a short time. The men once more began hustling to the rear, and Colonel Corcoran was captured by the oncoming Confederates. Sherman got away safely, still determined to reorganize his brigade, which he achieved three miles farther back, in the vicinity of Centreville. This, too, proved momentary, and his regiments soon became inextricably mixed with other units, as more and more men bolted in the direction of Washington, hoping to outdistance the Rebels, who were thought by many to be in hot pursuit.[28]

Confederate cavalry played a role early on, harassing the Union retreat, although their threat does not appear to have been a major factor, except for the effect upon the minds of terrified soldiers. Southern artillery fire struck along the turnpike too and blocked the bridge over Cub Run when it disabled a wagon crossing the stream. A traffic jam quickly developed at the bridge, as wagons, artillery pieces, caissons and frightened troops clogged the route to safety. Enraged and scared, men yelled and cursed as they found their path obstructed. Further complicating the mass exodus were numerous civilians who, in an oft told but important tale in understanding the Washington frame of mind, had come out to see the battle. Among them were several U.S. senators and ten or twelve congressmen, having chosen their places on the gently rolling hills, where they had hoped to witness the great clash of arms.

Some men, both politicians and the general public, had appeared with wives or lady friends, adorned in their Sunday best and carrying picnic baskets with wine or champagne to celebrate the anticipated triumph. Never mind that virtually nothing of the battle could be seen because of the ubiquitous haze of gun smoke. For the enthralled spectators, it was all a somewhat mysterious yet alluring pageant, hinting of danger and punctuated with a great deal of noise. They seemed to thoroughly enjoy the occasion, right up to the moment they suddenly realized that the Union forces were falling back toward Washington—fleeing in terror, and a portion of them rapidly turning into a wild, frantic mob.

Down from the hillsides then came the private carriages, transporting anxious civilians scrambling to make their escape. Some crowded right in with the mass of soldiers, ambulances, gun carriages and various encumbrances that seemed to be everywhere. Others struck out across the fields and hills, as did many of the troops, seeking a route less congested, even if longer and more rugged. The panic fed upon itself, with frightening rumors spreading rapidly. Most persistent was the cry that Rebel dragoons were bearing down upon the defeated Federals, slaughtering everyone they could run upon, including the civilians.[29]

Sherman remarked that he "saw very little evidence of [the army's] being pursued," but frightened imaginations were working creatively. At Centreville "came pouring in the confused masses of men, [who were] without orders or system." Sherman thought the scene "was as disgraceful as words can portray," but he also doubted "if volunteers from any quarter could [have done] better." The scenes of that July Sunday profoundly impressed him, both the battle and the beaten army fleeing in panic. "For the first time I saw the Carnage of battle," he wrote. The handful of guerrilla-like clashes with Indians that Sherman had experienced in Florida seemed like nothing in comparison with Bull Run. Men were "lying in every conceivable shape, and mangled in a horrible way," he told Ellen. Yet he seemed equally moved by the suffering and slaughter of large numbers of horses—"horses running about riderless with blood streaming from their nostrils . . . [while others] were lying on the ground hitched to guns, gnawing their sides in death." Sherman liked horses, and the widespread destruction of the big, innocent animals, forced by humans into a bloody butchery, had to be a disturbing sight, especially when experienced for the first time.[30]

Bull Run also left Sherman marveling that he himself had survived the battle. "I was under heavy fire for hours," he wrote Ellen, "brushed on the Knee & Shoulder—my horse shot through the leg, and was every way exposed and cannot imagine how I escaped." He did not anticipate surviving the war. "I never expect again to move you from Lancaster," he told Ellen a few days later. "The simple chances of war, provided we adhere to the determination of subduing the South, will . . . involve the destruction of all able bodied men of this Generation and go pretty deep into the next." He considered it "folly to underestimate the task," as the nation had been doing. "The Real war has not yet begun," he declared. "The worst will be down the Mississippi," and in the Deep South, he thought, "provided of course that we get that far."[31]

Sherman's Bull Run experience, as revealed in his letters to both Ellen and John, and in his memoirs, left him more keenly aware than ever of the alarming vulnerability of the United States, as well as the distinct possibility of Confederate success. "Probably a more gloomy day [accented by a slow rain setting in] never presented itself" than that which followed the battle, wrote Sherman, when "all organization seemed to be at an end." He feared that the American people "won't realize the magnitude of the opposition until we are whaled several times a la Bull Run." Yet time was a luxury the nation could not afford. If the Rebels took Washington, Sherman had no doubt that the Confederacy "would be an established fact" and quickly recognized "by all foreign nations." He believed that, fortunately for the Union, General Beauregard "committed a sad* mistake in not pursuing us promptly. Had he done so, he could have . . . gone into Washington." After more reflection on the battle, and the failure of the Confederates to pursue, Sherman changed his opinion. "I am now satisfied that the Southern army is not much better than ours—else Beauregard would certainly have taken Washington." The Rebel failure to move against the capital meant that they "must have suffered [heavy losses]." Those two statements were much closer to the truth.[32]

Nevertheless, the presumed inadequacies of the Southerners hardly compensated for the failings of the U.S. forces. The effect of the Bull Run disaster was very serious and no one knew that better, during the days of recrimination that followed the battle, than General-in-Chief Winfield Scott. The general disgustedly called himself "the greatest coward in America." He said that he deserved to be removed from command "because I did not stand up [to the pressure of the politicians and the press] when my army was not in condition for fighting, and resist [them] to the last." The troops, wrote Sherman, "are discouraged beyond measure." Many of the men were determined to go home, usually contending their term of enlistment was up, or that some kind of family emergency demanded their presence.[33]

"They claim to be only 3 months men," Sherman told John, "whereas the War Department claims their services for three years." He reported that some of his regiments were "in a state of mutiny," and he had been compelled to place about one hundred men in irons, imprisoning them on board a warship. Sunday, August 18, presented one of the worst threats that Sherman faced. A group of the volunteers were so mutinous that, he informed John, "I had my regulars all ready with shotted guns to fire on our own troops," some of whom were not only claiming a dis-

* Used in the archaic sense of very bad.

charge but refusing to obey orders and threatening to spike the artillery. "For some hours," he told Ellen, describing the same confrontation, "I thought I would have to give the order to fire, but they did not like the artillery, and have gone back to their duty."[34]

One of those tense and trying days after Bull Run did prove memorable in a welcome, positive manner. President Lincoln, accompanied by Secretary of State William Seward, appeared unannounced at Sherman's camp. "We thought we would come out and see the 'boys,'" as Sherman recalled the President saying. Learning that Lincoln planned to offer the troops words of encouragement, Sherman boldly suggested that the President should "please discourage all cheering, noise, or any sort of confusion; that we had had enough of it before Bull Run to ruin any set of men." What the nation needed now, said Sherman, "were cool, thoughtful, hard-fighting soldiers—no more hurrahing, no more humbug." He wrote that the President accepted his remarks well, "in the most perfect good nature."[35]

Lincoln then stood in his carriage before the assembled troops and, in Sherman's estimate, "made one of the neatest, best, and most feeling addresses I ever listened to, referring to our late disaster at Bull Run, the high duties that still devolved on us, and the brighter days yet to come." When the soldiers began to cheer, the President promptly checked them: "Don't cheer, boys. I confess I rather like it myself, but Colonel Sherman here says it is not military; and I guess we had better defer to his opinion." In conclusion, Lincoln declared, as commander in chief, that he was determined the troops should receive "everything that the law allowed" and urged the men to appeal to him personally if in any way they felt that they were wronged. "The effect of this speech," remembered Sherman in his memoirs, "was excellent."[36]

However, there was a captain who immediately came forward, availing himself of the President's offer to hear any man with a grievance. "Mr. President, I have a grievance," he stated, relating that Sherman, that very morning, had threatened to shoot him. Of course the officer, who was a lawyer, neglected to say that he was about to leave the army without a proper discharge and made an arrogant show of the matter in front of a group of soldiers. Sherman said Lincoln looked at the man and queried: "Threatened to shoot you?" The captain confirmed, "Yes, sir, he threatened to shoot me." The President then looked toward Sherman, "and stooping his tall, spare form toward the officer," according to Sherman, "said to him in a loud stage-whisper, easily heard for some yards around: 'Well, if I were you, and he threatened to shoot, I would not trust him, for I believe he would do it.'" A howl of laughter erupted, and the man beat a hasty retreat. When Sherman explained the case to Lincoln, the President remarked: "Of course I didn't know anything about it, but I thought you knew your own business best."[37]

From that day forward Sherman held a higher opinion of Lincoln. Through the war years his respect for the President would grow, and possibly enhanced his favorable memory of Lincoln's performance that summer day in 1861. Sherman, who had hardly ever been moved by any speaker, with the exception of Henry Clay, was obviously impressed by Lincoln, both his speech and his reply to the "grievance" case. That day certainly did not resolve all of Sherman's problems with the volunteers— "called by courtesy soldiers," as he once disparagingly referred to them when writing Ellen. Speeches rarely bring significant, permanent change. Presumably though, the President's impact on some of the troops proved beneficial. Clearly Sherman thought so.[38]

In August Sherman received a promotion to brigadier general of volunteers, confirming a rumor he heard several days earlier. Since some brigade commanders were expecting a demotion and General McDowell had been relieved of command in favor of George B. McClellan, the advancement in rank came as a bit of a surprise. "I have just sworn in as Brigadier General," he informed Ellen, "and therefore suppose I might as well admit the title." The promotion, however, did little to alleviate the gloomy, dark mood that had fastened itself upon him since the defeat at Bull Run. Fundamentally, he was mired in a deep-seated disgust that had been building up for some time.

The volunteers continued to provoke him. They were "the most destructive men I have ever known." People who had experienced their depredations, he declared, would prefer "government by the Czar of

Russia ... rather than our American Volunteer Army." Not even Goths or Vandals "ever had less respect for the lives & property of friends and foes." On August 17, because of the threats of mutiny, as well as the volunteers' never-ending grumbling and growling about clothing, shoes, beef, sick wives and more, Sherman told Ellen that "I have not undressed of a night since Bull Run." He supposed that he should "make a requisition for two wet nurses per soldier to nurse them in their helpless, pitiful condition."[39]

Having resisted returning to the army until he thought the new administration and the Congress were showing signs of taking the crisis seriously, Sherman was disappointed, both before and after Bull Run, as he observed widespread confusion and incompetence. "Out of this Chaos some order in time must arise, but how or when I can not tell." In the meantime, "the muddle," as he characterized the disconcerting mess in a letter to Ellen, gripped the nation's war effort. He feared that "our old Government may disintegrate and new Combinations" be formed. Kentucky and Tennessee, in this context, he considered critical. Sherman told John that unless the United States could control Kentucky and Tennessee, which he correctly viewed as a strategic entity, "it is a doubtful question whether the Federal Government can restore the Old Union."[40]

Even more basic, Sherman's long-standing distrust of democracy came to the fore. Democratic-republican government, as he analyzed the institution, was inherently weak when attempting to mount a war effort. "I doubt," he wrote Ellen, "if our Democratic form of Government admits of the organization and discipline without which our army is a mob." The volunteers are "all that we have got and God only knows the issue." Fortunately for the United States, "our adversaries have the weakness of slavery in their midst to offset our Democracy." He deemed it "beyond human wisdom to say which is the greater evil."[41]

Writing to his influential father-in-law, Sherman believed that "all should know that our defeat resulted from our own want of discipline & not from the superiority of our Enemy." He declared that "the defeat began with the Private soldiers [meaning volunteers], who would not reform their ranks or pay any heeds to our commands—I saw the colonels commanding, remonstrating and begging—I did so myself, and I heard McDowell plead with them to . . . make a new effort—but the men kept edging off in masses to the Rear." If the impression should "go down in history that the officers failed," he assured Ewing, then the analysis of Bull Run "would be an injustice and false." The volunteer soldiers must learn "that if at fault they will be held to account," just as, added Sherman, will be their officers. Otherwise, "if like Politicians we become afraid of the rank & file of our army, then our nation is at an End." The bottom line: the volunteers would have to become as good as regulars. In the meantime, he wrote John, he still felt "as one grasping in the dark."[42]

ABOUT THE MIDDLE of August, Sherman received a note from Robert Anderson, widely viewed in the North as a hero since Fort Sumter. Anderson wanted Sherman to meet him at Willard's Hotel in Washington. Sherman rode over and learned that Anderson had just been appointed commander of the Department of the Cumberland, headquartered in Louisville. He would soon be leaving for Kentucky, where events were thought to be approaching a crisis. Anderson wanted Sherman with him, "as his right hand." The objective was to marshal pro-Union forces, keep Kentucky in the Union, and try to assist the Federal men of Tennessee as well, especially in east Tennessee. Sherman was "perfectly willing to go." He wanted to get out of the Washington area, where mutinous volunteers and "clamors for discharge on every possible frivolous pretext" continued to plague him. Also, he had been wanting to go west, because he viewed the region and the mission as crucial, telling Ellen, "upon it may hang the existence of the present Government."[43]

Although Sherman was pleased to serve as Anderson's second in command, he did want a clear understanding that his role was not to be altered. Sherman informed Lincoln of "my extreme desire" to remain in a subordinate capacity. The President readily agreed, although surprised by his request. Lincoln was constantly badgered by generals seeking positions of top command. Apparently no one except Sherman had asked to be kept in a subordinate position. "Not till I see daylight ahead," he wrote Ellen, "do I want to lead." By late August, Sherman was on his way to the Bluegrass State. However, instead of relief, he was entering upon the most trying and embarrassing period of his Civil War career.[44]

Chapter Fourteen

"Crazy" in Kentucky

Sherman welcomed the Kentucky assignment. The Bluegrass State lay in the great strategic-logistic center of the war. Whichever power "controls the Ohio and the Mississippi will ultimately control this continent," Sherman wrote in a letter to Secretary of the Treasury Chase, on October 14, 1861. He had expressed the same conviction, in nearly identical words, to his brother John, as mentioned earlier. In fact, he stated this viewpoint many times, to various people. Any realistic military assessment of the war in the western theater would inevitably involve "the physical geography of the country." The Mississippi River, he declared, was "too grand an element to be divided, and all its extent [including the major tributaries] must of necessity be under one government." Sherman even apologized to his Louisianan friend Professor David Boyd for again stating the foregoing, "which we have said ... a thousand times." Because he expected that the Mississippi River would become "the grand field" of Union offensive operations, Sherman realized that Kentucky and Tennessee, united by rivers and railroads, as well as centrally located, were crucial to mounting a victorious campaign against the heart of the Confederacy. Above all, Kentucky was the key to Federal success in the western theater.[1]

Abraham Lincoln, soon after the conflict began, wrote, "I think to lose Kentucky is nearly the same as to lose the whole game." Sherman would have agreed. Elaborating on the issue, Lincoln said, "Kentucky gone, we can not hold Missouri, nor, as I think, Maryland. These all against us, and the job on our hands is too large for us. We would as well consent to separation at once, including the surrender of [Washington, D.C.]." Lincoln probably was right about the decisive impact if those three slave states had joined the Confederacy. One historian has calculated that Kentucky, Missouri and Maryland "would have added 45 percent to the white population and military manpower of the Confederacy, 80 percent to its manufacturing capacity, and nearly 40 percent to its supply of horses and mules." Those three states would also have contributed 120,360 more square miles to the Confederacy. Already the eleven states that seceded from the Union constituted some 726,721 square miles, an immense area considerably larger than all sixteen of the eastern and midwestern free states, which totaled 541,305 square miles. The sheer size of the Confederacy, when one thought about trying to subdue the region, had to give any sensible person pause—all the more if every slave state joined the new nation.[2]

Back in December 1860, Sherman advised his brother John, "twould be folly to coerce" in the event that all fifteen slave states seceded. "The only feasible plan," he wrote, "would be to make a compact confederacy of states that have common binding self interests to hold them together." Fortunately for the preservation of the Union, Kentucky, Missouri and Maryland remained loyal to the United States. So too did tiny Delaware; but composed of only three counties—two at high tide, according to the witticism—and consisting of less than 2,000 square miles, while located on the eastern periphery of the nation, that state was neither large enough nor in a position to be of much consequence. What a dramatic contrast was Kentucky—the most crucial of the border slave states for both the Union and the Confederacy.[3]

This was not because of the Bluegrass State's sizable population and territory, its numerous resources or its many ancestral ties with Virginia, which fostered "Southern" attachments and sympathies. While all of the above contributed to Kentucky's significance, the crux of the matter was the state's strategic location. One need only study a map and examine the course of the rivers and railroads, to understand the importance of Kentucky in the Civil War. Unlike any other war in American history, the Civil War was going to be fought along the rivers and the railroads. If the United States controlled Kentucky, it possessed the principal avenues, both waterways and railways, for invading and waging war against the heart of the vast western Confederacy. To lose Kentucky might not have been "to lose the whole game," but it would have made winning "the game" much more difficult.

For nearly five hundred miles, the Ohio River meanders along the northern border of Kentucky, winding westward toward its confluence with the Mississippi. Shortly before meeting the Mississippi, the Ohio is joined by two of its major tributaries from the south, the Cumberland and the Tennessee. The Cumberland River, in the hands of the Union, provided a route into the center of Tennessee at Nashville; the Tennessee River, broad and deep, penetrated across the Volunteer State to northern Alabama; while the great Mississippi, of course, pierced the Confederacy all the way to the vital port of New Orleans and on to the Gulf.

Nor was the steam-powered, smoke-belching Iron Horse a matter of small import when analyzing Kentucky's significance. From the major marshaling point of Louisville on the Ohio, the Louisville & Nashville Railroad was an obvious line of advance straight into the Confederacy at Tennessee's capital city. From Nashville, rail connections continued south to northern Alabama at Decatur, and southeast to Stevenson, Alabama, and on to Chattanooga, Tennessee, with all three towns located on the strategic, east–west running, Memphis & Charleston line—in other words, directly into the central South. Also, from Columbus, Kentucky, on the Mississippi River, the Mobile & Ohio rails extended south through Jackson, Tennessee, to a junction with the Memphis & Charleston at Corinth, Mississippi, and from thence ran most of the length of the Magnolia State before reaching a terminus at Mobile, Alabama. Not to be overlooked was the Memphis, Clarksville & Louisville Railroad, providing a link from Bowling Green, Kentucky, through west Tennessee to the Mississippi River at Memphis.

From a Confederate perspective, Kentucky was equally significant. If the Rebels could control the Bluegrass State, they would possess an innate defensive barrier at the Ohio River. The advantages of such a position can scarcely be overstated. "A Confederate Kentucky," wrote historian James Rawley, "would have thrown the southern frontier to the Ohio [River], fronting on the southern portions of Ohio, Indiana, and Illinois—where 2,600,000 persons had a sentimental attachment to the South. ... Kentucky's northern river boundary could afford a natural military frontier for the southern armies." The Confederates could then effectively blockade the Ohio River and, even more important, deny to the United States—whose military forces had to take the offensive, had to invade and conquer the Confederacy if they hoped to save the Union— any adequate military base, or feasible avenue of invasion. From the Appalachian Mountains in the east to the Mississippi in the west, the Federal armies would be stymied. For all these reasons the United States badly needed to possess Kentucky. The Rebels, then, conversely, would have no good way of saving the long and narrow state of Tennessee or the Mississippi River, or of stopping an invasion of the Deep South.[4]

Kentucky's situation, with both the United States and the Confederacy desiring control, was highly precarious and volatile. No border state was more deeply divided and ambivalent in her sympathies. Kentucky was supportive of slavery and enjoyed close ties with the South, yet she was strongly devoted to the Union and nourished a proud tradition of compromise—both of the latter personified by the late, legendary Henry Clay. Obviously, too, Kentuckians did not relish the prospect of their state's becoming a battleground.

Consequently, Kentucky tried to stay out of the war, and on May 20 issued a proclamation of neutrality. "In the long run," observed Bruce Catton, "this policy was bound to fail." Another writer termed the neutrality stand "preposterous." Perhaps neutrality was absurd, but from Kentucky's perspective it was also understandable; and initially the United States, as well as the Confederacy, respected her stand. Neither side wanted to commit any act that might push the state into the camp of the enemy. In the meantime, both sides prepared for, as they believed, the inevitable day when Kentucky's neutrality would come to an end.[5]

Kentucky recruits for the Union were gathered north of the Ohio River near Cincinnati, while Kentuckians favoring the Confederacy were being marshaled at a camp south of the Kentucky–Tennessee state line, near the Cumberland River. Within the state, the Kentucky State Guard (militia) was known to be pro-Confederate. Thus Kentucky Unionists soon formed their own militia, calling it the Home Guard. Men favoring the United States were greatly encouraged when the summer elections placed a clear majority of Unionists in both the U.S. Congress and the Kentucky state legislature. All the while the situation in western Kentucky, because of the vital rivers, grew more tense. If the Kentucky legislature declared for the Union, military force appeared to be essential to back up the decision.[6]

BY SEPTEMBER 1, Robert Anderson, George Thomas and Sherman had arrived in Cincinnati, where Sherman said "several prominent gentlemen of Kentucky [among them Joshua Speed, one of Lincoln's longtime, closest friends] met us to discuss the situation." The Kentucky state legislature was in session at Frankfort, and expected to take action in favor of the Union as soon as Anderson, a native Kentuckian, commanded a military force strong enough to ensure success against any Rebel challenges—which were widely anticipated. Anderson knew that somehow he had to get more troops. Before he and Thomas headed on to Louisville, where department headquarters would be established, Anderson sent Sherman to Indianapolis, Indiana, and Springfield, Illinois, in quest of soldiers. Conferring with Governor Oliver P. Morton of Indiana, Sherman found him "willing in a general way to help Kentucky," but all the new regiments, "as fast as they were mustered in," were being dispatched either to McClellan's army at Washington or Frémont's command in Missouri. At the next meeting, with Governor Richard Yates at Springfield, "I found the same general activity and zeal [as in Indiana]," remembered Sherman, but the new Illinois regiments were promised to Frémont. Thus Sherman pushed on to St. Louis, hoping for assistance from the nationally famous Pathfinder of the West.[7]

Sherman found the 1856 Republican presidential nominee "surrounded by sentinels," conducting himself as "a great potentate," but "very communicative." Sherman's negative opinion of Frémont, formed when they met in California, grew stronger. He wrote Ellen that Frémont "has called about him men who will swindle the Government and bring disgrace on us all." Sherman had known several of these people in California. He said they were "the very men" who were instigators of the Vigilance Committee in San Francisco. They were guilty of "open corruption" while in the Golden State, and Sherman declared they are "now the advisors of Frémont."[8]

Returning to the Planters' House, Sherman spied another California adventurer, "old Baron Steinberger," whom he purposely avoided. His presence, Sherman wrote, "recalled the maxim, 'where the vultures are, there is a carcass close by.'" Also, at the Planters' House, Sherman learned of "another Californian, a Mormon, who had the contract for a line of redoubts which Frémont had ordered to be constructed around the city." Profitable military contracts had drawn to St. Louis and Frémont, sarcastically commented Sherman, "some of the most enterprising men of California." Later reflecting that "in a very short time, Frémont fell from his high estate in Missouri," Sherman said he "suspected" the corruption of the Californians "can account for the fact." He might also have noted Frémont's Emancipation Proclamation in Missouri, which the President was forced to disavow when the Pathfinder arrogantly refused to retract his high-handed action. As for troops for Kentucky, Frémont was then totally focused on his own plans and problems. Eventually, he did order five regiments to Sherman.[9]

Sherman headed back east to Louisville, disappointed and displeased. "The great trouble," he wrote Ellen, "is that secessionists know they must fight, [while] the Union People look to the United States as some mythical power with unlimited quantities of men and money." If the nation could not, or would not, provide the essential men and armaments to fight for the vital state of Kentucky, he feared there was scant hope of saving the Union.

Nonetheless, major news was coming in from western Kentucky, and it was decidedly in favor of the United States. The Confederacy had brazenly violated Kentucky's neutrality. General Leonidas Polk took it upon himself to seize the town of Columbus, strategically located on high bluffs above the Mississippi River. Confederate President Jefferson Davis, who apparently possessed more political sense and concern than Polk, at least in this instance, ordered Polk to withdraw the troops from Columbus. But the Episcopal bishop turned general boldly refused. The predictable result was that Kentucky's aroused, Union-dominated legislature denounced the Rebel incursion and invited the United States to drive out the Confederates.[10]

Probably a Kentucky declaration for the Union would have occurred eventually anyway, but Polk's unauthorized and politically unwise movement was not even of military value. He had advanced into Columbus because he knew those bluffs, if strongly fortified, could prevent any Federal gunboats or transports from descending the river. Fearing that the Union forces might take Columbus, Polk determined to strike first. Columbus, however, was worthless to the Rebels unless they seized Paducah as well. The Tennessee River flows into the Ohio at Paducah, and was an obvious waterway into the heart of the Confederacy.

If the Confederates possessed both Paducah and Columbus, they could block a Union advance on either the Mississippi or Tennessee. The mouth of the Tennessee at Paducah actually was the key for both sides. If U.S. forces controlled it, the military value of Columbus to the Confederacy was negated, because as soon as the Federals moved south on the Tennessee, Columbus would be outflanked. Advancing on the Tennessee, as events in coming months demonstrated, was just as good as going down the Mississippi. Polk had intended to take Paducah as well as Columbus, but he allowed the Union forces at Cairo, Illinois, under the then unknown U. S. Grant, to steal a march on him and occupy Paducah. Polk should never have seized Columbus unless he simultaneously moved into Paducah.[11]

"On the day I reached Louisville," remembered Sherman, "the excitement ran high" due to the Confederate incursion and the Federal response. As a result, Sherman said Louisville "was full of all sorts of rumors." Most disturbing were reports that Simon Bolivar Buckner, a native Kentuckian from Munfordville on the Green River, was advancing on Louisville from Bowling Green, leading a formidable Confederate army. Although actually only 5,000 strong, Buckner's command was magnified by rumor to three times that many. The president of the Louisville & Nashville Railroad, former Secretary of the Treasury James Guthrie, received an alarming telegraph that one of his railroad bridges, only thirty miles south of Louisville, had been burned by the Rebels. General Anderson and Sherman listened as Guthrie informed them of the railroad's general vulnerability. "Several high and important trestles," spanned a great ravine just south of Salt Creek. If those were destroyed, Guthrie said months would be required to replace them. Also, at Muldraugh's Hill, just a little south of the vital trestles, reportedly lay a natural rampart covering Louisville. Sherman said "we all supposed that General Buckner, who was familiar with the ground, was aiming for [that strong position] from which to operate against Louisville." General Anderson ordered Sherman to secure possession of Muldraugh's Hill at once, before the Confederates could reach it.[12]

Collecting a mixed force of Home Guards and volunteers, numbering about 3,000 in all, Sherman boarded a train at midnight, and steamed south toward Muldraugh's Hill. Near daybreak, he reached the burned-out bridge over the Salt Creek, which forced the train to halt. Railroad hands went to work rebuilding the bridge, while Sherman sent a contingent of troops marching farther south to investigate the Louisville & Nashville's high trestles. Fortunately, they were all securely in place, and Sherman then pushed his entire command on to Muldraugh's Hill. He also learned that General Buckner had not even crossed the Green River. Nevertheless, he believed Confederate General Albert Sidney Johnston, who had recently assumed overall command of the Rebel forces in the west, was fortifying Bowling Green, "and preparing for a systematic advance into Kentucky." Sherman gave the Rebels far too much credit. "All the secessionists," he claimed, "are armed and flocking to Buckner's Command." In reality, Buckner was overestimating Sherman's forces almost as badly as Sherman had exaggerated Buckner's, while Johnston complained that Southerners "were not up to the revolutionary point." Lacking men, munitions and supplies, Johnston could not possibly launch an offensive.[13]

By October 1, Sherman's forces at Muldraugh's Hill were bolstered by fresh troops sent out from Louisville, and numbered between 4,000 and 5,000. Regardless, Sherman was ensconced in gloom. His command, organized in a two-brigade division, had little training and inadequate arms. About the lack of arms he constantly complained. He also believed that spies were in his midst, and newspapermen were a constant worry. The perennial discipline problem continued to aggravate. "The volunteers," he wrote his father-in-law, "are killing hogs, cattle, burning fence rails, and taking hay and wheat, all calculated to turn the People against us." The Kentuckians and Tennesseans "are all imbued with a bitterness that you can not comprehend and will jump at the chance to destroy us whom they now regard as northern hordes of Invaders." Expounding upon the perceived Southern superiority, he told Ellen that the enemy "swarm at Every point from Washington to Leavenworth . . . Superior to us in numbers and equipment."[14]

Little wonder that Sherman feared he would be cut off at Muldraugh's Hill, with the Confederates getting between him and Louisville and destroying the railroad trestles. He would then have to try to fight his way back to the Ohio River, through both enemy forces and a hostile populace. Exaggerating the Rebel numbers and the danger, while frustrated and obsessing about what he considered the woefully inadequate measures of the United States to counter the secessionists, Sherman wrote Ellen that he usually "was up all night." Not only was he suffering from sleep deprivation, but the weather in early October was "cold and wet," which likely would bring on asthma. Then things got worse. General Anderson resigned his position as head of the Department of the Cumberland, and Sherman had to take command. He was very upset, for unexpectedly he had the responsibility for all of Kentucky—and he was not up to the job.[15]

Anderson had resigned because he could not deal with the Kentucky situation. Like Sherman, he overestimated Confederate strength, while the inadequacies of the Home Guards and the Federal volunteers, in numbers, training and armaments, weighed heavily on his mind. Anderson's health was not good and growing worse. "The daily correspondence between General Anderson and myself," recalled Sherman, "satisfied me that the worry and harassment at Louisville were exhausting his strength and health." When Sherman relieved him, Anderson said that "he could not stand the mental torture of his command any longer, and that he must go away, or it would kill him." He had recommended Sherman to Washington as his successor, and the War Department so ordered.[16]

Once Sherman was suddenly elevated to command of the Department of the Cumberland, against his will and despite the President's promise that he could remain in a subordinate capacity, his dark mood turned yet more gloomy, his forecasts of doom more frequent. Knowing Lincoln, Sherman decided to write him directly. He said the Confederates "will make a more desperate effort [to control Kentucky] than they have . . . Missouri." The Union force to counter them, both those present and those expected, Sherman declared "entirely inadequate." He told John Sherman that "the South . . . must have Kentucky . . . [and had] already invaded the state with five times my forces." He even claimed, in that same letter to his brother, that "I am to be sacrificed." Addressing the governor of Ohio, Sherman stated that "never before was such [an inadequate] body of men thrust headlong into such danger."[17]

If Sherman were aware of the legendary meaning of the name Kentucky—"dark and bloody ground"—he probably would have thought the designation appropriate. "Some terrible [and no doubt bloody] disaster is inevitable," he told John, in still another prophecy of impending, decisive defeat in Kentucky. Just as the "dark and bloody ground" is apparently without foundation as the meaning of "Kentucky," so too Sherman's forecasts of a massive Southern advance would prove to be without substance. The Sherman of Kentucky was far from the confident, conquering general of the later war, a commander who could successfully lead 100,000 men against the enemy. Confederate Albert Johnston, if he could somehow have known Sherman's thinking in the fall of 1861, would have breathed easier.[18]

Johnston faced an awesome, perhaps ultimately impossible assignment. He commanded the vast Confederate Department Number Two,
which extended across hundreds of miles, from the Appalachian Mountains westward across the Mississippi River, and through Arkansas to
the Indian territory. The early run of Southern volunteers had dwindled
away by the fall, while Kentuckians never rose to the Confederacy in the
strength that many secessionists anticipated. Defending such a long line,
with inadequate numbers for the task, and those poorly armed (if armed
at all), called for extraordinary measures. Johnston's plan was simple
and effective. He feared that a Union advance would quickly uncover
the inferiority of his forces, so he put up a big bluff and hoped the Federals bought it. Sherman, and Anderson before him, as well as some other
Union officers, proved ideal subjects for the Confederate ruse.[19]

General Johnston had stationed most of the Southern regiments that
were east of the Mississippi River in one of three places: on the river bluffs
at Columbus; in front of Cumberland Gap, several hundred miles east of
the great river; and in the center, more or less, at Bowling Green. The
idea was for the Confederates to demonstrate aggressively in all three
areas. General Buckner, commanding the Rebels at Bowling Green,
astride the Louisville & Nashville Railroad, was quite active, mounting
seemingly menacing thrusts which, although bogus, convinced Sherman that a strong Confederate army was about to descend upon Louisville. He was sure that the enemy numbers were much greater than his.
Writing Salmon P. Chase to justify his requests for more supplies and
troops, Sherman admitted that he had no reliable information about the
plans of the enemy; nevertheless, he told the secretary of the treasury
that he expected the Rebels would first clear Kentucky of Federal forces,
and then threaten Cincinnati, before turning to approach St. Louis from
the east.[20]

Then in mid-October, only a few days after Sherman had replaced
General Anderson as commander of the Department of the Cumberland, he engaged in a fateful encounter with Secretary of War Simon
Cameron and Lorenzo Thomas, adjutant general of the army. Cameron
and Thomas arrived in Louisville after a trip to St. Louis investigat-

ing John C. Frémont's extravagant contracts and expenses. The idea of the incompetent Cameron, whose administration as secretary of war was blighted by waste and corruption, investigating anyone, even Frémont, is at once amusing and disturbing—a reminder of that long line of politicians who are primed to cast the first stones at others accused of faults similar to their own. Cameron and Thomas had intended to hurry on toward Washington, but Sherman insisted that they spend the night in Louisville, because he wanted to discuss military conditions in Kentucky, hoping to impress upon them the dire situation—"as bad as bad could be." Agreeing to stay the night, they headed to Sherman's room on the first floor of the Galt House, where the "excellent landlord," according to Sherman's appraisal, "sent us a good lunch and something to drink."[21]

Secretary Cameron, as Sherman remembered, "was not well, and lay on my bed" throughout their conversation. After some discussion about Frémont's situation in Missouri, as well as a touch of general conversation, Cameron was ready to hear about Kentucky. "Now General Sherman, tell us of your troubles," he instructed. Sherman said that he preferred to discuss their business in private. Cameron assured him, however, that all present are "friends"—even using the term "family," as Sherman recalled—and that "you may speak your mind freely and without restraint." Among those present was Brigadier General Thomas J. Wood of Kentucky, who later said that Cameron's response to Sherman's privacy request was "with some little testiness of manner." Also, the secretary did not mention that one "friend" was a newspaper reporter from the *New York Tribune*. His name was Samuel Wilkerson, an accomplished sycophant, whose ingratiating skills had succeeded in making him a favorite of Cameron.[22]

Sherman should have been skeptical about the unknown faces, and probably was. Nevertheless, he felt compelled to present Cameron with a full picture of the military state of affairs in Kentucky as he saw it. Apparently, he did not restrain himself in the least and proceeded to develop his gloomy analysis in considerable detail. He deplored the lack of suitable weapons. Most of the arms available were outdated and defective European muskets. He said that he had to have more and better equipment. Also, he argued that troop strength was far from adequate. He was defending a front of more than three hundred miles, but his forces were appallingly weak in comparison with those of McClellan and Frémont, whose fronts were only a third as long. When Cameron inquired how many soldiers he needed, Sherman gave the number that he and Anderson, when they came west, had agreed would be necessary to defend the Bluegrass State: 60,000. In order to take the offensive, however, Sherman said he would need 200,000 men.[23]

Cameron was shocked. "You astonish me!" he exclaimed. From where would such numbers possibly come? Sherman assured Cameron that Northerners would flock to the Union cause in great numbers if the War Department would stop discouraging their service by claiming that they were not needed. He thought too that some of the troops being sent to McClellan and Frémont should be reassigned to the Kentucky front. He declared that Kentucky's youth were hastening to join the Confederacy—the same story Cameron and Thomas would hear when they reached Frankfort and Lexington. That Kentucky's men were choosing the South was nothing more than a general impression. No one had assembled any data on the subject. Whatever Kentucky's potential Federal manpower base may have been, however, the numbers Sherman wanted most likely would require augmentation from outside the Bluegrass State.[24]

Sherman said that, before leaving Louisville, Secretary Cameron ordered all unassigned troops available in the region to Kentucky, told Lorenzo Thomas to make notes of their conversation and promised that he would further consider Sherman's requests when they got back to Washington. Cameron thought that Sherman, in large degree, had overestimated his needs. Worse—if *New York Tribune* reporter Samuel Wilkerson is to be believed—Wilkerson confided to correspondent Henry Villard that Cameron had concluded Sherman was "unbalanced and that it would not do to leave him in command." Only two weeks later the *New York Tribune* published the adjutant general's official report of Cameron's trip, with noticeable attention to the meeting with Sherman. Rival newspapermen believed the wily Wilkerson actually wrote the report, which Thomas signed, or at the least, composed portions of the document. Henry Villard thought the "broad insinuations that Sherman's mind was upset" bore the stamp of Wilkerson's hand. Sherman's estimate of 200,000 troops for offensive operations was cast in an absurd vein, while there was no mention of the 60,000 men he said would be sufficient for Kentucky's defense. In contrast to the portrayal of Sherman's nervous apprehensions and exaggerations, Cameron's supposed wisdom and calm demeanor were impressively presented.[25]

When Sherman read the report in the New York paper he was quite upset. He was yet more aroused upon learning that some of the men at his meeting with Cameron were newspaper people, particularly Samuel Wilkerson, the favorite of the war secretary. Visions of the California reporters who had plagued him during the banking years now resurfaced, reinforcing his view that the press could never be trusted. Indeed, Sherman believed newspapers not only were making a bad situation worse but actually constituted a threat to the preservation of the Union. He had a point. During the Civil War, newspapers frequently published information that was useful to the enemy—information sometimes acquired in deceptive and underhanded ways.

Sherman wrote Adjutant General Thomas on November 4, noting his awareness that "my estimate of the number of troops needed for this line, viz, 200,000, has been construed to my prejudice." He declared that "the country never has and probably never will comprehend" the force and numbers of the enemy and the strength required to defeat the Rebels. "Do not conclude, as before," he told Thomas in another letter two days later, "that I exaggerate the facts. They are as stated and the future looks as dark as possible." He also initiated the possibility of being relieved from command, if the War Department so desired.[26]

In months to come, Sherman's 200,000 troops for offensive operations would not seem much, if any, exaggeration. At the time, however, the figure was shocking to a lot of people. Furthermore, his calls for additional men and arms, and prophecies of impending doom if the quotas were not met, grew increasingly frequent, blunt and demanding, almost desperate. The more he obsessed about the situation, the worse it seemed, and the more unguarded became his dark pronouncements. Simultaneously, his rather eccentric behavior did not help his image. He seemed to talk, pace and smoke cigars incessantly. Long gone were the confident assurances to Ellen, when first traveling to California, that he had stopped smoking, never to resume. Typically he stayed up until 3:00 a.m., which was when the telegraph office closed, ready to pounce on any dispatches that might come in. Returning to the Galt House, he often continued to pace and smoke, before going to bed shortly before sunrise. His dress, never impressive, grew more slovenly. Sometimes he donned a stovepipe hat, calling yet more attention to his slender frame and unconventional ways. He might interrupt others when they talked, yet grew irritated if he himself were interrupted. The general impression he conveyed was that of an excitable yet distant personality, plagued by strange behavior and noticeable quirks.[27]

Sherman was taking himself and his command too seriously, and the mounting stress was destroying him. Ellen had once implored him, gently and tactfully: "Do write me a cheerful letter that I may have it to refer to when the gloomy ones come." Sherman retaliated: "How anybody could be cheerful now I can't tell." He probably reached his nadir in early to mid-November. He spoke to his brother John as if the Confederates were a species of supermen. "I have no doubt," he declared, that the Rebels are planning "a simultaneous attack on St. Louis, Louisville and Cincinnati. . . . They have the force necessary for success, and . . . the men capable of designing and executing it." This is an incredible statement, particularly coming from a man who, only two and one half years later, would prove himself a master of logistics in planning and leading the decisive Atlanta campaign. Why he, of all people, did not see the absurdity of such a pronouncement about Confederate offensive prowess is baffling. Continuing his morose and sullen epistle to John, Sherman expressed a "conviction . . . that our Government is destroyed, and . . . no human power can restore it."[28]

Then he told John of the green troops from Wisconsin and Minnesota who had just arrived in Kentucky without arms. "I can not but look upon it as absolutely sacrificing them," he declared. He saw "no hope [of their survival]. In their present raw and undisciplined condition," he considered them "helpless." Such striking concern for the untrained and unarmed is more understandable when assessed in the context of the recent bridge-burning mission Sherman had sanctioned in east Tennessee. In an effort to destroy Rebel rail transportation, Tennessee Unionists burned nine bridges, and heavily damaged five others. Sherman decided not to send Federal troops to their support, as originally intended, having concluded, because of perceived Rebel pressure along the Green River, that the risk to Kentucky's security was too great.[29]

The bridge burners were quickly apprehended by Confederate authorities and charged with treason, and several were hanged. Sherman felt responsible for their deaths. In a letter to John several weeks later, he wrote, "That the men . . . suffered death has been the chief source of my despondency." He believed that "I may be chiefly responsible for it." The execution of those men "weighed on me so that I felt unequal to the burden [of command in Kentucky], and gave it up. This horrid war," he proclaimed, "has turned human nature wrong side out."[30]

Those who know only the Sherman of hardhanded war—the Sherman of Memphis and of the destructive march through Georgia and the Carolinas, the man who could instruct a subordinate during the Atlanta campaign, "should you, under the impulse of natural anger, . . . hang the wretch, I approve the act before-hand"—miss the essential character of this complex soldier. He was indeed a sensitive man, naturally tender-hearted, who required time to accept and adjust to the mass bloodshed and inherent cruelty of war, particularly when he served as a leader. This was a significant, perhaps determining part of his difficulties in Kentucky.

Sherman was greatly relieved when Don Carlos Buell arrived in Louisville on November 15 to assume command of the Department of the Cumberland. As noted earlier, Sherman himself, in a despondent mood, had suggested the possibility of someone else's taking command in Kentucky; it was a responsibility he never wanted, as he reflected on Lincoln's promise that he could remain in a subordinate position. When George B. McClellan replaced the aged General Scott as overall

U.S. Army commander on November 1, Sherman's pessimistic messages led McClellan to send Colonel Thomas M. Key to report firsthand on the Kentucky situation. When Key concluded that the stress of command had overwhelmed Sherman, General Buell was sent to replace him. Sherman was ordered to St. Louis, where he would be under the command of Henry Halleck, his friend from California days, who had recently replaced Frémont.[31]

Sherman's deteriorating mental and physical state had already prompted an aide, Captain Frederick Prime, to send an urgent message to the Ewing home in Lancaster: "Send Mrs. Sherman and the youngest boy down to relieve General Sherman's mind from the pressure of business." Prime added the phrase "no cause for alarm," but obviously his words were inherently disturbing—all the more so in view of Sherman's recent depressing letters to his wife. Ellen went at once, along with sons Willy and Tommy, as well as her brother Philemon. She found her husband had eaten and slept very little for some time. Officers at headquarters clearly were worried about him, and Ellen concluded that he needed a long rest from his duties.

She sent a letter to John Sherman, telling him about Cump's situation. John responded with a strong message, written "with the freedom of a brother" he said, telling Cump in candid terms that his gloomy view of affairs was greatly overstated. Not only was he "in error," but also under the spell of "some strange delusions," and his mind was casting "a sombre shadow on everything." He had become "abrupt," and worse, "almost repulsive" in his dealings with others. It was as if John were trying to shake his brother back to reality—as John saw reality. When Sherman replied, he said, concerning the possibility he might be wrong, "I hope to God tis so," but immediately launched into a defense of his oft stated negative views.[32]

Ellen felt a little better about her husband's situation when General Buell relieved him. She still believed, however, that he needed several weeks of rest. Realizing that such a break was not about to happen—not immediately anyway—she and the boys headed back to Lancaster, while Sherman prepared to report for duty in the Department of the Missouri at St. Louis. Arriving in late November, he and Halleck exchanged greetings, probably genuinely pleased to see each other once more. Not surprisingly, the rumors of Sherman's Kentucky problems and vexations had preceded him.

Nevertheless, Halleck sent Sherman west to inspect the troops. He found the Union forces widely separated, located at Sedalia, Tipton and Jefferson City. The camp at Sedalia was nearly thirty miles from the troops at Tipton, for example—too far distant to render assistance in case of an attack. As in Kentucky, Sherman worried that the Rebels might strike at any moment. He ordered the men concentrated in a more defensible position, which was sound advice, and a step that Halleck eventually sanctioned. At the time, however, Halleck wired Sherman to make no movement without orders from him. Sherman complied, countermanding his own orders, and returned to St. Louis, as Halleck had instructed. There Ellen, having again become extremely worried about his health, awaited him. Halleck may have been motivated by the report of the departmental doctor, who claimed Sherman was unfit for command. "Perhaps also, even more so," as Basil Liddell Hart perceptively observed decades ago, Halleck "was nettled at the implication that his forces were left open to surprise." Halleck was a touchy fellow who, when crossed, could be vindictive. Whatever the motivations of "Old Brains," he wrote General McClellan, picking up on camp rumors and claiming Sherman had been "stampeded" by fear of the enemy, and that his presence was having a detrimental effect on the troops.[33]

When Sherman got back to St. Louis, a distressed Ellen implored him to take a break and rest. Halleck also recommended rest. Unknown to Sherman, he informed McClellan that Sherman's "physical and mental system" was broken, rendering him "for the present entirely unfit for duty." Reluctantly, Sherman requested a leave for three weeks and accompanied Ellen to Lancaster, and the rented house near her parents. Without question he needed rest, but the manner in which the leave developed, with his wife insisting on taking him home—the Ohio home located close to his father-in-law—was humiliating. Perhaps even the army could not provide the independence for which he yearned.[34]

As if recent events were not bad enough, the *Cincinnati Commercial* struck like a tsunami on December 11. GENERAL WILLIAM T. SHERMAN INSANE screamed the headline. "The painful intelligence reaches us, in such form that we are not at liberty to disclose it," declared the *Commercial*, "that General William T. Sherman, late commander of the Department of the Cumberland, is insane. It appears that he was, at the time while commanding in Kentucky, stark mad." The paper stated that Sherman once telegraphed the War Department three times in one day, requesting permission to retreat from Kentucky into Indiana, and claimed he frightened leading Union men of Louisville "almost out of their wits," with assertions that Louisville could not be held against "the overwhelming" Confederate forces. Also, the paper said, "The retreat from Cumberland Gap was one of his mad freaks." He was sent to Missouri, where "the shocking fact that he was a madman was developed by orders that his subordinates knew to be preposterous and refused to obey." It was "providential that the country has not to mourn the loss of an army, through the loss of mind of a general into whose hands was committed such vast responsibility," who now "has . . . been relieved altogether from command."[35]

That Sherman was embarrassed and distressed by the offending article is an understatement. "Among the keenest feelings of my life," he wrote the "Honorable Thomas Ewing" the day after the painful piece appeared, "is that arising from a consciousness that you will be mortified beyond measure at the disgrace which has befallen me—by the pronouncement in the Cincinnati Commercial that I am insane." Sherman felt certain that the accusation "will be widely circulated, and will impair my personal influence for much time to come, if not always." He was correct in assuming that the press attacks would spread around the nation.[36]

For a man like Sherman, long and justly proud of an excellent education at the U.S. Military Academy, the realization that his honor, one of the most cherished values of the West Point creed, had been soiled, embarrassing both him and his family, and whether deservedly or not, was deeply disturbing. One observes in Sherman's many letters the plethora of emotions that swept over him in the days and weeks following the publication of the stunning article, emotions that seem to have run the gauntlet from humiliation, regret, disappointment and despair to resentment, disgust, anger and hatred.

Perhaps there was some comfort in the knowledge that most of the allegations in the *Commercial* article were not true or were exaggerations. False was the charge that he telegraphed the War Department three times in one day requesting permission to withdraw across the Ohio River into Indiana. Never did he suggest retreating from Kentucky. That he frightened Louisville Unionists "almost out of their wits" is an exaggeration. Nor did any subordinate in Kentucky or Missouri ever refuse to obey one of Sherman's orders. As for his "mad freak" of retreating from Cumberland Gap, Sherman sensibly explained that "the retreat ... was not designed as a retreat, but to shift the position to another point to meet an expected contingency which did not happen." But the damage to Sherman's reputation had been done.

Of that fact he was distressingly aware. He told Ellen that "the idea of having brought disgrace on all associated with me is So horrible to contemplate that I cannot really endure it." He was especially concerned about "our Dear Children," and wrote brother John, "I am so sensible now of my disgrace ... that I do think I should have committed suicide were it not for my children." Thomas Ewing thought that Sherman should bring suit against the *Cincinnati Commercial* for libel. Ewing, in fact, was prepared to personally handle the case. John Sherman initially advised against legal action. He knew that his brother had made mistakes: overrating enemy forces, voicing unreasonable demands—even imprisoning a *Commercial* reporter for visiting troops after being denied permission to do so. However, after John actually read the *Commercial*'s accusations, he concurred with Thomas Ewing in advocating a lawsuit.

But Sherman shrank from the additional publicity that was sure to be associated with such a step. He preferred to keep quiet and ride out the "insanity" storm. He realized he had overstated the threat posed to Kentucky by the Rebels, although his judgment about the untrained, inadequately armed and poorly clad Union regiments was accurate. He never forgave the newspaper reporters for what he considered an attempt not only to embarrass him but actually to ruin his army career. Throughout the war he would keep reporters away as much as possible. He believed that many of the reporters, because they printed news useful to the enemy, were an insufferable obstacle to successful military operations.[37]

SHERMAN'S "INSANITY" in the fall of 1861 has been explained in various ways: manic depression, clinical depression, temporary insanity, recurring insanity and narcissistic personality disorder. Clearly, a number of stressful factors, combined with an unhealthy lifestyle, plagued him over a period of several months, finally culminating in mental and physical exhaustion. Sherman himself, looking back and analyzing his Kentucky difficulties, identified most of them.[38]

Sherman's problems began several months before the war, even prior to secession. He had been upset over the thought of fighting Southerners. On New Year's Day 1862, he wrote Ellen that "my former associations with the South have rendered me almost crazy, as one by one all links of hope were parted." Sherman required a long time to cope with his distress over breaking with the South.[39]

In another letter he told Ellen: "I certainly have not the same character I would have had, had I not lived so much in the South." Again he reaffirmed, as he made clear several times, that he had "wanted to Keep out of this war." He also told Ellen that "it does seem hard," while stationed in St. Louis, not to see close friends like James Lucas and Henry Turner, both of whom sympathized with the South. On January 8, he wrote John Sherman, "I have lived so much in the South, and have made my personal friends among [Southerners], that I no doubt have overrated not only the intensity of their feeling, but their strength, at the same time doubting that of the North."[40]

While Sherman knew that the Union possessed a huge potential advantage over the Confederacy in both manpower and all manner of war equipment—a fact he had expressed numerous times—he became convinced that U.S. leaders, as well as the American populace, did not grasp the magnitude of the secessionist challenge. The Bull Run defeat and, in Sherman's mind, the inadequate Federal response that followed were irrefutable evidence that the nation had not yet awakened to the crisis. Because Union war fervor was not up to the standard he deemed essential, Sherman grew increasingly discontent, testy and outspoken. He claimed that he did not want to lead, yet a major portion of his frustration arose from, as he later told his brother, "matters which seemed to me beyond my control." When he arrived in Kentucky, the problems were the same as in Washington, except that they seemed of greater degree—too few troops, and those men insufficiently trained and deficient in arms and equipment. Not to mention the threat of Rebel attack. He was also finding it hard to accept the carnage and cruelty of war, as his experience with the fate of the Tennessee bridge burners attested. The more he obsessed about the difficulties he faced, the more distressed he became, and the more eccentric were his actions.[41]

All the while, Sherman's health deteriorated. Night after night, week after week, as earlier referenced, he seldom retired until three or four o'clock in the morning; he then rose again within a short time. His diet was insufficient in quantity and quality. Smoking far too many cigars, he also "drank somewhat," as he admitted to his brother. He spent many hours hunched over a desk writing letters, while getting virtually no exercise, unless one counts his impatient pacing. Sleep deprivation, inadequate diet, heavy smoking, excessive alcohol, overwork, lack of exercise and constant worry constitute a formula for disaster, impacting both body and mind.[42]

Finally, another significant factor contributed to Sherman's collapse—and quite possibly it was the worst of all. He was convinced that he had failed at his chosen career: the army. The impact was devastating. "I am fully conscious," he told his brother early in 1862, "that in surrendering that [Kentucky] command I confessed my inability to manage it." He declared that the realization of that fact was "mortifying but true. . . . These thoughts so bore on me that they broke me down and I am not yet recovered."[43]

Sherman had experienced serious setbacks and major disappointments in the past, but nothing to compare with the military failure, and the nationwide public humiliation that followed. The California banking endeavor never brought the success initially envisioned, despite Sherman's hard work and business sense. The Wall Street project came to an end almost as soon as it got started, but through no fault of Sherman's. These really had been peripheral undertakings anyway, not his chosen profession. He had still sounded cocksure about the military when he earlier declared to Ellen that he "was fit for the Army but nothing else." And then he failed—abjectly failed, as he candidly admitted, where he had long expected to flourish. He had failed in the army "in the service of my country." Never before, and never again, would he experience a crisis that laid him so low.

DURING THE TIME that Sherman spent with Ellen and the children in December 1861, he ate better, slept more, rested from responsibility and experienced a measure of solace. Nevertheless he remained troubled. Ellen again broached the possibility of overseeing her father's saltworks. Sherman was not about to accept that alternative. Better to face his humiliation serving with the army, even in an embarrassingly reduced position. Departing for St. Louis shortly before Christmas to resume his military duties, he took note, perhaps with bitter amusement, of editor George Prentice's absurd praise in the *Louisville Journal*. Obviously attempting to atone for the insanity article being copied in his paper (while he was out of state, he claimed), Prentice declared that Sherman's "mind is probably unsurpassed in power and comprehensiveness, by ... any military man of our country." Sherman's "heroism [was] the equal of Richard the Lion-heart," and his actions at Bull Run had been "worthy of the greatest hero of any age."[44]

On December 23, General Halleck assigned Sherman to the command of Benton Barracks, a large base near St. Louis. He was to "organize, equip and prepare regiments" for an offensive campaign—a campaign that Sherman knew, of course, someone else would lead. The duty was important, but in Sherman's view demeaning after the command he had held in Kentucky. He remained gloomy, utterly displeased with himself, with thoughts of suicide crossing his mind. He also feared that the powerful congressional Committee on the Conduct of the War "will fix on me more than my share [of blame] in the Bull Run disaster," particularly after his failure in Kentucky and the newspaper claims that he was crazy. He continued to be plagued by thoughts of the embarrassment he had brought upon the family as well as himself. He felt "as though I should cast myself into the Mississippi," and cried out to Ellen, "Oh, that I could remove the last few months."[45]

Gradually, however, as Sherman worked effectively at Benton Barracks, he recovered his emotional stability and overall his health and attitude continued to improve. Sometimes he and Halleck discussed military affairs, conversations that were excellent therapy for Sherman. Halleck, whose Department of the Missouri would soon be expanded into the Department of the Mississippi, realized that Sherman's health was better and began to think about using him in a greater capacity. Also, without question, the shrewd Halleck was mindful of recent letters from Senator John Sherman and Thomas Ewing in strong support of General Sherman. Considering their influence in Washington, Halleck's own best interests appeared to coincide with Sherman's well-being. And Halleck well knew that a whole Sherman was too great a talent to remain sidelined. All the while, Ellen performed a nurturing role: "You *could not* disgrace anyone, for you could not do a dishonorable action," she wrote Sherman on January 8, 1862. Three days later, he promised her that he would "make an effort to get into the Field [again]," although he remained skeptical about being awarded a second chance.[46]

For Ellen and her family, as well as for John Sherman, Cump's Kentucky fate had been tragic. They still believed that he was capable of outstanding army service—truly significant achievements of far greater import than managing recruits at Benton Barracks, even if the St. Louis base was a huge marshaling center. Ellen now determined that she must do more than comfort and encourage her husband.

She would spearhead a campaign to vindicate Sherman's good name and restore him to a position worthy of his abilities. Ellen and he had experienced serious disagreements during their marriage, not the least of which concerned his army career. But if her husband was determined still to serve after all the trials he had been through, then Ellen decided that her duty, as a loyal wife, was henceforward to support him in every way possible. If Sherman believed that the Union should be preserved, and had determined to fight and likely sacrifice his life for it, then the Union would be her cause, too, with one important difference. For Ellen, whose devotion to her Catholic faith permeated all her views, the Union cause became a righteous cause, the Confederacy a manifestation of evil, Jefferson Davis "his Satanic majesty."

In early January, Ellen decided to go to the top on behalf of her husband. She penned a striking letter to the President. Describing Sherman's difficulties in Kentucky, she attributed the slanderous newspaper accounts to a conspiracy of army officers and reporters. Particularly, she implied that Lorenzo Thomas contributed significantly to Sherman's downfall. She hoped that Lincoln would somehow intervene "in my husband's favor and in vindication of his slandered name." When a number of days passed without any response, Ellen's patience grew thin.[47]

She determined to take her case to Lincoln in person. Thomas Ewing was about to travel to Washington on legal matters, providing an opportunity for Ellen to make the trip in company with him, and he was fully sympathetic with his daughter's mission. On January 29, Ellen and Thomas Ewing met with Lincoln, who received them warmly, and with praise for Sherman. Naturally, the President knew of the newspaper allegations but said that he had never thought Sherman, whom he remembered well, was insane. Lincoln "seemed very anxious," according to Ellen's letter to Cump that evening, "that we should believe that he felt kindly towards you." Ellen and her father left the meeting pleased with the President's attitude, even though he had not actually promised them anything. She assured her husband that he had powerful men working for him in the nation's capital, especially her father, her brother Tom and John Sherman. Furthermore, Edwin M. Stanton, who was a friend of Thomas Ewing, had just replaced the tainted Simon Cameron as secretary of war. Ellen prophesied that time would wear away the slander against her husband, after which "you will stand higher than ever." For Ellen's love and concern, Sherman was truly grateful, although he remained pessimistic about his future. Soon Sherman would get a second chance to prove himself, and as Ellen predicted, he would rise to "stand higher than ever."[48]

Chapter Fifteen

Triumphant in Tennessee

The campaign may be said to have begun at the Planters' House in St. Louis, on a winter night early in 1862. In his room on the second floor, Henry Halleck spread out a large map depicting the western theater of war. Present with General Halleck were Sherman and Brigadier General George W. Cullum, Halleck's chief of staff. The three were discussing plans for a Federal advance into the Confederacy as soon as preparations were complete and weather permitted. At issue was the point of attack. Cullum drew a line on the map, representing the Rebel defensive position across southern Kentucky and northern Tennessee.

The line stretched eastward from the Mississippi River at Columbus, Kentucky, through Forts Henry and Donelson on the Tennessee and Cumberland Rivers, and on to Bowling Green, Kentucky, north of Nashville on the Louisville & Nashville Railroad. "Now," asked Halleck, "where is the proper place to break it?" Sherman remembered that either he or Cullum replied with a fundamental axiom of military education: "*Naturally*, the center." Halleck then drew a line perpendicular to Cullum's line, and near its center. Halleck's line almost coincided with the course of the Tennessee River, and he said: "That is the true line of operations."[1]

Years later Sherman wrote that he had "always given Halleck the full credit for [the Tennessee River] movement, which was . . . the first real success on our side in the civil war." Such recognition surely was appropriate, for Halleck, as commander of the Department of the Missouri, did order the attack and would have borne the blame had it failed. Furthermore, as Sherman noted, "most people [then] urged the movement down the Mississippi River," but Halleck chose to target the Tennessee Valley. However, no Socrates was required to understand the potential advantages of a strike up the Tennessee River, and Halleck was not the only military man who favored the Tennessee.[2]

Most significant among the others were U. S. Grant, Charles F. Smith and Andrew H. Foote. Grant, the West Point veteran of the Mexican War, who afterward resigned from the army under a cloud of alleged hard drinking, had struggled with little success as a civilian, until getting another chance with the army when the Civil War began. Smith was a highly respected officer from the "Old Army," distinguished in the war with Mexico; Sherman had held him in high esteem since West Point days, when Smith served as adjutant of the military academy. Flag Officer Foote had been a navy man from his teens. Well into the sixth decade of an adventurous life, he epitomized a crusty old sea dog—except for being a zealous temperance advocate—and commanded the Western Flotilla. All three men favored an advance up the Tennessee, with an attack on Fort Henry, and they wanted to strike at once.[3]

Acting on Halleck's orders, Grant and Smith had recently staged a demonstration to deter the Confederates in western Kentucky from shifting forces eastward to oppose an advance by Buell on Cumberland Gap. While Grant's column marched toward Columbus, Smith's troops headed south for Fort Henry. Several miles north of the fort, on January 22, Smith boarded the gunboat *Lexington* for a probing foray against the fort. The gunboat fired several rounds, experiencing only a minimal response from the Rebel artillery before turning back downstream, where Smith rejoined his infantry division. Returning to Paducah, Smith reported to Grant that Fort Henry was highly vulnerable. Positioned on the Tennessee's east bank, on low ground a few miles south of the Kentucky state line, Fort Henry was dominated by the unfinished Fort Heiman, which stood on a much higher elevation across the river, and well within its artillery range. Also, the Rebels had no naval force with which to contest the Yankee flotilla. Possess Fort Heiman, declared Smith, and the capture of Fort Henry was assured.[4]

Grant wrote that Smith's report "confirmed views I had previously held, that the true line of operation was up the Tennessee and Cumberland Rivers." Flag Officer Foote, with whom Grant said he "consulted freely," offered enthusiastic support for such a campaign. When Grant laid the plan before General Halleck, he claimed that he "was cut short, as if my plan was preposterous." Grant soon renewed the Fort Henry proposal, seconded by Foote, who telegraphed Halleck advocating an advance up the Tennessee.[5]

General Halleck never considered the Tennessee River campaign "preposterous." Writing General-in-Chief of the Army McClellan on January 20, Halleck presented a succinct, convincing, prophetic argument in its favor—an analysis that would be difficult to improve upon. "The idea of moving down the Mississippi by steam is, in my opinion, impracticable, or at least premature. It is not a proper line of operation. . . . A much more feasible plan," he stated, would be to move up the Tennessee and Cumberland Rivers. "This would turn Columbus," a strong point which he declared could not be taken without "a terrible loss of life," and would also "force the abandonment of Bowling Green." The enemy at Columbus, unless he quickly retreated, would be "turned, paralyzed, and forced to surrender." This line of advance, Halleck correctly declared, "is the great central line of the Western theater of war, with the Ohio [River] . . . as the base and two good navigable rivers extending far into the interior of the theater of operations." Obviously Halleck favored the campaign. The general, wanting full credit for the operation, likely was irked that Grant and Foote were also advocating it.[6]

Halleck did have some other worries. He had been sick with the measles for more than a week during mid-January. Far worse, major problems continued to plague him throughout Missouri. Thus the general was hesitant—"too much haste will ruin everything," he had told Lincoln in reference to possible cooperation with Buell—to launch a major offensive on the rivers. Shifting troops across the Mississippi, a likely requirement for an advance in Kentucky, might mean the loss of Missouri. Much of Missouri was chaotic. Rebel guerrillas wreaked destruction, cutting down telegraph poles, tearing up rail lines, burning bridges, buildings and houses and terrorizing loyal Unionists. Further complicating the difficulties were "well mounted and well armed [Union] barbarians," as Brigadier General John M. Schofield called his German cavalry, who "plunder and rob friends and foes alike." Declaring them "a burning disgrace to the army and the Union cause," he finally succeeded in getting five of the most notorious "in irons."[7]

The whole disgusting, anarchic scene turned Halleck into an unapologetic advocate of hard war. Writing Thomas Ewing, who responded with sympathetic advice, he claimed "nothing but the severest punishment can prevent the burning of railroad bridges and the great destruction of human life." The army in Missouri, he declared, "is almost as much in a hostile country as it was when in Mexico." Halleck was determined "to put down these insurgents and bridge-burners with a strong hand." He fully expected "a newspaper howl [against him as] a bloodthirsty monster," but assured Ewing that "it must be done; there is no other remedy." He ordered that anyone cutting down telegraph poles or damaging rail lines be shot on sight, and "all persons found in disguise as pretended loyal citizens . . . giving information to or communicating with the enemy, will be arrested, tried, condemned, and shot as spies." In this respect, Halleck added, "the laws of war make no distinction of sex; all are liable to the same penalty." Missouri, he declared, must remain in the Union, whatever might be necessary to achieve that end. The rigorous, hardhanded war, which came to characterize Sherman's policy toward Confederate guerrillas when he occupied Memphis and west Tennessee later in 1862, probably stemmed to a degree from what he observed while serving under Halleck in St. Louis.[8]

Despite the ongoing difficulties in Missouri, Halleck concluded in late January that the time had come to launch the Tennessee River campaign. Grant had continued to prod him. More significant, President Lincoln, irritated by the continued failure of his generals to move against the enemy, issued an order on January 27 "for a general movement of the land and naval forces of the United States against the insurgent forces." The President designated February 22 (George Washington's birthday) as the date "for prompt execution of this order," and he specifically mentioned the armies he expected to advance, including "the army and flotilla at Cairo." Immediate action definitely seemed in Halleck's best interest. Advancing on the Tennessee required no cooperation with General Buell, whose Department of the Ohio did not extend westward beyond the Cumberland River. If Halleck's forces moved before Buell bestirred himself and could achieve success on the Tennessee, Halleck's chances of gaining overall command in the western theater would be greatly enhanced.[9]

Two days after the President's order, Halleck received a wire from General McClellan (which also went to Buell), informing him that information gained from a Rebel deserter revealed that General Beauregard had been ordered to Kentucky, accompanied by fifteen regiments from the Confederate army in Virginia. Beauregard, widely regarded in the Confederacy as the hero of Fort Sumter and Bull Run, whom some Southerners seemed to look upon as a one-man gang, was in fact heading west. But he was not bringing fifteen regiments with him. He was not even bringing one regiment. Nevertheless, if Halleck needed any more persuasion, the rumor that the "Napoleon in Gray" was headed west with Rebel reinforcements did the work. On January 30, Halleck wired Grant: "Make your preparations to take and hold Fort Henry. I will send you written instructions by mail." He penned his detailed orders the same day.[10]

THE UNION STRUCK on February 6, attacking Fort Henry with a combined land and water invasion force. Grant commanded about 15,000 men, organized in two divisions, under Charles Smith and John McClernand, an Illinois political general of Democratic persuasion. Disembarking some five or six miles north of the fort, beyond sight and range of the Rebel guns, Grant deployed his troops on both sides of the Tennessee. Smith was to advance on the west bank, seize incomplete and undefended Fort Heiman, bring up his artillery and fire across the river

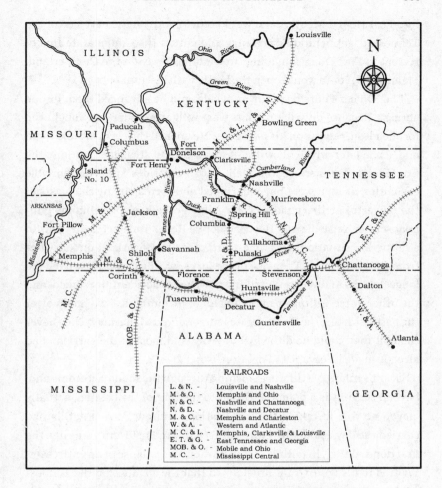

FORT HENRY, FORT DONELSON, SHILOH
OPERATIONS AREA

In February 1862, a Union army-navy offensive captured Fort Henry on the Tennessee River and Fort Donelson on the Cumberland River. Map by Jim Moon Jr.

into Fort Henry. McClernand would move south on the east side of the Tennessee, get behind Fort Henry and cut off the Confederate line of retreat to Fort Donelson, lying twelve miles away on the Cumberland. Meanwhile, Foote would open the battle with his gunboats.[11]

Flag Officer Foote had four ironclads, and he advanced them in line abreast. Because only their fronts were well armored, Foote fought the fort head-on, relying on his bow guns. He opened the clash around noon and, as he later wrote his wife, "it was a fearful struggle." Initially the Confederate gunners scored well, with both sides suffering horrible casualties, as men were burned, ripped and torn apart by the blasts of the powerful artillery pieces. The gritty Foote kept pressing his gunboats closer, regardless of the destructive Rebel fire. Fort Henry was in a desperate situation, with one-third of its fortifications under water from the rising river. Then one of the fort's two big guns, possessing the longest range and greatest striking power, was accidentally spiked; and the other burst, killing or mangling all of its gunners. Two hours after the battle started, the Confederates surrendered to the navy. They never thought they could hold the fort anyway, and most of the garrison had already made its escape to Fort Donelson.[12]

Grant's infantry still were sloshing through the muddy bottoms and, beyond serving as a potential threat to the rear of the bastion, actually played no role in taking the fortification. Andrew Foote's flotilla had carried the day. Suddenly it was a different war. Fort Henry was like the first domino that, in falling, sets in motion the collapse of an entire row. Writing to his wife, Grant proclaimed that the advance on the Tennessee River gave the Union "such an inside track on the enemy that by following up our success we can go anywhere." Without a doubt, breaking open the Tennessee River created a vast potential for carrying the war deep into the western Confederacy.[13]

Advancing up the Tennessee River, and thus paralleling the Mississippi River, proved just as helpful for Yankee strategic goals as moving down the Mississippi itself. In fact, control of the Tennessee was strategically preferable in some ways. The Union forces thereby flanked the Rebel stronghold on the Mississippi at Columbus, Kentucky, as well as severing the east–west transportation corridor of the Memphis, Clarksville & Louisville Railroad, which crossed the Tennessee only seventeen miles south of Fort Henry. The potential for even greater Yankee triumphs loomed ominously in the face of the Confederates. Union troops traveling the Tennessee River could soon threaten the vital Memphis & Charleston Railroad, the possession of which would mean that Confederate forces at Memphis were outflanked. The Rebels' entire Kentucky–Tennessee defensive position well might collapse under such multiple threats to their lines of communication. Barring a military miracle at Fort Donelson, the Confederates would likely be retreating into northern Mississippi and Alabama.

There would be no miracle. With the fall of Fort Henry, Grant's troops advanced overland against Fort Donelson, while Confederate General Albert Sidney Johnston abandoned Bowling Green, retreating through Nashville to northern Alabama, where he planned to concentrate his forces for a counteroffensive. However, Johnston ordered half of his troops to Fort Donelson in a forlorn hope of maintaining control of the Cumberland River and protecting Nashville from Union occupation. Ten days after the loss of Fort Henry, Fort Donelson also collapsed, following some hard fighting as well as considerable Confederate blundering, in a battle transpiring amid snow and sleet.

General Grant instantly became a Northern hero, popularly known as "Unconditional Surrender" Grant, a nickname stemming from his initials, when he denied any terms to the surrendering garrison and captured 12,000 to 15,000 Rebels. The Union forces thereby opened a second avenue of invasion, via the Cumberland River, into Nashville, which was the greatest storehouse, arsenal and centrally located transportation depot in the western Confederacy. On February 24, Nashville became the first Confederate state capital to fall to the Federals, ensuring the collapse of the entire Rebel defensive line in the region.[14]

The fall of Forts Henry and Donelson was the turning point of the war in the western theater, and arguably, in all the ramifications, the first turning point of the entire conflict. Historian B. Franklin Cooling well summarized the Union triumphs as "the expedition that broke open the war in the West." Stemming directly or indirectly from the capture of the forts, a series of Yankee victories followed—most dramatically and significantly at bloody Shiloh—which taken together, left the Confederacy struggling to survive. The wide-ranging military results were enhanced by the moral and political impact of catastrophic Rebel defeats: a deep discouragement in the South and a strengthened confidence in the North. Also, sometimes overlooked, is Basil Liddell Hart's concise, perceptive observation that the Union campaign not only "unlocked the gate into Tennessee," but additionally "closed the gate into Kentucky." The secessionist dream of establishing a northern boundary on the banks of the Ohio perished on the Tennessee and Cumberland Rivers in the winter of 1862. The Rebels would try to turn back time, notably in the late summer and early fall, when Braxton Bragg and Edmund Kirby-Smith advanced into Kentucky from central and east Tennessee. But they never came close to succeeding.[15]

FOR WILLIAM TECUMSEH SHERMAN, the campaign was the proverbial godsend. It put him back in the war in a big way. While Grant marched the infantry into position to invest Fort Donelson, and Foote confidently steamed up the Cumberland for a river assault on that fort, General Halleck placed Sherman in command of the District of Cairo, headquartered at Paducah, Kentucky, with orders to "send General Grant everything you can spare from Paducah and Smithland." Halleck knew his man well, for Sherman "was a born quartermaster"—a fact that goes far in explaining why Sherman ultimately became a master strategist. Energetically, Sherman began funneling men, food and all manner of supplies to Grant. Perhaps now another field command for Sherman was no longer out of the question. In fact, the day after the Federals captured Fort Donelson, Halleck wired Sherman that "we must now prepare for a still more important movement" and promised, "You will not be forgotten in this." As soon as John Sherman heard the good news, he offered his high-strung brother congratulations, and also urged him to "take my advice, be hopeful, cheerful, polite to everybody, even a newspaper reporter." John thought, "above all things," that Sherman must "be hopeful and push ahead. Active, bold, prompt, vigorous action," instructed John, "is now demanded."[16]

Sherman, without a doubt, fully realized the significance of what had just occurred on the rivers. He told Ellen that the campaign "is by far the most important event of this sad war," and soon wrote John, acclaiming "Grant's victory [as] most extraordinary and brilliant." He cautioned his enthusiastic younger brother not to infer too much from the triumph, however, stating that "the war is not yet over," and noting that he had "seen the captured men of Fort Donelson, and . . . [there is] none of them but hates the Yankees." He told his brother-in-law Charley Ewing, "The Mississippi must be possessed in its whole extent before the rebellion will be crushed." He was sounding more like the stable, competent Sherman of earlier days.[17]

Certainly not to be overlooked at this time is the relationship between Sherman and Grant, which began developing during Grant's investment of Fort Donelson. "During the siege," wrote Grant, "General Sherman had been sent to Smithland, at the mouth of the Cumberland River, to forward reinforcements and supplies to me. At that time," continued Grant, "he was my senior in rank and there was no authority of law to assign a junior to command a senior of the same grade." But clearly impressed by Sherman's attitude, Grant said "every boat that came up with supplies or reinforcements brought a note of encouragement from Sherman, asking me to call upon him for any assistance he could render and saying that if he could be of service at the front I might send for him and he would waive rank." Sherman was primed for the cheerful, prompt and vigorous action that his brother had declared "is now demanded." He was seeking a field command under Grant.[18]

By March 11, the Department of the Missouri and the western portion of the Department of the Ohio were consolidated into the Department of the Mississippi, with General Halleck assigned to command Buell's army, as well as his own victorious forces. Unity of command thus was achieved for the western offensive, and Sherman's star continued to rise. Halleck had already assigned him to command a new infantry division.

The drive southward on the Tennessee River from Fort Henry was also under way before Halleck became supreme commander in the West; however, Grant was not leading it, having run afoul of Halleck.[19]

Back in St. Louis, Halleck had experienced difficulty for several days in obtaining information from Grant. In part, the problem involved sabotage, when a telegraph operator of Rebel sympathies at Fort Henry intercepted several wires. Also, faulty organization of the military telegraph system contributed to the muddle, and the "green eyed monster" made an appearance as well. Jealous of Grant's recent glory and publicity, Halleck acted irresponsibly. Sherman, who of course was Halleck's friend, later wrote that the New Yorker "worked himself into a passion." Sherman thought that he should have exercised more patience.[20]

But the frustrated Halleck, never impressed by his ordinary-looking subordinate who wore an old slouch hat and habitually chomped on the butt of a cigar, dashed off an intemperate communication to Washington, detailing Grant's supposed faults, which seemed to be legion. Grant sent him "no returns, no reports, no information of any kind"; he had "left his command" without authority and ventured to Nashville; his army was as much "demoralized" by victory as was the Army of the Potomac by defeat at Bull Run; Grant gave "no regard to the future," and Halleck was "worn out and tired [of Grant's] neglect and inefficiency." The lowest blow came when Halleck referenced a rumor that Grant had "resumed his former bad habits"—a statement which Halleck well knew would be taken to mean that Grant was drinking to excess. Halleck proceeded to place Charles F. Smith in command of the Union troops marshaling at Fort Henry for the grand advance up the Tennessee River. Grant would remain on the sidelines.[21]

March was hardly a week old when a mighty Union armada, approximately sixty transports strong, loaded with soldiers, horses, armaments and supplies, steamed southward on the Tennessee. Marked by a long, black column of smoke rising above the valley, the line of steamers attracted attention for miles. By March 12, the vessels were docking at Savannah, Tennessee, a pro-Union town of about 600 people located on the east bank of the river, deep in the southern part of the state. The numerous transports drew up on both sides of the crowded stream, while General Smith established his headquarters at a white-brick mansion situated atop the bluff of the river. The owner of the house was William H. Cherry, a staunch Union man.[22]

Having learned that the Confederates were concentrating their forces at Corinth, Mississippi, General Halleck ordered Smith to break the Rebel rail communications both east and north of that vital crossroads, with the primary objective of destroying "the [Memphis & Charleston] railroad bridge over Bear Creek, near Eastport, Mississippi." Smith entrusted the Memphis & Charleston assignment to Sherman, of whom he thought highly, and who was the only West Pointer commanding a division, while Lew Wallace was ordered to break the Mobile & Ohio.[23]

Sherman embarked his division in nineteen steamboats, and moved up the Tennessee on March 14. Along the way he observed Pittsburg Landing, lying on the west bank of the Tennessee about nine miles south of Savannah. He learned from naval officer William Gwin, commanding the gunboat *Tyler*, that a good road ran southwest from Pittsburg to the railroad junction at Corinth. Pittsburg was the customary landing place for all manner of goods and materials shipped by river to and from Corinth, which lay only twenty miles distant. Gwin also told him that the superior guns of the *Tyler* and the *Lexington* had driven some Rebel field pieces from atop the hill at Pittsburg a couple of weeks earlier. Sherman feared that the Confederates might return and occupy the landing in force. Troubled too by the rising Tennessee, which was so swollen from recent rains that Pittsburg was then one of the few elevated points where soldiers could be disembarked, he sent back a request that General Smith deploy troops at Pittsburg in strength while he proceeded with the attempt to break the railroad.[24]

Cautiously moving up the river until he reached Eastport, Sherman observed Rebel batteries through his field glasses, with at least some infantry support nearby. Thus he "dropped back quietly to the mouth of Yellow River," a few miles below Eastport, and disembarked his troops at Tyler's Landing, Mississippi, slightly south of the Tennessee state line. Almost immediately Sherman's men, advancing southwest toward

Burnsville, began bogging down in the mud and rapidly rising water. The tiny creeks cutting across his line of advance toward the railroad had become surging, swirling torrents from the heavy rains. Some of the troopers who were spearheading the advance were unhorsed while attempting to swim their mounts across a rampaging creek. Several of the men were drowned.

An attempt to build a bridge was thwarted by water rising so fast that it covered the timbers which had just been positioned to support it. "The rain was pouring in torrents," remembered Sherman, and even sleet occasionally mixed with the rain, as the temperature dropped. The Tennessee River, at one period, rose fifteen feet in less than twenty-four hours. Disgusted, Sherman realized that to continue the mission might necessitate bridging every stream between the Tennessee and the railroad, a distance of nineteen miles. Scouts also reported that a Rebel force had been deployed to cover the railroad. Sherman ordered his men back to the boats and wrote "that we had to unharness the artillery-horses, and drag the guns under water through the bayous, to reach the bank of the [Tennessee]." Once more embarking his men, Sherman dropped downriver to Pittsburg Landing. He found that General Smith had ordered forward Stephen A. Hurlbut's division. Also, Smith instructed Sherman to go ashore with his division, and position it far enough back from the river that still other troops might encamp there.[25]

Lew Wallace's expedition fared better than Sherman's. Moving almost due west from Crump's Landing, which lay about four miles north of Pittsburg, his men struck the Mobile & Ohio rails at a trestle across Beach Creek. They tore up track for some distance, bending the rails and throwing them into the water. It was not worth the effort because the Confederates repaired the damage the next day. For his part, Sherman did not intend to give up the attempt to break the Memphis & Charleston, but on March 16, he conducted a reconnaissance south and west of Pittsburg Landing, and his findings had a far-reaching impact on subsequent events.[26]

Sherman made the reconnaissance in company with James Birdseye McPherson, with whom he initially became acquainted while pursuing his brief banking career in New York City. McPherson was a handsome young fellow who graduated first in the West Point class of 1853, and was then serving on Halleck's staff. He would play an increasingly important role as the war continued. Sherman wrote in his memoirs that he and McPherson moved out about ten miles toward Corinth and, questioning various people, concluded that the Confederates "were bringing large masses of men [by train] from every direction into Corinth."[27]

Sherman was "strongly impressed," as he reported at the time, with the relatively flat and elevated ground stretching approximately 2½ miles southwest from Pittsburg Landing. "The ground itself admits of easy defense by a small command," he observed, "and yet affords ample camping ground for a hundred thousand men." He thought "the only drawback" was limited docking space for the transports, especially with the water level so high. Only four or five steamboats could be moored at a time. Pittsburg was a natural defensive position, with the flanks protected on the north and west by Snake Creek and its tributary Owl Creek, and on the southeast by Lick Creek. Any enemy attack would have to come between those deep and swollen streams, through an opening of no more than three miles' width. Intrinsically formidable, the position, if properly developed, would have been impregnable. Even without entrenchments, and other enhancements, one historian of the campaign wrote, "At Shiloh, terrain was the key feature . . . that turned the tide toward Union victory on the Tennessee. . . . It is quite possible that the Confederates never actually had a chance to win at Shiloh."[28]

Regardless of the impressive terrain, Sherman was not recommending, as sometimes assumed, that the entire army be placed at Pittsburg Landing, even if he did note that there was enough room to accommodate 100,000 soldiers. In another report that same day he suggested that Union forces should be stationed also at Hamburg and Tyler's Landings to the south, as well as Crump's Landing to the north. Then the Federals, he said, "could move concentrically on Corinth or . . . any other point" along the Memphis & Charleston rails. "To advance on Corinth in force," he advised, "we should make use of several roads." Such width of deployment, based upon river communications and gunboat support, would leave the Confederates guessing about the route, or routes, of a Union offensive. The Rebels would also have no clearly defined target against which to concentrate if they did attack. But Grant, recently reinstated to command the expedition, decided to place all the troops at Pittsburg Landing, except for Lew Wallace's division at Crump's Landing. Grant thought of moving against Corinth by the most direct route, while Sherman believed the troops would "drag out too long on a single . . . road."[29]

Two factors had just combined to restore Grant to command. First, Halleck had backed down from his accusations against the victorious general. Challenged by Secretary of War Stanton, possibly after consultation with Lincoln, to either bring formal charges against Grant or cease making allegations, Halleck quickly reconsidered. He probably realized that attacking a man who had gained important triumphs for the nation, and had become a hero in the North, was not smart politics. Lamely he backpedaled, claiming that Grant had made satisfactory explanations and any problems with the general were inconsequential and in the past.[30]

Simultaneously with Halleck's willingness to restore Grant, General Smith had been forced to give up his command. Smith was the victim of what first appeared to be an inconsequential accident. He had slipped and fallen while getting into a rowboat, raking, as he himself described it, "the whole of the right leg—the shin and calf—with the seat." He noted that "the doctor fears injury to the bone." It was a painful misstep. The leg became infected, soon grew worse, and finally compelled the general to relinquish command while the buildup at Pittsburg Landing was in process. In about a month, Smith was dead.[31]

General Smith had been an aggressive commander, remaining eager, as before the attack on Fort Henry, to take the fight to the Rebels. While still in command at Savannah, he had written, "We are chafing like hounds in the leash to move at the enemy just in front but are forbidden by Halleck until the force is about doubled." Also, Smith had seen no reason for the army to be entrenched. "Our men suppose we have come here to fight," he said, "and if we begin to spade it will make them think we fear the enemy." Besides, Smith had boasted, "by God, I want nothing better than to have the Rebels come out and attack us. We can whip them to hell!" General Grant was of like mind with Smith, primed to get at the enemy as soon as possible.[32]

However, Halleck continued to apply a restraining hand on Grant, as he had on Smith. Halleck did not want any major movement against the Rebels until Don Carlos Buell's Army of the Ohio, marching overland from Nashville, could join forces with the troops under Grant. "Don't let the enemy draw you into an engagement now," Halleck ordered. He himself intended to come to Tennessee and "take personal command" for the offensive against the Confederates. Grant thus awaited the arrival of Buell and Halleck, maintained his headquarters at Savannah and looked upon Sherman as an informal field commander at Pittsburg Landing.[33]

Neither Grant nor Sherman nor any other senior Federal officer seemed concerned that the enemy might advance and attack the Union forces at Pittsburg. They completely misinterpreted the purpose of the Rebel buildup at Corinth, convinced that the Confederates were marshaling their forces to defend the Memphis & Charleston and the Mobile & Ohio crossroads. Nothing more. General Smith had expressed the common viewpoint in his colorful way. The Federals would have to advance on Corinth and "rout the badger out of his hole." Thus the army at Pittsburg spent its time drilling and training, preparing to take the offensive. Approximately 50 percent of the soldiers had never seen combat.

Since no one in authority worried about an enemy attack, the army's five divisions were scattered about the tableland without any tactical formation, with no semblance of a defensive line, and with the most inexperienced troops, Sherman's and Benjamin Prentiss's divisions, holding the advanced positions. Sherman gave orders that brigades should encamp facing west in order to be in line of battle when called to arms, and also that there should be no more than twenty-two paces between regimental encampments. But his orders were widely disregarded, and Sherman did not correct the situation. Worst of all, neither Sherman nor Grant made adequate provisions for outposting and patrolling that might have unmasked an enemy advance.[34]

On Thursday, April 3, as the Confederate Army moved out of Corinth, tramping northeast toward Pittsburg Landing and the Union Army, Sherman penned a letter to Ellen. He had not written to her for some time, explaining that he had been "pretty busy" in examining roads and rivers. "We are constantly in the presence of the enemy's pickets," he wrote, "but I am satisfied that [the Rebels] will await our coming at Corinth or some point of the [Memphis &] Charleston road." He noted also that "the weather is now springlike, apples & peaches in blossom and trees beginning to leave. Bluebirds singing and spring weather upon the hillsides." The next day he wrote his father-in-law, saying that the enemy had "strong Cavalry and Infantry pickets . . . almost to our very camp," but Sherman brushed these aside, assuring Thomas Ewing that they were "designed simply to carry notice back of an advance in force on our part."[35]

Sherman may have been unduly influenced by Grant's opinion that if the army faced any immediate danger—and Grant stated that he did not think the threat was real—it was Lew Wallace's division at Crump's Landing that might be targeted. On April 4, Grant wrote Sherman that he had received information indicating that the Rebels were sending a force to the hamlet of Purdy, "and it may be with a view to attack General Wallace." Grant said he had ordered W. H. L. Wallace, commanding the Second Division, to reinforce Lew Wallace, "in case of an attack, with his entire division, although I look for nothing of the kind, but it is best to be prepared." Then he directed Sherman: "Keep a sharp lookout for any movement in that direction,* and should such a thing be attempted, give all the support of your division and General Hurlbut's if necessary."[36]

Sherman responded on April 5, assuring Grant, "I have no doubt that nothing will occur today more than some picket firing. . . . I do not apprehend anything like an attack on our position." Reassured by Sherman, Grant wrote Halleck, "I have scarcely the faintest idea of an attack (general one) being made upon us, but will be prepared should such a thing take place."[37]

---

* Meaning to the west and north, for Purdy lay directly west of Crump's Landing.

....

STRIKING AT DAWN on April 6, the Confederate Army achieved a complete strategic surprise. In spite of their time-consuming, noise-making advance, the Rebels might even have gained tactical surprise had not Colonel Everett Peabody, a brigade leader in Prentiss's division, ignored his commander's ridicule, and sent out a reconnaissance patrol long before daylight. Groping their way in the early morning darkness, the Federals came up against the advancing enemy about a mile out to the south and west. They fought a delaying action for more than an hour, and sent a warning back to Peabody, who immediately mobilized his brigade. General Prentiss was incensed that Peabody sent forth an unauthorized patrol, which, alleged Prentiss, had brought on an engagement. In truth, Peabody's action prevented Prentiss's division from being taken by tactical surprise. Also, some soldiers in Sherman's camps had been stirred awake by the sounds of gunfire to the south. Everett Peabody died that day, and Prentiss became known as a hero of Shiloh, but he never saw fit to commend Peabody and merely listed the colonel as a brigade commander in his official report of the great clash.[38]

American history had never known anything like the ensuing battle at Pittsburg Landing. For two days, Federals and Confederates—more than 100,000 soldiers in all—waged a desperate, horrible struggle through fields, forests, orchards, ravines, creeks and swamps. At first, a Confederate victory seemed possible. The Rebels enjoyed the advantages of surprise and momentum, while several thousand Yankees fled from the field of conflict. (Sherman claimed in a letter to Ellen that "at least half [of my division] ran away.") But the Confederate attack did not develop as General Albert Sidney Johnston had envisioned. Confusion and misunderstanding plagued the Confederate high command. Compounding the difficulties was a poor attack formation, in which regiments, brigades and divisions became intermingled, sacrificing command control. The complex terrain presented yet more problems. And General Johnston was killed, generating controversy to this day about what impact his death had on the battle.[39]

The Union Army, however, weathered the initial shock of the Rebel onslaught. Many Federals fought bravely, effectively, and ultimately triumphantly. Sherman's faulty analysis of the enemy's intentions had contributed to the initial Confederate success, but once the battle was joined, no high-ranking Union officer fought better. Sherman made a three-hour stand at Shiloh Church that was immeasurably significant and afterward fought off, in tandem with McClernand's men, more enemy troops than were attacking the famous Hornets' Nest, as described in the prologue. When the U.S. forces succeeded in establishing a strong defensive line covering Pittsburg Landing as darkness came on, any chance of a Confederate victory was snuffed out. April 7 again saw fierce fighting, but the Federals had too many men and too much firepower. The forces in blue struck at dawn, drove the Grayclads back across the battlefield and forced them to retreat. The Confederates left a trail littered with equipment thrown away by exhausted soldiers as they tried to lighten their loads, while hard-jolting wagons transported as many of the wounded as possible, miserably piled in upon one another, some of them having lain in the rain all the night before.

On the morning of April 8, Sherman conducted a reconnaissance in force to determine, as Grant instructed, if the Confederates had retreated all the way to Corinth or still remained in the battle area. About five or six miles southwest of Pittsburg Landing, Sherman came upon Rebel cavalry at a place called the Fallen Timbers. Nathan Bedford Forrest, whom Sherman had probably never heard of at the time, commanded about 350 troopers there, drawn up on a ridge to protect the rear of the Confederate Army. Sherman reported that he looked across "a clear field, through which the road passed, and immediately beyond [was] a space of some 200 yards of fallen timber." Beyond the timber, he could see the enemy cavalry atop the ridge. Deploying two companies of the Seventy-Seventh Ohio as skirmishers, while posting the Fourth Illinois Cavalry on his flanks, Sherman aligned the rest of the Ohio regiment in attack formation a hundred yards behind the skirmishers, and moved toward the Rebels on the ridge.[40]

Forrest was significantly outnumbered, which Sherman may have guessed but did not know, for he could not see beyond the ridge. As the

Federal skirmishers began picking their way through the fallen timbers, Forrest sensed an opening and shouted to his men, "Charge!" He
led the way as his horse soldiers thundered toward Sherman's men.
Some of the Union skirmishers panicked and fled; others were blasted
by shotguns and pistols as the Southern horsemen rode them down.
"The enemy's cavalry came down boldly to the charge," as Sherman
described the scene, "breaking through the line of skirmishers, when
the regiment of infantry, without cause, broke, threw away their muskets and fled." As the infantry gave way, the Federal cavalry on the
flanks also fell into disorder. At once Sherman ordered the rest of
Colonel Jesse Hildebrand's brigade to form a line of battle in the rear,
"which was promptly executed," said Sherman, and "the broken infantry and cavalry rallied on this line."[41]

Forrest was so far in advance of his men, and so carried away by
the exhilaration of combat, that he galloped into the strong Union line
alone. He should have been killed. Yankees swarmed all about, trying
to shoot or drag him from his horse. A soldier did manage to place his
gun up against Forrest's hip and fire. The bullet lodged against his
spine, although it failed to unhorse him. As Forrest turned to escape, he
grabbed an Ohio soldier by the collar, swung the man onto the horse and
used him as a shield while he galloped away.

Sherman was amazed. Years later, he recounted how Forrest had
ridden very close to him and claimed that if the Rebel had not already
emptied his pistols, "my career would have ended right there." Forrest
recuperated at his home in Memphis, returning to duty three weeks
later, still carrying the bullet next to his spine. It was neither the first nor
the last time "that Devil Forrest," as Sherman came to call him, cheated
death, although perhaps never more spectacularly than at Fallen Timbers. Sherman gathered up his wounded, buried the dead and headed
back to his headquarters at Pittsburg Landing.[42]

Critics later claimed that General Grant should have pursued the
retreating Confederates, that he missed a great chance to inflict further
damage and possibly destroy the Rebel army. General John McClernand,
for example, actually wrote President Lincoln on April 14, claiming that

his division, "as usual, has borne or shared in bearing the brunt" of a two-day "terrible battle." Then he declared that it was "a great mistake" not to pursue the Rebels. After the war, Grant did say that he had wanted to pursue but could not bring himself to give such an order to "men who had fought desperately for two days, lying in the mud and rain whenever not fighting." Sherman reported that the troops were "fagged out," by the "hard fighting, exposure, and privation." In addition to Federal exhaustion, historian Stacy Allen convincingly summarized the "several tactical realities" that would have challenged any attempt at pursuit by the Union Army. Rapid pursuit by cavalry divisions or brigades was impossible, because such organizations did not exist. Any pursuit by infantry would have been greatly hampered by the shortage of horses, as hundreds had been killed and wounded, which meant that moving supplies of all kinds and hauling artillery would have prevented a major effort. Naturally defensive terrain, as demonstrated on a small scale by Sherman's experience would have provided the Rebels with good opportunities for ambush. Grant was right not to order a pursuit.[43]

The Battle of Shiloh was over—except for the burying of the dead, the suffering of the wounded, the anguish of those back home who would soon learn of their loved ones killed and maimed and the far-reaching strategic repercussions. The enormous casualties, which approached 24,000, according to historian Thomas Livermore's calculation, shocked both armies, as well as the nation. Each side counted more than 1,700 dead and 8,000 wounded, with those missing accounting for the remainder. On average in Civil War battles, about 15 percent of the wounded eventually died from their wounds. If that average holds for Shiloh, then a total of nearly 6,000 soldiers died. By far the bloodiest battle to that date, Shiloh presented a terrible preview of all the other major battles of the war that were yet to come. For the first time, men on both sides came to envision a measure of the war's eventual cost in suffering, death—and treasure.[44]

The consequences of the great battle cast a long and wide shadow. The strategic results were of greater significance, by far, than the horrendous casualty figures. The U.S. Army at Shiloh had turned back a major Southern counteroffensive, maintaining its position on the line of the Mississippi River, within a few miles of the Memphis & Charleston Railroad. In their bitter defeat on the west bank of the Tennessee, the Confederates surrendered the chance to stop a decisive Union drive, and possibly undo much of what the Yankees had achieved during the winter and early spring campaign. For the Federal Army, the path lay open to split the Confederacy along the Mississippi River, and that, in the long run, meant that the Rebels could never win the war. New Orleans author George Washington Cable dramatically wrote, "The South never smiled again after Shiloh."

ON APRIL 11, General Halleck arrived at Pittsburg Landing, taking command in person of the Union forces still recovering from the great clash. One of Halleck's first acts was to order Sherman "again to try to destroy the Memphis & Charleston Road, a thing," as Sherman wrote Ellen, "I had twice tried and failed." He embarked at once, on board the transports *Tecumseh*, certainly an appropriate name, and *White Cloud*, with a strike force of 100 cavalry and a brigade of infantry. Escorted by the gunboats *Tyler* and *Lexington*, he proceeded up the Tennessee about thirty miles to Chickasaw Landing, where the soldiers disembarked on the morning of April 13 and headed inland. This time Sherman was not to be denied. Driving off a Rebel guard estimated to be 150 strong, the Yankee force burned the Memphis & Charleston bridge spanning Bear Creek and, attacking with axes, destroyed about 500 feet of trestle across the swampy approach to the bridge as well as half a mile of telegraph poles. All Confederate railroad communication east of Corinth was severed.[45]

Sherman said "Halleck was delighted," because breaking that railroad "had been with him a Chief object." In his letter of April 14 to Ellen, Sherman enclosed a copy of Halleck's message to the secretary of war, which praised Sherman for "contributing largely to the glorious victory [at Shiloh]," and recommended that he be promoted to major general of volunteers to date from April 6. Understandably pleased, Sherman also sent a copy of Halleck's letter to John and declared to Ellen, "so at last

I Stand redeemed from the vile slanders of that Cincinnati paper." He knew that Ellen's father would be "pleased that I am once more restored to favor," and instructed: "Give him Halleck's letter & tell him I broke the Charleston Road." He could not resist slamming the newsmen. "I am sometimes amused at these newspaper reporters," he told Ellen, then explaining: "They keep shy of me as I have said that the first one I catch I will hang as a Spy." Sherman despised reporters, but his comments undoubtedly convey hyperbole. His sense of political reality was very much intact, as evidenced by his warning to an incensed, strongly opinionated Ellen: "For mercy's sake never speak of McClellan as you write."[46]

Ellen had become convinced that McClellan was plotting against the Union generally and Sherman in particular, having withheld the resources Cump had needed in Kentucky. In a letter of April 9, Ellen alleged that McClellan was connected with the Knights of the Golden Circle, a Northern organization in sympathy with the South. Guilty of treason, he planned for "our troops to be killed off by yellow fever when Summer comes on." Keenly aware that he himself had "committed a fearful mistake in Kentucky," Sherman thought it "a wonderful instance" that he had gotten an opportunity to recover. He did not believe that McClellan was a man of "malice or intention of wrong," but the victim of vicious rumors. He told Ellen, "Keep your own Counsel, and let me work for myself on this Line." Sherman thought it possible that McClellan might yet succeed in a big way, and if he then came to know Ellen's views, the general might move to "crush me."[47]

Sherman's letters to Ellen, more than those to John or anyone else, convey the deep impact Shiloh made on him, particularly the mental stress he experienced in coping with the sights of suffering and destruction—sickening sights that left an impression far more disturbing and profound than Bull Run. He descriptively wrote of not only the pathetic, mangled bodies of the dead and dying soldiers, but also "the horses! I think we have buried 2,000 since the fight, our own and the Enemy." He told her of "the wounded [men who] fill houses, tents, steamboats and every conceivable place." Sherman could "feel the horrid nature of this war," which "I never Expect ... to survive." He expressed a concern about what his older son, Willy, would know and think of him, particularly if indeed he died in the war. Instructing Ellen that she should read all accounts of his campaigns, he told her to "cut out paragraphs with my name for Willy's future Study—all *Slurs* you will hide away, and gradually convince yourself that I am as great a soldier as General Greene." Doubtless he referred to Nathanael Greene of the American Revolution.[48]

Sherman clearly was pleased to receive a letter from Willy after the battle, and in reply assured him that the message was "a first rate one." Gathering up several cannon and musket balls and a spur "from the boot of a dead Rebel Captain," he packed all in a box and addressed them to both Willy and Tom, cautioning the boys that some "have powder and you must keep them away from the fire, else they might burst and kill somebody." He wanted Ellen to "paste on them a little paper saying they were picked up near my tent on the Battle field of Shiloh."[49]

After Shiloh, all the Ewings and Shermans found great satisfaction in Cump's ascending military stature. Ellen's mother well expressed the family feelings when she told her daughter, speaking of Willy and Tom, "With what a just pride the dear Boys will always look upon the beautiful mementos of their Father's heroic bravery and victory at 'Shiloh.'" Despite the widespread, flattering acclaim Sherman enjoyed after the battle, he again became greatly agitated by newspaper reporters, who criticized Grant and others—above all, with the charge that the army had been caught by surprise on April 6. The trouble really started with Whitelaw Reid's sensational and mistake-prone account in the *Cincinnati Gazette* of April 14, which came down hard on Grant and was widely copied, or quoted in part, by many Northern papers.[50]

Actually, writing under the pen name "Agate," Reid treated Sherman quite well, presenting him as a hero of Shiloh, "dashing along the line ... and exposing his own life with the same freedom with which he demanded [the troops] offer of theirs." Sherman was not moved by Reid's favorable account of his actions and became particularly angry at the criticism of Grant. (Neither he nor Grant would ever admit the strategic surprise on the morning of April 6.) Sherman's disdain for "the most contemptible race of men that exist," as he caustically character-ized reporters, appears in many of the letters he penned in subsequent months. Of course Sherman well knew that if Grant was surprised, he himself was also open to the same criticism. That aggravating issue would involve both men in arguments for as long as they lived.[51]

Possibly neither Grant's nor Sherman's careers could have survived an admission of surprise at Shiloh, particularly in view of the unprec-edented casualties suffered by the Union Army, as well as the problems recently experienced by both generals. So persistent became the clamor of some Northerners, however, that President Lincoln telegraphed Halleck to check into the matter. When Halleck said the accounts of surprise "are utterly false," and the heavy casualties attributable to a hard-fighting Rebel army, Lincoln dropped the issue.

Whatever Halleck really thought about surprise, he was not inclined to criticize Grant again. Not after his rebuff from the secretary of war, and not after he himself had restored Grant to command before the battle. Neither was Halleck motivated to find fault with Sherman. He learned truly that no one contributed more to the eventual Union vic-tory than the lean redhead to whom Halleck had given command of a new division shortly before the great clash. Also, Halleck was enjoying a good relationship with Sherman's powerful family connections, both John Sherman and Thomas Ewing. He certainly was not about to bring their wrath down on himself. Finally, even if the army was surprised, Shiloh ended in triumph for the Union. Victory usually trumps all.[52]

Chapter Sixteen

THIS IS NO COMMON WAR

The Confederates had lost "a battle [they] simply had to win," as Bruce Catton wrote of Shiloh, "a crucial effort to save the Mississippi Valley." As the defeated Southern forces trudged back toward Corinth on April 8, the Confederacy suffered yet another blow. Island No. Ten, a major fortification in the Mississippi River near the Kentucky–Tennessee–Missouri boundary, was compelled to surrender. The great river thus lay open all the way to Fort Pillow, a strong point atop a Tennessee bluff only fifty miles north of Memphis. Unless the Rebels could hold Corinth, Fort Pillow would soon be cut off, as would the port city of Memphis.[1]

After Shiloh, morale and discipline in the Confederate Army deteriorated critically, and the atmosphere at Corinth—where thousands of wounded soldiers overwhelmed the houses, churches and public buildings—exacerbated the aura of defeat. If the Confederacy had not passed a conscription act shortly after the battle, extending all enlistments to three years, the army at Corinth likely would have suffered crippling losses. Even with conscription, several thousand men deserted. Beauregard did receive some reinforcements, increasing the army to more than 50,000. He began preparing an impressive line of entrenchments to defend the vital crossroads, realizing, however, that his numbers were not adequate for the task he faced. He called upon Richmond for still more reinforcement, with the dire warning that if defeated at Corinth, "we lose the Mississippi Valley and probably our cause."[2]

Meanwhile, General Halleck had begun assembling a massive force, eventually numbering more than 120,000 soldiers. Within a few days after arriving at Pittsburg Landing on April 11, Halleck issued an order reorganizing the whole army. He placed General Buell in command of the center. The left wing was led by John Pope, whose army was arriving at Hamburg Landing, following the surrender of Island No. Ten. George H. Thomas, Sherman's friend and classmate at West Point, who had served as his subordinate in Kentucky, took command of the right wing. Sherman's division was placed under Thomas. John McClernand commanded the reserve. General Grant, wrote Sherman, "was substantially left out," and named "Second in Command," a position depriving him of any actual command of troops. For more than a month, Grant remained without a command, but deeply aware, according to Sherman, of "the indignity, if not insult, [that had been] heaped upon him." Sherman claimed not to have been bothered by his assignment to serve under George Thomas.[3]

Eventually the dejected Grant decided that he might as well go home. He applied for a thirty-day leave of absence, which was approved. By chance Sherman dropped in to visit with Halleck, who mentioned that Grant planned to leave the next morning. Sherman knew Grant had been "chafing under the slights of his anomalous position" and, immediately after leaving Halleck, he rode to Grant's campsite. He found the general preparing to depart and pleaded with him to reconsider, telling how he himself had been overwhelmed by newspaper assertions that he was crazy, but the Battle of Shiloh had given him new life and "now [he] was in high feather." Some unforeseen event, Sherman argued, well might restore Grant to favor. Grant promised to wait awhile before leaving and not to depart without again communicating with Sherman. A few days later, Sherman got a message from him, stating that he would remain with the army. Sherman responded with congratulations, declaring that "you could not be quiet at home for a week when armies [are] moving . . . and rest could not relieve your mind of the . . . injustice . . . done [to] you." In urging Grant to stay, Sherman had rendered a major service to his country. His action also strengthened the growing friendship between the two; a respectful and trusting friendship that became invaluable in the future prosecution of the war.[4]

Not until three weeks after the battle of Shiloh did General Halleck begin advancing toward Corinth. On May 3, conveying aggressiveness, he telegraphed Secretary of War Stanton from Pittsburg Landing: "I leave here tomorrow morning, and our army will be before Corinth tomorrow night." Halleck's projection of a swift march proved absurd. Moving with extreme wariness, he told Stanton on May 13 that the Rebels were "strongly entrenched," with numbers "equal if not superior to ours." Clearly Halleck's information about the enemy's strength left a lot to be desired. His infinite caution did the rest, as he consumed a month advancing from the Shiloh battleground to the vicinity of Corinth, a distance of less than twenty miles.[5]

Sherman wrote in his memoirs that "the movement was provokingly slow." Every time that the army halted, entrenchments were prepared "even though we had encountered no serious opposition, except from cavalry, which gave ground easily as we advanced." Writing to Ellen on May 26, he touted the quality of the army, "now composed of all the best troops & men in the West and if we cannot conquer here we might as well give it up." It was a remarkable force, in some ways as impressive as any Civil War army assembled during the entire conflict.[6]

In addition to the numerical strength, Sherman, Grant, Thomas and Philip Sheridan were all present—the four men eventually considered the best high-ranking officers the U.S. Army produced. At hand too were James McPherson, William Rosecrans, James H. Wilson and others who were developing into outstanding leaders. Sherman's praise was hardly an exaggeration. The army's slow and cautious advance on Corinth did give Sherman an opportunity to drill and instruct his division. Always a restless, active man, he worked tirelessly, teaching and explaining to his troops any and all military details that a good soldier might need to know. Soon he would proudly inform Ellen: "My Division is now esteemed one of the best."[7]

Sherman's May 26 letter to Ellen is also memorable for a striking commentary about receiving his commission as a major general of volunteers. "I know not why it gives me far less Emotion than my old commission as 1st Lieutenant of artillery. The latter I knew I merited, this I doubt—but its possession completes the chain from cadet up, and will remain among the family archives when you and I repose in Eternity." In view of the embarrassment experienced in Kentucky, Sherman probably was more pleased than he admitted. Additionally, he was comforted that "Minnie is now old enough to remember," and he thought that "even the rest may Keep me in their memory should my career close with this [campaign], and I do feel in this fact great consolation."[8]

The big clash that Sherman, Halleck and many of the Federals expected was not to be. Beauregard, whose intelligence about Union strength was more accurate than Halleck's knowledge of the Rebel numbers, waited until the Yankees were poised to launch their assault and then, believing that he was outnumbered two to one, pulled out under the cover of darkness. "That night," remembered Sherman, "we heard unusual sounds in Corinth, the constant whistling of locomotives [which some assumed meant enemy reinforcements were arriving], and soon after daylight occurred a series of explosions followed by a dense smoke rising high over the town." Sherman, who like Halleck had overrated the Rebel numbers, wrote his brother John, "I cannot imagine why Beauregard has declined battle." But with gusto he exclaimed, "We want the Mississippi now, in its whole length, and a moment should not be lost."[9]

Thus in early June 1862, General Halleck's formidable army possessed Corinth, sitting on top of the greatest railroad prize in the western theater of the war. "Beauregard had saved his army," wrote historian Robert S. Henry, "but had been forced to give up another great slice of Confederate territory." With the Union Army holding Corinth, and occupying a substantial stretch of the Memphis & Charleston Railroad, both Fort Pillow and Memphis were doomed. Fort Pillow was evacuated immediately. On June 6, a Union flotilla under Flag Officer Charles H. Davis, which had quickly descended the Mississippi, appeared before Memphis. Davis soon destroyed some inferior Rebel gunboats and forced the surrender of the defenseless city.[10]

Already, near the mouth of "the Father of Waters," a U.S. naval expedition commanded by sixty-one-year-old David G. Farragut had taken New Orleans. The capture of the Crescent City, which occurred in late April, was a devastating blow to the Confederacy. The population was four times greater than that of any other Southern city. New Orleans was the wealthiest Southern municipality, boasted the largest sugar refinery in the world and was the capital of King Cotton and the foremost export port on the North American continent. Second only to New York in imports when the war began, New Orleans also served as the banking capital of the South. From Fort Henry and Fort Donelson on the Confederacy's northern border, to New Orleans on the southern, the decisiveness of the Union campaigning in the western theater during the winter and spring of 1862, which cost between 40,000 and 50,000 Confederate casualties, as well as immense territory and resources, would have seemed unthinkable back on New Year's Day.[11]

NOW IT WAS decision time for the U.S. Army at Corinth. What would be the next objective? Essentially, the Federals had pursued a two-pronged waterway assault on the western Confederacy: the main advance via the Tennessee River, and a complementary movement via the Mississippi River. South on the Tennessee the Yankees first struck, breaking open that vital waterway at Fort Henry, advancing to defeat the Confederate counteroffensive at Shiloh and proceeding to capture the Memphis & Charleston rails at Corinth. South on the Mississippi, they capitalized on the Tennessee successes, occupying the Columbus fortifications, reducing Island No. Ten and capturing Fort Pillow and Memphis, which were outflanked when the Rebels evacuated Corinth. But the advance on the Tennessee reached a dead end at the Memphis & Charleston Railroad. No longer did that waterway penetrate southward, laying off to the east in northern Alabama, where impassable shoals blocked farther navigation anyway.

Up to this point, the Mississippi Valley, with Farragut steaming up the great river to take New Orleans, constituted the prime target of

United States campaigning in the western theater. Sherman thought it should remain so. Whatever the goal, Sherman wanted the great bulk of the army at Corinth to continue operating as a unit. He declared in his memoirs that halting at Corinth and dispersing "the best materials for a fighting army that, up to that date, had been assembled in the West, [constituted] a fatal mistake." If General Halleck had "held his force as a unit," argued Sherman, "he could . . . by one move have solved the whole Mississippi problem." Sherman thought "from what [Halleck] then told me" that the general intended just such a campaign "but was overruled from Washington."[12]

At the time, Sherman refrained from any criticism of Halleck's actions. Only in letters to selected family members can one surmise what he really thought in 1862. Strongly he demurred to any overland advance against the Rebels. He wrote John Sherman that he did not think Halleck would attempt to follow the enemy, who had retreated to Tupelo, fifty miles south of Corinth. He said "pursuing overland . . . would be absurd." What Sherman wanted, of course, was control of the Mississippi River—all of it. On June 10 he wrote Ellen, "I think the Mississippi the great artery of America and whatever power holds it, holds the continent." A month later, declaring to Halleck that "I attach more importance to the West than the East," Sherman stated, "the man who at the end of this war holds the military control of the Valley of the Mississippi will be the man." In 1863 he would write, "The Valley of the Mississippi is America." On the decisive significance of the great river valley, Sherman's drum never missed a beat.[13]

But General Halleck decided, perhaps due in part to pressure from Washington, that he could defend the railroads, administer the occupied towns and cities and still move offensively with a portion of his command. The advance would not involve the Mississippi River, however. The decision was to turn east—turn east and move by the Memphis & Charleston Railroad. The objective was one of great political import, dear to the heart of President Lincoln. East Tennessee and its heavy population of Union sympathizers would be the goal—specifically, initially, Chattanooga. A small city of fewer than 5,000 people, Chattanooga was militarily significant for one very important reason. It was a natural passageway north and south, east and west. This was partially true because of the Tennessee River. More momentous, however, was the fact that Chattanooga was a major railroad town—not even Atlanta equaled it in this regard at the time. Thus General Buell began moving eastward with considerably less than one-half of the force that Halleck had led to Corinth.[14]

While the Lincoln administration might rightly regard east Tennessee Unionism and the railroads emanating from Chattanooga—northeast to Knoxville and Virginia, south to Atlanta, the Atlantic, and the Gulf, northwest to Nashville and Louisville, and west to Memphis—as strategic prizes, the big picture of the war in the western theater should not be forgotten. Sherman and many military leaders, including Grant, as well as the great midwestern political base from which the President himself hailed, regarded the reopening of the Mississippi as the primary war aim. Thus Buell's east Tennessee operation was a secondary effort when viewed in the larger context of western campaigning—a vital point in appreciating the Union war effort.

Shortly after Corinth fell, Sherman had been dispatched to Chewalla, fourteen miles to the northwest. There he began repairing the railroad, and trying to save anything of military value from half a dozen trains wrecked by the Rebels when they retreated to Tupelo. For the next few weeks Sherman's troops worked on the Memphis & Charleston at various places, attempting to repair and protect the rails to Memphis. "I had my own and Hurlbut's divisions about Grand Junction, Lagrange, Moscow, and Lafayette," he explained, "building railroad trestles and bridges, fighting off cavalry detachments . . . and waging an everlasting quarrel with planters about their negroes and fences—they trying in the midst of moving armies, to raise a crop of corn." The work was dangerous. Sherman said detachments of cavalry and guerrillas "infested the whole country," and noted that General Grant and his staff, en route for Memphis with "a very insignificant escort . . . came very near falling into the hands of the enemy."[15]

The problem of disease also loomed large. This was the first summer for the Union Army to campaign in the Deep South, experiencing extreme heat, sweltering humidity and, probably worst of all, insufficient clean water. "The sun is so hot," Sherman wrote Ellen in a letter from Moscow, "that many of our men fall down in the road and have to be hauled in wagons." He himself had been experiencing a "terrible headache, pains & lassitude, [and] for the first time in my life on a march I found myself unable to ride and had to use an ambulance." Years later, Sherman attributed the sickness to "a touch of malarial fever, which hung on me for a month." Attempting to reassure Ellen, he told her he got two straw hats from Memphis to more adequately protect his head from the heat. He also told her: "I am always discouraged when I come in contact with the People [who] all seem so deeply bitter. . . . Though they have lost all the River but Vicksburg, they are still as far from being subdued as . . . the first day of the Rebellion."[16]

While Sherman worked on the railroad, he continued a brouhaha with the lieutenant governor of Ohio, Benjamin F. Stanton, about the issue of surprise at Shiloh. Stanton had published an article in a newspaper in Bellefontaine, Ohio, that reiterated the substance of Whitelaw Reid's critical account of the battle, referenced in the previous chapter. Stanton decried "the blundering stupidity and negligence of the General in Command," wrote of the "intense feeling of indignation against Generals Grant and Prentiss" and claimed that the "general feeling amongst the most intelligent men with whom I conversed, is that they ought to be court-martialled and shot." When someone showed Sherman the article, his wrath grew white-hot.[17]

"The more I think of it, the more angry I become," he told Ellen, vowing that he would "get even with the miserable class of corrupt editors yet." Exchanging a number of heated letters with Stanton, over a period of several weeks, he charged upon one occasion that "your published statement is all false, false in general, false in every particular, and I repeat, you could not have failed to know it false when you published that statement." The clash with Stanton also dredged up bad memories of the press in California.[18]

Declaring to a friend that "the evil [had been] stripped bare in California, when adventurers and rascals with Penitentiary Degrees got possession of the Press and openly attempted to black-mail & browbeat Citizens," Sherman proclaimed that he had been "amazed at the meanness of [such] men . . . and . . . conceived a terrible mistrust of the Press." Furthermore, he added: "I hope this war will not end . . . until the Press is made to feel that they cannot libel and violate common decency without punishment."[19]

Fortunately for Sherman, Ellen and her father managed to restrain his pen when he initially dashed off a hotheaded, ill-considered message to Stanton, but first mailed it to the family for evaluation before publication. "I return your letter to Stanton, which Father took into his own hands," responded Ellen, "and desires you to reconsider & write with greater care as he says it is not only for the present time but for future history." Sherman accepted the wise admonition in a proper spirit and "modified [the letter] so as to be less belligerent & more in accordance with your father's views." He hoped to have the letter published in both Columbus and Cincinnati. Once Ellen and Thomas Ewing saw the revised version, they gave him their wholehearted support, Ellen reporting that "Father was very much pleased with it." Thomas Ewing in fact wrote an article defending Sherman, published in the *Louisville Journal*, which Sherman told Ellen was "complimentary more so than I deserve from such a high source."[20]

Ellen's fighting blood was really up. She was "so glad" to witness her husband's defiant stance, informing him that "Father says I must send [your letter] to the Editors in every direction." She promised to "send it North, South, East & West [naming prominent cities] . . . also to California & even to the Editors in the most obscure villages in the State." Yet Ellen cautioned that he must not be "too sweeping & too general" in his denunciations. She reminded him that some leading city papers, citing St. Louis and Louisville in particular, had criticized others at Shiloh "whilst praising you to the skies." Her advice was certainly sound. "Many of the Editors & their correspondents," she wrote, "admire you and you ought not in common politeness to repulse them all without distinction." John Sherman, whose take on the issue was a little different, added his straightforward advice about newsmen, asking his impetuous older brother, "Why can't you keep on good terms with them?" John declared that newsmen are "very useful if you allow them to be, but if not they have a power for evil that no one can stand against. I see no reason for you to quarrel." Sherman ceased the exchanges with Stanton only when General Halleck instructed him to do so. Writing to Phil Ewing, Sherman said that he was "very desirous of conforming to Halleck's wishes," agreeing with the general that "officers should not write for the papers, and it might have been better" had he never gotten into such a dispute.[21]

Halleck's intervention came in a letter primarily devoted to informing Sherman of a major command change. Halleck was going to Washington, having been summoned to become general-in-chief of the U.S. Army. President Lincoln had been disappointed with George McClellan's performance, generally and especially during the recent campaign against Richmond. The general's advance on the Rebel capital seemed so promising and yet ended in failure. John Pope had been called to replace McClellan as commander of the Army of the Potomac, while Lincoln chose Halleck to organize the overall Union war effort, east and west.

McClellan was incensed at the prospect of serving under Halleck, "whom I know to be my inferior." Sherman, on the other hand, deplored the loss of Halleck in the western theater. "I cannot express my heartfelt pain at hearing of your orders and intended departure," he wrote. Halleck had taken control in the Mississippi Valley "at a period of deep gloom," when Sherman felt that "our poor country was doomed to a Mexican anarchy, but at once rose order, system, firmness, and success." Sherman concluded: "You should not be removed. I fear the consequences." He wrote John that "the loss of Halleck is almost fatal." He considered Halleck "the only man yet who has risen to the occasion." Appreciative of Sherman's strong support, Halleck responded that he was "more than satisfied with everything that you have done. You have always had my respect, and recently you have won my highest admiration."[22]

While Sherman's praise of Halleck might be interpreted as effusive and self-serving, his words ring genuine. Sherman was a candid man

who often spoke his mind without mincing words. Not all people cynically calculate their every action and every utterance in an attempt to
advance themselves. That Sherman truly rated Halleck the best Union
general at this time is apparent in his letters to several family members,
particularly his brother John, Phil Ewing, Thomas Ewing Sr. and Ellen.
To Ellen, for example, he said that Halleck "ever astonishes me by his
sagacity," while he told Phil, in the course of briefly assessing several
generals, that "Halleck [is] the ablest man." Sherman also liked Halleck, and telling the general of the high esteem in which he held his commander was not out of character.[23]

Halleck's elevation to general-in-chief left Grant in command of west
Tennessee and northern Mississippi. Sherman became commander of
the District of Memphis, a clear indication that his problems in Kentucky were no longer of concern to either Halleck or Grant. His reputation seemed fully reestablished with the military people who mattered
the most. Pleased to be placing his headquarters at a major commercial port on the Mississippi, Sherman arrived with his troops on July
21. He found Memphis virtually a dead city. A number of prominent
citizens had taken flight, and many churches, businesses, schools and
even the theaters had shut down. Sherman ordered that everything be
reopened.[24]

"I caused all the stores to be opened," he wrote, and "churches,
schools, theaters, and places of amusement to be reestablished." He
reopened the saloons, licensing them in order to prevent the smuggling
of liquor into the city. "As to opening the Liquor saloons here," ran his
somewhat amusing explanation to Ellen, he claimed the deed "was done
by the city authorities to prevent the sale of whiskey by smugglers." As
far as we know, he said nothing to Ellen about the brothels, for which
Memphis was well-known, and which he permitted to remain open.
Both black and white prostitutes were available, and Sherman did not
believe that his responsibilities as a general included interfering with
the sexual activities of the troops.[25]

He also strengthened the police force, firmly established the city government and encouraged the people, despite their Rebel sympathies, to

return their city to life as it had been before the Federals arrived. Memphis would be under military occupation for the foreseeable future, but Sherman tried to convey a respect for civil government and the rights of all citizens. Writing Mayor John Park, he said that he was "glad to find in Memphis yourself & municipal authorities not only in existence," but exercising "important functions, and I shall endeavor to restore one or more civil tribunals for the arbitrament of contracts and punishments of crimes [for] which the Military has neither time nor inclination." Sherman expressed "unbounded respect for the civil law, Courts & authorities," pledging to do everything in "my power to restore them to their proper use . . . the protection of life, liberty & property." He wanted the Memphis police prepared for "any probable contingency," but also promised assistance by the army's provost guard if a problem arose that was beyond the strength of the city police to handle.[26]

Not surprisingly, Sherman zealously attempted to keep abreast of all activities in and around Memphis. "I traverse the city day and night," wrote the vigilant general. Not long after arriving in Memphis, he attended a church service, probably in part to create a ubiquitous sense of his presence. Accompanied by several staff members, he visited Calvary Episcopal, the leading church of that denomination in the city. After graduation from the U.S. Military Academy, Sherman seldom attended church anywhere. While at West Point, however, he had been compelled to go to Episcopal services each Sunday, which he well remembered. When the Memphis minister prayed the ritualistic Episcopalian prayer, he omitted the customary request that God's protection be with the President of the United States. Sherman caught the omission at once, having heard the prayer every Sunday at the military academy for four years. Immediately Sherman stood up, and in a loud voice recited the customary words on behalf of the President for all to hear, after which he sat back down. The next day, he informed the preacher that if he resumed praying for the President, the church would remain open. Otherwise, it would be closed. No doubt the minister recognized that Sherman was not a man with whom one should trifle. From that week forward, at least as long as Sherman commanded in Memphis, the preacher complied with his wishes. Once Sherman remarked to Ellen that the minister had "preached a real good Union sermon."[27]

Actually Sherman continued to attend services at Calvary Episcopal from time to time. Probably the main attraction was a woman whose singing he admired. On October 4, he wrote Ellen, "I have been to church 3 times—a young lady sings magnificently." All his life, he was attracted to women who could sing well. He wrote a letter to his eldest daughter, soon to turn twelve, telling Minnie about the young woman "who sings beautifully and I rather think I thought more of that than the Sermons." Declaring that "a sweet voice well cultivated is a gift which God alone can confer," he observed that all ladies, whether possessing "a good natural voice or not [should] try & sing," improving their voice "both to give pleasure to others & health to themselves." He also encouraged her to dance, particularly "the waltz, Polka & Schottische." Asserting that "Utility alone characterizes our American people," he claimed that "all other people study to please others & themselves." He urged her to study hard—naming several subjects including history and foreign languages—and suggested too that she play the guitar. He certainly wanted her to learn to ride a horse well. Instructing about self-image, the General stated that "modesty is the most beautiful feature in a young girl, but should not degenerate into bashfulness. Think yourself as good as any but never think yourself better than the poorest." Finally, Sherman told her that "if this horrid war should ever end, how happy we could all be in some good home at St. Louis or Leavenworth, or in California—Write to me often, and try and write like Mama—Nobody can write better than she."[28]

Relative to Catholicism, which Sherman knew would always be of interest to Ellen, he reported that he had been called upon by "the Sisters from St. Agnes Academy, the Elder of whom Sister Ann is well acquainted with you & your mother and asked many questions, among which, of course, did I say my prayers." Sherman said he replied that Bishop Joseph Alemany, who had been the first archbishop of San Francisco when he and Ellen lived there, and was a friend of the Ewings from earlier days in Ohio, "had specially exempted me because you were pious enough for half a dozen ordinary families. They were delighted with your zeal & also that I enabled them to get their supplies at a cheaper rate than they had hitherto done. I promised to call & see them, but doubt if I can find the time." He did find time, as one might expect, to encourage the Memphis theater, attending the performances whenever his work permitted, and he noted in a letter to Ellen in mid-December that the theater was crowded.[29]

One of Sherman's greatest problems was dealing with guerrillas. Southern insurgents infested the countryside around Memphis, as well as much of West Tennessee. They attacked communication lines, burned railroad bridges and trestles, ambushed small Federal patrols and preyed upon citizens known to be Union sympathizers, robbing, intimidating and terrorizing. Guerrillas also hid along the banks of the Mississippi River, firing on Union gunboats and merchant vessels. "There is not a garrison in Tennessee," Sherman wrote Treasury Secretary Salmon Chase on August 11, "where a man can go beyond the sight of a flag-staff without being shot or captured." He told Grant that "all the people are now guerrillas," saying that whenever "a small body [of troops] goes out [the insurgents] hastily assemble and attack, but when a large body moves out they scatter and go home." He told Halleck that "all the people of the South are now arming as partisan riders," and wrote Ellen that "the whole interior is alive with guerrillas."[30]

Sherman realized the impossibility of hunting down the actual perpetrators of guerrilla acts. Early on he concluded that the best response was a policy of collective responsibility. After an attack on a U.S. forage train killed one soldier and wounded several others, Sherman told Halleck, who had employed such a principle in Missouri, "I am satisfied we have no other remedy for this ambush firing than to hold the neighborhood fully responsible, though the punishment may fall on the wrong parties." He imprisoned twenty-five prominent men living in the vicinity of the ambush. Thus began a series of reprisals and collective punishments.[31]

Of all the guerrilla depredations during Sherman's Memphis tenure, nothing incensed him quite so much as when United States ships were attacked from the banks of the Mississippi River. He called such actions "inhuman and barbarous"; the perpetrators were "assassins," engaged in "an outrage of the greatest magnitude." In Sherman's mind, there was something very special, almost mystical, about the Mississippi. He spoke of the river as "the spinal column of America," convinced that it inherently assured the unity of the nation, "a physical refutation of sectionalism." The war to preserve the Union, in essence, was a war for control of the Mississippi. "The absolute destruction of Memphis, New Orleans & every city, town and hamlet of the South," he wrote a Memphis lady, "would not be too severe a punishment to a people for attempting to interfere with the navigation of the Mississippi."[32]

The act of retribution for which Sherman would be longest remembered in Memphis and west Tennessee came in late September 1862. Near the town of Randolph, in Tipton County, guerrillas fired on the Union steamer *Eugene,* an unarmed vessel with passengers aboard. Already incensed and frustrated by other attacks near Randolph, and on ships carrying women and children, Sherman sent the Forty-Sixth Ohio, Colonel Charles C. Walcutt commanding, to destroy the entire village, "leaving one house to mark the place." While burning the town, if Walcutt found any men "whom you suspect of guilt, bring them in, but no women or children." On September 26, Sherman reported to Grant that "the regiment has returned and Randolph is gone. . . . Punishment must be speedy, sure, and exemplary." The next day he ordered that for every boat attacked, ten Memphis families, selected by lot, would be expelled from the city.[33]

Memphis was shocked. Citizens, as well as Confederate officers, registered protests. Convinced that he was in the right, Sherman defended himself strongly. But once he thought his policy had restrained the insurgents—and probably disturbed by so much criticism—he suspended the expulsion order. A band of guerrillas then attacked two more ships, nearly capturing one of them, which barely managed to escape "with two dead and many wounded," according to Sherman. "The conduct of the guerrillas," he told Grant, "was fiendish in the extreme." Again Sherman dispatched the Forty-Sixth Ohio to exact retribution, leveling all the houses, and destroying the farms and cornfields for a distance of fifteen miles along the Mississippi, where the attacks had occurred. "This is done" said Sherman, to let the guerrillas know "that certain destruction awaits the country for firing on steamboats engaged in carrying supplies." He also renewed the expulsion order, reporting to Secretary of War Edwin Stanton on December 16 that forty people, their names drawn by lot, had been removed from Memphis. Sherman claimed that "the remedy struck at the Root of the Evil and no boat has been fired on since."[34]

Perhaps recalling his Florida experiences with the Seminole Indians, Sherman told a protesting lady that "we are not going to chase through the cane-breaks & swamps, the individuals who did the deeds, but will visit punishment upon the adherents of that cause which employs such agents." Which was the more cruel he wondered, for your partisans to "fire Cannon & musket balls through steamboats with women & children on board, set them on fire with women & children sleeping in their berth, and shoot down the passengers & engineers with the curses of hell on their tongues, or for us to say, the families of men engaged in such hellish deeds shall not live in peace where the flag of the United States floats."[35]

While in the throes of contending with guerrillas, Sherman assured his brother that "this is no common war," and declared to Grant that "all the South is in arms and deep in enmity." Convinced that "we cannot change the hearts" of the Southern people, Sherman forcefully asserted, "We can make war so terrible that they will realize ... however brave and gallant and devoted to their country, still they are mortal and should exhaust all peaceful remedies before they fly to war." John Sherman was supportive—"show no favor or even toleration to rebels"—although not as aggressively as Ellen, who sounded harsh like her husband. "I hope this may be not only a war of emancipation but also of extermination," she declared. "May we carry fire & sword into their states until not one habitation is left standing."[36]

Only a few days after Ellen penned those words, Sherman actually possessed a radiant new sword. Fifteen men from New York had sent him a splendid ceremonial sword, in honor of his service at the Battle of Shiloh. Eloquently he expressed his appreciation to the gentlemen who conveyed "to me in terms of marked respect a sword of uncommon value, of great beauty in design & magnificently executed." Sherman confessed himself "overwhelmed by the unexpected honor," while experiencing "a just pride in the terms of your letter and especially in contemplating the name of the donors among whom I recognize not only personal friends but merchants whose fame is coextensive with the dominions of our Glorious Flag." Such an august tribute "will nerve my arm and impel me to renewed exertions in the struggle yet before us." Naturally the Sherman and Ewing families viewed the gift as yet another recognition of Sherman's rising and deserved stature as a successful warrior. Maria Ewing wrote Ellen that Hugh Boyle and his wife "gave me a glowing description of the splendid sword, [which] must be Magnificent, but not more splendid & magnificent than the owner is deserving of."[37]

Meanwhile "the struggle yet before us" continued unabated, and Sherman was never free of the guerrilla issue while he commanded in Memphis. His constant problem with partisans dovetails with recent scholarship, which suggests that guerrilla activity in Tennessee and Kentucky was more extensive than previously thought, and perhaps comparable with Missouri and Kansas, states traditionally considered hotbeds of irregular warfare. To conclude, however, that Sherman became an advocate of total war as a result of his guerrilla experiences in the fall of 1862 would be excessive. More accurately, he recognized the dynamic, driving force of an evolving conflict, which propelled men toward greater ideological rigidity, accompanied by increasing bitterness and escalating brutality, ever more destructive of both life and property.[38]

Writing to his daughter about "how cruel men become in war," Sherman said, "It now requires all my energy to prevent our soldiers from robbing & plundering the houses and property of ... Enemies." He claimed that "our Enemies are even worse than we," and sadly spoke of old friends who "look on me as a Brutal wretch," and if given the chance "would now shoot me dead." Responding to Confederate General John

C. Pemberton, concerning guerrillas and reprisals, Sherman wrote that he knew Pemberton did not sanction some of the deeds perpetrated by Southern partisans, and then implored, relative to possible reprisals for unjustified and despicable Federal actions: "Do not make this war more vindictive and bloody than it has been and *will be in spite of the most moderate counsels*" [emphasis added]. In Sherman's mind, inevitably, the war would grow more ruthless.[39]

SHERMAN WAS ALSO troubled by the slavery question. The U.S. Congress had passed two Confiscation Acts—the first in the summer of 1861 and the second shortly before Sherman's arrival in Memphis—declaring that slaves employed in support of the Confederate war effort or owned by masters who were in open hostility to the United States were free. Sherman found hundreds of fugitive slaves at Memphis. He had no interest whatsoever in trying to determine their status, under the Confiscation Acts, as slave or free. Nor did he conceive it his duty, believing that such work was the prerogative of the judiciary. He simply decided that if they remained in the city—and he did permit them to leave if they chose—then they must work. Slave labor would benefit the Union Army, while simultaneously depriving the Confederacy.[40]

Initially Sherman employed the majority of the slaves, approximately 1,300 males, in building Fort Pickering, a fortification overlooking the Mississippi River. Designed to guard the land approaches to Memphis, the fort was already under construction when Sherman arrived. Several hundred more blacks were put to work on the levee, loading and unloading boats; eventually about 1,000 served as teamsters and cooks. "All such negroes will be entitled to rations," he ordered, and "will be supplied with necessary clothing and [chewing] tobacco at the rate of one pound per month." Records of their labor would be kept, but no wages were to be paid "until the courts determine whether the negro be slave or free." Sherman anticipated that "a fair and equitable settlement [for loyal slave owners and freedmen] would be made at the 'end of the war.'" He also forbade any Federal soldier from hiring a slave as a personal servant.[41]

Clearly Sherman regarded the Confiscation measures as vexatious, which several of his letters reveal—particularly those to John. The U.S. government, in his view, was freeing slaves without addressing the consequences, either for the army or the blacks. He considered the government's action a typical procedure of blundering politicians, who failed to understand the practical aspects of their policies. Some of the freedmen could be put to work, but certainly not all, not even the majority. He wrote John that "no army could take care of the wants of the host of niggers, women & children that would hang about it, freed without the condition attached of earning their food and clothing." Sherman said he had already employed "the labor of negroes as far as will benefit the army." All others encumbered his forces. The army's wagon trains already were "a horrible impediment, and if we are to take along & feed the negros who flee to us for refuge, it will be an impossible task. You can not solve this negro question in a day."[42]

Then, on September 22, President Lincoln announced the preliminary Emancipation Act, to become effective on the first day of January 1863. That very day Sherman wrote his brother, "Are we to free all the negros, men, women, and children? Whether there be work for them or not?" The following day he addressed the provost marshal general of St. Louis: "I foresee much trouble as winter comes, to the women & children. Does Congress intend to feed & care for all the negroes? Is it not a task too great to be undertaken? These are serious questions and I can get no . . . word of advice from Washington." A week later Sherman again vented his frustration in a letter to John: "The President declares negros free, but makes no machinery by which such freedom is assured. I still see no solution of this Great problem except in theory." Sherman rightly foresaw that increasing numbers of refugee blacks—men, women and children—would constitute a tedious problem and a serious encumbrance upon Union military operations.[43]

Equally distressing to Sherman was the presence of numerous Northern merchants engaged in trading with the enemy. The single greatest commercial problem was the exchange in cotton. Sherman said "hundreds of greedy speculators flocked down the Mississippi, and resorted to all sorts of measures to obtain cotton." He claimed "swarms of Jews" were involved. Southerners selling the precious commodity demanded payment in gold, about three hundred dollars per bale, said Sherman, who had no doubt that the gold provided military supplies for the Confederacy. Thus he prohibited the purchase of cotton with gold, silver or treasury notes. Discovering that cotton could also be bought with salt, he forbade that exchange too, defining salt as contraband of war because of its use in curing meat for the Rebel armies.[44]

Sherman wrote Ellen on August 5, explaining that when he got to Memphis "the town was full of Jews & speculators buying cotton for gold, silver and treasury notes, the very thing the Confederates wanted, money." He had stopped all that exchange, and expected to be "universally abused by the Northern merchants." Sarcastically he declared, "I have no doubt the surrender of Memphis was made knowing that our People for the sake of a little profit would supply them the very thing they stood in need of." Later in August, he told her, "I see the Cincinnati papers are finding fault with me again." Then he claimed, "Cincinnati furnishes more contraband goods than Charleston, and has done more to prolong the war than the state of South Carolina." Not a merchant there, he claimed, "but would sell salt, bacon, powder & lead, if they can make *money* by it. . . . The cause of war is not alone in the nigger, but in the mercenary spirit of our countrymen." In a letter to Colonel William H. H. Taylor, Sherman wrote, "'Commerce must follow the flag' sounds well, but in truth commerce supplies our enemy the means to destroy that flag & the Government whose Emblem it is."[45]

Sherman's cotton policy did not stand. Just as Grant's order barring Jews from trains heading south was immediately overturned, so too Sherman found his prohibition of cotton purchases with gold and silver swiftly rebuked in Washington. By the summer of 1862, the Northern manufacturers had geared up to equip the Union armies with all manner of goods made from cotton fiber, the production of tents being a high priority at the time. Cotton was available in the South and the U.S. government intended to get it. With the growing demand, both manufacturers and speculators knew that big profits were likely, as government contracts for war materials proliferated. As ever in war, some men thought only of getting rich or richer—legally or illegally—and the number of American millionaires would increase many times over during the conflict, while hundreds of thousands of men suffered and died. With disgust Sherman wrote Ellen, "our people seem to measure everything by the money they can make."[46]

The reversal of Sherman's cotton order came from the secretary of war. Perhaps to cushion Stanton's rebuff, General Halleck told Sherman that "tents for the new levies can not be furnished till we get more cotton, and hence the absolute necessity of encouraging that trade just now. Money is of no more value to the rebels than cotton," the general dubiously claimed, "for they can purchase military munitions with the latter as well as the former." Halleck ignored the obvious fact that a ready market for Southern cotton at a high price in gold greatly facilitated the acquiring of munitions in the South, both the ease and the quantity. Certainly Halleck, like Sherman, had no choice but to accept Stanton's decision. He speculated that the policy would be changed "as soon as we get enough cotton for military purposes." Sherman's view, expressed to Adjutant General Lorenzo Thomas, was that "if the policy of the government demands cotton, order us to seize and procure it by the usual operations of war." Writing to John, Sherman revealed his anger: "The mercenary spirit of our people is too much and my orders are reversed and I am ordered to encourage the trade in cotton and all orders prohibiting Gold, Silver & Notes to be paid for it are annulled by orders from Washington." Bitterly he concluded, "but what are the lives of our soldiers to the profits of the merchant?"[47]

Smuggling was also a problem. Confederate sympathizers, in league with Northern men whose greatest goal was gaining wealth, continually sneaked military supplies out of Memphis. These quickly found their way to the Southern armies. In an effort to stop this traffic, Sherman restricted all trade to five major roads, with travel during daylight hours only, without exception. These roads were constantly monitored by Federal soldiers. However, many other roads led in and out of the city. Although some of these were little more than rough trails and paths, they served the purpose for smugglers. Guarding all of them was impossible. Even the checkpoints on the five designated trade routes were not always effective. Some guards were deceived by ingenious methods of concealing medicine, ammunition, salt, whiskey and other contraband.

Sherman discovered "a handsome city hearse" in a Mississippi barn, with a coffin containing "a fine assortment of medicines" that had been smuggled out of Memphis under ruse of "a first-class funeral." Guards sometimes could be bribed to allow forbidden items to pass. Considerable success was enjoyed by Southern women in moving illegal goods, because guards were reluctant to search females thoroughly, particularly to search under their skirts. All Sherman's work to curtail smuggling achieved only mixed results. Doubtless his efforts slowed the contraband, but he reported that "in spite of all efforts smuggling is carried on. . . . I am satisfied that salt and arms are got to the interior somehow."[48]

FAMILY LIFE back in Ohio—both the Sherman and the Ewing families— never seemed very far away from Cump, nor lacking for problems. Early in the war, Sherman had placed Charley Ewing, the youngest of Ellen's brothers, in the U.S. Thirteenth Infantry, the regiment Sherman initially was to command, but never did. Charley eventually found himself guarding prisoners in Illinois. He had not seen combat, feared the war would be over before he ever got into action and wanted to serve with Sherman. Ellen, her father and Charley were not going to be satisfied until Charley joined Sherman in some capacity. Following Shiloh, Sherman spoke to Halleck about the matter, more than once, at last obtaining the general's assurance that several companies of the Thirteenth, including Charley's, had been ordered to join Sherman's command.[49]

Several weeks passed, however, and the Thirteenth remained in Illinois, with Charley shifted from guard duty to mustering in new troops, after Ellen went to see the governor of Ohio about what she termed her brother's "ignominious post." Ellen considered the mustering assignment as nothing more than a stopgap measure, and continued urging her husband to do something about Charley's plight. Sherman was irritated by the pressure, writing Charley that already he had done "all a gentleman should do" in attempting to help, and declared that "your father [and] Ellen have written me some 500 times on this one subject." But because Charley seemed "so deeply offended" at him, Sherman promised that "I will do what I would not do for myself; go behind Halleck and enquire of his adjutant what has been done. If Halleck find it out," Sherman said, "my influence with him is gone," for he would think that Sherman must have "doubted his word and promise." He concluded the letter by stating: "We cannot change the inveterate hatred of these [Southern] People," and thus Charley "need not be uneasy. You will get your belly full of fighting." In early December, the Thirteenth Infantry, and Charley, arrived in Memphis. By then Ellen was working to get her brother Phil assigned to Sherman.[50]

Meanwhile, a long-festering source of tension between Ellen and Sherman's sister Elizabeth resurfaced. At issue was control of the house that had belonged to Sherman's mother. When Elizabeth decided to move out, Ellen wanted to live there, but Elizabeth intended to rent the place. Sherman had a strong claim on it, having contributed significantly to the support of his mother, also giving Elizabeth $2,000 when she was in dire need and allowing her, with John's consent, to live there for several years until her financial condition improved. Spurred on by Ellen, Sherman contended with his sister for some time. He wrote John to help him. Sherman seemed particularly incensed that Elizabeth had rented the house to a preacher. Finally he did succeed in securing the place for Ellen and the children, beginning in the spring of 1863.[51]

Ellen also wanted to visit her husband in Memphis. Sherman did not like the idea, telling her that "in spite of my injunctions, several families have come to Memphis to see their husbands, but I do not wish you to come." Clearly he did not like setting an example of that which he opposed. Sherman said that "military camps are no place for ladies," a sentiment he repeated in letters to Ellen, brother-in-law Phil and John Sherman. Only when he thought John was coming to Memphis for a short visit did he relent, writing that Ellen might accompany John.

His brother eventually decided not to make the trip, but Ellen came anyway. She stayed for nearly a month, bringing the children, except for Minnie and Willy, who were away at school. She lodged some of the time at the Gayoso House, already a Memphis landmark dating from 1842, featuring an impressive Greek Revival portico with wrought-iron balconies overlooking the Mississippi, and offering amenities available nowhere else in the city, such as marble tubs, silver faucets and flush toilets. While visiting his father, six-year-old Tommy became "a corporal" in one of the companies, fitted with a little uniform which he "wore . . . like a real soldier," according to Sherman. He was disappointed that Willy did not get "a chance to see a large army." One evening, several of Sherman's officers appeared, conducted a ceremony and presented the General with a fine sword. Ellen knew by Sherman's response that he was deeply gratified by such "attachment and confidence on the part of his tried and valued officers." She also observed that he was thin, and "more wrinkled than most men of sixty"; however, he was "so cheerful and well," she wrote John, that she "ceased to lament the evidences of time & care."[52]

By early December, Ellen had returned to Ohio. Sherman was preparing to begin a campaign against the Confederate stronghold at Vicksburg. Feeling good about his service in Memphis, he enthusiastically wrote Ellen, "I feel I have achieved perfect success"—an exaggeration, obviously, but he had done a creditable job in a difficult situation, perhaps as good as reasonably could have been expected. He told Halleck, "I think Memphis is now the best and most complete base of operations on the Mississippi." He recognized that he was popular with his officers and men, and even some of the Memphis people. While he knew as well as anyone that he was not engaged in a popularity contest, the esteem he enjoyed boosted his confidence.

During his Memphis tenure Sherman took steps to assist the poor. "Generosity and benevolence to the poor and distressed are characteristics of good soldiers," he wrote to his regimental and company commanders on October 30. He said that "many poor families in and about Memphis" were in need of wood, clothing and food. Declaring that the

United States government "provides all these to our soldiers bounte-
ously," Sherman instructed that every company, "by the exercise of reasonable economy," should save a portion of their allotment and give the
surplus to the poor. He set up a Central Relief Committee, where "bread,
flour, meat, rice, coffee, sugar, or anything needed by poor and sick families," would be received and "distributed to the worthy." This program
enhanced the popular image of both the army and its commander, as
well as helping the needy families.

Sherman does not seem to have regretted missing the Battle of
Corinth. In early October the Confederates had tried to regain that vital
crossroads. Hoping to deceive the Union defenders, a Rebel army moved
north, as if to march into Tennessee several miles west of Corinth. The
Confederates then turned back and attacked the town from the northwest. The Federals were prepared, however, and prevailed after a hard-
fought two-day battle in which about 20,000 men were engaged on each
side. Sherman did regard the effect of the clash as "very great," because
it ensured continued Union control of west Tennessee, and he wrote
Grant that the confidence of Southern sympathizers in Memphis had
been "shaken . . . awfully."

What Sherman really wanted, as many times he had indicated, was
"to stick to the Mississippi," and he eagerly looked forward to a major
military campaign on the great river. Plainly, the main obstacle blocking
United States control of the Mississippi was the fortress at Vicksburg.
In Sherman's mind, no military objective of the war was of such importance at that time as reducing Vicksburg, and thereby clearing and
securing navigation of the Mississippi all the way to the Gulf of Mexico.
Comparatively, Port Hudson, standing some miles south of Vicksburg,
would present a minor annoyance once the formidable bastion at Vicksburg was in Federal hands. Sherman was primed to get on with the job.[53]

Chapter Seventeen

THE STRONGEST PLACE
I EVER SAW

The great Confederate citadel stood high atop massive, unscalable bluffs that overlooked the Mississippi, the first high ground below Memphis that lay on the east bank of the river. Towering two hundred feet above the Mississippi, and bristling with many heavy guns sited both on the heights and at water level, the Vicksburg fortress dominated a hairpin curve of the mighty river as it streamed southward along the base of the precipice. The finest army that Sherman or Grant ever commanded could not have landed below those heights and taken the stronghold by assault from the riverfront.

As for the land side—north, east and south—the terrain everywhere was ideal for defense. The Walnut Hills, on which the fortress rested, were cut by numerous ravines and gullies. Those ravines, sometimes forty or fifty feet deep and running in various directions were snarled with thick, entangling brush and fallen timber. Confederate engineers skillfully enhanced the natural defenses with extensive earthworks, strengthened with abatis, and providing excellent fields of fire. Despite the formidable Rebel land defenses, the only hope of taking Vicksburg was with a large army moving against it on the solid ground east of the fortress, while naval vessels, supported by infantry, were positioned to choke off any possible supplies and reinforcements from the trans-Mississippi, as Confederate territory west of the river is frequently designated.

The importance of Vicksburg was not only that it dominated the legendary river. Vicksburg was also the sole railroad and river junction between Memphis and New Orleans. Through Vicksburg ran the western Confederacy's single east–west rail connection with the trans-Mississippi. The Vicksburg, Shreveport & Texas line extended west of the river, while the Southern Mississippi Railroad ran east from Vicksburg to Jackson, there intersecting the north–south railroad to New Orleans, before continuing east through Meridian. At Meridian, the Southern Mississippi crossed the Mobile & Ohio rails coming south from Corinth. Control of the Mississippi River certainly was the Union's top priority, but breaking the Rebel east–west rail connections through Vicksburg would by no means be a minor achievement.

The U.S. military forces, both army and navy, required time and experience to fully appreciate the difficulties inherent in attempting to reduce the Vicksburg bastion. Their learning process began during the late spring and early summer of 1862. Some Union leaders then anticipated—not very realistically in historical hindsight—that Vicksburg would fall to the combined naval forces of David Farragut, steaming upriver from New Orleans, and the fleet of Charles Davis moving downriver from Memphis. Had not Farragut taken New Orleans, and received the surrender of Baton Rouge and Natchez, while Davis forced the capitulation of Memphis? Army assistance might not even be necessary to capture Vicksburg. General Halleck wrote Secretary of War Stanton on June 12, "If the combined fleets of Farragut and Davis fail to take Vicksburg, I will send an expedition for that purpose." On June 25, Halleck again wrote to Stanton: "It is hoped that the two flotillas united will be able to reduce [Vicksburg]."[1]

Beginning the last week of June, the naval commanders made a determined effort to subdue the mighty fortress. Their combined strength boasted more than two hundred guns and a score of mortars, with which they bombarded the Confederate citadel day after day. The Rebel stronghold showed no sign whatsoever of cracking. In fact the Southern heavy batteries fiercely dueled the Federal naval guns on at least equal terms. At one point Farragut and Davis engaged a crude Confederate ironclad,

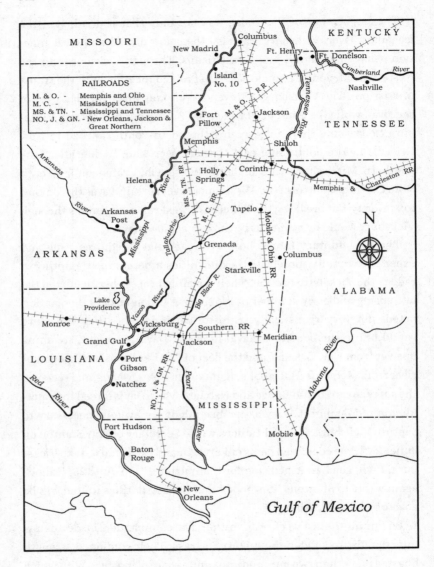

VICKSBURG OPERATIONS AREA

By late 1862, the capture of Vicksburg became the primary Union objective in the western theater of the war. Map by Jim Moon Jr.

called the *Arkansas*, which unexpectedly emerged from the mouth of
the Yazoo River and caused quite a stir as its ten guns damaged more
than one of the Union vessels. Farragut was disappointed that he did not
destroy the ship, but within a few months her failing engines compelled
the crew to blow her up in order to prevent capture.[2]

Realizing that naval guns alone could never overcome Vicksburg,
Farragut put to work the 3,000 soldiers he brought with him from New
Orleans in an attempt to divert the channel of the Mississippi River. The
plan was to dig a canal, out of range of the fortress guns, which would
change the course of the river, leaving Vicksburg high, dry and useless
in blocking the Mississippi. But the great stream refused to cooperate, while hundreds of Yankees, both sailors and soldiers, were dying
of disease. The river level was also falling and Farragut rightly feared
his deep-draft ships might be stranded. In late July he gave up the campaign, heading downriver, while Davis steamed northward. Halleck had
long since committed his forces elsewhere and, as noted earlier, Lincoln
had summoned him to Washington as general-in-chief of all the armies.[3]

Thus the daunting task of reducing Vicksburg fell upon the shoulders
of Grant, supported enthusiastically by Sherman. After Farragut and
Davis ended their campaign to take the fortress, the Rebels continued
to strengthen its defenses. The Confederates also reclaimed control
of the Mississippi River from Vicksburg to Port Hudson, a distance of
perhaps 120 miles in a straight line—some 200 miles when measured
by the winding river. The Red River emptied into the Mississippi not
far north of Port Hudson, while the railroad from Texas ran eastward
through Shreveport and on to Vicksburg. Both by water and rail, all
manner of supplies and munitions could be transported to the armies
of the western Confederacy as long as that great stretch of the Mississippi remained in Southern hands. Actually, Confederate supplies from
west of the Mississippi never reached the quantities that President Lincoln and some other Americans assumed. But perceptions, whether
correct or erroneous, often motivate action, and Vicksburg was widely
perceived as a great gateway through which poured war materials from
the trans-Mississippi. From the Union perspective, that gateway must

be sealed off, simultaneously securing the great river for United States trade and transportation.[4]

Sherman, as anyone aware of his reverence for the Mississippi River might expect, had been urging General Grant to move against Vicksburg ever since Grant took command when Halleck departed for Washington. Sherman favored advancing an army down the Mississippi Central Railroad, thereby keeping constant pressure on the Confederate Army in the northern part of the state, while another Union force moved south on the Mississippi, to the mouth of the Yazoo.[5] Flowing from the northeast, the Yazoo emptied into the Mississippi about ten miles north of Vicksburg. From a landing on the Yazoo, Sherman believed the Federals could advance successfully against the Vicksburg fortifications. Convinced that the majority of the enemy forces that could defend Vicksburg were north of the Tallahatchie River, a tributary of the Yazoo, Sherman wrote Grant on October 21: "Now is the time to strike at the Yazoo and the Mississippi Central." Of course Grant knew as well as Sherman that Vicksburg must be taken at some point, but he did not act until well into November.[6]

Grant was understandably reluctant to take aggressive action against Vicksburg—or anywhere else, given his history with General Halleck—until he was positive he had both the approval of Halleck and the necessary forces and supplies to ensure success. During the first two weeks of November, several communications between Grant and Halleck give insight to Grant's perspective. Particularly significant are the exchanges of November 10 and 11. Responding to a query from Grant about reinforcements, Halleck told him that new regiments would soon be arriving in Memphis from Illinois, Ohio and Kentucky. "Memphis," said General Halleck, "will be made the depot of a joint military and naval expedition on Vicksburg."[7]

Grant had been hearing rumors that John A. McClernand was raising an army, with the approval of President Lincoln, for operations on the Mississippi against the Vicksburg fortress. "Am I to understand," Grant asked Halleck on the evening of November 10, "that I lie still here [his headquarters at La Grange, Tennessee] while an expedition is fitted out from Memphis, or do you want me to push as far south as possible? Am I to have Sherman move subject to my order, or is he and his forces reserved for some special service?" Halleck, like Grant and Sherman, was no advocate of a non–West Point politician such as McClernand leading a campaign to reduce Vicksburg. Halleck gave Grant the clearance for which he no doubt had hoped: "You have command of all troops sent to your department, and have permission to fight the enemy where you please." On November 14, Grant shared with Sherman the information Halleck had sent about the mounting of an expedition from Memphis against Vicksburg, also noting "the mysterious rumors of McClernand's command."[8]

The next day Grant sent a brief order to Sherman: "Meet me at Columbus, Kentucky, on Thursday next. If you have a good map of the country south of you, take it up with you." Sherman embarked on a steamboat and headed north from Memphis. Grant explained that he intended to move against the Confederate forces commanded by John Pemberton in north Mississippi, which were entrenched on a line south of the Tallahatchie. James McPherson, who commanded the Union troops at Corinth, was to rendezvous with Grant at Holly Springs, Mississippi, coming up on his left flank, while Sherman, leaving a proper garrison in Memphis, would advance into Mississippi with the majority of his command and join up on Grant's right flank. The initial objective would be Pemberton's army; the ultimate objective, said Grant, was to reduce Vicksburg and open the navigation of the Mississippi River.[9]

The plan may not have been all that Sherman wanted, but the important thing was that Grant had decided to take action—action pointing toward reducing the fortress at Vicksburg. Sherman was pleased and, hurrying back to Memphis, he prepared to move out as soon as possible. In late November Grant advanced down the Mississippi Central Railroad, while Sherman moved southeastward from Memphis, leading approximately 16,000 soldiers and drawing close to Grant's troops as both forces neared the Tallahatchie River. Pemberton refused to engage, retreating farther into the interior of the state. The weather turned bad, with pouring rain, streams swollen and difficult to cross, while some roads were nearly impassable. Grant revised his plans, especially after learning that Halleck's interest now focused on Vicksburg, with a campaign projection somewhat reminiscent of Sherman's. "Your main object," Halleck instructed on December 5, "will be to hold the line from Memphis to Corinth with as small a force as possible, while the largest number possible is thrown upon Vicksburg with the gunboats." On December 7, Halleck clearly gave Grant a green light to proceed: "You will move your troops as you may deem best to accomplish the great object in view."[10]

Grant summoned Sherman to meet him at Oxford, Mississippi. On an overall basis, Grant now favored the plan Sherman had advocated: a two-pronged advance by land and river against Vicksburg. Sherman was to return to Memphis, marshal all the new regiments arriving from the Midwest, many of which John McClernand was directing south, and with 40,000 men (the number Grant quoted to Halleck) proceed down the Mississippi by steamboat to move against Vicksburg from the Yazoo. The entire gunboat fleet, under the command of David D. Porter, would cooperate with the army. Meanwhile, Grant would advance to keep pressure on Pemberton's army, preventing the Confederate general from sending reinforcements to the Vicksburg defenders, whom Sherman and Grant anticipated would be outnumbered. Sherman's forces were to enter the Yazoo, land at a suitable disembarkation point and ascend the Chickasaw Bluffs southeast of the river. After gaining the plateau east of Vicksburg—considered the best ground from which to attack—Sherman would seize the great citadel from the rear. It was hoped that Nathaniel P. Banks would be advancing from the south, placing yet more pressure on the Rebels. Essentially, the Vicksburg campaign would be the one Sherman favored, and Sherman himself was being positioned as the key leader in taking the formidable bastion.[11]

While Sherman's troops had maneuvered in north Mississippi, discipline problems among the soldiers, although not as bad as they once had been, continued to aggravate him. One soldier wrote his wife about the General's coming upon some troops who had appropriated an elegant carriage from a nearby plantation. They were enjoying their fine mode of transportation, as they traveled down the road in a style to which they likely were not accustomed—certainly not since they had been in the army. Sherman probably had no particular concern about who might be the owner of the carriage and the horses pulling it. The problem, as he saw it, was the manifestation of a lack of regimen in his command. Men on the march who acted like these troops could not be depended upon to do their duty in battle. At once Sherman ordered the men to get down from the carriage. When one of them refused, Sherman became enraged, grabbed a rifle from a soldier near at hand and perhaps would have shot the defiant fellow, but the weapon was not loaded. Thereupon he resorted to a measure that made more sense than shooting a soldier anyway. Unhitching the four horses that pulled the carriage, he forced the men to get into the harness and pull the carriage back to the plantation from which they had stolen it.[12]

Sherman was also annoyed by soldiers pretending to be sick. "In course of time we may get an army," he sarcastically remarked to brother John, but for the present, he claimed that "at the moment of Marching a fearful list of sickness develops and one fourth [of the Army] has to be left behind. . . . The Great Evil is absenteeism," he wrote, "which is really Desertion & should be punished with Death." Sherman was back in Memphis by December 13, where he learned of the bloody, awful repulse suffered by the Army of the Potomac at Fredericksburg, Virginia. Ambrose Burnside had launched frontal assaults against the virtually impregnable Rebel position on Marye's Heights, costing the Union forces almost 13,000 casualties. Many observers thought the outcome of such a battle was clearly foreseeable, and Sherman predicted to John that General McClellan "will be recalled [to command] sooner or later." Sherman still held a favorable opinion of McClellan's ability, although Ellen continued to see him, as noted previously, in a dark light. She informed her husband: "Father writes that Secretary Stanton told him you were 'by far the best general we have—administratively and in the field'—So do not provoke me again by putting yourself below McClellan."[13]

By the time Ellen penned those words, Sherman was already on his way down the Mississippi to attack Vicksburg, armed with a carte blanche order from Grant to reduce "that place in such manner as circumstances and your own judgment may dictate." Sherman had written John, "The move is one of vast importance, and if successful will remove the chief obstacles to the navigation of the Mississippi." Sherman well knew that he had a tough assignment. Several factors bothered him, and he told John that "things are not exactly right." Grant commanded east of the Mississippi, Samuel R. Curtis west of the river and Admiral Porter on the river itself. "All ought to be under one head" he said, acknowledging unity of command, one of the nine principles of generalship recognized today by the U.S. Army. As the action developed, however, it involved neither Grant nor Curtis in any direct or meaningful manner. The relationship between Sherman and Porter, who would have to work effectively with each other if the mission were to succeed, was the critical factor. Only on the eve of the expedition did the two men meet for the first time. Fortunately, they liked each other. Porter was a few years older than Sherman. A longtime navy man who had gone to sea when he was ten, he spoke his mind readily and had a hearty manner about him—if he approved of you. Sherman and Porter meshed perfectly, experiencing no problems in coordinating army-navy operations.[14]

Sherman was also concerned about keeping in touch with Grant. Rail and river communication would be long, time-consuming and uncertain, while communication by land was basically unreliable. "The Country is full of Guerilla Bands so that the couriers cannot be relied on across the country 75 miles," he informed John. Telegraph lines, while instantaneous, were highly vulnerable—and sometimes were cut by a single person. Probably Sherman and Grant would be unable to communicate, a situation both anticipated. All Sherman could do, realistically, was try to reach Vicksburg by a designated date—December 25—which Grant would be expecting as he maneuvered to pressure Pemberton's Confederates. Sherman knew too that he was not going to have 40,000 troops, telling John, after he saw the new regiments in Memphis, "I cannot count on more than 30,000." He would have that many only after picking up a 10,000-man division under Frederick Steele at Helena, Arkansas.[15]

"The preparations were necessarily hasty in the extreme," Sherman wrote in his memoirs, "but this was the essence of the whole plan, viz., to reach Vicksburg as it were by surprise," he claimed, "while General Grant held in check Pemberton's army . . . leaving me to contend only with the smaller garrison of Vicksburg and its well-known strong batteries and defenses." Actually, surprise was unrealistic, and both Sherman and Grant had to know it. Nearly seventy troop transports steaming down the Mississippi, carrying approximately 32,500 men, and accompanied by a gunboat fleet—"a magnificent sight," according to Sherman—could not escape detection. Furthermore, when snipers fired on the vessels from a small settlement on the eastern shore, Porter's gunboats shelled the town, and Sherman landed troops who burned some buildings in the area. Long before Sherman reached the Yazoo, the Confederates knew that large numbers of Federal troops were moving south on the Mississippi. And they had to know that Vicksburg was the only possible objective that warranted such an impressive force.[16]

While undeniably both Sherman and Grant were in a hurry for the Vicksburg expedition to weigh anchor, their true motivation was to thwart John McClernand's plans to take command of the operation. This Grant confessed in his memoirs: "I feared that delay might bring McClernand, who was [Sherman's] senior and who had authority from the President and Secretary of War Stanton to exercise that particular command. . . . I doubted McClernand's fitness; and I had good reason to believe that in forestalling him I was by no means giving offense to those whose authority to command was above both him and me." Grant knew that General Halleck also distrusted McClernand's abilities. He knew too that Halleck held Sherman in high regard. Both Halleck and Grant were determined that Sherman would lead the expedition against Vicksburg.[17]

The inception of the campaign did indeed involve a bit of a surprise, although the Confederates were not the ones victimized. John McClernand, having just married the sister of his deceased wife, arrived in Memphis shortly after Christmas. Accompanied by his new spouse, as well as the bridal party, McClernand expected that he would at once assume command of the troops he had raised, and with them set forth to reduce Vicksburg. Instead, he learned to his consternation that William Tecumseh Sherman had embarked for Vicksburg on December 19, taking with him all the men who were available. McClernand was convinced that he had been betrayed. "Either accident or intention," he wrote the President, had thwarted the plans, as well as allegedly undermining the authority of both Lincoln and Stanton. A few days later, he decried "the clique of West Pointers who have been persecuting me for months." The major villain, he eventually concluded, was Halleck. On December 30, McClernand steamed after Sherman, on the *Tigress*, still accompanied by his new bride and her party, as well as an amazing gaggle of forty-nine staff officers. McClernand's high-handed bungling in the weeks to come contributed greatly toward establishing the term "political general" as a byword for military incompetence.[18]

ON THE EVENING of December 20, Sherman arrived at Helena, Arkansas, where he picked up Frederick Steele's division the next morning. From upriver came a disturbing report. Union soldiers arriving in Memphis after Sherman departed said that Grant's newly established forward supply depot at Holly Springs had been captured. "I hardly know what faith to put in such a report," he wrote Grant, "but suppose whatever may be the case, you will attend to it." Unfortunately, the report was true; worse, Holly Springs was not the whole story. The Rebels had struck in both Mississippi and Tennessee. Confederate Major General Earl Van Dorn's cavalry swept around Grant's eastern flank and destroyed the great supply base, while Nathan Bedford Forrest's troopers tore up nearly fifty miles of railroad and telegraph lines north of Jackson, Tennessee, also burning a large quantity of provisions. Grant had to pull back. With the railroad wrecked, he could not bring up more supplies for some time. Nor could he get word to Sherman. The Rebels were free to send reinforcements to Vicksburg, and they did.[19]

Sherman faced a tough decision. He knew nothing of the destruction in Tennessee, and the information about Holly Springs was unconfirmed. If the Holly Springs report were not true, and Sherman halted

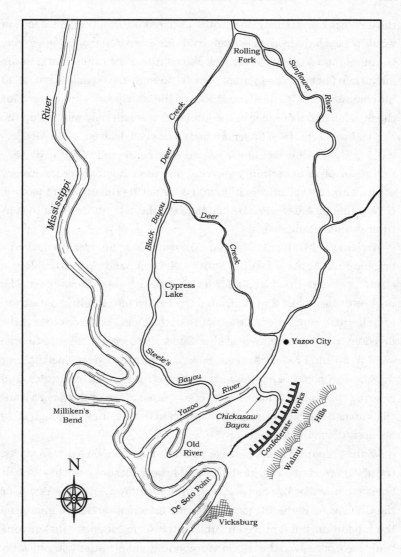

CHICKASAW BAYOU AND STEELE'S BAYOU OPERATION AREA

U. S. Grant's first offensive against Vicksburg envisioned Sherman advancing by water to attack the Confederates at Chickasaw Bayou (Chickasaw Bluffs). Map by Jim Moon Jr.

the advance based solely on unsubstantiated information, his decision would at best be judged excessively cautious. Even if the report were true, Grant might deal with the setback and continue the campaign. If in the meantime Sherman had pulled back to Memphis, he would have failed his commander. Also, the troops aboard the transports were primed for the mission and a number of the gunboats were already moving up the Yazoo. Furthermore, if Sherman halted or even delayed, John McClernand quite possibly would arrive and take command. War, by its very nature, involves uncertainty and risk. Sherman did not have the luxury of awaiting further information and considering the matter at leisure. Given what he knew when he had to make the call, his decision to continue is understandable.

Arriving at Milliken's Bend on Christmas Day, Sherman detached a brigade from Andrew Jackson Smith's division, sending it to break up a stretch of the railroad leading from Vicksburg toward Shreveport. The next morning, while Smith awaited the return of the railroad destroyers, Sherman proceeded to the mouth of the Yazoo with his other three divisions, commanded by Brigadier Generals Morgan L. Smith, George W. Morgan and Frederick Steele. Several gunboats had steamed upriver days before, penetrating the narrow Yazoo for some fifteen miles, and clearing the muddy water of torpedoes (mines). One of the navy's ironclads struck a torpedo and sank in less than ten minutes, although all of her crew did manage to escape.[20]

While preparing a safe passage for Sherman's men on the transports, the naval vessels also scouted for suitable landing sites, which were few. Sherman never before had seen the wild, swampy area of the Yazoo, or the Chickasaw Bluffs. He gathered some information before mounting the expedition, but it proved insufficient. It seems doubtful that anyone could have perceived the region's foreboding complexities without actually seeing them firsthand—all the more so when such maps as Sherman possessed were inadequate. "Low boggy ground, with innumerable bayous or deep sloughs," to quote Sherman, mingled with dense woods covered by Spanish moss, and stretched for miles along the Vicksburg side of the Yazoo.[21]

After conferring with Porter and learning that the Yazoo above the mouth of Chickasaw Bayou was not yet cleared of mines, Sherman disembarked his troops at Johnson's Plantation, a parcel of cleared ground in a swampy area on the south bank of the river, approximately a dozen miles upstream. The place was not ideal, but perhaps as good as anything available. On December 27 and 28, Sherman personally reconnoitered the whole area, attempting to determine the best ground for an attack. The region was cut up by bayous. "We get across one only to find ourselves on the bank of another." Both days saw widespread heavy skirmishing, and sniper fire presented a danger everywhere. In fact, a sniper took out one of Sherman's division commanders.

"During the general reconnaissance of the 28th, Morgan L. Smith received a severe and dangerous wound in his hip," recounted Sherman, "which completely disabled him." Sherman feared that Smith's wound would prove fatal, but he did survive. Sherman regarded Smith as one of his best officers. He also mourned the loss of William Gwin, commander of the ironclad *Benton*. Sherman had worked with Gwin back in March on the Tennessee River, in attempting to break the Memphis & Charleston Railroad. He told Ellen that Gwin was "my favorite in the fleet." In a sharp engagement on the Yazoo, Gwin insisted that a commander's place was on the quarterdeck, not the armored pilothouse. Struck by a solid shot in the chest and arm, which left a lung exposed and badly injured, while ripping away most of the arm—"the most fearful wound I ever saw," said Porter—Gwin lingered in pain for a few days before finally relieved by death. "We of the army," wrote Sherman, "had come to regard him as one of us."[22]

By Monday morning, December 29, Sherman was ready to attack. He estimated the enemy's total forces at 15,000—approximately twice their actual number, although more Confederates were arriving daily. Positioned on high ground atop the Chickasaw Bluffs, the Rebels also held a shelf of land extending along the base of the bluffs. With a road running along the shelf, some fifteen to twenty feet above the swampy lowland, and another road paralleling it at the top of the bluffs, the Southerners could quickly shift their defensive strength to any threatened point. Also, about a mile and a half from the Yazoo, Sherman's forces, before they could assault the Confederates on the bluffs, first confronted the formidable natural obstacle of Chickasaw Bayou. The bayou, said Sherman, "was impassable except at two points—one near the head of [the] Bayou ... and the other about a mile lower down." The entire area, Sherman declared, "was as difficult as it could possibly be from nature and art." He decided, as recorded in his memoirs, "to make a show of attack along the whole front, but to break across the bayou at the two points named." One of the approaches, he reported, was across a narrow levee and the other over a sandbar. Both presented the enemy with an excellent killing field.

Brigadier General David Stuart, now leading Morgan Smith's troops, was to launch one of the primary attacks, while George Morgan's division made the other. Sherman ordered demonstrations against both flanks, while Andrew Jackson Smith's command, as a further diversion, was to move out on the road leading from Johnson's Plantation toward Vicksburg. When Sherman pointed out the ground where General Morgan was to attack, Morgan confidently asserted, according to Sherman: "General, in ten minutes after you give the signal I'll be on those hills." Division commander Frederick Steele reported that Morgan told him that "within thirty minutes" he would possess "the heights to a moral certainty"—bold words soon to be proven ingloriously empty.[23]

Sherman gave the attack signal at noon, his batteries opening a heavy artillery fire along the whole line. General Morgan, however, did not even get across the bayou, let alone assault the hills beyond. A brigade led by Brigadier General Frank Blair Jr. did make it across the bayou, but was devastated by Rebel artillery and rifled musketry. Another brigade moved out in a wrong direction and never came close to getting across the bayou. Men who did manage to cross, and charge to the base of the bluffs, were pinned down, surviving by, in Sherman's words, "scooping out with their hands caves in the bank, which sheltered them against the fire of the enemy, who, right over their heads, held their muskets outside the parapet vertically, and fired down. So critical was the position," he concluded, that "we could not recall the men till after dark, and then one at a time."[24]

The attack had resulted in a bloody repulse, accomplished nothing and inflicted only minimal casualties on the Rebels. Sherman always believed that General Morgan handled his division incompetently, costing the Federals any chance of success, but he said nothing critical of Morgan in his official report, even though he was urged to do so by Frank Blair. "Our loss is about 1800, —say 300 killed, 400 taken prisoner, and over a thousand wounded," Sherman estimated shortly after the attack. His figures were not far off, except for the number of U.S. soldiers killed, later calculated at 208. Confederate casualties totaled 207, of which 63 were killed. Sherman was not ready to give up, however. Consulting with David Porter, who agreed to cooperate, Sherman decided to move one of his divisions upstream to Haynes's Bluff and launch a diversionary attack against the Confederate right flank. If the Rebels dispatched reinforcements to that flank, Sherman hoped, with his other divisions, to break through their weakened line in the center.[25]

Frederick Steele's division was loaded aboard the transports for the diversionary endeavor. But early on the morning of January 1, 1863, a fog "so thick and impenetrable that it was impossible to move," settled on the Yazoo, and the effort had to be abandoned. Rain also began falling. Sherman noticed watermarks on trees "ten and twelve feet above their roots." He envisioned the entire region's quickly becoming a quagmire, and his whole expedition literally mud-bound. No word had been heard from either Grant or Banks, and Sherman thought the sound of trains coming and going at Vicksburg probably signaled the arrival of enemy reinforcements. He was right. "I was forced to the conclusion," he reported, "that it was not only prudent but proper that I should move my command to some other point." On January 2 and 3 the rain came down in torrents. Sherman felt sure that he had escaped the swamps of Chickasaw Bayou in the nick of time, "for now water and mud must be forty feet deep there."[26]

Nevertheless, Sherman agonized that his first independent combat operation, and his first major attack, had ended in failure. While George Morgan's ineffective leadership played a part in the disaster, Sherman's greater problem was the awful terrain. Although his total forces significantly outnumbered the Confederates, the nature of the ground over which the attack was made prevented him from using his superior forces to advantage. Moving across narrow and open ground, before they could even assault the bluffs, the Union sacrificed mass at the points where they hoped to break through the enemy defenses. Unless Sherman could have devised some way to strike the Rebels in flank, both with surprise and force, it is doubtful that he, or any other commander, could have won the battle. But with the enemy holding the high ground, a surprise attack anywhere would have been well nigh impossible. The terrain was so formidable in favor of the Southerners that quite conceivably Sherman never actually had a chance of defeating the Confederates at Chickasaw Bluffs.

"Well, we have been to Vicksburg," Sherman wrote Ellen, "and it was too much for us, and we have backed out." He knew that "People at a distance" would ridicule the failure, but confidently asserted that "nobody who was there will." He spoke of "the natural strength" of the position, offering some details supportive of historian John Keegan's recent, perceptive assessment that basically Sherman "had been defeated by geography." In a letter to his brother, Sherman spoke of the criticisms he must face from the press, also elaborating, as he had to Ellen, on the difficulties, many involving the terrain, that any commander would confront in attempting to overcome Vicksburg. However, he still acknowledged that "Vicksburg must be reduced," and then declared, "It is the strongest place I ever saw, both by nature and by art."[27]

The Ewing and Sherman families, not surprisingly, were unequivocally supportive of the General upon learning about the defeat. Maria Ewing probably expressed the consensus family opinion when she wrote Ellen of Sherman's wisdom and skill in retiring when he did and thereby saving his army. Maria thus touched upon one of Sherman's developing strengths—he could recognize when he was beat. Unlike some commanders in the heat of a battle, Sherman possessed a cool objectivity and, valuing the lives of his soldiers, would not keep throwing more men into a losing fight. Maria also elaborated interestingly, "Who could have imagined the strength of the enemy?" she asked, "their immense numbers, their defenses, ... their fortifications—surely their Master, the devil, has helped them." Vicksburg, she asserted, "had always been proverbial for its wickedness," and Maria had long heard that the river city, with its infamous red-light district along the waterfront, was the devil's own "headquarters." There was "great cause to thank God" for Sherman's safe deliverance from that wicked place.[28]

If God had saved Sherman from the devil's own den, Maria Ewing's son-in-law still had to deal with John McClernand. The Illinois political general arrived at the mouth of the Yazoo to take command just as Sherman was withdrawing his forces in defeat. The timing, for the volatile redhead, could hardly have been worse. Already low in spirit, the occasion proved bitter indeed. Sherman disliked McClernand intensely, declaring to brother John that the man was consumed "by a gnawing desire for fame & notoriety." Without a doubt, McClernand was an obnoxious character; still, Sherman likely would have been a bit more indulgent of the man's faults had he been a West Pointer and not a politician.[29]

Sherman next voiced his disappointment in the President. "Mr. Lincoln intended to insult me and the military profession by putting McClernand over me," he charged in the January 17 letter to his brother, "and I would have quietly folded up my things and gone to St. Louis, only I know in times like these all must submit to insult and infamy if necessary." Had the President "ordered a soldier here," he continued, "I would not have breathed a syllable of complaint, but to put a politician who claims a knowledge he Knows he does not possess & who envies the earned reputation of every subordinate" was unacceptable. "I never dreamed," he told John, "of so severe a test of my patriotism as being superseded by McClernand." Sherman assured Ellen, however, that he did "submit gracefully" when McClernand took command. His deep respect for military protocol would not have countenanced any inappropriate behavior. Ellen's view about the appointment of McClernand was that Lincoln "ought to be impeached as an imbecile."[30]

McClernand named his new command the Army of the Mississippi and organized it in two corps, one under George Morgan and the second under Sherman. While McClernand did not blame Sherman for the Chickasaw Bayou defeat—writing War Secretary Stanton that Sherman "has probably done all in the present case that anyone could have done"—his appointment of Morgan to lead a corps had to be galling to Sherman, coming as it did in the wake of that officer's poor performance on the Yazoo. From McClernand, Sherman learned that Grant was not advancing on Vicksburg, having retreated after the attacks on his supplies and communications. Sherman surmised that Confederate reinforcements truly were arriving at Vicksburg, just as he had thought. The wisdom of his decision to pull back from the Yazoo seemed confirmed. As for McClernand, Sherman did not think he had "any definite views or plans of action." McClernand spoke only "in general terms, of opening the navigation of the Mississippi, 'cutting his way to the sea,' etc., etc., but the *modus operandi* was not so clear."[31]

Since McClernand did not have a specific objective in mind, Sherman made a suggestion. Several days earlier the Union steamboat *Blue Wing*, heading south on the Mississippi with a cargo of mail and ammunition, had been captured by a Rebel gunboat near the mouth of the Arkansas River. The Arkansas emptied into the Mississippi on the west side of the great river, about halfway between Memphis and Vicksburg, and Sherman had learned that the enemy gunboat came from Fort Hindman (also known as Arkansas Post and as Post of Arkansas), a base about forty miles up the Arkansas. Sherman argued in favor of an attack on Fort Hindman, contending that Federal operations against Vicksburg would be harassed and hindered as long as the Confederates were free to steam down the Arkansas River and attack the Union supply line on the Mississippi. Sherman wanted permission to move up the Arkansas with his corps, and "clear out" Arkansas Post. Success would also offset, to a degree, Sherman's failure on the Yazoo—although he certainly was not about to mention such a face-saving motive to McClernand—and boost the morale of the troops.[32]

McClernand seemed uncertain about Sherman's proposal, according to Sherman, who then suggested that they put the matter to Admiral Porter, whose gunboats and transports would be essential to such

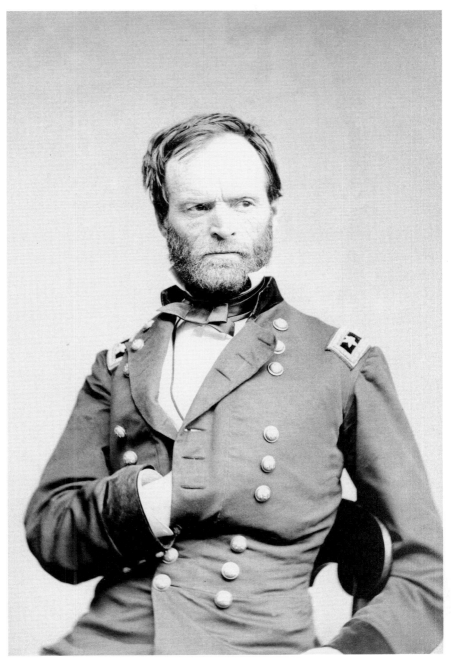

William Tecumseh Sherman in 1864. He had become nationally famous and was approaching the zenith of his army career.

Ellen Ewing Sherman, in her midforties, portrayed by G. P. A. Healy. Her marriage to Sherman in 1850 proved difficult from the first.

John Sherman, William Tecumseh's younger brother by three years, became a successful lawyer and politician.

Thomas Ewing was Sherman's affluent and influential foster father, and eventually his father-in-law.

The sons of Thomas and Maria Ewing (from left): Hugh Boyle, Phil, Tom Jr. and Charley.

The first son of William Tecumseh and Ellen, Willy, who died of fever at nine after visiting his father's Mississippi headquarters following the fall of Vicksburg.

Sherman's daughters (from left): Lizzie, Rachel, Elly and Minnie.

Thomas Ewing Sherman, the General's second son, pictured with his father in 1865.

Sherman near Atlanta, sitting tall and straight in the saddle, a short time before the fall of the city.

Sherman and his generals (from left): Oliver O. Howard, John A. Logan,
William B. Hazen, Sherman, Jefferson C. Davis, Henry W. Slocum,
Joseph A. Mower and Francis P. Blair.

Sherman on the Great Plains as a member of the Indian Peace Commission.

an operation. Porter's esteem for Sherman remained strong despite the Chickasaw Bayou repulse. The admiral thought Sherman "managed his men most beautifully" and attributed the defeat to Grant's inability to carry out the original plan, the inadequate leadership of some subordinates and the rain, which had "drowned [Sherman's] army out of the swamps." Sherman and Porter had already talked about the possibility of attacking the Rebel fort. McClernand readily agreed to a meeting with Porter, whom he and Sherman aroused about midnight, aboard his boat the *Black Hawk*, anchored at the mouth of the Yazoo. Porter soon decided, if he had not already done so, that he did not like John McClernand any better than Sherman did. "McClernand has just arrived," Porter wrote Andrew Foote on January 3, "and will take command; Sherman, though, will have all the brains." Sherman claimed that at one point during the midnight meeting he had to pull the admiral aside and calm him down, so incensed was Porter at McClernand. Eventually the three men reached an understanding, and McClernand approved the operation to reduce Fort Hindman. McClernand also decided, which Sherman never had in mind, to go along himself and take the whole army.[33]

On January 10, the troops were landed three or four miles below the fort. During the night following, which Sherman said was "bitter cold," although bright from the light of the moon, he made a personal, "close up" reconnaissance of the enemy position. Hiding behind a stump about 4:00 a.m., he heard a Rebel bugler "sound as pretty a reveille as I ever listened to." Returning to his command, Sherman said he moved all the corps into "an easy position for assault." The plan was for Porter's three ironclads to open the fight, blasting the fort from the waterfront; they hoped this would silence the Confederate guns, thereby saving the infantry, declared Sherman, from artillery fire along the "only possible line of attack."[34]

At 1:00 p.m. on Sunday, January 11, the gunboats opened fire and the army batteries immediately joined in the barrage. After a short time, Sherman ordered his artillery to cease firing and sent the infantry columns forward. His corps advanced on the right side of a road leading to the rear of the fort, while Morgan's corps moved on the left. The intervening ground between the Federals and the Rebel fort was approximately one-third of a mile. With the exception of a few gullies, the ground was generally level, offering little cover other than some trees and scattered logs. Nevertheless, "the troops advanced well under a heavy fire," declared Sherman, and slowly but relentlessly drew closer to the enemy's position.

Pounded from the river by the naval guns, while observing large numbers of Union infantry steadily crawling closer, many Confederates became convinced that further resistance was useless. Southern brigade commander Robert R. Garland, reported that between 4:00 and 4:30 p.m., the Union batteries and gunboats "had complete command [of his location], taking it in front, flank, and rear at the same time, literally raking our entire position." As the Federals readied for a final rush against the fort, an enemy soldier appeared on the parapet, waving a large white flag. "Numerous smaller white rags appeared," remembered Sherman, and the Rebels surrendered. Their total casualties were more than 5,500, the great majority of whom became prisoners. Northern casualties numbered 1,061, with 134 of them killed.[35]

The Confederate fort was rife with confusion as the surrender took place. Not all of the Rebels had been ready to give up, and some blamed Robert Garland for instigating the surrender without proper authorization from Thomas J. Churchill, his commanding officer. Apparently what really happened was that a number of soldiers simply decided, more or less simultaneously, that the time to raise the white flag was at hand. They proceeded to do so, and the action became contagious. But, wrote Sherman, "there seemed to be a good deal of feeling among the rebel officers against Garland," and consequently, the Confederate colonel asked Sherman whether he could stay the night with him. Sherman readily consented and then borrowed "a battered coffee-pot with some coffee and scraps of hard bread" from one of his soldiers. "I made coffee [and we] ate our bread together," remembered Sherman, "and talked politics by the fire till quite late at night."[36]

The Union triumph at Arkansas Post "was not a battle, but a clean little 'affaire,'" he told Ellen. Obviously pleased with the success, whatever it might be called, he overreached a bit, as he asserted, "This relieves our Vicksburg trip of all appearances of a reverse, as by this move we open the Arkansas and compel all organized masses of the Enemy to pass below the Arkansas River, and it will also secure this flank when we renew our attack on Vicksburg." Additionally, whenever the water level of the Arkansas rose, the capital at Little Rock would be open to the destructive fire of Federal gunboats. Turning to family news, Sherman noted that Charley Ewing had been under fire for some time. Presumably Ellen's brother was at last seeing all the action he desired. As for Sherman—whose war experience had now exceeded a year and a half—he offered a revealing comment about the perils of battle, declaring to his wife that "when danger is present, I feel it less than when it is in the remote future, or in the past," an assessment consistent with the cool demeanor that seemed always to characterize him in the heat of an engagement.[37]

Sherman continued to be unimpressed by John McClernand. He saw him on board the *Tigress* soon after the capture of Fort Hindman, and the political general was "in high spirits." Repeatedly McClernand exclaimed, "Glorious! Glorious! My star is ever in the ascendant!" While McClernand spoke in complimentary terms of the army, he "was extremely jealous of the navy," observed Sherman. Tired and hungry, Sherman was unappreciative of McClernand's self-congratulatory hurrahing. The exuberant Illinois politician said that he "had a man up a tree," observing the action as it unfolded and promised he soon would "make a splendid report" about the battle. Sherman did not think much of the report, saying it "almost ignored the action of Porter's fleet," which Sherman believed had played the major role in the victory. "The Admiral led his fleet in person," remembered Sherman, "and his guns silenced those of [the] Fort." Shortly after the engagement, he wrote John, "The Gunboats were handled beautifully and without them we would have had hard work; with them it was easy." Not to give Porter due credit, in Sherman's view, was the petty act of a little man. "McClernand is unfit [to command]," he declared to Ellen, "consumed by an inordinate personal ambition."[38]

For the record, McClernand did send Porter a two-sentence, congratulatory message, noting "the efficient and brilliant part taken by you, as commander of the Mississippi Squadron, in the reduction today of the Post of Arkansas." Sherman was certainly right, however, about McClernand's neglect of the navy in his official report. That report, fully nine printed pages in the *War of the Rebellion* records, scarcely mentions Porter's contribution. Other aspects of McClernand's report surely irritated Sherman as well. McClernand reported that Sherman "exhibited his usual activity and enterprise," while George Morgan had "proved his tactical skill and strategic talent"—quite a remarkable turnaround for a man whose recent performance at Chickasaw Bayou, in the appropriate words of historian Steven Woodworth, had been "nothing short of abysmal." Morgan, like McClernand, was a politician and a Democrat.[39]

Sherman always said that the attack on Arkansas Post originated with him. Writing to General Ethan Hitchcock, his friend from California days, he declared on January 25, "I planned & executed the move on the Post of Arkansas, but another had arrived at the critical moment [to] take the honor." Also, conveying his displeasure with the President's management of the war, Sherman told Hitchcock that he would "be rejoiced if Mr. Lincoln shall say '*Young* man we can do without you go home.' Indeed I would." Although Sherman never mentioned McClernand by name, the letter to Hitchcock clearly demonstrates the humiliation and disgust he had experienced when the Illinois politician superseded him. "There is no happiness to me in this mass of selfishness & I believe I serve my country with as pure a feeling as actuates any mortal, though I despise many of the tools that rule & control me." Sherman also had written both Ellen and John, declaring unequivocally that he proposed the Arkansas Post expedition. "I led the columns, gave all orders, and entered [the fort]," when McClernand then "came along and managed the prisoners & the captured property."[40]

To the utter annoyance of Sherman, John McClernand claimed to be the author of the attack on Fort Hindman. Early in his official report of that action, McClernand wrote, "I sailed . . . in execution of a purpose, the importance of which I suggested to General [Willis A.] Gorman at

Helena, December 30, on my way down the river. That purpose was the reduction of Fort Hindman, . . . which formed the key to Little Rock, the capital of . . . Arkansas." Just possibly, General Gorman himself might have inspired the idea of moving up the Arkansas. On December 19, a week before McClernand reached Memphis, Sherman wrote Grant that General Gorman "proposes to move all his forces from Helena to Napoleon at the mouth of the Arkansas." He could then be positioned either "to bring all his men to Vicksburg or act up the Arkansas."[41]

Regardless of McClernand's claims, the evidence favors Sherman as the driving force behind the Arkansas expedition. When General Grant, upon learning of the Fort Hindman venture and thinking that it was conceived by McClernand, called it "a wild goose chase," Sherman wrote his friend explaining the value, in his judgment, of eliminating the Rebel fort. If the Arkansas Post attack actually originated with McClernand, it's doubtful whether Sherman, given his disdain of the Illinois politician, would have written in defense of the mission. Brigadier General Frank Blair's corroborative statement to Sherman on February 1 is persuasive, all the more because Blair's attitude toward Sherman was somewhat testy at the time. "I am well aware," Blair wrote, "that you planned and in great measure executed the move against Arkansas Post, and I have not failed to say what I knew of it on proper occasions."

Furthermore, the very fact that Sherman became obsessed with the issue of credit tends to confirm his initiation of the venture. He was the man who, after the disappointing repulse on the Yazoo, felt deeply the need to reap something positive from the expedition—as his January 12 letter to Ellen conveyed. John McClernand was not the general who had suffered a defeat. When Sherman realized that McClernand himself would take the army up the Arkansas and seize the credit for the victory—a triumph that Sherman had conceived and intended to engineer—his anger boiled. As early as January 4, several days before the success at Arkansas Post, he wrote Ellen that he had proposed attacking the fort, and said that he was on the way to do so even as he wrote. Finally, Admiral Porter's statement in a February 3 letter to Sherman is forthright and convincing: "As to the Arkansas Post affair, it originated with yourself entirely, and you proposed it to me on the night you embarked the troops, and before it was known you had been relieved and that General McClernand had arrived."[42]

Obviously, the question of who proposed the attack on Arkansas Post is of no consequence whatsoever in the broad picture of the Civil War. The significance lies in the further exacerbation of Sherman's pronounced contempt for McClernand. It was as if the general now symbolized everything that was wrong with the way that the conduct of the war had evolved, both militarily and politically. As we have seen, Sherman criticized McClernand scathingly in letters to family members. He also lashed out at the deplorable judgment, as he saw it, of a president who would appoint such an unqualified man to a high military position. Seething with rage, he talked recklessly about leaving the army, writing Ellen that "the President's placing McClernand here, and the dead Set to ruin me for McClernand's personal Glory, would afford me a good chance to Slide out and escape the storms and troubles yet in reserve for us." Again he wrote: "Should I conclude to quit, I will go to Memphis and then to St. Louis. That is the best harbor to bring up in." The talk of "quitting" really alarmed Ellen.[43]

She feared—after Sherman's defeat on the Yazoo, the elevation of McClernand and the wild assertions about leaving the army—that her husband might be slipping back into the despairing mind-set that overwhelmed him in Kentucky. However, there were major differences this time. Sherman was neither suffering self-doubt, which basically ended with Shiloh, nor experiencing a debilitating embarrassment, as in the Kentucky meltdown. Rather, in early 1863, Sherman was driven by anger—a deep-seated anger that the war might be lost by incompetent, partisan politicians, amateur generals, undisciplined volunteer soldiers, lying, self-serving news reporters and a nation either ignorant of or unwilling to pay the price demanded by victory. Sherman was angry, too, because he felt powerless in the face of potential disaster; that anger, above all, was fueled by the presence of John McClernand. But, McClernand's ever ascending star was about to be dimmed.

Chapter Eighteen

The River of Our Greatness Is Free

On January 30, 1863, Ulysses S. Grant officially took command of the expedition against Vicksburg. McClernand's "Army of the Mississippi" ceased to exist. Grant headed the Department of the Tennessee, and the forces he would lead against Vicksburg became known as the Army of the Tennessee. William Tecumseh Sherman was to command the Fifteenth Army Corps, while James B. McPherson would lead the Seventeenth Corps. McClernand's authority was limited to command of the Thirteenth Corps, "charged with garrisoning the post of Helena, Arkansas, and any other point on the west bank of the river it may be necessary to hold south of that place." Grant thus put the Illinois political general in the backwater of the movement against the great Confederate fortress. His key lieutenants would be Sherman and McPherson.[1]

Grant minced no words in a message to the Department of War on February 1. "If General Sherman had been left in command here, such is my confidence in him that I would not have thought my presence necessary. But whether I do General McClernand injustice or not," declared Grant unequivocally, "I have not confidence in his ability as a soldier to conduct an operation of the magnitude of this one successfully." Grant added, "In this opinion I have no doubt . . . I am borne out by a majority of the officers of the expedition, though I have not questioned one of them on the subject." Grant knew that Admiral Porter was of like mind, having "written freely [meaning relative to McClernand] to the Secretary of the Navy," and requesting that his message be shown to Secretary of War Edwin Stanton.[2]

John McClernand wasted not an instant in protesting Grant's take-over, although framing his message as a request for clarification. He claimed to have "projected the Mississippi River expedition," as well as being "assigned to the command of it," allegedly by the President. Was he now to be "entirely withdrawn from it"? Patiently, briefly and firmly, Grant replied to McClernand the next day, "I will take direct command of the Mississippi River expedition, which necessarily limits your command to the Thirteenth Corps." McClernand was not ready to give up. Boldly he asserted his "right to command the expedition," in justice to himself "as its author and actual promoter." He requested Grant to forward all their correspondence on the subject to "the General-in-Chief, and through him to the Secretary of War and the President."[3]

Grant did forward the papers as McClernand, whose attitude bordered on insubordination, had requested. Grant was confident that his assumption of command would be upheld. Back on January 12, General Halleck had instructed Grant, "You are hereby authorized to relieve General McClernand from command of the expedition against Vicksburg, giving it to the next in rank or taking it yourself." Grant surely was pleased to have such authority, although he realized the timing was not then right to move against the political general. News of the triumph at Post of Arkansas had brought praise of McClernand in Illinois and the Midwest. Also, Grant wanted to gather more information. When he took action, he intended to do so from a position of sufficient strength, and he did. There would be no intervention from Washington.[4]

Sherman was pleased, of course, when he heard the news, having urged Grant, as had Porter, to take command of the Vicksburg expedition. He would have experienced even more satisfaction if McClernand could have been removed altogether from the army. Sherman was concerned that the scheming politician might yet find a way to undermine Grant and reclaim the leadership of the movement against Vicksburg. Moreover, the demotion of McClernand did not resolve other issues that continued to plague Sherman. The lack of discipline among the national volunteers, never far removed from his thoughts, was again brought to the fore in mid-January by the wanton burning of Napoleon, the village at the mouth of the Arkansas River.[5]

"I went in person to direct the extinguishment of the fire in Napoleon," Sherman recounted, but "it was impossible to put it out." It was "impossible to find out the incendiary," he continued, declaring that "no man in the army has labored harder than I have to check this [unruly] spirit in our soldiers." He stated that "we all [the army] deserve to be killed unless we can produce a state of discipline when such disgraceful acts can not be committed unpunished." The defiant troops were still very much on Sherman's mind when he wrote General Hitchcock a week after Napoleon was burned: "Plunder, arson & devastation mark the progress of our armies," he said. "Houses are fired under our very feet & though hundreds know . . . who did it, yet the commanding General can not get a clue." He asserted that soldiers made no distinction between friends or foe. "Even Negroes are plundered of their blankets, chickens, corn meal & their poorest garments." Sherman wanted a disciplined army, and he certainly was not yet the legendary destroyer of Southern property—the monstrous devil of Georgia and the Carolinas—if indeed he ever actually became that man.[6]

Sherman was also stewing once more about the treatment he received from the newspapers. He did expect the reporters to blame him for the Chickasaw Bayou defeat. He predicted it in numerous letters. Many newsmen sought to assess blame whenever failure attended a mission, both to attract readers, and because they seemingly operated on the premise that defeat meant that the army commander was at fault. These facts Sherman knew. Possibly, however, he was not prepared for the reappearance of the "i" word. While the *Chicago Tribune* called for Sherman to be removed from command, the *New York Times*, in mid-January, spoke of the General's "insane ambition," his "madness" and the "insane attack" at Chickasaw Bluffs. Equally bad, both because of Sherman's family connections, and the widespread influence of Cincinnati papers in the lower tier of midwestern free states, the *Cincinnati*

Gazette, quoting another paper, claimed that on the Yazoo expedition Sherman had to be restrained in his stateroom "perfectly insane."[7]

Undoubtedly Sherman himself brought on some of the newspaper problems, because of the high-handed manner in which he tried to restrain reporters while characterizing them as liars and spies. On the other hand, the all too frequent bias and inaccuracy of their reporting was deeply upsetting, and reporters sometimes, as Sherman charged, printed information that was valuable to the enemy—which, in Sherman's definition, made them spies. His continuing personal war with the press, spiking again in early 1863, was yet another reason for the anger that motivated him to talk, once more, about quitting the army.[8]

Both the Ewings and the Shermans were worried that he might do just that. They became even more concerned—Ellen was nearly frantic—upon learning that he had written James Lucas and Henry Turner. "Among all the infamous [newspaper] charges," Sherman told his two St. Louis friends, "none has give me more pain than the assertion that my troops are disaffected, mutinous and personally opposed to me. This is false, false as hell. My own division will follow me anywhere." Then came Sherman's shocking request: "If you see a chance for me to make a living, I would be much obliged for an early notice." Thomas Ewing wrote his son Hugh Boyle, who by 1863 was serving with Sherman, "General Sherman was badly used by the President in placing that wooden-headed McClernand over him. He talks of resigning, but this will not do." Such an action, declared Sherman's father-in-law, would be "a terrible mortification to his family and friends and a triumph to his enemies. See him," Ewing instructed Hugh, "and tell him how strongly we all feel on the subject."[9]

John Sherman gave his brother "particular fits," as the General described John's reprimands upon hearing the talk of resignation. John said such an action would harm the family, and fail the country, the troops and his fellow officers in a time of crisis. Cump must not be defeated by newspaper correspondents and "the thoughtless interference of a fool President & by the jealousies of a few rivals." If he resigned from the army, critics would see the act as proof of the incapacity of which they accused him. Ellen was equally straightforward, even more blunt about her husband's quarrels with the news media and his threats to leave the army. With a level head, but clearly exasperated, she wrote about the newspapers, "You cannot do anything *unaided* against them & there is *not one* man in power who will unite with you against them. So dear Cump give up the struggle & suffer them to annoy you no longer."

Three days later, relative to quitting the army, Ellen demanded, "Do you not see that you would thus be giving your enemies—the correspondents—the triumph they wish. *They will then have written you down.*" Soon Ellen was writing yet again, expressing an understanding of and sympathy with Sherman's frustrations about the newsmen, but pleading with him not to leave the army: "If you abandon your country & her cause when so few are competent & willing to serve, I shall then indeed be distressed." Wisely she reminded her husband that he labored in the service of his country. Admiring how he always had been "guided by duty and principle," and had long withstood "the combined assaults of the unthinking and the malicious," Ellen could not bear the thought that now, after all the trials he had weathered, he would succumb. "I tremble lest you have already resigned." If he had, she begged him to recall his resignation. "I implore you by all that you hold sacred and dear not to encourage [such a] thought one moment longer."[10]

Perhaps if Grant had not taken command of the Vicksburg operation and McClernand had been allowed to lead the expedition, Sherman actually would have resigned. Clearly the family took his threats to quit seriously. His loyalty to the Union never wavered, but dealing with McClernand and news reporters may have brought Sherman to the brink of stepping down. He did not leave the army, of course, although he continued mentioning the possibility in several letters into the spring of 1863. He did decide to court-martial a newspaper correspondent, Thomas W. Knox of the *New York Herald*, on charges of being a spy. The espionage charge was based on the idea that information about the Federal Army, appearing in Northern papers, soon made its way into the Confederate press, becoming readily available to the Rebel army. Sherman sought to make an example of Knox, hoping that other reporters—

"the most contemptible race of men that exist"—would be cowed by such an action.[11]

Knox was chosen because Sherman considered his account of the Chickasaw Bluffs defeat both highly inaccurate, which it was, and particularly damaging, due to his paper's widespread influence. The New York City papers were the leaders of the industry, and the *New York Herald* was then the single most important paper in the nation. Sherman harbored a particular dislike of Knox, whom he found arrogant and overbearing.[12]

Sherman had already orchestrated a recent, notable court-martial, in which he charged Colonel Thomas Worthington of the Forty-Sixth Ohio Infantry with insubordination and drunkenness. Sherman truthfully claimed that for a while he patiently shielded Worthington, refusing to take action against the officer because of "his West Point name, the sake of his family, & my belief that his own sense of Right" would in time lead to a change in the man's behavior. But Worthington only grew worse. He was frequently drunk, and his critical pronouncements about Halleck, Grant, Sherman and others became increasingly obnoxious. When Worthington focused on Shiloh and the issue of surprise, and even began to publish his views, Sherman concluded that he "had forborne too long," and preferred charges against the colonel.[13]

In a letter to his father-in-law, Sherman claimed that he gave Worthington "a good court, 13 high impartial officers," and that the trial was "long, fair, and perfect," after which the court found Worthington guilty and he was cashiered. Worthington probably deserved a court-martial, but he hardly received the "fair and perfect trial" that Sherman asserted. Sherman brought the charges, selected the "impartial officers" of the court and himself testified against Worthington. Sherman had become a powerful man, with influential military and family connections, and the members of the court would have known that he wanted Worthington kicked out of the army. When President Andrew Johnson reviewed the case a few years later, he granted Worthington an honorable discharge. The man did not go away quietly, criticizing Sherman to anyone who would listen, even after Sherman became general-in-chief of the army.[14]

The Worthington court-martial was a relatively inconsequential affair, however, when compared with Sherman's action against Thomas Knox. Never before in American history had a newspaper correspondent been subjected to a court-martial—and never again has such a thing occurred. Even though Knox was a civilian, he was in a war zone, where civil courts were not functioning. Before the Civil War, the U.S. Army had devised military commissions to try civilians accused of military crimes in a war zone. Sherman hoped to establish a strong precedent that any civilian following an army was subject to military law. When Knox realized that Sherman was really out to get him—even if Sherman, as he assured both his brother and Admiral Porter, "did not want the fellow shot"—the reporter decided that his situation called for some major groveling.[15]

First claiming ignorance of Sherman's order forbidding civilians to accompany the expedition against Vicksburg, Knox said he learned of the prohibition only after the army landed on the banks of the Yazoo. His *New York Herald* account of the battle at Chickasaw Bluffs admittedly had been based upon "exceedingly limited" sources of information. With later access to the "orders, plans, and reports" of the operation, he had realized "to my regret that I labored under repeated errors," which had led to a number of "misstatements." Actually, Sherman's "plans and orders" could not possibly have been "more full and complete." Never had Knox seen plans "so admirably calculated to cover every contingency." The failure to achieve the objective could not possibly be attributed to any shortcoming of Sherman. "Deeply deploring" his errors, in what he grandiosely termed a "history" of the Yazoo operations, Knox stated that he had since become "fully convinced of [Sherman's] prompt, efficient, and judicious management of the troops . . . from [the expedition's] commencement to its close." Altogether, Knox did a fine job of prostrating himself before Sherman. He simply had dug too deep a hole from which to crawl out. Sherman was in no mood to be lenient. Knox's forthright admission of authoring such a sorry piece may have served to incense Sherman more. Probably Knox could never have appeased Sherman regardless of what he said.[16]

Thus the court-martial proceeded, convened at Young's Point, Louisiana, on February 5, 1863. Three charges were brought against Knox: providing intelligence to the enemy, engaging in espionage and disobedience of Sherman's orders. Sherman testified against Knox for two days and was the only witness for the prosecution. On February 18, the court acquitted Knox of the first two charges, but found him guilty of violating Sherman's order banning civilians from the Yazoo expedition. As punishment, Knox was banished outside of army lines and ordered not to return on pain of arrest and imprisonment.[17]

Sherman was far from satisfied. He had wanted Knox convicted as a spy, and he wanted the man to serve time in prison. Neither happened, and worse, the President decided to revoke Knox's banishment if Grant, as Sherman's commanding officer, would approve. Lincoln had received a testimonial from some reporters and congressmen, requesting him to reverse the judgment of Knox's court-martial. Trying neither to offend the newspapers nor the army—at least not any more than necessary—the President allowed Knox to visit Grant's headquarters, but whether or not he could stay within army lines was for Grant to determine.[18]

Grant responded by immediately taking the offensive against the reporter: "You came here first in positive violation of an order from General Sherman," Grant charged in his letter to Knox. "You attempted to break down his influence with his command. . . . You made insinuations against his sanity, and said many things which were untrue" about one of "the ablest soldiers and purest men in the country." Although Grant normally "would conform to the slightest wish of the President," he declared that "my respect for General Sherman is such that in this case I must decline, unless General Sherman first gives his consent to your remaining."[19]

Grant had chosen to leave the decision to Sherman. It was an action for which Sherman was long grateful, and one that undoubtedly served to bind the two generals ever closer to each other. As for relenting, and permitting Knox to stay within army lines, such a thought was anathema to Sherman. "Come with a sword or musket in your hand . . . and I will welcome you as a brother and associate," read his message to Knox, "but come ... as the representative of the press ... and my answer is, Never."[20]

Knox realized that Sherman had won. He was finished as a reporter in the western theater. He soon left Grant's headquarters and headed to the eastern theater, where he continued to work as a war correspondent. Ironically, if Sherman had not succeeded in banishing him from the Vicksburg campaign, Knox probably would have spent time in prison— a Confederate prison. Within a short time after he was banished, three reporters boarded a Union ship that attempted to run past the Vicksburg batteries. The powerful Rebel guns blasted the vessel apart. The reporters were captured, and spent more than a year and a half in an enemy jail. Knox later said that he certainly would have been accompanying them, except for the wrath of Sherman. When Sherman heard about the fate of the reporters—who initially were thought to have perished—he allegedly exclaimed: "Good! We'll have news from hell before breakfast." Such a growling response is the kind of utterance he well might have made.[21]

Sherman remained in a foul mood whenever he spoke of reporters, and he continued to bash them mercilessly in his letters to family. Ellen apparently feared that he might become physically violent with a correspondent. She warned him against losing his temper, and possibly taking the life of "a poor wretch unfit for earth." Often in home letters, Sherman employed his rapier pen to relieve stress and frustration, but he remained angry that he had not achieved total victory against Knox.[22]

Although Knox had escaped prison, Sherman accomplished his general purpose. The reporters had been cowed. They knew henceforward that they had to be very careful when they dealt with Sherman, if they expected to continue their work. In campaigns to come, he would succeed in totally controlling and stifling the press. While he maneuvered to implement his antipress views, Sherman assured Murat Halstead, the editor of the *Cincinnati Commercial*, who had come out strongly in his favor, "I am no enemy to freedom of thought, freedom of the 'Press' and speech." Sherman's court-martial of Knox dramatized the danger that war always poses to freedom of the press—all the more so because Sherman sincerely thought of himself as a champion of the United States Constitution. But he could not see, or would not see, that his stand against the press constituted a threat to the nation's founding document, which he so revered.[23]

FORTUNATELY FOR SHERMAN and the army, he could not spend all of his time and energy warring against the press. By mid-March, the campaign against Vicksburg, *"the hardest problem of the war"*—as Sherman characterized the Rebel fortress in a letter to his friend Edward Ord—was heating up once more. Sherman's Fifteenth Corps, upon the orders of Grant, had been struggling to deepen and widen the canal that Admiral Farragut began digging the year before. When Farragut departed, the canal was hardly more than a shallow ditch traversing the base of De Soto Point, the narrow, low-lying Louisiana peninsula directly across the great river from Vicksburg. The idea was that a formidable ditch, sufficiently wide and deep, would initiate a new channel for the Mississippi River. At some point, so ran the thinking, the mighty current of the river would be drawn to the massive ditch, as if it were a magnet. Thus the force of nature, in the form of the Mississippi, would inevitably take control, and finish the work of scouring out a new channel that would bypass the Vicksburg bastion.[24]

Sherman never had much faith in the project, although he did loyally try to make it work. In truth, Grant did not think much of the idea either, but the project fascinated Lincoln, who wanted Grant to pursue it. A major difficulty of the scheme was that the canal's northern end led out of a virtually stagnant backwater, where the Mississippi's powerful current could have no erosive effect. Furthermore, even if the river had followed the new channel, the issue of the Vicksburg fortress still would not have been resolved. Sherman explained the difficulty in his February 22 letter to Ord: "The canal we are digging here does not Solve the problem, for the lower end of the Canal, although below Vicksburg, is not below the Walnut Hills, which are fortified for four miles below the outlet of the canal." The outlet was within range of the Vicksburg guns, and nothing could prevent the Rebels from marshaling still more guns farther south along the bluffs, if necessary to continue commanding the river.[25]

Sherman's men were also having to battle high water. The river just kept rising, as heavy rains inundated the region. Louisiana bayous were flooding in the rear of Sherman's corps, and he had to throw up a levee along the west side of his big ditch to prevent being totally washed away. "The canal here is worthless," he wrote John in early March, "and the Country is so overflowed with water that we are roosting on a narrow levee." In a letter to Ellen, he deplored the canal's slow progress, blaming it on "the rain & liquid mud," and noted the "water above, below, and all round." The rain at times was torrential, leaving the roads "simply quagmires"; and he told Ord, "We have no ground here even to bury our men save the levee."[26]

At least Sherman had been removed from the enemy's line of fire for several weeks while he pursued the canal project. Ellen had to be pleased about that. Charley Ewing had written her that Sherman unnecessarily exposed himself in battle. Ellen told her husband that Charley said "at Arkansas Post you took the worst possible position for your own preservation." Sherman responded, "I know better than Charley where danger lies, and where I should be." At Arkansas Post the enemy could sometimes see him and, he readily admitted, "of course they fired at me." However, in expressing his responsibilities as an army leader, as well as a sense of fair play, Sherman declared, "Soldiers have a right to See & Know that the man who guides them is near enough to See with his own Eyes, and that he cannot see without being seen."[27]

On the lighter side, Sherman seemed rather amused at some of Ellen's comments about their children, especially the girls. He remarked on his wife's "excessive vanity about Elly," who was not yet four years old, and observed that he thought Ellen's "discussion of their future husbands is a little remote." Nonetheless, he slipped into a nostalgic, sentimental mood as his mind turned to their oldest child, twelve-year-old Minnie. "It seems but a day since Minnie came to New Orleans a baby, and you went back in the *Tecumseh*, and I am hourly reminded of the event by seeing the self-same *Tecumseh* plying about, looking rather old and seedy."[28]

As for the war, no doubt Sherman felt like the canal work constituted little more than marking time, until "sooner or later," as he wrote Colonel Benjamin H. Grierson, "we must get on shore & fight it out." Grant also pursued two other projects in hope of getting around the Vicksburg guns. One began at Lake Providence, Louisiana, fifty miles upriver from Vicksburg, and only a short distance west of the Mississippi River. The concept was to open a channel from the Mississippi into the lake, from which a number of interconnected streams (and swamps) eventually led into the Red River. If this agonizing route could be made passable for gunboats and transports, then the Federals could steam down the Red River to its mouth, and turn up the Mississippi. Approaching the Rebel fortress from the south, the army could be landed on solid ground east of the river, with a supply line behind it.[29]

The project was given to James McPherson's Seventeenth Corps. Like Sherman with his canal, McPherson faced a tough assignment. The roundabout route involved a distance of approximately 450 miles. Securing such a long supply line, assuming the route could be made practicable for ships in the first place, would not be easy. And the project demanded a major construction effort, as much of the distance from Lake Providence to the Red River was filled with trees, which had to be cut down far enough below the water that ships could pass safely over the stumps. Initially Sherman thought the Lake Providence idea more promising than his canal, but after weeks of toil, the route would finally be given up as a lost cause.[30]

Still another idea called for cutting the Mississippi River levee approximately two hundred miles above Vicksburg, at a place called Yazoo Pass, on the Mississippi side of the river. Union boats could then steam into Moon Lake, from which a narrow, torturous route led to the Coldwater River, which fed into the Tallahatchie, a stream eventually joining the Yalobusha, which in turn finally connected with the Yazoo. The hope was to land the army, after a 250-mile water trek, on solid ground east of the Yazoo, and a relatively short distance north of Vicksburg.

Grant decided to give it a try. When the army engineers blew a hole in the levee, "a miniature Niagara went boiling through Yazoo Pass," in the words of Bruce Catton, and an impressive expedition headed eastward into the waterway. Navy gunboats were in the lead, followed by transports carrying the infantry. But the route quickly became extremely difficult, filled with snags. The stream turned sharply, frequently and sometimes confusingly, while a powerful current made steering difficult. Rebels were soon at work, felling trees across the route. Swamp areas proved nearly impassable, and the Union vessels, on some days, did well if they made two and one half or three miles. Then, at the confluence of the Tallahatchie and the Yalobusha, the Federals confronted little Fort Pemberton, an unimpressive Confederate structure. Alongside their fort, the Southerners had sunk the captured *Star of the West*, of Fort Sumter fame, in order to block the Tallahatchie channel. Fort Pemberton mounted only one rifled gun and a few smaller pieces—but they were enough.[31]

Already the problems presented by the treacherous waterway had nearly stopped the expedition. The tiny fort finished the job. The stream was so narrow that the gunboats could not mass their firepower. They had to approach the fort one at a time, and the Confederate guns more than held their own. The Federal infantry might have stormed the little bastion, except that the water channels and mosquito-infested swamps were deep, and there was no dry ground on which infantry could land and mount an assault. The Union soldiers, who outnumbered the Confederates in the fort by a wide margin, were useless in such exasperating circumstances. Thus the Yazoo Pass idea reached an inglorious end, and the vessels began withdrawing.

In the meantime Admiral Porter, who had been studying his charts and personally exploring several creeks and bayous, had come up with yet another route for landing the army on firm ground east of the Yazoo, from which a short advance on Vicksburg would be feasible. Porter soon sold the project to Grant, taking the general for a reconnaissance run over the first stretch of the proposed waterway. Grant, who had earlier been hopeful for the Yazoo Pass route, now turned his enthusiasm to the Steele's Bayou expedition, as the project came to be known. He ordered Sherman, more than ever his favorite subordinate, to support the maneuver with a division. Sherman cooperated fully, pleased to get away from the futile canal, "where the Mississippi threatened to drown us." He continued to think, however, as he told Ellen, "the original plan was best: Grant to come down by Land—Banks to come up and me to enter Yazoo." Readily admitting the difficulties of "cooperation at such distances and over such long lines," he still wanted to try the plan again, with more strength and more careful planning. At the moment, however, he threw himself wholeheartedly into the support of Porter's new idea.[32]

The plan would take advantage of the remarkably high water flooding the bayous, creeks and rivers. Porter declared, in his naval history of the war, "that land usually dry for miles in the interior . . . had seventeen feet of water over it." The water was deep enough for the ships, whether gunboats or transports, and could be expected to remain at adequate depth for a sufficiently long period. After first ascending the Yazoo for a few miles, the expedition would turn north into the mouth of Steele's Bayou, a sluggish stream whose entrance was so dense with overhanging trees that, as Porter wrote, it "could scarcely be made out." But when the obstructions were cut away, a wide pass "showed itself, lined out with heavy trees." Proceeding up Steele's Bayou for some forty miles (and Porter had not reconnoitered beyond Steele's Bayou), the flotilla would turn eastward through Black Bayou, which soon joined Deer Creek, on which the northward trek was to be resumed, until its confluence with a lazy stream called the Rolling Fork. This bayou led southeastward, and eventually connected with the Sunflower River, which in turn led straight south and finally emptied into the Yazoo. The winding, agonizing course encompassed about two hundred miles, but it avoided Fort Pemberton and reentered the Yazoo well above the powerful Confederate batteries at Haynes's Bluff.[33]

Porter was convinced that he had found the answer to reducing the Vicksburg fortress. On Sunday, March 15, "one of the most remarkable military and naval expeditions that ever set out," according to Porter's description, got under way. The admiral himself led the voyage with five of his best ironclads, followed by four mortar boats and four tugs. Porter was aboard his flagship *Cincinnati*, accompanied by a pilot who claimed to know all about the country. Cheered with hope, Porter declared, "It was all fair sailing at first." Sherman took his troops up the Mississippi to a point where the river bent eastward to within a short distance of Steele's Bayou. There disembarking, the infantry tramped across a marshy stretch of land for a mile or so and boarded transports that had followed Porter's war vessels. Porter was forging ahead with the gunboats, and the transports, once Sherman's men were on board, steamed northward in the wake of the admiral.[34]

"The expedition went along finely," Porter reported, "until it reached Black Bayou." There the passageway narrowed, the appearance of the water lived up to its ominous name and the trees grew more dense, with thick branches meeting overhead, only a few feet above the gunboats, and banging destructively against their superstructure. Trees blocking the passageway, some of them two feet in diameter, had to be pushed over by the ironclads, while crews worked to cut away the branches above. "It was terrible work," Porter said. The pilot assured him that once they got a little farther, the route would become better. The admiral observed that "it certainly could not get worse." But he was wrong: it got a lot worse. The pilot proved to be a fraud, who had never seen the place. The armada's advance, on March 16, slowed to a crawl.[35]

The next day saw more of the same. If Porter chanced to remember that it was St. Patrick's Day, he well might have wondered, when snakes dropped onto the *Cincinnati*'s deck from the low-lying branches as the ironclad ran into them, if that grand saint of the Emerald Isle who drove the serpents from Ireland had subsequently inflicted the reptiles upon the Mississippi Valley. The gunboats, in fact, knocked loose many creatures that had taken to the trees in an effort to avoid the high water. Coons, rats, mice, lizards and even wild cats landed on the decks from time to time. A few sailors drew duty with brooms, ordered to sweep the animal life over the side of the boats, as well as to remove the limbs of decayed trees, which often fell on the decks. An officer on the *Cincinnati* who was keeping a private journal observed that "the first dry land ... since we left the Yazoo is now on our right." Soon black people by the hundreds, according to Porter, flocked to see the novel sight of the gunboats struggling through the trees. They said the whites had fled their plantations upon the approach of the Federal vessels.[36]

The situation continued to get worse as the gunboats kept doggedly at their excruciating voyage up Deer Creek. Porter, at best, made no more than half a mile an hour. Then the Rebels began setting fire to thousands of bales of cotton that were piled on both sides of the stream. The passageway between the burning cotton became obscured with smoke and extremely hot. Told by a black man that the cotton would likely burn two days, maybe three, Porter decided to press on. The heat was so intense that paint on the boat blistered, and the admiral sought relief inside a small deckhouse covered with iron. He said breathing the smoke "was even worse than the heat." Some of the crew who failed to find shelter were scorched. About the time the *Cincinnati* had passed through the cotton fires, there was a startling crash, which some first thought was an earthquake. In the dense, stifling smoke, no one had seen the span of a partially submerged bridge, laying directly ahead. The heavy gunboat had smashed right through it.[37]

Eventually the ironclads took out three or four more bridges. Finally approaching Rolling Fork, the admiral found that, "for a distance of 600 yards, a bed of willows blocked the way." Steaming ahead and hoping for the best, because Porter realized that "it would have taken weeks to remove the willows," the *Cincinnati* was soon brought to a halt, with willow withes snagged in her rough iron, and also fouling the paddle wheels. Crewmen worked day and night with saws, knives, chisels and cutlasses to cut the ship loose. As the Federals slowly extricated themselves from the willows, with "the Negroes helping us eagerly," according to the *Cincinnati* officer's journal, the Rebels were gathering strength, hoping to capture the gunboats.[38]

Confederate sharpshooters armed with Whitworth rifles began picking off sailors. The Southerners also felled trees across the channel ahead of the gunboats to block their advance. A Union patrol captured a handful of enemy soldiers, who claimed the Rebels were landing two batteries and a large party of infantry only a few miles away. Porter was already experiencing enemy artillery fire, and scouts sent ashore confirmed that Rebel infantry were approaching. "I was also informed that the enemy were cutting down trees in our rear to prevent ... our escape. This," reported the admiral, with remarkable understatement, "looked unpleasant."[39]

He now faced the very real possibility of being trapped—unless Sherman, miles behind with the infantry, could somehow come up in time to ward off disaster. The more vulnerable wooden transports, with a superstructure taller than the gunboats, had fallen behind, as they experienced great difficulty in navigating the clogged waterways. But Sherman appeared to be Porter's only chance of saving his valuable ironclads. The admiral could no longer go forward and, unless help came quickly, his gunboats would have to be scuttled. Along with other problems, he had been, as he afterward expressed his plight, "checkmated by the willows."[40]

Porter obviously needed to get word of his predicament to Sherman at once. A black man volunteered to carry the message (unfortunately, the courageous fellow is known today only as "Mr. Tub," the name recorded by Porter). The admiral scribbled a brief note on a piece of paper, gave his messenger directions and hoped that somehow he would get through to Sherman. He did, delivering Porter's plea for help after dark, probably sometime around midnight. "The Admiral stated," Sherman recalled, "that he had met a force of infantry and artillery which gave him great trouble ... killing the men who had to expose themselves outside the iron armor [in order] to shove off the bows of the boats, which had so little headway that they would not steer. He begged me," Sherman continued, "to come to his rescue."[41]

Sherman responded instantly. He had about 800 men with him, under command of Colonel Giles A. Smith, brother of Morgan Smith—with whom he had pushed on for some distance ahead of the main body of his division. He ordered Colonel Smith, with his troops, to start at once, rapidly work his way along the east bank of Deer Creek to the gunboats and to then assure Porter that he would be "coming up with every man I could raise" as fast as possible.[42]

Sherman said "the night was absolutely black" as he took a canoe and paddled some four or five miles down Black Bayou, until "luckily" he came up on the transport *Silver Wave*, which was bringing up two regiments of his infantry. Also gathering several parties of soldiers, who had been at work along the bayou, Sherman loaded them into an empty coal barge, towed by a navy tugboat, and headed back up the bayou, with the tug and barge leading the way, and the *Silver Wave* following. It was a wild ride in the early morning darkness, at a speed faster than normally would have been attempted during daylight, with the transport "crashing through the trees, [which carried] away pilot-house, smoke stacks, and everything above deck," according to Sherman. Even so, the pace was slowing as more obstacles were encountered. He decided to put his men ashore and push through the canebrakes on foot, "carrying lighted candles in our hands," until the dawn.[43]

Meanwhile, Admiral Porter prepared for the worst. Guns were loaded with grapeshot and canister. The men were to sleep at the guns, ready to repel Confederates when they attempted to board. "Everything outside," ordered Porter, should be "covered with slush [to make it as slick as possible], save our shot for the artillery." The vessels must be defended "to the last," he declared, "and when we can do no better, we will blow them up." Whatever happened, Porter knew his ironclads must not fall into the hands of the enemy. Such a fate would be far more than an embarrassment. The ironclads would give the Rebels a naval strength never before enjoyed, put a new complexion on the war for control of the Mississippi, and delay the reduction of Vicksburg for weeks, possibly months. The survival of the gunboats very likely depended upon Sherman bringing up his infantry in time to drive off the enemy.[44]

Through the morning hours, "knowing that moments were precious," as Sherman said, he and his troops generally moved at double-quick time, occasionally resting briefly, as they followed the same route that Giles Smith had taken. "Being on foot myself," Sherman declared, "no man could complain." More than once the pace was slowed when they had to wade through swamps, where Sherman said the water came above his hips. He thought that the soldiers "were glad to have their general and field officers afoot, but we gave them a fair specimen of marching, covering about twenty-one miles by noon." The time must have been around 1:00 p.m. when at last they neared the gunboats. Porter wrote that just then "a large body of Confederate troops were seen advancing directly through the woods . . . while the sharpshooters in redoubled numbers opened fire on the fleet not more than fifty yards distant." Porter steeled himself for a desperate defensive stand, when suddenly a great din of musketry arose from the woods, as the head of Sherman's column came upon the Confederates. The enemy seemed to be taken totally by surprise, and soon began pulling back. "Sherman arrived," wrote Porter, as he generously gave credit where credit was due, "just in the nick of time."[45]

Only moments before, an officer who had found a horse and realized that his commander ought to have a mount, had offered it to Sherman. The General swung up on the animal bareback and rode triumphantly along the levee, while sailors who gathered on the decks cheered him "most vociferously" as he went by. Porter thought that the sailors received Sherman "with the warmest cheers he ever had in his life." For a general who loved the theater, it had to be thrilling, as well as satisfying, that he had been able to bring the army up before it was too late. But Sherman had also exposed himself to enemy sharpshooters, if any were still within range. One wonders if Ellen, always concerned about her husband unnecessarily placing himself in harm's way, ever learned about that climactic ride.[46]

He got away with it safely though and approaching Porter, according to the admiral, demanded how he ever "got into such an ugly scrape?" The General also demanded, although of course he already knew, "Who in thunder proposed such a mad scheme?" He declared, according to Porter, "This is the most infernal expedition I was ever on." It probably was but, with the infantry at hand for protection, Porter was able, having unshipped the rudders, to back his ironclads downstream until eventually, upon reaching a broader channel, he succeeded in turning them around and heading back to the Yazoo.[47]

On Tuesday, March 24, as the retreat continued, rain came down hard, as it did throughout much of the night. Some enemy troops followed the gunboats for a time, occasionally shooting at them from a distance, but with no hope of penetrating Sherman's defensive screen. Many blacks were following, too. A naval officer observed that they "form a motley group indeed, of all ages and sexes, the lame, the halt, and the blind, as well as the stalwart and active." They were "in high glee—'going to freedom, sure,' they say." Their presence troubled Porter, who wrote, "I much fear that terrible scenes will be enacted in the district through which we went. The slave there has been told that he is free, and more than any place . . . [they] seem determined to maintain what, to them, seems a most precious boon. I do not blame them, for slavery exists in the worst form in the valley of the Mississippi."[48]

By Wednesday the twenty-fifth, the Rebel pursuers had given up, and the Union infantry, knowing they had gotten away safely, were for a time "strewed all along the bank," some cooking and others amusing themselves in various ways. Aboard the *Cincinnati*, the journal keeper described one of the infantry "games," in which a soldier upon the back of a mule—and in the buff—would first attempt to force the animal to swim the stream, then "endeavor to climb a steep bank upon the opposite side; some twenty of them have already tried this feat and failed, still others try." Without a doubt, both army and navy were thankful to see the futile Steele's Bayou expedition come to an end.[49]

Steele's Bayou was the last attempt to get around the guns of Vicksburg by some convoluted water route. Admiral Porter, in a portion of his report to Secretary of the Navy Gideon Welles, which he marked confidential, declared, "There is but one thing now to be done, and that is to start an army of 150,000 men from Memphis via Granada,* and let them go supplied with everything required to take Vicksburg. Let all minor considerations give way to this and Vicksburg will be ours." While praising Sherman—"No other general could have done better or as well as Sherman"—Porter commented bluntly, and a bit unfairly: "Had General

---

* Spelled Grenada in the twenty-first century.

Grant not turned back when on the way to Granada he would have been in Vicksburg before this."[50]

Sherman was of like mind about the water routes, as he reported to army headquarters. Regarding the original objective of "finding a practicable point on the east bank of the Yazoo whereon to disembark my corps, I pronounce it impossible by any channel communicating with Steele's Bayou." In a letter to Ellen from "near Vicksburg," on April 10, he stated, "The only true plan was the one we started with. This Grand Army should be on the Main land, moving south along the Road & Roads from Memphis, Holly Springs, and Corinth, concentrating on Granada, thence towards Canton where the Central Road crosses Big Black, and then on Vicksburg." He thought that the gunboats and a smaller army should be at Vicksburg, "and on the first sign of the presence of the main force inland ... should attack here violently." This had been the plan at Oxford "in December last, is my plan now, and Grant knows it is my opinion." Cautioning that only Ellen and her father should know his judgment, he warned that Thomas Ewing "must not write to the War Department as from me." Sherman closed the topic forthrightly: "It is my opinion that we shall never take Vicksburg by operations by River alone."[51]

GENERAL GRANT HAD no intention of returning the army to Memphis, however. Politically, he considered such a move unacceptable. Politicians, reporters, indeed the general public, would view it as a retreat—even worse, a defeat. John McClernand's political clout might finally bring about the removal of Grant from command. A representative of the War Department, Charles A. Dana, arrived in early April, officially to investigate the paymaster department of the western theater, but actually to report on Grant for the benefit of Stanton and Lincoln. This Grant fully realized, as did Sherman, who wrote his brother John that Dana "is here I suppose to watch us all."[52]

Both Grant and Sherman received the man cordially, cultivating his goodwill. Dana was an intelligent fellow who, once he got to know the generals, and understood what had been occurring and why, soon became one of their strongest supporters. Adjutant General Lorenzo Thomas had shown up about the same time as Dana, on a mission to recruit blacks for the army, although rumors spread that he too was present to observe Grant. Undoubtedly Thomas—if he developed a negative view of Grant, and whether he had been instructed to keep an eye on the General or not—could be expected to express his opinions to Washington. As for recruiting blacks to serve in the Union Army, Sherman, predictably, was not pleased. "I would prefer to have this a white man's war, & provide for the negro after the Storm has passed," he told Ellen, "but we are in a Revolution and I must not pretend to judge. With my opinions of negros, and my experience, yea prejudice, I cannot trust them yet." At the moment, though, dealing with Vicksburg remained Sherman's number one concern.[53]

Of course Grant knew that conventional military strategy was exactly what Sherman and others advocated. But with good reason, he feared that going back to Memphis, arguably a sound military maneuver, well might result in his being relieved of command. Sherman's thinking was more along the lines that politicians, newsmen and the public "would just have to take their medicine," to employ a common expression. He seemed unwilling to acknowledge the political reality. Yet had McClernand—that "dirty dog, consumed by a burning desire for personal renown," as Sherman referred to him in a letter to John—been summoned to replace Grant, Sherman would have been enraged. If Grant and Sherman could have been given an IQ test, Sherman would have scored higher than Grant. Nor did Grant possess the fund of knowledge that Sherman had amassed. But Grant, fortunately, evaluated the political situation more rationally than his chief lieutenant. Additionally, Grant's perception of the Vicksburg campaign's military intangibles, which involves a phase of intelligence difficult if not impossible to measure even today, was about to be proven superior, if success be the test, to that of Sherman.[54]

Grant's decision was to march the army south on the Louisiana side of the river and cross the Mississippi some twenty-five or thirty miles downstream from Vicksburg, in the vicinity of Grand Gulf. While the

Army of the Tennessee marched, Admiral Porter would daringly run a number of his gunboats and transports down the Mississippi, directly past the Vicksburg batteries under the cover of darkness. The losses from the powerful, well-positioned Confederate guns might be heavy, but considering the end to be achieved, they would be justifiable. Porter agreed to make the run, although emphasizing to Grant that once south of Vicksburg, there could be no return for any reason. To ply slowly north against the strong current while taking scores, and possibly hundreds of hits from the Confederate guns, would ensure disaster, even for ironclads. Grant was not concerned about a return trip. He believed that enough vessels would succeed in making the run to ferry the army across the river, from which point, operating on dry ground, the infantry at last would be able to close in on Vicksburg from the south and east.

Sherman fully expected the plan to fail, and again urged Grant to take the bulk of the army back to Memphis and march on Vicksburg by way of Granada. He also wanted Grant to call upon McPherson and McClernand to express their strategy as well—and in writing. Knowing that the highly regarded McPherson opposed Grant's plan, Sherman probably hoped that if he and "Mac," as he fondly called McPherson, were both on record against the move, then Grant might reconsider. Even if not, at least John McClernand, whom Sherman believed had no real plan of action in mind, would be on record, whatever his opinion, and unable to later claim that he had favored a different strategy. However, Grant had made his decision. Sherman supported him fully, telling John that "it is my duty to cooperate with Zeal and I shall."[55]

By mid-April, Grant was ready to make the move. On the night of April 16, "the desperate and terrible thing," as Sherman memorably characterized the daring mission, got under way. Stealth was the key word, when Admiral Porter gave the signal to move out on that moonless but starry night. Orders had been issued that lights must be extinguished aboard all the ships, and the coal in the furnaces should be "well ignited, so as to show no smoke, that low steam should be carried, that not a wheel was to turn except to keep the vessel's bow down river, and to drift past the enemy's works fifty yards apart." Six ironclads headed the procession, with Porter's flagship *Benton* in the lead. The single wooden gunboat, for its own protection, was lashed to the starboard side of an ironclad. Three transports, loaded with supplies, followed the ironclads, with a seventh ironclad bringing up the rear. Most of the vessels had coal barges lashed to their starboard side. Concluding the parade was an ammunition barge. If blown up by enemy fire, it was hoped that damage to the ships ahead would be avoided.[56]

Porter's flagship silently drifted past the first Confederate battery "without receiving a shot," recalled the admiral, but as she came up on the next battery, the Vicksburg, Shreveport & Texas Railroad station, located on the right bank of the Mississippi, was set afire, with more fires soon blazing forth on both sides of the river, and lighting up the ships, "as plainly as if it was daylight." Still the Rebel batteries did not open fire for several precious moments. The Confederates had been taken by surprise, as a number of artillery officers were attending a ball in one of Vicksburg's finest mansions. Once alerted, they got to the river defenses as fast as they could. Just as Porter was beginning to think that he might have somehow gotten incredibly lucky, a spectacular, hellish scene— "grand in the extreme," he said—suddenly burst upon him.[57]

The guns of Vicksburg had come alive, and soon were thundering all along the waterfront. Porter's flotilla, as ordered, headed at once to the Mississippi shore, increasing speed and returning fire, as they blasted the buildings along the docks. The admiral's tactic caused many of the Rebel heavy guns, positioned thirty or forty feet above the river, to overshoot his vessels. It was difficult to depress the muzzles enough to strike boats hugging the Vicksburg shoreline. For all the sound and fury, Porter said that the damage was relatively minor, as the weak points on the sides of the boats "were mostly protected by heavy logs, which prevented many shots and shells going through the iron." Sherman had taken up a position on a yawl, "out in the stream" below Vicksburg, and a little beyond range of the enemy guns. Fearful that a great many casualties would be suffered, he had ordered that four yawls should be "hauled across the swamps, to the river below Vicksburg, and manned with soldiers," ready and waiting to pick up the wounded. The scene he witnessed was unforgettable. He thought the fires on both sides of the river, the roar of cannon, the bursting of shells and the transport *Henry Clay*, which became a blazing, floating wreck, drifting helplessly with the current before she went to pieces and sank, "made up a picture of the terrible not often seen."[58]

Actually, the run past the batteries was a great success. Not a gunboat had been lost, even if some were rather badly beaten up, and only the *Henry Clay* was sunk. Another that had been disabled was taken under tow by an ironclad and pulled safely through. Only fifteen men, according to Porter, were wounded, and no one was killed. Sherman picked up the pilot of the downed transport, who was clinging to a piece of wreckage. When Porter's flagship arrived beyond the guns, Sherman climbed aboard, yelling, "Are you alright, old fellow?" Learning both that Porter was fine and that the crew had suffered only minimal injuries, he enthusiastically offered congratulations and observed that Porter had done much better in front of Vicksburg than when he had been "grounding on willow-trees" during the Steele's Bayou expedition. Sherman then proceeded to visit the other ships, extend his congratulations and express his pleasure that they had come through safely. After all, particularly since Steele's Bayou, he had become rather a favorite of the navy, as well as the army. He was a tough and demanding general, but he seemed to like mingling with the men, and he conveyed a genuine concern for their well-being. He was on his way to becoming the military's beloved "Uncle Billy."[59]

Soon Grant prepared for another run down the river, this time with six unescorted transports, which were loaded with hay, corn, medical supplies and other provisions. Only a few nights later, with army volunteers manning the vessels because their civilian crews refused to take the risk, the ships drifted south with the current until the enemy opened fire. Then they poured on the steam. Some of the ships were badly mauled, although all except one got through: the *Tigress*, former headquarters ship of Grant at Shiloh, and McClernand more recently, went down. Nevertheless, all the other vessels were usable, if only as barges to be towed across the river as ferryboats for Grant's soldiers. Meanwhile, the Army of the Tennessee, McClernand's corps in the lead, laboriously advanced through swamps and bayous, on the west side of the river, for nearly fifty miles to the vicinity of New Carthage. It was slow going, as the troops worked, slogged and tramped along, moving toward a rendez-vous with Porter's transports. McPherson's corps was to follow McCler-nand, with Sherman bringing his corps up last.[60]

After Porter's gunboats and transports had run past the Vicksburg batteries, Grant hurried south in order to be at hand when the army began crossing the river to the Mississippi shore. The general also con-tinued his efforts to confuse John Pemberton, who remained in charge of defending Vicksburg. Already Sherman, acting upon Grant's order, had sent Frederick Steele's division far up the Mississippi, on an expe-dition through the Delta to Greenville. The objective was to divert Con-federate attention from the army's march south. It was also another chance to show the enemy what to expect when U.S. vessels traveling the Mississippi were fired upon. "Greenville has been a favorite point from which to assail our passing boats, and one object of your expedi-tion," Sherman instructed Steele, "is to let the planters and inhabitants on Deer Creek see and feel that they will be held accountable for the acts of guerrillas and Confederate soldiers who sojourn in their coun-try for the purpose of firing on our passing boats." By the time Steele departed from Greenville some three weeks into April, little was left of the town other than charred remains. Much of the outlying area was devastated, too.[61]

Sherman and Steele both believed that "the stores necessary for a family should be spared," and Sherman, always concerned about mili-tary discipline, thought that "it injures our men to allow them to plunder indiscriminately the inhabitants of the country." He said that soldiers "will become absolutely lawless unless this can be checked." Yet he him-self continued to employ a policy that was difficult, if not impossible to control. He wrote Steele, who wanted to aid the suffering at Greenville: "Whatever restitution you may make to the families along Deer Creek ... will meet my hearty satisfaction."[62]

The foray into the Delta, which did get Pemberton's attention, was not the only diversion that Grant inaugurated. On April 27, the Union commander sent a message to Sherman suggesting that he create a diversion up the Yazoo River. The Rebels still had strong fortifications along the Yazoo, at Snyder's Bluff, Drumgould's Bluff, and Haynes's Bluff. If Pemberton should think that there was no longer any danger on the Yazoo, he just might send reinforcements south to Grand Gulf. A convincing feint by Sherman, up the Yazoo, would probably hold those Confederates in place. But Grant said he was "loth" to order his friend to carry out the diversion, explaining that "it would be so hard to make our own troops understand that only a demonstration was intended, and our people at home would characterize it as a repulse. I therefore leave it to you whether to make such a demonstration." Grant had expressed his wishes with sensitivity—and perhaps with cunning.[63]

Sherman's response the next day was exactly what Grant wanted. Did Grant think that Sherman cared what the newspapers might say! He assured his commander that he would "make as strong a demonstration as possible." He would ensure that the troops fully understood the purpose, so as not to be disturbed when they were pulled out. As for the people back home, they could find out the truth "as they best can; it is none of their business." Grant was engaged in "a hazardous enterprise, and for good reasons, wished to divert attention; that is sufficient to me, and it shall be done." In cooperation once more with the navy, K. Randolph Breese commanding the flotilla, Sherman took Frank Blair's division up the Yazoo aboard ten transports, accompanied by eight gunboats, for an "ostentatious" foray at Haynes's Bluff.

For two days the gunboats dueled with the Rebel artillery, while Sherman's soldiers engaged in animated skirmishing, after which Sherman returned his men to Young's Point for the march to join up with Grant. Sherman claimed that the Yazoo diversion, "made with . . . pomp and display . . . completely fulfilled its purpose." Bruce Catton agreed, writing that "Confederate Pemberton was completely taken in," believing he was about to be attacked from the north. Recently historian Michael Ballard concluded that "Sherman's troops did a poor job of selling their attack, and the Confederates suspected a diversion." At the least, Sherman presented Pemberton with yet another enemy movement to ponder. He was already sorely confused, earlier thinking that Union ships heading south from Memphis, together with the abandonment of the Yazoo Pass and Steele's Bayou expeditions, signified Grant was pulling back to Tennessee.[64]

By the time that Porter ran the Vicksburg batteries, another Union diversion was under way. In mid-April, Colonel Benjamin Grierson, commanding about 1,700 cavalry, rode out of La Grange, Tennessee, heading south into the heart of Mississippi. A thirty-six-year-old of average size, Grierson had been a music instructor and band organizer before the war. He disliked horses, having been kicked in the face by a pony when he was a boy, which left a lifelong disfigurement. After unsuccessfully protesting his assignment to the cavalry (for he hoped to serve in the infantry)—and unlikely as it might seem—he became an outstanding commander.

Grierson's daring operation developed into one of the truly spectacular raids of the war, and well may have been the single most effective diversion in aid of Grant's crossing downriver from Vicksburg. For more than two weeks, the Union troopers rode, passing east of Jackson, tearing up over fifty miles of railroad track, cutting telegraph wires, destroying bridges and all manner of war supplies, while generally wreaking havoc and successfully avoiding Confederate efforts to run them down. After covering approximately 500 miles, they arrived safely within Federal lines at Baton Rouge, having suffered only minimal casualties. Grierson, like Lord Byron, he wrote his wife, had awakened one morning "to find myself famous." The real significance of Grierson's ride was not the damage his troopers inflicted upon the enemy, but rather the impact the bold foray had on General Pemberton's thinking. For several crucial days, Pemberton seemed to be focused as much on Grierson's cavalry as he was on Grant's army.[65]

And Grant needed a few extra days. Plans to cross the Mississippi River were not proceeding as fast as he and Admiral Porter had intended. If Pemberton should awake to the imminent danger he faced and mass his forces to resist a Union landing in the Grand Gulf region, the Army of the Tennessee could be in serious trouble. The delay, in no small degree, was attributable to John McClernand, commanding the lead corps in the Union advance. He seemed not to grasp the necessity of hurrying, which frustrated Porter. Writing Grant that the run past the Vicksburg guns had been demoralizing to the Rebels, Porter warned, "Don't give them time to get over it." Pointedly he stated: "I wish twenty times a day that Sherman was here, or yourself." When Grant joined up with Porter, he was not at all pleased by what he observed of McClernand's performance. With Grant was Charles Dana, who reported, "The first thing which struck us on approaching the points of embarkation [for the crossing to the east bank] was that the steamboats and barges were scattered about in the river and in the bayou as if there were no idea of the imperative necessity of the promptest possible movements."[66]

Furthermore, although Grant had ordered that officers must leave behind their horses and baggage, "McClernand carries his bride along with him," Dana wrote the secretary of war, "with her servants and baggage." Grant at once sent for McClernand, discussed with him the proposed attack "and ordered him to embark his men without losing a moment." Grant then departed to deal with other business. Yet, by dark the next evening, "not a single man or cannon had been embarked." Instead, McClernand had held an afternoon review of the Illinois troops in honor of visiting Governor Richard Yates, who delivered a speech—as did McClernand, naturally. "At the same time," observed Dana, "a salute of artillery was fired, notwithstanding that positive orders had repeatedly been given to use no ammunition for any purpose except against the enemy."[67]

The problem was that John McClernand, although he wore shoulder straps, was a politician. He consistently manifested an arrogant sense of entitlement which often—the author is inclined to say usually—characterizes that profession. McClernand differed from others of the breed only in setting an exceptionally high degree of self-centered conduct. Perhaps if the man had been a competent military officer, Grant, Sherman, McPherson, Porter and others might have been more tolerant of his obnoxious behavior. But as Dana observed, McClernand's "exceeding incompetency" became ever more evident. Dana eventually reported to Stanton that McClernand was not fit even to command a regiment. By that time, the Illinois politician had proven beyond a doubt that he was not qualified to command a corps.[68]

By April 29, Grant finally was ready to go, having succeeded in getting about 10,000 men of McClernand's corps aboard the transports and barges. The plan was to have the navy silence the guns at Grand Gulf, then rapidly land the infantry under cover of Porter's guns and carry the enemy fortifications by storm. Grant was mounting a formidable amphibious endeavor. For nearly 5½ hours, according to Grant, Porter pressed the attack, but to no avail. When Grant afterward went aboard Porter's flagship to confer with the admiral, he remembered that "the sight of the mangled and dying men which met my eye as I boarded the ship was sickening." Situated upon a high bluff, Grand Gulf appeared "as defensible upon its front as Vicksburg and . . . would have been just as impossible to capture by a frontal attack."[69]

Grant and Porter soon agreed upon another plan. The invasion force would move several miles farther south, while Porter's gunboats, transports and barges would run past the Grand Gulf defenses under cover of darkness. Porter would then carry the infantry across the river some distance below Grand Gulf. The question was where to land, and Grant sent an intelligence gathering patrol across the river, with sharp-eyed staff member James Wilson among the group. The soldiers found a sympathetic slave. The man said that Bruinsburg, a little village about forty miles south of Vicksburg, was the best landing spot, because it provided a good road leading eastward to Port Gibson and on to Jackson. Grant was convinced.[70]

On the morning of April 30, McClernand's corps and one division of McPherson's corps, a total of approximately 25,000 men, landed on the east bank of the Mississippi River and began tramping inland toward Port Gibson. "I felt a degree of relief scarcely ever equaled since," explained Grant in his memoirs. "I was now in the enemy's country, with a vast river and the stronghold of Vicksburg between me and my base of supplies. But I was on dry ground on the same side of the river with the

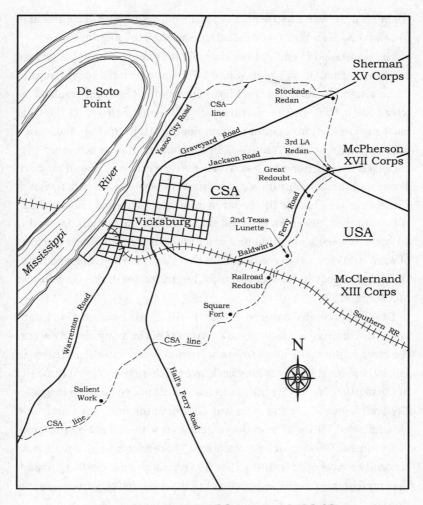

VICKSBURG MAY 18–JULY 4, 1863

On May 19, and again on May 22, Grant attempted to take Vicksburg by assault. Map by Jim Moon Jr.

enemy." Grant won a battle near Port Gibson, defeating a detachment of Rebels from Grand Gulf, and called for Sherman to join him.[71]

His redheaded friend did not share Grant's sense of relief. Sherman still feared that Grant's plan would fail. While he did expect Grant to make a safe lodgment on the Mississippi shore, "the real trouble," he wrote Ellen, "will be the maintenance of the army there." If the Confederate destruction of Grant's supply depot at Holly Springs had caused him to pull back into Tennessee in December, "how much more precarious is his position now below Vicksburg, with every pound of provision, forage and ammunition to float past the seven miles of batteries at Vicksburg, or be hauled thirty-seven miles along a narrow, boggy road." If Grant failed, Sherman believed that McClernand, a man possessing an "over-towering ambition and utter ignorance of the first principles of war," would be left in command. In that case, Sherman assured Ellen, "you may expect to hear of me at St. Louis, for I will not serve under McClernand."[72]

But Sherman also assured Ellen, "I will do all I can to aid Grant." With his commander and a substantial part of the army already across the river, while many more troops were moving to join them, Sherman knew there must be no turning back, even if there were "great difficulty in the matter of food." He fully anticipated this in a warning to Brigadier General James M. Tuttle, who was commanding one of his divisions. He cautioned Tuttle to "give the subject your whole attention [because] every ounce of food must be economized." Like Sherman, Grant also was certainly concerned about supplies for the troops and, contrary to popular myth, Grant never intended to cut loose completely from a supply line.[73]

On May 3, Grant reported to General Henry Halleck from near Grand Gulf: "The country will supply all the forage required for ... an active campaign, and the necessary fresh beef. Other supplies will have to be drawn from Milliken's Bend. This is a long and precarious route, but I have every confidence in succeeding in doing it." The very same day, Grant instructed Sherman to send a wagon train to Grand Gulf, filled with rations. "The road to Vicksburg is open," he told Sherman, and all they needed were "men, ammunition, and hard bread—we can subsist our horses on the country, and obtain considerable supplies for the troops." On May 6, Grant informed Halleck: "I will move as soon as three days' rations are received, and send wagons back to the Gulf for more to follow." Three days later, Grant wrote Major T. S. Bowers, acting assistant adjutant general, that he "wished to impress upon the generals remaining on the Louisiana side of the Mississippi . . . that the wagon road from Milliken's Bend . . . should be shortened by every possible means. . . . Meanwhile, all possible exertion should be made to keep the army supplied by the present route." Grant ordered that "hard bread, coffee, and salt should be kept up anyhow, and then the other articles of the rations as they can be supplied."[74]

When Sherman arrived east of Grand Gulf, and saw the situation firsthand, he sent Grant an urgent message to hold up, declaring on May 9 that "this road will be jammed as sure as life if you attempt to supply 50,000 men by one single road." Grant responded, "I do not calculate upon the possibility of supplying the army with full rations from Grand Gulf. I know it will be impossible without constructing additional roads. What I do expect, however, is to get up what rations of hard bread, coffee, and salt we can, and make the country furnish the balance." Grant had decided that the army would live partially off the land, with wagon trains bringing up such essential supplies as medicine, ammunition and some rations. As the thing turned out, the army lived in great part off the land, Sherman later reported, "and received little or nothing till our arrival" in front of Vicksburg. Grant's offensive maneuver had taken Pemberton by surprise. Grant now possessed the initiative and he fully intended to keep it. "A delay," he told Sherman, "would give the enemy time to reinforce and fortify." Grant planned to move rapidly, and that is why he also decided not to cooperate with Nathaniel Banks, whose roundabout campaigning—whether he meant to join forces with Grant, invest Port Hudson or pursue some other objective—seemed lacking in focus.[75]

And move Grant did, quickly advancing northeast toward Jackson, about sixty miles distant. General Pemberton, perhaps more confused than ever, anticipated that Grant would march at once on Vicksburg.

Instead the Union commander swept between Pemberton's army and the Confederate forces assembling at the capital. On May 13, Confederate General Joseph Johnston arrived from Tennessee to take command at Jackson, but his 6,000 men were not nearly enough to hold back Sherman and McPherson, who drove the Southerners out. Grant had successfully interposed his army between Pemberton and Johnston. He aimed to keep their forces separated, and he did.

After destroying railroads and war installations in Jackson, including "the arsenal buildings, the Government foundry, the gun-carriage establishment ... and a very valuable cotton factory," according to Sherman's report, Grant turned the army westward, marching against Pemberton, whom he planned to force back into Vicksburg. Grant had approximately 30,000 men up, and Pemberton fought him twice, with a strength of about 20,000, first at Champion's Hill, and again the next day at the Big Black River. Afterward the Confederate general retreated into the Vicksburg fortifications, where his total forces then numbered some 31,000.

By May 19, Grant had Vicksburg surrounded, holding a line from the Mississippi south of the town, to the Chickasaw Bluffs and the Yazoo River on the north. A full supply line was at once reestablished with the Mississippi River via the Yazoo, and all of the troops soon had rations issued to them. The strength of the Union Army would shortly reach 40,000, with more troops arriving from Memphis. Sherman's Fifteenth Corps held the right of the line of investment; McPherson's Seventeenth Corps was in the center; and McClernand, with the Thirteenth, held the left. It was too late for Johnston and Pemberton to unite their forces. Grant seemed to have everything going his way, and Sherman could at last join with his commander in experiencing a sense of relief.[76]

Riding with Grant along the Chickasaw Bluffs, from which the two generals gazed down upon the muddy Yazoo, Sherman said that, as Grant recalled the substance of his remarks, "up to this minute he had felt no positive assurance of success." But now he had come to believe that this "was ... one of the greatest campaigns in history." While Vicksburg was not yet captured, "and there was no telling what might happen before it was taken," nevertheless, "whether captured or not," Sherman declared that Grant had conducted "a complete and successful campaign." He accomplished what Sherman had believed could not be done; indeed, Grant possessed the essential qualities of an outstanding commander.[77]

But taking Vicksburg did prove difficult, more so than either Sherman or Grant expected when first they invested the Rebel citadel. Supposing that Vicksburg's defenders were demoralized after the defeats suffered at Champion's Hill and the Big Black River, General Grant ordered an assault on May 19. One vigorous attack just might break the Confederates decisively and conclude the campaign. The Rebels held high ground, however, along terrain naturally contoured for defense, with deep ravines and gullies running in varying directions, while their entire position had been strengthened by excellent fieldworks. In many places the Southerners could lay down a heavy crossfire, as well as frontal fire. Nevertheless, Grant had seen the Rebels break at the Big Black, despite fortifications, and he hoped for the same result. Sherman's Fifteenth Corps, located northeast of Vicksburg, and closer to the enemy line than either McPherson or McClernand, would make the main effort.[78]

The objective was Stockade Redan, a Confederate strongpoint blocking the grimly named Graveyard Road at the point where the road entered the Vicksburg defenses. For several hours Union artillery blasted both sides of the triangular-shaped bastion, the apex of which faced toward Sherman's troops. The Yankee bombardment enshrouded the area with smoke but did little damage to the target. The guns ceased firing about two o'clock, and the cheering Federal infantry advanced on both sides of Graveyard Road. Courageously struggling forward against a lethal enemy fire, they got within less than a hundred yards of the redan, but could go no farther. Pinned to the ground, the Union soldiers blazed away at the Rebels during a long afternoon.

When they began running low on ammunition, both enemy fire and the rough terrain made it difficult to bring up more. The dire need for ammunition led to a dramatic act of heroism by one of the youngest soldiers in the Federal forces. When fourteen-year-old Orion P. Howe, a drummer boy with the Fifty-Fifth Illinois regimental band, realized that ammunition was desperately needed at the front, he gathered up all he could carry and successfully dashed forward to supply it. He made more than one trip, and was stopped only when, having been wounded in the leg, he spotted Sherman astride his horse on the Graveyard Road, and shouted to the General that the Fifty-Fifth Illinois needed more ammunition. Sherman ordered the boy to the rear at once, for treatment of his injury, also assuring the youngster that he would get the ammunition forward to the regiment. In recognition of his actions in that critical situation, Howe was awarded the Medal of Honor, the youngest recipient during the Vicksburg campaign.

But Sherman's assault had failed; his Fifteenth Corps suffered more than 900 casualties. Neither McPherson nor McClernand accomplished anything of importance. The Southerners, behind strong fortifications, had fought with renewed determination. During the next two days the Union troops edged in closer to Vicksburg's defenses. Perhaps the next attack, across a shorter distance, with less time under fire, would be triumphant. This time the entire army, deployed on a three-mile front, would simultaneously advance against the Rebel fortress.

The new assault, with Grant, Sherman, McPherson and McClernand synchronizing their watches, began at 10:00 a.m. on May 22. Once again, the primary objective for Sherman's forces was Stockade Redan. Instead of advancing in line of battle, however, Sherman attempted a different tactic. His men were to charge in narrow column, as fast as possible, up Graveyard Road toward the Rebel fortification. Leading the assault were 150 volunteers, carrying scaling ladders, planks and other equipment. They were to cross the protective ditch in front of the redan and put the scaling ladders in position for the soldiers following, whose assignment was to climb the right side of the citadel. At the same time, a diversionary attack would be launched some distance farther away. The volunteers were engaged in a virtual suicide mission, and Sherman properly called them the "forlorn hope."

They did manage, at a terrible cost of blood and life, to lay planks across the ditch, and place the scaling ladders against the side of the redan, but a murderous fire from the defenders prevented the attack from succeeding. Among the Medals of Honor awarded at Vicksburg, more than half went to members of the "forlorn hope." Despite a "gallant" attempt (Grant's word), the Union effort to storm the Vicksburg defenses had been thrown back all along the lines. Sherman was with Grant when a staff officer from McClernand rode up with a message. McClernand reported that "he had gained the enemy's entrenchments at several points," needed reinforcements and called for Sherman and McPherson to renew their attacks. Grant was very skeptical about McClernand's claim, but when he repeated his request, Grant sent a reinforcing division from the Seventeenth Corps, and ordered Sherman and McPherson to attack again.[79]

Sherman said he then ordered another assault at 3:00 p.m., which proved "equally unsuccessful and bloody." McPherson's renewed effort met with the same result. McClernand's report was false; he had gained nothing of significance, and the new attacks cost hundreds of additional casualties. Sherman and McPherson were furious, as was Grant. The commander thought seriously of relieving McClernand immediately but then decided to wait until Vicksburg fell. While siege operations progressed—for Grant did not intend to attack again—he would closely supervise all of McClernand's operations, and "place no reliance upon his reports," according to Charles Dana, "unless otherwise corroborated." It was following the May 22 fiasco that Dana wrote Stanton that McClernand was not even capable of commanding a regiment.[80]

As events developed, McClernand, ever full of himself, finally went too far, even for Grant's patience. Near the end of May, McClernand issued an order, which actually was not an order at all, but a congratulatory address to the Thirteenth Corps—which soon appeared in the newspapers, first in St. Louis. McClernand credited his corps with spearheading the Vicksburg campaign, and in essence accused "General McPherson and myself," as Sherman wrote Grant, "with disobeying the orders" of the commanding general on May 22, in not assaulting and allowing the enemy "to mass his forces against the Thirteenth

Army Corps alone." Sherman pronounced the accusation a "monstrous falsehood," which it was.[81]

On June 18, Grant relieved McClernand of command, and assigned Edward O. C. Ord to take charge of the Thirteenth Corps. Sherman did not exaggerate when he wrote his brother that the "riddance" of McClernand "was a relief to the whole army." Charles Dana made sure that Secretary of War Stanton understood that while "the congratulatory address . . . is the occasion of McClernand's removal, it is not its cause." The cause was "his repeated disobedience of important orders, his general insubordinate disposition, and his palpable incompetence for the duties of the position." All the more was Grant's action fully justified, Dana pointed out, because if Grant should be disabled and McClernand ascend to command the Army of the Tennessee, the result would be "the most pernicious consequences to the cause."[82]

FOR SIX WEEKS following the May 22 assault, the Union army besieged Vicksburg, steadily pressing the approach trenches closer and closer to the Rebel defenses. General Grant drew more troops from Memphis, bolstering his total forces to some 75,000. Food inside the enemy lines grew increasingly scarce, and the suffering became intense. "All day and night," Sherman informed Ellen, "continues the sharp crash of the Rifle and deep sound of mortars & cannon hurling shot & shells at the doomed city." Sherman wrote that he pitied "the poor families in Vicksburg," where women and children "are living in caves and holes underground whilst our shot & shells tear through their houses overhead." Vicksburg had to be "a horrid place," he said, "yet the People have been wrought up to Such a pitch of enthusiasm that I have not yet met one but would prefer all to perish rather than give up."[83]

One day in the latter part of June, while visiting his outposts and pickets, Sherman came up on a farm where he found "a bevy of women," awaiting the fate of their husbands and sons who were penned up in Vicksburg. He gave Ellen a brief summary of the encounter: "Do, oh do General Sherman spare my son, in one breath and in another," the mother proclaimed "that Lincoln was a tyrant and we only Murderers, Robbers, plunders and the defilers of the houses and altars of an innocent & outraged People." She and all the women "were real secesh, bitter as gall & yet Oh do General Sherman protect my son." Several of the women began crying, "and Dolly [Sherman's horse] & I concluded to go into the more genial atmosphere out in the Fields & Woods." Sherman expressed his doubt that "History affords a parallel of the deep & bitter enmity of the women of the South. No one who sees & hears them but must feel the intensity of their hate."[84]

Meanwhile, Grant had been troubled by rumors that Confederate General Joe Johnston was accumulating forces with which to come to the aid of Vicksburg. Grant sent Sherman to deal with the Johnston threat—if it should actually develop. On June 27, Sherman wrote Ellen from Bear Creek, twenty miles northeast of Vicksburg: "I am out here studying a most complicated Geography and preparing for Joe Johnston if he comes to the relief of Vicksburg." Sherman sounded confident, saying that he had been riding "a great deal" as he examined the terrain, "and think I know pretty well the weak and strong points of this Extended Line ... and if Johnston comes I think he will have a pretty hard task to reach Vicksburg."[85]

Johnston did not come, and by July 1, Grant's lines had been pushed so close to the enemy that in some places only a few yards separated the antagonists. Grant gave orders to prepare for an assault on July 6, with good reason to believe that this time the army would be successful in smashing through the Confederate fortifications. It did not come to that, as the starving and demoralized enemy, some almost in mutiny, surrendered on July 4. Three days later, the Rebels at Port Hudson, upon learning that the Vicksburg bastion had capitulated, surrendered to Nathaniel Banks, who had finally arrived to place that fortification under siege. Sherman regretted that he did not have the opportunity to march into Vicksburg with Grant for the surrender ceremony, but he immediately sent hearty congratulations when Grant informed him on July 3 that Pemberton was about to capitulate. "Telegraph me the moment you have Vicksburg in possession," he instructed. "If you are [already] in Vicksburg, Glory Hallelujah, the best fourth of July since 1776." On July 4, he wrote Grant, "The telegraph has just announced to me that Vicksburg is ours. . . . I can hardly contain myself," declared the effervescent general, "on this most glorious anniversary of the birth of a nation."[86]

And to Ellen he soon wrote, "I want to hear from you after you hear of the fall of Vicksburg. I have bet you will get tight on the occasion. . . . Well I confess a saint would be justified in sinning on such a Fourth of July as we have just passed through." Also, in his letter to Grant on July 4, Sherman victoriously declared that "the river of our greatness is free as God made it." With the United States totally possessing the Mississippi, the hardest problem of the war, in Sherman's assessment, had at long last been resolved, and he obviously felt that his wife, devout Catholic though she was, should "get tight" in celebration of the inimitable triumph.[87]

Chapter Nineteen

WHY WAS I NOT KILLED
AT VICKSBURG?

On July 5, 1863, Sherman jubilantly saluted the fall of Vicksburg as "the event of the war thus far;" and years later he exalted the Vicksburg triumph as "the most *decisive* event of the whole war." The U.S. Army had split the Confederacy along the great Mississippi and that victory, in the long run, meant that the Southern Confederacy could never be a viable nation. Sherman really wanted to be present for the surrender ceremony—"I did hope Grant would have given me Vicksburg and let someone else follow up the enemy inland," he wrote Ellen—but Grant ordered Sherman east, across the Big Black River, to drive away Joe Johnston's army. Sherman was reinforced by Ord and the Thirteenth Corps, and John G. Parke's Ninth Corps. "The weather," remembered Sherman, "was fearfully hot, and water scarce. Johnston . . . in retreating had caused cattle, hogs, and sheep to be driven into the ponds of water, and there shot down; so that we had to haul their dead and stinking carcasses out to use the water." Nevertheless, by July 10 the Rebel army had retreated into Jackson, and the next day Sherman, who had no intention of assaulting the strengthened enemy entrenchments, placed the city under siege.[1]

Steadily his forces expanded their lines along the enemy flanks, pressing the siege and shelling the capital city day and night. Sherman claimed that the Confederates "burned nearly all the handsome dwellings round about the Town, because they gave us shelter, or to light up the ground, to prevent night attacks." Then, during the night of July 16–17, Johnston evacuated the city, successfully carrying off most of his supplies and men. He also set fire to a block of commisary stores that he could not remove. Sherman said that the Union troops, in spite of guards posted, "widened the Circle of fire so that Jackson, once the pride and boast of Mississippi, is now a ruined town." Sherman pursued Johnston's army briefly, ensuring that the enemy got "a good Start," and continued withdrawing, rather than halting some miles east of the capital. He told Admiral Porter that the weather remained extremely hot, the dust stifling, and water scarce. "I would ruin my command," he declared, if he were to mount a serious pursuit.[2]

Actually Sherman had little or no interest in pursuing Johnston anyway. Instead, he concentrated on breaking up the railroads radiating from the capital. For a distance of sixty miles to the south, forty miles to the north, and ten miles to the east, his forces wreaked havoc. In addition to rails, Sherman's men destroyed locomotives, rolling stock, bridges and trestles. Four thousand men were at work smashing rails and equipment in the city itself. "Jackson," he assured his brother John, "will never again be a point where our enemy can assemble and threaten us on the river." Perhaps inevitably, some of the parties sent out to destroy the railroads broadened their work of devastation, rendering the countryside "terrible to contemplate."[3]

Yet Sherman fully realized, as he told his friend Ord, that "this Jackson movement . . . was simply a postscript" to the Vicksburg triumph. "A real conclusion," he declared in a letter to David Stuart, had been gained at Vicksburg. The magnificent campaign, in his appraisal, was the turning point of the awful conflict. He wanted to savor the moment, however briefly, because he regarded it as without equal. He soon penned a letter to Thomas Ewing, claiming that "Grant, myself, and McPherson . . . [had] been smart enough to direct our efforts to the critical 'Line of operations'—the 'strategic directrix' of the North American Continent," and thus had achieved "one of the Stupendous works of this war." He also "confessed" to his father-in-law that he had a feeling of "some pride" in the accomplishment.[4]

"No event in my life," he wrote Admiral Porter on July 4, "could have given me more personal pride or pleasure than to have met you today on the wharf at Vicksburg—a 4th of July so eloquent in events as to need no words or stimulants to elevate its importance." Sherman, of course, was not able to be present upon that grand day; but finally, taking control of Jackson, he and a group of his officers got a real chance to celebrate the great triumph—and in the capital of Mississippi. On the night of July 18, at the governor's mansion, which somehow had escaped harm, Sherman said that "we had a beautiful supper and union of the generals of this army." He wrote David Porter, "I assure you that the 'Army and Navy Forever' was sung with a full and hearty chorus." He also told Porter, "To me it will ever be a source of pride that real harmony has always characterized our intercourse, and let what may arise, I will ever call upon Admiral Porter with the same confidence as I have in the past." With Sherman and Porter composing a command tandem, army-navy relations could hardly have been better. Neither man evidenced any tolerance, other than a bit of good-natured banter, for interservice rivalry.[5]

On July 20, Sherman's forces started back toward Vicksburg, the destruction of the railroads having been accomplished to the General's satisfaction. However, the malicious conduct of some soldiers continued to trouble him. "The amount of plundering and stealing done by our army makes me ashamed of it," he confided to Grant. The difficulty, often the impossibility, of determining guilt for random, wanton actions frustrated a commander like Sherman, who sought a well-disciplined army. He was a controlling personality who pursued perfection, yet he was learning that he had to accept a degree of unruliness among his troops.[6]

At the Big Black River Sherman's Fifteenth Corps went into camp along the west bank, while Ord's Thirteenth Corps continued on south to Natchez. Grant had offered Natchez to Sherman, but he wanted to relax a bit and thought the city would present more problems than the rural area along the Big Black. "Were we to go to Natchez," he wrote his brother-in-law Phil, "it would be one endless strife about run away Negros, plundering and pillaging soldiers, and I am sick and tired of it."

Parke's Ninth Corps was ordered north to Kentucky, where it became a part of the Army of the Ohio. McPherson's Seventeen Corps remained in and around Vicksburg, while Grant went to New Orleans for a few days in order to confer with Nathaniel Banks.[7]

Sherman's troops lay about eighteen miles east of Vicksburg, whence abundant supplies arrived by railroad. "My own headquarters was in tents in a fine grove of old oaks," he wrote, and the Thirteenth Regulars provided his headquarters guard. "All the camps were arranged for health, comfort, rest and drill," said Sherman. Enthusiastically he told John: "I have the handsomest camp I ever saw, and should be glad to have visitors." The railroad came within four miles of his tent, "and I have its exclusive use, & a telegraph, at my elbow."[8]

Not surprisingly, Grant, Sherman and McPherson all received major promotions for their leadership in the Vicksburg campaign. Grant was elevated to major general in the regular army, while Sherman became a brigadier general in the regular army, as did McPherson. On August 4, General Halleck wrote to Sherman: "If you continue, my dear General," declared Old Brains, "as you have begun, no one at the end of the war will have a more brilliant record." Hugh Boyle Ewing wrote his father, "The army is confident that Cump can defeat anybody. His praise is on every tongue." The setback at Chickasaw Bayou was a thing of the past. The confidence gained at Shiloh had been vindicated and strengthened by the success at Vicksburg. "My children & children's children will now associate my name with their Country's History," Sherman proudly wrote his father-in-law. As for Ellen's brothers, the General wrote to her, "Tell your father that both Hugh and Charley stuck close to their duties and earned their honors without my aid. I give them no advantage not due their rank." (Charley was now a captain, serving on Sherman's staff, while Hugh had become a brigadier general following the Battle of Antietam in September 1862.) A gregarious Sherman longed to share the triumph with his family. However, while he granted many of his soldiers a furlough, he denied himself such a privilege, believing that a commander should remain with his corps.[9]

If he was going to see Ellen and the children they would have to come to Mississippi. Convinced that he had a healthy camp, he invited Ellen to bring the children and visit him on the Big Black. The family could enjoy an ideal retreat for the late summer. He told Ellen's father, "I have no apprehensions on the Score of health and the present condition of my command satisfies me on this score." Ellen's mother, who had been ill for several weeks, having undergone two surgeries, seemed much better, thus easing Ellen's mind about leaving Maria for a while. "I am over-joyed with your letter, dearest Cump," she responded on July 26. "I feel so impatient to be off that I can scarcely keep quiet." Requesting that he write at once about the necessary details of the trip, Ellen prayed, "God grant that nothing may occur to mar the happiness we anticipate."[10]

"I DREAMED THAT Willy crept into my bed and lay up softly to me," Sherman had written Ellen on May 2; expressing his "disappointment at waking in my narrow cot and discovering the illusion—I saw him as plainly as possible." Willy was his namesake and the son he favored. According to Ellen, Willy had "thinned off, grown taller, and resembles you very much." Maria Ewing agreed; she thought Willy's likeness to Cump was "so striking." Probably pleased to learn that his son's appear-ance increasingly resembled his own, Sherman already believed that he related well to Willy. During the siege of Vicksburg he wrote the nine-year-old, "It occurred to me that you would like to have a fishing pole from the Battle Field, so I had a dozen [cane poles] cut ... and sent to Lancaster." He instructed Willy to give one to his brother, another to Tommy Ewing, and then distribute the rest among his friends, telling them they were gathered from the Vicksburg battlefield. "Each cane is therefore a precious memento," declared the General, convinced that Willy "would prefer them to any book, or toy bought with money."[11]

If Sherman favored Willy over Tom—and his partiality was evident to Ellen, who cautioned him to mask his feelings—the child to whom he most often wrote letters was Minnie. Perhaps this was because Minnie was the oldest. Maybe it was because she had been away from him for so much of her life, having remained with her grandparents in Ohio while Sherman lived in California. He still addressed her as "Dear Little Minnie," although Ellen informed him that "Minnie is taller than I, and so mature in look and manner that you would almost forget that she is only twelve and imagine your daughter of marriageable age, could you see her now." Sherman was delighted when Ellen arrived at his camp in mid-August, accompanied by Minnie, Lizzie, Willy and Tom. He had hoped to see four-year-old Elly, and two-year-old Rachel as well, but Ellen thought that bringing the youngest children would make the trip too difficult. Ellen's description of Minnie's appearance and manner proved no exaggeration, and Sherman pronounced his eldest, "although only in her thirteenth year ... a beautiful woman."[12]

Sherman and Ellen lived in two large hospital tents, "one of which is our parlour," Ellen informed her mother, while the children occupied smaller tents nearby. Sherman was both surprised and pleased to see how well the children got along with one another, and all seemed to be healthy. Routinely, the family rose with the sun, ate breakfast and proceeded with a full day of activity. Willy was very interested in army affairs, more so than the other children. Often he rode on horseback with his father to observe a military drill or review. He learned the manual of arms, and the Thirteenth Regiment made him an honorary sergeant. Sherman was delighted. Minnie, too, liked horseback riding with her father, which certainly pleased the General.[13]

On Sunday, September 6, Sherman took Ellen and the children into Vicksburg "to see the Fortifications ... and all the points of interest." The children zealously gathered up bullets and fragments of shot and shell, until they realized they were overloaded and needed to be more discriminating. Ellen wrote her mother that "Vicksburg is the most forlorn, desolate looking place I have ever dreamed of." Nevertheless, she went into the city a number of times, taking the children with her and passing time with Mrs. Grant, whose children were about the same age as Ellen's. The Grants were spending the late summer in a shady residence overlooking the Mississippi. Occasionally Ellen and the children had dinner at General McPherson's headquarters, who seemed pleased to host them. Altogether, Ellen and the children experienced a very agreeable time while visiting Sherman's camp. There was the bonus of enjoying a reunion with Ellen's brothers, Hugh Boyle and Charley, as well as, for Ellen, the regular attendance at mass with chaplain J. C. Carrier, a priest from Notre Dame, Indiana.[14]

During those rather idyllic summer days following the magnificent triumph on the Mississippi, and the great, simultaneous victory in southern Pennsylvania at Gettysburg, the end of the war may well have appeared to be drawing near. West of the Allegheny Mountains, where the border between Union and Confederacy stretched for hundreds of miles, the Southerners clearly were losing the struggle. By the fall of 1863, the United States had won West Virginia and much of Missouri, Kentucky and Tennessee, along with parts of Arkansas and Louisiana. The Federals had occupied strategic islands around the 3,500 miles of Rebel coastal perimeter; penetrated major, vital rivers; and above all, gained control of "the Father of Waters." They had also fastened an ever tightening blockade on the Southerners. Yet cruelly, despite the obvious reality that the Confederacy was going down, economically and militarily, the appalling struggle was far from over. Although critically wounded, the Rebels remained extremely dangerous.

On September 19 and 20, the Confederate Army of Tennessee, under Braxton Bragg, which General William Rosecrans had skillfully maneuvered out of middle Tennessee, suddenly rose up in north Georgia near Chickamauga Creek, an Indian name said to mean "river of death," and delivered a sledgehammer blow against the United States forces. Strengthened by two divisions of James Longstreet's corps from Virginia, the Rebel army struck the Union right center about noon on the second day of the battle. Through a confusion of orders, an entire Federal division had just pulled out of the Yankee line. The Rebel attack hit that precise point, a gap nearly a quarter mile wide that had been opened up by the Union mistake. The Southerners, massed in great force for the assault, stormed through the gap and split the Army of the Cumberland in two. Rosecrans, and much of the army, panicked and fled for Chattanooga.

Fortunately for the Union, George Thomas, hailed ever afterward as "the Rock of Chickamauga," sustained his position on the left wing, while marshaling reserves led by Gordon Granger, together with remnants from the disintegrated right and center, to form a new line along the ragged elevation of Snodgrass Hill. Holding on through several hours of fierce fighting, Thomas's stand saved the U.S. Army from destruction. As sunset approached, Thomas withdrew the troops to Chattanooga and the Confederates did not pursue.

No battle of the war, relative to time of fighting and numbers engaged, was more bloody than Chickamauga. In absolute terms, the three-day clash at Gettysburg saw the greatest number of casualties, totaling 51,000, according to the long accepted figure. Chickamauga, with nearly 35,000 casualties in two days, recorded slaughter at the same rate as Gettysburg—and that when total Yankee strength going into Chickamauga numbered approximately 25,000 fewer than Gettysburg, while Southern forces were nearly 10,000 fewer. But the Confederacy's bloody victory, at a cost of at least 18,500 casualties, held little strategic meaning, because Chattanooga remained in Union hands. The Rebels soon advanced to the northern point of Lookout Mountain, while their main force entrenched on Missionary Ridge. A third, much smaller group settled in at Brown's Ferry, across the bend of the Tennessee River west of Chattanooga. Rosecrans's besieged army was denied supplies by river, railroad and wagon road, and faced the prospect of starvation unless relieving forces came to the rescue.[15]

"The first intimation I got of this disaster was on the 22nd of September," Sherman said, when he got an order from Grant to "dispatch one of my divisions immediately into Vicksburg," from whence it would proceed at once to Chattanooga. The following day Sherman met with Grant. After reviewing several "alarming dispatches" (Sherman's words) from Halleck, Grant decided that Sherman and his entire corps should head for Chattanooga. Traveling by riverboat to Memphis, Sherman would then move eastward, repairing the Memphis & Charleston Railroad, according to Halleck's instructions, as he marched.[16]

Plans were made for Ellen and the children to accompany Sherman to Memphis, and then continue upriver to Ohio. Neither Ellen nor

Minnie was well when they boarded the steamer *Atlantic*. Ellen had developed a severe headache, and Minnie was running a high fever. Both parents were concerned, because Minnie obviously felt very sick. But Willy, who got on the *Atlantic* carrying a small, double-barreled shotgun, with his father teasing him "about carrying away captured property," became critically ill—actually, fatally ill with typhoid fever. His distraught mother, still suffering from the excruciating headache, stayed at his bedside, dipping linens in water to place on her son's hot forehead, while the steamer slowly churned northward. Finally docking at Memphis on the morning of October 2, the Shermans immediately took a carriage to the Gayoso Hotel, where General Sherman carried Willy up the stairs to their rooms. The boy died at the Gayoso on the evening of October 3, 1863.[17]

"The blow was a terrible one to us all, so sudden and so unexpected," recalled Sherman in his memoirs. Soon after Willy's death, writing to General Grant, Sherman confided to his friend that the tragedy "has affected me more than any other misfortune could. I can hardly compose myself enough for work," he admitted, yet vowing that he "must and will do so at once." He telegraphed General Halleck that the loss of Willy "is more to me than words can express," but assured the general that he would not let his boy's death "divert my mind from the duty I owe my country." Also sharing his grief with Admiral Porter, Sherman said that Willy "was my Pride & Hope of Life," and now, he declared, "I must work on purely . . . for love of country and Professional Pride." He told his brother John that Willy "somehow was more to me than the other children, because he was with me in California and was so wrapt up in me down here."[18]

It is the letters to Ellen, though, that fully reveal the devastating impact that Willy's death had on Sherman. "Sleeping—waking—everywhere I see Poor Little Willy," he wrote Ellen on October 6. "His face & form are as deeply imprinted on my memory as were deep seated the hopes I had in his future. . . . I will always deplore my judgment," he declared, "in taking my family to so fatal a climate at so critical a period of the year." To this theme, with its implications of guilt, the troubled father would return again and again. He told his wife that he had followed her home in his mind, estimating the hour when "all Lancaster would be shrouded in gloom to think that Willy Sherman was coming back a corpse." While he would "go on to the End," he also wrote that "the Chief stay to my faltering heart is now gone."[19]

Four days later, while still at the Gayoso, and shortly before leaving for Chattanooga, Sherman admitted: "I still feel out of heart to write. The moment I begin to think of you & the children, Poor Willy appears before me as plain as life." Sadly recounting memories of the child in San Francisco, Leavenworth and "running to meet me with open arms at Black River, & last, moaning in death in this Hotel," Sherman said that "at times I cannot realize the truth so dreamlike, and yet I know we can never see his bright, honest face again." Although acknowledging that "the world moves on," yet he was tormented to "see ladies & children playing in the Room where Willy died, and it seems sacrilege." Then followed the self-blame: "Why should I ever have taken [the family] to that dread Climate? It nearly kills me to think of it. Why was I not Killed at Vicksburg," he cried, probably returning to his belief that he would not survive the war, "and left Willy to grow up to take care of you?"[20]

Sherman attempted to alleviate his grief by plunging into his work, a solution that had helped with problems in the past. But for months to come, despite heavy military demands, many of the letters he wrote to Ellen made mournful reference to the child who had been his favorite. Ellen too wrote letter after letter to her husband in which she sorrowed for Willy. She feared that she had taken too much pride in the boy, thus experiencing her own peculiar sense of guilt. She took solace in her faith, certain that the precious child now resided in heaven. "Two months ago yesterday, dearest Cump," she wrote on October 16, "we arrived at your camp on the Big Black, and what have we not gone through since then! I realize now that . . . we really live only in our home above. Earth would be insupportable to me," she declared, "did I not feel Willy was near me in spirit and hears my prayers. . . . Innocent, guileless heart." Again she pleaded for her husband to accept Catholicism, thereby ensuring an ultimate reunion with their beloved son.

However, the Catholic Church had never been, and never would be, acceptable to Sherman. The church was fine for Ellen, and he would never attempt to undermine her faith, but he simply was not a believer. He continued to immerse himself in the memory of Willy, partially because, for Sherman, memory now constituted the sole reality; also, because he sought to assuage his own feelings about selfishly exposing the boy to a dangerous climate. In a very real sense, Sherman did not want to put Willy's death behind him. He even decided that Sam, a horse of his that Willy liked to ride while he was in Mississippi, should be sent to Ellen in Lancaster, and he instructed her to "see that he is taken good care of." Not surprisingly, he did not want Willy's body to stay in Ohio—that state to which Sherman never intended to return "if I can avoid it"—and in 1867, the child's remains would be reinterred in St. Louis.[21]

But in October 1863, despite his personal misery, Sherman knew that he had to get on with the war. "Since Poor Willy's death I have felt more than ever my natural desire to slide out into obscurity," he wrote Ellen's brother Phil. Yet "the moment I cast about to See how I could get away," he continued, "it seems impossible for all naturally & by habit come to me for orders & instructions. . . . I seem to possess a knowledge of men & things, of Rivers, Roads, capacity of trains, wagons &c. that no one near me even professes to have." Some readers might interpret those words as shameful braggadocio. While Sherman was not immune to penning an occasional self-congratulatory little essay, this was not one of those times. His self-appraisal was matter-of-fact and basically accurate; and, in fact, right then the logistics of the Memphis & Charleston Railroad, which Halleck wanted repaired, were troubling him.[22]

"I don't like this railroad," he wrote General Grant; "it lies parallel to an enemy's country, and they can break it when they please." He predicted that the rails "will be cut the moment I get east of Bear Creek." The distance from Memphis to Chattanooga is more than three hundred miles. Sherman did not have enough men to repair and defend the railroad, and also reinforce the besieged troops at Chattanooga—nor did he have the time required for such a project. "To depend on a road so precarious as this [for supplies and troop transportation] would tie us down to localities that can have no material influence on events." He was absolutely correct. The odd thing is that General Halleck, who was no stranger to the region and its problems, wanted the railroad secured. His view is all the more puzzling considering the crisis at Chattanooga. Sherman instead, as he wrote Grant, wanted "to move about and learn to live on the corn and meal of the country." A hundred miles east of Memphis, the Tennessee River might serve as a partial communications line for his eastward trek; still farther east, the railroads from Nashville to the Alabama towns of Decatur and Stevenson could be of assistance. But to rely primarily on the Memphis & Charleston Railroad for supplies, especially the long stretch from Memphis to the Tennessee River, was not practical. Sherman's logistical concepts were evolving and broadening since his Vicksburg experiences, and he knew that the movement to Chattanooga could not be sustained by any one railroad. His troops would have to forage liberally on the Tennessee–Alabama countryside.[23]

Sherman soon had more reason to dislike the Memphis & Charleston Railroad. On Sunday morning, October 11, he, his staff, the headquarters detachment and their horses steamed eastward from Memphis aboard a special train. It was the day after he had written to Grant expressing his concerns about the railroad. At the Collierville depot, about twenty-five miles out, the train most likely would have run into a Rebel ambush if it had been an hour or so later. Fortunately, Sherman and the 250 men with him arrived in the nick of time to reinforce the small Collierville garrison and fend off an attack by Rebel cavalry, who otherwise would have gained control of the railroad. Sherman took command of course, and "for three or four hours," according to his recollection, the battle continued until the Confederates broke away, as a larger body of Sherman's troops began arriving from Memphis.[24]

During the fight, Sherman conducted himself in his customary bold manner, and one of the Collierville garrison, fearing for his safety, admonished the General to take cover. Sherman bluntly told the sergeant to mind his own business. The concern of Ellen and other family members that he frequently exposed himself to danger is well founded. This, however, was the style of Sherman's leadership, both to accurately determine the tactical situation he faced and to inspire confidence in the men he commanded. Evidently the Collierville clash, although small, was a hard fight. "The enemy closed down on us several times, and got possession of the rear of our train," reported Sherman, "but our men were cool and practiced shots ... and drove them back." Confederate artillery "knocked to pieces our locomotive and several of the cars, and set fire to the train;" he continued, "but we managed to get possession again, and extinguished the fire." The Rebels captured several horses, including Dolly, Sherman's favorite mare. Doubtless he was thankful that he had left Sam at Memphis for the trip to Ohio, or he too might have been captured. When Sherman told Ellen about Dolly's fate, he added: "I have the satisfaction to know She will break the neck of the first Guerrilla that fires a pistol from her back."[25]

Sherman spent the day after the Collierville engagement in repairing damages to the railroad and getting a train ready for the trip into Corinth. While he refrained from criticizing Halleck, he strongly disagreed with the policy of spreading out soldiers in many small garrisons to protect the Memphis & Charleston from Rebel cavalry and guerrillas. The railroad still could be broken by a determined enemy, who might either strike it where no troops were present or overwhelm stationary garrisons with surprise and superior numbers. "A dozen men can break it any night," declared Sherman. Because the railroad was highly vulnerable, Sherman even wanted to abandon Corinth, which he considered of little value to the Union at the time. If it was later needed, he believed the Federals could retake the town with a minimum of effort.[26]

When Sherman's train finally pulled into Corinth, he heard an exciting rumor that a major change of leadership was in the works, with General Grant to become a theater-wide commander in the west. Feeling sure the rumor was true, Sherman dashed off a message to Grant, urging his friend: "Accept the command of the great army of the center; don't hesitate. By your presence ... you will unite all discordant elements and impress the enemy in proportion. All success and honor to you." The rumor was correct. Under date of October 16, General Orders No. 337, President Lincoln directed that the Armies of the Ohio, the Cumberland

and the Tennessee would constitute the Military Division of the Mississippi, under command of U. S. Grant. Within a few days, as Sherman doubtless expected, Grant turned over his old command, the Army of the Tennessee, to Sherman. Grant also removed General Rosecrans from command of the Army of the Cumberland, replacing him with George Thomas, whose orders were to defend Chattanooga "at all hazards." Famously, the Rock of Chickamauga replied, "We will hold the town until we starve."[27]

Meanwhile, Sherman remained busy "pushing forward the repairs to the railroad bridge at Bear Creek, and in patching up the many breaks between it and Tuscumbia." River transports loaded with provisions, under protection of gunboats dispatched by Admiral Porter, awaited him at the Tennessee River, which became, with the water level rising, a more reliable communications line than the railroad from Memphis. Nevertheless, Sherman increasingly encouraged his troops to live off the countryside. He himself liked moving about the open country, believing that such a life was healthier for the men than residing in camp. Also, forage consumed by the Union was thus denied to the enemy. Sherman was pleased by the way the soldiers took to the task. "I never saw such greedy rascals after chicken and fresh meat," he said. "I don't think I will draw anything for them but salt," he mused. All the more, he disliked the time-consuming repair of the railroad, which he really did not need anyway.[28]

Much to Sherman's satisfaction, on October 27, the railroad work abruptly came to an end. The General was sitting on the porch of a house in northeast Mississippi when he saw a man approaching, "a dirty, black-haired individual, with mixed dress and strange demeanor." The fellow was a "Corporal Pike," and he described, "in his peculiar way" remarked Sherman, how he had come down the Tennessee River in a canoe, "fired at all the way by guerrillas," until he reached Sherman's advance troops at Tuscumbia. There General Frank Blair had directed him on to Sherman, for whom Pike carried a message from General Grant at Chattanooga.

"Drop all work on the Memphis & Charleston Railroad," Grant

ordered; "cross the Tennessee and hurry eastward with all possible dispatch toward Bridgeport, till you meet further orders from me." A reenergized Sherman was soon across the river, directing the Fifteenth Corps, commanded by Frank Blair since Sherman became the army commander, toward Chattanooga, and usually riding at the head of the troops. James McPherson remained in command of the Seventeenth Corps at Vicksburg, and Stephen Hurlbut's corps remained at Memphis. Corporal Pike, "a singular character," said Sherman, obviously intrigued by the man, was provided with a horse, and accompanied the General for a time. When they parted company, Sherman told Pike that if ever he could do him a personal service, to let him know.[29]

The march eastward was slowed by the large number of wagons. Sherman's mission being the relief of Chattanooga, he supposed, naturally, that the wagons might be required to provision the troops. He did not want to leave them behind, or start them back toward Memphis, for fear that the Rebels would capture them. Pushing on ahead of his troops during the last miles of the journey, Sherman reached Bridgeport, Alabama, approximately thirty miles from Chattanooga, during the night of November 13. The main body of the Fifteenth Corps was not far behind him, and considering the drag caused by hundreds of wagons, the troops had made good time. The loss of Willy continued to plague Sherman, who wrote Ellen from Bridgeport: "I cannot banish from my mind Poor Willy." Speaking of what "a good boy" the youngster was, Sherman tried to find some consolation as he declared that Willy "knows how we loved him, and if he sees us now, he knows how we mourn his absence."[30]

A dispatch from Grant awaited him at Bridgeport, ordering that Sherman push on to Chattanooga at once, leaving his troops to follow as soon as possible. Grant wanted Sherman's input about the plans for raising the siege, which were being discussed by Grant, Thomas and the other generals, particularly since Grant expected Sherman's command to play a major role in the coming engagement. Sherman arrived in Chattanooga on November 14, where Grant, in the presence of several generals, welcomed him heartily. Grant offered him a cigar and, indicating a rocking chair, instructed his red-haired friend to "take the chair of honor." Sherman responded, "Oh no! That belongs to you, General." But Grant, who was two years younger than Sherman, insisted that he take the rocker, explaining that he believed in showing a "proper respect to age." Since Grant "put it on that ground," declared Sherman with good nature, "I *must* accept."[31]

The last time Sherman saw Grant, the latter had been hobbling around on crutches, suffering considerable pain from a bruised and swollen leg. The injury had been sustained in a fall from a horse during his trip to New Orleans after the Vicksburg triumph. Grant's leg was still a problem when he had to make the trip into Chattanooga, especially during the last sixty torturous miles of the journey. The only way into the Union lines at that time was up the Sequatchie Valley and over Walden's Ridge on a rough, circuitous road that army trains laboriously traversed in carrying a trickle of supplies to the Federals. Grant and his staff had struggled into Chattanooga on October 23, contending with heavy rain for a portion of the distance.[32]

Arriving damp and dirty at the headquarters of General Thomas, Grant slumped down in front of a fire and lit a cigar. Probably, based on the last miserable stretch of his trip, he had already decided on the first order of business. When he learned that hardly enough ammunition existed for even one day of battle, saw the half-starved soldiers, along with hundreds of dead mules and horses, and was informed that the army was down to quarter-rations, while armed guards prevented hungry soldiers from stealing the little food available for the animals, there could be no doubt that the top priority was opening up a supply line—a cracker line, as Grant called it. William F. "Baldy" Smith, a contentious but capable West Pointer, proposed a bold plan to do just that. Grant liked it, and after riding with Smith, Thomas and other officers on an inspection tour, he issued orders for action as soon as possible.[33]

The crux of the plan was to capture Brown's Ferry, on the Tennessee River west of Chattanooga. If the Union forces seized that ferry, they could open a direct supply line into Chattanooga from Bridgeport. Stealth and surprise were the basic ingredients of Smith's daring plan. From three directions U.S. forces would converge on Brown's Ferry,

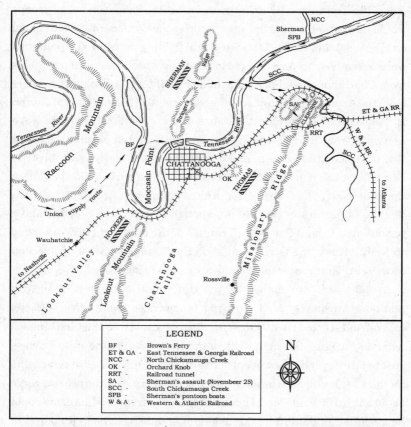

AREA OF SHERMAN'S CHATTANOOGA OPERATIONS

Grant intended for Sherman to play the decisive role at Chattanooga, paving the way for Thomas and Hooker to move against Rebel positions farther south. Map by Jim Moon Jr.

establishing a beachhead on the west bank of the river. Under cover of darkness, one column of infantry would march overland, west across the narrow neck of Moccasin Point, while a second group would float down the Tennessee River in pontoon boats. The river-borne troops would make the assault, hoping to surprise the Confederate force posted on the west bank of the Tennessee, and holding on while the pontoons were assembled to provide a bridge across which the reinforcements from Chattanooga could be brought up rapidly. A third column, soldiers from the Army of the Potomac under command of Major General Joseph H. Hooker, had the greatest distance to travel. Following the railroad eastward from Bridgeport, these men would march around the south side of Raccoon Mountain, and during the night, close up on Brown's Ferry from the rear. Combining forces, the Yankees would then drive the Rebels out of Cummings Gap, a passage through Raccoon Mountain (for the Confederates had not put enough troops there to withstand a serious attack), and thus secure control of the road from Brown's Ferry to Kelly's Ferry, the latter located on the Tennessee, west of Raccoon Mountain. The cracker line would be open to Bridgeport.

At 3:00 a.m. on October 27, the Union flotilla of more than fifty pontoon-transports, each carrying on average twenty-five soldiers, cast off and started silently drifting downstream from the Chattanooga wharves, hugging the right bank of the river for the nine-mile journey. Just before daylight, they swept across the river and landed at two points on the west bank, one the gorge at Brown's Ferry, and the other a gorge about a third of a mile farther downstream, from which the enemy could be assaulted in flank. The Confederates should have been prepared to give the Union a very tough battle for such strategic ground. Yet, not only were the Rebels surprised, they did not have near enough troops with which to contest the assault.

While Joseph Hooker did not arrive in time for the fight at Brown's Ferry, his absence was of no consequence. The Federal forces from Chattanooga surprised, outflanked and outnumbered the Confederates. The battle was little more than a sharp skirmish, probably lasting less than thirty minutes, after which the Southerners retreated. A second fight, at

Wauhatchie a few days later, guaranteed the Federal communications line. The Rebels had lost their greatest advantage—the ability to deny food, military supplies and reinforcements to the enemy. The Union Army was soon eating better. Numerical strength, once Sherman and Hooker arrived, approached 70,000, while Confederate Braxton Bragg depleted his fighting force to about 40,000, sending Longstreet's men to Knoxville in a futile attempt to capture that city.[34]

Such was the situation when Sherman's troops marched into Chattanooga via the recently opened cracker line. Grant wanted to attack the Rebels as soon as Sherman could get his men into position. The plan called for Hooker on the right and Thomas in the center to create diversions against, respectively, the Confederates at Lookout Mountain and their center on Missionary Ridge. Sherman was assigned the main task, to cross the Tennessee River several miles upstream from Chattanooga, and assault the northern end of Missionary Ridge, breaking the enemy's right flank, and then advancing south along the ridge to cut the Rebel line of retreat. Grant, who was feeling pressure from Washington to aid Ambrose Burnside at Knoxville, believed that an attack against Missionary Ridge, even if it did not succeed, would so alarm the Confederate commander that he would recall Longstreet's troops.[35]

But Sherman failed to move his forces into attack position fast enough to satisfy Grant. Probably Sherman, considering his pronounced prejudices about politics, both civil and military, was not fully in tune with Grant's concern about pleasing Washington. Also, Willy's recent death continued to have a depressing and numbing impact on him. Clearly he did not initially realize his commander's impatience with him. Only when Grant sent Sherman a crisp order, through John A. Rawlins, Grant's chief of staff, saying that Sherman must leave his wagon trains behind, avoid any further delay "and move up at once" did Sherman grasp Grant's agitation. Charles Dana wrote, "Grant says the blunder is his; that he should have given Sherman explicit orders to leave his wagons behind; but I know, . . . that no one was so much astonished as Grant on learning they had not been left, even without such orders."[36]

Sherman wasted no time in acting to set matters right with his commander. "I need not express how I felt," he responded, "that my troops should cause delay." Promising that he would attack Missionary Ridge the next morning, November 24, he stated, "No cause on earth will induce me to ask for longer delay, and tonight, at midnight, we move." Hidden near the mouth of North Chickamauga Creek, which emptied into the Tennessee River about seven or eight miles northeast of Chattanooga, Sherman's men began quietly filing into pontoon boats, 116 of them, early on the morning of the twenty-fourth. "Be prompt as you can, boys; there's room for thirty in a boat," said Sherman in a hushed voice, as he stood close at hand in the darkness. Some of the men were startled when they realized the General was right beside them. Within minutes, an assault force of more than 1,000 soldiers was afloat in the swift current of the Tennessee, heading downstream for four miles, toward a landing on the east bank of the river, just below the mouth of South Chickamauga Creek. Rifles loaded but not capped, as insurance against a noisy blunder that would alert the enemy, the Federals achieved complete surprise and captured the Confederate pickets, except for one man who managed to escape.[37]

As soon as the day dawned, a gloomy, overcast and misty morning, some boats were taken from the work of ferrying men across the river— Sherman reporting that several thousand troops were already ashore on the east bank, and a small steamboat had come up from Chattanooga to help with the ferrying—and used in the construction of a pontoon bridge. Planned and built under the immediate supervision of "Baldy" Smith, the 1,350-foot-long span was in place across the Tennessee by noon. Sherman was delighted, praising "the genius and intelligence of General William F. Smith." He reported, "I doubt if the history of war can show a bridge of that extent . . . laid down so noiselessly and well in so short of time." And despite the Rebel picket who got away, no enemy counterattack had developed.[38]

Sherman then moved to the attack, three divisions strong, against the right flank of the Confederate Army positioned on the northern end of Missionary Ridge. Or so he thought. Advancing in a light, drizzling rain, Sherman had Brigadier General Morgan Smith's division leading on the left of the Blueclad formation, while Brigadier Generals John E. Smith and Hugh Boyle Ewing led the center and right divisions. Perhaps it looked like a demanding assignment as the men began ascending the hill. They moved cautiously. But nothing more than Confederate outposts were present and the Yankees encountered little resistance. According to the estimate of a Union soldier, the Rebels were only 200 or 300 strong and "retired hastily and in some disorder." Sherman said that "at 3:30 p.m. we gained, with no loss, the desired point."[39]

In reality, his three divisions had just overwhelmed an undefended hill—except for the enemy outposts. Sherman's men were atop Billy Goat Hill, as it is known today. That prominent knoll was one of several heights clustered in the general vicinity, but stood completely apart from Missionary Ridge. Sherman's position then lay about a mile or more, separated by a deep ravine, from the northern end of Missionary Ridge— a section of the complex ridge that was called Tunnel Hill because of the railroad tunnel passing through it. Little wonder that Sherman had a mistaken concept of the terrain. The northern extremity of Missionary Ridge, near the Tennessee River, actually is not a ridge at all, having expanded from the narrow, rugged line that defines most of its length, to a confusing eruption of eminences, knolls, and hilly outcroppings. A few days earlier, Sherman, Grant, Thomas and "Baldy" Smith had viewed the area where Sherman was to attack, although, for security against detection, their vantage point had been on the west bank of the Tennessee. From there it was impossible to tell that the ridge was not continuous and that a series of knobs existed north of Tunnel Hill. If Sherman had ordered a reconnaissance on the east bank of the river, his plans to surprise the Rebels when he crossed might well have been compromised. Besides, the only maps he possessed showed the ridge to be continuous. His misconception of the terrain is fully understandable.[40]

Hardly an hour of daylight remained when Sherman's men reached the top of Billy Goat Hill on that short, murky, miserable day. Sherman's planning and execution of the river crossing had been excellent, and at the moment when his troops gained the height of Billy Goat Hill, Confederate General Patrick Cleburne had only a portion of one brigade entrenching between Sherman and the railroad tunnel. Obviously Sherman did not, and could not have known that fact. In a valuable study of the struggle for Chattanooga, historian Wiley Sword faulted Sherman for "his absence from the forward positions before darkness fell on [November] twenty-fourth." However, even if Sherman had fully grasped the true lay of the terrain at that late hour, there was not sufficient time to both mount a reconnaissance in force (which might or might not enlighten his decision about what to do next) and then possibly launch an assault against the Rebels—unless he were willing to consider a risky night attack across rugged and unfamiliar ground.

There was no reason to think that the Confederate defenders in Sherman's front were relatively few. The reasonable expectation was that the Southern forces would be massing for a counterattack in an effort to save the key point of their entire battle line. Shortly before noon, Grant had sent Sherman a message, saying that a "considerable movement [of enemy troops] has taken place on top of the ridge toward you." On the far left of Sherman's position, the brigade of Giles Smith had engaged in a firefight with Rebel troops whose strength was unknown. "The enemy felt our left flank about 4 p.m.," Sherman reported, "and a pretty smart engagement with artillery and muskets ensued ... [and] Smith was severely wounded." Furthermore, Sherman and his men needed rest, having been up all night. The General had to make a decision quickly, and he determined, while a bit of daylight yet remained, to entrench a defensible position. Given what Sherman knew when he had to make the call, it was a reasonable decision.[41]

During the night of November 24, and the early morning of the twenty-fifth, Patrick Cleburne, with William J. Hardee's assistance part of the time, occupied and fortified Tunnel Hill with his division, reinforced by two brigades and two regiments. The night was unusually dark due to an eclipse of the moon lasting about two hours. Cleburne's only mention of the eclipse involved the delay that it caused. He did an outstanding job of positioning the Rebel defenders in spite of the darkness, establishing clear fields of fire in some areas, and was also able to put both frontal and enfilade fire at a few points. The thirty-five-year-old general from County Cork, Ireland, once a British soldier, already had proven he was unsurpassed as a division commander in the Rebel army. He was preparing to demonstrate that fact yet again.[42]

WHILE SHERMAN'S FORCES were crossing the Tennessee, and attempting to gain a lodgement on the Confederate northern flank, another Union advance had been progressing eight miles away. Major General "Fighting Joe" Hooker, leading more than 10,000 troops, had moved against the Confederates at the base of Lookout Mountain. The Southerners were outnumbered about four or five to one, and soon withdrew to Missionary Ridge. Some of Hooker's men ascended the mountain, disappearing in the mists as they climbed. On the morning of November 25, the United States flag flew from atop Lookout Mountain. The clash was romanticized as the "Battle Above the Clouds."

Hooker's lead division commander, Brigadier General John W. Geary, whose veterans of Gettysburg had climbed the mountain, dramatically wrote his wife that "this feat will be celebrated until time shall be no more." General Grant was not impressed, and later said that the battle of Lookout Mountain "is all poetry." Union domination of Lookout Mountain did assure control of the railroad into Chattanooga from the west, and that was an important achievement. The Confederate strength, however, still lay along the line of Missionary Ridge, where Grant looked to Sherman for decisive results on the northern end of that elevation at Tunnel Hill.[43]

The struggle for Chattanooga came to a climax on Wednesday, November 25, a day that dawned hazy but turned clear and sunny during the morning. General Grant, still intending to hammer the Rebel right flank, sent orders that Sherman should attack at break of day. Sherman was in the saddle early, riding from left to right, and "catching as accurate an idea of the ground as possible by the dim light of morning." About seven o'clock he sent skirmishers forward and a heavy picket firing began, although he did not attack until ten or ten-thirty. Sherman decided to assign the main assault to Brigadier General Hugh Boyle

Ewing's division. "I guess, Ewing, if you're ready you might as well go ahead," Sherman reportedly told his brother-in-law between puffs of his cigar, but "don't call for help until you actually need it."[44]

As bugles sounded the advance, Ewing had Brigadier General John M. Corse's brigade, reinforced with one of Joseph A. Lightburn's regiments, lead the attack. The men moved straight toward the northern face of Tunnel Hill. On Corse's right flank, the brigade of Colonel John M. Loomis would advance along the west base of the ridge, turn when nearing the tunnel and join in the assault. Two brigades from John E. Smith's division were to follow in the rear of Loomis. Ewing's third brigade, commanded by Colonel Joseph R. Cockerill, was to remain in reserve, while Brigadier General Morgan L. Smith's division tramped along the eastern base of the ridge, hopefully within supporting distance of Corse's left flank.[45]

The Union troops moved forward with confidence. These soldiers were the proud conquerors of Vicksburg and they fully expected to take Tunnel Hill. But they faced a daunting task, engaging in a severe and bloody trial that raged over the next several hours. Corse's spearheading brigade steadily ascended the narrow, northern end of the ridge, which sloped up gradually toward the Rebel position. The Blueclads assaulted "with a fearlessness and determination that was astonishing," reported Colonel Charles C. Walcutt, who led the brigade after Colonel Corse was badly wounded, and they drove close to the Confederate entrenchments before the force of their effort was spent.[46]

Sherman has taken criticism for launching his main effort with a single brigade. Presumably the narrowness of the ridge at its northern end was the reason for striking with one brigade only. Actually, there was sufficient space for a two-brigade assault, and the General, if he knew that, should have so ordered. The result, however, likely would have been the same. The Southerners, at any given point, could rapidly mass as many defenders as the attackers whom they confronted—and fighting from entrenchments always awarded defenders with a decided advantage.

Meanwhile, the Union right-flank brigade of Colonel Loomis crossed several hundred yards of open fields, where the men were exposed to artillery fire from above the tunnel and on the ridge. Approaching the railroad track leading to the tunnel, they engaged in an intense firefight with two enemy regiments. These Rebels, having spotted the Yankees advancing, had scrambled down the ridge, one regiment on each side of the railroad. Loomis gradually applied more pressure, especially with artillery, after bringing up a section of a battery to support the advance of his left flank. When at last the Confederates withdrew and climbed back up the ridge, Loomis turned and began ascending the ragged elevation near the tunnel. But the Rebels took advantage of interior lines, and quickly shifted more troops to that threatened sector. The Union soldiers encountered a heavy, direct fire of rifled musketry. Stymied, they went to ground, seeking whatever cover the rough ridge presented.[47]

Neither the advance of the primary Union attack force under Corse nor the right-flank brigade led by Loomis had presented any real threat to the Confederate grip on Tunnel Hill. The great problem for Sherman throughout the frustrating struggle was that, although he had about 30,000 troops, compared with fewer than 10,000 Confederates, he never found a way to deploy his superior numbers effectively at the actual points of fighting. Several times the Federals climbed the ridge either in a somewhat helter-skelter fashion, or one brigade behind the other, with the trailing brigade never getting into action until the preceding was overwhelmed.[48]

Late in the afternoon, when at last Union pressure from several brigades actually threatened to carry Tunnel Hill—or so some Confederate officers feared—General Cleburne launched a bayonet counterattack with brigade strength. The Blueclads were taken by surprise, with the weight of the Rebel charge striking them in front, while one regiment simultaneously assaulted their right flank. The fury of the Confederate onslaught was overwhelming. The Federals retreated, a number of units in confusion, and some triumphant Southerners pursued them all the way to the base of the ridge. At this point, with little daylight remaining, Sherman undoubtedly knew that he could not take his assigned objective.[49]

Sherman was not at his best on November 25. However, few students of Sherman's military career have given sufficient weight to the fact that not only was he up against the best Rebel division (and that unit reinforced) in the Army of Tennessee, and one led by the best division commander in that army, but he was also contending against General Terrain—which was even worse. General Terrain can be the single most powerful determinant in a military campaign, and at Tunnel Hill the terrain had a tremendous impact. "Perhaps the solution was a coordinated assault that hit the ridge on the end and both sides at once," wrote Steven Woodworth in a perceptive analysis, "but that would be maddeningly difficult to accomplish, since the attackers would be out of sight of one another, separated by the broad, rugged base of the ridge, while the defenders had a compact, open, yet sheltered position on their hilltop."[50]

While Sherman seethed with frustration as he contemplated defeat, General Grant grew increasingly uneasy. Grant stood with General Thomas atop Orchard Knob, about three miles southwest of Tunnel Hill. He did not know Sherman's actual situation, although he and other Union officers believed, mistakenly, that they had seen Confederate reinforcements moving northward along the crest of Missionary Ridge to strengthen the Rebel flank. Grant did know that Fighting Joe Hooker had not made any progress against the enemy's southern flank. Very little daylight remained in which to fight. Grant decided that he must do something at once to help Sherman's attack succeed. He ordered General Thomas's Army of the Cumberland to advance and carry the enemy rifle pits at the base of Missionary Ridge. Grant hoped this action would so threaten Bragg's center that he would draw troops from his right flank to secure the heart of his line, thus relieving the pressure on Sherman.[51]

Grant issued his attack order at half past three, remembered Lieutenant Colonel Joseph S. Fullerton. Upon the firing, in rapid succession, of six guns from atop Orchard Knob, Thomas's troops, four divisions strong, were "to move forward and take the rifle-pits at the foot of the ridge." A little before four o'clock, the attack-signifying field pieces sounded with a deafening roar, and the Yankees stepped forward, a solid mass more than two miles in width, tramping toward the ragged ridge, a mile or more distant. Quick time became double-quick, and finally many soldiers broke into a run. Not stopping to fire a single volley at the Confederates, the Blueclads swept into the rifle pits, shooting and bayoneting the Southerners. Some Federals shouted, as if in retribution, "Chickamauga! Chickamauga!" Elated by their triumph, many men yelled and screamed, and fired into the clusters of Rebels who were retreating up the side of the ridge. Others, perhaps not in as good shape physically, simply milled about, trying to catch their breath after the exhausting charge and hand-to-hand fighting. Confederate dead and wounded lay all about, the bloody evidence of apparent Union victory.[52]

Then suddenly, everything seemed to go wrong. Confederates midway up the slope, or positioned near the crest, began shooting at the Yankees as fast as they could load and fire. Rebel artillery also began to zero in on Thomas's men. The Federals scrambled for cover, but precious little was to be found. The trenches just won became a death trap as Grayclad infantry and artillery blasted them with devastating results. "Terrible was the effect of this fire on the dense lines of the enemy," recalled a Confederate officer who observed the havoc from atop the ridge while his guns fired murderous barrages of canister at the Yankees below.[53]

General Grant had blundered, not foreseeing the dire circumstances in which the charge to the rifle pits would leave the Union soldiers. Ironically, in his haste to aid Sherman, Grant impulsively launched an assault that placed the center of his army in an untenable position. With Sherman repulsed at Tunnel Hill, Hooker's forces stalled to the south, and the Army of the Cumberland entangled in a slaughter pen at the base of Missionary Ridge, no one in the Union Army, from a general to a private, should have expected that the final moments of the battle for Chattanooga were at hand. What was about to happen could not have seemed likely, and certainly not in quite the manner that the spectacular event suddenly and rapidly unfolded. If the Yankees hoped to escape from the bloody mess in which they were trapped at the rifle pits, they would have to seize the ridge. Thus developed an all-out assault on the center of the enemy line atop the rugged elevation—a charge born of anger, desperation and the instinct of war-wise combat veterans, both officers and common soldiers. In a grand, never-to-be-forgotten surge, the Yankees stormed up the ridge to gain the victory—and save themselves from Grant's destructive blunder.[54]

As the mad rush up the steep ridge began, Grant, Thomas, Gordon Granger and various staff officers watched in astonishment from atop Orchard Knob. Then Grant, seemingly convinced that he was observing a full-fledged disaster in the making, became angry. Turning to Thomas, he demanded: "Who ordered those men up the ridge?" Thomas replied that he did not know, but certainly not him. Grant next put the question to Granger, who said that "they started up without orders." Perhaps seeking to lighten the tenseness of the moment, Granger added, "When those fellows get started all hell can't stop them." Anticipating that the attack would fail, Grant muttered something to the effect that somebody would pay for the debacle. And then, as the rays of late afternoon sunlight penetrated between patches of gun smoke, playing upon glistening bayonets, swords, and rifle barrels along a two-mile sweep across the western side of the ridge, Grant and the others watched the totally unexpected unfold.[55]

The Union assault carried the very center of the presumably impregnable Rebel position. From many places along the height of the ridge, and seemingly in near simultaneous triumph, the American flag and Yankee regimental flags were spotted waving in the cold wind. Brigadier General Thomas Wood always argued that his division was the first to reach the top, and he marshaled an impressive array of eyewitness testimony to that effect. The magnificent charge was so sudden, and had seemed so unlikely, that afterward Federal soldiers thought the surge up Missionary Ridge constituted one of the most dramatic and grand pageants of the war. In Union legend the assault came to seem almost invincible. The telling and retelling of the epic achievement, which sometimes bordered on the mystical and providential, magnified Federal courage and significantly contributed to a misunderstanding of how it all happened.[56]

Actually, the western face of Missionary Ridge, along with its natural defensive strengths of height and ruggedness, also presented the Confederates with major difficulties. Long and very narrow, the ridge seems hardly to crest on the western side before starting to decline on the east; and at no point is it wider than six hundred feet, at times not even one hundred feet across. Winding, rising and falling, and marred at places by deep ravines, the crest is not easily traversable ground. The Rebels could not quickly reinforce a threatened point. Worse, most of the Grayclad entrenchments at the top of the ridge were poorly positioned. Placed along the physical crest rather than the "military" crest—meaning that they were situated upon the topmost geographic line rather than along the highest line from which the enemy could be seen and fired upon— this blunder put the Rebel infantry at a great disadvantage, because they could not lay down any effective frontal fire or flanking fire until the enemy was nearly upon them.

The Confederate commanders made other mistakes as well. For examples, places existed along the complex, uneven ridge where no single line would have been sufficient; two or more positions were necessary to give adequate fields of fire to the flanks as well as straight ahead. Also, from the first, there was confusion about what would be expected from the troops in the rifle pits at the base of the ridge. The Rebel disadvantages were not insurmountable, but their officers probably never expected a Federal assault anyway. Consequently, some key Confederates failed to seriously analyze the deceptively complicated terrain they might be called upon to defend. They likely never realized, until it was too late, that the ridge provided the attackers with cover for most of their climb up the steep slope. Equally unfortunate for the Grayclad defenders, they seemed unmindful of the strength inherent in a well-developed position along the military crest. All in all, the Southern defense of the center of Missionary Ridge was thoroughly muddled, and thus the onrushing Army of the Cumberland overwhelmed the Rebel line to win the battle.[57]

SHERMAN LEARNED THE NEWS of victory from Grant soon after dark. The commanding general's message is revealing, indicating the "spin" that he would put on the Union achievement. Referencing "the handsome manner" in which Thomas's troops carried the ridge, Grant then assured Sherman that he could "feel a just pride, too, in the part taken by the forces under your command in taking, first, so much of the same range of hills, and then in attracting the attention of so many of the enemy as to make Thomas' part certain of success." In other words, Thomas had succeeded because, as Grant declared in his official report, the Confederates "in desperation to defeat or resist the progress of Sherman," weakened their center on Missionary Ridge, thus enabling the fulfillment of "Thomas' part" in the battle plan. Grant's rather amusing version of the victory merits his own pronouncement, previously noted, about the fight at Lookout Mountain, when he declared it "is all poetry."[58]

As for Sherman, who undoubtedly sought to avoid any admission of failure, Grant's message probably served as a welcome, thought-provoking stimulant. At once Sherman seized a golden opportunity to simultaneously praise Grant's leadership, associate himself strongly with Grant's success, reinvent the plan of battle according to his commander's faulty analysis and thereby, rather ingeniously, wipe out his failure to take Tunnel Hill. Soon after the battle, Sherman boastfully wrote Grant, declaring that "no man could have held his army after our combinations were made." Later he commented that Chattanooga "was a great victory—the neatest and cleanest battle I was ever in—and Grant deserves the credit of it all."

Whenever Sherman talked about the fight for Chattanooga in the days and years to come, he consistently misrepresented the battle plan. In his memoirs, for example, Sherman alleged that the objective was to pressure the Rebel flanks "so that Thomas's army could break through [the enemy's] center." The whole plan "succeeded admirably." General Grant, in his memoirs, likewise misrepresented the battle plan, asserting that the engagement had been fought according to his orders, and stating that the plan called for "the Army of the Cumberland to assault in the center." Loyal to each other, Sherman and Grant provide a strikingly instructive lesson in analyzing generalship. Just as they never admitted surprise at Shiloh, they always insisted that the fighting at Chattanooga had all gone according to Grant's plan.[59]

In truth, many of the generals at Chattanooga, both Yankee and

Rebel, were not particularly impressive during that complex engagement. The significant factor, irrespective of the generalship, was that the military forces of the United States had gained a decisive victory. The human cost was great, a total of 5,824 Union casualties, although not nearly so large as in the September defeat at Chickamauga. Viewed strategically, the losses were acceptable. The vital railroad center of Chattanooga rested securely in Federal hands, and a campaign into the heart of Georgia, based on railroad communications, would be possible in the coming spring.[60]

Sherman was ready for a rest, and so was his army, following the long trek from Memphis and the struggle for Chattanooga. General Grant, however, knew that something must be done to relieve General Burnside at Knoxville. The pressure from Washington was strong. On the very day that the Union troops overran the center of Missionary Ridge, General Halleck telegraphed Grant, shortly before noon: "I congratulate you on the success thus far of your plans. I fear that General Burnside is hard pressed, and that any further delay may prove fatal. I know you will do all in your power to relieve him." President Lincoln, along with good words about Chattanooga, had also prodded Grant that same morning: "Remember Burnside."

Once again, Grant called on Sherman, ordering him on November 29 to march for Knoxville. Burnside and his troops were under siege, and believed to be on the verge of starvation. Grant had earlier sent Gordon Granger heading northward with 20,000 troops, but he confided to Sherman that "I have no faith in his energy and capacity to manage an expedition of the importance of this one. . . . I shall have to send you. Push as rapidly as you can to the Hiwassee and determine for yourself what force to take with you from that point. . . . In plain words, you will assume command of all forces moving [to the relief of Burnside.]."[61]

Sherman did not want the assignment, but he had no choice and proceeded at once to carry out the orders of his commander. The march to Knoxville was hard, punctuated by miserably cold weather. "Indeed, on our way up," remembered Sherman, "I personally was almost frozen, and had to beg leave to sleep in the house of a family at Athens." Cold weather came early that fall, heralding the onset of an unusually severe winter. On December 8, Sherman wrote Ellen that he was "pretty well worn out by the hard marching and exposure."[62]

Considering the trying conditions they faced on that tramp to Knoxville, with clothing and shoes wearing thin at best, Sherman and his men made good time. "With the head of my infantry column, I reached Marysville [Maryville], about fifteen miles short of Knoxville, on the 5th of December," he wrote, and there received news from Burnside that "Longstreet had raised the siege, and started in retreat . . . toward Virginia." Sherman halted his army, and on the morning of December 6, he and Granger, along with several staff officers, rode into Knoxville.

Approaching the city, Sherman observed a large pen in which were gathered "a fine lot of cattle," which he thought "did not look much like starvation." To his surprise, Sherman found General Burnside and his staff occupying "a large, fine mansion, [and] looking very comfortable." Soon all sat down to a good roast-turkey dinner, "with clean table-cloth, dishes, knives, forks, spoons, etc., etc.," remarked Sherman. "I had seen nothing of this kind in all my field experience." The facts were that Longstreet had never completely invested Burnside's position, and from Union sympathizers, the Federal troops had received a good supply of beef, bacon and cornmeal. They never faced starvation, and Sherman regretted that he had pushed his men so hard in coming to the "rescue."[63]

Returning from Knoxville via an understandably "leisurely" march (Sherman's word), Chattanooga was reached on December 16, after which his troops proceeded to take up winter quarters in north Alabama. Grant established headquarters in Nashville, leaving General Thomas at Chattanooga, in command of the Department of the Cumberland. Sherman was making plans to spend Christmas with his family in Ohio, but first he joined Grant at a meeting in Nashville. Sherman had been contemplating a destructive raid from Vicksburg through Jackson, and on to Meridian, Mississippi, tearing up railroads, destroying crops, warehouses, arsenals and all manner of military supplies. He thought such a raid would be a formidable strike against Rebel guerrillas, a setback to civilian morale and a blow against enemy molestation of Union navigation on the Mississippi. Sherman also wanted a similar strike by Nathaniel Banks, on the west side of the river. Grant found Sherman's arguments convincing and gave his consent.[64]

Sherman was in Nashville for two nights, December 20 and 21. After completing their business on one of the nights, he and Grant, along with several other generals, headed to the theater to take in a performance of *Hamlet*. Nashville theaters often offered some excellent productions, but this was not such an occasion. Sherman thought, as did many in the audience, that the actors were butchering their roles. When Sherman, according to General Grenville Dodge, became rather loud in his negative remarks, Grant suggested that they leave. Apparently determined that the night not become a total loss, Sherman wanted to find a restaurant where they could get some oysters. They did find the oysters, but ironically, because of the military curfew, the proprietor felt compelled to cut short their repast.[65]

On December 22, Sherman headed to Louisville, and from there on to Lancaster, arriving on Christmas Day. "With General Grant's consent," he wrote Halleck, "I have come here for a few days to comfort my family, almost heart-broken at the death of our oldest boy and at the declining health of Mr. and Mrs. Ewing." Ellen was expecting another child in the spring, and still grieving deeply over the loss of Willy. While father and mother doubtless found some consolation in being together, the tragedy of the boy's death still weighed heavily upon both. The short visit left Sherman in a gloomy mood when time came to return to duty.[66]

Chapter Twenty

ONE HUNDRED THOUSAND
STRONG

The winter of 1863–1864 "opened very cold and severe," according to Sherman, who well remembered the raw weather during his march to Knoxville in early December. The frigid conditions continued through the Christmas season with little sign of moderation. On a numbing New Year's Day Sherman left Lancaster, en route for Memphis, to begin preparations for his destructive foray across the state of Mississippi. Minnie accompanied her father as far as Cincinnati, in order to return to Mount Notre Dame, the convent school where she had been studying.[1]

The night was bitter cold when their train steamed into the Cincinnati depot. It was about 4:00 a.m. when he and Minnie got to the 340-room Burnet House, then the pride of Cincinnati, easily identifiable by its great dome, and called by the *Illustrated London News* "the finest hotel in the world." They tried, apparently without success, to start a fire, and then slept together to keep warm. A few days later, aboard the U.S. *Juliet*, a small gunboat that Admiral Porter made available for Sherman's trip down the Mississippi, he wrote Minnie: "I can not tell you how bad I felt to leave you alone at that school in Cincinnati, but it is so important that you should now be studying that I could not help it." Writing to Ellen soon after, he said that "Minnie acts somewhat like Willie, with that simple confidence that is very captivating."[2]

Sherman's journey to Memphis proved to be a dangerous ordeal. At Cairo, Illinois, which he had reached by train from Cincinnati, he found the Mississippi almost icebound. "With the utmost difficulty we made our way through [the ice]," he wrote in his memoirs, "for hours floating in the midst of immense cakes, that chafed and ground our boat so that at times we were in danger of sinking." At last he reached Memphis on January 10, and he wrote Ellen that the winter at Memphis was as severe as in Ohio. People who knew the river expected floating ice to reach the Gulf of Mexico, "which will be an extraordinary phenomenon."[3]

In contrast to the Memphis weather, many of the citizens gave Sherman a warm reception. "People here have crowded about all day," he informed Ellen on January 11, "and seem disappointed that I am not coming here to stay." The mayor and a group of leading citizens honored him with a banquet at the Gayoso on January 24. Realizing that he would be called upon to speak, he assured Ellen that he would be careful, "as I know full well there is a clique who would be happy to catch me tripping." He wrote his brother John that he dreaded the dinner "more than I did the assault on Vicksburg."[4]

Sherman actually enjoyed the banquet, "which was really a fine affair," he proudly told Ellen, noting that "the hall of the Gayoso was crammed and the utmost harmony prevailed." He sent her a copy of the newspaper *Argus*, which reported his speech "about right," and then he declared that his remarks were well received, in fact "vehemently applauded." He also sent John a copy of the *Argus*, while warning him against the *Bulletin* for its inaccuracies. Telling John that he could not "speak from notes, or keep myself strictly to the points," nevertheless, he had no doubt that "the effect of my crude speeches is good," which he delivered with a manner "in earnest and language emphatic."[5]

A few days later, in another letter to Ellen, Sherman claimed that he "was not aware of the hold I had on the people [of Memphis] until I was there this time." He told her that "every time I went into a theater or public assembly there was a storm of applause." Such adulation is subtly addictive. Perhaps Sherman would have been wise to recall his own words, when he earlier cautioned his friend Grant against the lustrous plaudits ensuing from the conquest of Vicksburg, and memorably proclaimed that "this glittering flattery will be as the passing breeze of the sea on a warm summer day."[6]

Sherman's time in Memphis kept him busy, both tending to affairs of the Army of the Tennessee and preparing to sally forth from Vicksburg to Meridian. "Today my pen has been going for ten hours," he told Ellen in one of his letters, "and I have signed the death warrant of several soldiers, two negros & one Guerrilla, all for murder & hard crimes." Sherman's major concern was preparing the formidable raid he would lead into enemy territory. Although the Confederacy had been split down the Mississippi River, Sherman thought that the severance should be broadened and secured against any future Rebel encroachment upon that vital artery.[7]

His primary interest focused on the area east of the river. If this region were safe against Rebel attacks upon American shipping, Sherman believed the trans-Mississippi would be of minor consequence. He had previously explained to John: "We are killing Arkansas & Louisiana. ... All the people are moving to Texas with their negroes & cattle—Let them go—Let the back door open, & let them have Texas. Admit an irreconcilability of interest & character, but assert the absolute Right to the Valley of the Mississippi, and leave malcontents to go freely to Texas." Sherman considered Texas little, if any better than Mexico, which he despised. Abandoning Texas would be good riddance for the nation. Once the secessionists of Arkansas and Louisiana joined the Texans, he predicted that "their pugnacious propensities will be aimed at Mexico."[8]

By late January, Sherman's plans for his marauding expedition were complete. He had put together a force of more than 20,000 infantry, consisting of two divisions from Stephen Hurlbut's command in Memphis and two divisions from James McPherson's Seventeenth Corps in Vicksburg. Upon Sherman's instructions, McPherson had sent out spies who learned the enemy's location and approximate strength. While in Memphis, Sherman had ordered Brigadier General William Sooy Smith to form a cavalry command of about 7,000 troopers. At the same time that Sherman's infantry marched from Vicksburg toward Meridian,

Smith's cavalry would ride south from Memphis, also striking straight for Meridian.[9]

On January 28, the General was once again aboard *Juliet*, the now familiar little gunboat that had brought him safely through the ice. He was "bound for Vicksburg in a fog," as he told John, while hurriedly writing to several family members. He informed Ellen, "I expect to leave Vicksburg in a very few days, and will cut loose all communications, so you will not hear from me save through the Southern papers, till I am back to the Mississippi." As might be expected, he spoke again of Willy, and declared that his heart had been "too much wrapped up" in the boy. Admitting also that he had been "too partial to him," he then denied his wife's recent observation that he had been slighting Lizzie in favor of Minnie. After asserting, as he shifted to another topic, that "I have had my share [of military campaigning] but cannot avoid the future," he again, perhaps wistfully but also unrealistically, brought up California. Surely he knew that Ellen's temper would flare, but nevertheless, he wrote that if he could be certain of employment, he would go to California "this spring, but I fear my motives would be misconstrued."[10]

He also composed a letter to Minnie. "Time passes so fast ... and my life is such a turmoil," he wrote her, "that it is only in the quiet of night that I can think of my dear Children that Seem to me dearer and dearer." He felt compelled to tell her "how much I think about you, and how anxious I am that you should improve the few years that remain to you of Childhood." In a short while, "I will go out to the Big Black where we were so happy last summer, when you and Willy used to ride with me." Maybe he would escape death once more, he said, but if not, he assured her that he was comforted by the faith that she would think of him always.[11]

Sherman's restless, perceptive mind seemed relentlessly engaged in analyzing national affairs, political and military, economic and social—and also racial. On the last day of January, he wrote a long letter to the assistant adjutant general of the Army of the Tennessee, in which he crafted an impressive, succinct summation of how the war began and developed, as well as revealing his hopes and vision for the eventual resolution of the tragic conflict:

I know that Slave owners, finding themselves in possession of a species of property in opposition to the growing sentiment of the whole Civilized World ... foolishly appealed to War, and by skilled political handling they involved ... the whole South.... Some of the Rich & slaveholding are prejudiced to an extent that nothing but death & ruin will ever extinguish, but I hope that as the poorer & industrial classes of the South realize their relative weakness, and their dependence upon the fruits of the earth & the good will of their fellow men, they will not only discover the error of their ways & repent of their hasty action, but bless those who persistently have maintained a Constitutional Government strong enough to sustain itself, protect its citizens, and promise peaceful homes to millions yet unborn.[12]

The letter he wrote to his brother on January 28 addressed similar issues. Sarcastically he admitted "the right of secession," explaining that "men may expatriate themselves" from the nation. They may go anywhere, even to Madagascar he mused, "but they can not carry with them the ground." He also would like to see the abandoned plantations "pass into new hands, even that of negros, rather than to speculators with Contract negros whom they treat as Slaves." Considering Sherman's view of blacks as inferiors, such a statement is rather remarkable.[13]

By February 3, 1864, the rush of letter writing ceased, and Sherman's march got under way. He had succeeded in maintaining secrecy, and his own soldiers were not sure where they were going. In the hope of confusing the Rebels, he spread stories that the destination was Mobile. "The expedition is one of celerity," he explained in his orders, and "all things must tend to that [end]." Not a single tent, "from the commander-in-chief down," was to be carried. "I will set the example myself," he declared to Ellen. Most significant, Sherman was going to operate without any supply line, while conducting a major raid deep into enemy territory, and covering about three hundred miles round trip. In addition to what the men could carry in their haversacks, they would live on rations transported in three wagons allotted to each regiment and, as Sherman had said when journeying from Memphis to Chattanooga, "the corn and meal of the country." Gathering food from the Southern countryside would serve a double purpose, denying it to the Confederate military. When a woman complained of Yankees raiding her meat house, Sherman said the men needed the meat, and Southerners, because they had initiated the war, "must bear the consequences."[14]

On February 6, Sherman's troops marched into Jackson—for the third time in less than a year. "I am here again and a new burning has been inflicted on this afflicted town," he wrote Ellen the next day. A number of buildings were torched, although the statehouse and the courthouse did survive. As Sherman's columns headed for Meridian, a distinct path of devastation unfolded east of the capital. Several towns suffered almost total annihilation, as flames and smoke marked the route of the Blue-clad columns. Sometimes the Southern cavalry, as it fell back before the Union advance, destroyed supplies that might benefit Sherman's forces. Most of the havoc, however, was attributable to the Federals.[15]

By February 14, the General was in Meridian. He had expected to encounter enemy infantry, but Leonidas Polk, the Confederate "bishop-general," had pulled his troops out and retreated into Alabama. "I scared the Bishop out of his senses," Sherman boasted to Ellen with obvious relish. His only opposition was Rebel cavalry, which he easily brushed aside. He gave his men a day of rest and then put them to work destroying anything of military value.[16]

The top priority was the two intersecting railroad lines, the north–south Mobile & Ohio, and the east–west rails from Jackson to Selma. Thousands of men were assigned to work on the railroads, tearing up miles of track, burning the ties and bending the rails; they also destroyed bridges, trestles, rolling stock and locomotives. In addition to the railroads, Sherman's men wrecked the town and its environs, burning depots, storehouses, hospitals, hotels, offices, sawmills and the arsenal. The General would report that Meridian "no longer exists." He started back to Vicksburg on February 20, the day that Ellen's mother died. Sherman, of course, would not know about Maria's passing until after he returned to Vicksburg.[17]

At the time he left Meridian, Sherman was very concerned that he had neither seen nor heard from Sooy Smith. Hoping to learn something about the cavalry's fate, he extended his return march, circling to the north for a number of miles before heading west. But Smith was nowhere near. Farther to the north, at Okolona, Mississippi, he had encountered Nathan Bedford Forrest. Although the Confederate troopers were significantly outnumbered, Forrest attacked aggressively and triumphantly. When the battle was over, Smith had lost nearly 400 men. He had also lost any desire to further engage with Forrest and headed back toward Memphis.[18]

Sherman was angry when at last he learned of Smith's retreat. "I am down on William Sooy Smith," he told Ellen. "He could have come to me, I know ... and had he," Sherman claimed, "I would have captured Polk's Army, but the Enemy had too much Cavalry for me to attempt it with men afoot." He had also wanted to destroy Forrest and was convinced that Smith had the strength of force with which to do it. "In this we failed utterly," he declared, "because General ... Smith did not fulfill his orders ... as contained in my letter of instruction to him of January 27th ... and my personal explanations to him at the same time." Based on the account in his memoirs, Sherman never again placed any military confidence in Smith.[19]

Except for the failure of Smith's mission, Sherman was pleased with the Meridian expedition. He had no doubt that Confederate military operations west of Meridian would be far more difficult than before, while Union transportation on the Mississippi River would be less vulnerable. Of inestimable importance for future operations, Sherman now had firsthand convincing evidence that he could lead an army through the heart of Rebel territory, living off the land with no supply line whatsoever, and the enemy could not stop him. Grant had moved from the Mississippi River, south of Vicksburg, with only a skimpy supply line, to place the Rebel fortress under siege, and then reestablish full river communications with the north. Now Sherman had marched a much greater distance without any supply line. The impact on Southerners in his path had to be devastating. They had witnessed Union forces going wherever they pleased, and destroying anything they chose.[20]

As Sherman rode toward the Big Black River on his return to Vicksburg, his thoughts again focused upon Willy, his "almost too loved boy," about whom he said to Ellen, "I yet can dream of him as still alive." Crossing the Big Black, and seeing "the ruins of our old camp," he recalled how "Willy ran to me, his whole heart beaming in his face." The General could hardly realize "that I should never see him again." Aboard the steamboat *Westmoreland*, churning up the Mississippi toward Memphis, Sherman wrote of Willy's "pure & brave Spirit [which] will hover over this Grand Artery of America." In words charged with emotion, he declared, "I want to live out here & die here also, and don't care if my grave be like De Soto's in its muddy waters." Sherman would soon be on his way to Georgia, however, and he would not again see the Mississippi's "muddy waters" until the war was over.[21]

BY THE SPRING of 1864, the United States military forces had succeeded in delivering a number of massive, strategically crippling blows against the Confederacy. From Fort Henry, Fort Donelson and Nashville on the secessionists' northern border to New Orleans on the southern, the Union campaigning inflicted enormous casualties and recovered an immense amount of Rebel territory. Most of the Federal achievements were never to be overturned, even briefly, and none permanently. The war for the Union, a noble and inspiring cause, had broadened significantly into a fight for the emancipation of the slaves, an objective equally noble and worthy, as well as destructive of the Confederacy's fundamental raison d'etre.

In addition, at the little Pennsylvania town of Gettysburg, the U.S. Army had thrown back a formidable Rebel invasion, led by the South's most able general, in the bloodiest clash of the war. This huge, spectacular engagement in time engendered, as historian Stephen Woodworth recently observed, "the myth that it was somehow the turning point or decisive battle of the Civil War." Actually Vicksburg, as historian Gary Gallagher declared in a sesquicentennial article, "loomed far larger in 1863 than did Gettysburg." The conquest of Vicksburg meant that Sherman's "Grand Artery of America," securely under Federal control, guaranteed an immutable division of the western Confederacy, from its receding northern border to the Gulf of Mexico.[22]

Even when the Southerners achieved a great but costly victory at bloody Chickamauga, the triumph proved strategically barren. The United States had also established an ever tightening naval blockade around the 3,500 miles of Confederate coastline, a stranglehold that the Southerners' diminutive navy could never hope to break. And the once strongly held Confederate faith that, if nothing else, foreign intervention would secure their independence, seemed by 1864 relegated to the growing catalogue of Rebel might-have-beens.

Yet after three years of struggle, the outcome of the war had not been determined. Many square miles of the Confederacy's vast heartland were still intact. The determination of the Southern people to resist "Yankee domination" had not been broken. The Rebels still had two major armies poised to continue the fight. Although the Confederacy was obviously diminished and weakened, it appeared to be far from willing to quit. Unquestionably, Sherman realized those facts. Shortly after his destructive foray across Mississippi, he wrote that "the Devils seem to have a determination that cannot but be admired—No amount of poverty or adversity seems to shake their faith—niggers gone—wealth & luxury gone, money worthless, starvation in view within a period of two or three years, are causes enough to make the bravest tremble, yet I see no signs of let up . . . the masses determined to fight it out."[23]

Thus as the spring of 1864 drew nigh, the United States had once again to gird itself for battle, once more to take the offensive and carry the war to the Southerners—invade and conquer. The Confederacy had only to defend and maintain in order to succeed, but the North had to *win* the war. It would be a hard and demanding year. "All that has gone before is mere skirmishing," prophesied Sherman in a mid-March letter to Ellen.[24]

Romantic illusions of the glory of war were long gone, destroyed by the ubiquitous reality of suffering and death. While the United States had a much larger manpower pool from which to recruit soldiers than did the Confederacy—where approximately one-half of the Southern white male population between the ages of eighteen and thirty was being killed or maimed—the fact that the Union percentage of casualties was not as high as the Rebels seemed of little comfort when fathers and husbands, sons and brothers, and friends were being killed and crippled. No war in the nation's history had been like it—not even close.

And the war was becoming ever more brutal. Sherman was familiar with Carl von Clausewitz's *On War*. Whether from digesting Clausewitz or reflecting upon his own firsthand experience, or both, Sherman well understood that war has a natural dynamic, a dynamic toward ever more violence. This natural trend became exacerbated in 1864, fueled by the pressure of thousands of former slaves serving in the Union army. Southern whites, with the approval of Jefferson Davis, viewed those blacks as fugitive slaves, and their white officers as instigators of slave insurrections. Some Confederate soldiers had no intention of taking any black prisoners. Naturally the former slaves could be expected to retaliate, once they learned, and they soon did, of such racially charged Rebel behavior.[25]

The most famous Confederate massacre of black troops took place on April 12, 1864, fifty miles north of Memphis, at Fort Pillow. Sherman was not at all surprised. "Of course Forrest & all southerners will Kill them and their white officers," he wrote his brother John. He also expected more such barbarity, declaring "it is inevitable." No other case received the publicity of Fort Pillow, but Sherman was right in anticipating that similar and equally despicable events would follow. Already he could testify of deeply disturbing acts by some Southerners. On the very day of the Fort Pillow massacre, and before he knew about it, Sherman wrote General Lorenzo Thomas: "I heard a young lady in Canton [Mississippi], educated at Philadelphia, who was a communicant of a Christian church, thank her God that her negroes, who had attempted to escape into our lines at Big Black, had been overtaken by Ross' Texas brigade and Killed. She thanked God and did so in religious sincerity." Sherman then declared: "All the people of the South ... unite in this, that they will Kill as vipers the whites who attempt to free their slaves, and also the 'ungrateful slaves' who attempt to change their character from slave to free."[26]

The war's violence grew in other ways too. More property—increasingly civilian as well as military—would be torched in 1864 than the previous year. Guerrilla depredations became more widespread and intensified in brutality. Prisoners of war were seldom exchanged anymore. The parole system had broken down after Vicksburg, when Confederate parolees returned to the Rebel army without being exchanged for Union prisoners. Any slim possibility of renewing the parole system ended when African-Americans began serving in the Federal army, because Southerners adamantly refused to exchange captured blacks. Prisons became more crowded, ravaged by disease, and many men did not survive.[27]

The great conflict, as might be expected, demanded still more soldiers. Union veterans were strongly encouraged to reenlist, with the promise of a thirty-day furlough, a four-hundred-dollar bounty and other inducements. Among the Federal's western armies, a high percentage of the soldiers did choose to see the war through to the end. Bounties were also being paid to new men who joined up. Some received Federal, state and local bounties, all of which could amount to a sizable sum. Sherman strongly disliked the bounty system of raising troops. Cynically he claimed that "we have less sense even than the Mexicans, paying fabulous bounties for a parcel of boys & old men, and swelling our Muster Rolls, but adding nothing to our real fighting Strength." Sherman believed, however, that more soldiers and larger armies were imperative to win the war, even if some of the new troops were "boys & old men." The nation "can not put forth too much of an army this year," he wrote his senator brother on April 5, declaring "the war is not yet over by a d——d sight." In another letter he warned: "Don't you delude yourself that [the conflict] is even approaching an end." He stated that 1864 "may be the Crisis of the War." In a letter to Minnie, he wrote that 1864 would "either raise our Country's fame to the highest Standard or sink it to that of Mexico."[28]

IN TRUTH, 1864 became the decisive year of the great struggle. On March 17, a momentous, war-changing event occurred. U. S. Grant was appointed general-in-chief of all the armies of the United States, with the exalted rank of lieutenant general. No one in the nation's history had been elevated to lieutenant general since George Washington (Winfield Scott's three stars represented a brevet, or honorary, rank, rather than an official one). While there were several lieutenant generals in the Rebel armies, Grant was the only one in the Federal forces. At last there would be unity of command, with Grant directing the overall war effort, east and west. Sherman was genuinely pleased with the decision. After observing Grant's military capacity for two years, he had concluded that his friend was the single most able Union general.

Writing at once to congratulate the new general-in-chief, Sherman felt compelled to offer advice about one matter. "Do not stay in Washington," he urged. Sherman feared that Grant might not be able "to stand the buffets of intrigue and policy." Grant should direct operations from the western theater, where Sherman believed that the war's decisive campaigning had been unfolding. "I tell you the Atlantic slope and Pacific shores will follow [the Mississippi Valley's] destiny as sure as the limbs of a tree live or die with the main trunk!" Earnestly he implored Grant, "For God's sake and for your country's sake, come out of Washington!"[29]

Grant was more politically discerning than Sherman gave him credit for being, and he fully realized that President Lincoln and the U.S. Congress—not to mention public opinion—expected him to maintain his headquarters in the east, and oversee the military operations against the formidable Confederate Army of Northern Virginia led by Robert E. Lee. That army still lay uncomfortably close to Washington. Sherman should have understood this. Possibly he was so focused on the war in the west that he was blind to the reality of politics in the east. Perhaps his longtime disdain for politicians benumbed him to the necessity of working with and pleasing men whom he basically considered inferiors.

Whatever the nuances of Sherman's strongly worded, heartfelt exhortations for Grant to remain in the west, he obviously had set aside his own self-interest. If Grant went east, Sherman would be the odds-on favorite to succeed him, thus rising to command all the Union armies in the west. Nevertheless, Sherman sincerely admonished Grant not to go east. When he realized that Grant's decision was irrevocable, he then wrote brother John, "Give Grant all the help you can," he urged. "He will expect your friendship—We are close friends. His simplicity and modesty are natural & not affected." He also warned John, "Don't disgust him by flattery or importunity," and declared that "Grant is as good a leader as we can find. . . . His character more than his Genius will reconcile Armies and attach the People."[30]

Thus Sherman succeeded to the command of the vast Military Division of the Mississippi, embracing the Departments of the Ohio, Cumberland, Tennessee and Arkansas. Meanwhile, the new general-in-chief wasted no time in devising and implementing a grand, coordinated spring offensive on all fronts. The Confederacy's two major armies would be the primary objectives: Robert E. Lee's Army of Northern Virginia, then encamped near the Rapidan River, and the Army of Tennessee, positioned in northwest Georgia near Dalton, and led by Joseph E. Johnston, who had succeeded Braxton Bragg following the Rebel defeat at Chattanooga. Grant envisioned subsidiary campaigns as well, intending to keep pressure on all Rebel forces, east and west. He himself would be the key general in the east, and Sherman in the west. Grant summoned Sherman to meet him in Nashville, where they would discuss strategy face-to-face.

Although they were together for several days at the Tennessee capital, the two generals never got a chance to talk at length. Sherman then accompanied Grant to Cincinnati, but conversing on the train proved unsatisfactory as well. Finally they checked in at the Burnet House, broke out maps and discussed their plans in detail. The two men had the whole war in their hands. Years later, Sherman pointed out Parlor A, and stated that the campaign began right there. "He was to go for Lee and I was to go for Joe Johnston. That was his plan. No routes prescribed.... It was the beginning of the end." Thus the Burnet House, and particularly Parlor A, became a hallowed site of the Civil War. There the Grand Army of the Republic held meetings for years.*[31]

More specifically, Grant planned to ride with the Army of the Potomac, which he left under the command of George Gordon Meade. "Lee's army will be your objective point," he told Meade. "Wherever Lee goes, there you will go also." There too would go Grant, who was well aware of Confederate hopes for military gains in 1864, gains sufficient to strengthen war weariness in the North, and possibly lead to the defeat of President Lincoln in that fall's election. By this stage of the conflict, the defeat of Lincoln very possibly constituted the only realistic chance for the Confederacy yet to achieve success. Grant intended to overwhelm the enemy armies and end the war before the presidential election. If that goal proved impossible, he and Sherman would, at the least, apply unrelenting pressure, east and west, against the Rebel armies. Any important Southern military gain must be made impossible.[32]

"You I propose to move against Johnston's army," Grant instructed Sherman, "to break it up, and to get into the interior of the enemy's country as far as you can, inflicting all the damage you can against their war resources." Grant added: "I do not propose to lay down for you a plan of campaign, but simply to lay down the work it is desirable to have done, and leave you free to execute it in your own way." Sherman assured the general-in-chief that he would "not let side issues draw me

---

* The great hotel, which had opened the same year and month that Sherman and Ellen married and through the decades hosted some truly significant people, including Abraham Lincoln, survived into the mid-1920s, when it was torn down to make way for an office building—perhaps symbolizing the era when President Calvin Coolidge famously declared "the business of the American people is business."

off from your main plans, in which I am to knock Joe Johnston, and to do as much damage to the resources of the enemy as possible." Reflecting their understanding in Cincinnati, Sherman vowed: "I will ever bear in mind that Johnston is at all times to be kept so busy that he cannot in any event send any part of his command against you or Banks."[33]

Sherman referred to Major General Nathaniel Banks, who was another "political general." A former speaker of the U.S. House of Representatives, Banks was a facile chameleon throughout the course of his political career: twice a Democrat, once a Know-Nothing and twice a Republican. Although he had no military experience, his political clout gained him a commission as major general of volunteers. In the spring of 1864, he commanded the Department of the Gulf. Grant and Sherman had to work with the man, for Banks enjoyed the support of President Lincoln. They intended for Banks to open a subsidiary attack against Mobile at the same time that Sherman launched his campaign against Joe Johnston in north Georgia, if not before. Once he captured Mobile, Banks was to drive northward toward Montgomery, prevent Confederate forces in Alabama from reinforcing Johnston and open a supply line from the Gulf of Mexico that could help sustain Sherman's striking force of 100,000 men.[34]

On April 10, Sherman wrote Grant: "If Banks can at the same time carry Mobile and open up the Alabama River, he will in a measure solve the most difficult part of my problem, viz., 'provisions.'" But Sherman, having spent two days in New Orleans with Banks after the march across Mississippi, was not impressed by the man. Banks was then preparing to lead an expedition up the Red River to Shreveport and beyond, for which Sherman lent him two divisions, specifying that they must be returned to him for the Georgia campaign. The Red River expedition was slow getting under way, however, as Banks prepared for the establishment of a civil government in Louisiana and invited Sherman to participate in a grand inauguration of the governor. Sherman was put off. "I regarded all such ceremonies as out of place at a time when it seemed to me every hour and every minute were due to the war." He left, clearly with no intention of depending on Banks for significant help. "Georgia has a million of inhabitants" he wrote Grant. "If they can live, we should not starve. If the enemy interrupt our communications, I will be absolved from all obligations to subsist on our own resources, and will feel perfectly justified in taking whatever . . . we can find."[35]

If Sherman had placed any faith in the Mobile campaign he would have been sorely disappointed, for it never even got under way. The Lincoln administration decided that Banks should first lead a joint army-navy expedition up the Red River into western Louisiana and eastern Texas, thus making a show of force to impress French Emperor Louis Napoleon III, who had sent an army into Mexico. Banks could simultaneously seize Southern cotton for wealthy men in the North. "The Real Power that controls us," Sherman declared in a letter to his father-in-law, in a statement strongly reminding how little war ever changes, "is a swarm of men who are trying to make money."[36]

The Red River campaign was a debacle. Approximately thirty-five miles south of Shreveport, Banks's advance was stopped at Sabine Cross-roads. Admiral Porter wrote Sherman that only the fighting of Andrew Jackson Smith's command, on loan from Sherman, "saved Banks from utter rout." Ultimately retreating back down the river, Banks almost lost Porter's gunboat flotilla to the falling water level above Alexandria. Only the ingenuity of Wisconsin Colonel Joseph Bailey, who ingeniously devised a dam and created a chute deep enough to float the ironclads, saved Banks from a humiliating disaster. Obviously Banks failed to awe Louis Napoleon. Perhaps eventually more concerned with trying to extract cotton, he managed to seize very little.

Banks did not get back to New Orleans until it was far too late to move against Mobile. Some 15,000 Rebel troops from Alabama were free to reinforce Johnston in north Georgia, which they did, and Sherman gained no supplies from the Gulf. Nor did Banks return the soldiers Sherman had lent him. Particularly, Sherman wanted back the division commanded by Andrew Jackson Smith, which he regarded as one of his best. "As I before stated," he wrote Banks, "I must have A. J. Smith's troops as soon as possible. I beg you will expedite their return." Banks refused to release the borrowed veterans, thereby compelling

Sherman to rethink the way he had intended to launch the north Georgia campaign.[37]

Two political generals, Franz Sigel and Benjamin F. Butler, also headed subsidiary operations in Virginia. Sigel, attempting to destroy a major source of Confederate rations in the Shenandoah Valley and disrupt Rebel communications with the western Confederacy, blundered to defeat at the Battle of New Market. Butler, commanding about 35,000 troops, approached Richmond from the east and south, seemingly with a realistic chance to capture the Confederate capital. However, General Beauregard, leading approximately half as many men as Butler, drove the Union forces onto a peninsula known as Bermuda Hundred, which was formed by the confluence of the James and Appomattox Rivers. The Rebels entrenched across the opening of the peninsula, trapping Butler's army "as if," in Grant's stinging, oft quoted words, "it had been in a bottle strongly corked." All three subsidiary campaigns came to naught, leaving the great weight of defeating the Confederacy primarily upon the armies directed by Grant and Sherman.[38]

WHEN THE TWO GENERALS discussed war plans at Cincinnati in March, Sherman also got a chance to visit briefly with Ellen, who came in from Lancaster. With his wife expecting another baby soon, quite probably they talked about what to name the child. Already they had concluded, if the new arrival were a boy, that they would not call him Willy. Only a few days before, Sherman had written Ellen, "On reflection, I agree with you that [Willy's] name must remain sacred to us forever. He must remain to our memories as though living, and his name must not be taken by any one. Though dead, he is still our Willy and we can love him as God only knows how we loved him."[39]

After spending two days in Cincinnati, Sherman was back in Nashville by March 24, preparing for the great spring campaign. He would be commanding the largest U.S. armed force that had been assembled in the western theater since General Halleck's advance on Corinth following the battle of Shiloh. He would be striking deep into the South-

ern heartland. The objective, in tandem with Grant, was nothing less
than the final defeat of the Confederacy. Understanding fully what was
at stake, Sherman was determined not to fail. First, he started for the
front, traveling by rail in a special car, to confer face-to-face with his
principal generals: James McPherson, commanding the Army of the
Tennessee, George Thomas, commanding the Army of the Cumberland,
and John Schofield, leading the Army of the Ohio. They rendezvoused in
Chattanooga.[40]

"We had nothing like a council of war, but conversed freely and
frankly," remembered Sherman, who emphasized that preparations
must be made at once. He fixed May 1 as the date "when all things should
be ready." Sherman realized that "the great question of the campaign
was one of supplies," a daunting responsibility, basically resting upon
his shoulders. In addition to the needs of 100,000 fighting men, he must
provide for 35,000 supporting animals—not to mention the thousands of
men required to operate, maintain and defend the railroads and supply
depots. Returning to Nashville, his chief depot for stockpiling essential
supplies, the General was busy with preparations through most of April.

Fortunately, in this all-important aspect of war, Sherman had no
superior in either the Union or the Confederate military—and perhaps
no equal. Tennessee's capital, he noted, "was itself partially in a hostile
country," and the city's large warehouses and railroad equipment had
to be well protected. Nashville was not the beginning point, though.
The routes of supply would come from the Ohio River at Louisville, via
the Louisville & Nashville Railroad, and the Cumberland River, which
joined the Ohio west of Louisville, and both routes had to be guarded.
Protecting supplies en route to Nashville, however, was relatively easy
when compared with the rail lines from Nashville to Chattanooga, the
forward base for Sherman's forces. Between Nashville and Chattanooga,
a distance of 136 miles according to Sherman, "every foot of the way . . .
had to be strongly guarded against the acts of a local hostile population
and the enemy's cavalry." Some allowances had to be made too for train
wrecks, which were not an uncommon occurrence.[41]

Sherman estimated that to be reasonably certain of adequate supplies, he needed 130 cars, holding ten tons each, to reach Chattanooga every day. "Even with this calculation," he wrote, "we could not afford to bring forward hay for the horses and mules, nor more than five pounds of oats or corn per day for each animal." This amount was considerably less than the commonly accepted daily requirement of food and forage, which Sherman placed at twenty pounds for a horse. A man, he said, "can get along" with only two pounds. Sherman was banking on finding adequate fields of wheat and corn, plus a good deal of grass, as he advanced into Georgia. Beef cattle would be driven on the hoof. The soldiers would march.[42]

When Sherman wrote of protecting the rails "every foot of the way" from Nashville to Chattanooga, he exaggerated but little. Two railroads were available for the run to Chattanooga: the Nashville & Decatur line, which joined the Memphis & Charleston at Decatur, Alabama, and thence east to Chattanooga; and the Nashville & Chattanooga line, which met the Memphis & Charleston at Stevenson, Alabama, significantly farther east than Decatur. Obviously, as a glance at the angles instantly reveals, the Nashville & Chattanooga road was the shorter of the two. Both railroads were highly vulnerable targets for the Rebels to attack.

On the Nashville & Chattanooga line there was an important bridge only twelve miles southeast of Nashville at the little town of Antioch. From Antioch to LaVergne, the rails crossed several trestles. Then came major bridges over Stones River, Duck River, and the Elk River. Just south of Cowan, Tennessee, stretched a tunnel, 2,228 feet long, which was certainly an inviting target. South of the tunnel, the grade declined steeply, presenting more destructive opportunities. Once beyond Stevenson, Alabama, the Memphis & Charleston was exceedingly vulnerable, crossing a lengthy bridge at Bridgeport, Alabama, before traversing high and rather fragile trestles on the thirty-mile approach into Chattanooga. The Nashville & Decatur route was similarly vulnerable—even more so in fact, because it covered a considerably longer distance.[43]

The crucial work of defending the Union's indispensable line of communication would be coordinated from Nashville, with the largest numbers of troops, by order of General Sherman, stationed at Nashville, Murfreesboro, Columbia, Decatur and Stevenson, "from which places they can be rapidly transported to the point of danger." Smaller reserves were to be placed "judiciously" at other points, from which they could be quickly shifted wherever necessary. An infantry regiment, for example, was to be stationed at Tullahoma, and two regiments at Bridgeport. A great number of block-houses, capable of withstanding the blasts of artillery, were constructed at various weak points. The Nashville & Chattanooga line had about fifty blockhouses, manned by a total of 1,400 soldiers. These forces, numbering about 25 men per blockhouse, were expected to "hold their ground . . . against any cavalry force until relief comes." (Sherman was most concerned about Nathan Bedford Forrest.) The blockhouses must be prepared to fight "to the last," he said, to "save the time necessary for concentration." The Nashville & Decatur line was also heavily defended by blockhouses, although Sherman naturally preferred the shorter Nashville & Chattanooga route whenever possible.[44]

Not only did Sherman have to provide adequate numbers of guards, stationed at many points; also, crews of qualified workmen, with essential equipment and tools, had to be located at strategic points, ready to rapidly repair any damage, whether from accidents, natural causes or the destructive efforts of the enemy. These squads had to be versatile, capable of dealing with bridges, trestles, tunnels, creek crossings, rails and roadbeds. Furthermore, Sherman needed additional locomotives and rolling stock. The sixty locomotives and six hundred cars available when he took command were inadequate for stockpiling any surplus. He wanted one hundred locomotives and a thousand cars. With the approval of the secretary of war, he began accumulating rolling stock and engines from Northern railroads as fast as possible.[45]

Sherman also issued a general order limiting the use of the cars to "essential articles of food, ammunition, and supplies for the army proper, forbidding any further issue to citizens, and cutting off all civil traffic." This order engendered considerable protest. Even President Lincoln, upon receiving requests from poor people of Union persuasion in east Tennessee, telegraphed Sherman inquiring whether he could not modify his orders. The General respectfully refused, stating that the railroads "had but a limited capacity, and could not provide for the necessities of the army and the people too." No doubt Sherman took delight in denying use of the railroads to the press and to ministers. He noted that "every regiment has its chaplain and there is no necessity at all for these wandering preachers, who are a positive nuisance." Refusing their request with relish, Sherman declared that the railroad was "purely for military freight. 200 pounds of powder or oats are worth more . . . than that amount of bottled piety." Sherman vowed not to give in, although the "preachers clamor & the Sanitaries Wail."[46]

Supervision of the railroads was centered in Nashville. When Sherman took command, Colonel Daniel C. McCallum was the overall director and general manager of western military railroads, having been appointed by Grant. Sherman retained McCallum, who supervised a Department of Transportation, led by Colonel Adna Anderson, that actually operated the supply trains. Colonel William W. Wright managed a Department of Construction, charged with the repair work essential to keep the roads functioning. Sherman's goal was to stockpile a large quantity of supplies in both Nashville and Chattanooga—sufficient that even if his long communication line were seriously damaged, between either Louisville and Nashville or Nashville and Chattanooga, he could continue to supply his forces for several weeks while repairs were made. "Ordinary prudence dictated . . . an accumulation at the front," he said. Once the campaign began, Sherman's advancing forces obviously would depend upon an ever lengthening supply line. The Western & Atlantic Railroad, running from Chattanooga to Atlanta, would quickly come into play. Sherman's railroads would never be out of commission long, and he gave Colonel Wright high marks—"a wonderfully ingenious, industrious, and zealous officer, and I can hardly do him justice"—for his demanding, and often difficult repair work.[47]

Although Sherman was pushing hard to be ready for the beginning of the campaign, he occasionally found time for his favorite diversion, the theater. Offered a private box at the New Nashville Theater, the General declined, preferring to be, as one contemporary wrote, "surrounded by his boys in blue, laughing and applauding . . . with as much gusto as any in the audience." General Wesley K. Clark recently observed that "Sherman cemented his reputation with the troops through his sheer personal competence and presence on the battlefield. Whether it was demonstrating the proper way to construct a fascine, or showing up at the front personally to reconnoiter, Sherman earned his men's trust and admiration . . . as someone with enormous personal competence." Sitting in the audience with his soldiers at the theater surely contributed also to the popularity he enjoyed with the men. While Sherman undoubtedly realized that fact, the General, at least by this stage of the war, genuinely liked being in the midst of his troops.[48]

Sherman's favorable stature had been increasing back home too, as well as in the eyes of the men he commanded. He was not yet "lionized" on a par with Grant, but his fame was spreading. A "Miss Bailey" had recently requested a lock of his hair. He told Tom Ewing Jr. that he referred her first letter to his redheaded orderly "whose modesty was so shocked that his face outrivaled in brilliancy his brick top." When Miss Bailey wrote a second time, Sherman said he answered, sending her an autograph, "and describing my hair as red, bristly & horrid—I think she is satisfied to leave my locks out of the cluster of flowers to be made up out of the hairs of the Great men of the day. Such nonsense is repulsive to me."[49]

He assured Tom that by May 1 he intended "to have a host as vast & terrible as Alaric led into Rome." Already Southerners were in dread of his coming. Some Confederate officers, politicians, newsmen and even clergymen claimed Sherman was about to bring upon the South both brutal Northerners and hordes of savage former slaves. A Southern paper asserted that the "northern barbarians" respected neither life nor virtue, and "our wives and daughters are reserved for a fate even worse than death." Southern men must arise, "strike" and exterminate "such living demons!"[50]

No doubt some despicable characters marched among Sherman's "vast & terrible" host, but neither free blacks nor former slaves were a part of that throng. Sherman's army was composed totally of white men.

While preparing for the advance into Georgia, the General found time to express, more than once, his negative attitude about African-Americans serving in the Union Army. "I think the negro question is run into the ground," he wrote John Sherman. Of course he had no choice but to accept the destruction of slavery, "and whatever the proper authorities resolve on I must do," but like many army men, he did not believe that blacks would make good soldiers. He would not have them in combat roles, either for offensive or defensive purposes, if he could avoid it. "We ought not to engraft a doubtful element in the army *now*," he declared, for "it is too critical a period." Of necessity some men "must work & raise corn," he said to John, so "why not use in a great measure the negro labor we have Captured, instead of scattering it and dissipating it in a poor quality of soldiery and in raising cotton."[51]

Sherman had another objection to enlisting African-Americans in the Union Army. Mobilizing blacks offered Northern whites yet another way to avoid serving their country. Already they might purchase an exemption or hire a substitute. Sherman believed, as he told his brother, that "every man in the United States" should fight for his country. Recruiting blacks was "the means by which Massachusetts and other states can dodge their share." Stating that "our own soldiers have prejudices," he wrote that "these are aroused by the foolish squabbles of Governors to show that they have given their quotas." Filling state quotas through the enlistment of blacks irritated Sherman as much as the bounty system of raising troops.[52]

Regardless of what Sherman thought of blacks serving in combat roles, the General knew, above all, that his forces must be ready to move by May 1. Writing to Grant from Nashville on April 24, Sherman felt confident. "Supplies are the great question," he declared, then affirming, "I have materially increased the number of cars [arriving] daily." From an average of 65 to 80 railcars coming into Nashville per day when he began, the number had grown impressively: 193 on April 23, and 134 the next day. He estimated that 145 cars daily "will give us a day's supply and a day's accumulation."[53]

The number of Union soldiers available for the campaign was also impressive, although the total was not as great as Sherman desired. The failure of Banks to return the soldiers Sherman loaned him, plus a sizable number of men not yet returned from furlough, reduced the command he had originally anticipated by some 15,000 to 20,000. Nevertheless, Sherman still would lead a grand force, 100,000 strong. The Army of the Cumberland, commanded by Major General George Thomas, was the largest army by far: 60,773 men, and 130 guns. Major General James McPherson's Army of the Tennessee numbered 24,465, with 96 guns, while Major General John Schofield's Army of the Ohio (basically only a corps in size) weighed in with 13,559 men and 28 guns. The grand aggregate was 98,797 troops and 254 guns. The opposing Confederate forces, known as the Army of Tennessee (not to be confused with the Federal Army of the Tennessee), would begin the struggle with a force of approximately 55,000, soon strengthened by some 12,000 to 15,000 additional troops.[54]

In late April, Sherman removed his headquarters from Nashville to Chattanooga and prepared to take command in the field. Several hundred miles distant, northeast across the rugged mountains of Carolina and Virginia, Grant was poised with Meade and the Army of the Potomac, ready to move across the Rapidan River, in hope of flanking the Rebel army. At last the stage was set and both major military forces of the United States were positioned to launch campaigns simultaneously, west and east. "The weather is beautiful," Sherman wrote Ellen on May 4, "and the army is in fine condition." The beginning of the end was at hand.[55]

Chapter Twenty-One

I KNEW MORE OF GEORGIA THAN THE REBELS DID

Sherman opened the campaign with 25,000 of "the best men in America," as he characterized the Army of the Tennessee, marching in the hope of striking a decisive blow. He intended to surprise the Confederates by rapidly turning their left flank and cutting the vital Western & Atlantic Railroad at Resaca, a dozen miles south of Dalton. With the Rebel supply line from Atlanta broken, the Southerners would have to fall back from their imposing fortifications at Dalton and fight Sherman's superior numbers under far less favorable, and possibly disastrous, circumstances. While McPherson and the Army of the Tennessee maneuvered to smite the railroad, the armies of Thomas and Schofield were to press forward, strongly feigning a frontal attack against the formidable enemy position. Thus Sherman would avoid "the terrible door of death that Johnston had prepared for [the Union forces] in the Buzzard Roost."[1]

The unsavory name of Buzzard Roost was a local designation for Mill Creek Gap, where the Western & Atlantic Railroad passed through the long, high and precipitous Rocky Face Ridge, just northwest of Dalton. The Confederate Army had strongly entrenched along Rocky Face, occupying a nearly unassailable position for several miles north and south of Buzzard Roost. The ridge was a rugged, narrow eminence— not more than ten to thirty feet wide at the top, according to the diary of Confederate Captain Samuel T. Foster—rising about seven hundred

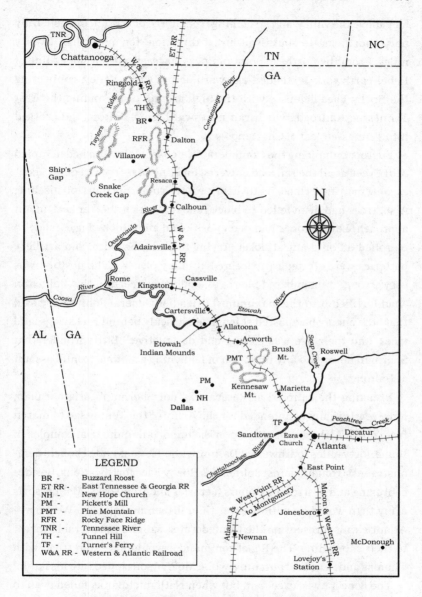

FROM CHATTANOOGA TO ATLANTA

In early May 1864, Sherman launched a 100,000-man offensive in northwest Georgia. Map by Jim Moon Jr.

feet above the valley, and stretching from north of Dalton, in a generally north-northeast to south-southwest direction, for more than twenty miles. From the northern point of Rocky Face, a well-developed line of Rebel earthworks extended eastward across Crow Valley, connecting the Rocky Face defenses with the high ground commanding the East Tennessee Railroad, which ran northward from Dalton, and crossed into Tennessee east of Chattanooga.[2]

Further enhancing the Confederate defenses, Johnston had dammed Mill Creek at all the railroad culverts, forming "a sort of irregular lake," as Sherman described it, to help protect some portions of his line. Also, trees had been felled to block roads by which the Yankees might approach. Large stones had been positioned atop Rocky Face, ready to be rolled off onto any attackers trying to scale the ridge, and artillery batteries were strategically located at many places. "The position was very strong," remembered Sherman, and he was certain that Johnston "had fortified it to the maximum." Brigadier General John Geary said that "the enemy had posted skirmishers thickly behind rocks, logs, and trees, and their fire was galling and destructive." Little wonder that Sherman never had any intention of launching a serious frontal assault at Dalton.[3]

Breaking the railroad at Resaca was not Sherman's original plan, however. Initially he intended for the Army of the Tennessee to march from north Alabama directly upon the important industrial complex of Rome, forty miles southwest of Dalton, while Thomas and Schofield demonstrated strongly against Johnston's Rocky Face fortifications. Besides capturing and destroying Rome's factories and ironworks, McPherson's army then would be within fewer than fifteen miles of the Western & Atlantic rails, presenting the Confederates with an insufferable threat to their supply line. The Rebel commander would have to retreat, with Thomas and Schofield pursuing, while McPherson ripped into his flank.[4]

The concept was excellent, but when Nathaniel Banks failed even to attack Mobile or return the troops Sherman lent him, the plans had to be altered. Sherman had envisioned McPherson's seizing Rome with a 35,000-man force. Deprived of both the veterans still on furlough, and the men withheld by Banks, the strength of the Army of the Tennessee was, as noted earlier, less than 25,000. Also, Banks's nonperformance on the Gulf freed Leonidas Polk's forces in south Alabama and Mississippi. Probably those Rebels would be moving north, possibly striking the relatively isolated Army of the Tennessee, and maybe in tandem with detachments from Johnston's army. Sherman, uncomfortable with such a scenario, prudently decided against the march on Rome. Instead, he would keep McPherson's forces closer to Thomas and Schofield. McPherson would strike through Snake Creek Gap, a pass in Rocky Face Ridge several miles south of the Confederate fortifications, which would place him only a few miles from the Western & Atlantic Railroad at Resaca.[5]

Actually, General Thomas had proposed the march through Snake Creek Gap, having learned about the pass a few months earlier, when some of his forces were skirmishing with the Rebels west of Rocky Face Ridge. He recommended that Sherman assign his Army of the Cumberland to flank Johnston through the gap. Possibly Sherman, during his explorations in the region as a young lieutenant, might have come across Snake Creek Gap. The passage of more than twenty years, however, would have taxed even Sherman's remarkable memory and eye for terrain. Whether Sherman already knew about the gap or not, he liked Thomas's idea, except that he realized the Army of the Cumberland was too large and unwieldy for the assignment. For whatever reason, he did not give Thomas any credit for the concept.[6]

The smaller Army of the Tennessee, as Sherman well knew from his own recent experience in leading the outfit, could be expected to march rapidly, while still possessing sufficient strength to strike powerfully. Furthermore, with the Army of the Cumberland positioned immediately in front of Johnston's fortifications, the withdrawal of 60,000 men seemed quite likely to destroy any possibility of maintaining secrecy. McPherson's forces, on the other hand, were not yet occupying a part of the Union lines. Thus the Army of the Tennessee stood a good chance of striking the Western & Atlantic before Johnston realized what was happening. Factoring into Sherman's decision as well, which Brigadier

General Jacob D. Cox, who commanded one of the three divisions in the Army of the Ohio pointed out, was "the desire to have the greater strength of the Army of the Cumberland at the center," thereby solidly covering his rail communications and the forward base at Chattanooga.[7]

With good reason, Sherman believed that he had a winning plan; he was confident that his favorite, McPherson, would get the job done. McPherson's orders were to break the railroad and then take up a strong defensive position at the mouth of Snake Creek Gap. When the Confederate commander, learning that his supply line had been cut, began falling back, with Thomas and Schofield in pursuit, McPherson would attack the Rebels in flank. With a little luck, Sherman just might deal Johnston's army a deathblow with his very first maneuver.[8]

Johnston anticipated that Sherman would strike from the north, moving against the right front of the Southern defenses. Not only was the Confederate general totally wrong about Sherman's scheme of attack, he had also "completely ignored Snake Creek Gap," leaving it undefended. Sherman's plan seemed to be coming together beautifully—even more so than he could have known. McPherson's advance units, having moved through Ship's Gap and Villanow, reached Snake Creek Gap late in the evening of May 8. On the following morning, the Army of the Tennessee emerged from the gap's eastern mouth, easily driving off a Confederate cavalry brigade and moving toward Resaca.[9]

"I got a short note from McPherson that day (written at 2 p.m. when he was within a mile-and-a-half of the railroad, above and near Resaca)," remembered Sherman, "and we all felt jubilant." Sherman triumphantly exclaimed, "I've got Joe Johnston dead!" Indeed, he very nearly did. The exuberant Union commander renewed his orders to Thomas and Schofield to be prepared for "instant pursuit of . . . a broken and disordered army, forced to retreat by roads . . . east of Resaca, which were known to be very rough and impracticable."[10]

But the dream of a brilliant and decisive triumph, as rather often with dreams, came suddenly to an unexpected and disappointing conclusion. The Army of the Tennessee's advance units, within less than half a mile of the Western & Atlantic tracks, came under infantry fire heavier than McPherson had anticipated. Haunted by the unknown, perhaps a nightmare vision of Johnston's speeding large numbers of troops to attack him while he was separated from the rest of Sherman's command, McPherson pulled back into the safety of Snake Creek Gap. When Sherman learned that his preferred subordinate had failed to break the railroad his spirit sank. "Well Mac," he admonished the Army of the Tennessee's commander when again they stood face-to-face, "you missed the opportunity of your life!"[11]

Sherman recognized that McPherson, in falling back to the gap, had been "perfectly justified by his orders"—except that McPherson had been ordered to break the railroad first. Clearly Sherman felt that McPherson had not been as aggressive as he should have been. Years later he wrote in his memoirs, with a touch of exaggeration, that McPherson "could have walked into Resaca . . . or he could have placed his whole force astride the railroad above Resaca, and there have easily withstood the attack of all of Johnston's army, with the knowledge that Thomas and Schofield were on his heels." Sherman, of course, was the beneficiary of hindsight when writing his memoirs, having observed Joe Johnston's actions throughout all of the campaign. Knowing the history of Johnston's movements may well have influenced Sherman's claim in his memoirs that Johnston, rather than attacking McPherson in position on the railroad, would have retreated eastward, and "we should have captured half his army and all his artillery and wagons at the very beginning of the campaign."[12]

The strike through Snake Creek Gap was McPherson's first significant assignment as an army commander. General Wesley Clark pertinently observed that command in war has to be learned "the only way it can be learned—by experience." Perhaps with greater experience, McPherson would have acted more aggressively, and Sherman's turning maneuver would have brought an unqualified triumph at the inception of the campaign. When it failed to do so, the plan became a subject for second-guessing—as might be expected. General Schofield, in his memoirs published after Sherman's death, claimed in defense of his West Point classmate that McPherson's force "was entirely too small for the work assigned it." Not that the Army of the Cumberland was the answer. Declaring Thomas's command "unwieldy and slow," and too large for such an endeavor, Schofield wrote that Sherman's best move would have been to strengthen McPherson's maneuver "with a corps of Thomas' army in close support." Also, he said that Johnston's railroad should have been seized and held, not merely broken.[13]

The most severe castigation of Sherman's Snake Creek Gap maneuver was presented by the historian Albert Castel in a 1992 history of the Atlanta campaign. Contending that Sherman's "first and by-far-greatest mistake was not to execute Thomas's original plan of operations," Castel proclaimed that "had 'Slow Trot' Thomas, as some members of Sherman's entourage disparagingly call him, been in command of the Union army in Georgia, the North probably would have won the campaign in less than a week." What General Thomas might or might not have accomplished remains forever unknowable, but Castel's flat-out confidence in Thomas is questionable. Larry Daniel, in a history of the Army of the Cumberland, offered a thought-provoking comparison with the earlier Tullahoma, Tennessee, campaign: "In that instance, Thomas seized Hoover's Gap, but then squandered his success and subsequently stalled, thus giving the Confederates time to withdraw to Tullahoma. If Thomas performed sluggishly with one corps, would he [at Snake Creek Gap] have acted more boldly with three?"[14]

While both Stones River and Chickamauga offered compelling evidence of Thomas's prowess as a defensive commander, the general's offensive credentials were murky. The Army of the Cumberland's celebrated assault at Missionary Ridge, for example, was neither planned nor ordered by Thomas. There was no good reason, in the spring of 1864, for Sherman to think of Thomas as a better offensive commander than McPherson. Given Sherman's familiarity with McPherson and the Army of the Tennessee, as well as the Army of the Cumberland's bulk and positioning, his decision to assign the turning maneuver to McPherson was reasonable and understandable. And nearly 25,000 veteran infantry was not a paltry force for such a mission. Admittedly, as Schofield later contended, strengthening the Army of the Tennessee with supporting troops from Thomas—even one division—would have provided McPherson with significant reinforcement. Sherman simply never thought that "Mac" needed assistance.

McPherson's march very nearly succeeded and probably would have if he had pressed forward as Sherman expected. Brigadier General John W. Fuller, commanding the lead brigade as it advanced to break the railroad, contributed a revealing summation: "The skirmishers had already reached a position from which they commanded the railroad, and the battalions were close behind, with every prospect of beating the small force sent out by the enemy to counteract our movements. Here, however, General McPherson deemed it prudent to halt ... and to withdraw ... immediately to the mouth of the gap in our rear." McPherson should have realized, as Sherman had reminded, that Johnston "cannot afford a detachment strong enough to fight you," without having to deal with an overwhelming Federal force at his back. The overly cautious action of McPherson, who graduated first in his West Point class, was not foreseeable, and Sherman should not be faulted for something no one could have prophesied.[15]

Sherman soon ordered most of his forces to move through Snake Creek Gap, straight for Resaca. Only Oliver O. Howard's Fourth Corps, Army of the Cumberland, along with a division of cavalry, were left in front of Buzzard Roost to watch Johnston's army. Moving out on May 10, most of the Yankee troops reached Snake Creek Gap by the evening of May 12. While Sherman's men tramped southward on the west side of Rocky Face, Joe Johnston and his chief subordinates remained perplexed about the Union commander's intentions. Not until May 12 did Johnston realize that Sherman was marching around his left flank. The Confederate commander would likely have faced a dire situation, despite McPherson's failure to carry out his mission, had not Leonidas Polk's reinforcements from Alabama and Mississippi—some 15,000 troops—begun arriving in Resaca the day before Sherman got there.[16]

Awakened at last to the danger of being trapped north of Resaca and the Oostenaula River, Johnston moved rapidly southward to join up with Polk's forces. Total Rebel strength then numbered approximately

65,000, organized into three corps, commanded by William Hardee, Lieutenant General John Bell Hood and Leonidas Polk. Johnston occupied a formidable line, extending in a rough, crescentlike shape from the Oostenaula west of Resaca to a point northeast of town. Potentially, he still had a major problem. Two sizable rivers, the Oostenaula and the Conasauga, were at his back. Sherman approached Johnston's new position with the Army of the Ohio on the left, the Army of the Cumberland in the center and the Army of the Tennessee on the right.[17]

General Schofield climbed up a hill to the rear of his troops, discovered that portions of the enemy's main line of defense were visible and sent a courier to inform Sherman of the vantage point. The commanding general soon appeared, accompanied by George Thomas, Joe Hooker and several staff officers. All of them scrambled up the hill to survey the Southerners' works, only to be greeted by an enemy shell crashing through and exploding in the branches of a dead tree. Schofield said everybody scattered to find cover except for Sherman and Hooker. He claimed the two men drew themselves to full height, as if totally unconcerned with danger, and strode around the top of the hill in silence, each waiting, thought Schofield, for the other to first seek shelter. At last, "as if by some mysterious impulse," they simultaneously marched to the rear, the event convincing Schofield that personal relations between the two were not good.[18]

Sherman had no more intention of attacking the Rebel defenses at Resaca, which appeared to be strongly manned at all points, than he did at Buzzard Roost. Sergeant Andrew McCornack, serving with the 127th Illinois Volunteer Infantry Regiment, who knew something about assaulting enemy fortifications—having won the Medal of Honor for the Forlorn Hope effort against Stockade Redan on May 22, 1863, at Vicksburg—declared in a letter to his father that the Rebel defenses at Resaca "were better than they had at Vicksburg."[19]

Sherman quickly decided on another turning movement. He sent a division of the Army of the Tennessee trekking for Lay's Ferry, several miles southwest of Resaca. Brigadier General Thomas W. Sweeny's division of the Sixteenth Corps was ordered to establish a bridgehead on the south bank of the Oostenaula, thereby placing the Yankees within a short distance of Johnston's crucial railroad. As Sweeny maneuvered to carry out his mission, Sherman closed in against Resaca, although making no attempt to actually assault the enemy's fortified works. On May 14 and 15, booming artillery and the din of musketry reverberated for miles through the north Georgia hills, while the Army of the Tennessee managed to gain a ridge overlooking the town, from which its field artillery commanded the Western & Atlantic bridge over the Oostenaula. The Grayclads attempted, unsuccessfully, to regain the position.[20]

For men in the ranks, the fortunes of soldiering sometimes varied remarkably. Sergeant Eugene A. "Casey" McWayne, also serving with Andrew McCornack in the 127th, wrote the "folks at home" that on May 10 he "had a good time; went fishing, caught some Bull Points [bullheads?] and an eel." May 14 and 15 presented quite a contrast. McWayne's regiment charged up a hill in the face of enemy fire, drove the Rebels back and dug in at the top. McWayne claimed that Brigadier General Giles Smith ordered their colonel "to hold that hill if he lost every man in doing so." Soon, wrote McWayne, "the Rebs charged [attempting to recover the high ground], but were repulsed with a heavy loss."[21]

Andrew McCornack essentially confirmed McWayne's account of the regiment's action at Resaca, writing that in attempting to recover the hill, "the Rebs formed five columns deep and made for us." When General John A. Logan, commanding the Fifteenth Corps, saw the heavy Confederate force advancing, he exclaimed, according to McCornack, that "the first brigade is gone to hell." However, McCornack proudly reported, "We took it cool ... gave them 4 or 5 rounds, and you ought to [have seen] the Johnny Rebs run." Assuring his parents and sisters that he was "well, tough, & hearty," McCornack urged the family to send him "some fine cut chewing tobacco," as well as "a good hat." He did not care how much the hat might cost, because he expected soon to get paid. "They owe us four months [pay] now," added the sergeant.[22]

While the mass of the Union Army pressed hard against the Southerners at Resaca, Sweeny's division proceeded with the cross-river assault near Lay's Ferry. The assignment was not easy though, as soldiers struggled, under fire, to carry heavy boats to the launching point and then rowed, twenty men to a boat, across the Oostenaula to secure a landing site on the south bank. But the demanding operation did succeed, placing Sherman in position once more to imperil the Rebel line of communication. As soon as Johnston realized that he was being flanked again, he pulled out of Resaca under cover of the early morning darkness on May 16, burning the railroad bridge over the Oostenaula, and heading southward in rapid retreat.[23]

Sherman has been faulted by historian Richard McMurry for not making "a serious effort [at Lay's Ferry] to cut off Johnston north of the Oostenaula or trap him on the north side of that stream with his back to the river." Surely that possibility crossed Sherman's mind—although probably not for long. Lay's Ferry would have presented a more difficult maneuver than Snake Creek Gap. To again take Johnston by surprise would have seemed unlikely, while bridging the Oostenaula and placing a major force on its south bank before Johnston could react was a greater challenge than merely marching through Snake Creek Gap. Also, with McPherson's failure fresh in mind, Sherman would not have been inclined to give him a more difficult assignment.[24]

Nor would he have entrusted the taxing mission to Schofield or Thomas. The Army of the Ohio was too small for such a job, even if Sherman had sufficient confidence in Schofield's ability to do the work, which, at best, is questionable. After the Snake Creek failure, Sherman was not about to immediately follow it with a more difficult maneuver, regardless of who might direct the action.

Already Sherman had flanked the Southerners out of two strong defensive positions in less than two weeks. Confidently, he put his three armies in immediate pursuit of the Rebels. Sherman had seized the offensive, a key principle of generalship long recognized by the U.S. Army, and he had no intention of relinquishing it. General Thomas advanced directly south along the Western & Atlantic railway. The Army of the Ohio and Joe Hooker's Twentieth Corps, which Sherman detached from the Army of the Cumberland, composed the left flank of the march, while James McPherson's Army of the Tennessee became the right flank. Sherman's forces were spread out across several miles, east and west of the railroad, forging ahead with a bold self-assurance epitomized by the commander himself.[25]

"So eager was [Sherman] to bring on a battle in the comparatively open country north of the Etowah [River]," wrote Jacob D. Cox, the division commander in the Army of the Ohio, "that he ordered his subordinates not to hesitate to engage the enemy without reference to supports, feeling sure that he could . . . concentrate with rapidity enough to secure the victory." Cox said that Sherman's "apparent carelessness was a calculated audacity, willing to take some risks for the sake of tempting his adversary to a general engagement." Sherman wanted very much, as he wrote Schofield on May 18, to "bring Johnston to battle this side of the Etowah . . . even at the hazard of beginning battle with but a part of our forces."[26]

Meanwhile, farther to the south, at Confederate headquarters, General Johnston had been experiencing increasing pressure to turn and fight the oncoming Yankees. If he kept giving up huge chunks of territory without a major battle, would he not ultimately destroy the morale of his forces? Richmond was prodding him to attack, and his senior corps commander, William Hardee, urged him to make a stand at Adairsville. But Johnston did not like the look of the terrain. Again he retreated, only this time armed with a plan to mass his forces against a smaller, relatively isolated segment of Sherman's host.

Johnston's concept for battle was excellent, pivoting on a simple divergence of the road. He believed that Sherman would divide his large forces at Adairsville, sending part on the road to Cassville, and the remainder down the road to Kingston. The Rebel commander intended, with the weight of his army, to attack the smaller of Sherman's advancing columns while it was separated from the other. Johnston sent Hardee's corps, with most of the cavalry and the army's wagon trains, directly south to Kingston, skirmishing heavily with Sherman's pursuers in the hope that the Union commander would believe that the main body of the Confederates was retreating toward Kingston. Simultaneously Hood and Polk, with their corps, hurried down the Cassville Road and prepared for the ambush. The plan was for Polk to launch a head-on attack, while Hood struck the Federals in flank.[27]

Sherman proceeded as the Confederate commander hoped. Convinced that Johnston was heading to Kingston, Sherman was perplexed about the reason. "All the signs continue of Johnston's having retreated on Kingston," Sherman told Schofield, "and why he should lead to Kingston, if he designs to cover his trains to Cartersville [a town on the Western & Atlantic about six miles south of Cassville] I do not see." Nevertheless, he assured Schofield, "in any hypothesis our plan is right." Sherman had sent the main portion of Thomas's army, along with McPherson on his right flank, directly toward Kingston, while Hooker's Twentieth Corps was veering southeast to Cassville, with Schofield on Hooker's eastern flank.[28]

Everything seemed to be developing favorably for Johnston's attack. The recent arrival of Polk's cavalry division and Samuel G. French's infantry division had boosted total Rebel strength above 70,000, possibly as high as 74,000. It was the largest army that the western Confederacy ever marshaled. Hood and Polk were massed to assail Schofield and Hooker, while Hardee had positioned his corps to block Thomas and McPherson from rendering any assistance to their comrades.

"I lead you to battle," proclaimed Johnston in an ostentatious address on the morning of May 19, which was read at the head of each regiment. "The greatest enthusiasm prevailed in our ranks," reported Colonel Ellison Capers of the Twenty-Fourth South Carolina Infantry, "as the men and officers saw the army formed for battle." Every moment of that hot, fateful morning seemed to be building to an inevitable and major engagement. Then suddenly chance took a hand.[29]

While maneuvering to strike an unsuspecting Schofield, about 10:30 a.m., General Hood discovered that Yankee cavalry were approaching on a road off to his right. The Federal troopers were totally unexpected, for a recent Confederate reconnaissance to the northeast had not revealed any signs of the enemy. Hood had no idea either how large the Union force might be or whether infantry were coming on immediately behind the cavalry. To launch an assault when his own command might be attacked from the flank and rear was unthinkable. Quickly Hood halted his advance, deployed skirmishers to engage the Federals on his right flank, sent word of the alarming enemy presence to Johnston and began falling back toward Cassville. Albert Castel declared that the surprise appearance of the Federal cavalry on Hood's right flank "unknowingly ... saved the Union column that was moving down the Adairsville Road from a damaging if not devastating attack."[30]

That afternoon, Johnston drew up his army, as he later reported, "in what seemed to me an excellent position—a bold ridge immediately in rear of Cassville, with an open valley before it." Hardee's corps held the left, with Polk in the center and Hood on the right. Hardee advised Johnston to wait and see whether Sherman would attack. However, Polk and Hood soon claimed their lines would be enfiladed by Union artillery on the morrow, and "urged [Johnston] to abandon the ground immediately." Once more the Rebel commander retreated, crossing the Etowah on May 20. He reported it was "a step which I have regretted ever since."

Confederate Brigadier General Arthur Manigault remembered, "To our great surprise, and to the disgust of many, at midnight we received the order to retire, and at two o'clock, our division drew out as noiselessly as possible, and bringing up the rear of our corps, took up the line of march for the railroad crossing at the Etowah River." The retreating Southerners burned the railroad bridge as soon as they were across, but Sherman's hardworking repair crews, as at Resaca, wasted no time in reopening the vital span. General Howard described how Sherman, while working at his headquarters in Kingston on May 22, became irritated by the ringing of a church bell, and sent a guard to arrest the bell ringer. When the man was brought into his office, Sherman looked up from his writing and asked abruptly: "What were you ringing that bell for?" The man replied: "For service. It is Sunday, General." Sherman responded: "Oh! Is it? Didn't know it was Sunday. Let him go."[31]

SHERMAN WAS ECSTATIC. "The Etowah ... is the Rubicon of Georgia," he declared on May 23. The campaign was not yet three weeks old, and not only had the Confederates twice been maneuvered out of formidable defensive positions, while retreating nearly fifty miles, but Sherman's Yankees were also across two of the three major rivers between Chattanooga and Atlanta: the Oostenaula and the Etowah. Only the Chattahoochee remained, and the Union commander believed, as he spiritedly told Ellen, that soon he would be putting "the best army in the country" across it. "We are all in motion like a vast hive of bees," Sherman asserted in his effervescent style, "and expect to swarm over the Chattahoochee in a few days." Chief Quartermaster and Brigadier General Robert Allen, who was visiting Sherman's headquarters, observed that "officers and men are in the highest spirits and confident of success." Allen also noted Sherman's words, with pleasure no doubt, that "no army in the world is better provided."[32]

Besides the obvious success of forcing the Rebels south of the Etowah, Sherman had already secured the industrial town of Rome and the Noble Iron Works. Joe Johnston's retreat then handed Sherman the Etowah Iron Works as well, which were located near Cartersville, and allowed the Union forces to continue building a lethal momentum. Sherman ordered Schofield to destroy those works, along with some nearby flour mills, which was quickly accomplished. In Richmond, Jefferson Davis became still more concerned about how much farther his Georgia commander intended to fall back before ever making a stand. Sherman seemed fully in control, gaining more territory more readily than expected. Perhaps reflecting the thinking of many Federals, Private Jacob Dickason, Twenty-Fifth Wisconsin Volunteer Infantry, wrote his brother on May 22: "I feel in hopes the war will come to a close by fall." Dickason was correct—for him personally. He died of disease on August 31, 1864.[33]

Sherman was soon on the move again. "I knew more of Georgia than the Rebels did," the Union commander later blurted. He knew that he did not want to attack Joe Johnston's new position at Allatoona Pass, through which ran the Western & Atlantic Railroad and the pike to Atlanta. Sherman explained that two decades before he had stopped to see some Indian mounds on the Etowah River and, staying in the vicinity for several days, had also noted the Allatoona Pass. He remembered that it "was very strong, would be hard to force, and resolved not even to attempt it." Instead, he decided "to turn the position by moving from Kingston to Marietta *via* Dallas."[34]

The small town of Dallas lay about fifteen miles south of the Etowah River—measuring in a straight line from the site of the Indian mounds—and about eighteen miles west of the Confederate's new supply base on the Western & Atlantic at Marietta. Sherman's turning maneuver would force the Southern commander to abandon his impressive defensive position in the Allatoona region, or otherwise Sherman soon would be marching against his railroad communications, and threatening to cut him off on the north side of the Chattahoochee River. Sherman anticipated that Johnston well might "fall behind the Chattahoochee."[35]

On May 23 Sherman initiated his grand turning maneuver, a movement broader and more daring than at Dalton or Resaca. Quite possibly he would be operating "independent of the railroad for twenty days." He did not seem at all worried about leaving his rail communications. In addition to fully packed army supply wagons, and "beef on the hoof," Sherman would also "rely on getting much meat, and forage, and vegetables" from the countryside through which his forces would be passing. General Thomas and the Army of the Cumberland advanced by the direct middle route, with Schofield on the left of Thomas, while McPherson's hard-marching Army of the Tennessee swung widely to the right of Thomas, in order to approach Dallas from the west. Sherman rode with Thomas.[36]

He hoped again to take Johnston by surprise, but this time the Confederate cavalry quickly warned their commander that Sherman's forces were on the move. Instead of falling back to the Chattahoochee, as Sherman thought likely, Johnston directed the Confederate Army south and west toward Dallas, to intercept the Yankee threat of turning his flank. Captain Sam Foster, reflecting the disgust of Southerners with retreating, recorded in his diary: "We travel in a southwest direction, but none of us have any idea where we are going. . . . Some say we are going to Florida and put in a pontoon bridge over to Cuba." By midmorning of May

25, the Confederate forces were positioned to block Sherman's advance. They defended a line facing generally north by northwest, with Hardee's corps on the left near Dallas, Polk's corps on Hardee's right flank, while Hood's corps, the last to leave Allatoona lest Sherman send a force down the railroad, lay to the right of Polk. Hood covered a key crossroads marked by a Methodist church known as New Hope.[37]

The brutal struggle that soon erupted along the Dallas–New Hope Church–Pickett's Mill line, has been characterized by some writers as hardly more than heavy skirmishing. Historian James Reston Jr., in *Sherman's March and Vietnam*, discounted all the fighting in the Atlanta campaign except Resaca, Kennesaw Mountain and three engagements around Atlanta as merely "maneuver, usually Johnston fortifying the high ridges and Sherman bypassing them to the west." Sherman biographer Lloyd Lewis made reference to "three days' skirmishing around New Hope Church," thus dismissing the subject in less than half a sentence. Actually the intense, savage fighting on this line, and the large number of casualties, fully justified the designation by which many of Sherman's men later referred to the encounters: "the Battle of the Hell Hole."[38]

On the morning of May 25, Fighting Joe Hooker's Twentieth Corps, Army of the Cumberland, led the Union advance. Tramping along the road to Dallas, the Federal soldiers were steadily approaching the crossroads at New Hope Church, where Hood's corps was drawing up for battle. In the center-front of Hooker's corps marched John Geary's division, with Daniel Butterfield's division moving on a country road to Geary's left and rear while Alpheus Williams led the division on Geary's right. Geary's troops advanced on the better road, by the shortest route, and were the first to strike the enemy, and that unexpectedly. Around noon, his skirmishers became heavily involved with those of the Grayclads. General Geary, a veteran of Chancellorsville, Gettysburg, Wauhatchie (where his son Edward had been killed) and Chattanooga, reinforced his skirmishers and ultimately deployed all three of his brigades before his division began gradually forcing the Rebels to give ground.[39]

Geary was really worried. "From prisoners captured we learned that Hood's entire corps was in our front," reported the brigadier, "and Hardee's not far off in the direction of Dallas. My division was isolated, at least five miles from the nearest supporting troops, and had been sustaining a sharp conflict with the enemy for four hours. Close in my front was an overwhelming force." Joe Hooker, who was with Geary at the time, ordered him to dig in on a ridge that, in Geary's words, "appeared advantageous for defense." A slight barricade of logs was hastily thrown up, and skirmish lines "deployed to a greater extent than before, and ordered to keep up an aggressive fire," hoping to deceive the Confederates "as to our weakness."[40]

About this time Sherman got involved. His idea of the tactical situation was quite different from Geary and Hooker—and he was wrong. Sherman believed he was on Johnston's left flank. Apparently Sherman's mind had locked in on a preconception of how his turning maneuver would play out. He did not think Johnston could have so quickly shifted his forces to counter the Union advance, and impatiently he ignored the evidence to the contrary. From studying a map Sherman had recognized the importance of the crossroads at New Hope Church, and he wanted it seized at once. When informed of Geary's situation, Sherman thought it had been exaggerated. Reluctantly consenting to a delay while Williams's division came up to join Geary's, Sherman told a staff officer, "Let Williams go in anywhere as soon as he gets up. I don't see what they are waiting for in front now. There haven't been twenty rebels there today."[41]

By five o'clock Williams's division was at hand, with Butterfield arriving about the same time. All three divisions were rapidly deployed for attack in columns of brigades (meaning one behind another), a massed formation devised for penetrating power. The brunt of the Federal assault was met by Alexander P. Stewart's division. Stewart had three brigades deployed along a low ridge at the crossroads, while holding a fourth in reserve. Two of the three front-line units managed to throw up breastworks. Sixteen artillery pieces supported them, some of which were angled for cross-firing. Confederates who were not protected by breastworks scrambled for whatever cover they could find, even tomb-stones in the church cemetery.

Although the Yankees outnumbered the Rebels approximately three to one, their assault failed to break through the Southern line. The in-depth attack formation presented a narrow front of only one brigade for each division. Thus the majority of the Union soldiers were not in position to shoot at the enemy, nullifying their superior numbers. The Confederate front was about the same width as that of the Blueclads, enabling the strongly positioned defenders to mount, according to General Geary's report, "a very heavy artillery and musketry fire [which was] ... heavier than in any other battle of the campaign in which my command was engaged." A Southerner wrote in his diary that the continuous volleys of small arms, coupled with the earsplitting cannonading, constituted "the heaviest firing I ever listened to."[42]

The intense Confederate fire had an unnerving effect upon some Northerners, as is evident from the report of Lieutenant Colonel James C. Rogers, commanding the 123rd New York Infantry in Alpheus Williams's division. Rogers said his regiment advanced until "close under the enemy's guns ... so near that by lying on the ground nearly all [the grape and canister] passed over it harmlessly." There his unit lay until a relieving regiment came up, but the fresh regiment "scarcely had formed in front," reported the lieutenant colonel, "when the enemy's battery, which had been silent for a few minutes, opened again." As a result, the newly arrived regiment suddenly "rushed in disorder to the rear," said Rogers, with "all attempts to stop them ... even with a line of bayonets, proving useless." Williams's command was the hardest hit of Hooker's divisions at New Hope Church, taking a total of 870 casualties.[43]

Union Captain John W. Tuttle memorably recorded a disquieting scene of disorientation, suffering and destruction. He said that thousands of men were crowding forward, without any semblance of organization, as they attempted to relieve those who had been fighting. The soldiers relieved came swarming back, adding to the mass of confusion, amd Tuttle thought "nearly everybody was swearing at the top of his voice." For approximately three hours the fierce struggle continued, as twilight faded and night came on. The night was "intensely dark," remembered General Geary, who said that "a very severe thunderstorm, with cold, pelting rain, added to the gloom," while the "fitful flashes of lightning" momentarily illuminated the dead, dying and wounded. Geary said that casualties in his division, although lighter than Williams's division, came to a total of 376. General Hooker, for all three of his divisions, reported casualties at New Hope Church of 1,665, probably a minimal figure. Confederates were convinced that the true number was considerably higher.[44]

Joe Johnston, for example, who placed Southern casualties at about 450 killed and wounded, reported that the Union loss was at least 3,000. "No more persistent attack or determined resistance has anywhere been made" was the assessment by Rebel General Stewart, who observed that "the enemy's fire was very heavy, [but] passed over the [Confederate] line to a great extent," thus accounting for the relatively few Southern losses, which he placed between 300 and 400, while reporting Hooker's losses "at from 3,000 to 5,000." Johnston's and Stewart's reports of Federal casualties are almost certainly too high, but they do call in question the accuracy of Hooker's numbers.[45]

After the carnage was over, Sherman acknowledged in his report that "a hard battle" had been fought at New Hope Church. He never admitted, however, that a Confederate division held the crossroads well before Hooker's attack. Perhaps Sherman always believed that there had not been "twenty rebels there today," when he ordered Hooker to secure the crossroads at the church. All generals, even the great ones, make mistakes. If Sherman came to realize that he had been wrong about the Rebel presence at New Hope Church—and he probably did—he would not have been inclined to admit that fact, particularly if it meant acknowledging that Hooker had been right.[46]

On the day after the battle at New Hope Church there was constant skirmishing, but no major fighting. From the day's action, Sherman determined that the enemy line stretched for four or five miles, and he could discover no significant gaps to exploit. By early morning of May 27, he decided to turn the right flank of the Confederate position. The maneuver would place his forces between the Southerners and the Western & Atlantic, thus enabling him to reopen communication with the railroad. Sherman's choice to lead the march was General Howard. While Howard trekked for the Rebel flank, with Thomas Wood's division from the Fourth Corps, along with units from the Fourteenth and Twenty-Third Corps, Union troops all along the front were to keep up an aggressive demonstration to pin down the Southern army.[47]

The Confederates posted on the Grayclads' right flank were Patrick Cleburne's 5,000-man division, one of the hardest-fighting units in the Rebel army, as they had proven at Chattanooga and elsewhere. Howard's march was discovered almost as soon as his troops began moving out, and the Southerners continued to monitor the Federal progress throughout the day. If the Confederates needed any help in keeping track of the Yankees, they had only to listen for periodic bugle sounds, because one Union brigade commander, attempting to keep his troops going in the right direction through the thick forest, instructed the buglers to frequently sound their pieces. As the day wore on, Cleburne simply shifted his forces farther to the east, while Joe Johnston sent additional troops to back him up if necessary.

The Union march carried across very rugged terrain, which proved fatiguing to traverse, and at times almost impassable. Thomas Wood, directing his three-brigade division, with Brigadier General William B. Hazen's Second Brigade in the lead, said the men moved "through dense forests and the thickest jungle, a country whose surface was scarred by deep ravines and intersected by difficult ridges." Lieutenant Colonel Joseph Fullerton wrote in his journal about the difficult, confusing and at times near impenetrable terrain: "1 p.m., have advanced about one mile and a half, and country rolling and covered with timber and undergrowth; can see nothing fifty yards in front." Fullerton also noted that the day was "very hot."[48]

General Howard did not know where he was. Anyone who has examined the terrain over which his forces were struggling will not be surprised by the comment he sent to General Thomas: "No person can appreciate the difficulty of moving over this ground unless he can see it." Howard's march was delayed by periodic reconnoitering, followed by still further trekking to the left. Uncertain of where the Confederate right flank was located and perplexed about his own location, Howard continued his groping, frustrating, eastward tramp. At last, after advancing a total of approximately three miles, Howard concluded that his march had probably overlapped the right flank of the enemy. He prepared to attack.[49]

"I am now turning the enemy's right flank, I think," he reported to General Thomas at 4:35 p.m. Howard was badly mistaken. His attack, made in the vicinity of Pickett's Mill, along Little Pumpkinvine Creek, with Hazen's brigade going in alone, struck a veteran, well-positioned enemy. Hazen had thought his men would be the spearhead for an assault in columns of brigades. Then he heard Wood say: "We will put in Hazen and see what success he has." Howard seemed to agree, with a nod of his head—perhaps a mere acquiescence—but whatever, the thing was done. Hazen found the Rebels in force, occupying high ground, covered by breastworks, "which extended to our left farther than we could see," as Fullerton recounted in his journal.

Cleburne's troops, according to Fullerton, "not only opened a murderous fire from their front line of works, but also terrible cross-fires from both flanks." Only when the remnants of Hazen's brigade were falling back did Wood and Howard send in another brigade, which soon shared the same fate as Hazen's. From beginning to end, the Union attack was an uncoordinated, piecemeal effort. The Federals never came close to deploying their overall superiority of numbers. Pat Cleburne reported that as the Yankees "appeared upon the slope," his men "slaughtered them with deliberate aim." He said some of his officers, "who have seen the most service," testified that the piles of dead "were greater than they had ever seen before."[50]

Southern Captain Sam Foster, fighting with Hiram B. Granbury's Texas brigade, wrote in his diary that at sun rise the next morning "I beheld that which . . . I hope never [to] see again, dead men meet[ing] the eye in every direction." Foster said that "in one place I counted 50 dead men in a circle of 30 feet of me." He observed that "it seems like they nearly all have been shot in the head." Stating that he had seen many dead men during the war, as well as wounded men mangled in varied ways, Foster declared that he "never before saw anything that made me sick, like looking at the brains of these men did." He noted that Generals Johnston, Hardee, Cleburne and Granbury "all say that the dead are strewn thicker... than at any battle of the war." General Johnston, while reporting that the total number of Confederate killed and wounded was about 450, claimed that the Union dead, "except those borne off, were counted at 600." He thus estimated "the whole [enemy] loss at 3,000 at least."[51]

General Howard acknowledged that Union "losses were very heavy, being upward of 1,400 killed, wounded and missing in General Wood's division alone." (Wood specified his division's casualties at 1,457.) General Hazen said that when he was forced to retreat, his brigade had lost 500 men. A soldier afterward asked Hazen about the location of his brigade, and the veteran general reportedly replied, with tears in his eyes: "Brigade, hell, I have none!" With a well-earned reputation as a hard-fighting officer and a capable leader, no one knew better than the disgusted Hazen that the battle had been a badly managed affair. Little wonder that Ambrose Bierce, a young writer-to-be of notable stature, who was then serving in Hazen's brigade, later recorded a scathing account of May 27, which he entitled "The Crime at Pickett's Mill."[52]

In bitter retrospect, the Battle of Pickett's Mill is tragic, because Sherman had sent orders to cancel the attack. But Howard did not get the word in time. Probably the reason that Sherman decided against the attack is revealed in a message that he sent Schofield at five o'clock on that terrible day: "It is useless," he declared, "to look for the flank of the enemy, as he makes temporary breast-works as fast as we travel." Sherman, in his official report, did not say much about New Hope Church, and nothing at all about Pickett's Mill. In his memoirs, he characterized New Hope Church as "a drawn battle," never mentioning Pickett's Mill. At the time, Sherman wrote General Joseph D. Webster at the Nashville headquarters of the Military Division of the Mississippi, claiming that "Johnston tried to head us off at Dallas, but did not succeed." Continuing his brief summation, Sherman declared that "in all encounters we had the advantage. All is working well. You may give this publicly."[53]

After Pickett's Mill, Sherman knew that he needed to get back to the Western & Atlantic. His maneuver had not taken Johnston by surprise—which was key to the whole endeavor. There was no rational expectation of breaking through the enemy line. The army wagons, because of distance and poor roads, were falling behind in sustaining Sherman's troops, and even if he now succeeded in turning Johnston's left flank, the Southerners would be positioned to cut him off completely from the railroad. Logistically, he had no other choice, and began preparations, as Basil Liddell Hart wrote, "to side-step eastward toward the railroad."[54]

Joe Johnston, however, thought he saw an opportunity to strike Sherman's left flank. Whether the idea originated with Johnston or John Bell Hood is unclear, but Hood drew the assignment. Conducting a slow and arduous night march of a half dozen miles or more, Hood then discovered that the Yankee flank was no longer "in air," as the Rebel cavalry scouts had earlier reported. Hood halted and informed Johnston of the latest cavalry intelligence. Reluctantly the Confederate commander called off his intended assault.[55]

But Johnston's hopes for a successful counterattack soon rose anew, based on reports that Sherman's western flank was vulnerable. Union troops in the Dallas area were thought to be pulling back and moving northward. Johnston ordered General Hardee to send in a division, develop the situation and attack if the circumstances seemed inviting. William B. Bate's division was selected for the probing mission. Confident that the Yankees were in an exposed situation, Bate ordered a brigade forward to the attack, with the others to follow if indeed the Federals were vulnerable. They were not. The lone Rebel brigade quickly found itself facing a superior enemy force. Once Bate realized the Union strength, he immediately tried to cancel the attack, but without success, as two more Southern brigades took up the assault.[56]

Union Sergeant Robert G. Ardry, 111th Illinois, described the Confederate charge and the resulting slaughter in a letter to his father. The

Federals had entrenched after nightfall, he said, "and we covered the clay over with brush and they [the Rebels] did not know that we had anything of the kind. They came up bravely, and when within 75 yards, and our skirmishers all in, the word fire was given." Ardry declared: "Our line for ¼ of a mile was one sheet of fire," which broke the enemy lines, "but they rallied and on they came ... but we just more than shot them down." Admitting that "we had all the advantages," the sergeant said the Rebels suffered terribly, and he estimated they lost 3,000 killed and wounded.[57]

The Southerners had made a fearless but futile effort. "The Rebs charged on our works ... four times," according to Andrew McCornack, "but were driven back with a heavy loss." The "Battle of Dallas ... is practically a mirror image of Pickett's Mill," validly observed Albert Castel, "with the Confederates ... being the ones to make a valiant but bumbling and bloody assault ... [that] was utterly unnecessary."[58]

Thus ended the brutal, sanguinary fighting on the Dallas–New Hope Church–Pickett's Mill line, fighting in which Sergeant Casey McWayne thought that "the Rebs have been the most desperate ... that we have ever fought them." These battles also heralded a marked change in the nature of the western campaigning. Beginning with the "Hell Hole" experience and continuing through the battles for Atlanta, both Yankees and Rebels quickly threw up defensive works whenever and wherever they halted. Soldiers entrenched to a degree previously unmatched. Another significant, tactical lesson presented itself during these grim clashes at New Hope Church and Pickett's Mill. Both attacks were made in columns of brigades, a formation that, in a rugged, heavily wooded country against an entrenched enemy, "had little, if any advantage over a single line of equal front," as Jacob Cox explained. He pointed out that the column "could not charge with the *ensemble* which could give it momentum [to break through the enemy line], and its depth was therefore a disadvantage, since it exposed masses of men to fire who were wholly unable to fire in return." Not everyone immediately grasped the lesson, of course, but that fact did not make the reality any less manifest.[59]

....

WHEN SHERMAN GOT BACK to the Western & Atlantic in early June, he had failed to realize his ambitious goals of gaining the railroad farther to the south at Marietta and maneuvering the Rebels back to the Chattahoochee. Johnston had adeptly countered his determined flanking effort, and in the fighting on the Dallas–New Hope Church–Pickett's Mill line, Sherman's forces had suffered greater casualties overall than the enemy. Yet strategically, Sherman had gained another triumph. He had flanked the Confederates out of an apparently impregnable defensive position covering the Western & Atlantic at the Allatoona Pass, which, after all, had been the primary objective when he initiated the turning movement. He had drawn some fifteen miles closer to Atlanta and compelled Johnston to relinquish another hunk of Georgia. Undeniably, Sherman remained in control of the campaign.

Chapter Twenty-Two

I WANT A BOLD PUSH
FOR ATLANTA

On June 3, Sherman's forces began entering Acworth, a Western & Atlantic town located a number of miles south of the Allatoona Pass, where the General decided to establish his headquarters. It was the same day that General Grant launched a grim and costly frontal assault against Lee's army east of Richmond, at a place called Cold Harbor. The Army of the Potomac suffered 7,000 casualties during the attack, most of them in less than thirty minutes, and "Cold Harbor" became a Civil War byword for senseless slaughter. Grant later said that he regretted the attack more than any he ever ordered. Although Grant had driven the Rebel army to the outskirts of the Confederate capital, the Union forces had suffered an average of nearly 2,000 casualties per day since the inception of the campaign. The thirty-day total of well over 50,000 men was several times the losses of Sherman's command during the same period.[1]

Sherman defended his friend, whom some critics characterized as "Butcher" Grant, telling Ellen that "Grant's Battles in Virginia are 'fearful but necessary.'" He said "immense slaughter" was required to prove that "our Northern armies can & will fight." Yet Sherman was not about to risk his own forces on such a scale, because "at this distance from home we can not afford the losses of such terrible assaults as Grant has made." Sherman was far deeper into enemy territory than Grant, and in the event of defeat or crippling losses, he would face correspondingly greater difficulties in extricating his army. This fact surely weighed on Sherman's mind as the campaign progressed. It limited his offensive flexibility, and largely dictated a campaign of maneuver—with all maneuvers governed, to some degree, by the parameter of the railroad.[2]

Sherman was not going up against Robert E. Lee. But otherwise, his campaign was the more challenging endeavor in Grant's two-pronged strategy for crushing the Rebels with unrelenting, simultaneous pressure against their two major armies. Being so much farther into enemy territory than Grant—who could rely on short and secure communications— Sherman depended on a single-track railroad, some 350 miles long, for many essential supplies; and those rails grew longer with every advance. He knew that if his railroad communications failed, the campaign would fail, and Grant's strategy for winning the war would fail.

"There was great danger, always in my mind," Sherman later recalled, "that [Nathan Bedford] Forrest would collect a heavy cavalry command in Mississippi . . . and break up our railroad below Nashville." Sherman expressed this critical concern to his brother, saying that "my long and single line of railroad to my rear, of limited capacity, is the delicate point of my game." He told Ellen: "Thus far we have been well supplied, and I hope it will continue, though I expect to hear every day of Forrest breaking into Tennessee." He had ordered an expedition against Forrest from Memphis, hoping to "give him full employment."[3]

Forrest did find full employment. In northeast Mississippi at Brice's Cross Roads, he clashed with the Union forces from Memphis, but the result was not at all what Sherman had sought. News came from Secretary of War Stanton on June 14: "We have just received from General [Cadwallader] Washburn a report of battle between [Samuel] Sturgis and Forrest, in which our forces were defeated with great loss." Stanton added that Washburn claimed, "Forrest is in pursuit." The report was not exaggerated. Brilliantly handling his smaller command, the Confederate cavalry leader utterly routed the superior Union forces. Sherman replied that he could not understand how Forrest, with only his cavalry, could have defeated 8,000 Federal troops, of which a substantial portion were infantry.[4]

Sherman told Stanton that he would have the Sturgis expedition critically examined, and if Sturgis was at fault, "he shall have no mercy at my hands." Perplexed, he said of Sturgis's defeat: "I can not but believe he had troops enough. I know I would have been willing to attempt the same task with that force; but Forrest is the very devil, and I think he has got some of our troops under cower." He assured Stanton that he had two officers at Memphis, Andrew Jackson Smith and Joseph A. Mower, who "will fight all the time." Sherman concluded that keeping Forrest off his vital rail line required spending some serious money, and probably taking heavy casualties. The redheaded commander believed he had no alternative.[5]

Determined to deal with Forrest decisively, Sherman declared to Stanton: "I will order them [Smith and Mower] to make up a force and go out and follow Forrest to the death, if it cost 10,000 lives and breaks the treasury." While Sherman never succeeded in killing Forrest, his expeditions from Memphis accomplished the Union objective. He kept the Rebel commander so busy in Mississippi that he was not able to attack the Yankee rail communications in Tennessee. Strategically, Sherman would continue to win "the delicate point" of his game.[6]

The Federal commander also got an assist from the enemy. Joe Johnston, Jefferson Davis and Braxton Bragg, military advisor to the Confederate president, all knew that striking hard at Sherman's railroad and inflicting major destruction should be a high priority. There the agreement ended. Davis and Bragg thought that Johnston's own cavalry forces were strong enough both to cover the Army of Tennessee's flanks and break Sherman's railroad. Johnston firmly demurred, believing that he should keep all of his cavalry close at hand, and convinced that the Southern cavalry in Mississippi and Alabama, under the overall command of Stephen D. Lee, was better positioned for such work anyway. However, Johnston had no authority over Lee's forces, and Jefferson Davis, the only power who might have intervened, did not. Lee was not inclined to send his cavalry elsewhere while Northern expeditions from Memphis were sallying forth into the region where he commanded. Consequently, while Confederate raiders did break Sherman's rail lines occasionally and briefly, they never launched a truly strong effort with the potential of dealing out severe, long-term destruction upon the Federal rails.[7]

While Sherman at Acworth mulled over his next move, the Union armies enjoyed a short respite from the hard marching and fighting of late May. Andrew McCornack told his family, "The boys are all in good spirits." The general opinion of the troops was that "this campaign will end the war." McCornack hoped it would, but added, "I have not got that idea yet." He believed "old Billy T.," as he fondly referred to Sherman, was more than a match for the Rebels. Seeing Sherman on May 30, he declared, "He is along the lines all the time." McCornack closed his June 8 letter with "I must clean up my shoot[ing] stick [rifled musket] and stew some green apples."[8]

If McCornack and "the boys" were all in good spirits, it was in spite of the nasty weather, which soured the attitude of some men, both Yank and Reb. June had brought rain, "continuously for seventeen days," according to General Howard, turning the roads into quagmires. Sherman told Ellen that the rain not only came down hard but sometimes cold, and one day he wrote Grant that the rain was pouring "as though it had no intention ever to stop."[9]

Still, by June 11, the hardworking Union repair crews had the rails open to Big Shanty, a little town south of Acworth. Sergeant McCornack noted that "we get full rations of everything now," and again declared his faith in "old Billy T., who is a bit too sharp" for Johnston. "He always flanks him," appreciatively observed McCornack. Another heartening development was the arrival of Frank Blair's corps, 10,000 strong, which made up for the casualties suffered during the May campaigning. "My army is stronger today than when I first sallied forth from Chattanooga," Cump assured Ellen. He declared, "Every man in America should be aroused, and all who will not help should now be put in petticoats & deprived of the Right to vote."[10]

Sherman relished another piece of good news. Upon learning that a son, Charles Celestine Sherman, had arrived, he told Ellen: "I am glad that you are over the terrible labor," and hoped "it is the last you will have to Endure." He was "pleased to know the Sex of the child, as he must succeed to the place left vacant by Willy, though I fear we will never again be able to lavish on any one the love we bore for him." Once more Sherman repeated what he had already said several times: "I agree with you that we should retain Willy's name vacant for his memory, and that though dead to the world, he yet lives fresh in our memories."[11]

Sherman's mind often ran to thoughts of Willy. Only a few days later, writing Ellen again, he fervently expressed his hopes for the newborn: "May the child grow up and possess the courage, confidence and kindness of heart of our poor Willy." Sherman declared that "I would gladly surrender all the honors & fame of this life if I could see him once more in his loving confidence & faith in us, but we must now think of the living & prepare them for our Exodus." He closed with a striking acknowledgment of the hatred with which Southerners regarded him: "I know the country swarms with thousands who would shoot me & thank their God they had slain a monster." Yet he asserted, and perhaps truthfully, that he had been "more kindly disposed to the People of the South than any general officer of the whole army."[12]

Meanwhile, on the night of June 4, Joe Johnston had fallen back to a new line, which ran from Brush Mountain, east of the Western & Atlantic, to Lost Mountain on the west, with Pine Mountain standing out in a salient near the center. Hood's corps held the Rebel right, Hardee's corps the left, and Polk's corps was in the middle. From atop Pine Mountain, Confederate officers had a good view of Sherman's forces, which had advanced beyond Big Shanty and pressed close to the Southern lines. By June 14, recalled Sherman, "the rain slackened, and we occupied a continuous line of ten miles, entrenched, conforming to the irregular position of the enemy, when I reconnoitered with a view to make a break in their line." Passing Pine Mountain, he spotted a group of Grayclads on the height, brazenly viewing the Union position. Because of the distance, Sherman could not tell who they were, not even, he wrote in his memoirs, if they were officers. "How saucy they are," he remarked, and ordered artillery fire placed on the summit to compel the enemy to take cover.[13]

Not only were the men atop the mountain Confederate officers, they were the commander of the army, and two of his three corps commanders, along with several staff officers. They had been cautioned that Federal artillery was zeroed in on the height. Sherman's order to open fire was quickly obeyed, and the first shot was a near miss—which sent Johnston, Hardee and indeed everyone except Leonidas Polk scrambling for cover. Polk moved more slowly, and either the second or third shot struck the bishop-general in the mid-to-upper body. He died instantly. Polk's mangled remains were carried down the hill, and Johnston's forces mourned the loss of the corps commander whom many Confederates respected as a strong moral force in the army.

Polk's military competence is another matter. Steven Woodworth wrote that the shot which killed Polk "was one of the worst shots fired for the Union cause during the entire course of the war." Polk was worth more to the Federals while ineptly commanding Rebel troops than he was dead. I largely agree with Woodworth's assessment: "Polk's incompetence ... had consistently hamstrung Confederate operations west of the Appalachians, while his special relationship with the president made the bishop-general untouchable."[14]

Both during and after the war, Southerners who damned Sherman as if he were the devil personified spread the story that the Union commander himself had sighted the gun and pulled the lanyard to fire the shot that killed Polk. This accusation is ridiculous. Yet the death of Polk seemed not to trouble Sherman in the least. He seldom related well to men of the cloth, regardless of their denomination. He wrote General Halleck: "We killed Bishop Polk yesterday, and have made good progress today." It was the kind of statement that unreconstructed Rebels would later relish as evidence of Sherman's cruelty.[15]

General Hardee had advised Johnston to abandon Pine Mountain, pointing out that Union artillery commanded the height. This was the reason the Confederate generals were examining the area when Polk was killed. Within a short time Johnston pulled the Rebel army back another two or three miles, contracting his line into a ragged semicircle centered on Kennesaw Mountain and covering the Western & Atlantic north and west of Marietta. William Wing Loring, who was temporarily leading Polk's corps, occupied the center, with Hood on the right astride the railroad while Hardee's corps held the left flank. The new position appeared stronger than the one just abandoned—probably as strong as any Johnston had held since the campaign began.[16]

Sherman contemplated his next move with some frustration. He stretched out his lines, probing to see if he might turn the Southern flanks, particularly the left flank, the better to threaten the Rebel rail line at Marietta. With the application of sufficient Yankee pressure, Joe Johnston might yet retreat to the Chattahoochee. While McPherson extended his lines eastward and Thomas held the center, Sherman sent Schofield, reinforced by Hooker's corps, feeling for the enemy's western flank. The movement by Schofield and Hooker got Johnston's attention.

The Rebel commander pulled Hood's corps from his eastern flank, temporarily manning the position with dismounted cavalry, and sent Hood's infantry hurrying westward along the rear base of Kennesaw Mountain in an effort to block the Union turning movement. Perhaps assuming that he had outflanked the flankers, Hood, without any reconnaissance, impetuously decided to attack. The Yankees enjoyed superior numbers, and Schofield had his Blueclads defending a ridge behind quickly improvised breastworks. The resulting clash, known as Kolb's Farm (also called Culp's Farm), cost the Confederates approximately 1,000 casualties.[17]

Private Noah G. Hill, 123rd New York, penned a letter to his father describing the battle, in which his regiment had been posted as skirmishers, well in advance of the main Union line. About 5:30 p.m., according to Hill, all hell broke loose, "and they came near getting me." He gave an interesting account of the Rebel attack, writing, "We were so close to them [when on the skirmish line] that we could hear them talk. They were in the bushes, and we were in front of them about six rods, when [their officers] gave the order to go forward. We all jumped up and fired, and then fell back fast. We laid some of them low you can bet." Hill said the Confederates then mounted three, maybe four charges, and he was thankful when at last they "gave it up" after having suffered "a great slaughter." Southern casualties were about three times as many as the Northern. Hill's letter is stamped: "God Save the Union."[18]

The Battle of Kolb's Farm further fueled the bad blood between Sherman and Hooker. Late in the afternoon of June 22, Hooker sent a brief message to Sherman: "We have repulsed two heavy attacks and feel confident, our only apprehension being from our extreme right flank. Three entire corps are in front of us." Sherman knew there were only three corps in Johnston's entire army. Beyond a doubt, all three were not in front of Hooker, and Hooker's concern about the right flank (whatever precisely Fighting Joe may have had in mind) seemed to Sherman an unwarranted insinuation, directed at Schofield, that he was not doing his job.[19]

The following morning Schofield was with Hooker, near the point where their commands joined, when Sherman rode up in the pouring rain. All three men stepped inside a little church close at hand, where Sherman handed Schofield Hooker's message of the previous afternoon. According to Sherman's account in his memoirs, Schofield "was very angry, and pretty sharp words" passed between him and Hooker. Sherman said Schofield claimed that the Confederate attack struck his troops before Hooker's, and "offered to go out and show me that the dead men of his advance division ([Milo S.] Hascall's) were lying farther out than any of Hooker's." After Sherman was dead, Schofield wrote in his memoirs that he "did not remember" being particularly angry, although he said Sherman was.[20]

Sherman rode away from the church with Hooker, telling him "that such a thing must not occur again," in a reprimand "more gentle than the occasion demanded." From that time, claimed Sherman, Hooker "began to sulk." Sherman said that Hooker came "from the East with great fame as a 'fighter,' and at Chattanooga he was glorified by his 'battle above the clouds,' which I fear turned his head." Hooker was "jealous of all the army commanders, because in years, former rank, and experience, he thought he was our superior."[21]

DESPITE HIS IMPRESSIVE successes in forcing Johnston to give ground, Sherman grew increasingly impatient. For a few days following the engagement at Kolb's Farm, the two armies faced each other in what progressively seemed like a stalemate, while their artillery, as if symbolizing a deadlock, roared all along the lines day and night. One Union soldier thought the sound similar to "a continual long roll," and said that Kennesaw presented "a magnificent spectacle" at night, as "sheets of white flame" poured forth from the Southerners' guns on the mountain, while shells rose from the Federal batteries, "like so many rockets," and arched toward the enemy on the heights. Above the scene were "weird, unearthly reflections on the clouds."[22]

A few days earlier, Sherman had written General Halleck that he was studying the Confederate position "and am now inclined to feign on both flanks and assault the center. It may cost us dear, but in results would surpass an attempt to pass around. . . . If by assaulting, I can break his line," Sherman concluded, "I see no reason why it would not produce a decisive effect." By June 24, Sherman had made his decision, and issued an attack order for the twenty-seventh.[23]

It was the first time in the campaign that Sherman ordered a frontal assault against a position that he knew was fortified—a thing that, as he previously stated several times, he was not going to attempt, because the casualties would be too heavy. On June 5, for example, he had written Halleck, "I will not run head on [against the enemy] . . . fortifications." A week later he told Halleck, "We cannot risk the heavy losses of an assault at this distance from our base." His change of mind came only after days of mulling over several tormenting factors. He worried, as from the onset of the campaign, that if he did not press Johnston strongly enough, the Confederate commander might send reinforcements to Lee's army. A lengthy standoff along the Kennesaw Mountain line just might prompt Johnston to dispatch aid to the hard-pressed Army of Northern Virginia. A stalemate, whether from the perspective of Sherman's own campaign or the possible impact on Grant's, was simply unacceptable.[24]

Sherman also seemed concerned that flanking maneuvers might be undermining the combat effectiveness of his forces. Confiding to Grant that McPherson had been "a little over cautious" at Snake Creek Gap, he said his "chief source of trouble" lay with the Army of the Cumberland. "A fresh furrow in a plowed field," he claimed, would cause them to entrench. Again and again he had tried to make the point that "we must assail . . . we are on the offensive." He closed by assuring Grant, "You may go on with full assurance that I will continue to press Johnston as fast as I can . . . inspire motion into a large . . . and slow (by habit) army."[25]

Still another factor heavily weighing on Sherman's mind was the difficulty he had been experiencing in trying to get around the Rebel flanks. Making his point with exaggeration, Sherman told Halleck that "Johnston must have full fifty miles of connected trenches, with abatis and finished batteries." Stymied in his effort to turn the enemy's western flank at Kennesaw, he was not willing to again cut loose from the railroad for a wide-ranging turning movement, like he did in getting around the Allatoona Pass—especially with the roads, many of which were poor under the best of conditions, in even worse shape from days and days of rain.[26]

Sherman also learned, thanks to McPherson's probing efforts, that when Hood marched westward to check the flanking threat of Schofield and Hooker, Loring's Rebel corps had then shifted eastward to cover a portion of the entrenchments vacated by Hood. Overall, the Confederate line was stretched thin, extending for a distance of some eight miles. Sherman believed it must be relatively weak somewhere. If he suddenly struck at Johnston's apparent strength, aggressively attacking in the center of those fortified heights—a tactic from which previously he had altogether refrained—the Southern commander might be taken aback. Surprise, one of the most important principles of generalship, sometimes achieves results far out of proportion to both the strength committed and the effort expended. Doubtless Sherman remembered the startling triumph at Missionary Ridge, when Union infantry, storming a presumably impregnable height, surprised the Rebels and thoroughly routed them. Victory on such a scale at Kennesaw might send the enemy in pell-mell retreat to the Chattahoochee.[27]

The thought of appearing predictable to Johnston was on Sherman's mind as well. In his campaign report, he wrote, "An army to be efficient must not settle down to a single mode of offense." He did not want the Rebel commander believing that William Tecumseh Sherman would never attack a defensive position head-on. Possibly dovetailing with this concern, he knew that some critics described him as "not a fighting general." A frontal attack on Kennesaw would go far in negating any criticism that he would never do anything except maneuver.[28]

Sherman decided that the assault would go in against the left center of the Confederate position. If he "could thrust a strong head of column through at that point, by pushing it boldly and rapidly for two and one half miles, it would reach the railroad below Marietta, [and] cut off the enemy's right and center from its line of retreat." Thus Sherman convinced himself that a frontal assault against the Kennesaw defenses was a sensible endeavor. The General wrote that he consulted with all three army commanders, who agreed that the Union lines could not be prudently stretched out any longer, and "therefore there was no alternative but to attack 'fortified lines,' a thing carefully avoided up to that time." All may have agreed that the Federal lines were stretched to the maximum. They probably did, according to Schofield's memoirs, but Sherman's facile pen too readily swept onward, asserting that his lieutenants also favored a frontal assault.[29]

The sun rose in a cloudless sky on Monday, June 27, 1864, heralding the onset of a hot and humid day. At eight o'clock the Federal artillery, more than 200 guns strong, began a roaring bombardment of the enemy mountainside, which continued for approximately a quarter hour. "Hell has broke loose in Georgia, sure enough!" yelled a Southerner as the Union barrage got under way. When the Yankee guns ceased, the Blue-clad infantry moved to the attack. One corps of the Army of the Tennessee struck two-mile-long Kennesaw Mountain itself, going in primarily against Pigeon Hill, the lowest of the three peaks defining Kennesaw. Another corps, from the Army of the Cumberland, assaulted Johnston's lines about a mile farther to the right. Simultaneously, elements of the Army of the Tennessee demonstrated against the Rebel eastern flank, and Schofield's Army of the Ohio feigned an attack against the enemy's left flank.[30]

By mid-to-late morning both assaults, after suffering significant losses, had failed to break through the formidable Confederate entrenchments. Among the mortally wounded was Colonel Daniel McCook, Sherman's former law partner. Early in the afternoon, Sherman asked General Thomas, "Do you think you can carry any part of the enemy's line today?" Sherman said he would order another effort if Thomas thought he could succeed. Thomas replied that the Rebel works were "exceeding strong; in fact so strong that they can not be carried by assault except by immense sacrifice . . . even if they can be carried at all." Bitingly, he concluded, "We have already lost heavily today . . . one or two more such assaults would use up this army."[31]

Sherman reported that Union casualties were "nearly 3,000, while we inflicted comparatively little loss to the enemy." McPherson reported a loss of about 500, while Thomas suffered casualties of approximately 2,000. Sherman did not ignore General Thomas's remark that "one or two more such assaults would use up this army." Pointedly, he replied that "our loss is small, compared with some of those [in the] East. It should not in the least discourage us. At times assaults are necessary and inevitable." Later he sent a follow-up: "Go where we may, we will find the breast-works and abatis, unless we move more rapidly than we have heretofore."[32]

Regardless of such a declaration to Thomas about the usefulness of assaults, Sherman, after Kennesaw, had no intention of making another. In his message to Halleck on the night of June 27, he stated, "I can press Johnston and keep him from re-inforcing Lee, but to assault him in position will cost us more lives than we can spare." Clearly Sherman misjudged the situation when he ordered the attack at Kennesaw—although no more than other commanders of renown have sometimes done, like Grant at Cold Harbor, or Lee at Malvern Hill or Gettysburg. Fortunately, Sherman's casualties were not comparable to the losses in those futile attacks. Kennesaw became prominent, not because of Union casualties, which relative to Grant's campaign were, as one historian expressed the matter, "the small change of everyday operations." Rather, Kennesaw Mountain is strikingly conspicuous because Sherman, after an established pattern of maneuver, suddenly attempted a frontal assault—and then never tried one again.[33]

While the Kennesaw lines were stronger than Sherman thought they might be, his assaulting columns did carry to within a few yards of the enemy trenches at some places. He telegraphed Halleck: "The assault I made was no mistake." If the attack "had . . . been made with one-fourth more vigor . . . I would have put the head of George Thomas' whole army right through Johnston's . . . lines on the best ground for go[ing] ahead, while my entire forces were well in hand on roads converging to my then object, Marietta." Sherman markedly claimed, "Had [Brigadier General Charles] Harker and [Colonel Daniel] McCook not been struck down so early, the assault would have succeeded, and then the battle would have all been in our favor, on account of our superiority of numbers, position, and initiative."[34]

Just possibly the attack may have come nearer succeeding than Sherman's critics have admitted. Thomas wrote Sherman at 6:00 p.m. on June 27: "Both General Harker and Colonel McCook were wounded on the enemy's breast-works, and all say had they not been wounded, we would have driven the enemy from his works." Sherman and Thomas may be dismissed by some as proverbial Monday morning quarterbacks. Yet sometimes the issue of battle, like a sporting event, actually is determined by a single, perhaps even marginal factor. Change that factor and the conclusion may be different—although probably not at Kennesaw.

General Howard observed that the Confederate position was stronger, both naturally and artificially, than Cemetery Ridge at Gettysburg. Also, the narrow-fronted assault formation, in brigade columns, negated Union strength. Command leadership was significantly weakened, not only by the mortal wounding of Harker and McCook, but by incompetence and fear in some instances as well. William Farries, a combat-wise sergeant in the Army of the Cumberland, bitterly assessed the Kennesaw battle: "Our division was so poorly handled that the Rebs repulsed us with but little trouble." Declaring that he "never saw men fall so fast in all my life," the sergeant said the Southerners "had a cross fire on us with both artillery and musketry, and instead of being ordered forward on the 'double quick,' we were halted and told to lie down. What they [the officers] were waiting for I could never ascertain." Farries said the men finally "got up and ran back to our breast-works without orders. Our loss," he cuttingly concluded, "will show whether the men acted rightly or not." A mile to the east, where the Army of the Tennessee attacked, Casey McWayne told of a major who, having ordered his company to advance, soon headed for the rear. A captain took command, but uncertain what to do, ordered a halt, leaving the men desperately seeking cover from the intense Confederate fire.[35]

Whatever Sherman, in the depths of his soul, really thought about his chances of victory at Kennesaw, he had the good sense to realize that any opportunity he may have had to break Johnston on those heights was gone forever. However tough he sometimes sounded, Sherman was genuinely concerned about sparing the lives of his soldiers to the greatest degree consistent with success, and he did not want them to pay the price of risking another attack like June 27. Writing Ellen soon afterward, he deplored "the awful amount of death & destruction that now stalks abroad," while decrying the war's impact on his own psyche: "I begin to regard the death & mangling of a couple thousand soldiers as a small affair, a kind of morning Dash—and it may be well that we become so hardened."[36]

But Sherman was not a man who easily became "so hardened" to death, whether death among the forces he commanded, or his family and friends; and this the context of his many letters clearly reveals. Writing Minnie on the same day that he penned the above to Ellen, and mentioning her new baby brother, he seized the chance to speak again of Willy: "I fear we all loved Willy too much to let another supply his place." He confided that he thought Lizzie "is destined to be a Stay at home, whilst you and I will be gad abouts." Then he assured Minnie that "I will keep my promise to you, if you stay another year at your present school, to take you myself to New York, and give you a year at the best Seminary I can find there." Yet he immediately added, "I ought not to make many promises, for I daily see too many officers buried by the road side, or carried to the rear maimed and mangled to count on much of a future."[37]

....

SHERMAN WAS PLEASED to learn that Schofield, in making a demonstration against the Southern left at Kennesaw, had actually prepared the way for a smooth resumption of his flanking maneuvers. Taking advantage of the enemy's preoccupation with defending against the assaults of McPherson and Thomas, Schofield had pushed forward Jacob Cox's division for some two miles, gaining a position from which to threaten Johnston's line of retreat. Sherman quickly made plans to exploit the opportunity. "Satisfied of the bloody cost of attacking entrenched lines," he later wrote, "I at once thought of moving the whole army to the railroad at a point (Fulton) about ten miles below Marietta, or to the Chattahoochee River itself." This would mean cutting loose from the railroad again, for several days, and Sherman remarked that "General Thomas, as usual, shook his head, deeming it risky to leave the railroad."[38]

A confident Sherman had made his decision, however, issuing orders to bring forward provisions and forage to fill the army wagons with ten days of supplies. Prudence dictated that Schofield's small Army of the Ohio should be reinforced immediately. Thus Sherman sent McPherson's Army of the Tennessee swinging to the right, not only to strengthen Schofield, but also because he wanted McPherson's hard-marching force to spearhead the turning movement. He anticipated that Johnston, once he realized that Sherman's strong flanking arm was nearer to Atlanta than he, would fall back from the Kennesaw line, to defend the railroad and the river.[39]

McPherson's move got under way on July 2, and the Confederate commander, who soon detected the march, realized that he must either retreat or come out of his Kennesaw entrenchments and attack Sherman in the open field. Sherman said he would welcome the latter but did not expect it to happen. As he anticipated, and even sooner than expected, Joe Johnston once more chose to retreat. Again the Union commander had flanked the Grayclads out of a very formidable position. During McPherson's march, a disgusted Rebel soldier, taken prisoner by the 103rd Illinois Infantry, memorably voiced his vexation at Sherman's strategy: "Sherman'll never go to hell," he growled; "he will flank the devil and make heaven in spite of the guards." Many of Sherman's soldiers had a different take on their commander's flanking maneuvers. Writing the "folks at home," Sergeant McWayne remarked, "If you-ns could see we-uns, you would think we live bully. Dog-'on if we don't. We find but few folks at home. They say (those that we see) that 'you-ns flink our men, so they have to fall back.' Bully for the 'flink,' I say! It saves a great many hard fought battles."[40]

Sherman was up "by the earliest dawn of the 3rd of July," training a large, tripod-mounted glass on Kennesaw, and watching the army's pickets cautiously making their way up the mountainside. Once at the top, he saw the Union soldiers excitedly running along the crest. The Confederates were gone. Animated by the thought that Johnston's forces were out in the open and possibly vulnerable to his superior numbers, Sherman acted immediately. "I roused my staff, and started them off with orders in every direction for a pursuit . . . hoping to catch Johnston in the confusion of retreat, especially at the crossing of the Chattahoochee River."[41]

Not for a moment did Sherman imagine that Johnston might throw up fortifications, with the Chattahoochee at his back. The pursuit, however, was not nearly aggressive enough to satisfy the fired-up commander. Not only was the infantry advance too cautious. Worse, when Sherman rode into Marietta, soon after the enemy rear guard had moved out, and learned that most of the Blueclad cavalry, which was expected to be leading the pursuit under command of Kenner Garrard, was either stalled in the town or still coming up, he was enraged. "Where's Gar'd?" he roared. "Where in hell's Gar'd?" When Garrard appeared, Sherman had little interest or time for the cavalry commander's explanations of tardiness. With strong language, he hurried Garrard forward, incensed that Johnston might already be escaping across the waterway.[42]

To his surprise, Sherman soon learned that Johnston had simply fallen back to a formidably entrenched position on the north bank of the Chattahoochee, which covered the Western & Atlantic Railroad crossing and several pontoon bridges. From a vantage point in the second story of a house on the Federal picket line—where he admitted being very nearly shot, as the structure was "perfectly riddled with musket-balls," and even hit by cannon shot—Sherman evaluated the enemy position. Later he pronounced it "one of the strongest pieces of field fortification I ever saw."[43]

Extensive abatis, deep ditches and impressive redoubts indicated that the line had been under preparation for some time. From a slave who managed to hide for hours under a log, and at last escape into the Union lines, Sherman learned that approximately 1,000 slaves had prepared and strengthened the position. The main enemy defenses extended along the north bank of the Chattahoochee, both right and left of the railroad bridge, for about six miles. Cavalry and pickets monitored both flanks beyond the main line, while artillery, and occasionally a fort, were placed at fords and ferries. Johnston hoped that his massive bridgehead would prove both impregnable to frontal assault, and invulnerable to any flanking maneuver that Sherman might attempt. Sherman said "the case" needed to be "studied a little."[44]

Meanwhile, the strange episode of newspaper reporter DeB. Randolph Keim had been unfolding. Sherman had forbidden newsmen to accompany his armies. Surprisingly he made an exception in the instance of Keim, probably because the reporter informed him that he was a friend of James McPherson. All went well for a while, and the only information that appeared in Northern newspapers about Sherman's campaign was very general in nature—and to the effect that success attended his every endeavor. Sherman himself, as previously noted, at times framed harmless information for public release. Then an article appeared in the *New York Herald*, dated June 23, 1864, which apparently came from Keim and revealed that Sherman could read the enemy's signal code. Understandably, Sherman was infuriated, for he knew the Confederates managed to acquire Northern papers as quickly as he did. General Thomas was equally incensed, and told Sherman that he thought "Keim should at once be executed as a spy."[45]

Assured by Thomas that "Keim is not harbored in the Army of the Cumberland, and I know not where he is," Sherman sent an order to McPherson to arrest Keim "and have him delivered to General Thomas to be tried as a spy." Sherman instructed McPherson: "Let this be done at once, for publishing in a New York paper . . . that our signal officers can interpret the signals of the enemy." McPherson arrested Keim and sent the man to Thomas; but also, for whatever reasons, McPherson interceded with Thomas on behalf of the reporter. Thomas concluded that because of McPherson's "recommendation of leniency of punishment . . . I will have him sent north of the Ohio River, with orders not to return to this army during the war."[46]

How much, if anything, Sherman knew about the exchanges between McPherson and Thomas, and what he thought about the banishment, seem impossible to determine. Whatever Sherman thought, he apparently did not pursue the matter. At least Keim was gone, and Sherman doubtless came away from the incident fully convinced that no reporter should be trusted. For his part, Keim revealed no animosity toward Sherman, later writing a favorable assessment of the General's life. Perhaps Keim, after the passage of some years, held no grudge against Sherman.[47]

During late June and early July, although focused on the Confederates at Kennesaw and then at the Chattahoochee, Sherman was growing increasingly concerned about Ellen's well-being. After learning from her brother Phil about the birth of their son, as earlier noted, Sherman had received no letter from Ellen herself. Knowing her health had been fragile, he became all the more worried after receiving a letter from Phil's wife, indicating that Ellen had been seriously ill after the delivery of the child. He wrote Phil, telling him that he had not received a letter from Ellen in more than two months, and that "she never before neglected to write as now." He said the mails "are pretty regular," and the telegraph "is to my tent." Declaring that "I hear from all parts of the world daily, but can get nothing from Lancaster," he implored his brother-in-law, "If Ellen be really too unwell to write, I wish you would see that someone tells me the truth for I have enough care & responsibility without the uneasiness . . . from absolute silence at home."[48]

Supplying and directing 100,000 men at war, while campaigning deep into enemy territory, constituted an awesome responsibility. Regardless of family concerns, Sherman knew he had to get on with the task at hand.

The General was a quick study, particularly when the issue involved military maneuvering. He soon formulated a good plan to resolve the Chattahoochee problem. Rightly expecting "every possible resistance" to a crossing, he decided "to feign on the right, but actually to cross over by the left."[49]

With McPherson's army, Sherman mounted a strong and convincing demonstration downriver from the Western & Atlantic bridge. McPherson's forces reached the Chattahoochee below Turner's Ferry, while Major General George Stoneman's cavalry rode several miles farther, to a point opposite Sandtown, which was nearly ten miles, as the crow flies, south of the railroad crossing. The troopers aggressively pretended to be searching the river for a place to cross over. Naturally the Confederate cavalry watched the Federal activity, both infantry and cavalry, as best they could from the Chattahoochee's opposite bank.

Joe Johnston knew—as Sherman well knew he would know—that McPherson's Army of the Tennessee usually led the Union flanking maneuvers. A detailed report by one of Johnston's staff officers had identified seven potential downstream crossings, places where the north bank of the river would provide the Federals with good approaches and favorable ground for covering artillery fire. Also, the aggressiveness of Stoneman's troopers apparently confirmed what the Confederate commander was already assuming. Furthermore, if Sherman crossed downstream in his approach to Atlanta, he would be positioned to break Johnston's communications to the west. General Johnston was thinking exactly what Sherman wanted him to think.[50]

While Stoneman and McPherson strove to hoodwink Johnston downstream, Kenner Garrard took his cavalry nearly twenty miles upriver from the Western & Atlantic, all the way to Roswell, as he searched for a suitable crossing. Sherman really wanted something closer, however, and John Schofield, making a reconnaissance of the Chattahoochee for several miles north of Pace's Ferry, decided that the place where Soap Creek emptied into the river was favorable for a surprise. The enemy held the opposite bank with only a light force. Schofield thought he just might get across the Chattahoochee before the Rebels knew what was happening. Sherman thought so too. Schofield wanted to reconnoiter more fully, but Sherman had learned that the main body of the Confederate cavalry was a number of miles downstream on the Rebel left flank. The time for action was at hand. He ordered Schofield to cross as soon as possible, drive away the defenders, throw up entrenchments and lay a pontoon bridge.[51]

On July 8, at half past three in the afternoon, Schofield struck. He took the Rebels totally by surprise. By night he was on the high ground beyond, strongly entrenched, with two good pontoon bridges finished, and was prepared, if necessary, to resist an assault by a large enemy force. It was probably the best piece of work that Schofield contributed during the entire campaign, and it was accomplished "without the loss of a man."[52]

The totality of surprise is dramatically attested by the unfinished letter of a Confederate soldier to his wife, which was found in the enemy campsite. The Southerner wrote that he was "almost as free from peril as if he were at home on his plantation; that the solitude about them was rarely broken, even by the appearance of a single horseman on the opposite side of the river." The letter ended in the middle of a sentence, likely broken by the sudden emergence of twenty pontoon boats from the mouth of Soap Creek, loaded with Union soldiers pulling rapidly for the Rebel side, while Federals who had silently scrambled across a submerged fish dam farther upstream began leveling flanking fire against the astonished defenders. Simultaneous musket fire, quickly enhanced by artillery fire, struck them from the north bank of the river. The entire operation came together precisely as planned, and only a few Confederates escaped.[53]

Farther up the Chattahoochee, Garrard's cavalry captured the town of Roswell, although not in time to prevent the Rebel cavalry from burning the bridge across the swollen stream. Roswell was an important manufacturing center where several textile mills produced cloth for the Confederacy. Garrard wasted no time in torching the buildings, "the utter destruction" of which, said Sherman, meets with "my entire approval." The flag of France was prominent above one structure, and

Garrard reported: "Over the woolen factory the French flag was flying, but seeing no Federal flag above it, I had the building burnt."[54]

Sherman assured him that he had done the right thing. In fact Sherman authorized his cavalry officer specifically about the alleged French owner: "Should you, under the impulse of anger, natural at contemplating such perfidy, hang the wretch, I approve the act beforehand." To his credit, Garrard did not hang anyone. Among the workers he took into custody were 400 women, whom Sherman sent north of the Ohio River, to be "turned loose to earn a living where they won't do us any harm." As for Roswell, a Union soldier penned a summary remark that the village had been "a very pleasant little town, . . . but now is a mass of ruins."[55]

Although the capture of 400 women received a great deal of attention, the really significant war news was that Sherman's forces were across the Chattahoochee, the last of the three major river barriers separating the Yankees from Atlanta. Schofield had led the way, and more Federals soon followed. Brigadier General Edward McCook ordered a detachment of his cavalry to cross at Cochran's Ford, not far from Schofield's bridgehead. The endeavor proved quite remarkable and, in a sense, amusing. The water was deep and the men crossed the river "naked, with nothing but guns, cartridge-boxes, and hats," according to McCook's report. Once on the south bank, the nude Federals drove off the Confederates, and captured several of them. "They would have got more," claimed McCook, "but the rebels had the advantage in running through the bushes with clothes on." The brigadier declared the event "a very successful raid for naked men to make." McCook also reported that "citizens say the enemy were totally unprepared for a crossing on this flank." Sherman's decision to cross upstream was vindicated.

With Union troops across the river in strength, and thousands more soon to follow, Johnston abandoned his extensive fortifications during the night of July 9–10. He withdrew to the south bank of the river, burning the Western & Atlantic bridge, and the wagon bridge, as well as destroying the other bridges by which his army had crossed over. Pausing briefly at the entrenchments previously prepared on the south bank, Johnston soon pulled back to a line behind Peachtree Creek, a westward-flowing tributary of the Chattahoochee. There the Confederate forces were positioned fewer than five miles from the center of Atlanta.[56]

By any objective analysis, the event was another triumph for an elated Sherman. "I think in crossing the Chattahoochee as I have, without the loss of a man," he wrote Phil Ewing, "I have achieved really a creditable deed." General Thomas had told Sherman that he dreaded crossing the Chattahoochee "more than any one thing ahead." When Thomas learned, continued Sherman, "that I had Schofield across, fortified and with two pontoon bridges laid, he could not believe it." Sergeant William Farries jubilantly wrote, "We have got old Johnston and his 'Graybacks' across the [Chattahoochee] river. ... If Johnston intended to make a stand between here and Atlanta, he would have tried to prevent us crossing the river." Thousands of celebrating Union soldiers soon jumped naked into the river, noisily splashing about, as they relished their first leisurely bath in a long time—and their commander plunged in with them.[57]

Obviously there was no joy in Atlanta, which learned at once that Johnston's army had been maneuvered from the Chattahoochee, falling back to the outskirts of the city. People old and young, many of them women, packed essentials onto wagons, along with whatever precious items took up minimal space, and hurried away. Many children made an exit in company with the women, as well as a few men—most too old to fight. Others escaped by train, heading for Macon, Augusta or wherever to avoid Sherman's armies. Newspapers pulled out, except the *Appeal*—originally the *Memphis Appeal*, before fleeing the Union occupation of Memphis.[58]

The fictitious Aunt Pitty Pat's memorable exclamation in Margaret Mitchell's *Gone With the Wind* rings as if it might actually have been historical, and marvelously fitting: "Yankees in Georgia! How did they ever get in?" Sherman was sure enough "in," and right on Atlanta's doorstep. From atop a hill, he could see the roofs of the city's buildings. What now, Southerners wondered, would Joe Johnston do? Their general had retreated all the way from northern Georgia, at Dalton's Rocky Face Ridge, to the northern edge of Atlanta, without ever launching a major attack against Sherman's forces. Would he now finally strike? Or would Atlanta, a city that at the beginning of 1864 was second to none as a Confederate war-production center, rail crossroads and prominent symbol of Southern resistance, be abandoned to the forces of General Sherman without an all-out fight?

The most recent performance of the Confederate commander, regardless of perspective, was neither satisfactory nor encouraging. Johnston's formidable Chattahoochee line had been devised for defense by a relatively small force—only one or two divisions—in order to permit the Confederates in strength either to strike the Yankees as they attempted to cross the river or isolate and bludgeon any force that did reach the south bank. Johnston possessed the interior line of communication for rapidly massing against a Union crossing. But Johnston did not anticipate an upstream crossing by Sherman, and was slow to react. He was initially uncertain where the enemy was crossing, and then came the issue of whether the Blueclads were merely feigning. Doubtless Johnston was also troubled by the counsel of John Bell Hood, who thought the entire army should be withdrawn to the south bank of the Chattahoochee.[59]

Even after the Confederate commander withdrew to Peachtree Creek, he still might have attacked Sherman. "Here Johnston lost probably the greatest opportunity of the campaign," declares one historian. For several days after Johnston pulled back to the Peachtree line, Sherman's forces were divided, some north and some south of the Chattahoochee, and spread out over a front of twenty miles. An aggressive Confederate commander might have recrossed Peachtree Creek, taking advantage of the opportunity. But by this stage of the campaign, Sherman understood his opponent. He was confident that Johnston, positioned on a south side elevation overlooking Peachtree, was not about to recross that stream and attack.[60]

Jefferson Davis feared that he too understood Joe Johnston, and that the general was likely to give up Atlanta without waging a decisive battle. At the direction of Davis, Braxton Bragg arrived in Atlanta by train to confer with Johnston. Before Bragg even saw Johnston, he sent Davis an ominous dispatch, saying that "indications seem to favor an entire evacuation of this place." In another message, Bragg told Davis, "Our army is sadly depleted. . . . I find but little encouraging." On July 15, Bragg sent the president another depressing dispatch, noting that "nearly all available stores and machinery are removed, and the people have mostly evacuated the town." After visiting twice with Johnston, Bragg wrote Davis, "I cannot learn that he has any more plan for the future than he has had in the past." This disturbing summation would not have been difficult for Davis to believe, and very likely it triggered his July 16 dispatch to Johnston, in which he demanded, "I wish to hear from you as to present situation, and your plan of operations so specifically as will enable me to anticipate events."[61]

Johnston replied promptly, but the message could hardly have been more discouraging. "As the enemy has double our number, we must be on the defensive," he stated. "My plan of operations must, therefore, depend upon that of the enemy. It is mainly to watch for an opportunity to fight to advantage. We are trying to put Atlanta in condition to be held for a day or two by the Georgia militia, that army movements may be freer and wider." Every sentence was disturbing. Perhaps Davis had already made the decision to remove Johnston from command; perhaps he still wavered until he read the above and realized that Johnston must be replaced immediately if there were any hope of saving Atlanta.[62]

He issued an order removing Johnston from command on Sunday morning, July 17. "As you have failed to arrest the advance of the enemy to the vicinity of Atlanta . . . and express no confidence that you can defeat or repel him, you are hereby relieved from the command of the Army and Department of Tennessee." Johnston was to turn over command of the army immediately to John Bell Hood. Nearly a quarter century younger than Johnston, Hood had been maimed and weakened from war wounds. A limp, useless left arm had hung by his side since Gettysburg, and he had lost his right leg at Chickamauga. He hobbled with a crutch to support the stump of that amputated limb. Prior to the Atlanta campaign, he had built a reputation, and deservedly so, as a fighter, and that reputation served him well as he recuperated in Richmond, where he came to be regarded as a Confederate hero.[63]

The crippled general's rise to command, however, is the essence of irony. "He was not," observed the historian Tom Connelly, "the simple man some considered him to be." From the time Hood became a corps commander in the Army of Tennessee, he sent letters to Richmond, "all of which were damaging to Johnston," declared Connelly. Hood's letter of July 14 to General Bragg spoke of the army having had "several chances to strike the enemy a decisive blow." Deploring the failure "to take advantage of such opportunities," Hood declared that he "regard[ed] it as a great misfortune . . . that we failed to give battle to the enemy many miles north of our present position." Astonishingly, in light of the facts, he claimed that he himself had "so often urged that we should force the enemy to give us battle as to almost be regarded [as] reckless by the officers high in rank in this army, since their views have been so directly opposite." While acknowledging that "our present position is a very difficult one," he strongly asserted that "we should not, under any circumstances, allow the enemy to gain possession of Atlanta." Hood claimed he favored attacking the enemy, "even if we should have to re-cross the river to do so."[64]

Hood's letter is filled with misrepresentation. The assertion that he often urged battle is simply not true. Hood advised Johnston to retreat at Adairsville, at the Etowah River, at Kennesaw Mountain and at the Chattahoochee. Little wonder that the term "lying" was employed by Hood's most careful biographer. Bragg evidently favored the removal of Johnston before he even arrived in Atlanta, and Bragg was no friend of William Hardee, who as the senior corps commander was the only likely successor to Johnston other than Hood. Thus Bragg accepted Hood's version of the campaign, according to which Hood's many attempts to give battle to the Yankees had been stymied; and Bragg's reports to Jefferson Davis apparently proved compelling, in influencing the Confederate president's determination to both remove Johnston and replace him with Hood. An alliance of Hood and Bragg, however unlikely it might have seemed in some respects, had gained for Hood the command for which he was angling.[65]

Meanwhile, Sherman's decision to cross the Chattahoochee above the Western & Atlantic Railroad and move on Atlanta from the north and east proved to be the best possible choice. He never intended to attack Atlanta directly. Rather, as he informed Halleck, he planned to make a circuit of the city, "destroying all its railroads." Johnston then, with his communication lines broken, would most likely abandon Atlanta. Otherwise the Confederate commander must either accept a siege or come out of his fortifications and attack. If Sherman struck the enemy railroads by initially moving on Atlanta from the west, he would have to take his forces away from his own railroad for an indeterminate period of time. But if he advanced from the north and east, Sherman's armies could remain between the Rebel forces and the Union communications.[66]

While Sherman prepared to march on Atlanta, he wanted Johnston to think that the major Union advance on the city would come from the west. Thus he had sent Major General Lovell H. Rousseau from Nashville deep into Alabama, at the head of 2,000 cavalry, to attack the Confederate rail lines connecting Georgia with Alabama and Mississippi. Simultaneously, George Stoneman rode southwest of Atlanta, charged with destroying the Atlanta & West Point Railroad in the vicinity of Newnan. Rousseau did his work well, at least for cavalry, tearing up some twenty miles of track. The damage by Stoneman was minimal, but the two raids did help focus Confederate attention on the western side of Atlanta. Also, for several days McPherson's Army of the Tennessee, following Sherman's instruction, kept up a demonstration downstream from the Western & Atlantic bridge, as if positioning there to cross the Chattahoochee and advance on Atlanta from the west. Actually, when fully prepared, Sherman would shift McPherson's infantry rapidly upstream, swinging behind the Army of the Cumberland, to cross the Chattahoochee at Roswell, and march to break the railroad east of Atlanta in the vicinity of Decatur.[67]

If Sherman ever had any doubt about the wisdom of striking at Atlanta from the north and east, it was dispelled by mid-July, when Grant and Halleck warned him that Robert E. Lee well might send 20,000, maybe even 25,000 reinforcements to Johnston. Lee could not feed the men he had, and did not need all of them to hold his strong fortifications anyway. If Confederate reinforcements were sent from Virginia, they surely would be coming in by rail from east of Atlanta, the only line secure from Union interdiction. Sherman should therefore, advised Grant and Halleck, destroy the railroad as far to the east as possible, prepare a good defensive position to hold if reinforcements did join the enemy at Atlanta and mass "as large an amount of supplies as possible . . . at Chattanooga." Grant promised "a desperate effort . . . to hold the enemy without the necessity of so many men," thus permitting him to help Sherman with reinforcements.[68]

Actually, Sherman was way ahead of Grant and Halleck in anticipation and preparation. An hour before midnight on July 16, he telegraphed Halleck: "I had anticipated all possible chances and am accumulating all the stores possible at Chattanooga and Allatoona." Sherman still had 100,000 soldiers, and did "not fear Johnston with reinforcements of 20,000, if he will take the offensive; but I recognize the danger arising from my long [supply] line and the superiority of the enemy's cavalry in numbers and audacity." He said nothing about establishing a defensive line, but rather assured his friend that on the morrow he would be advancing "toward Decatur and Stone Mountain, east of Atlanta." He sent a copy of the message to Grant.[69]

Sherman regarded Allatoona "of the first importance," and two days earlier he had stated that "it is a second Chattanooga; its front and rear are . . . [easily defended] and its flanks are strong." He had directed that major supplies be accumulated there, which "would make a raid to our rear less to be feared, giving us the means of living till repairs could be made." Sherman was also massing supplies at Marietta, another place he fortified. And he told McPherson: "I want everything done that is prudent and necessary at Roswell to make it a kind of secondary base for operations against Atlanta." Obviously Sherman did not exaggerate when he assured General Halleck that he had been anticipating all possible contingencies.[70]

Sherman never used the word "logistics," a term that came into prominence only during World War II, but he was a master of the subject. Because of Sherman's genius in managing logistics, he was able to supply his armies, as well as feed the thousands of animals those forces required, while seizing and maintaining the offensive against the Rebel army. The closer he drew to Atlanta, the longer grew his line of communications, and the more impressive was his achievement.[71]

"Your operations thus far have been the admiration of all military men," General Halleck assured Sherman, "and they prove what energy and skill combined can accomplish, while either without the other may utterly fail." Halleck then summarized the war situation in the eastern theater, where Grant had failed to achieve the success for which all had hoped when the spring campaigning began. Noting that "we have just escaped another formidable raid on Baltimore and Washington," the general declared that Grant "would not believe that [Confederate Richard] Ewell's corps had left his front till it . . . had already reached Maryland." Consequently Grant had to dispatch a corps to drive the raiders from the vicinity of the nation's capital.

Halleck, who never thought highly of Grant, then confided: "I fear Grant has made a fatal mistake in placing himself south of James River. He can not now reach Richmond without taking Petersburg, which is strongly fortified, crossing the Appomattox and re-crossing the James." Grant had thus opened Washington, D.C., to Confederate raiders. "I hope," Halleck observed darkly, "that we may yet have full success, but I find that many of Grant's general officers think the campaign already a failure." Never mentioning the immense casualties that Grant's forces suffered, which had contributed hugely to a pronounced and growing national war weariness, Halleck stated, as if groping for a brighter note in conclusion: "Perseverance, however, may compensate for all errors and overcome all obstacles."[72]

Grant had not won the war in Virginia. The only prospect of significant military success by midsummer of 1864 seemed to rest solely with Sherman, which at this point he surely realized. On July 18, he told Thomas that McPherson—having swung behind Schofield and Thomas on a swiftly executed fifty-mile march from the Federal right to the extreme left—had reached the railroad east of Atlanta, at a place two miles from Stone Mountain. There he was busily tearing up track and telegraph lines. Sherman instructed Thomas: "I want a bold push for Atlanta and have made my orders, which, I think, will put us in Atlanta or very close to it." He commented, not yet knowing that Hood was in command: "It is hard to realize that Johnston will give up Atlanta without a fight, but it may be so. Let us develop the truth."[73]

Within a short time Sherman learned from a newspaper out of Atlanta, which was brought in by a spy, that John Bell Hood had just replaced Johnston. Thomas, McPherson and Schofield had all known Hood at West Point. Schofield and McPherson had been his classmates, and Thomas was one of Hood's instructors, and later his commander in Texas. "What sort of a fellow is he?" Sherman asked Schofield, who replied: "He'll hit you like hell, now, before you know it." All three generals agreed that Hood, in Sherman's summary words, "was bold even to rashness." Sherman said he "inferred that the change . . . meant 'fight.'" At once he alerted all his forces, cautioning every division commander "to be always prepared for battle in any shape." As his three armies converged toward Atlanta on July 19, Sherman said that they met "such feeble resistance that I really thought the enemy intended to evacuate the place." How wrong he was.[74]

HOOD INDEED REALIZED that his elevation to command meant "fight"— just as Sherman and the Federal generals anticipated, and just as all Confederates looked for Hood, in the words of a Richmond paper, "to drive back Sherman and save Atlanta." On July 20, Thomas's Army of the Cumberland was closing down on the city from the north, while McPherson had swung wide to approach from the east. Schofield advanced on McPherson's right flank, and a gap of nearly two miles had developed between Schofield's right and Thomas's left. Hood hoped to strike Thomas, whose army was overly extended along a six-mile front, as he crossed Peachtree Creek, which was not easily fordable. Union reinforcements, because of the distance between Schofield and Thomas, would not be readily available to assist the Army of the Cumberland.

The situation did seem promising for the Rebels—if the attack could have been made earlier in the day.[75]

Hood's plan called for an assault by two of the army's three corps, but the new Confederate commander did not order the attack to begin until one in the afternoon. Because of confusion and defensive adjustments necessitated by the rapid advance of McPherson's army, the Southern attack was not launched until nearly four o'clock, and then it was poorly managed. Hood primarily blamed corps commander Hardee for having "failed to push the attack as ordered." Later praising Alexander Stewart for "carrying out his instructions to the letter," while his corps "nobly performed their duty," Hood claimed Hardee, although leading "the best troops in the army, virtually accomplished nothing." Still sulking after being passed over for command of the army, Hardee did perform sluggishly. His biographer concluded that Peachtree Creek was "one of Hardee's poorest performances." Hood himself, however, was not without blame, and particularly must be faulted for inadequate command control.

When the Confederates finally attacked, much of Thomas's army was already across Peachtree, and some of the Yankees were beginning to throw up entrenchments. Although taken by surprise, the Army of the Cumberland rose to the challenge, and Thomas handled his forces well. The battle raged for the better part of three hours before Hood became convinced that the attack had failed. He withdrew into the outer line of Atlanta's fortifications, less than 2½ miles from the city center. Confederate casualties were at least 2,500, and probably more; the Army of the Cumberland suffered a loss of 1,600.[76]

Following the Peachtree clash, Sherman thought Hood likely would abandon Atlanta—as he earlier expected of Johnston. Sherman had not yet adjusted to the pronounced difference between the two generals. While the Army of the Cumberland fought north of Atlanta, McPherson's Army of the Tennessee had continued maneuvering to turn the Confederate right flank, and close in on the city from the east. On the morning of July 21, as Sherman sought to eliminate the gaps between his advancing forces, McPherson's troops succeeded in capturing a conspicuous bald hill, from the crest of which they gained a good view of Atlanta.

The Southerners tried to recover the height, but the Federals held on tenaciously, and a brutal fight ensued. The Grayclads "rallied and made repeated attempts to regain possession of the hill," reported Union General Frank Blair, "in all of which they were unsuccessful and suffered considerable loss." Confederate General Cleburne said the engagement was "the bitterest" of his life, while Rebel brigadier James Smith reported that a Yankee battery enfiladed his position from a range of about 800 yards, and delivered the most "accurate and destructive cannonading" he ever witnessed. Incredibly, a single shot killed seventeen of the eighteen men who composed one of the companies in the Eighteenth Texas.

As the battle intensified, Cleburne feared that his right flank was going to be turned. Desperately he fought, and at last reinforcements arrived. Unable to reclaim the high ground, the Rebels did maintain their front east of Atlanta. Federal guns, however, began shelling the city, which was within easy range from the bald hill. During the afternoon, Union troops observed Confederate regiments moving through Atlanta in a southern direction. Sherman concluded that Hood was pulling out of the city, as he anticipated, and he issued orders for a pursuit.[77]

Strongly attuned to the warnings from Halleck and Grant about Rebel reinforcements from Virginia, Sherman's primary focus was on the Augusta railroad east of Atlanta. He wanted it "absolutely and completely destroyed, every tie burned and every rail twisted." The cavalry was not getting the job done to his satisfaction. Thus he decided that McPherson's Sixteenth Corps should be assigned the task. McPherson, however, was convinced that Hood meant to attack, and that the Rebels marching southward intended to strike on the morrow—most likely targeting the left flank of the Army of the Tennessee. McPherson did not believe his former classmate would simply abandon Atlanta without any further effort to defend the city.[78]

On the morning of July 22, Union observers from atop the bald hill noticed, and the advance of skirmishers revealed, that the Grayclads had not relinquished Atlanta. Orders to pursue were cancelled. McPherson felt virtually certain that Hood was preparing to attack. Because Garrard's cavalry had been sent to bust up the railroad eastward, the Army of the Tennessee's left flank was "in the air," and McPherson was anxious to have the Sixteenth Corps posted on that flank, a move he had recently ordered. Fortunately, Sherman agreed to allow the Sixteenth Corps to remain in place until afternoon when, if no enemy assault had occurred, McPherson would assign it to the job of wrecking the railroad. Sherman also informed McPherson that as soon as the road to Augusta was broken up, he intended to shift McPherson's "whole army around by the rear to Thomas' extreme right," and destroy Hood's communications to the south.[79]

McPherson, as events soon confirmed, was absolutely right about Hood's plan. The Confederate commander had quickly realized, as Sherman maneuvered to turn his eastern flank, that he must either attack again or retreat and lose Atlanta. He chose to attack, convinced that this time he must deal with McPherson's army, which was the most threatening of Sherman's forces. By the afternoon of July 21, Hood believed that McPherson, having captured the bald hill from the crest of which he could shell Atlanta, was on the verge of flanking his entire line, breaking the vital Macon railroad supply route south of the city, and thus rendering Atlanta untenable. Hood also had information indicating that McPherson's left flank was exposed, which could only have strengthened his decision about where to strike. Despite William Hardee's less than stellar performance at Peachtree Creek, Hood had little choice but to select Hardee's large and experienced corps to spearhead a demanding and desperate attack.[80]

"With visions of [Stonewall] Jackson's flank move at Chancellorsville," to quote historian Tom Connelly, Hood sent Hardee's corps on a grueling, fifteen-to-eighteen-mile night march, with the objective of attacking McPherson's left flank and rear at daylight on July 22. As soon as Hardee's strike "succeeded in forcing back the enemy's left," Hood explained, then Major General Benjamin F. Cheatham's corps would join the battle and assail McPherson's army in front. Hood never intended a simultaneous attack by Hardee and Cheatham. Again, however, the Southern forces were plagued by confusion, as well as weariness, not to mention the heat and humidity. Some Rebels looted the Five Points area as they passed through the city. Hardee's march was not at all "a very simple one," as Hood misleadingly said in his memoirs. Through no fault of Hardee, the attack could not be launched until afternoon. When at last in position, the assault was made in a disorganized, piecemeal fashion. The historian Albert Castel summarized Hood's plan as attempting "to do too much with too little in too short a time." But Hood did launch a terrible battle.[81]

HIGH NOON HAD come and gone without a Confederate attack, and James McPherson, sitting in the shade of an oak grove, where he and a number of officers had eaten lunch, prepared an order, as he had promised Sherman, directing the Sixteenth Corps to proceed with the railroad-wrecking assignment. Suddenly he heard firing break out on the army's left flank, apparently signaling a major enemy strike at the very place he had expected. McPherson mounted up at once and rode toward his threatened lines. The Sixteenth Corps was right where it needed to be in order to meet the initial Confederate attack. Timing and chance had ruled in favor of the Union Army. McPherson's railroad order, which he had given to a staff officer for delivery, arrived in the hands of Grenville Dodge, the Sixteenth Corps commander, just as the Rebels attacked. If the Southern assault had been launched earlier, even an hour earlier, all of the Sixteenth Corps would not have been on site, and if it had come an hour or more later, a significant number of Federals would have already marched away to work on the railroad.[82]

The reality, which the Confederates discovered only when they attacked, was that McPherson's flank was not "in the air." In fact, the Federals could hardly have been better positioned to blunt the enemy's opening assault. The fatigued Southerners, after struggling through dense woods, extensive briar patches, thick underbrush, an expansive slimy morass and other obstacles, delivered an uncoordinated attack, which the Yankees smashed with heavy musketry and artillery fire. McPherson had arrived in time to watch approvingly from high ground as the Sixteenth Corps threw back the first assaults by two of Hardee's divisions.[83]

But Hardee had more infantry coming up, and the battle was far from over. McPherson soon learned that a gap, approximately a half mile long, existed between the Sixteenth and Seventeenth Corps. He wanted that gap closed as soon as possible. Since the Sixteenth Corps was firmly holding its ground, McPherson chose to ride across the gap, reconnoitering for himself, as he headed toward the Seventeenth Corps. Some Confederates had already advanced into the gap, however, and as McPherson rode through a heavily wooded area, well ahead of most of his staff, he ran up on a number of Rebels. Ordered to halt, McPherson instead wheeled his horse around and tried to escape. Several Southerners fired and one of their shots killed him.[84]

Sherman was shocked. "The suddenness of this terrible calamity would have overwhelmed me with grief," Sherman wrote in his campaign report, "but the living demanded my whole thoughts." Quickly Sherman dispatched a staff officer to the Army of the Tennessee's senior corps commander, General John Logan, commanding the Fifteenth Corps, to inform him of what had happened. Known by the soldiers under his command as "Black Jack" because of his swarthy complexion, Logan could inspire his troops with his own fighting spirit. Sherman instructed him to "assume command of the Army of the Tennessee ... hold stubbornly the ground already chosen ... especially the [bald] hill gained ... the night before." The army's left flank was to be rapidly refused, swinging it back to the southeast from the bald hill, and thereby blunting the Rebel turning movement. Sherman assured Logan, in Logan's words, "that whatever assistance I might need would be furnished," and one of Schofield's brigades was dispatched toward Decatur to help protect the wagon train and the army's rear.[85]

Blazing, roaring and slaughtering, the savage clash consumed the remainder of the day and became known as the Battle of Atlanta. The most determined and vicious Southern attacks fell upon the Seventeenth Corps and the Fifteenth Corps. Brigadier General Giles Smith, recently elevated to command the Fourth Division of the Seventeenth Corps, vividly described how his troops fought off furious attacks from the front, flank and rear. "The first attack, sweeping around our left, and attacking suddenly in the rear, might have thrown any veteran troops into confusion," reported Smith, "but at the command, they promptly took the other side of their works and fought with great coolness." Smith stated that four times during the battle, his troops "were compelled, by attacks in their rear, to change from one side of the works to the other, and change front twice to repel assaults from the left, thus occupying seven different positions during the engagement, besides minor changes of a portion of the command." The fighting was desperate, sometimes hand to hand. Smith testified that during one attack, which lasted about three-quarters of an hour, "men were bayoneted across the works, and officers with their swords fought hand-to-hand with men with bayonets." After seven hours of fighting, Smith triumphantly concluded: "I consider their attack an entire failure." [86]

Sergeant Casey McWayne, fighting in the First Brigade, which General Smith had led before becoming Fourth Division commander, essentially confirmed Smith's account of the battle. The clash on July 22 was "a hand-to-hand fight," McWayne wrote his mother and sisters. He described how General Smith effectively handled their division, "fighting the Rebs in front of him till he drove them back, then got on the opposite side of his works, and fought the Rebs in his rear until he repulsed them. Then, getting back on the other side and fighting them again, [he battled] until he had been back and forth over his works six different times." McWayne also testified matter-of-factly that the Confederate casualties were severe. "We buried 2,420 Rebs," he declared, "and sent over under a flag of truce . . . 800 dead, which makes 3,220 dead Rebs that we know of, and how many they got off we do not know."[87]

About midafternoon the Fifteenth Corps, located on the right flank of the Army of the Tennessee, came under heavy attack when Hood ordered Benjamin Cheatham's corps into the fight. General Logan reported that the Confederates launched "a most desperate assault, [which] broke our line and captured the [four-gun] battery of [Captain Francis] DeGress on the right of the Second Division." Another Union battery at once opened fire on the horses of DeGress's battery, killing the animals so that the Southerners could not carry off the guns. DeGress, who barely managed to escape being captured, reported that thirty-nine horses of his Battery H, First Illinois Light Artillery, were killed, testimony to the awful butchery that humans inflicted upon helpless animals when fighting their wars. Lieutenant George Echte, commanding Battery A of the First Illinois, reported fifty-five of his horses "were killed and captured, mostly killed." Such mutilation of the big animals must have set hard with men like Sherman. Beyond a doubt, it added immensely to the horrors of a Civil War battleground.[88]

When the Confederate attack penetrated the Fifteenth Corps, General Logan was still with the Sixteenth Corps on the army's left flank, where he had ridden soon after taking command. Sherman, however, was near at hand, observing the development of the battle from close to his headquarters at the Howard House (called after a Thomas C. Howard, who occupied the structure). Responding to the breakthrough, Sherman ordered division commander Charles R. Woods to change front at once and strike the Confederates in flank. He also summoned General Schofield to bring forward all his available batteries. Schofield said the batteries responded "at a full gallop," and he gave a memorable account of "witnessing Sherman's splendid conduct."[89]

A trained artilleryman, Sherman seized the chance to become personally involved in throwing back the Rebel assault. According to Schofield, Sherman "led the batteries in person to some high, open ground *in front of our line* near the Howard House, placed them in position and directed their fire, which from that advanced position enfiladed the parapets from which our troops had been driven, and which the enemy then occupied." Schofield declared that "with the aid of that terrible raking fire . . . Union troops very quickly regained the entrenchments they had lost." At that critical moment, the troops also received major assistance from Logan.[90]

Having learned of the fierce Southern attack on the Fifteenth Corps,

Black Jack Logan came galloping back to his old command, leading two brigades for a counterattack. Nearing the breakthrough point, he was "visible for half a mile in almost any direction." The soldiers could see him coming, his long dark hair streaming as he rode. The general was waving his hat and yelling, with a strong voice that carried above the noise of battle, "McPherson and revenge boys!" Shouts of "Black Jack! Black Jack!" rose from hundreds of soldiers. They surged forward, drove the Rebels back and also recovered the artillery, to the great joy of DeGress. Sherman said DeGress had been "in tears" earlier, lamenting the loss of his favorite guns.[91]

While the battle continued until dark, with the Southerners renewing the attack and striving to take the bald hill, the Union forces held firmly. When the July 22 clash was over, the Federals had suffered 3,722 casualties, the most sustained in any of the battles around Atlanta. Confederate losses were considerably greater, but also more difficult to assess, having been estimated from a low of 5,500 to twice that number. Sherman reported "the enemy sustained an aggregate loss of full 8,000 men." General Logan placed the Rebel casualties higher, "at least 10,000." General Cox concurred, stating that "no ingenuity of figuring can reduce the enemy's total loss below the ten thousand at which Logan put it."[92]

Sherman had chosen to let the Army of the Tennessee "fight this battle almost unaided." Perhaps he wanted, as historian Shelby Foote suggested, "McPherson's veterans [to have] the honor of avenging his fall." Sherman also asserted in his memoirs that "if any assistance were rendered by either of the other armies, the Army of the Tennessee would be jealous." Without question, rivalry between the armies existed, particularly involving the Army of the Cumberland and the Army of the Tennessee. The struggle for Chattanooga had been a major catalyst. The Army of the Tennessee, then commanded by Sherman, envisioned itself as coming to the "rescue" of the Cumberlanders after the defeat at Chickamauga. However, the Army of the Cumberland executed an illustrious, legendary charge up Missionary Ridge, which won the battle. During the Atlanta campaign, various incidents had exacerbated the rivalry. "It was unfortunate," as Basil Liddell-Hart stated, "that a commander-in-chief should pander to it." Unfortunate, but not particularly surprising, and certainly an understandable manifestation of human nature. Sherman clearly favored his former command, wanting it to reap the greatest honors and glory of the campaign. Also, Sherman had greater confidence in the Army of the Tennessee than in either of the other armies. He fully believed that it would win the battle.[93]

But Sherman's bias was not the only reason he did not call upon the others for reinforcements. Shifting troops, particularly from the Army of the Cumberland, because of distance and terrain, would have been time-consuming. They well might not have arrived in time to be of any help. Schofield said he favored a counterattack against the left flank of the Rebel assault, with "my reserve [force] and Thomas's," but claimed Sherman told him that "he had asked Thomas to send some troops . . . and the latter had replied that he had none to spare." Sherman made no mention of any counterattack proposal by Schofield, declaring that he sent orders to Schofield and Thomas to press the enemy in their front and, if possible, make a lodgment in Atlanta. The Rebels, reasoned Sherman, must have weakened their lines in order to concentrate troops for an attack. Ordering Schofield and Thomas to press the Southerners in their front was an obvious response. However, Sherman said that both generals "reported that the lines to their front, at all accessible points, were strong . . . and were fully manned."[94]

Generally considered, Sherman had handled the battle well. Hearing heavy firing on the Army of the Tennessee's left flank, which likely signaled the onset of a full-scale engagement, Sherman sent reinforcements to that threatened sector. That they proved to be unnecessary is not indicative of a bad decision. On the contrary, Sherman knew that McPherson both expected Hood to strike that flank, and had sought to strengthen it. When severe firing erupted and intensified on the left, Sherman was reasonably certain that McPherson had surmised correctly. Sending reinforcements to the left flank and rear was an obvious move.[95]

When later in the day the Southerners broke through the line of the Fifteenth Corps, Sherman acted decisively, ordering a division to attack the Confederates in flank, while he himself directed an enfilading artillery fire against them. General Jacob Cox, who observed Sherman in battle several times, thought that Sherman's "mind seemed never so clear, his confidence never so strong, his spirit never so inspiring . . . as in the crisis of some fierce struggle like that of the day when McPherson fell in front of Atlanta."[96]

ON THE DAY after the battle, Sherman and his staff rode along the lines of the Army of the Tennessee, stopping from time to time to say a few words to the soldiers, who cheered him enthusiastically. Thanking the troops for their determined stand, he expressed his grief over McPherson's death—in a sense grieving with the soldiers, who also held McPherson in high esteem. "His death occasioned a profound sense of loss," wrote General Oliver Howard, "a feeling that his place can never be completely filled." Without a doubt Sherman, who wept when McPherson's body was recovered and brought to his headquarters, experienced that "profound sense of loss," for he knew McPherson better than did Howard—or anyone else in the army. Sherman also knew that an emotion-draining task lay before him.[97]

He had to write Emily Hoffman, McPherson's fiancée in Baltimore, a burden all the more difficult because back in the spring Sherman had refused McPherson's request for a furlough to marry her. Due to the impending campaign, Sherman felt that he could not grant his friend's request. He wrote Miss Hoffman a letter at that time, expressing his regret, and closed with the admonition: "Be patient and I know that when the happy day comes for him to stand by your side . . . you will regard him with a high respect & honor that will convert Simple love into something sublime & beautiful." That "happy day" would never come, and Sherman felt compelled to write what surely was one of the most difficult letters he ever composed.[98]

Delaying two weeks before framing the trying message, Sherman declared, "I yield to none on earth except yourself the right to excel me in lamentations for our Dead Hero." He cried out, "Why oh! Why should deaths darts reach the young and brilliant instead of older men who could better have been spared." Writing at some length of his associations with and admiration of McPherson, Sherman then recounted the circumstances of his death and closed by vowing that "while life lasts I will delight in the memory of that bright particular star which has gone before to prepare the way for us more hardened Sinners who must struggle on to the End." Emily Hoffman's staunchly pro-Southern family had never approved of McPherson. "I have the most wonderful news—McPherson is dead," reportedly remarked one of the family upon learning of his death, a comment said to have been heard by the young woman. Emily Hoffman allegedly went to her bedroom, and with food and water brought to her door, spoke to no one, and did not come out for a year. She never married.[99]

Sherman could not delay the choice of a permanent successor to McPherson. Black Jack Logan had done a good job in the heat of battle. General Thomas, however, in the words of Sherman, "remonstrated warmly against my recommending that General Logan should be ... assigned to the command." Thomas supported Oliver Howard for the position, preferring a professional soldier. Also, Thomas had experienced problems with Logan, and did not have a comfortable relationship with the Illinois volunteer general. Sherman certainly was not going to elevate Joe Hooker, with whom he had been dissatisfied for some time. Forthrightly Sherman expressed his opinion of Hooker in a letter to Ellen, characterizing the man as "envious, imperious, and a braggart." Frank Blair, also a politician of course, would have been less acceptable for the command than Logan.

Sherman decided to give the job to Howard, a West Point man who had been seasoned by hard fighting in the eastern theater. He offered an explanation in his memoirs: "I knew we would have to execute some most delicate maneuvers, requiring the utmost skill, nicety, and precision." Sherman was about to change the direction of his advance, as he had told McPherson shortly before he was killed. Sherman intended to send the Army of the Tennessee in a wide, circular, northern sweep around Atlanta, from the east to the west side of the city—then thrusting southward in an attempt, ultimately, to cut Confederate communications. Undoubtedly, although it was a tough decision, Sherman felt better with a West Pointer directing the army's maneuver. And because of General Thomas's attitude, harmony in the high command eliminated Logan.[100]

The choice of Howard had major repercussions. Joe Hooker was furious at the appointment, unfairly blaming Howard for his own debacle at Chancellorsville. He immediately requested to be relieved as commander of the Twentieth Corps. General Thomas "heartily recommended" compliance, and Sherman approved, telling Ellen, "This ought to damn him, showing that he is selfish & not patriotic." General Logan was deeply disappointed at being passed over, for he realized that he was more than adequate in a battle. Sherman well knew that he needed Black Jack to continue leading the Fifteenth Corps and sought to soothe his feelings with a frank letter extolling Logan's invaluable service to the Army of the Tennessee, as well as Sherman's own sincere recognition of, and confidence in, his combat leadership.

"No one," said Sherman, "could have a higher appreciation of the responsibility then devolved on you so unexpectedly [when McPherson was killed] and the noble manner in which you met it." How much influence, if indeed any, this good, diplomatic letter had upon Logan's decision to stay in the army is impossible to determine. Black Jack did resume command of the Fifteenth Corps and continued to lead it with distinction. After all, the Illinois politician had vowed to serve until the Southern rebellion was defeated. But from that time forward, Logan nursed a resentment toward West Point officers, especially Sherman, and as a powerful figure in the U.S. House of Representatives following the war, he would present problems for Sherman.[101]

While Sherman wrestled with the issue of McPherson's successor, he was relieved, at long last, to receive a letter from Ellen. Dated July 20, the lengthy message revealed that his wife's health had improved and conveyed considerable family news. Relative to the death of his older brother James, Cump remarked that "he was a good fellow, but John Barleycorn was too much for him." Succinctly he updated Ellen about the campaign: "We have Atlanta close aboard as the Sailors say, but it is a hard nut to handle. . . . I must gradually destroy the [rail] Roads which make Atlanta a place worth having. . . . Two out of three are broken and we are maneuvering for the third." Naturally he lamented the loss of McPherson, since Ellen knew and liked the young general, who had been very kind to Willy when she visited Vicksburg.

Sherman was a bit frustrated that Ellen, after years of wangling to live near her parents in Lancaster, was contemplating moving away. "I prefer you should stay at Lancaster at whatever sacrifice of feeling or personal convenience til we can see daylight ahead in this war. But if you will go," he advised, "better to Cincinnati than Notre Dame." Medical attendance at Notre Dame, the Indiana town with Minnie's school and a university, would be no better than Lancaster, and "if I get killed, which is not improbable at any moment, you will of course be compelled to live at Lancaster. . . . I daily pass death in the most familiar shape and you should base your calculations on that event." But Ellen seemed to have her mind set. Sherman did consent to her leaving Lancaster, no doubt with reluctance, and told her, "I will not preach Economy anymore." Despite his advice, she soon moved to Notre Dame.[102]

Meanwhile, in the predawn hours of July 27, the Army of the Tennessee began moving to the west side of Atlanta, intending to strike south against the Macon & Western Railroad, the last important communication route for Hood's army. The railroad branched at East Point, about a half dozen miles down the line from Atlanta, with one set of tracks then running southwest to Montgomery, Selma and Mobile, while the other continued to Macon and southeast to Savannah. Late on the morning of the twenty-eighth, as the Fifteenth Corps trudged up a ridge where a Methodist meeting house known as Ezra Church was located, Hood attacked once more—the third time in nine days—marshaling two of his army's three corps for the onslaught.[103]

Sergeant Andrew McCornack was out on the skirmish line, and saw "the Rebs coming in heavy force . . . about noon." He said, "We gave them the best we had in the wheelhouse, but still they came." McCornack thought his whole company was about to be captured, for they were nearly surrounded at one point as they fell back to the Federal line of battle. "The Rebs kept hollering, 'Halt, you son of a bitch,' but I could not see it, and got away alright, and joined the regiment, which was pouring volleys into them the best they knew how." Thus began for McCornack the Battle of Ezra Church, which he declared "the hardest fight I ever saw."[104]

The Union troops, holding high ground, were well positioned to throw back the first assault, and when the Rebels re-formed and struck again, some of the Federals had managed to partially dig in. The determined enemy charges brought severe pressure on the Yankee line, whereupon General Logan assertively raced along the front, roaring above the din of battle, "Hold 'em! Hold 'em!" He called on the Sixteenth and Seventeenth Corps for reinforcements, and six additional regiments joined the fray. Thinking that Hood had weakened his Atlanta lines, Sherman ordered Schofield and Thomas "to make an attempt to break in," but he said that "both reported they found the parapets very strong and fully manned." Darkness brought an end to the clash. Hood had been beaten, and again suffered heavy losses.[105]

In his family letters after the Ezra Church engagement, Sergeant Casey McWayne commented that "we have had some very hard fighting lately." In a matter-of-fact style he said, "We kill a great many Rebs in the fights—now more than ever, because they come out from their works, and charge our men, which is useless for them. For they do not do any good, only get their men slaughtered." McWayne presented a macabre description of the fighting's aftermath, stating that "in burying the Rebs, [who] smelled so, [the men] got a rope and put [it] around their necks, and 4 or 5 got a hold and started with [them], drawing them up in line, just as they [do when] they lay R. R. ties." McWayne told his father that sometimes they "set the contrabands [former slaves] at work," dragging off the dead Southerners "to be buried by hitching a rope around their necks, and four or five start off on a trot, as they call it."[106]

On July 31, Sherman summarized the casualties of Peachtree Creek, Atlanta and Ezra Church in a letter to his brother John, claiming that in "each of these battles we killed as many as our entire casualties." He calculated the total Rebel dead, buried by the Union troops, as 4,700, "and the wounded . . . make the loss over 20,000—we have taken near 3,000 prisoners." He noted that the weather had been "dreadfully hot," and that he did not think Hood would attack again. Of course, Sherman had not thought Hood would attack again after the Battle of Atlanta. He had difficulty grasping the Confederate commander's willingness to see his men "slaughtered"—as Sergeant McWayne so well characterized the result of Hood's assaults.[107]

Both Sherman and Howard, who were together shortly before the Ezra Church clash began, praised General Logan. Sherman's report lauded him for "conspicuous" leadership during the battle, while Howard lavishly wrote that Logan "was indefatigable, and the success of the day is as much attributable to him as to any one man." Unquestionably, Black Jack was continuing to lead with illustrious success, but what he really thought of Sherman is revealed in a letter to his wife, saying that at the Battle of Ezra Church "I had the hardest fight of the campaign . . . and gained a great and complete victory, but will get no credit for it. West Point must have all under Sherman, who is an infernal *brute*." Logan was a smart man who, regardless of his bitterness toward Sherman, assured his wife that "the good sense of it is for me to say not a word but go on and do my duty to my country." That he did.[108]

During the weeks following Hood's three failed attacks, Sherman gradually extended his well-entrenched lines for miles along the west side of Atlanta, in an attempt to reach the Confederate railroad. A veteran remarked, "If digging is the way to put down the rebellion, I guess we will have to do it." Although the Federal entrenchments eventually stretched for about ten miles, Hood countered by extending the Rebel defensive lines farther and farther. Sherman could not reach the railroad with his infantry, writing Halleck that "I do not deem it prudent to extend more to the right." He also made unsuccessful attempts to cut the rail line with cavalry, and George Stoneman's command of about 600 troopers was captured. Sherman was growing impatient and frustrated that he could neither turn the Rebel flank nor, as his men skirmished daily and sometimes heavily with the Southerners, could he identify a suitably weak place to assault. What Sherman could and did do was pound Atlanta with artillery.[109]

On August 7, he told Halleck he would make "Atlanta too hot to be endured. . . . One thing is certain, whether we get inside Atlanta or not, it will be a used-up community by the time we are done with it." New long-range guns were hauled down the railroad from Chattanooga, and on August 9, the General wrote Halleck that "I threw into Atlanta about 3,000 solid shot and shell today, and have got from Chattanooga four 4 and ½ inch rifled guns, and will try their effect." He proposed to Howard, "Let us destroy Atlanta and make it a desolation." That same day he told Grant he intended "to expend about 4,000 rifled shot into the heart of Atlanta."[110]

The Union guns daily blasted both the enemy's defensive works and the city proper. Some civilians were still inside Atlanta, but for all Sherman knew, Hood might have refused to order them out in the hope that their presence would deter the bombardment. A Federal soldier remarked that one Sunday he could see "women walking around on the Rebel works, dressed up in their Sunday go to meeting clothes. . . . Our cannon could have started them off. . . . But the boys . . . had more respect for the ladies [than to fire at them]." He quipped that "if they were in favor of disunion, they may be in favor of union before this month is out."[111]

Secretary of War Edwin Stanton, diligently keeping abreast of Sherman's situation and aware of the general's frustrations, sent him a strongly reassuring message. "Do not imagine that we are impatient of your progress; instead of considering it slow [which Sherman seemed concerned about in a recent letter to Stanton], we regard it rapid, brilliant, and successful beyond our expectations. Take your time," Stanton declared, "and do your work in your own way. This Department is only anxious to afford you every assistance within its power." While the bombardment proceeded, Sherman conceived another plan to get at the Rebel-held railroad south of the city. On August 10, he shared his thinking with Grant: "I may have to leave a corps at the [Western & Atlantic] railroad bridge [over the Chattahoochee], well entrenched, and cut loose with the balance and make a desolating circle around Atlanta."[112]

This was essentially what he did, beginning the move on the night of August 25. "It was one of Sherman's greatest strengths as a general," observed historian Steven Woodworth, "that when the situation in front of him required bold action, he took it." Sherman left the Twentieth Corps, under command of Major General Henry W. Slocum, strongly entrenched on the north side of Atlanta, astride the Western & Atlantic rails at the Chattahoochee bridge. With the rest of the Army of the Cumberland, as well as his two other armies—"reduced to fighting trim"— Sherman cut loose from his supply line and struck southwest in a broad turning march to break Hood's last, vital rail communications. "Lookout for me about St. Marks, Fla., or Savannah, Ga.," he told Halleck, "if I should . . . be cut off from my base."[113]

Sherman's plan worked beautifully; the Army of the Tennessee reached the Atlanta & West Point rails on August 28. After a day of destructive work on that road, General Howard pushed the army eastward toward the Macon & Western at Jonesboro, approximately twenty miles south of Atlanta. Confederate cavalry fired the bridge over the Flint River, but Logan's Fifteenth Corps, which was leading the march, arrived in time to extinguish the flames. Crossing the stream about dusk on August 30, Logan's men dug in immediately on a low-lying ridge approximately a half mile from the railroad. Meanwhile, Thomas and Schofield were about to make lodgments on the Macon & Western several miles nearer to Atlanta.[114]

For some time General Hood remained puzzled about Sherman's intentions—perhaps in part because of Joe Wheeler's greatly exaggerated claims about the destruction he had wrought on Sherman's railroad. Actually the damage Wheeler inflicted was minimal. At one point Hood seems to have thought that Sherman was withdrawing across the Chattahoochee, masking the movement by feigning an attack on the railroads. Also, he wondered whether Sherman was preparing to attack Atlanta from the west. When at last Hood discovered that some of Sherman's forces were about to strike the Macon & Western at Jonesboro, he sent General Hardee, with two of the army's three corps, on what proved to be a futile mission to defend those indispensable rails. About three in the afternoon on the last day of August, the Confederates attacked and were thrown back in the Battle of Jonesboro. "The Johnnies lost awful heavily," wrote Sergeant McCornack, who said that the enemy "came within twenty steps ... [and] I had just as good shots as ever I did at a rabbit." His description was not magnified. Captain Samuel D. McConnell of the badly depleted Seventh Florida Infantry thought the Rebel assault at Jonesboro was "sheer hell." Afterward McConnell was in despair, no doubt sensing that the loss of Atlanta was at hand. Southern casualties at the Battle of Jonesboro totaled 2,500, perhaps more, while General Logan reported casualties of fewer than 200 in the Fifteenth Corps.[115]

BY SEPTEMBER 1, Confederate manpower had been severely depleted as a result of Hood's assaults, while the Yankees had finally gotten control of every railroad into Atlanta. Hood really had no choice but to give up the city. Late in the afternoon of the first, the Grayclad evacuation of Atlanta began, with Alexander Stewart's corps and the Georgia militia tramping southeastward down the McDonough Road. The last troops to clear the city fired the military warehouses and army property that could not be hauled away. Over eighty freight cars, about one-third of which were loaded with ammunition, were set ablaze, sometimes resulting in rapid detonation of shells; and sometimes in huge explosions, as whole caches of gunpowder discharged and lit up the night sky. General Hardee, with the Rebel forces at Jonesboro, slipped away during the night, and eventually joined up with Hood and the remainder of the Army of Tennessee at Lovejoy's Station, about half a dozen miles farther south.[116]

For a time on the afternoon of August 31, and during the following day, Sherman's superior numbers had been located between the two segments of Hood's army. General Thomas proposed that while Schofield and Major General David S. Stanley's troops destroyed the railroad on September 1, he be allowed to swing the Army of the Cumberland east and south to pin the Confederates at Jonesboro between his Cumberlanders and the Army of the Tennessee, with results, declared Thomas,

that would be "eminently beneficial." Sherman was skeptical, telling Thomas that he wanted to see "the first step in the enemy's game,
after he knows we [the mass of the Union Army] are between him and
Atlanta." He believed that "the sooner we get all of our army together in
close order the better." Actually Sherman came up with a more tightly
conceived plan of attack for September 1. He hoped, with a direct route,
to strike the northern flank of the Rebels who faced the Army of the Tennessee. David Stanley and U.S. Brigadier General Jefferson C. Davis were
the key actors, but Stanley, who was to come up on Davis's left flank, was
late. An exasperated Sherman dispatched staff officers to hurry Stanley
on and finally even sent General Thomas to bring up Stanley's troops.
"Had [Stanley] moved straight on by the flank, or by a slight circuit to
his left, he would have inclosed the whole ground occupied by Hardee's
... [men]," who could not, Sherman asserted, "have escaped us; but night
came on, and Hardee did escape."[117]

Nevertheless, Sherman had Atlanta and, on September 2, his lead
elements moved into the city. Sherman said that before giving official
notice of the triumph to the army in general orders, he wanted to be sure
that General Thomas was made aware of the wonderful news. According to Sherman, the usually reserved Virginian reacted by snapping his
fingers, whistling, "and almost dancing." As word spread rapidly among
the Union armies, Sherman recalled that shouts, "wild hallooing, and
glorious laughter" arose from the men in the ranks. And Sherman sent
General Halleck a wire that became at once famous: "Atlanta Is Ours,
and fairly won."[118]

Chapter Twenty-Three

IT'S A BIG GAME, BUT I
KNOW I CAN DO IT

When the mighty fortress at Vicksburg had fallen in 1863, and the United States once more controlled the great Mississippi, Sherman realized, as he then wrote Thomas Ewing, that his name would forever be associated with the nation's history. In comparison with the Atlanta triumph, however, Vicksburg had served as a mere springboard. With the conquest of Atlanta, Sherman's fame skyrocketed. The entire country had been following the Georgia campaign, and the victory news unleashed a wave of celebration and praise. "Sherman's taken Atlanta!" cried the newboys, and a grateful republic rejoiced. Suddenly Sherman was truly famous.[1]

General Grant wrote Sherman that "I feel you have accomplished the most gigantic undertaking given to any general in this war, and with a skill and ability that will be acknowledged in history as unsurpassed, if not unequaled." General Halleck said the campaign was "the most brilliant of the war." The *New York Herald*, often critical of Sherman in the past, lauded the Atlanta achievement as "cyclopean." President Lincoln ordered 100-gun salutes fired in a dozen major cities in honor of "the brilliant achievements of the army under command of Major General Sherman . . . and the capture of Atlanta." As Charles Francis Adams Jr., the great-grandson of John Adams and grandson of John Quincy Adams, who was an officer in the Army of the Potomac, listened to the artillery salute fired in honor of Sherman's triumph, he was moved to write his mother: "How superbly Sherman ... has handled that army." Speaking of "the boldness, the caution, the skill, the judgment, the profound military experience and knowledge of that movement," Adams then asserted, "Unquestionably it is *the* campaign of this war."[2]

While the Vicksburg campaign strategically climaxed a series of far-reaching Union victories in the western theater, and signaled the ultimate doom of the Confederacy by splitting it in half and reopening the Mississippi in its entirety to Union gunboats and transports, the South fought on. The Grayclads hoped somehow—perhaps war weariness in the North, foreign intervention, the genius of Lee, the hand of fate—to reverse the disastrous course of the Confederate war effort. But with the capture of Atlanta, Sherman had struck a blow equally as, if not more, devastating to the Rebels than Vicksburg. The Atlanta triumph, both in military substance and political and psychological timing, was a tremendous Union victory. Sherman had directed 100,000 men into the heart of the Confederacy, defeating one of the two major Southern armies, and capturing the most important rail center in the Deep South. The triumph provided an electrifying boost to Union morale, and just when Grant's costly campaign in Virginia—which was initially expected to achieve a decisive result—seemed to have reached a bloody stalemate.

Furthermore, the fall of Atlanta struck a near crippling blow against the Confederate spirit, convincing many a Southerner that the war could not be won. Still worse for Southern morale, when coupled with the reelection of Abraham Lincoln in the 1864 presidential race, the capture of Atlanta seemed to assure that the Confederate cause was lost. The Rebels had looked hopefully to the United States election, thinking that the defeat of Lincoln would signify the collapse of Northern support for the war and lead to peace negotiations and a recognition of Southern independence. "Sherman had saved Lincoln," asserted Basil Liddell Hart, "and by saving him sealed the fate of the South." Other historians agree.[3]

But to proclaim that the Atlanta triumph "saved Lincoln" may be claiming too much for the impact of Sherman's victory, great as it was;

after all, the President did win 55 percent of the popular vote. On the other hand, Lincoln himself seemed quite doubtful, less than two weeks before the conquest of Atlanta, that he would be reelected—writing that it was "exceedingly probable" that he would not win. Some Republican leaders were still working to oust him as the party's nominee, convinced he could not be reelected. John Sherman wrote Cump in late July, claiming that "the conviction is general that Lincoln has not the energy, dignity, or character to either conduct the war or to make peace." John said "a popular ticket would be Grant and Sherman," an idea that Sherman instantly dismissed: "Fortunately, we are not candidates."[4]

It is a common saying that "timing is everything," and sometimes human affairs do seem so disposed. The climax of Sherman's Atlanta campaign occurred early enough that many of his soldiers could be furloughed to return home and vote in crucial states, like Illinois and Indiana, where absentee voting by soldiers was not allowed. This was important because an overwhelming number of Union troops—78 percent of all Federal soldiers, and fully 86 percent of Sherman's forces—voted for Lincoln. Not only the soldiers' votes, but their influence with the folks back home, while impossible to quantify, undoubtedly worked to the benefit of the President.

The capture of Atlanta also came in time to generate a surging sense of military triumph as the populace contemplated going to the polls. "To the vast majority of Northerners," historian Albert Castel stressed, "the fall of Atlanta means that the war can be won—indeed that it *is* being won." Major General Philip Sheridan's devastation of the Shenandoah Valley that September and David Farragut's recent triumph at Mobile Bay did not arouse Northerners like the capture of Atlanta had. No one can know how many voters, because of the Atlanta success, decided to vote for Lincoln rather than either staying at home or voting for Democratic nominee George McClellan. It is sensible to assume that some did, for Sherman's victory changed the bleak atmosphere in the North. General Sherman had won a military victory whose political consequences—ironically, considering his hostility toward politics—were as great as, probably greater than, any other campaign of the war.[5]

In addition to what the Atlanta campaign did for the nation, it also showcased Sherman's military talent. First and foremost was the logistical triumph. With a precarious single-track railroad, extending four hundred miles across Kentucky, Tennessee, part of Alabama and north Georgia, Sherman had supplied 100,000 fighting men with the necessities for making war. Those vulnerable rails had to be protected, obviously, from inevitable enemy attacks. When the Rebels did break the railroad, as was certain sometimes to occur, Sherman's repair crews were qualified for any challenge, even building major new bridges and trestles. Also, while the rails were broken, his forces could still operate, because he had stored sufficient supplies at key depots.

The General was fully aware of the magnitude of the achievement, as evidenced by his letters to Thomas Ewing. On August 11, he had written Ellen's father that "for 100 days not a man or horse has been without ample food, or a musket or gun without adequate ammunition. I esteem this a triumph greater than any success that has attended me in Battle or in Strategy." The accomplishment "has not been the result of blind chance [for] at this moment I have abundant supplies for twenty days, and I keep a Construction Party in Chattanooga that can in ten days repair any break that can be made to my rear." He also maintained "a large depot of supplies at Chattanooga & Allatoona . . . fortresses which no cavalry force of the enemy can reach, and in our wagons generally manage to have from ten to twenty days supply." After Atlanta, Sherman felt he had both achieved his potential and measured up to the stature of his father-in-law. With obvious satisfaction, he wrote Ewing on September 15, declaring that his foster father had "lived to See the little red-headed urchin not only handle an hundred thousand men, smoothly and easily, but fight them . . . at a distance of hundreds of miles from his arsenals and sources of supply." Sherman indeed had directed a sparkling achievement, and his bragging to Ewing is understandable.[6]

The Atlanta campaign had also proven that Sherman was a master of maneuver warfare. Time and again he successfully performed turning movements, enabling him to maintain the offensive initiative, avoid the enemy's strongpoints, exploit the enemy's vulnerability and largely determine the course of combat, thus presenting his opponent the undesirable choice of retreating or accepting battle at a disadvantage. "Successful maneuver requires," as set forth by the United States Army, "flexibility in organization, administrative support, and command and control." Maneuver may also be interrelated, as it was in Sherman's Atlanta campaign, with other principles of generalship, particularly offensive action, economy of force and surprise.

Sherman was at his best when he flanked the Confederates at Snake Creek Gap, surprising Johnston and forcing the enemy commander to give up his formidable defenses, long in preparation, at Rocky Face Ridge. His maneuver at the Chattahoochee River was also masterly, deceiving Joe Johnston by feigning a downstream crossing and then executing a bloodless success on the enemy's eastern flank, which turned Johnston out of another strong position. Yet again, Sherman deftly shifted the Army of the Tennessee from the northwestern side of Atlanta to the eastern side, striking south toward Decatur, and placing his forces astride a vital enemy railroad. These and other well-conceived flanking movements highlighted the campaign.[7]

Sherman's logistical genius, and his cool prowess for successfully maneuvering his forces to avoid the big, costly battles and yet achieve his objective, are among the most significant reasons that he has long been more relevant than other generals of the American Civil War. Of course there have been criticisms. Sherman, some have alleged, failed to carry out Grant's primary campaign order. From Washington, D.C., on April 4, Grant had instructed his chief lieutenant: "You I propose to move against Johnston's army, to break it up, and to get into the interior of the enemy's country as far as you can, inflicting all the damage you can against their war resources." While Sherman had not destroyed the Southern army, it suffered severely in the fighting around Atlanta after Hood became the commander. The heavy Confederate losses could not be easily replaced. Although Sherman did not "break it up," he had gained an impressive tactical victory in forcing the Rebel army out of Atlanta. More to the point, Grant's orders essentially constituted a general guideline, rather than a demand for a one-two punch in a specific order. As Grant explained: "I do not propose to lay down for you a plan of campaign, but simply to lay down the work it is desirable to have done, and leave you free to execute it in your own way." Grant surely realized that many factors would influence the development, direction and emphasis of the north Georgia campaign. He trusted Sherman to make adjustments for inevitable, unforeseeable events, as well as executing decisions which could be faced only once the campaign got under way.[8]

When Sherman responded to Grant on April 10, he projected a campaign of turning movements that would force the Confederate Army back to Atlanta, which he said "is about as far ahead as I feel disposed to look." Sherman's basic focus was strategic, expressed in the promise that "I will ever bear in mind that Johnston is at all times to be kept so busy that he can not in any event send any part of his command against you." Grant certainly understood what Sherman planned, and he neither objected nor sought to make modifications. It is important to keep in mind that Grant and Sherman had already discussed their plans in person, and at length, when they conferred in Cincinnati only a short time prior to the early April correspondence.[9]

As the campaigning progressed, the city of Atlanta inevitably loomed more and more significant, serving as the base of supplies for the Confederate Army falling back upon it, and as an increasingly powerful symbol of Southern resistance to the Yankee invader. Sherman sometimes acquired Confederate newspapers, which proclaimed the absolute necessity of defending Atlanta for military, political and morale reasons. Doubtless Sherman sensed, as he advanced closer and closer to Atlanta, that capturing the city would inflict great damage, in Grant's words, "against [the Confederate] war resources," both material and psychological. Simultaneously Northern spirits were lifted. The Union perception of the Atlanta victory instantly confirmed the great importance of Sherman's triumph. He had become a national hero.

THE QUESTION FACING Sherman was what to do next. He had witnessed appalling numbers of people killed and wounded, and he still could see no end to the war and its horrendous loss of life. While serving in Mississippi, he had led an army from Vicksburg across the state to Meridian and back, as a means of conducting psychological warfare against the South. Primarily he destroyed property of military value, but inevitably a significant amount of private property was razed as well. Sherman became convinced that inflicting casualties, however lurid the numbers might be, would never be as effective as attacks on the Southern psyche through the destruction of property—and obviously this kind of warfare would also spare the lives of his men. He had conducted the Mississippi campaign without a supply line, carrying provisions in his wagons, heavily supplemented by foodstuffs taken from the enemy. Now he was thinking about the same type of campaign, except that this time it would be on a much greater scale.

Mulling over the possibility of marching far deeper into Georgia, Sherman began to correspond with Grant about future operations. On September 10, Grant invited Sherman's ideas, telling him that "as soon as your men are sufficiently rested and preparations can be made... another campaign should be commenced. We want to keep the enemy constantly pressed." Sherman was "perfectly alive to the importance of pushing our advantage to the utmost"; however, he did not think further operations dependent upon the railroad were feasible. The number of soldiers required to protect it was already at a maximum. On the other hand, if the navy could control "the Savannah River as high as Augusta, or the Chattahoochee as far up as Columbus," then Sherman declared, "I can sweep the whole State of Georgia."[10]

Within a few days Sherman was thinking more daringly, and in larger focus. If the Union fleet could be sent to the mouth of the Savannah River, he assured Grant, "I would not hesitate to cross the State of Georgia with 60,000 men, hauling some stores and depending on the country for the balance." Speculating about how the enemy might react to such a march, Sherman projected possible countermeasures that he likely would take. He closed by saying: "If you can whip Lee, and I can march to the Atlantic, I think Uncle Abe will give us twenty days leave of absence to see the young folks." Sherman well realized that Grant, as general-in-chief of the United States armies, with oversight of the grand strategy for the war, was the only man whom he needed to persuade about the value of such a campaign in order to get the permission he sought. Sherman pursued the subject at every opportunity.[11]

But in the latter part of September, General Hood moved around Sherman's right flank, leading the Confederate army west and north to strike the Western & Atlantic Railroad in Sherman's rear. Leaving one corps to hold Atlanta and defend the Chattahoochee bridges, Sherman moved north on October 3 and 4, with about 45,000 troops, and gave chase to Hood, whose men were already ripping up the railroad from Big Shanty to Acworth. When the Southerners pushed on northward, Sherman guessed correctly that they were heading for his large supply depot at the Allatoona Pass. By signal flags from atop high gound, he ordered the division of Brigadier General John Corse, at Rome, to reinforce the Allatoona garrison at once. A fierce fight resulted, with each side suffering more than 700 killed, wounded or missing. Then proceeding north to Dalton, Hood took the surrender of an 800-man railroad garrison, about 600 of whom were blacks. The prisoners were forced to tear up railroad track, and evidence points to the blacks being badly treated. Several were executed.[12]

When General Hood then marched westward into north Alabama, Sherman decided to give up the chase. Characterizing Hood as an "eccentric" man, he remarked that "he can turn and twist like a fox and wear out my army in pursuit." Sherman had no idea what Hood might do next. The Confederate commander's movements worried General George Thomas, who was back in Nashville tending to affairs of the Department of the Cumberland. Thomas thought, correctly as matters developed, that Hood well might be planning to invade Tennessee and march on Nashville. The truth was that Sherman had no desire to follow Hood, wherever the Rebel commander might go. As he later said, he was "strongly convinced of the wisdom of my proposition to change the whole tactics of the campaign." He wrote Grant: "Why will it not do to leave Tennessee to the forces which General Thomas has, and the reserves soon to come to Nashville, and for me to destroy Atlanta and . . .

march across Georgia to Savannah or Charleston, breaking roads and doing irreparable damage? We can not remain on the defensive."[13]

Sherman and Grant exchanged telegrams throughout October and into November, discussing Sherman's proposed campaign. Sherman advocated destroying the railroad from Chattanooga to Atlanta, and then "striking out with wagons for Milledgeville, Millen, and Savannah." If he did continue to maintain the railroad, he said it would cost a thousand men monthly, "and will gain no result," while the "utter destruction of [Georgia's rail] roads, houses, and people will cripple their military resources.... I can make the march," he confidently declared, "and make Georgia howl." Naturally Grant informed General Halleck and War Secretary Stanton (and through Stanton the President) of Sherman's proposed march. Stanton told Grant that Lincoln "feels much solicitude" about Sherman's plan, "and hopes that it will be maturely considered."[14]

Grant himself raised several issues. Like Thomas, he worried that Hood would march into middle Tennessee and declared that "he ought to be met and prevented from getting north of the Tennessee River." Thinking, as he typically did, of trying to destroy enemy military forces, Grant said, "If there is any way of getting at Hood's army, I would prefer that." Sherman replied strongly. If he were "to let go Atlanta and North Georgia and make for Hood," he was convinced that "no single army can catch him," and worse, "Jeff Davis' cherished plan of making me leave Georgia by maneuvering" would have succeeded, and "the whole effect of my [Atlanta] campaign will be lost." On the other hand, if Sherman were "to move through Georgia, smashing things to the sea," he believed that Hood would follow him. "Instead of being on the defensive [Atlanta and the railroad], I would be on the offensive; instead of guessing at what [Hood] means to do, he would have to guess at my plans." Again Sherman declared, "We cannot now remain on the defensive." If Hood did move toward Nashville, Sherman thought Thomas had a force strong enough to stop him, as he assured both Grant and Halleck.[15]

Another concern on Grant's mind was that Sherman might be "bushwhacked by all the old men, little boys, and such railroad guards as are still left at home." Sherman was not worried. He intended to lead an army 60,000 strong, made up of "only the best fighting material." He could take care of himself against any force the enemy might possibly bring against him. Grant had also raised the issue of preparing a coastal base to supply Sherman's forces, but Sherman assured him that his men would need no supplies. Everything they required would be taken from the countryside. Exuding confidence, he wrote on October 22, "I will subsist . . . luxuriously."[16]

He wrote General Halleck that the "movement is not purely military or strategic, but it will illustrate the vulnerability of the South." Sherman believed that when the rich planters "see their fences and corn and hogs and sheep vanish before their eyes," they will finally realize "what war means." He also told Halleck that "it is overwhelming to my mind that there are thousands of people abroad and in the South who will reason thus: If the North can march an army through the South it is proof positive that the North can prevail in this contest." The march would be "a demonstration to the world . . . that we have a power which Davis cannot resist."[17]

Sherman had determined to bring the war home to the South in a devastating and unforgettable manner. To cavalry commander James Wilson he ominously said, "I . . . propose to leave a trail that will be recognized fifty years hence." He was thinking beyond any general of his day. The most effective way to end the conflict was to destroy the support base, both material and psychological, of the Confederate war effort. He would strike hard at railroads and all war-production facilities; but additionally, in marching wherever he pleased, living off the countryside, and demonstrating that no one could stop him, he would be leveling a terrible blow against civilian morale, and through the civilians against Southern military morale.[18]

"Man has two supreme loyalties—to country and to family," declared Basil Liddell Hart. Stating that with most men the family is the stronger loyalty, he contended that so long as their families are safe, men "will defend their country, believing that by their sacrifice they are safeguarding their families also." However, when the family itself is in danger, then "the bonds of patriotism, discipline, and comradeship are loosened."

This was the devastating impact of Sherman's march, that in taking the war home to the Southern populace, he simultaneously and inescapably struck at the will of the Confederate soldier to continue fighting. For years to come many Southerners, while never convinced that the United States had been right in prosecuting the war, would live with a sullen memory of Northern military might, and that largely because of Sherman's awful, sixty-mile-wide swath of destruction through Georgia and the Carolinas.[19]

After weeks of considering Sherman's arguments for the campaign, Grant's concerns for his safety and success subsided. Sherman got the backing he wanted. "On mature reflection," Grant wrote Stanton, "I believe Sherman's proposition is the best that can be adopted." Assuring the secretary of war that both Thomas and Sherman would be strong enough to meet whatever challenges developed, Grant declared: "Such an army as Sherman has (and with such a commander) is hard to corner or capture." To his credit, Grant had concluded that Sherman was right in not pursuing Hood, because General Thomas, with the force Sherman had left with him, would be able to deal with Hood if it became necessary. Just as Sherman had contended, Grant echoed his thinking on November 2, writing that "I do not really see that you can withdraw from where you are to follow Hood, without giving up all we have gained in territory. I say, then, go as you propose." Five days later Grant telegraphed: "I think everything here [the administration] favorable now. Great good fortune attend you. I believe you will be eminently successful."[20]

Sherman fully realized that the campaign would be a demanding one, and if he failed, the critics would swarm like vultures after a fresh kill. Probably, however, his confidence had seldom been greater. On the last day of October, he told a new staff officer, Henry Hitchcock, an observant young man who would keep a valuable diary throughout the march, "It's a big game, but I can do it—I *know* I can do it."[21]

SOON AFTER SHERMAN captured Atlanta he evacuated the civilian population from the city, allowing "no trade, manufactories, nor any citizens there at all," and telling General Halleck that "if the people raise a howl against my barbarity and cruelty, I will answer that war is war, and not popularity seeking." Sherman had no intention of allowing his forces to be burdened with caring for civilians, which "absorbs the attention of officers in listening to everlasting complaints and special grievances that are not military." He noted too that poor residents of a war-torn city would compel the army "sooner or later to feed them or see them starve under our eyes."[22]

The civilian removal policy at once generated an outcry, as Sherman had anticipated. Leading the protesters was General Hood, with whom Sherman engaged in an intense, fiery correspondence. The mayor of Atlanta, strongly supported by two councilmen, entered into the controversy as well. Sherman defended his decision astutely, being more knowledgeable about military practices, precedents and history than Hood or the others. In response to Mayor James M. Calhoun's plea that the policy generated "consequences appalling and heart-rending," Sherman declared that "war is cruelty and you can not refine it. . . . You might as well appeal against the thunder-storm as against these terrible hardships of war [which] . . . are inevitable." The removal of the civilians was affirmed in Washington. Halleck wrote Sherman that his actions were "fully approved by the War Department. Not only are you justified by the laws and usages of war in removing these people, but I think it was your duty to your own army to do so."

While corresponding with Grant, and contemplating his next move after the fall of Atlanta, Sherman conversed with three Confederates, former members of the U.S. Congress, who came into Atlanta under a flag of truce. He tried to convince them to persuade the governor of Georgia, Joseph E. Brown, that he should use his influence and power to take Georgia out of the war. The three men knew how much Georgia had already suffered, and Sherman promised that if the governor and other officials would cooperate, and pull Georgia out of the Confederacy, he would spare the state any more destruction. Nothing came of the proposal, and Sherman probably never expected anything from it, but it says something about the General's desire for the war to be over.

On November 10, he wrote his son Tom that while the people acclaimed him a great general, and he had achieved "what the People call fame & Glory," he would rather, if somehow it were possible, "come home quietly and have you & Willy meet me at the cars than to hear the shouts of the people."[23]

By mid-November, Sherman's forces had destroyed the railroad and telegraph communications for most of the distance back to Chattanooga and were poised to strike out from Atlanta "to ruin Georgia," as Sherman had earlier, vigorously summarized the objective. Before departing the city, however, he ordered the destruction of everything that might possibly benefit the enemy. Already Atlanta had suffered major punishment, some of the devastation inflicted by the Confederates, who in preparing to defend the city, had stripped suburban houses of wood for fortifications and had burned others to clear fields of fire for artillery and musketry. When later forced to evacuate Atlanta, the Rebels demolished the Atlanta Rolling Mill; torched buildings containing supplies they were unable to remove; and set fire to ordnance-filled freight cars, the explosions of which leveled several nearby structures and set fire to others.

But Sherman, of course, inflicted more damage than the Confederates. When he brought the war to Atlanta's doorstep in midsummer—ominously telling Halleck that the city would be "a used-up community when we are done with it"—his long-range artillery bombardment, day and night for several weeks, had rained indiscriminate death and destruction. A woman was struck by a shell fragment and killed while ironing clothes in her house. A small girl was hit and killed by a shell at a street intersection. An African-American barber, standing outside his shop, died when struck by a ricocheting shell fragment. Others died in similar, random circumstances. Houses, factories and stores burned. Dust and smoke polluted the atmosphere. Young Carrie Berry, whose tenth birthday came in August, wrote in her diary: "How I wish the Federals would quit shelling us and we could get out of the cellar and get some fresh air." Once the bombardment did cease, and the Yankees occupied the city, various structures were dismantled as the soldiers sought wood to build huts for shelter.

Then finally, two and a half months after Atlanta fell, and immediately before marching south and east across Georgia, General Sherman wreaked destruction upon the city yet again. This time, in terms of property damage, the devastation was the worst ever. All military resources were to be destroyed, and these were broadly defined. A large force under the direction of Captain Orlando M. Poe, Sherman's chief engineer, did the work, They torched the railroad depots, the roundhouse, the machine shops, foundries, merchant mills and arsenals. Machinery that could not be destroyed by fire "was most ingeniously broken and made worthless." One of the machine shops, which had been used by the Confederates as an arsenal, contained piles of live shells that detonated when flames reached them, and created a night, recalled Sherman, "made hideous by the bursting of shells, whose fragments came uncomfortably near" the house where the General was staying. The fires spread to a block of stores, and Sherman recorded that "the heart of the city was in flames all night," but added that the fires "did not reach . . . the great mass of dwelling-houses." In years to come, some Southerners claimed that Sherman brutally burned Atlanta to the ground, a charge that is often taken for granted.

Certainly Sherman did not intend that private dwellings, churches, hospitals and other nonmilitary facilities should be destroyed. Colonel William Cogswell, in command of the provost guard, was charged with enforcing the orders against indiscriminate arson, even if it meant "shooting on the spot all incendiaries." Cogswell's assignment proved virtually impossible. His guards could not be everywhere, and they were concentrated in the downtown areas. Some soldiers had their own ideas of how Atlanta should be treated, and "a careful and selective destruction" was not what they had in mind. They wanted to burn the whole city, and clearly the provost guard could not stop every one of them. Some men who wanted to torch all of Atlanta claimed to be retaliating for the Confederate burning of Chambersburg, Pennsylvania.

There were also men in the grip of alcohol, and excited beyond control by the prospect of themselves contributing to the great conflagration. In fact, some drunken soldiers, in defiance of orders, had been setting fires

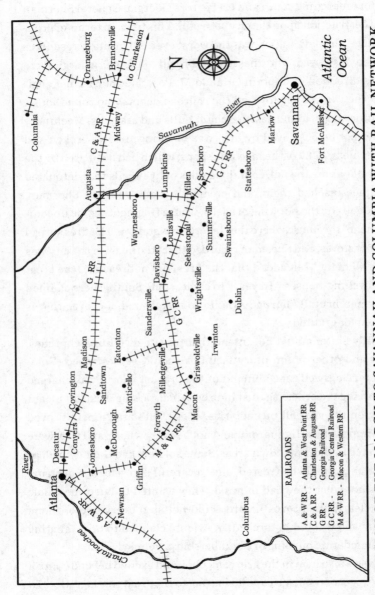

REGION OF THE MARCH TO SAVANNAH AND COLUMBIA WITH RAIL NETWORK

On November 16, 1864, Sherman moved out of Atlanta with 60,000 men, heading southeastward on the march to the sea. Map by Jim Moon Jr.

for several days before the burning authorized by Sherman actually took place. There is no doubt that many residences—perhaps a great many—and some business buildings that were of no military value whatsoever were destroyed in spite of Sherman's intentions and instructions to save them. And regardless of the General's earlier evacuation orders, some civilians still remained in the city.

Martha Quillen watched as a line of burning structures drew nearer to her home. She could "hear the wild shouts" raised by Union troops, who carried blazing torches as they approached closer and closer. Fully expecting her house to be set fire, she gained a last-minute reprieve, only because some Federal officers decided to establish a headquarters in her parlor, and thus posted guards to protect the place from the arsonists.

A sergeant in the First Michigan Engineers and Mechanics got caught up in setting fires to houses. When about to torch one home, a little girl came up and pleaded with him "not to burn our house." Looking into his face and calling him "Mr. Soldier," she inquired, if he did torch the house, "Where are we going to live?" The sergeant said he dispensed with the torch and left, for he no longer "had the heart" to burn the place.

Carrie Berry was still in the city, her father having remained there because he was doing some work for the Union Army. Carrie thought it looked like the whole of Atlanta was on fire when the Federals left. Marauding Yankee soldiers, wrote the ten-year-old, "behaved very badly." She added that "nobody knows what we have suffered." And Martha Quillen remarked that she hoped no one "will ever expect me to love Yankees."

The truth is that when Sherman's forces left Atlanta, the city had suffered severe damage, although determining the precise extent of the loss seems impossible. It is equally true, as Sherman himself indicated, that the whole of Atlanta was not destroyed. Nor was the General alone responsible for all of the devastation that did take place. Nevertheless, the name "Sherman" would come to symbolize that terrible time in Atlanta, when a deep and lasting scar, which rankles to this day, was created in the hearts of many Southerners.[24]

....

WITH THE SMOKING RUINS of Atlanta at his back, Sherman set out through central Georgia on the morning of November 16, "to demonstrate the vulnerability of the South," as he explained his objective to General Thomas. He would "make its inhabitants feel that war and individual ruin are synonymous terms." Even those who were not victims, "who did not suffer from the march," observed historian Joseph T. Glatthaar, "had to realize that they were just as vulnerable to such destructive marches." Railroads, factories, farms, all manner of supplies and many private houses would be destroyed, with Sherman making a mockery of Confederate President Jefferson Davis's recent assertion, while visiting the Rebel army, that the Yankees would have to retreat from Georgia or starve, and predicting that the retreat would be "more disastrous than was that of Napoleon from Moscow."[25]

Far from retreating, Sherman was advancing with an army of more than 62,000 men, the great majority of whom were infantry, numbering 55,329. The cavalry command was 5,063 strong, while the artillery arm numbered 1,812 men, and sixty-five guns. The entire force comprised experienced and physically hardened troops, who were grouped into two wings of approximately equal numbers. The right wing was commanded by General Oliver Howard, and the left by General Henry Slocum, with Howard's wing made up of the Fifteenth and Seventeenth Corps, while Slocum's wing was composed of the Fourteenth and Twentieth Corps. The two wings would follow separate routes, although roughly paralleling each other, as each advanced in two corps columns, a formation that enabled Sherman to present a wide front, sometimes as much as sixty miles. This was a good configuration for confusing the enemy about the army's destination, as well as for foraging and wreaking destruction. It was in fact the same type of formation that he used back in the winter when marching across Mississippi.[26]

Howard's right wing led off to the southeast along the Macon & Western Railroad, as if heading for Macon, while Slocum's wing marched directly east through Decatur, along the Georgia Railroad, initially following a path leading in the direction of Augusta. The immediate objective was Milledgeville, the capital of Georgia, which lay about one hundred miles distant from Atlanta, and more or less in the middle between the two diverging lines of march that led out from that destroyed town. The plan was for the left and right wings gradually to converge toward Milledgeville on a trek that was expected to take approximately a week, with the troops covering about fifteen miles a day, while destroying anything of value to the Confederate war effort. Sherman and his staff rode away from Atlanta with Slocum's wing. "We turned our horses to the east," remembered Sherman, and "Atlanta was soon lost behind the screen of trees, and became a thing of the past." He recalled the day as "extremely beautiful, clear sunlight, with bracing air." The good weather did not last however, as rain and drizzle soon made the roads slick and muddy. Sherman also noted "a 'devil-may-care' feeling pervading officers and men, that made me feel the full load of responsibility, for success would be accepted as a matter of course, whereas, should we fail, this 'march' would be adjudged the wild adventure of a crazy fool."[27]

Sherman's orders for the campaign are engaging, conveying a determination to preserve secrecy about the army's destination, immediate and ultimate, and a confidence that both officers and men would follow his lead without question. They would be advancing "for a special purpose," he told them, which was "well known to the War Department and General Grant." He stated that it was sufficient for the army to know that the mission "involves a departure from our present base, and a long and difficult march to a new one." Their objective was "to strike a blow at our enemy that will have a material effect in producing what we all so much desire—his complete overthrow."[28]

The army was instructed to "forage liberally on the country during the march," but in a systematic manner. Authorized foraging parties were to be organized by each brigade commander, and led by "discreet officers," who would gather "corn or forage of any kind, meat of any kind, vegetables, corn-meal, or whatever is needed by the command." Only during a halt or camp might individual soldiers seek "turnips, potatoes, and other vegetables, and . . . drive in stock [that was] within sight of their camp." The regular foraging parties would gather the bulk of necessities, with a goal of keeping the wagons supplied with "at least ten days' provisions."[29]

As for horses, mules and wagons, which obviously would be required in large number, Sherman said "the cavalry and artillery may appropriate freely and without limit" from Georgia's inhabitants, "discriminating, however, between the rich, who are usually hostile, and the poor or industrious, usually neutral or friendly." He did not anticipate any difficulty in finding whatever his army needed, because he had studied the 1860 census data and planned to travel through some of the most bountiful agricultural counties in the state. Although everything of military value to the enemy was to be destroyed, only corps commanders were entrusted with the power to burn private houses, cotton gins, mills, etc.—and for them Sherman laid down a general principle. Wherever "the army is unmolested, no destruction of such property should be permitted"; however, he said that if guerrillas, bushwhackers or any inhabitants offered resistance, then the corps commanders were ordered to respond with "a devastation more or less relentless according to the measure of such hostility."[30]

Major Henry Hitchcock enthused that "Sherman's plans are splendid." The army did carry them out in the main, although certainly not to perfection. Sherman later admitted: "No doubt many acts of pillage, robbery, and violence, were committed by these parties of foragers ... for I have since heard of jewelry taken from women, and the plunder of articles that never reached the commissary; but these acts were exceptional and incidental." Sherman's characterization of such plundering as "exceptional and incidental" goes too far in minimizing the facts. The excesses certainly were not limited to foragers. At Madison, some fifty miles out from Atlanta on the Georgia Railroad, the Twentieth Corps entered the town, and Union Captain David P. Conyngham declared that "pillaging went on with a vengeance." He said "stores were ripped open," and soldiers grabbed whatever appealed to them. "Cellars of rich wine were discovered and prostrate men gave evidence of its strength." When a milliner's store was sacked, the captain claimed that soldiers decorated their caps and horses with ribbons, "and the negro wenches, too, came in for a share of the decorative spoils." Major Hitchcock observed that problems often developed because widespread straggling took place. Stopping soldiers from going into houses was a particularly futile task. Such an endeavor, declared Hitchcock, would "require a guard for every house." The fictitious but unforgettable Scarlett O'Hara in *Gone with the Wind*, blasting a Yankee bummer with "Pa's pistol" on the staircase at Tara, seems appropriately realistic. Sherman himself remarked that stragglers "are harder to conquer than the enemy."[31]

Relative to the legitimate foraging parties, there seemed to be, in Sherman's remarkable words, "a charm about it that attracted the soldiers, and it was [considered] to be a privilege to be detailed on such a party." He said the men would return "mounted on all sorts of beasts, which were at once taken from them and appropriated to the general use; but the next day they would start out again on foot." Without doubt, many wild and dangerous scenes erupted all across the wide swath cut by Sherman's two wings, as the foragers scoured the countryside in search of provisions. "At and near every farm house we hear constant shooting," reported Major Hitchcock—shooting indicative, particularly, of the men killing pigs and chickens. Not surprisingly, the exuberant and often careless soldiers sometimes shot themselves, or one another. "It is reported tonight," wrote Hitchcock on November 19 "that two of our men were killed today, and three wounded, all accidentally," while they were foraging.[32]

Sergeant Casey McWayne offered some intriguing insights about the march. He said that the troops lacked for nothing, in spite of all the Georgians' efforts at concealment. He described how the inhabitants "would tie their horses & mules in swamps, drive their cattle, sheep, and hogs onto islands in their swamps," and bury all their "clothes, corn, salt, & pork, jewelry, money . . . —well, in fact, everything they had in the house except themselves. But they were found by the Damned Yankees after all." McWayne explained that whenever the men discovered soft ground, they would take the ramrods from their rifled muskets, run them into the ground until they struck something solid and then begin digging. "I dug up a valise on a plantation," he wrote, "and found $1,630 in Confederate money."

Then he recorded an event that he thought his family would find amusing. While hunting around one plantation, and finding some fresh dirt, the soldiers pushed their ramrods down and struck what they thought was probably a board. As they began digging, suddenly a voice from beneath yelled: "Hold on, let me *out*, I will surrender." When the men got a grip on the board and pulled it up, "there was a Johnny. He had dug a hole in the ground, placed a board over it, with a hole in it—so he could get air—then covered it over with dirt, but was careful to keep the hole open to get a supply of fresh air." McWayne speculated that "this was done by the women folks, I suppose," and concluded: "You may bet he was a scared Johnny."[33]

The Second Minnesota's Judson W. Bishop recorded another scene of soldiers probing a plot of recently dug-up ground near a farmhouse. Some ladies watched with considerable interest from the veranda as the men retrieved a box, removed the top and found the remains of a dog, which instantly rebuked them, said Bishop, "with an odoriferous protest that reached their consciences by the most direct route." Immediately they replaced the lid and returned the animal to its burial ground. One of the women then remarked that "poor Fido was not resting in peace . . . that day," for this was "the fourth time he had been resurrected since morning."[34]

Obviously Union troops seeking food and animals (and sometimes plunder) were not welcomed by Georgians who found themselves in the path of the Yankees. One woman, standing by the porch of a shack with two small boys, watched a soldier carrying off two of her chickens, while just beyond him a column of Union soldiers tramped by. "Our men will fight you as long as they live," she bitterly declared, "and these boys will fight you when they grow up." On another occasion, a well-dressed woman is said to have walked up to a Union column as it marched and spit on a soldier. The men retaliated by burning her house. Near Milledgeville, Rebel cavalry surprised Federal foragers and a gunfight erupted inside a home. When a Yankee seized a woman as a shield, she called for the Rebels to kill him, even if they shot her. One man got a clear shot at the forager's head, and the woman, splattered with brains and blood, survived.

Sometimes, not surprisingly, vindictive and ridiculous charges were aimed at Sherman. A rumor spread that the General received one-fifth of everything the foragers took. One woman claimed that Sherman collected gold watches and had stolen over two hundred by the time he left the South. Another woman, whose farm had been overrun, addressed a nasty letter to Mrs. Sherman, inquiring if the General had told her about the mulatto girl accompanying him, who was "spoken of by the Negroes ... as Sherman's wife." Historian Burke Davis wrote that he had never found any other claim that Sherman had a black mistress. Whether Ellen actually received the letter is unknown.

While many a Georgian condemned the Yankees for ravaging the countryside, it should be noted that the Confederates often treated Southerners just as badly, if not worse. Major General Joseph Wheeler's Rebel troopers had a fearsome reputation. Retired merchant John W. Pitts told some of Sherman's staff that "the Confederates were a great deal worse than our men, that they pillaged and plundered everybody, and the inhabitants dreaded their coming."[35]

But Sherman's destructiveness could be terrible. On a cold November 22, a day punctuated by, in Sherman's words, "a high, raw wind," the General came up on a plantation north of Milledgeville that soon got a full dose of Union vengeance. The property belonged to former Georgia governor Howell Cobb, a prominent politician who had served as Speaker of the U. S. House of Representatives and secretary of the treasury before becoming a strong secessionist and a major general in the Confederate Army—"one of the *head devils*," according to Major Hitchcock. "Of course we confiscated his property," remembered Sherman, "and found it rich in corn, beans, peanuts and sorghum-molasses."

Perhaps Sherman was particularly incensed by the story of an aged African-American. The General was sitting with his back to a fire, taking a drink of whiskey and smoking a cigar, when a black man approached, trembling with fear. Hitchcock said Sherman "talked kindly—reassured him, etc." When Sherman asked why he trembled, he said "that he wanted to be sure that we were in fact 'Yankees.' . . ." The black man then told about a group of Rebels, disguised as Federals, who went among the African-Americans, coaxing them to abandon the plantation. When they got several committed to leave, the whites flogged those blacks until they were nearly dead. The elderly black initially was about as scared of Sherman as he was of the Rebels, for he had been assured that Sherman and his men were savages who would burn the slaves alive. He was greatly relieved when he realized Sherman would not harm him. Indeed, when the Federal troops passed through Conyers, a woman admitted to some of Sherman's staff that she had told her slaves that the Yankees "shot, burned, and drowned negroes" in Atlanta, both young and old. Sherman told the African-Americans to help themselves to whatever supplies they wanted from Howell Cobb's plantation, also instructing the soldiers to do likewise. That night huge bonfires consumed the fence rails, while both slaves and soldiers carried off an immense quantity of provisions. Sherman gave orders that as soon as he left, everything was to be burned, sparing only the slave quarters, which the blacks needed for shelter. Like their commander, many of the men in Sherman's army realized that slavery was at the root of the rebellion. Thus a great host of them were ready to pillage and burn the mansions of the planter aristocracy, as well as destroying anything that symbolized slavery—auction blocks, slave pens, whipping posts, even dogs used to hunt escaped slaves.[36]

November 22 is also notable for the clash at Griswoldville, the only actual battle during Sherman's trek to Savannah. Believing that Sherman would target the munitions factories at Augusta, the Confederates marshaled troops in the Macon area, and sent them marching for Augusta to strengthen its defenders. Unfortunately for the Southerners, the Rebel force was mainly composed of older men and young boys (some not even fifteen) and led by an incompetent commander. Their route to Augusta crossed the path of Sherman's cavalry northeast of Macon. The Yankees quickly brought up infantry, deployed in a good defensive position, and the Rebel commander foolishly ordered a frontal assault.

The Union forces, armed with Spencer repeating weapons, cut down the attackers as they tried to come across an open field. The slaughter left 51 Confederates dead, and nearly 500 wounded, compared with 13 dead Federals, and fewer than 100 wounded. Some of the Yankees were very distressed upon realizing they had been shooting boys and old men. An Indiana private, walking over the field after the battle, wrote that the scene "was a terrible sight." He told of a fourteen-year-old boy with a broken arm and leg and near him "cold in death, lay his Father, two Brothers, and an Uncle." An Illinois soldier wrote "I hope we will never have to shoot such men again." The Southern effort, tragically for those involved, was totally in vain, for Augusta was not on Sherman's agenda anyhow—perhaps because he thought it would be heavily fortified, and its reduction would require too much time and bloodshed. Also, after securing Savannah, he hoped to march into South Carolina, and Augusta could again serve as a decoy.[37]

On November 23, Sherman and his escort rode into the capital of Georgia, preceded by the Twentieth Corps; later in the day, the entire left wing was united in and around the city. All of the right wing was near Gordon, only twelve miles away from Milledgeville. "First act of drama well played, General!" began Henry Hitchcock's diary entry for that day. General Beauregard's call, from many miles away at Corinth, Mississippi, for Georgians to "Rally around your patriotic Governor and gallant soldiers!" was to no avail. Georgia's capital had been captured without the Northerners firing a single gun in its conquest. Governor Brown, having stripped the governor's mansion of rugs, drapes, dishes and silver, had fled before Sherman arrived. Numerous citizens also left. The Georgia legislature did pass a *levée en masse*, making every able-bodied man between sixteen and fifty-five liable for military service, and then it too fled. Sherman rode to the governor's mansion, placed two planks across two camp chairs to form a crude desk and set up his headquarters. Anna Maria Green, a twenty-one-year-old resident, was overwhelmed: "We were despondent," she wrote, "our heads bowed and our hearts crushed—the Yankees in possession of Milledgeville. The Yankee flag waved from the capitol—Our degradation was bitter."[38]

Several Union regiments were detailed to destroy the arsenal, the depot, factories and storehouses in Milledgeville. Although it was not ordered, Hitchcock said 270 bales of cotton were torched. The wrecking of railroad track, perhaps needless to say, also continued. Sherman himself had given instructions about how to destroy rail lines. A large group of men, as many as an entire regiment, would line up along one side of a railroad track. Upon command, all would bend over in unison, grasp the wood ties at one end, raise them up and flip both ties and rails over, which broke the ties loose from the rails upon crashing to the ground. The ties were then gathered in piles, set on fire, and the rails heated over them until they were red-hot in the middle. At that point the rails were twisted into spirals, or twisted around trees. Sometimes the twisted rails were formed into the gigantic letters US and left in a conspicuous location. Sherman emphasized the importance of twisting the rails, because repairing them would entail reheating and rerolling at rolling mills, a very scarce facility in the Confederacy. He demanded that there be no exceptions to the twisting form of destruction.

The statehouse was spared. A number of men, some of them officers, "in the spirit of mischief" said Sherman, gathered in the legislative hall and amused themselves by electing a speaker, declaring themselves the duly constituted representatives of Georgia and repealing the state's ordinance of secession. "I was not present at these frolics," recalled Sherman, "but heard of them and enjoyed the joke."[39]

One of Sherman's staff officers, George Ward Nichols, noted that while many of Milledgeville's citizens had made an exodus from the city, the African-Americans "welcomed our approach with ecstatic exclamations of joy: 'Bress the Lord! tanks be to Almighty God, the Yanks is come!'" Many were sure that the Day of Jubilee had arrived, and eagerly shouted "Jubilee! Jubilee!" They had learned of the Old Testament practice, following forty-nine years of toil, that slaves were freed in the fiftieth year—the year of Jubilee. Some of the bolder blacks hugged soldiers, as they praised and thanked them for bringing the Jubilee.

A few days later, Union soldiers would read in a Savannah paper about a grand ball held in the Georgia capital while Sherman was there. The piece alleged that only black and mulatto women were present to dance with the Yankees. No one in the Union Army knew anything about such an event. Another tale making the rounds among Southerners had it that the Federals threw a ball in Macon, and that General Howard led the first dance with a black woman as his partner. Howard was not even in Macon, and the city was never occupied, even briefly, by Union troops; and obviously no Federal ball was held there. General Howard, who came to be known as "the Christian General," because of his pious ways—which Sherman occasionally found rather irritating—was quite upset by the implications that were easily read into such a story. Major Hitchcock expressed his disgust numerous times about "the most atrocious lies" that were spread about the conduct of the Yankee forces— "our uniform cruelty, our killing all the women and children, burning all the houses, forcing the negroes into our army in the front rank of battle, etc., etc." He said that everywhere such stories were systematically and persistently circulated—alleging that Sherman actually ordered such terrible acts and his whole army carried them out—and the lies were believed, "even by intelligent people."[40]

Without question, numerous white Georgians were ready to believe the worst about Sherman's Yankees, but it is equally clear that many African-Americans did not accept the awful tales. They frequently told Sherman and his staff of brutal treatment that had been inflicted upon them—and the evidence, such as terrible whelts on their skin, was sometimes plain to see. At a farm near Milledgeville Major Hitchcock recorded in his diary: "The negroes here ... say they have been habitually punished by flogging, not only with strap, but with handsaws and paddles with holes—and salt put in the wounds." They also told about "a famous 'track-hound' (blood-hound) at the next house, nearby, used to hunt runaways." George Nichols, with Sherman's permission, went to the house and had a soldier shoot the hound. Hitchcock reported that Nichols "says the darkies there were in great glee over it. No wonder."[41]

The Federals heard from various sources that bloodhounds were widely used for hunting escaped Union prisoners, blacks fleeing slavery and even Confederate deserters. One Union escapee from the infamous Andersonville prison, upon being recaptured, was reportedly first beaten with a musket, and then thrown to a pack of bloodhounds, which ripped him apart horribly, resulting in his death. Because of such reports of brutality, some Yankee soldiers shot any bloodhound they came upon.[42]

The harsh attitude that African-Americans at times exhibited toward their owners took some Federals by surprise. Major Hitchcock remarked about the bitterness of a black woman named Louisa, who was a household servant of a planter named Joseph B. Jones. She said that Jones, a planter-politician and prominent Methodist, "used to declare that he would wade in blood knee-deep before the Yankees come here," but four days earlier he had fled to Savannah, leaving his sick wife and children. The possibility of burning the plantation house came up in their conversation. "'It *ought* to be burned,' she said bitterly." When Hitchcock asked why, Louisa replied: "'Cause there has been so much devilment here, whipping niggers most to death to make 'em work to pay for it.'" Questioned if Jones had ever whipped her, Louisa indicated that she had gotten off lightly: "He never struck me but twenty cuts since he owned me these fifteen years." She continued to speak, however, about Jones's savage ways toward other blacks, saying that "he has whipped plenty of niggers with paddle and strap too."[43]

Sherman often took time to talk with the African-Americans. Sometimes he was seeking information. Unlike the earlier days, when he had little confidence in intelligence gleaned from slaves, he now sought them. "I don't want a white man" he told some officers whom he sent out to find a black. "I need some reliable information about roads and bridges." They brought in an elderly black man with whom Sherman talked a long time. Staff officer George Nichols wrote that "General Sherman has never lost an opportunity of talking with and advising the negroes who come to our camp." Henry Hitchcock was impressed by the way the General handled these occasions. He described him as dealing with the blacks frankly, in a manner not overly familiar, and yet putting them at ease as they conversed. In fact, Hitchcock complimented Sherman's manner in dealing with white Southerners as well as black,

IT'S A BIG GAME, BUT I KNOW I CAN DO IT

saying "the General talks 'mighty well'—frank, almost blunt, but ... always to the point and *never over-bearing* nor rude." Sherman invariably advised African-Americans to stay where they were, rather than following the army. If they volunteered, he would permit able-bodied young men to serve as teamsters, or in the pioneer (engineer) corps, but never for combat troops. He explained that the army could not provide for families, women, children, older men and the aged. Neither food nor transportation was anywhere near adequate for such a following. Nevertheless, eventually there were thousands of contrabands trudging along in the wake of Sherman's forces. "The Darkies come to us from every direction," observed a Union private, despite the fact that "General Sherman has tried in every way to explain ... that they had better stay on the plantations until the war is ended." Bringing along bundles and bags of clothing and various necessities, such as cookware, many of the effervescent blacks seemed unmindful of the hardships and dangers, particularly the rivers and swamps they would have to confront in the days ahead.

On November 24, Sherman moved on from Milledgeville, his troops continuing to march in two parallel wings, foraging, destroying and skirmishing, often clashing with Rebel cavalry, sometimes with a small command of infantry. While men suffered and died on both sides, the casualties were relatively few. The Union forces mostly proceeded at will—"treason fled before us, resistance was in vain," the famous song "Marching Through Georgia" later proclaimed—as the Grayclad strength was insufficient to do more than pester the Yankee advance. The general direction of the march was southeast, but the left wing under Slocum was still spread out far enough to the north that the Confederates could not discount Augusta as Sherman's objective—tending to confirm, in the minds of some Southerners, what they had believed since the start of the campaign. Levying a swath of devastation across the Georgia landscape, the men passed through such towns as Sandersville, Sparta, Warrenton, Tennille Station, Wrightsville, Davisboro, Louisville, Swainsboro, Summertown, Sebastopol, Scarboro, Statesboro, Waynesboro, Birdsville and Lumpkin's Station.

At Sandersville, a Union soldier wrote to his family: "We ... completely ransacked the whole town, only left the citizens unmolested. It was done to retaliate for burning a bridge and resistance of the day before." No doubt some citizens would not have considered themselves "unmolested." A woman in Sandersville described how Yankee soldiers tramped into her home, stealing china, silver, linens and food, while others shot all the hogs, cows and chickens they did not take with them. Few indeed were the towns that did not experience some damage, and a number suffered severely. When the Federals moved into Louisville, where much of the business district was burned, Brigadier General Judson Kilpatrick's cavalry, reinforced by a division of infantry, struck out northeast toward Waynesboro on November 29, making a feint toward Augusta. They tore up sections of the railroad between Augusta and Millen, and devastated a large area that afterward was called "the burnt district," by Georgians in and near the region.

As the Union forces drew closer to Savannah, the enemy opposition became even weaker than it had been. The right wing under Howard was moving primarily in the direction of Millen, a town about sixty-five miles northwest of Savannah, where Sherman arrived on Saturday, December 3. Close to Millen lay Camp Lawton, a Confederate prison facility, the horrors of which were witnessed by a great many Union soldiers. The camp provided no shelter from the weather, and the prisoners had dug into the ground as they sought relief from the elements. Prisoners were confined within a very limited space, with deadlines beyond which the guards would shoot anyone who ventured past. According to some sources, there was no pure water available. Food, at best, was far from adequate. A lot of men had died, and hundreds of graves were evident. The fleeing Confederate guards had left a number of dead prisoners unburied. "Everyone who visited this place," wrote a Federal officer, left with "a feeling of hardness toward the Southern Confederacy he had never felt before."

Those troops who did not see Camp Lawton soon heard about it, and some men met up with former prisoners who told of the misery and mistreatment they had endured. More than ever, many soldiers in the Federal Army felt completely justified as they inflicted destruction and distress upon the Southerners. Sherman ordered Frank Blair, commanding the Seventeenth Corps, to make the destruction of Millen "'tenfold more devilish' than he had ever dreamed of, as this is one of the places they have been starving our prisoners."[44]

AS THE GREAT RAID progressed, and despite Sherman's wishes, the number of African-Americans who followed the army constantly increased. Many of the blacks would suffer and die. Racial conflict made the situation worse. While some Union soldiers sympathized with the plight of the contrabands, others resented their presence, even considered them responsible for the coming of the war and treated them badly. Among several distressing, deplorable incidents, the most merciless involved the refugees who were following the Fourteenth Corps, commanded by Brigadier General Jefferson C. Davis of Indiana. The five-foot-eight-inch Davis was a contentious personality, perhaps best remembered for a deadly confrontation two years earlier with Major General William Nelson in the lobby of the Galt House Hotel in Louisville.

Nelson, who was a loud, profane bully of a man, standing six foot five and weighing over three hundred pounds, took "delight in hectoring the officers and men of his command," according to an Indiana soldier. After more than one altercation, Davis challenged Nelson to a duel. The big man refused and reportedly slapped Davis with the back of his hand, whereupon the enraged Davis procured a pistol and shot and killed Nelson in the hotel. Few seemed to regret Nelson's death, but it was alarming that a general could be murdered without his murderer's ever being brought to trial. Davis himself, it should be noted, was not a favorite with the soldiers he commanded on the march across Georgia, mainly because he developed a reputation for coming down hard on foraging violations.[45]

Early in December, Davis's Fourteenth Corps came up to Ebenezer Creek, a deep rapid-flowing stream that was a tributary of the Savannah

River. Ebenezer is a Biblical name, from the first book of Samuel, and literally means "stone of help"—ironic, in view of ensuing events. The army's pioneers laid down a pontoon bridge more than one hundred feet long, on which the Yankee soldiers crossed over the dangerous waters, along with their animals, artillery and wagons. The contrabands were not allowed to follow, for Davis had issued orders that the bridge was to be taken up as soon as the troops were across the rushing current.

Hundreds of African-Americans looked on with dismay and anguish as the bridge was removed. When they heard that Confederate cavalry was coming up behind them, panic ensued. Many men, women and children rushed into the water. Some managed to swim across, while others, either unable to swim or weak swimmers, were overcome by the swift-flowing stream and drowned while desperately seeking places to ford. Rebel cavalry, according to Federal soldiers—some of whom tried to help the blacks get across—then slew a number of the refugees while rounding up others, presumably to return them to slavery. An Indiana chaplain acridly blamed Jefferson C. Davis, calling him a man "without one spark of humanity in his makeup," while an Illinois colonel, who witnessed the horrible event, later said that "across the stretch of twenty years my soul burns with indignation . . . as I recall it." That was not the only time that Davis, a man of proslavery sympathies, took action detrimental to contrabands. Accounts of the despicable affair appeared in Northern papers soon after Sherman's forces reached Savannah. Although Sherman was several miles from the scene, his well-known opposition to enlisting blacks in the army brought criticism that Davis simply reflected Sherman's own racism.[46]

On December 9, about the same time as the wretched Ebenezer Creek incident, Sherman and his staff were riding with the right wing of the army, drawing near Savannah, when they noticed that a column of the Seventeenth Corps had turned out of the main road and was marching through the fields. Close by, in a fence corner, stood a group of soldiers. Sherman rode up, sensing that something was amiss. He learned that mines had been buried in the road by the Rebels, one of which had exploded, killing a horse and wounding several men. A lieutenant of the

First Alabama Cavalry (Union) whose time of service had just expired suffered the worst wound. His right foot had been torn off by the blast, and much of the flesh on the leg was blown away. He lay on the ground, very pale, waiting for a surgeon to amputate his leg.[47]

Sherman wrote in his memoirs: "This was not war, but murder, and it made me very angry." No doubt it did, as it did many others. General Blair, commanding the Seventeenth Corps, had ordered up a squad of Confederate prisoners to clear out the mines. These Rebels arrived shortly after Sherman did, and "begged hard," according to Sherman, for the Union commander to override Blair. But Sherman reiterated Blair's order and told the prisoners, said Hitchcock, that "their people had put these things there to assassinate our men ... and they must remove them; and if *they* got blown up he didn't care." Hitchcock, who sometimes recorded reservations and occasionally criticism of Sherman decisions that he considered overly harsh, declared that "he did exactly right" in this case. Working *"very carefully,"* in the staff officer's emphasized words, the prisoners managed to uncover the rest of the mines without incident.[48]

During the next couple of days, Sherman's entire force approached Savannah's defensive works, the Fourteenth Corps coming up on the far left, with its flank brushing the Savannah River. The Twentieth Corps formed on the right of the Fourteenth, with the Seventeenth Corps advancing to the right of the Twentieth, while the Fifteenth came up on the army's extreme right. "As soon as it was demonstrated that Savannah was well fortified," Sherman decided not to attack, but to lay siege to the city. The first step "was to open communication with our fleet," he said, "which was supposed to be waiting for us with supplies and clothing in Ossabaw Sound," about twenty miles south of Savannah. Rations had become rather meager during the last quarter of the march. The soldiers were ready for something other than rice, which had been the only food found in abundance for several days.

Standing in the way of Federal contact with the navy was an earthen fortification known as Fort McAllister. Sherman ordered General Howard to attack and capture it. Howard gave the assignment to William Hazen's division, and Sherman later said that he personally gave Hazen his orders. Fort McAllister had its heavy guns pointing out to sea, and fewer than 300 men to defend it from the rear. In less than thirty minutes Hazen's command overwhelmed it. The route to the U.S. Navy, and the supplies that Sherman's forces needed, was open. The march to the sea was triumphant.[49]

Major Hitchcock wrote his wife a long letter right after the fort fell, in which he lavished praise upon Sherman: "He is the man of the war as to military genius." General Hazen observed that Sherman was still seething about the Rebels mining the road. Upon meeting George W. Anderson, the captured Confederate commander of the fort, Sherman criticized the use of mines as inhuman and barbarous, and mocked the vaunted idea of "Southern Chivalry." Many of Sherman's army were probably thinking along the lines of Casey McWayne. Writing the "dear folks at home" from a plantation that was owned by a Miss Mary Henderson south of Savannah, McWayne declared, "I tell you, Old Pap [Sherman] has done well for us on this march. After we had taken Fort McAllister it opened a place for hardtack to run in. . . . Some of the boys have been down and got some oysters already. I will write again [as] soon as we take Savannah. It will not be long." Sherman himself, obviously amused, wrote Ellen about an army foraging party, moving toward Ossabaw Sound in a boat, that met a steamer coming up the Ogeechee River and hailed her. The foragers were told that the ship carried Major General John G. Foster, in response to which a soldier blurted: "Oh H——l, we've got 27 Major Generals up at Camp. What we want is hardtack."[50]

Sergeant McWayne was right about Savannah. The capture of the city was only a matter of time. In fact, Sherman wrote General Halleck on the day Fort McAllister fell, "I regard Savannah as already gained." Just over a week after the fort was subdued, Confederate General William Hardee and his 10,000-man garrison pulled out of the city, crossing into South Carolina before Sherman closed off the escape route. If Hardee had been trapped in Savannah, Sherman most likely would have attempted to starve the city into submission. He did not want a costly

assault, nor the employment of artillery, for he had fond memories of
Savannah's homes and gardens.

As it was, the gracefully appointed city was spared the agony of a siege,
and Sherman rode into Savannah on December 21. The next day he sent
the President a telegram which would be long remembered: "I beg to
present you, as a Christmas gift, the city of Savannah, with one hundred
and fifty guns and plenty of ammunition, and also about twenty-five
thousand bales of cotton." Casey McWayne was also in a festive mood,
writing his mother and sisters about the seafood repasts in which he was
indulging: "We are having oysters & fish aplenty—oysters in the shell,
of course, for we have to rake them out of their beds ourselves. . . . Just
think of having an oyster supper any time you please, and just as many
as you please."[51]

Lincoln responded to Sherman's gift on the day after Christmas:
"Many, many thanks for your Christmas gift—the capture of Savannah."
Admitting that he "was anxious, if not fearful" of the result when Sherman set forth from Atlanta, the President acknowledged that because
"none of us went further than to acquiesce," the honor of the great success "is all yours." Not only did Sherman's triumph "afford the obvious
and immediate military advantages," but it also demonstrated "to the
world that your army could be divided, putting the stronger part to an
important new service," while the lesser contingent still possessed sufficient power to vanquish Hood's army at Nashville, all of which, declared
Lincoln in his memorable style, "brings those who sat in darkness to see
a great light."[52]

Even his critics had to appreciate what Sherman had accomplished.
Waging war successfully, by its very nature, involves risk. Sherman,
who had matured to see his military chessboard—recalling Napoleon's
famous remark at Borodino—more clearly than most generals ever do,
had become a master at calculating risks. Depending upon General
Thomas to deal with Hood was an acceptable risk, because Sherman
knew that when Andrew Jackson Smith's reinforcements arrived in
Nashville, the Union would have a numerical advantage over the Confederates. Sherman considered his own risk relatively minimal, for

although he would be operating deep in enemy territory, and without a supply line, he was leading a seasoned army through a region where food was plentiful for the taking, and he knew that the Rebels could not possibly match his strength of arms. The great damage that he expected to inflict, and indeed did inflict, upon the Confederate psyche made the risk imminently justifiable.

Sherman took up residence and established his personal headquarters in the elegant mansion of Charles Green, a wealthy British banker and cotton merchant. Initially Sherman had gone to the Pulaski Hotel, located at the corner of West Bryan and Bull Streets, about which he had known when serving in the region as a young lieutenant. He found the hotel keeper ready to welcome the General and his staff as boarders. When Sherman informed him "that we were not in the habit of paying board," the keeper's ardor for accommodating the General waned perceptively. While Sherman considered the situation, Green came up and offered his house.

"At first I felt strongly disinclined to make use of any private dwelling," remembered Sherman, "lest complaints should arise of damage and loss of furniture, and so expressed myself to Mr. Green." Green realized, naturally, that if Sherman stayed with him, no harm was likely to come to his home. Upon Green's insistence, and observing that "a most excellent house it was in all respects," Sherman accepted his offer. Henry Hitchcock observed that the structure was "the finest house in the city," an appraisal not exaggerated. Sherman wrote Ellen on Christmas Day that "the house is elegant & splendidly furnished with pictures & Statuary—my bedroom has a bath & dressing room attached which look out of proportion to my poor baggage." A few days later he spoke of "the magnificent mansion [in which he was] living like a Gentleman."[53]

Fortunately Charles Green's imposing residence still survives. Green had arrived in Savannah from England when he was in his midtwenties and by 1850 possessed "a fleet of several ships that were traveling back and forth from Savannah to Liverpool on a continuous basis." In that year, he began construction of a regal, Gothic Revival home, which cost a total of $93,000, when completed four years later. The arresting exterior, constructed of brick, stucco and stone, is highlighted by an exceptional front entrance, and complemented by three bay and four oriel windows. Three pairs of doors mark the front entrance. The outer doors are massive, and fold back on each side to form two small closets. The second pair is louvered, and the third pair is adorned with glass panels. Both the second and third pairs may be slid into the wall, as one determines according to the weather. William Howard Russell, an English journalist who visited Savannah while covering the war in 1861, recorded of the 7,300-square-foot main part of the house: "Italian statuary graced the hall," while "finely carved tables and furniture, stained glass, and pictures from Europe set forth the sitting rooms."[54]

Located right beside Green's residence was St. John's Episcopal Church. Christmas Day fell on Sunday, and Sherman observed the occasion at St. John's. A clergyman inquired if the General had any objections to prayers for special persons, as required by the diocese of Georgia. Sherman responded that they should "certainly pray for Jeff Davis" and added, "Certainly pray for the Devil too. I don't know any two that require prayers more than they do." The minister at St. John's, noted Major Hitchcock, omitted the prayer for the President of the United States. Sherman, however, remained silent. During the afternoon, Sherman enjoyed seeing a number of children playing in the park nearby, and later he remarked "with great pleasure and feeling," according to Hitchcock, about the presence of those children.[55]

On Christmas evening Sherman presided at a military-style, "family dinner-party" in the Green mansion. All present were officers except Green, who made his china and silver available for the occasion. George Nichols had "secured three or four lovely turkeys and sundry other good things," while Colonel Henry A. Barnum contributed "some very good wine," which had been given to him by grateful wine merchants, at whose stores he had placed guards. The festivities began appropriately with a toast to Sherman, who responded with "a little speech, patriotic, modest, and pointed," said Major Hitchcock. Later, when Green "made as happy a little after-dinner speech as I ever heard," Hitchcock reported that Sherman proposed that they drink to Charles Green's health—most fittingly, since Green, even if he had originally favored the Confederacy, had proven himself a hospitable and pleasant host. At that point Hitchcock said he withdrew for the night, "fearing a little, I confess, that [the toasts] might become too lively, but [he admitted] in that I was mistaken." The major pronounced the evening "as quiet and pleasant a Christmas dinner as one could wish—away from home."[56]

It had been a good Christmas, and actually Sherman himself had received something of a Christmas gift on December 24. It came in the form of a most welcome letter from General Grant. Long before Sherman reached Savannah he was planning, once his army was resupplied by sea, to sally forth into the Carolinas, particularly laying waste to South Carolina. Ultimately he intended to move into Virginia and join forces with Grant. Sherman believed he would thus strike a greater blow against the will of the Confederacy to continue the war than he had in Georgia. But upon reaching the Atlantic, a message from Grant awaited him, dated December 6, in which the general-in-chief contended that "the most important operation toward closing out the rebellion will be to close out Lee and his army." Therefore Grant instructed Sherman to establish a seacoast base, leave his artillery and cavalry, along with enough infantry to secure the base, come with the bulk of his infantry by sea and join up with Grant "to close out Lee."[57]

Although disappointed, and convinced that Grant's idea was not the best strategic move, Sherman loyally indicated at once that he would take steps to join Grant as soon as sufficient transport vessels became available. Marshaling enough ships would take time. Meanwhile, in several letters to Grant, he carefully and diplomatically set before the general-in-chief the Carolina campaign which he envisioned. On December 18, for example, he wrote Grant, "With Savannah in our possession, at some future time, if not now, we can punish South Carolina as she deserves, and as thousands of people in Georgia hoped we would do."

Sherman then firmly declared, "I do sincerely believe that the whole United States, North and South, would rejoice to have this army turned loose on South Carolina, to devastate that State in the manner we have done in Georgia." In another letter, written right after Sherman gained possession of Savannah, he pointedly told Grant, "I have now completed my first step, and should like to go on to you via Columbia and Raleigh, but will prepare to embark as soon as vessels come. Colonel [Orville E.] Babcock will have told you all, and you know better than anybody else how much better troops arrive by a land march than when carried by transports." He said that "the capture of Savannah ... gives us a magnificent position in this quarter; and if you can hold Lee, and if Thomas can continue as he did [at Nashville] ... I could go on and smash South Carolina all to pieces, and also break up [rail] roads as far as the Roanoke. But, as I before remarked, I will now look to coming to you as soon as transportation comes."[58]

Once again Sherman succeeded in convincing Grant, as he did before the march to the sea, to approve a campaign that he himself strongly favored—and this time the approval necessitated changing Grant's own concept of their best military move. It is to Grant's credit that he realized, spurred in part by the victories of Schofield and Thomas at Franklin and Nashville, that Sherman's plans for a major raid through the Carolinas promised the greatest military dividends. His message sanctioning Sherman's Carolina foray, which reached Sherman's headquarters on Christmas Eve, first congratulated the General "on the successful termination of your most brilliant campaign," which Grant stated that he would not have entrusted "to any other living commander." Discussing the war both east and west, and conveying his change of mind about Sherman joining him, Grant offered the interesting opinion that "Lee is averse to going out of Virginia, and if the cause of the South is lost he wants Richmond to be the last place surrendered. . . . It may be well to indulge him until we get everything else in our hands." Again congratulating Sherman "upon the brilliant results of your campaign, the like of which is not read of in . . . history," Grant said that he subscribed himself "more than ever, if possible, your friend."[59]

The message was surely a gratifying one for Sherman, and he responded the same day, thanking Grant for "the handsome commendation you pay my army," and expressing his pleasure "that you have modified your former order." He assured Grant that he felt "no doubt whatever as to our future plans," and, presenting a number of specifics, he declared that "I left Augusta untouched on purpose: because now the enemy will be in doubt as to my objective point after crossing the Savannah River, whether it be Augusta or Charleston, and will naturally divide his forces." Sherman planned to ignore both cities and march for the state capital at Columbia. Sherman critics sometimes claim his declaration about purposefully bypassing Augusta when heading for Savannah, is a mere after-the-fact explanation, devoid of any validity. However, since Sherman fully intended to take the war to South Carolina, it is reasonable to assume that he would have been thinking ahead to that campaign.[60]

Also on Christmas Eve, Sherman wrote Halleck that he was "very glad that General Grant has changed his mind about embarking my troops for the James River, leaving us free to make the broad swath . . . through South and North Carolina." Significantly he declared, "I attach more importance to these deep incisions into the enemy's country, because this war differs from European wars in this particular. We are not only fighting hostile armies, but a hostile people, and must make old and young, rich and poor, feel the hard hand of war, as well as their organized armies." Affirming that his march through Georgia "has had a wonderful effect in this respect," Sherman addressed the far greater impact that he now foresaw in the Carolinas: "The truth is the whole army is burning with an insatiable desire to wreak vengeance upon South Carolina. I almost tremble at her fate, but feel that she deserves all that seems in store for her." Noting that "many and many a person in Georgia" wanted his army to strike at South Carolina, Sherman said he looked upon Columbia "as quite as bad as Charleston, and I doubt if we shall spare the public buildings there as we did at Milledgeville." Years later, in his memoirs, Sherman strikingly emphasized his view of the Carolina campaign: "Were I to express my measure of the relative importance of the march to the sea, and of that from Savannah northward, I would place the former at one, and the latter at ten." Yet, as so often with famous concepts, the march to the sea gained the lion's share of dramatic publicity—and thus it has been ever since.

The march to the sea, "at least in popular imagination," wrote historian Noah Andre Trudeau, "was seen as a defining moment in American history." For the first time, a vast region had been scorched and despoiled, and war taken to women, children and the aged. Some have said the march was "total war"; others have disagreed, basically differing about how "total war" should be defined. Whatever the march may be called, Sherman's intentions were clear: destroy anything of military value to the Confederacy, while subjecting Southern civilians to the inevitable depredations inflicted by a large army tramping through their country and living off the land. To Sherman, bringing the war to civilians would bring the war to an end sooner: "The simple fact that a man's home has been visited by an enemy makes a soldier in Lee's or Johnston's army very, very anxious to get home to look after his family and property." While Sherman had not ordered the destruction of civilian property, he did not seem particularly troubled when it happened. His attitude about the fate of houses abandoned by their owners is noteworthy: "I don't want them destroyed," he said about vacated houses, "but do not take much care to preserve them." The very nature of Sherman's march guaranteed that private property, to some degree, would be destroyed. This the General undoubtedly realized.

In the context of war—and especially "total war," or anything akin to it—the issue of rape should not be ignored. The number of rapes committed by Sherman's men during the march to the sea will never be known, but unquestionably some sexual assaults did occur. The evidence indicates, however, and probably surprisingly to some people, that the attacks were not many. In searching army court-marshal records, Joseph T. Glatthaar found only one instance of the army prosecuting soldiers for rape during the march to Savannah. Glatthaar also observed that "most officers and men alike abhorred this sort of conduct and . . . some officers even issued standing orders to shoot on the spot any soldier found abusing citizens." Union officers Henry Hitchcock and Harvey Reid, concerned about such despicable acts, made numerous inquiries on the subject, and both men concluded that very few women were raped during the march. Noah Trudeau noted that only one victim of rape actually became known by name. Pertinent also is the fact that while Georgians accused Sherman's army of many things after the war—thievery, robbery, arson, wanton destruction, and all on a widespread scale—rape was seldom among their charges.[61]

WHILE SHERMAN ENGAGED in preparing his army to "smash South Carolina all to pieces," as he wrote Grant, he was forced to deal with some other issues. He remarked to Ellen that "Savannah would be an agreeable place to me [if he were] less burdened with the cares of armies, women, cotton, negros and all the disturbing Elements of this war." Actually, the army presented little problem. He kept the troops busy with drill, inspections and parades. Writing to General Grant on the last day of the year, he said, "The people here seem to be well content as they have reason to be for our troops have behaved magnificently. You would think it Sunday, so quiet is everything in the City day & night." Five days into the new year, he assured Ellen that "it is wonderful how smoothly all things [military] move for they all seem to feel implicit faith in me, not because I am strong or bold, but because they think I know everything." In another message Cump again told her, "the soldiers think I know everything," and added that they think "they can do anything." He also wrote his wife that "The soldiers manifest to me the most thorough affection, and a wonderful confidence." Sherman was proud, but his assessment was accurate.[62]

A large number of women called on Sherman, and he thought they came much as they had at Memphis, "disposed to usurp my time more from curiosity than business. They had been told of my burning & Killing till they expected the veriest monster." Among Savannah's prominent ladies who came to call were the wives of Confederate generals Hardee, Gustavus W. Smith and Lafayette McLaws. When the Southern forces evacuated the city, the generals left letters for Sherman, requesting that he see to the welfare of their families, letters that the ladies presented to him. Of course Sherman intended to see that no harm befell them, and he was pleased that "eyes were opened," as leading citizens, male and female, came to realize that "the Vandal Chief," as Sherman referenced himself, actually was not the murdering villain that many had supposed. But when he inquired about people he had known in his younger days, he observed that "it marks the Sad havoc of War," for most were either "gone or in poverty."[63]

Major Hitchcock wrote his wife that many of Savannah's leading men who visited the General "say openly that the C. S. A. is 'played out,'" but Sherman told Ellen that he found a number of women who were "as haughty and proud as ever." Both Hitchcock and George Nichols were impressed by the way "the General's new-found colored friends" came by the hundreds to see "Mr. Sherman." Nichols said that since Sherman's arrival in the city, "he has kept open house for all who choose to call upon him, white or black," and declared of his relationship with the blacks, that Sherman's "great heart has overflowed in kindly counsels to these poor people." Hitchcock wrote in greater detail. The morning that Sherman entered Savannah, Hitchcock related that the General rode immediately to the riverbank and climbed up to inspect a signal station on the roof of a warehouse. By the time the General got back down to the street, a crowd of African-Americans had gathered "who pressed round him to welcome him and shake hands and tell him how long they had watched and prayed for his coming."[64]

Once Sherman moved into Green's house, Hitchcock wrote that for several days "there was a constant stream of [blacks], old and young, men, women and children, black, yellow and cream-colored, uncouth and well-bred, bashful and talkative—but always respectful and well-behaved—all day long, anxious to pay their respects and to see the man they had heard so much of, and whom . . . God had sent to answer their prayers." Frequently a dozen, or even twenty came at a time. Hitchcock testified that regardless of what the General was doing, he "always had them shown in at once," and greeted them "in his off-hand—though not undignified way—'Well, boys,—come to see Mr. Sherman, have you? Well, I'm Mr. Sherman—glad to see you'—and shaking hands with them all." Hitchcock remarked, obviously pleased by Sherman's interaction with the blacks, that the whole scene, "I dare say," would have been "highly disgusting ... to 'a refined Southern gentleman.'" He said "the General gives them all good advice—briefly and to the point, telling them they are free now, have no master nor mistress to *support*, and must be industrious and well-behaved, etc."[65]

Probably Sherman's utter disgust with the pronounced sense of entitlement and the arrogant rebelliousness of the planter-politicians who rent the Union and brought on "this terrible war," softened his attitude toward the former slaves of those despicable men, even though he did consider African-Americans his inferiors—just as he did Native Americans and Mexican-Americans. He likely was touched by the way the blacks seemed almost to worship him. Perhaps something akin to a sense of noblesse oblige motivated him. Whatever precisely his racial mind-set, General Sherman seemed to treat the blacks with respect and kindness.

This fact, however, did not remove the political problem he had created for himself in opposing the recruitment of blacks for the army. On December 30, General Halleck warned him "in this private and friendly way," that ill winds were brewing against him in the nation's capital. "While almost everyone is praising your great march through Georgia, and the capture of Savannah," nevertheless, Halleck declared, "there is a certain class having now great influence with the President ... who are decidedly disposed to make a point against you. I mean in regard to 'inevitable Sambo.'" Their charge was, in Halleck's words, "that you have manifested an almost *criminal* dislike to the negro, and that you are not willing to carry out the wishes of the Government in regard to him, but repulse him with contempt!" Worst of all, Halleck referenced the charge that Sherman had cut bridges in his rear, "causing the massacre of large numbers [of blacks] by Wheeler's cavalry." Would it not be possible, now that Sherman was in possession of Savannah and there was no fear of inadequate supplies for his army, to reopen "avenues of escape [into Savannah] for the negroes, without interfering with your military operations?"[66]

Sherman may have wondered just where Halleck himself actually stood on the issue, for the General did express his warning message in strong, even aggressive terms. Clearly Sherman was aggravated by the accusations. The "cock-and-bull story of my turning back negroes that Wheeler might kill them is all humbug. I turned nobody back." As for Union General Jefferson C. Davis at Ebenezer Creek, he had taken up the pontoon bridge, said Sherman, "because he wanted his bridge." From a military view, Sherman considered Davis's action justified. He also told Halleck that neither Davis nor General Slocum believed that Wheeler's troops killed any blacks. Sherman then declared himself "the best kind of a friend to Sambo. . . . They gather around me in crowds, and I can't find out whether I am Moses or Aaron, or which of the prophets; but surely I am rated as one of the congregation." He added that it was difficult "to tell in what sense I am most appreciated by Sambo—in saving him from his master, or the new master that threatens him with a new species of slavery. I mean State recruiting agents."[67]

In 1863 the United States had begun conscripting men for military duty, declaring every able-bodied male citizen aged twenty to forty-five eligible for service and assigning each congressional district a quota to be raised, based on its male population minus the number of men who had already served. If the quota was not filled by volunteers, the necessary number would be drafted. State officials strove to stimulate volunteering and thus avoid the stigma of conscription. Some ruthless and greedy men saw an opportunity, through "recruiting" blacks in the South, to meet assigned quotas in Northern states, enabling more white men to avoid military service and picking up the bounties being paid for new recruits.

Sherman was incensed by the unscrupulous actions of "avaricious recruiting agents" from the New England states. In answer to a letter from Salmon P. Chase, the recently appointed chief justice of the United States, who was concerned about Sherman's treatment of blacks, the General wrote, "You can not know the acts and devices to which base white men resort to secure negro soldiers, not to aid us to fight, but to get bounties for their own pockets, and to diminish their quotas [of white soldiers] at home." Describing them in his memoirs as "ravenous State agents," Sherman told of Colonel Joseph C. Audenreid, his aide-de-camp, finding "at least a hundred poor negroes shut up in a house and pen" in Savannah—the state agents waiting for nightfall to stealthily convey them from the city, having told the African-Americans that they did not have any choice. They had to become soldiers!

George Nichols stated that "negro men have rushed frightened to General Sherman's headquarters begging for protection from the 'land-sharks,' who, it appears, have seized all the able-bodied negroes they could lay their hands upon, and locked them up until they could be mustered into the service." Nichols characterized Sherman as "exceedingly angry" when he learned what was happening, and said "the General at once gave orders to have the negroes released, threatened the recruiting agents with severe punishment if violence was again used, and assured the negroes that they were free to go where they liked for work, and . . . could become soldiers if they chose, but . . . would not be forced into the army." Sherman declared in his letter to Chief Justice Chase, "Every negro who is fit for a soldier, and is willing, I invariably allow to join a Negro regiment, but I do oppose and rightfully too, the *forcing* of negros as soldiers."[68]

On January 11, Secretary of War Edwin Stanton and several other dignitaries arrived in Savannah. Officially, Stanton came to confirm United States control of the city and to deal with the cotton issue. As to cotton, Sherman assumed a firm stance. "I have taken all the Cotton as prize of war," he wrote Ellen, "30,000 bales, equal to 13 millions of dollars, much of which is claimed by English merchants." He disregarded their claims, "on the ground that this Cotton has been notoriously employed to buy cartridges & arms, and . . . Ships, [for Rebels] and was collected here for that very purpose." He added that "our own merchants are equally *Culpable*," an assessment undoubtedly true in some cases, for both trading with the enemy and general war profiteering had become rife during the conflict.[69]

Sherman told Secretary Stanton that he had been approached "by all the consuls and half the people of Savannah on this cotton question, and my invariable answer has been that all the cotton in Savannah was prize of war, and belonged to the United States, and nobody should recover

one bale of it with my consent." Cotton had been "one of the chief causes
of the war," and Sherman thought that it should help pay the expenses
of the war. He declared that "all cotton became tainted with treason
from the hour the first act of hostility was committed against the United
States, some time in December, 1860—and that no bill of sale subsequent
to that date could convey title." He ordered that every bale of cotton be
thoroughly marked with identifying information. However, Secretary
Stanton, according to Sherman's account, changed this and "ordered the
obliteration of all the marks; so that no man, friend or foe, could trace
his identical cotton." Sherman used the term "Strange" in describing
Stanton's action, writing that claims were later filed for "three times
the quantity actually captured" and that "reclamations on the Treasury
have [since] been *allowed* for more than the actual quantity captured."[70]

Strange indeed, but the cotton issue was a relatively minor concern
for Stanton. His basic interest actually was Sherman's relations with
the African-Americans. Wasting no time, the war secretary met with a
delegation of blacks at Sherman's personal headquarters on the evening
of January 12. He had asked the General to arrange the interview, and
Sherman invited the men he considered the most intelligent and knowledgeable, mainly Baptist and Methodist preachers. Twenty came, meeting in Sherman's upstairs room at the Green mansion. Garrison Frazier,
a sixty-seven-year-old Baptist minister and former slave who had saved
enough gold and silver to buy freedom for himself and his wife, was
selected as their primary spokesman. Among the questions put to the
group, one of the most significant concerned how the men thought they
could best take care of themselves and assist the United States Government in maintaining their freedom. The response was that they would
need land "to till by the labor of the women, and children, and old men—
and we can soon maintain ourselves and have something to spare."
In regard to assisting the U.S. government, they said that their young
men should enlist in the service of the government, and "serve in such
manner as they may be wanted."[71]

As the meeting progressed, George Nichols, who was present much
of the time, said that Sherman often stood by the fireplace, occasion-

ally entering into the discussion. When Stanton wanted to ask the group about Sherman, the General left the room. What the secretary of war then heard was, without exception, complimentary of Sherman. He was a man, they said, set apart "in the providence of God," to accomplish the work that was in their interest—a man who "should be honored for the faithful performance of his duty." They thought it "probable" that he had not met Stanton himself "with more courtesy than he met us." He was "a friend and gentleman" in whom they had confidence. Their interests "could not be in better hands." When Sherman reentered the room, there was discussion of several general subjects, upon which Adjutant General Edward D. Townsend did not take any notes. Nichols said the conversation lasted "until the small hours of the morning," and added that he doubted whether twenty white ministers could have been found in any Northern city who could have represented "so much common sense and intelligence as these men." If Stanton hoped to confirm Washington criticisms of Sherman's alleged mistreatment of African-Americans, the black leaders surely disappointed him.[72]

Sherman soon drafted, with Stanton's approval (and probably his initiative), Special Field Orders No. 15, which "reserved and set apart [land] for the settlement of the negroes now made free," along the southeast coast, from Charleston south to the St. Johns River in Florida. The land was divided into forty-acre plots on which the black refugees were to be settled. Although not mentioned in the order, Sherman also allowed mules, which the army had confiscated during the march, to be used by the freedmen. Thus the phrase "forty acres and a mule" came into being. The order also "provided fully for the enlistment of colored troops" in the military service of the United States. On the land allocated for the African-Americans, which encompassed the sea islands and "abandoned rice fields along the rivers for thirty miles back from the sea . . . no white person whatsoever, unless military officers and soldiers detailed for duty," would be allowed to reside. The "exclusive management of affairs" was assigned solely "to the freed people themselves, subject only to the U. S. Military authority, and the acts of Congress."

Sherman had to be pleased, at least for the time being, because the policy promised to alleviate the problem of blacks following his army, as well as being a seemingly good solution for the refugees themselves. Perhaps Sherman also found a measure of satisfaction in turning over abandoned plantations to the former slaves. However, the order would be overturned after the war, and most of the land returned to white ownership. Sherman indicated no disapproval. In fact, he wrote in his memoirs, that the military "did not undertake to give a fee-simple title; and all that was designed . . . was to make temporary provisions for the freedmen and their families during the rest of the war, or until Congress should take action." What some had seen as an opportunity for the former slaves to gain permanent control of a plot of land was not to be realized.[73]

Chapter Twenty-Four

Taking the War to the Braggart Carolinians

While in Savannah Sherman renewed contact with his family, although he did not receive a letter from Ellen until January 4. On Christmas Day, in a message to Minnie, he wrote, "Tell Mama if she is at South Bend [Indiana] that I have written to her twice at Lancaster, as I have not yet heard whether She has actually moved up to Notre Dame." He had "not even heard if the baby got well of the Cold with which he was suffering at the time I left Atlanta." His fears for the child were soon confirmed. Receiving letters from Ellen's father, his brother John and his brother-in-law Hugh Boyle Ewing, and reading an obituary in the *New York Herald*, he learned that Charles Celestine Sherman died a few days short of six months, and was buried in South Bend. Writing to Ellen the next day, Sherman said he "had hoped that the little fellow would *weather* the *ailment*, but it seems he too is lost to us, and gone to join Willy." Telling Ellen that he had not heard from her since reaching the coast, he speculated that his wife might "be so grieved at [the child's] death you Cannot write to me." When at last he heard from her, he responded understandingly of "the deep pain and anguish through which you have passed in the . . . sickness of the little baby I never saw."[1]

In her deep sorrow, Ellen again called upon her husband to accept the Roman Catholic religion. "My greatest comfort," she declared, "would be to know that you my dear husband were blessed with the faith which sanctified your children." If Cump should die "without the faith," he would "leave us miserable the rest of our lives with a weight of sorrow . . . which no worldly influence can dissipate." How he could live since Willy's death "without the faith," she could not conceive, for her own suffering since the boy died had been "more than I could have borne without its consolations." She also revealed her plans for Tommy, their sole surviving son. Ellen was enrolling him in the Academy at Notre Dame, in the hope that he would someday become a priest.[2]

Sherman ignored Ellen's Catholicism plea and indicated that he was concerned about her mental well-being. "I fear somewhat your mind will settle into the 'Religio Melancholia,' which be assured is not of divine inspiration, but rather a morbid state not natural or healthful." Regarding Tommy, he said, "I will risk his being a Priest—of course I should regret such a choice and ask that no influence be let to produce that result." His respectful request, in view of Ellen's obsession with Catholicism, conveys a touch of amusement—if the issue were not so serious. Stating unequivocally that he opposed Tommy becoming a priest, Sherman said he "is too young for even the thought." The General could hardly have been more wrong.[3]

Ellen was also badgering him again about advancing the military interests of her brothers. She wanted Cump to recommend Charley for promotion to brigadier general. She declared that she would "not . . . take no for an answer," and claimed that he "owe[d] it to him"; otherwise, Charley's relationship to Sherman "would be a disadvantage to him." Sherman refused and patiently explained to his wife that if her brother became a brigadier general "at the expense of Colonels who have commanded Brigades in half a dozen battles," over a period of two or three years, such a promotion "would be a gross injustice . . . which I cannot commit." Too, Ellen wanted Sherman to allow Hugh Boyle to rejoin Sherman's forces. Hugh had left Sherman in the spring of 1864, when he was leading a division, to take command of the District of Louisville.

Sherman told Ellen at the time that Hugh was making a mistake. He said that "so far as the war goes he might as well be in Ohio." Now Sherman had no command to give him, unless he displaced some competent and loyal general who had been with him for a long time. "I think Hugh made his choice ... and should content himself as he best may," Sherman wrote Phil Ewing. "It is only by being just to all present," Cump explained, "and preferring only the Zealous officer, that I maintain such a hold on my army. I never absent myself an hour, and cannot overlook it in others." Hugh, however, convinced himself that Sherman had treated him shabbily and quite possibly never forgave him. For that matter, Ellen had a difficult time getting beyond her husband's "fastidious views," as she once called his stance about Hugh.[4]

During the time in Savannah, Sherman learned that a movement was under way in Ohio to recognize and reward him for his military success. Some favored giving him a farm near Cincinnati or a house in the city. Others wanted to collect a large sum of money for him. General Grant, himself a recipient of public favors, hoped to do something in recognition of Sherman's "great Capacity as a Soldier," which was demonstrated "by his unequaled campaign through Georgia." Calling Sherman "one of the greatest purest and best of men," Grant wrote his father, seeking to get the elder Grant involved in inaugurating a "Subscription to present to Mrs. Sherman a comfortable furnished house" in Cincinnati. Grant observed that Sherman "is poor," and declared that he "always will be, but he is great and magnanimous."

Hearing that several prominent Ohioans were engaged in a campaign to raise money for Sherman, Grant wrote the leaders, commending the project and assuring them that history "holds no record of Sherman's superior, and of but few equals." The General pledged to give $500. He added that General Rufus Ingalls, his army's chief quartermaster, was "equally alive ... to the eminent services of General Sherman," and would be giving $250 to the fund.[5]

Sherman speculated about the Ohio endeavor in a letter to his brother-in-law Phil Ewing, indicating that he would prefer to receive interest-paying bonds, because he was not a farmer, and a house seemed pointless, for he could not "imagine any contingency of life that would keep me in Cincinnati longer than a day." He said that he really did not want to accept any tribute, but felt rather compelled to do so, because "Ellen calls for so much money that at times I have nothing ahead." In the same vein he wrote John Sherman, "I don't save anything, for Ellen's expenses have been and are heavy—Mine are comparatively light." The Ohio campaign eventually resulted in the Cincinnati testimonial committee presenting Sherman with a monetary award of $10,000 in gold. It would not be the only peoples' gift to the triumphant general.[6]

Also while still in Savannah, Sherman was troubled to learn of a movement in the U.S. Congress to promote him to lieutenant general, the same rank Grant held. At once Sherman wrote his brother, instructing John to use his influence to stop the bill. "I will accept no commission that would tend to create a rivalry with Grant," he told John. "I have all the rank I want, and on the score of pay," declared that "as long as I can Keep out in the woods My family can live on my pay, about $550 a month." He also wrote Grant, telling the general-in-chief that he had sent word to John to stop the bill. He wanted nothing to disrupt the "perfect understanding" between the two. "I would rather have you in Command than *anybody* for you are fair, honest, and have at heart the same purpose that Should animate all." Grant replied in kind, declaring that "no one would be more pleased at your advancement than I" and promising that if he were subordinate to Sherman "it would not change our personal relations in the least." Seldom in the history of war has a close relationship between top generals equaled that of Sherman and Grant.[7]

As Sherman contemplated marching through the Carolinas, he was pleased to learn that Fort Fisher, which controlled access to Wilmington, North Carolina, had fallen to the forces of General Alfred H. Terry, ably assisted by the navy under Admiral Porter. Earlier, General Benjamin Butler, infamous to Southerners since his occupation of New Orleans, and no favorite among many professionally trained Union generals, had been removed from command after he mucked up an attack on the fort. Since Butler had bragged that he would reduce the strongpoint without wasting soldiers' lives—which many (Sherman among them) considered to be a studied aspersion aimed at Grant—Butler's fiasco seemed all the worse. Federal lives indeed had been spared, but Butler failed utterly. Soon after Grant dismissed Butler, General Terry succeeded in capturing the fort.

"The capture of Fort Fisher has a most important bearing on my campaign," Sherman wrote Grant, "because it gives me another point of security on the sea board." In journeying across the Carolinas, Sherman could not predict what contingencies might develop. Knowing that Fort Fisher was in Union hands provided additional comfort if unforeseeable difficulties arose. He was also pleased that Terry took the fort "because it silences Butler, who was to you a dangerous man. His address to his troops on being relieved, was a direct, mean & malicious attack on you, and I admire the patience & skill by which you relieved yourself & the Country of him." Furthermore, Sherman "rejoiced that Terry was not a West Pointer . . . belonged to your army, and . . . had the same troops with which Butler [failed]—Porter is in high glee."[8]

Responding to a letter from Porter, Sherman himself was evidently in high spirits about the sacking of General Butler: "I am rejoiced that the current of events has carried Butler to Lowell, [Massachusetts,] where he should have stayed and confined his bellicose operations to the factory girls." Assuring Porter that his command soon would be moving north from Savannah, the General declared that "the braggart Carolinians will find in our Western boys a different kind of metal." Sherman's army was ready for the march and like the soldiers, the General was eager to proceed. "My health is good," he told his brother, "and Save a little Rheumatism in my right arm during the last march," Sherman affirmed that "I do not feel any older." Nearing his forty-fifth birthday, he still possessed his red hair and red beard—"no gray hairs yet." Knowing, as he wrote Halleck, that "the whole army is crazy to be turned loose in Carolina," Sherman was primed to get on with the job.[9]

AT THE BEGINNING of February, after several days of delay because of bad weather, the campaign got under way. Again the army was composed of two wings, commanded by Generals Howard and Slocum, and was essentially the same force, 60,000 strong, that had marched from Atlanta to Savannah. Black Jack Logan, who had gone to Illinois after the capture of Atlanta for political campaigning, was present once more, in command of the Fifteenth Corps. General Howard's right wing, consisting of the Fifteenth and Seventeenth Corps, was basically the Army of the Tennessee, as the Sixteenth Corps had been merged into the Fifteenth and Seventeenth after Logan left Atlanta. Sherman would usually ride with the right wing, alternating between the Seventeenth and the Fifteenth Corps, and more often with the Fifteenth.

Upon departing Savannah, Howard's wing at first seemed to be marching toward Charleston, while Slocum's left wing, made up of the Fourteenth and Twentieth Corps, appeared to be trekking toward Augusta. Both movements were feints, intended to puzzle the Confederates about Sherman's real objective, the South Carolina capital of Columbia. Gradually Howard's right wing swung to the northwest, drawing closer to Slocum's columns. Only when both wings appeared to be moving nearer to each other, and advancing in a more northern direction, did it become increasingly evident that Sherman's forces actually were heading for Columbia.[10]

For several days the Confederates were confused by Sherman's deceptive maneuvering. His cunning designs actually were enhanced by the attitude of many Charlestonians, who believed, as Rebel General Hardee wrote Jefferson Davis, "Charleston is the Confederacy, and to save Charleston they are willing that Lee should give up Richmond, or any other section of the Confederacy." That Sherman would ignore Charleston seemed inconceivable to many of its residents. Also, Sherman's beguiling movements received assistance from Rebel engineers, who thought it impossible, in the dead of winter, to march across miles and miles of swamps, interspersed with numerous channels of icy water, and traversing immense and dense areas of trees, vines and thickets—which characterized southern South Carolina. They found it hard to believe that Sherman's forces, campaigning without a supply line, would advance on Columbia.[11]

Even after the Southerners realized that Sherman was marching toward Columbia, they had only limited forces with which to oppose him. Wade Hampton, who returned from Virginia to help defend his home state, along with William Hardee and Fighting Joe Wheeler, would be leading the Confederate troops, which Sherman believed numbered about 15,000—a reasonably accurate estimate. In overall command was General P. G. T. Beauregard. Sherman knew that their forces "could hardly delay us an hour," he later wrote. He was somewhat concerned—"the only serious question" as the campaign began—that Lee might elude Grant, slipping away and marching south to intercept his advance, and making junction with the remnants of Hood's army that had escaped from Tennessee after the Battle of Nashville. If Lee should get away from Grant, Sherman was relying upon his friend to give chase and come up in the rear of Lee's forces.[12]

Sherman might face a much greater military challenge in the Carolinas than in the march across Georgia. Consequently he arranged for the navy to provide several points of security along the coast, in the event that a crisis developed. Otherwise he was confident, even if he would be traveling more than four hundred miles. He proceeded with the same arrangement for foraging and marching as during the trek to Savannah. The weather, not surprisingly, proved more severe than during the march to the sea. Heavy rain came down frequently, and the temperature was colder. Thomas W. Osborn, an artillery officer who kept a diary, wrote that "the nights are chilly, in truth very cold, and we require a large amount of clothing to make us comfortable."[13]

Osborn also noted, on February 2, that General Slocum's left wing was not advancing at the pace Sherman expected. "General Sherman is in high temper," wrote the officer, "and orders a halt until the left wing comes up." Sherman's "nervous temperament and sarcasm are now at their highest pitch, and all who are acquainted with him keep at a respectful distance." Osborn declared that it mattered not if one were a major general or a private, one would be wise not to "tamper" with Sherman at such a time. Significantly, Osborn was not being critical of Sherman. Actually his sympathies were with the commander. He feared that Slocum lacked "the ability and energy to cope with what he has on his hands." In fairness to Slocum, he faced greater problems in crossing the badly flooded Savannah River than did General Howard.[14]

Once on the move again, Sherman's forces soon approached the first of many menacing swamps, some of which were quite wide, and traversed by numerous river channels. Thomas Osborn recorded fascinating details about these obstacles, writing that Whippy Swamp Creek was three-quarters of a mile wide, with seven streams running through it. He said that another swamp was a mile across, "with the water running in thirty five different streams." Yet another had "sixteen clear and fine running streams, on an average of fifty feet wide and from one to two hundred feet apart." When he came upon one that was "only a quarter of a mile wide," he found the river running in nine streams, "and considerably deeper" than most that were crossed. Generally speaking, the swamps varied from knee deep to above a man's waist. Sometimes Sherman rode through, and sometimes he dismounted and waded along with the soldiers.[15]

The Confederates burned all the bridges, filled the roads with fallen timbers, skirmished with Sherman's advance and sometimes fortified the opposite side of a swamp or river, hoping to pick off some of the approaching Federal troops. They always refused a full-scale fight, pulling out when the superior Yankee troops threatened to flank them, if not before. Rumor spread that General Hardee, with 30,000 Rebels, awaited the Union forces on the far side of the Salkehatchie River, determined to make a desperate and bloody stand. It was just that—a rumor.

Obviously Sherman's pioneer organizations, often composed heavily of blacks, were of immense value, working continuously to construct roads and bridges across the swampy low country. They laid down literally miles and miles of corduroy roads, so that the artillery and supply wagons could advance with the infantry. And many of the infantry found themselves called upon to assist with the hard, heavy, filthy work. Great numbers of trees had to be felled, sheared of limbs and dragged to the passageway where they were laid side by side to form the rough road. Sometimes the mud was so thick and oozy that logs had to be laid on top of one another, several layers thick, before the primitive roadway became passable.[16]

It was a week into February when some of Sherman's troops reached Midway—a tiny town of five houses and a depot—located on the Charles-

ton & Augusta Railroad, about halfway between the two cities. The foraging party, which was about five miles ahead of the oncoming infantry,
at once recognized the importance of the railroad. They began throwing
up defensive works to hold it until the army could get up, and sent one of
their number back to inform the leading infantry division of their prize.
General Howard was riding with the Seventeenth Corps and beginning
to deploy the lead division in readiness for a possible battle at the railroad, when he saw a man approaching, "and riding as hard as he could."
Drawing near and recognizing Howard, the soldier called out, "Hurry
up, General; we have got the railroad!" He promised that the foragers
would "hold it against any force until you come up." Sherman later summarized the amusing situation: "While we, the generals, were proceeding deliberately to prepare for a serious battle, a parcel of our foragers, in
search of plunder . . . actually captured the South Carolina Railroad."[17]

As soon as the Union troops arrived in strength, they set to work on
the rails, giving them a spiral twist so they would have to be melted and
run out again, thus thoroughly destroying them for a distance of more
than forty miles. Only after the Union troops finished eradicating the
rails, and resumed the march toward Columbia, could the Rebels be reasonably sure that Sherman was moving on Columbia and not Augusta.[18]

Sherman wrote that the extensive destruction of the Charleston &
Augusta Railroad was done "partly to prevent any possibility of its restoration and partly to utilize the time necessary for General Slocum to get
up." Because Sherman hoped to keep up the delusion, as long as possible,
that the Union Army might yet turn west, he ordered Judson Kilpatrick
to demonstrate strongly with his cavalry in the direction of Augusta.
On February 11, with Slocum's wing finally near, Sherman resumed the
march toward Columbia. The path of each corps could be traced by columns of smoke, black and sometimes quite dense, rising from burning
houses, barns, business establishments, warehouses, cotton, turpentine
mills and fences. Only churches and schoolhouses survived. Sometimes
not even those escaped the vengeful torching of the Yankees. "The country behind us is . . . an utter desolation," declared a Union officer.[19]

Joseph T. Glatthaar, in his campaign study, stated that Sherman's troops burned a dozen towns on their march to Columbia. Sherman acknowledged that he made no particular effort to rein in the troops. An officer on General Slocum's staff claimed Sherman instructed Slocum that he need not be as careful about private property in South Carolina as in Georgia. The more destroyed the better, said Sherman, for the people of South Carolina were more responsible than anybody else for bringing on the conflict, and "should be made to feel the war." Sherman understood his army's emotions, and wrote that "I saw and felt that we would not be able longer to restrain our men as we had done in Georgia." He also claimed that he did not want the army's "vigor and energy . . . impaired," because he expected "bold and strong resistance at the many . . . rivers that lay across our path." Glatthaar concluded that "only at Orangeburg was there any suggestion that someone other than the Union army had begun the fire, and even then soldiers admitted that their comrades had plundered the town nonetheless."[20]

The burning of Orangeburg occurred because, according to George Nichols of Sherman's staff, the Confederates, preparing to retreat as the Federals approached, torched a large amount of cotton belonging to a Jewish merchant in order to keep it from falling into Sherman's hands. Ironically, Sherman would have destroyed the cotton anyway. The enraged merchant then burned his own store, apparently expecting the fire, fueled by a high wind, to burn the entire village—which it did. Both the Rebels and the merchant left town as the fire raged. Nichols noted that Sherman and Howard put soldiers to work in a futile attempt to extinguish the flames.[21]

Nichols also provides a compelling example of the disdain with which some Northerners viewed the Southern planter-aristocracy. His diary entry on February 12 states: "Tonight we are encamped upon the place of one of South Carolina's most high-blooded chivalry—one of those persons who believed himself to have been brought into the world to rule over his fellow-creatures, a sort of Grand Pasha." Nichols then penned a brief but devastating assessment of the "peculiar institution": "As near as I can ascertain," he charged, "it has been the effort of the South Carolina master to degrade his slaves as low in the scale of human nature, and as near the mules and oxen which he owns in common with them, as possible." He then added that "the evidences of the heartlessness and cruelty of these white men" had caused his "blood to boil."[22]

BY MID FEBRUARY, most of Sherman's forces had waded, slogged, corduroyed, foraged, fought and burned their way to the outskirts of Columbia. South Carolina's capital, picturesquely situated at the meeting of the Broad and Saluda Rivers, whose waters there formed the Congaree, had a population of less than 10,000 when the war began. The conflict swelled that number to approximately 25,000. Many of the streets were a spacious one hundred feet wide, lined with impressive trees, such as large magnolias, and accented by sizable, expensive homes. Considered one of the safest places in the Confederacy because of its remote site, the Confederate government printed money in Columbia, while bankers in various locations, most notably Charleston, had moved valuable assets there. The three banks of antebellum days had grown to more than fifteen. Columbia's production of munitions became one of its largest industries, and important railroads served the capital's transportation needs. Many Southerners who lived in areas perceived as more vulnerable to Yankee intrusion had sent all manner of treasured possessions to Columbia for safekeeping. Even large caches of expensive wines, brought in by blockade runners, had been transported to the city for protection. Then suddenly, Sherman's forces were drawing near the city.[23]

Blacks in Columbia seemed to know, or at least believe, that Sherman was heading for the capital before the whites realized it. Their praises for Sherman were voiced too often for the liking of some whites, who set up a whipping post in the city and severely flogged several of the blacks whom they considered too outspoken. Understandably, such abuse left many blacks bitter and primed for vengeance when Federal forces arrived. Another group ready to wreak violence was Union prisoners of war, who had been brought from Charleston and incarcerated at the state lunatic asylum. When the Rebels, upon the approach of Sherman, moved the prisoners to the railroad depot for transportation elsewhere, a number of them managed to escape. Having been mistreated by their captors—more than one prisoner had been shot for no apparent reason—some of those men were ready to burn South Carolina's capital to the ground.[24]

For days, rumors had circulated among Sherman's troops that Columbia was being strongly fortified, with Rebel forces concentrating there, and even male citizens being conscripted to help man the trenches. Major Confederate leaders were indeed present: P. G. T. Beauregard, Joe Johnston, Wade Hampton and Joe Wheeler. There was, however, no troop concentration achieved. The Confederates, in their determination to protect Charleston and Augusta, had few men for Columbia. After Southern sharpshooters fired at the Federals for a time—which was answered by Union artillery shelling the city—the Rebels soon decided to leave. Sherman was approaching from three directions, with overwhelming numbers, and the railroads from the capital to Charleston and Augusta were already in his hands. Before the Rebels pulled out, all the cotton bales were taken from the storehouses and piled in the main streets. Apparently Joe Wheeler's cavalry then set the cotton on fire, and they also continued to aggrandize their fearsome reputation for wanton destruction by plundering a number of stores. Some civilians, white and black, joined in the looting. Sherman said that the railroad depot and a large storehouse were also "burned to the ground." It was a prelude of much worse to come.[25]

Beauregard, Johnston, Hampton and the Confederate troops abandoned Columbia during the night of February 16 and the early morning of the seventeenth. The city's mayor, T. J. Goodwyn, accompanied by the aldermen, quickly came out and surrendered the capital to Sherman. Perhaps an hour before noon on the seventeenth, Sherman and his staff, along with General Howard and his staff, were riding through the main streets of the city. Cotton was still burning fiercely in some areas, and Yankee soldiers, along with civilians, worked to extinguish it. Thomas Osborn, who wrote his account of that triumphant day on the very next morning, declared that "the negroes went into demonstrations of delight which I have never before seen equaled. They ran, shouted, yelled, danced, and cut up curlicues generally."

George Nichols stated that the welcome the African-Americans gave Sherman "was singular and touching. They greeted his arrival with exclamations of unbounded joy."A great many of them wanted to shake the General's hand—"which he always gladly gives to these poor people." He was also met by escaped Union prisoners, who "had been secreted in the town by the negroes." Nichols said he had never seen Sherman's "face beam with such exultation ... as when he took those poor fellows by the hand and welcomed them home—home to the army, to protection, to the arms of their brave comrades." (Sherman and his soldiers, during the march to the sea, as earlier noted, had been deeply touched by the despicable facilities for Union prisoners in Millen, Georgia.)[26]

One of the escaped prisoners, S. H. M. Byers of the Fifth Iowa Infantry, handed Sherman a paper to read when he had time. The General soon discovered that while a prisoner, the officer had written a song entitled "Sherman's March to the Sea," which a group of the prisoners liked to sing. There were five stanzas, each followed by the chorus, the words of which were:

> Then sang we a song of our chieftain,
>   That echoed over river and lea;
> And the stars of our banner shone brighter
>   When Sherman marched down to the sea!

Sherman was so impressed that he sent for Byers, making him one of his staff officers, and the two men established a relationship that lasted for the remainder of their lives.[27]

Sherman placed General Howard in charge of Columbia and ordered him to "destroy the public buildings, railroad property, manufacturing and machine shops," but to "spare libraries, asylums, and private dwellings." Some of the soldiers decided the occasion warranted celebrating with liquor, of which there was a huge amount available. Doubtless the Northerners would have found the alcohol without assistance, but blacks and even some whites either brought out whiskey in buckets and bottles for the troops or happily guided them to the places where the booze was stored. Sherman observed, as he rode along the streets, "that several of the men were evidently in liquor," and called the matter to Howard's attention for appropriate action. The problem, however, considering the soldiers' mood, and the availability of unlimited alcohol—Sherman said he found 120 caches of whiskey in one cellar alone—only became worse.[28]

Meanwhile, Mayor Goodwyn directed Sherman to the house of Blanton Duncan, a lawyer who had fled with the Confederates. The mayor proposed that Sherman use the Duncan house as his quarters. The General found it satisfactory and settled in. A little later in the evening, the mayor returned with a message that there was a lady in the city who said she was a friend of Sherman. Inquiring as to her maiden name, Sherman realized the woman was the sister of James Poyas, the young man with whom he frequently hunted when stationed at Fort Moultrie in 1845, and whose family he recalled as "extremely hospitable." In fact he had been hunting with James Poyas when he suffered an excruciatingly painful injury, as his galloping horse failed to clear a fallen log and crashed violently to the ground, jamming a double-barreled gun into Sherman's armpit. Quite possibly the rheumatism recently troubling his right arm stemmed from that nasty accident, which had required months to heal.[29]

Sherman went at once to renew acquaintance with the friend from days long past. He had given her a book about watercolor painting, an art of which both she and he had been quite fond. He soon learned that the volume likely saved her house. Earlier in the day, Union soldiers had appeared, began chasing chickens and ducks in the yard and then entered the lady's house, evidently bent on taking anything they wanted. She immediately produced the book, inscribed to her by Sherman when he was a lieutenant. Telling the Union officer in charge of the soldiers that she was a friend of his commanding general, she demanded that he stop his men from pillaging. The officer examined the signature, then turned to the others and declared: "Boys . . . that's Uncle Billy's writing, for I have seen it before." He ordered the looting stopped and arranged for guards to protect the place. Sherman said he and the lady had a long visit. He admired how she had handled the menacing situation. When he rode out of Columbia a few days later, he had a hundred pounds of ham and a large quantity of rice delivered to her house.[30]

Returning to his quarters that night, Sherman lay down to rest, only to notice shortly thereafter a bright light flickering on the wall of his room. It was the startling reflection of fire. The mysterious Biblical writing on the palace wall, "Mene, Mene, Tekel, Upharsin," which the prophet Daniel interpreted as a signal that the end of King Belshazzar's reign was imminent, comes readily to mind—as if the flickering reflection upon Sherman's wall symbolized the fast-approaching fate of Columbia. All the more as high winds had arisen and buffeted the city for hours. Several buildings were on fire, much of the smoldering cotton had been rekindled and the conflagration was spreading. According to some historical accounts, and in the thinking of many Southerners both then and now, Sherman's savage army burned Columbia to the ground. Joseph Glatthaar wrote: "Just as Sherman's troops burned a dozen towns en route to Columbia, so they torched the capital."[31]

Actually the situation seems more complex. Sherman, as previously noted, had ordered that all private dwellings, as well as libraries and asylums, should not be harmed. He personally assured more than one resident that while several public buildings would be destroyed, the homes of citizens would be safe. There is ample evidence that the General, many of his officers and a lot of the troops worked to stop the spread of the fires. At the same time, however, there were Yankees bent on wreaking as much destruction as possible. A number of escaped prisoners of war were equally determined to set fire to all of the city. One of those men later claimed that he alone had torched seventeen houses. Even if he exaggerated, his baneful intentions are clear. A number of blacks joined in as well, plundering and burning. Some soldiers and civilians (including escaped civil prisoners), became intoxicated, which made the scene all the more dangerous. Several men who were dead drunk burned to death. The violent windstorm, frequently gusting with galelike force, whirled flaming debris through the air—some of which Sherman said was carried for five or six blocks—and spread the conflagration over still more of the city.[32]

George Nichols, who was with Sherman much of the time, wrote that "the central part of the city, including the main business street, was in flames, while the wind ... was driving the sparks and cinders in heavy masses over the eastern portion of the city, where the finest residences were situated. These buildings ... were instantly ignited" and soon "the conflagration was raging in every direction." The mansion of Wade Hampton was among those that went up in flames. Thomas Osborn reported that Union troops, trying to bring the fires under control, were arresting all men who were on the streets "and very frequently had to use force." Many were shot. Osborn claimed that *"forty* of our men were killed in this way."[33]

In some public buildings the Confederates "had stored shot, shell, and other ammunition," according to Nichols, "and when the flames reached these magazines we had the Atlanta experience again." Explosions sent "huge columns of fire shooting heavenward, the red-hot iron flying here and there." Sometime between midnight and two or three in the morning, the fierce wind finally subsided and the fire was contained. Otherwise the entire city would have been in ashes. Even so, a great many buildings were destroyed. Sherman said the fire "burned out the very heart of the city, embracing several churches, the old State-house, and the school ... of the very Sister of Charity who had appealed for my personal protection." While the high wind prevailed, "it was simply beyond human possibility" to stop the fires from spreading.[34]

The new statehouse, which was not completely finished, did survive, and a bunch of soldiers enjoyed a merry time there. About forty men gathered in the Senate chamber, organized themselves as the South Carolina legislative body and unanimously "repealed" the state's ordinance of secession—an ordinance unanimously passed in December 1860. They also "officially" censured John C. Calhoun, hurled inkstands and other objects at a bust of the famous politician and finally adjourned with provision to reconvene at the capital of North Carolina.[35]

When the army took up the march again on February 20, Thomas Osborn estimated that three-fourths of Columbia had been burned and every railroad into the town destroyed for approximately thirty miles.

For the rest of his life, Sherman would be denounced by many Southerners for intentionally and barbarously destroying Atlanta and Columbia. A decade later, for example, the Louisville *Courier-Journal*, in a ridiculous article, charged that Sherman had supervised the burning of Columbia's Ursuline Convent, watching with "demonic satisfaction" as the structure went up in flames.[36]

The truth is that when Sherman first entered the city, the convent's Lady Superioress (Sherman's term), who once taught in a school that Minnie attended, sent a message to Sherman appealing for protection. He told Charley Ewing, who was Roman Catholic, to visit and assure Sister Baptista Lynch that there would be no destruction of private property in Columbia. Unfortunately, the convent was located near where the fires started and could not be saved. The next day Sherman visited Sister Baptista, expressing his regret for the loss, and told her to select a suitable place for the young girls. She chose the Methodist Female College and Sherman gave his approval.[37]

Clearly Sherman never intended to destroy private property in Columbia; neither was he nor anyone else, Union or Confederate, exclusively responsible for the conflagration that wiped out so much of the city. In his official report, Sherman charged responsibility for the fire to Wade Hampton. He strongly disliked (despised may not be too strong a term) Hampton. And Confederates, whether upon the orders of Hampton or Wheeler, or their own initiative, did set fire to cotton bales that contributed to the great fire. However, as just described, many men played a role in the terrible event. Years later, speaking to a crowd of Union veterans, Sherman claimed: "Had I intended to burn Columbia... there would have been no concealment about it." Considering the General's character, that statement is credible.[38]

As the army left Columbia, it was followed by a large column of blacks fleeing slavery, whose numbers continued to grow on a daily basis. There were also many white refugees along, some of them Unionist in sentiment, who feared the vengeance of their neighbors. Others sought to escape forced service in the Rebel army, and doubtless all worried about the future if they stayed in the devastated capital. A number of Jews were denied the right to travel with the army, allegedly because they had loaded down the military transportation with their trunks.[39]

Osborn said that shortly after Sherman's army headed northeast from Columbia, some Confederate officers were captured, among whom were a principal and a second on their way to fight a duel that apparently, in some manner, involved a lady. David Conyngham, who told of the incident as well, said that "being chivalrous and obliging," the Federals "made every effort to catch the [other antagonist] in order to let them finish their little affair of honor in our presence, but failed." Osborn also said that "two of our men were found today (February 22) with their brains beat out, and from all appearances had been captured and then murdered." During the Georgia campaign some Union soldiers had been murdered after being captured, but on the march from Columbia to North Carolina, such atrocities became much more common.[40]

General Judson Kilpatrick, commanding the Union cavalry, reported to Sherman on February 22 that eighteen of his men had been murdered after they surrendered, their bodies mutilated and marked "Death to all Foragers." Sherman replied that foraging was clearly within the laws of war; the murder of soldiers who surrendered was not. He instructed Kilpatrick that the enemy's action "leaves no alternative; you must retaliate man for man. . . . Let it be done at once." Sherman got still another message from Kilpatrick, saying that the bodies of twenty-one Federal infantrymen had been found in a ravine, stripped of their clothing and their throats cut.[41]

Sherman sent a message to Wade Hampton, overall commander of the Confederate cavalry, on the following day: "It is officially reported to me that our foraging parties are murdered after capture and labeled 'Death to all Foragers.'" Citing two incidents of such atrocities, with the number killed, Sherman said he had ordered a like number of Confederate prisoners killed. "Personally I regret the bitter feelings engendered by this war," he wrote, and declared, "I merely assert our War Right to Forage," which he called "a war right as old as history." Hampton replied a short time later, livid with rage, saying it was the right of every Southern white to kill any Union forager as he would "a wild beast," and vowing that he would shoot two Yankee soldiers for every Confederate that Sherman's men killed.[42]

No one knows how many atrocities were committed as the hatred of each side for the other escalated, but the situation reached its worst during Sherman's march across northern South Carolina. In early March, he crossed the state line into North Carolina, and told Ellen, "South Carolina has had a visit from the West that will cure her of her pride and boasting." South Carolina would never forget Sherman's "visit," but his assessment, relative to pride and boasting, was overly optimistic. When compelled to face failure, prideful, boastful people are strongly inclined to rationalize and blame others and/or circumstances beyond their control. Sherman also declared that "the importance of this march exceeds that from Atlanta to Savannah."[43]

This was true. He proved, as he wrote Secretary of War Stanton, that "no place in the Confederacy was safe" from his army. He had bludgeoned the Southern will to resist the military strength of the United States. He had destroyed any realistic hope of ultimate Confederate success, and the people of the South realized that the Confederate armies could not protect them. The signs of Rebel collapse, material and psychological, were unmistakable and ubiquitous. Even Southern soldiers in the army of Robert E. Lee were impacted—disheartened by the news of Sherman's relentless forces moving at will, and laying waste at will, first across Georgia, and then through the Carolinas. He had brought the war, in devastating fashion, to the home of secession. His correspondence with various people during the late summer and early fall of 1864, and through his days in Savannah, contains a number of warnings that the war will likely drag on for some time. Once having devastated South Carolina, however, and moving relentlessly through North Carolina, such assertions cease. Sherman realized the conflict was nearly over.[44]

In North Carolina he wrote General Slocum that "it might be well to instruct your brigade commanders that we are now out of South Carolina and that a little moderation may be of political consequence to us in North Carolina." Sherman knew that a significant number of North Carolinians were Unionists. Others were disillusioned about the Confederacy, and perhaps ready to acknowledge Union supremacy. He instructed General Kilpatrick, "Deal as moderately and fairly by the North Carolinians as possible, and fan the flame of discord already existing between them and their proud cousins of South Carolina. There never was much love between them."[45]

Although final victory was drawing near, the situation was still very dangerous for all concerned. In fact, while General Kilpatrick was heading for Fayetteville, North Carolina, he came close to being captured or killed. Small of stature and quite ordinary in appearance, Kilpatrick nevertheless possessed a well-earned reputation for romantic adventures. George Nichols fittingly observed that Kilpatrick's face "is expressive of determination and daring." Indulging his passions, even though he knew that Rebel cavalry were in the general vicinity, Kilpatrick spent the night of March 9 in a house with a young woman from Columbia. Fortunately, he was awake in the early morning hours, wearing underclothing and a nightshirt, when he spotted enemy cavalry approaching. Abandoning uniform, pistol, horse and the woman, he dashed for safety, with the house serving to screen him from the view of the oncoming Confederates. Finding a stray horse, as fate smiled upon him, he rode away bareback. His companion, who is said to have been a beautiful woman, was rescued from possible harm by a Rebel cavalryman. He escorted her away from the ensuing turmoil and found a hiding place for her.[46]

While Sherman was marching through the Carolinas, the Confederates were desperately marshaling manpower in the hope of somehow striking a crippling blow against his forces. The remnants of Hood's defeated army, under the command of Alexander Stewart, arrived to strengthen the troops under Hardee and Hampton, along with other soldiers who were gathered from coastal garrisons. Joe Johnston, upon the advice of General Lee, was restored to command. With a total of no more than 25,000 men of all arms, Johnston faced a near impossible task. Sherman believed the Rebels were too weak and scattered to present any serious threat to his plans.

On March 11, he entered Fayetteville, North Carolina, which had been evacuated by Hardee's troops as the Union forces drew near. Sherman established his headquarters at the United States arsenal that the Southerners had been using since 1861. Because both Fort Fisher and the port of Wilmington were in Federal hands, Sherman was once more in contact, via the Cape Fear River, with the coast and the U.S. Navy. He took the opportunity, as he informed Grant, "to clean my columns of the vast crowd of refugees and negroes that encumber me. Some I will send down the river in boats & the balance . . . to Wilmington by land under small escort."[47]

George Nichols estimated that the total number of refugees who had followed the army since it left Savannah "could not have been less than twenty-five thousand," of which he said that "a very large proportion are negroes, chiefly women and children." Reflecting upon the army's difficulties in marching across the Carolinas, Nichols declared that "the fact of its accomplishment with twenty-five thousand . . . helpless human beings, devouring food and clogging every step onward, will remain one of the marvels of military operations." Nichols clearly revealed his sympathies for the African-Americans: "God help the poor creatures! They endured suffering and exposure in pursuit of freedom, and . . . have attained that boon at last."[48]

Notable among the white refugees heading for the coast from Fayetteville was General Kilpatrick's companion on the night when the Southern cavalry almost caught him. Marie Boozer was her name, and she was accompanied by her mother and younger sister. As Sherman left Fayetteville on March 15, he destroyed the arsenal and several public buildings. George Nichols claimed that private property "has been respected to a degree which is remarkable." Sherman continued to trek northeastward, riding initially with Slocum's left wing and advancing toward Goldsboro, from where he would have a railroad available to the coast. At Goldsboro he planned to link up with General Schofield's Twenty-Third Corps, accompanied by two divisions from the Tenth Corps, under Alfred Terry. Upon the orders of Grant, Schofield had been transported from Tennessee to North Carolina, covering some 1,400 miles by rail and water, and was moving to rendezvous with Sherman at Goldsboro.[49]

When Joe Johnston had been restored to command, he was ordered to concentrate all the Confederate forces available and "drive Sherman back." He struck on March 19, attacking Sherman's left wing about twenty-five miles southwest of Goldsboro, at a little place called Bentonville. He hoped to deliver a severe blow against a segment of Sherman's forces before the rest of his troops could render assistance. Sherman, who at the time was riding with his right wing, specifically the Fifteenth Corps, was taken by surprise, having supposed, as he later told Grant, that "all danger [of a Rebel attack] was passed." He referred to a sharp fight Slocum had with some 6,500 of Hardee's troops near a road junction at Averasboro on March 16, after which the Southerners withdrew and joined up with the rest of Johnston's forces a few miles to the rear.[50]

Johnston hit one of the Yankee divisions hard at Bentonville, but the Rebels were halted by a Federal counterattack. Johnston then took up a defensive position and hoped that the Federals would make an assault. On March 20, Sherman was at hand, and the rest of his forces were arriving, which gave him nearly a three-to-one advantage in manpower. Perhaps at that point he might have destroyed Johnston's army, but he chose not to attack. However, on March 21, the aggressive Joseph Mower, commanding the First Division of the Seventeenth Corps, broke through the Confederate left flank, penetrated deeply and threatened Johnston's only line of retreat. Sherman had a great opportunity to administer a deathblow to Johnston's forces, but instead ordered Mower to pull back to the line of his corps.[51]

"I think I made a mistake there," Sherman said later, "and should rapidly have followed Mower's lead with the whole of the right wing, which would have brought on a general battle, and it could not have resulted otherwise than successfully to us, by reason of our vastly superior numbers." But at the time he had to make the decision, Sherman was not thinking in terms of waging battle. In fact, he told Slocum the day before, "I would rather avoid a general battle if possible." While he had good reason to believe that his army was significantly greater in strength than Johnston's, he could not be sure what the difference might be. He wanted first to rendezvous with Schofield if forced to confront the Rebels in a full-scale engagement.[52]

Actually, the bottom line is that Sherman saw no need for fighting a general battle at this stage of the war anyway. In gaining a great triumph his army would inevitably suffer casualties. Even if the Confederate losses proved significantly more than the Union's, that would be little consolation if there were no good reason to have fought the battle in the first place. Sherman knew that his marches had devastated great parts of Georgia and the Carolinas, hammering both the ability and the will of the Confederacy to continue prosecuting the war. He had written his father-in-law on the last day of 1864, saying that his army "will march to certain death if I order it, because they know & feel that night & day I labor to the end that not a life shall be lost in vain." More than ever, when the terrible conflict was so near the end, Sherman wanted to spare the lives of his soldiers as much as he possibly could.[53]

By nightfall of March 21, Johnston realized that holding his position any longer had become too dangerous, and he withdrew under cover of darkness, retreating in the direction of Raleigh. He concluded about Sherman: "I can do no more than annoy him." The Battle of Bentonville, the only significant effort to stop Sherman's march, cost the Confederates nearly 3,500 casualties, with 240 killed. Union losses were about 1,500, of whom 194 were killed.[54]

ENCOUNTERING NO FURTHER opposition, Sherman's forces triumphantly marched into Goldsboro with flags flying and bands sounding patriotic aires. The junction with Schofield and Terry dramatically signaled the successful climax of the Carolina campaign, for Sherman now had approximately 90,000 troops at hand. He was strong enough to deal with any conceivable Confederate move by Johnston or Lee, even if Lee should manage to escape Grant and join forces with Johnston—a then highly unlikely scenario. The proud general stated: "We had in midwinter accomplished the whole journey of four hundred and twenty-five miles [from Savannah] in fifty days," and had reached Goldsboro "with the army in superb order, and the trains almost as fresh as when we started from Atlanta." He declared that the endeavor was "one of the longest and most important marches ever made by an organized army."[55]

While at Goldsboro Sherman devoted a lot of time to writing letters, both official and personal. In a letter to Minnie on March 24, he remarked that the hour was almost midnight, "and I have written nearly thirty long letters, but have a great many more to write." These letters provide priceless insights to his thinking at the time. "I would like to march this army through New York just as it appears today, with its wagons, pack mules, cattle, niggers and bummers," he wrote Ellen, "and I think they would make a more attractive show than your fair." He referred to his wife's participation in organizing a U.S. Sanitary Commission fair, to be held at Chicago in June, for the relief of soldiers and their families. Ellen had requested that Cump send her anything of value that might be used in raising money. He told her that he had nothing worthwhile to contribute and added, "I don't much approve of ladies selling things at a table," but said that he did not object to her helping organize and manage the proceedings. Eventually he did send her the Confederate flag that had flown over the statehouse in Columbia.[56]

As a truly national military hero, Sherman's name was being frequently alluded to in connection with the presidency of the United States. It was a natural, probably inevitable development, considering that four of the sixteen presidents—Washington, Jackson, Harrison and Taylor—had been generals. Sherman, however, had no interest whatsoever in that exalted office. Responding to a letter from a lawyer in St. Louis, the General indulged his love of hyperbole: "You may tell *all* that I would rather serve 4 years in the Singsing Penitentiary than in Washington & believe that I could come out a better man. If that ain't emphatic enough, use strong expressions and I will endorse them."[57]

Informed that the *New York Tribune* had recently characterized him as an abolitionist, Sherman seemed delighted to respond that "a nigger as such is a most excellent fellow, but he is not fit to marry, to associate, or vote with me, or mine." Regarding the right to vote, Sherman replied to Chief Justice Chase, who had reprimanded him about the language he employed in reference to African-Americans. Sherman not only opposed blacks voting, but arrestingly added, "Indeed it appears to me that the right of suffrage in our Country should be rather abridged than enlarged." Clearly, in Sherman's judgment, not all white males deserved to vote, either.[58]

He also got off a letter to Commodore Thomas Turner, who had written to offer his congratulations on the march to Savannah. Thomas was a brother of Henry S. Turner, Sherman's business associate and close friend before the war. Henry was a Southern sympathizer, whom Sherman had been out of contact with for about two years. He had learned that Henry and his wife lost two sons in the conflict, one serving in the Confederate Army, and the other with the Union forces. In responding to the commodore, Sherman spoke at length of his friendship with Henry, and said that "the loss of his notice . . . has been to me the Source of much pain. I fear he believes all the absurd stories people tell of me." The letter had the effect for which Sherman no doubt hoped. Thomas Turner contacted Henry, who soon wrote Sherman a good letter, which led to the reestablishment of their warm relationship.[59]

Sherman penned another interesting letter, to the governor of California, Frederick F. Low, who wrote to express the thanks of the people of California for the triumphant campaigns in which Sherman and his forces engaged. Sherman assured Governor Low that every soldier of his army "will feel a new pride when he is assured that far off on the golden coast of the Pacific . . . our fellow citizens have hailed our progress through this land whose inhabitants had well-nigh brought our Government to ruin and infamy." Closing in rather memorable style, Sherman declared, "I bid you be of good cheer, for there are . . . brave men . . . who are determined that the sun, as he daily reviews our continent from the Chesapeake to San Francisco Bay, shall see a united people, and not a bundle of quarreling factions."[60]

By March 26, Sherman laid aside his pen. Repairs on the railroad from Goldsboro to New Bern were finished, the army would soon be fully resupplied by rail, and he could head for City Point, Virginia, to confer with Grant in person. Leaving Schofield temporarily in command of the troops, Sherman took along two staff officers, and rapidly made his way to meet with the general-in-chief on March 27 and 28. Brigadier General Horace Porter, an 1860 West Point graduate, who had been on Grant's staff for the past year, said that when the steamer transporting Sherman up the James River docked, "Sherman . . . jumped ashore and was hurrying forward with long strides to meet his chief." Greeting each other enthusiastically, Sherman and Grant stood "with their hands locked in a cordial grasp, uttering earnest words of familiar greeting." Proceeding to Grant's headquarters, Sherman received a hearty welcome from Julia Grant as well. He took a seat close to the fire and, with Grant and his wife and several officers listening, "gave a most graphic description of the stirring events of his march through Georgia."[61]

Porter assessed the presentation as "the more charming from the fact that it was related without the manifestation of the slightest egotism." He declared, "Never were listeners more enthusiastic; never was a speaker more eloquent. The story, told as he alone could tell it, was a grand epic related with Homeric power." Eventually, after about an hour, Grant interrupted, telling Sherman that President Lincoln was at hand, aboard the *River Queen*, "and I know he will be anxious to see you." Grant suggested that they visit the President before dinner, to which Sherman readily agreed. Lincoln greeted Sherman graciously and enthusiastically, obviously very pleased to see him. "He was full of curiosity," remembered Sherman, "about the many incidents of our great march, which had reached him officially and through the newspapers, and seemed to enjoy very much the more ludicrous parts." The President was rather worried about the army in Sherman's absence, but the General assured him that Schofield was fully capable of managing any problem that might arise. With plans made to visit with Lincoln again the next day, the generals returned to Grant's headquarters and sat down to discuss military plans.[62]

"'Perhaps you don't want me here listening to all your secrets,' remarked Mrs. Grant," according to Porter's account. Sherman, who was obviously enjoying himself, glanced at Julia and asked Grant if he really thought they could trust her. When Grant immediately expressed doubt, Sherman turned his chair toward Mrs. Grant. Declaring that he had some questions for her, he claimed that her answers would determine whether or not she could understand their plans well enough to betray them to the Rebels. Assuming a grave tone, Sherman proceeded in "a manner which became more and more amusing," wrote Porter, asking her "all sorts of geographical questions about the Carolinas and Virginia." At once entering into the spirit of the occasion, Julia replied with answers indicating little or no knowledge of rivers, mountains, etc. (Actually, having studied the maps at her husband's headquarters, Julia Grant possessed a good geographical knowledge of the war theaters.) "In a short time," continued Porter, "Sherman turned to his chief, who had been greatly amused . . . and exclaimed, 'Well, Grant, I think we can trust her.'" The generals proceeded with their conversation.[63]

The next morning, Admiral Porter arrived at Grant's headquarters, and he and Sherman visited for a time. Particularly, Porter wanted to know about the swamps and overflowing rivers that had confronted Sherman in the Carolinas. The two also reminisced about the swamps they contended with in Mississippi. After a conversation of a quarter of an hour or so, Sherman and Porter accompanied Grant to President Lincoln's ship. No one else was present as the four men met in the upper salon of the *River Queen*. "After the general compliments," wrote Sherman, "Grant inquired after *Mrs.* Lincoln."[64]

Grant's wife, when Sherman and Grant returned from seeing the President the previous day, was disturbed to learn that neither general had asked about Lincoln's wife. The omission was a faux pas, a serious one in Julia Grant's estimation, and Grant intended to rectify the miscue at the first opportunity. In response to Grant's query, the President went to his wife's room, returned "and begged us to excuse her," recalled Sherman, "for she was not well." Probably Mary Lincoln was still upset by the rough ride that she and Julia Grant experienced in an army ambulance shortly after she first arrived at City Point—as well as what followed.

Lincoln, Grant and several officers had ridden ahead on horseback, so as not to be late for a scheduled review of troops, while the two women, accompanied by Horace Porter, made their way over a corduroyed road. At one point Mrs. Lincoln was lifted off her seat, and the jolt jammed her head against the top of the wagon. She then insisted on getting out and walking, but Porter, observing that the mud was knee deep, convinced her that such a course would be worse than the ambulance. Mary at last reached the parade grounds, presumably in a foul mood, to find not only that the review was under way but—far worse in her mind—that the wife of General E. O. C. Ord, who was an attractive woman, was riding beside the President in the place that she would have occupied. Mary mounted a distressing, vile tirade against Mrs. Ord, and continued to manifest her anger at dinner later that evening. She likely was still agitated when the President told Grant, on the morning of the conference, that Mrs. Lincoln was not well. Little wonder too that Julia Grant had wanted her husband to ask about the well-being of Mary Lincoln.[65]

Proceeding with the meeting, the President and the three military men engaged in an informal discussion of the issues facing the nation as the war neared its conclusion. Grant told the President that he planned to move at once around the Rebel flank and cut Lee's army off from the Carolinas. If Lee should move first, Grant promised to be in hot pursuit, while Sherman assured the President, according to Horace Porter's account, that "in such a contingency his army, by acting on the defensive, could resist both Johnston and Lee until Grant could reach him." The Rebels then "would be caught in a vise," from which no escape would be possible. Lincoln seemed deeply concerned about the possibility of another bloody battle and hoped that such might somehow be avoided. Grant and Sherman realized, of course, that the issue was not in their hands—as no doubt Lincoln himself was fully aware.[66]

Sherman wanted to know what, once the war ended, was to be done with the Rebel armies and their political leaders. Lincoln was strongly inclined toward a lenient policy. He wanted, in Sherman's words, "to get the men composing the Confederate armies back to their homes, at work on their farms and in their shops." He had no desire for retaliation. "Let them have their horses to plow with, and, if you like, their guns to shoot crows with." In the President's second inaugural address, he had spoken of "malice toward none," and "charity for all." Sherman later recalled those words, and said Lincoln seemed to him the very embodiment of a benevolent spirit, as he spoke of how he hoped to deal with the defeated South.[67]

As for the fate of the Confederate political leaders, Horace Porter recorded that the President "intimated, though he did not say so in express terms, that it would relieve the situation if they should escape to some foreign country." Lincoln, understandably, was not about to say such a thing in public, but it was clear that, unlike a lot of people in the North, he did not intend or desire revenge against Jefferson Davis and the others. The President again expressed apprehension about Sherman's being away from his army. Once more Sherman assured him that Schofield could cope with any situation that might occur. Sherman added that he was starting back to Goldsboro right after noon. When he left Lincoln, whom he would never see again, Sherman wrote in his memoirs that he "was more than ever impressed by his kindly nature," and he declared that, "of all the men I ever met," Lincoln "seemed to possess more of the elements of greatness, combined with goodness, than any other."[68]

John Sherman had come down from Washington, and he accompanied his brother back to Goldsboro for a short visit. The two discussed family matters as well as affairs in the nation's capital. Sherman remained in an exuberant mood as he reflected upon his success. "The last march from Savannah to Goldsboro," he wrote Ellen, "is by far the most important in Conception and Execution of any act of my life." He rejoiced as he continued to receive "the highest compliments from all quarters." Grant was "the same enthusiastic friend. Mr. Lincoln . . . was lavish in his good wishes, and since Mr. Stanton visited me at Savannah, he too has become the warmest possible friend." (Within a month Sherman surely rued such a thought about Stanton.) Continuing to revel in his most recent triumph, the General spoke of his deceased son, by then a year and a half in the grave: "Oh, that Willy could hear & see—his proud little heart would swell to overflowing."[69]

Thinking of Minnie and Lizzie, Sherman vowed again—"if I live"—to certainly "redeem my promise to Minnie to send her, and Lizzie too, to the best school I can find in New York next year." He assured Ellen that he had recently written to both Minnie and Lizzie, promising to get off a letter to Tommy soon as well. John Sherman was advising that Ohio's contribution in honor of Cump's military successes should be used to secure a homestead for Ellen. John had indicated that Ellen preferred that the money be used for that purpose. The General thought it better to wait until the war is over, "and determines my fate," before making a decision about a homestead. "Still," he told his wife, "if you want a home in Cincinnati, I shall not object."[70]

Sherman had to get on with the war. Preparing to take the offensive against Johnston's forces, he wrote Thomas Ewing Sr. that again he would be trusting to maneuver, "which wins better than rough fighting." The conflict was finally and rapidly drawing to a close. South of Petersburg, Virginia, Grant, with overwhelming numbers at his command, was extending the Federal lines farther to the west, compelling the inferior Rebels to stretch out and weaken their defenses. At some point, and soon, Grant would either break through the thin Confederate line or turn Lee's right flank and cut off any possibility of escape. At nightfall on Sunday, April 2, General Lee pulled his troops out of the doomed Petersburg fortifications and tramped westward, with the soldiers spread out on several roads as they headed toward Amelia Court House. There Lee hoped to find badly needed supplies. Grant pursued on a more or less parallel route to the south, aiming to block Lee's path and compel him to fight at a great disadvantage or surrender. Federal forces quickly moved into both Richmond and Petersburg.[71]

When Sherman heard this news, he wrote Grant that he was "delighted and amazed at the result of your move to the south of Petersburg." He declared that Grant's "perseverance and pluck . . . would make Wellington jump out of his coffin." Meanwhile, General Lee had reached a dead end. With no supplies available at Amelia Court House and superior Union forces marshaling to both the east and west, Lee surrendered the Army of Northern Virginia to Grant at Appomattox Court House on April 9. Five days later, Joe Johnston asked Sherman for an armistice.

April 14 was also the day that actor John Wilkes Booth fatally shot President Lincoln at Ford's Theater, as the President watched a presentation of *Our American Cousin*. The assassination of Lincoln was an event, in the words of historians E. B. Long and Barbara Long, that "will remain vivid as long as the history of the United States is known."[72]

Chapter Twenty-Five

A SOLDIER OF RENOWN

On the morning of April 17, Sherman was about to board a train at Raleigh, North Carolina, for a short ride to negotiate with Joe Johnston, when he received a telegram from Edwin Stanton informing him that the President had been assassinated. Secretary of State William Seward and his son had been attacked about the same time as Lincoln and were seriously injured. The secretary of war warned Sherman that he had "evidence that an assassin is also on your track." Sherman ordered the telegrapher not to reveal the awful news to anyone. He planned to return from a noon meeting with Johnston by late afternoon, and at that time would break the stunning news to his officers and the army.[1]

A few miles out from Durham Station, Sherman and Johnston met in a small farmhouse belonging to James Bennett and his wife, readily granted to use as the site of the conference. The two generals had never seen one another before that day, "but we knew enough of each other," thought Sherman, "to be well acquainted at once." All staff officers remained outside the house. The Bennetts withdrew into a little log structure nearby. "As soon as we were alone together," Sherman said he showed Johnston the dispatch announcing Mr. Lincoln's assassination. Observing the Confederate general closely, Sherman declared that he made no attempt to conceal his distress. Johnston condemned the act unequivocally and said he hoped that Sherman did not think the Confederate government had instigated it. Sherman assured him that he did not believe Johnston, Lee or any Confederate military officers would have condoned an assassination. He "would not say as much for Jeff Davis," and other "men of that stripe"—a remark that angered Davis when he heard about it. Sherman was impressed by Johnston's concern about Lincoln's death. Johnston looked upon the loss as a blow to the people of the South who, he said, "had begun to realize that Mr. Lincoln was the best friend the South had."[2]

The two generals discussed the impact of the assassination on the country generally, and on the armies. Sherman worried about the effect on his troops in Raleigh. Many Union soldiers revered Lincoln and Sherman feared that some might seek vengeance on the North Carolina capital and the surrounding areas. Johnston seemed fully aware of the delicate situation with which Sherman would have to deal. The generals were in complete agreement that any further fighting was to be avoided if at all possible. Johnston wanted to not only surrender his army, but also arrange terms to cover all Confederate forces. Like Sherman, he seemed quite troubled about the possibility of the Southern armies breaking up and waging guerrilla actions. Sherman questioned whether Johnston had the authority to negotiate on such a broad scale. Admitting he did not at that moment, Johnston believed he could procure such power from Jefferson Davis. The generals agreed to meet again the next day at noon, at the same place. Their conversation had been "extremely cordial," in Sherman's words. He then hurried back to Raleigh, hoping that word of the President's assassination had not leaked out while he was gone.[3]

It had not. Before making an announcement to the army, Sherman stationed heavy guards in Raleigh, and ordered his generals to see that order was maintained. "The general commanding announces, with pain and sorrow," read Special Field Orders No. 56, "that on the evening of the 14th instant, at the theater in Washington City, his Excellency, the President of the United States, Mr. Lincoln, was assassinated." Telling of the attempt to kill Secretary of State Seward and his son, Sherman stated, "It is believed, by persons capable of judging, that other high officers were designed to share the same fate. Thus it seems that our enemy, despairing of meeting us in open, manly warfare, begins to resort to the assassin's tools." While confident that "the great mass of the Confederate army would scorn such acts," Sherman considered the assassination "the legitimate consequence of rebellion against rightful authority." Union men, he concluded, "must now be prepared for . . . assassins and guerrillas; but woe unto the people who seek to expend their wild passions in such a manner, for there is but one dread result!"[4]

The announcement was powerful and memorable, the last statement packed with emotion. Perhaps Sherman might have chosen a less rousing thought on which to end, but he had little time to formulate the announcement, and he surely wanted the army to have no doubt that their commanding general had been deeply moved, both by the President's death and the manner in which he died. "I doubt if, in the whole land, there were more sincere mourners over [Lincoln's] . . . sad fate then there were in . . . Raleigh," Sherman wrote of his army. Soldiers gathered "in little squads, silent or talking in subdued but bitter tones," observed Major Hitchcock, "many . . . weeping like children." General Howard remarked that "the grief is . . . completely depressing amongst the officers." He saw generals shedding tears when they spoke of Lincoln.[5]

Some angry soldiers sought to strike out in retaliation. Thomas Osborn stated that it was only "with considerable difficulty that the army has been restrained from acts of revenge." The most serious threat was mounted by about two thousand men from General Logan's Fifteenth Corps. Billeted just outside of Raleigh, a mob began marching toward the city, bellowing threats to burn the capital. As they approached, General Jacob Cox, whose troops were guarding Raleigh, watched anxiously, wondering what the next few minutes might bring. Then Black Jack Logan galloped up and ordered his men to turn back. They halted momentarily, then resumed moving toward the city. Only when Logan, raising his booming voice, threatened to open artillery fire on them with canister, did the soldiers finally obey his order and return to camp.[6]

During that evening, and early the next morning, Sherman sought the advice of his generals before again meeting with Johnston. "Without exception," Sherman said, they all advised him "to agree to some terms" that would end the conflict. "If Johnston made a point of it," they even thought Jefferson Davis and his cabinet should be permitted to escape from the country. Black Jack Logan, according to his biographer, "was most vocal in favoring surrender on almost any terms." Frank Blair, also a politician, was of like mind. Sherman remarked that "either Logan or Blair" insisted that, if necessary, "we should even provide a vessel to carry [Davis and company] . . . from Charleston to Nassau."[7]

On the morning of April 18, Sherman again boarded a railcar, in company with most of his personal staff, and steamed to Durham Station, where he and Johnston once more rendezvoused at the Bennett house. Johnston assured him that he had indeed gained the authority to surrender all the Confederate armies. In return Johnston wanted an assurance of the political rights of Confederate officers and soldiers. This, he contended, would be very helpful in gaining their acceptance of the surrender terms.[8]

Only a few days earlier Sherman had written General Grant, praising his surrender terms with Lee as "magnanimous and liberal," and saying that he would "of course grant the same" to Johnston when the time came. Reiterating that intention on April 15, Sherman promised Grant that he would "be careful not to complicate any point of civil policy." Unfortunately, whatever his motives, Sherman proceeded to do the very thing he had pledged not to do. He did say to Johnston that Lincoln's amnesty proclamation of December 1863 was still in force, and that it guaranteed surrendered soldiers would receive a full pardon, which restored their rights of citizenship. Johnston insisted that Confederate officers and men were alarmed and, regardless of the Lincoln proclamation, the surrender terms needed to address the issue.[9]

Johnston also wanted to bring John Breckinridge, who was nearby, into their deliberations. Sherman objected. The former vice president of the United States was then serving as Confederate secretary of war, and Sherman contended that he and Johnston were engaged in a military convention. Johnston countered that Breckinridge was also a major general in the Confederate Army, and his input could be valuable. Sherman relented and the Kentuckian joined the discussion. He soon confirmed what Johnston had contended about the uneasiness of Southern soldiers and officers regarding their political rights after surrender.[10]

Not long after Breckinridge joined them, Sherman walked to the door and called for his saddlebags, which a staff member quickly brought to him. He produced a bottle therefrom and offered Johnston and Breckinridge a drink. The latter is said to have "poured out a tremendous drink, which he swallowed with great satisfaction." Possibly Sherman felt the two Southerners were ganging up on him and sought to create a more congenial atmosphere through imbibing a little alcohol. During the negotiations, Sherman reportedly shoved back his chair and blurted something to the effect: "Who is doing the surrendering anyhow? If this thing goes on, you'll have me sending a letter of apology to Jeff Davis." And then again, perhaps Sherman himself simply wanted a drink, and politely offered the others one as well. Breckinridge's alcoholic pleasure was short-lived, however. When Sherman, working intensely on composing the surrender terms, poured himself another drink, he then corked the bottle without passing it on. While Joe Johnston attributed the sleight to absentmindedness, Breckinridge was incensed, later telling Johnston that "no Kentucky gentleman would ever" have done such a thing.[11]

When Sherman finished writing the surrender document, he felt great pride and confidence in the achievement. It was, he assured Grant and Halleck, "an absolute submission of the enemy to the lawful authority of the United States, and disperses his armies . . . in such a manner as to prevent their breaking up into guerrilla bands." Because both Johnston and Breckinridge "admitted that slavery was dead," Sherman claimed he "could not insist on embracing it in such a paper, because it can be made with the states in detail." Sherman said that as he wrote, he recalled his conversation with Lincoln at City Point and composed terms that "concisely expressed his views and wishes." Admiral Porter, who was with Sherman at City Point, declared that "Sherman would not, and could not have been censured," for his surrender terms if the conversation between Lincoln and the General had been known. Porter asserted that "Mr. Lincoln, had he lived, would have acquitted the General of any blame."[12]

Whether Porter was right about Lincoln or not, the fact remains that Lincoln was dead, and Sherman had plunged into delicate and controversial issues. He had entered into terms of a political nature. His document recognized the existing state governments in the South, effective as soon as their members took an oath of allegiance to the United States. Where conflicting state governments existed, the U.S. Supreme Court would determine which should be recognized as legitimate. His terms sanctioned the reestablishment of Federal courts in the South, and guaranteed the "political rights and franchises" of the Southern people, "as well as their rights of persons and property." The terms seemed even to leave a possibility of recognizing the Confederate war debt. Sherman also indicated that no one was to be punished "by reason of the late war, so long as they live in peace and quiet."[13]

No doubt Sherman believed that he was acting in the best interests of the nation, and in the spirit of the assassinated president. But many in the North believed that, at the least, major Confederate political and military leaders should be punished, the franchise denied to all who had supported the Confederacy and freedom, including the right to vote, assured for the former slaves. Whatever Sherman, Johnston and Breckinridge might think about slavery being "dead," Southern plantation magnates had long defined slaves as "property," the right of which Sherman's surrender terms guaranteed. When the document reached Washington, the brouhaha was on.

Secretary of War Stanton rose like a viper and struck vehemently at Sherman. Long aggravated by Sherman's negative attitude toward blacks serving in the army, or toward their being placed on an equality with whites, Stanton led a charge to reject Sherman's surrender terms, as well as discredit and embarrass the General. At a hastily arranged meeting of Andrew Johnson, the newly sworn-in president, as well as the cabinet and General Grant, the terms were officially disavowed, while the conversation even entailed implications of disloyalty on the part of Sherman. Stanton reacted as if Sherman had penned an unalterable treaty rather than a proposal to be duly considered. In Stanton's impassioned denigration of Sherman, "there were echoes of Ebenezer Creek," in the words of one historian, as well as Stanton's controversy with the General in Savannah.

Stanton bluntly ordered Grant to give notice of the government's disapproval to the General. He told Grant that "the instructions given to you by the late President Abraham Lincoln on the 3rd of March by my telegraph of that date, addressed to you, express substantially the views of President Andrew Johnson and will be observed by General Sherman." The secretary of war ordered Grant to "proceed immediately" to Sherman's headquarters, "and direct operations against the enemy." Since Lincoln's death, Edwin Stanton, as his biographers Benjamin P. Thomas and Harold Hyman concluded, "was indeed in virtual control of the government," and he was essentially ordering Sherman removed from command.[14]

Stanton's March 3 telegram, conveying Lincoln's instructions about negotiating with Lee, stated that Grant was "not to decide, discuss, or confer upon any political question. Such questions the President holds in his own hands, and will submit them to no military conferences or conventions." Unfairly for Sherman, Stanton neither sent him a copy of Lincoln's instructions nor conveyed to him the substance of Lincoln's message, which obviously he should have done if he expected it to be followed. When Sherman conferred with Johnston, uppermost in his mind was the conference with Lincoln at City Point, where the President spoke of lenient terms of capitulation and the opportunity of arranging the surrender of all Confederate armies in such a manner as to forestall the breakup of Rebel forces into guerrilla bands. As some critics have asserted, Sherman's disdain for politicians and his own sense of importance as a military conqueror should be factored into any evaluation of his motivations in authoring the lenient surrender terms. These, however, were not primary.[15]

Even General Halleck, whom Sherman had long considered a friend, provided Stanton with information that, whether Halleck so intended or not, could be readily analyzed to Sherman's detriment. Halleck, recently

placed in charge of Virginia and the section of North Carolina not occupied by Sherman's forces, wired Stanton on April 22; from "respectable
parties" in Richmond, he told Stanton that he had learned the president of the Confederacy, "and his partisans" were trying to escape with
a "very large" cache of "gold plunder, to go to Mexico or Europe." They
hoped "to make terms with Sherman or some other Southern commander," and Halleck concluded that "Johnston's negotiations look to
this end."

Four days later, Halleck, who by then knew that Sherman's surrender
terms with Johnston had been overturned, sent another message to Stanton, which was even more disparaging to Sherman. Halleck had ordered,
acting upon Grant's instructions (which were unknown to Sherman),
that General George Meade and the Army of the Potomac should move
into North Carolina and block the retreat of Johnston's forces. Also,
George Thomas, George Stoneman and James Wilson, all under Sherman's command, should "pay no regard to any truce or orders" of Sherman. It was as if no negotiations had ever occurred between Sherman
and Johnston. When Sherman learned of Halleck's role in "the deadly
malignity" perpetrated against him, he never forgave the man. Halleck
eventually apologized for his message to Stanton. Sherman refused to
accept the apology, and bitterly declared that when warned of an assassin being on his trail, "I little dreamed he would turn up in the direction
and guise he did."[16]

Stanton, for his part, continued to spew a massive dose of venom against
Sherman. His letter of April 22 to Major General John A. Dix in New
York, who commanded the Department of the East, strongly intimated
that Sherman, in Sherman's later summation, was "a common traitor
and a public enemy," whose subordinates had been instructed to disobey
his "lawful orders." The letter got into the hands of newspapermen—as
Sherman correctly believed that Stanton intended—and was published in
many Northern papers. "To say that I was merely angry . . . would hardly
express the state of my feelings," Sherman wrote in his memoirs. "I was
outraged beyond measure." While undoubtedly Sherman had over-
stepped his authority, he did not deserve to be treated in the way that the

impetuous Stanton had branded his motives, and then spread the awful implications far and wide. "I do think that my rank, if not past services," Sherman declared in a letter to Grant on April 28, "entitled me at least to the respect of keeping secret what was known to none but the cabinet until further inquiry could have been made."[17]

Sherman of course had known nothing about the hullabaloo in Washington until Grant, acting on Stanton's orders, arrived at his headquarters on April 24. Tactfully and carefully, Grant explained some aspects of the situation but did not share the full story. Although the two generals talked at length, Grant did not reveal that Stanton had ordered him to take over Sherman's army. Neither did Grant inform Sherman of the impassioned cabinet meeting—during which Grant had remained silent while Stanton raged against Sherman. Considering Stanton's frame of mind, Grant well may have thought that silence was the path of wisdom in that situation. There was no mention of the charges that Sherman intended to allow Jefferson Davis to escape from the country nor the rumors that Sherman planned to seize power and become a dictator. (Attorney General James Speed seemed to believe this, at least for a time.)

Sherman remained calm and reasonable as he and Grant conversed. At once Sherman notified Joe Johnston that the terms had been disapproved in Washington and the truce was terminated. Since both wanted an end to the war, they soon met again at the Bennett house and signed a new document that closely emulated Grant's surrender terms with Lee. Grant was pleased and returned to the capital. Having listened to Sherman's point of view, Grant was incensed at the manner in which Stanton had dealt with him. The actions of the secretary of war, and those who supported him, were "infamous—infamous! After four years of such service as Sherman has done—that he should be used like this."[18]

Grant immediately composed an explanatory message to Stanton, designed to restore confidence in Sherman, who had acted upon "what he thought was precedent authorized by the President." It was a good telegram, clearly indicating that Sherman had acted in good faith and had taken steps at once to set matters right when informed his terms were

unacceptable. But Stanton was in a white-hot fury. Just three words—
"Your dispatch received"—constituted the sole recognition that the secretary of war made of Grant's message. Caustically Stanton inveighed:
"The arrangement between Sherman and Johnston meets with universal disapprobation. No one of any class or shade of opinion approves it.
I have not known as much surprise and discontent at anything that has
happened during the war." His last sentence declared, "The hope of the
country is that you may repair the misfortune occasioned by Sherman's
negotiations."[19]

Stanton then proceeded to delete the portions of Grant's telegram
that explained Sherman's motivations and attitude. He released a mere
two sentences to the press, which omitted any indication that most of
Grant's message had been expunged. The highly misleading publication simply read: "I reached here [Sherman's headquarters] this morning, and delivered to General Sherman the reply to his negotiations
with Johnston. Word was immediately sent to Johnston terminating
the truce, and information that civil matters could not be entertained
in any convention between army commanders." Historian Burke Davis
stated that the full copy of Grant's telegram was hidden away in Stanton's files—found only after the secretary of war died.[20]

As yet unaware of the unscrupulous machinations of Stanton, Sherman wrote him on April 25 and actually stated: "I admit my folly in
embracing in a military convention any civil matters, but unfortunately
such is the nature of our situation that they seem inextricably united,
and I understood from you at Savannah that the financial state of the
country demanded military successes, and would warrant a little bending to policy." Sherman added another sentence explaining further his
negotiations with Johnston, after which he closed with a protest that
after "four years' patient, unremitting, and successful labor, I deserved
no reminder such as is contained in the last paragraph of your letter [of
April 21] to General Grant. You may assure the President I heed his suggestion." Stanton was in no mood to listen to any explanations. Regardless of the General's admission of "folly," the conclusion of his letter was
surely not to Stanton's liking. But the secretary of war was so aroused

that even if Sherman had said nothing about what he "deserved," it probably would have made no difference whatsoever.[21]

On April 26 Sherman and Johnston returned yet again to the Bennett house. The generals were as eager for peace as ever. Nevertheless, reaching an agreement proved difficult. The most troublesome issue concerned the status of the surrendered Confederates. While acknowledging that Grant's terms to Lee were generous, Johnston considered them inadequate. Neither food nor transportation had been provided to help Lee's paroled soldiers return to their homes. As a result, their homeward path had become a trail of robbery and violence. Johnston, understandably, did not want this to happen with his troops, and in this respect contended that he should receive better terms than Lee. Sherman could see his point but was convinced that the administration in Washington would not approve any terms except those that Grant gave Lee. The fruitless discussion went on for some time, until Sherman decided to call in General Schofield and see if he had any suggestions about solving the knotty problem.[22]

Schofield proved to be very helpful. After Johnston's surrender, he would be in command of a force to maintain order in North Carolina. While Sherman took most of the Union troops to Washington, Schofield would be administering the details of Confederate demobilization. He assured Johnston that he would do everything possible to avoid the situation the Southern general feared. Field transportation would be lent to the troops for the journey to their homes. Every brigade or separate body of men would retain a number of arms equal to one-seventh of its effective strength, which could be used, if necessary, to defend themselves against guerrillas and bushwhackers. Private horses and other private property of both Confederate officers and men would be retained by them. Transportation by water from Mobile or New Orleans would be provided for troops from Arkansas and Texas. The Union army would also furnish 250,000 rations to Johnston's troops.

Both Johnston and Sherman were satisfied with such an arrangement. Schofield then wrote the terms, essentially the same as Lee received at Appomattox, except for the additional provisions to get the troops home in as orderly a manner as possible. Johnston and Sherman placed their signature upon the document, Johnston remarking "I believe that is the best we can do." Sherman returned to Raleigh and conferred with Grant, who soon approved the revised terms with his signature. Staff officer George Nichols interestingly remarked that "Johnston has been induced to surrender quite as much by the discontent and threats of his own soldiers as by the Federal force. . . . Johnston has pursued the only wise course left open to him."[23]

WITHIN A SHORT TIME, Sherman would learn the full extent of Stanton's actions. His rage against the secretary of war then fully matched that of Stanton toward him—if any difference in degree existed, Sherman's wrath exceeded that of Stanton. Sherman wanted nothing more to do with the man. Before leaving by water for a short inspection trip to Savannah, he met with about a dozen of his generals at the governor's mansion in Raleigh. Among those present was Major General Carl Schurz, who wrote that "I witnessed a scene which I shall never forget." Sherman, declared Schurz, "paced up and down the room like a caged lion and . . . unbosomed himself with an eloquence of furious invective which for a while made us all stare." Schurz said that Sherman "lashed the Secretary of War as a mean, scheming, vindictive politician, who made it his business to rob military men of the credit earned by exposing their lives in the service of their country." Those who attacked Sherman were "a mass of fools not worth fighting for." He "railed at the press, which had altogether too much freedom; which had become an engine of vilification." Schurz, who admired Sherman, was not particularly concerned about the outburst in the presence of his generals, but feared that "a similar volcanic eruption in public" might seriously damage the General's standing "before the people."[24]

When Sherman had realized that a number of newspapers across the country were attacking him, he worried that his military career, having just reached its zenith, might well be destroyed by the clamor of his old enemy, the press. Such a fate was not about to occur. Some significant newspapers supported Sherman strongly; the influential Ewing family, along with Senator John Sherman, rallied behind him, and the negative outcry, which was never as widespread as the General feared, fizzled and failed. Victory is a formidable ally, which usually trumps all opposition, and Sherman's triumphs ruled the day—which was the most important factor in this unseemly affair. Sherman's troops were fiercely loyal to their commander, and the Northern people were primed to celebrate the end of the great war. The majority of the nation was in no mood to discard the conqueror of Atlanta and the leader of the march to the sea, whose great military achievements were fresh in their minds. In early May, his brother-in-law Tom Ewing wrote Sherman, "There is an almost universal feeling of indignation, manifest in the press & everywhere else, at the conduct of the Government towards you." Sherman remained a hero.[25]

It took him a good while to cool down, however, as well as time to realize that his army career was far from ended. He vented his anger in a number of letters to various people. Probably no accusation disturbed him more than the charge of insubordination leveled against him by the *New York Times*. "I have never in my life questioned or disobeyed an order," he declared to General Grant, "though many and many a time have I risked my life, my health, and reputation in obeying orders, or even hints, to execute plans and purposes not to my liking. It is not fair," he raged, "to withhold from me plans and policy . . . and expect me to guess at them, for facts and events appear quite different from different stand-points." He thought "a great outrage has been enacted against me by Mr. Stanton and Mr. Halleck. . . . My officers and men feel this insult as keenly as I do," he stated, and declared that he intended to treat Stanton "with scorn and contempt . . . for I regard my military career as ended." Whatever might happen in the future, he hoped "to stay with my army until it ceases to exist, or till it is broken up and scattered to other duty." He concluded, "The lust for Power in Political minds is the strongest passion of Life, and impels Ambitious men (Richard III) to deeds of Infamy."[26]

"Washington is as corrupt as Hell," he exclaimed in a letter to Ellen. He intended to "avoid it as a pest house." As so often when he was upset, his thoughts turned westward. He knew of a people who would not treat him in such a manner, he stated to General Logan—"the West, the Valley of the Mississippi, the heart & soul, and future strength of America, and I for one will go there." Still smarting from Stanton's actions in late May, Sherman again lashed out at politicians: "I am not a politician, never voted but once in my life, and never read a Political Platform. If spared I never will read a Political Platform or hold any Civil office whatsoever."[27]

ON APRIL 30, Sherman headed for Savannah, leaving his corps commanders to lead the army's march northward from Raleigh. He planned to rejoin the troops at Richmond, and from there accompany them the remainder of the way to Washington for a final grand review. Upon arriving in Savannah, he ordered that large quantities of food and other supplies should be distributed to Georgia's suffering people. General James Wilson, acting on Sherman's orders, soon was issuing 250 bushels of corn per day to civilians and, by June, meal and flour were being dispensed copiously in Atlanta. It was as if Sherman intended to prove, as more than once he had said, that he was indeed a true and generous friend of the South.[28]

After a short visit in Savannah, Sherman sailed back up the coast to rejoin his army. In the harbor at Morehead City, North Carolina, where his journey was delayed by a storm, he visited with Chief Justice Chase, who had come south to study the issue of African-Americans being permitted to vote. Sherman jumped at the chance of telling Chase why he was "not prepared to receive the negro on terms of political equality." Black suffrage would "arouse passions and prejudices at the North," including the prejudices of "our own armed soldiers." (Only a few Northern states allowed blacks to vote.) As for Southerners, most were adamantly opposed to giving the vote to blacks, and Sherman believed such a policy could not be sustained.

The South was a vast region, as Sherman was well qualified to point out, and many of its people could not be reached by United States military forces. The U.S. Army, he declared, "cannot combat existing ideas with force." Why not "imitate the example of England in allowing causes to work out their gradual solution?" He concluded his little lecture strongly with a reminder for Chase, relative to force: "That you may study the chances of changing the tone and character of a people by military occupation . . . I invite your attention to the occupation of Spain by Napoleon's best armies from about 1806 to the close of his career."[29]

Sherman was still seething about Stanton. The General had written a hard-hitting attack on the secretary of war, which he intended to publish, even if it would "soon lead to the closing of my military career," and he showed it to the chief justice. Chase was disturbed at the thought of the nation's possibly losing such a commander as Sherman, as well as the General's aggressive and bitter attitude toward Stanton. While the chief justice was certainly no friend of the secretary of war, he did not think the publication of Sherman's piece was wise and persuaded him to lay aside any public denunciation of Stanton. Chase's daughter, traveling with her father, recalled portions of Sherman's conversation with the chief justice. Particularly, she remembered Sherman's claiming that if Lincoln had lived, "I should never have been insulted in this fashion! We neither of us are the kind to kick an enemy after he is conquered." She also described Sherman's face as "red with indignation as he strode up and down the cabin like an enraged lion."[30]

But certainly not all was gloom and doom. "At Savannah, Charleston, Wilmington, and Morehead City," reported the General to Ellen, "officers, soldiers, sailors and citizens paid me . . . honored respect, especially my old soldiers, more especially when they heard they were down on me at Washington." When Sherman rejoined his army outside of Richmond, he was inundated by officers and men who greeted him warmly. He wrote Ellen that "they received with shouts my public denial of a Review for Halleck." General Halleck, explained Sherman, had ordered Slocum's wing to enter Richmond and pass in review before him. "I forbade it," Cump with relish declared to Ellen. "Tomorrow I march through Richmond with Colors flying & drums beating, as a matter of Right and not by Halleck's favor, and no notice will be taken of him personally or officially. I dare him to oppose my march."[31]

Sherman did not exaggerate about the loyalty of his troops, or their disdain for Halleck. A soldier of the Thirtieth Illinois would not believe that Sherman made any mistake, "until I know all about it," and apparently did not particularly care anyway: "I'd rather fight under him than Grant, and if he were Mahomet we'd be devoted Mussulmen." When Halleck posted guards at the roads into Richmond, many of Sherman's men were enraged, ready to shoot their way into the Virginia capital. One group of men from the Eighty-Fifth Indiana did throw the guards into the James River and proceed into the city.[32]

On May 11, after Grant had given him the required orders, Sherman marched his army across the James and into Richmond, having told Halleck that he preferred they not meet, and warning the general to stay out of sight, lest his presence should bring on violence. Ignoring Halleck's headquarters, Sherman and his triumphant forces audaciously tramped through the capital. Ellen, initially taken aback by Cump's mild terms to Johnston, was now altogether in step with her husband. Attributing his leniency to a pure and merciful heart and learning of the injustice inflicted by Stanton and Halleck, she wrote Sherman on May 17 that she was "truly charmed to find that you have had so good an opportunity of returning the insult of that base man Halleck." She had "not felt so much pleased with anything since the fall of Savannah—since 'Sherman marched down to the Sea.'" Climactically she exuded, "I would rather have seen that defiant parade through Richmond than anything else since the war began."[33]

For a long time back, Ellen had not cared for Halleck, but Sherman, over a span of many years, considered him a close, personal friend, a man in whom he placed his trust. Their relationship dated from Sherman's first days in California. He now felt betrayed. Once he wrote Halleck that he had lain awake all night contemplating Halleck's actions, and concluded he could not "consent to the renewal of a friendship I had prized so highly, till I can see deeper into the diabolical plot than I now do." He never saw deeply enough; the friendship was never renewed.[34]

After resting for a day on the north side of Richmond, Sherman began marching for Washington. The Virginia battlefields arrested the army's attention. Sherman swung back and forth, riding from corps to corps, and taking in many of the sites. Gruesome evidence of murderous struggle were all about—a landscape marred by extensive entrenchments, trees blasted by artillery fire and riddled by musket balls, burned-out houses marked by still-standing chimneys, numerous skeletons of soldiers, some never buried, others dug up from shallow graves by animals. Sherman was intensely moved. In a letter to James E. Yeatman in St. Louis on May 21, 1865, he wrote, "I confess, without shame, I am sick and tired of fighting—its glory is all moonshine; even success the most brilliant is over dead and mangled bodies, with the anguish and lamentations of distant families, appealing to me for sons, husbands, and fathers."[35]

On May 17, the army reached Alexandria, and there encamped on the outskirts of Washington. Upon learning that a grand parade was soon to be held, during which President Johnson and the cabinet would review both the eastern and western armies, Sherman wrote John Rawlins, the army chief of staff in Washington, that his forces would be ready, "though in the rough. Troops have not been paid for eight or ten months, and clothing may be bad, but a better set of legs and arms can not be displayed on this continent." Bitter about the way he had been treated by Stanton, and aware of rumors flying that he planned to take over the government, Sherman told Rawlins to "let some one newspaper know that the vandal Sherman is encamped near the canal bridge. . . . Though in disgrace, he is untamed and unconquered."[36]

On May 20, Sherman met with Grant, and also visited with President Johnson and all his cabinet, except for Stanton. Sherman was really pleased by the President's warm greeting. With arms outstretched Johnson reportedly said, "General Sherman, I am very glad to see you— very glad—and I mean what I say." Sherman wrote, "He was extremely cordial to me, and knowing that I was chafing under the censures of the War Department, especially of the two war bulletins of Mr. Stanton, he volunteered that he knew of neither of them till seen in the newspapers." The secretary of war, Johnson said, "had shown [them] neither to him nor to any of his associates in the cabinet till they were published." Such a gratifying message from the President could only have strengthened and hardened Sherman's animosity toward Stanton.[37]

There was further irritation. The powerful congressional Committee on the Conduct of the War summoned Sherman to testify about the surrender terms he had forged with Joe Johnston. Sherman wanted to put off his appearance until after the grand review, but the committee, chaired by the radical Ohioan Ben Wade and dominated by radicals, insisted that he come before them at once. Motivated by goals essentially political, the radical Republicans viewed President Lincoln's early actions about Reconstruction of the Southern governments as too liberal and hoped to show that Sherman's disavowed surrender terms actually emanated from Lincoln. On May 22, Sherman was questioned for several hours. Articulately and defiantly, he stood his ground while refraining from losing his temper. He managed to denounce both Stanton and Halleck with convincing arguments, testifying that "my chief object" in negotiating with Johnston was to keep his army from scattering into guerrilla bands. When pressed about the conference with Lincoln, Sherman was evasive, saying as little as possible, and claiming that "nothing specific and definite" had been said in regard to peace terms with the Confederacy while also declaring that, "had President Lincoln lived, I know he would have sustained me."[38]

Sherman's strongest attack against Stanton concerned the war secretary's March 3 telegram to Grant, conveying Lincoln's wishes relative to negotiating with Lee, about which Sherman, as noted earlier, had no knowledge. Stanton had used it against him unscrupulously, implying that Sherman had violated the President's clear instructions. "I was not in possession of [the telegram]," Sherman declared to the committee and devastatingly added that "I have reason to know that Mr. Stanton knew I was not in possession of it." He also charged that Stanton, during his visit in Savannah, had indicated to him that civil matters should be dealt with, and thus Stanton's public attacks on him, in tandem with Halleck, constituted "an act of perfidy." The general lashed out at Halleck in equally aggressive terms, especially striking at Halleck's April 26 dispatch, where Sherman's generals had been instructed not to obey his commands.[39]

Undoubtedly Sherman was pleased when at last he could get on with the grand review, scheduled for May 23 and 24. On the first day, General George Meade's eastern army proudly marched from the Capitol, paraded along Pennsylvania Avenue, with their bands triumphantly sounding martial airs, and continued past the reviewing stand where the President, cabinet members and general officers watched the spectacular event. It was, by any standard, a great show, and an immense crowd took it in. While Sherman was aware that the easterners made a few basic marching errors, he worried that his own rough westerners, scheduled for the next day, might not do as well.

At least he had resolved one issue. Both Black Jack Logan and Oliver Howard wanted to ride at the head of the Army of the Tennessee in the grand review. Logan, of course, had taken command of that army when James McPherson was killed and led it to one of the most important victories in the Atlanta campaign. Although Sherman then picked Howard as permanent commander, and he directed the army to Savannah and through the Carolinas, Howard had recently been named to head the Freedmen's Bureau. Sherman chose Logan to replace Howard and Black Jack had just assumed command. Howard contended, however, that because he had headed the army since Atlanta he should lead it in the great parade. Sherman requested that he relinquish that honor, arguing that it would mean "everything" to Logan, while Howard, as a Christian, wouldn't "mind such a sacrifice." Sherman knew his man. Howard submitted, probably feeling better about his "sacrifice" because Sherman asked the one-armed general to ride side by side with him at the head of all the troops.[40]

The morning of May 24 was "extremely beautiful," according to Sherman's recollection, "and the ground in splendid order for our review. The streets were filled with people to see the pageant, armed with bouquets of flowers for their favorite regiments or heroes, and everything was propitious." Sherman was pleased that Ellen, with their son Tommy and her father, was present for the grand occasion. Markedly unlike his typical rough and unkempt appearance when campaigning, General Sherman on this day was smartly arrayed in full military regalia.

Most of his troops had never seen their commander looking so clean and sharp, and even his horse was adorned with wreaths on its big neck. "Old Glory" seemed to be fluttering everywhere, all around the Capitol and along the parade route. Regimental bands were poised to add their martial strains for the festivities, Sherman having decided not to allow any music from civilian groups, which he believed had created some of the marching problems he observed among Meade's men. "Punctually at 9 a.m.," Sherman wrote that "the signal gun was fired, when in person, attended by General Howard and all my staff, I rode slowly down Pennsylvania Avenue, the crowds of men, women, and children densely lining the sidewalks, and almost obstructing the way."[41]

Following closely behind Sherman and Howard came Logan, at the head of the Fifteenth Corps, Army of the Tennessee, whose "swarthy coal-black hair gave him the air of a native chief," observed Horace Porter. Equally arresting was Sherman's red hair, with the sun shining upon it, as he rode with hat in hand. Wondering how well his troops were marching, the General finally turned in his saddle and looked back. While some of the men wore new uniforms, others had only their heavily worn clothing, and not a few were barefoot. Sherman's concern, of course, was not their clothing, but how they were marching. "The sight was simply magnificent. The column was compact, and the glittering muskets looked like a solid mass of steel, moving with the regularity of a pendulum." Years later he declared, "I believe it was the happiest and most satisfactory moment of my life." Carl Schurz, who said that because of his experiences he had developed "a profound abhorrence of war," could not help but be impressed. "I must confess," he wrote, "when I saw those valiant hosts swinging in broad fronted column down Pennsylvania Avenue, . . . Sherman's bronzed veterans—the men nothing but bone, muscle and skin—their tattered battle-flags fluttering victoriously over their heads in the full pride of achievement, my heart leaped in the consciousness of having been one of them. It was a spectacle splendid and imposing beyond description."[42]

Sherman turned again to the front and proudly continued to lead the procession, riding side by side with Howard. When Howard fell back

a pace or two, Sherman motioned for the general to move up alongside him. Fittingly preceding each division of white soldiers were the
black pioneer units, "armed with picks and spades," symbolic of the
essential labor they had performed during Sherman's campaigns—
the only African-Americans that he allowed to serve with his forces.
They "marched abreast in double ranks," wrote Sherman, "keeping
perfect dress and step, and added much to the interest of the occasion." Near Lafayette Square someone called Sherman's attention
to William Seward, the secretary of state, still recovering from injuries suffered in the assassination conspiracy. He was sitting in an
upper window of a brick house, heavily bandaged and feeble from
his wounds, as he watched the victory parade. Sherman turned, rode
a few steps in Seward's direction and waved his hat. "He recognized
the salute," remembered Sherman, "returned it, and then we rode on
steadily past the President, saluting with our swords. All on his stand
arose and acknowledged the salute."[43]

Having passed the reviewing stand, Sherman turned into the gate of
the White House grounds, dismounted and went up on the stand, where
he greeted Ellen—whom he had not seen for a year and a half—her father
and Tommy. Then he shook hands with President Johnson, General
Grant and all the cabinet members except Stanton. "As I approached Mr.
Stanton, he offered me his hand," Sherman declared, "but I declined it
publicly, and the fact was universally noticed." Writing General Schofield in North Carolina, Sherman said the grand review "came off in
magnificent style, and . . . Stanton offered to shake hands with me in the
presence of the President but I declined." Clearly Sherman was delighted
to snub Stanton at that auspicious moment. "I then took my post on the
left of the President, and for six hours and a half stood, while the army
passed in the order of the Fifteenth, Seventeenth, Twentieth, and Fourteenth Corps. It was, in my judgment," remembered the General in his
memoirs, with understandable satisfaction, and perhaps pardonable
egotism, "the most magnificent army in existence."[44]

Many of the officers and men in Sherman's forces, aware of their
commander's difficulties with the secretary of war, felt much the same

as their leader did about Stanton. Sometimes they made a spectacle of themselves, "especially when a little in liquor," as Grant said. Two days after the grand review, a group of officers were at Willard's Hotel, "drinking and discussing violently the conduct of Mr. Stanton," according to Grant's report to Sherman. From time to time, one of them would leap up on the counter and lead the others in giving "three groans for Mr. Stanton," and then take another drink. In addition to the Sherman-Stanton issue, Grant was concerned about maintaining control over the huge number of soldiers camped around the capital, especially considering the rivalry between the eastern and western forces. He told Sherman of his conversation with General Christopher C. Augur, who commanded the Department of Washington. Augur declared, in Grant's summary words, "when the men of the different armies meet in town, if drinking, they are sure to fight." Augur was right. "What we want is to preserve quiet and decorum," Grant told Sherman, until the men could be paid and discharged. He expected Sherman to take whatever steps were necessary to enforce discipline.[45]

Sherman acted at once, hastening to see General Augur. Finding that the general was not in his office, he consulted with the officer of the day and provost-marshal, requesting them "as a favor to me to arrest and imprison any officer or man belonging to my command who transgressed any orders, rules, or regulations of the place, more especially for acts of drunkenness, noise or rowdyism." Sherman then rode the streets until midnight, observing the situation. "I thank you for leaving the matter of orders to my management," he told Grant, "and I . . . assure you nothing offensive shall occur of any importance. Such . . . things as a tipsy soldier occasionally cannot be helped, but even that shall be punished according to 'local orders.'"[46]

More irritating to Sherman than rowdy soldiers were the reports circulating in Washington that Democrats, particularly that wing of the party which had opposed the war, wanted Sherman as their presidential candidate in 1868. His conflict with Stanton had fueled the speculation. No doubt it was difficult for anyone, above all politicians, to believe that an immensely popular person like Sherman, who was in a position to make a formidable run for the presidency, actually had no interest whatsoever in doing so. While Sherman never intended to be a candidate of either party, he wrote Grant that he considered it "an insult . . . that copperheads who opposed the war or threw obstacles in the way of its successful prosecution," wanted him as their standard-bearer. "I would like Mr. Johnson," he wrote Grant, "to believe that the newspaper gossip of my having Presidential aspirations is absurd . . . and I would check it if I knew how."[47]

By this time, although still angry at Stanton and Halleck, Sherman realized that he had come through the aggravating episode with his military reputation fully intact—in the opinion of many Americans. "Mr. Johnson has been more than kind to me," he wrote General Schofield on May 28, "and the howl against me is narrowed down to Halleck and Stanton." Two days later, Sherman posted Special Field Orders No. 76, an appropriate and moving farewell address to his army, and thus quietly concluded his role in the war. "He had won great renown as a soldier, and an immense popularity all over the Northern country," observed Carl Schurz in his *Reminiscences*. "This he knew," Schurz declared of Sherman, "and he thoroughly relished it."[48]

Indeed he did. In the years to come, many societies and public organizations made Sherman an honorary member, and he would attend their gatherings with pleasure. His appearances at the theater, which were frequent whenever he was not out on the Great Plains, or some other place where such entertainment could not be had, were often greeted by the orchestra striking up "Marching Through Georgia," while the audience stood and applauded the General's arrival. At any social occasion, for as long as he lived, he would be received as an honored guest.

Sometimes he did grow weary of strangers who approached him on the street or the train or wherever they happened to come upon him. Soon after the war, he wrote his brother John that he had thought about making a trip to Detroit to see an old friend, "but am bothered by people in traveling so much that I prefer to be quiet till the people run after new gods." Within a short time, he predicted, new issues would drop him "out of memory." He was wrong. The Civil War was too big, and he himself had become too big for that to happen. If the people did find "new gods," they never ceased venerating the old god. Sherman's fame would endure, and when it involved formal occasions, set social pieces or gatherings of Civil War veterans, especially the Army of the Tennessee, these the General would always, as Carl Schurz said, "thoroughly relish."[49]

IN EARLY JUNE, Sherman took Ellen and Tommy to New York. Newspapers hailed his arrival in the city, and large crowds gathered to see the illustrious, controversial, red-haired general with the fascinating Indian middle name. The Shermans lodged at the Twenty-Third Street mansion of William Scott, the widower of a cousin of the General who hosted a reception in Sherman's honor. Many prominent men and women came, eager to be identified, if only briefly, with a hero. In addition, the General would soon learn, if he did not already know, that a remarkable number of women, sometimes young as well as older, would now welcome his company—one of the prices of military fame. At forty-five, Sherman was still slim, his stomach flat, and although his face was wrinkled, he manifested a ruggedly handsome appearance. Physical attractiveness made his fame all the more alluring. Young women would sometimes greet him with a kiss. Numerous women of all ages would seek him out, simply because he was now viewed as one of the nation's greatest men.[50]

Next it was on to West Point for a short visit at the military academy. Winfield Scott, architect and leader of the magnificent Mexico City campaign in the 1840s, who was then in his late seventies, embraced Sherman with gusto, thanking God that "you have lived to see this day and that I, too, have lived to see it." Sherman shook hands with many of the cadets, and delighted in telling them what the school had been like when he was there. In the future, the General would return time and again to West Point, for he was comfortable there, and he knew that more than any experience of his life, the military academy had defined his being. "I was fit for the Army but nothing else," he had remarked in the late 1850s. Actually that was not true, but it was true that Sherman never *wanted* any career other than that of a soldier, and finally he had succeeded at his chosen profession, probably to a greater degree than he ever dared to dream.[51]

Resuming the journey, which developed into sort of an informal victory tour, they headed for Chicago and the Sanitary Fair, held for the benefit of soldiers who were suffering and impoverished by the war, in which Ellen played a prominent role. Sherman remained in Chicago for about two weeks, speaking at the fair and upon several other occasions, including at the theater, where he addressed a receptive audience from his opera box. Naturally, since South Bend, Indiana, lay near by, he and Ellen visited with two of their children, who were in school there.

During the following weeks, he spoke at least once in every city that he visited, and in Cincinnati, the *Enquirer* claimed that he received "the largest ovation . . . paid to any distinguished man during the war." Sherman was bothered, however, to find that people everywhere were focused on the march to Savannah, while relatively ignoring the Carolinas, which he considered both a more significant campaign, and more difficult. "The march to the sea," he told John, "seems to have captivated everybody, whereas it was child's play compared with the other." He was right. Confederate engineers, as earlier noted, never expected Sherman to take the route he did, for they considered it a near impossible undertaking in winter. Regardless of Sherman's judgment and wishes, the nation remembered the march to the sea, and thus it ever would be.[52]

But Sherman could have the personal satisfaction of knowing that in the Atlanta campaign, with his mastery of logistics and maneuver warfare, as well as in the marches through Georgia and the Carolinas, he had developed a new understanding of the most effective way of waging the war, and the least costly in terms of the lives of his soldiers.

While the General's informal, triumphant tour unfolded, the country had been divided into five military divisions. Sherman was assigned to command the Military Division of the Mississippi, soon to become known as the Military Division of the Missouri. It constituted a vast territory, approximately one-third of the country, extending west of the Mississippi River, and north of Texas, all the way to the Rocky Mountains and northward to Canada. Sherman's headquarters would be in St. Louis, hundreds of miles away from Washington, that city he detested. He was pleased to be looking to the development of the great western part of the nation. He believed that many a former soldier would be doing the same. Returning home after the war, they would "find their places occupied by others ... and that they themselves had changed." They would "naturally," he thought, turn to "the great West," rather more "stimulated than retarded by the danger of an Indian War."[53]

With a touch of excitement and anticipation, Sherman prepared to make his home in St. Louis. The many friends who welcomed him back, including Henry Turner, raised $30,000 to buy him a house. When Sherman selected a fine, impressive structure at 912 Garrison Avenue, which cost some $24,000, his generous friends deposited the rest of the money in his bank account. While Sherman initially seemed to be taking both his fame and the inevitable postwar adjustments in stride, Ellen found that being the wife of a national hero was not all to her liking. She complained of being "stared at," as well as being the subject of "odious comparisons." The women admiring her husband irritated her: "Of course, every good looking young fashionable thinks it a pity so distinguished a man could not have her for his wife instead of the worn down old woman before her." Ellen said that she had "always known that Cump must succeed if health were spared him & I therefore feel no particular elation at his present success, although the country seems wild with joy." In coming years, Ellen would increasingly dwell upon negative factors, as she interpreted them, and to a great degree reject a social life other than her concerns for family and the Catholic faith, with its promise of a better life after death.[54]

As for the General, within a few months he was once again feeling economic pressures. In a letter to his longtime friend E. O. C. Ord, Sherman confided: "I almost regret that instead of accepting a Big House," on which the property taxes were very heavy, "I had not awaited my chance to choose a house in some more quiet and cheap place." He complained also of not being able to use the free public schools, "for which we are all taxed," and instead was "compelled [meaning because of Ellen] to use

Catholic schools which are very costly." When the last of his children, Philemon Tecumseh, who like his father would be called Cump, was born in early 1867, Sherman felt still more financial strain. "My pay is now about $1,070 a month," he wrote his brother John, declaring that "I can barely get along and could not live here except that I received a house as a present." Soon after, he concluded that he could not send Minnie to school in New York, because it would be too expensive.[55]

WHEN SHERMAN TOOK command of the army on the Plains, he said that "my thoughts and feelings at once reverted to the construction of the great Pacific Railway." Chartered by the U.S. Congress during the war, construction was already under way when Sherman assumed his new post. He determined to place the resources of the army behind this momentous project. In October, he and his chief aides, Joseph Auden-reid and Lewis M. Dayton, along with a few others, took a train out to Omaha, pulled by an engine named the "Major General Sherman," to celebrate the completion of the first sixteen miles of track and assure the builders personally that he "would afford them all possible assistance and encouragement." He was pleased that General Grenville Dodge, his highly valued compatriot in arms during the Civil War, was the railroad's chief engineer, having resigned from the army to take that position.

During the winter of 1866, Sherman made a trip to Washington, lobbying for President Johnson to create new military departments within the Division of the Missouri, to better protect the railroad workers from Indian attacks. "Every time they build a section," Sherman promised, "I'll be on hand to ... see that it is properly built." He exaggerated but little. Over the next couple of years he often headed west from St. Louis, both to check on the railroad and further familiarize himself with his immense territorial command. On May 10, 1869, the tracks of the Central Pacific, building eastward from California, and the Union Pacific, building westward from Omaha, were joined at Promontory, Utah. General Dodge paid tribute to Sherman, by then general-in-chief of the army, whose "continuous active aid, with that of the Army, has made

you a part of us and enabled us to complete our work in so short a time."
The highest point on the railroad, west of Cheyenne, Wyoming, which
was, according to Stephen Ambrose, 8,242 feet in elevation, making it
"the highest point of any railroad anywhere," was christened "Sherman
Summit."[56]

The other of Sherman's major responsibilities while commanding the
Division of the Missouri concerned the Native Americans. A long, often
violent and mostly sad relationship between the European settlers of
North America and the Indians, as the Europeans and their descendants
called them, reached a deplorable climax in the years following the Civil
War. An ultimately disastrous Indian policy had been pursued earlier,
during the administrations of Andrew Jackson and his chosen successor, Martin Van Buren. Most of the Indians east of the Mississippi had
been driven westward, beyond the great river, with treaty-guaranteed
promises of a permanent territory of their own, forever free of white
encroachment. Understandably, the Native Americans did not want to
leave their ancestral homelands, favored by heavy forests, ample rain-
fall and abundant game, to endure a lengthy, difficult journey ("the trail
of tears") to a relatively dry and barren region, where the Indians of the
Great Plains already roamed a vast area as they tracked the buffalo to
support their way of life. But the eastern Indians were given no choice.
The white man demanded their land.

Then, after the Civil War, a rapidly expanding, aggressive, white
American civilization began another, big encroachment upon the allegedly "permanent" and guaranteed Native American territory. Farmers, sheepherders and cattlemen headed west, encouraged in part by
the Homestead Act, passed during the war, which provided 160 acres
of free land to anyone living on and working that land for five years.
Large numbers of former soldiers, as Sherman expected, decided to go
west. So too did prospectors, seeking a gold strike—perhaps another
discovery like the California bonanza—or a silver strike, or some
other precious mineral. The building of the transcontinental railroads
employed many men, and a lot of them took up permanent residence in
the West. White hunters were attracted by the huge number of buffalo,

which supplied food and clothing for the Plains Indians. These hunters killed the great animals, which were easy targets, because of so-called sport—also for buffalo hides—and to clear the way for the railroads (a buffalo herd might sometimes block a train for hours). Many white men, looking upon Native Americans as inferior beings (the proverbial "savages") seemed to have no qualms about intruding upon Indian territory whenever they might be so inclined. The Indians naturally felt betrayed, concluding that the white man could not be trusted, and armed clashes—sometimes instigated by the whites, sometimes by the Indians—became inevitable.

Sherman found himself in a very frustrating position. On the one hand he was expected to protect the white settlers from the Indians; on the other, he was charged with defending the Indians against white infringement upon their territory. Evenhanded action proved very difficult, for often it was impossible to know, with reasonable certainty, just what had occurred and who was responsible. Some whites blamed any violence on the Native Americans, fostering all manner of rumors, and sometimes actually stirring up trouble in the hope of enlisting the army against the Indians. Sherman was not easily fooled and realized that the Indians at times were falsely accused. If he declined to take sides with the whites, some criticized him severely. When a group of Denver citizens burned the General in effigy, he wrote John, "I am of course held responsible by the frontier people for not rushing to war because of occasional depredations, some of which have been committed by white men." About the same time, he told Ord that some Indians "cannot resist the chance to take a scalp & steal a few fresh horses." Then, he said, "a few scattered cases of this kind become Exaggerated till war is regarded as sure to come."[57]

The General's task was amplified by the vastness of the territory he commanded, coupled with an inadequate number of troops with which to keep order across more than a million square miles of harsh landscape. Once he remarked: "It is these awful distances that make our problem out here so difficult." Nevertheless, he vowed that "little by little" he would get the job done. As for the size of the army, in the summer of 1866 Congress authorized a total force of some 57,000 officers and men—dramatically down from approximately one million during the Civil War. Obviously no one thought it necessary, once the Confederacy was defeated, to keep a million men under arms, but the 57,000 was reduced to about 25,000 by 1869, and so it would remain until the Spanish-American War. This force was charged with assuring stability during Reconstruction in the South, manning 255 forts and posts all over the nation and dealing with the Indian country. At the beginning of Sherman's tenure as commander of the Military Division of the Missouri, he had about 25,000 men available, a number that gradually declined over the next several years. The Native American population was probably 250,000.[58]

In the summer of 1867, Congress created an eight-man Peace Commission to address the Indian issues. Four members were civilians, including Nathaniel G. Taylor, the federal government's commissioner of Indian Affairs, and four were military men, among whom Sherman was of course the most prominent. The other generals were Alfred Terry, William S. Harney and Christopher Augur. The group met with various Indian representatives, at several sites, during 1867 and 1868. Sherman seems to have become increasingly pessimistic about the ultimate fate of the Indian. At North Platte, Nebraska, where the commission was scheduled to meet with a number of Cheyenne and Sioux, Sherman wrote Ellen that the night before the conference, "the Indians got on a big drunk and are not now in condition to have their talk." He then declared, "I guess we will have to give them a good ducking in the Platte and then proceed to business," adding that "the more I see of them, the more satisfied I am that no amount of sentimentality will save them the doom in Store for them."[59]

In the spring of 1868, Sherman and Samuel F. Tappan, one of the civilian members of the Peace Commission, headed into southeastern New Mexico to confer with the Navajos. Sherman detested New Mexico. "I want to see this country lay hold of Mexico again," he was fond of saying, "and thrash her till she promises to take those damned territories [Arizona as well as New Mexico] back again." He denounced the New Mexicans as "a mixed band of Mexican, indian & negro," inferior to any of those three races "if pure." Perhaps Sherman's intense feelings against New Mexico made him more inclined to sympathize with the Navajos.[60]

As usual, Sherman traveled south to meet the Navajos with very little escort, like he did all over his vast division, remarking to Grant that four armed men could make their way anywhere in New Mexico. Interestingly, while on the trek to see the Navajos, Stewart Van Vliet, his good friend since West Point days, who well knew Cump's habits, wrote him a letter. Van Vliet was worried about the way Sherman continually exposed himself to danger. "I want to see you out of that Indian country," Van Vliet implored, "for you expose yourself so unnecessarily with insufficient escort, that I am always afraid that you will 'go under' on one of your trips." Now, if Grant became president, which would elevate Sherman to general-in-chief of the army, Van Vliet declared that "I don't want you to lose the chance through the instrumentality of some rugged Indian." Sherman was not about to change his well-established practices. Maybe, having survived the Civil War, in which he had expected to be killed, he had developed something of a sense of invincibility. Perhaps even more, he genuinely liked the freedom of roaming over the great western territories in the company of only a handful of soldiers. And clearly he felt there was not much danger.[61]

The Navajos, formerly a numerous people, had been compelled to leave their home country four years earlier, travel several hundred miles and resettle on a reservation known as the Bosque Redondo, meaning "the Round Forest." Sherman said it was nothing but "a mere spot of green grass in the midst of a wild desert." There was hardly any wood available, the water was foul, and the soil poor. The Navajos had worked hard, but the first year worms ate the corn crop, also again the next year, and the third year a hailstorm destroyed the crop. Sherman told his senator brother: "We found 7,200 Indians there ... abject and disheartened." They were living in miserable poverty, dejected and without hope. Sherman suggested the possibility of going east into Indian Territory, where he promised that the army would protect them. The Navajos were not interested in going east, or anywhere else except back to their ancestral homeland, centered in the northwestern corner of New Mexico. Sherman mulled over the matter. The next day, he told them that they could go home, and within approximately a month the Navajos were once again in their ancestral country. It was a good thing that Sherman did for them. They have fared better than most of the Native American peoples.[62]

Samuel Tappan was impressed and heaped high praise on Sherman: "Congress and the people are glad to leave it [the Indian issue] to you.... Your march to the sea and your settlement of our Indian issues so far, gives you a prestige that no one else has or ever will have in this country." Tappan spoke the truth—at that point in time. However, Sherman's compassion for the Navajos would never be equaled in his dealings with any other Indians. In the fall of 1868, he wrote John, "The Indian War on the plains need simply amount to this.... All who cling to their old hunting grounds are hostile and will remain so until killed off." He predicted: "We will have a sort of predatory war for years, every now and then be shocked by the indiscriminate murder of travelers and settlers, but the country is so large ... that we can not make a single war and end it."

The U.S. troops, who were widely scattered, "have daily chases and skirmishes," he said, "sometimes getting the best, and sometimes the worst, but the Indians have this great advantage—they can steal fresh horses ... and drop the jaded ones. We must operate each man to his own horse." But Sherman believed that he knew how to deal with the Native Americans. He would take the war to the Indians during the winter, "and when winter starves their ponies, they will want a truce *and shan't have it* [emphasis added], unless the civil influence compels me again, as it did last winter." Shortly before writing John, when trouble with the Cheyenne and the Arapaho had erupted once more, the General told Ellen, "Probably in the end it will be better to kill them all off." Samuel Tappan and others whose sympathies lay with the Indians would soon be upset by Sherman's plans for any Native Americans who refused to be confined to a reservation.[63]

During the years when Sherman commanded the Division of the Missouri, he was called more than once to the nation's capital. In the fall of

1866, he received a summons from President Johnson. The issues were a diplomatic mission to Mexico and a high-stakes political struggle in Washington. The President was engaged in a heated controversy about Reconstruction in the South, and regarded Secretary of War Stanton as a spy for the radical Republicans who opposed Johnson's policies. Johnson knew that the outspoken Sherman's views of the Southern question were akin to his own and broached the possibility of the General's replacing Stanton. Obviously Sherman had no love for Stanton, but neither did he intend to leave his western post for a cabinet position. The Mexican mission gave Sherman a way out of the problem.[64]

President Johnson wanted General Grant to escort the newly appointed American minister to Mexico, Lewis D. Campbell of Ohio, to his new assignment. They would be on a quest to establish a good relationship with Benito Juárez, the self-proclaimed president of Mexico. Juarez was favored by many Mexicans in the hope of ridding their country of Louis Napoleon's puppet government, which had been established during the American Civil War, and propped up by some 20,000 French troops. The presence of General Grant clearly would constitute a statement that the United States wanted the French out of Mexico. While Grant, and presumably all Americans, were against the French presence south of the border, the army's general-in-chief, then being widely promoted as the next Republican candidate for the presidency, had no intention of leaving the country—particularly not when he suspected that Johnson was trying to remove him from the political limelight. When Sherman met with the President, he knew, having already talked with Grant, that his friend was not going to travel to Mexico. After making that fact clear to Johnson, Sherman himself volunteered to accompany Campbell if the President so wished. He did, likely thinking that was the best solution for which he could hope, and thus Sherman sailed for Mexico on what proved, from the first, to be a useless trip.[65]

"Campbell is quite an inferior man" was Cump's appraisal in a letter to Ellen. He said that Campbell "drank so much the first two days out . . . that I got from him a promise of abstinence." Sherman did it by means of a mutual pledge, "so that I can not now take my usual *nooning*. But it makes no difference," he assured his wife, for he was never addicted to liquor, and "would have been ashamed to meet French and Spanish officers with a Drunken Minister as our National Representative." Matters only got worse upon reaching Mexico, because they searched in vain for President Juárez, "who is . . . away up in Chihuahua for no other possible purpose than to be where the devil himself can not get at him." Sherman had "not the remotest idea of riding mule back a thousand miles in Mexico to find its chief magistrate." While he believed that the French occupation of Mexico should be terminated, he told John that he would "deplore anything that would make us assume Mexico in any shape—its territory, its government, or its people."[66]

Disappointed in Lewis Campbell and disgusted with the trip generally, Sherman came back to the United States ahead of Campbell, intending to be home in St. Louis by Christmas. He journeyed by way of New Orleans, where he saw several old friends and stayed with General Phil Sheridan. Then traveling by rail, he came northward through Mississippi and Tennessee, meeting a number of former Confederates who wanted to visit with him along the way. As for Lewis Campbell, who came into New Orleans a few days after Sherman left, his public drunkenness in the Crescent City, said to have occurred for three nights in a row, became a serious embarrassment, which even the arrival of Campbell's daughter did not arrest. Appalled when he heard of Campbell's spree, Sherman wrote Thomas Ewing Sr. that he was "sometimes amazed that our Government should entrust delicate business" to such men—a sentiment he also expressed to Ellen.[67]

Sherman was back in St. Louis by Christmas, and soon prepared to celebrate New Year's Day, an occasion he always enjoyed, by holding an open house. Ellen, expecting the birth of a child any day, was in no condition, physically or mentally, to preside as hostess. The General was delighted to have his daughter Minnie, less than a month away from her sixteenth birthday, act in place of her mother and receive with him a host of guests in the parlor from eleven in the morning until nine in the evening. Ellen was pleased that Minnie could "relieve me of a duty that is irksome." The birth of Philemon Tecumseh Sherman, on January 9, 1867, led Ellen to remark to her father that "Cump is much pleased with his boy, and well he might be," she added, "for the child is strong and healthy and exactly like him." She observed that "Cump attempts to alter his tone of voice when he speaks to him (if there is no one about), and assumes a tender and persuasive tone, but," she concluded, "he makes a horrible failure of it."[68]

Although the occasion of Philemon Tecumseh's birth was a happy one for Sherman, it did dredge up melancholy memories of Willy, as had his recent trip through Mississippi. In March, he traveled to Lancaster and removed Willy's body, to be transferred to a new grave, at Calvary Cemetery in St. Louis, where Sherman himself intended to be buried. He also had Charles Celestine's remains transferred there. Not long afterward, he wrote Ord: "Ain't you haunted by the thousands of ghosts that flit about those deep and tangled ravines that make up Vicksburg? . . . It was Vicksburg that cost me my Willy, and I can not but feel that it must be an unpleasant spot."[69]

That spring, Sherman rewarded his daughter Lizzie for making good grades at school, taking her and a few of her friends for a several-hundred-mile excursion on the Union Pacific. The ride was completed without difficulty, but right after Sherman got back to St. Louis, Indians struck several stagecoach stations, attacked a surveying party and hit the Union Pacific Railroad in northern Colorado. Immediately heading west again to assess the damage and the general situation, Sherman realized that an all-out war against the Indians still was impossible, because of the inadequate number of troops he had available. Nor could he possibly protect every white settlement. As soon as he struck the Indians in one place, they would ride for another, usually and wisely refusing to fight except when they could set up an ambush or in some manner gain an advantage.[70]

Despite the possibilities of a dangerous confrontation with Native Americans, Sherman remained enthusiastic about taking guests for a ride on the railroad. He could be quite persuasive. Already he had been west with his brother John, during August and September of 1866. Two summers later, he was very pleased when General Grant, who did indeed become the Republican candidate for president in 1868, said that he wanted to take a trip west with him. In mid-July, joined by Phil Sheridan, the three generals, with their aides, struck out for Denver. It was a memorable trip. Frequently they stopped, speaking from the rear platform of the train, as they addressed the people who gathered to see the most famous U.S. generals of the Civil War. Probably never had the spectators witnessed so much high-ranking brass, all the more notable because one of the generals might soon be elected president of the United States.[71]

Sherman seemed most content, however, when traveling throughout the great West in the company of a small escort, as he so frequently did, especially while commanding the Division of the Missouri, and sometimes even after becoming the army's general-in-chief. One of his letters to Ellen conveys a great deal about his feelings during such trips. He wrote her that "in this wild roving about, camping by the side of some stream with pickets out to give alarm if necessary & mules picketed close in, there is a charm that can not be described or reasoned about." Biographer Lloyd Lewis, perhaps perceptively, although risking an overly romantic assessment, suggested that these years were "the Indian summer of his life as a campaigner," like one last "mild return of the hardships that in four strenuous years had become delights." Once more, "when all but the pickets were asleep," Sherman could rise and "stand by the dying bivouac fire," reflecting upon the war, an experience like nothing else in his life had ever been, or ever could be again. As Faulkner later expressed it in *Requiem for a Nun*: "The past is never dead. It's not even past."[72]

The General's western excursions, to some degree, probably served as a coping mechanism for the most profound, emotional-psychological experience of his life. By twenty-first-century estimates, 750,000 men died in the Civil War; many of the wounded were maimed for life. It seems humanly impossible not to be scarred permanently, mentally, by four years of unrelenting exposure to such mayhem. Perhaps Sherman, strongly girdled by military fame, may occasionally have engaged in a bit of romanticizing about the war. But likely this would have been an infrequent indulgence, for deep in his heart he always knew what the awful thing had really been like.

The western trips also served as an escape from the emotional and financial irritants of home life. While Sherman genuinely cared for his wife, he clearly considered her a hypochondriac and found her reticent nature, which became more pronounced with years, a troubling contrast with his own expansive personality. He also realized that he did not, and never would, make enough money to support the lifestyle of his family. Moreover, when back east, Sherman himself liked, at least occasionally, to partake of the good life. With respect to Ellen, he sometimes seemed not to realize how hurtful something he said might be or, worse, possibly, he simply did not care—almost as if he were just thinking aloud, uttering something that was sure to be disturbing, but was perhaps nothing more than a fantasy. More than once, for instance, he told her that he felt like abandoning his job, joining an Indian tribe and wandering the prairies.

When Congress, in the summer of 1866, created for Grant the rank of general of the army, Sherman was elevated to Grant's old rank of lieutenant general, which approximately doubled his pay. When Grant became the President, Sherman rose to full general. Still money was scarce. Ellen demonstrated considerable patience with her husband's ways, but occasionally she lashed out, as in a sarcastic commentary to her father. Cump had "missed his calling when he took a civilized wife, as nature made him for the spouse of a squaw." If he actually did go to live among the Indians, "should they give him any power," she declared that he would "kill off by severity and want of . . . Kindness . . . the unfortunate doomed tribe."[73]

Sherman's western trips may have made him feel more separated from Washington and the political posturing and maneuvering he so detested about both parties. But he frequently told his brother John what he was thinking about national concerns. Doubtless he would have liked for people to accept his judgments, but he was not possessed of a temperament to actually participate in the political process. To his credit, he realized that fact. Besides, he considered action in the political arena to be beneath him.

On one of the most important and controversial issues of the day, for example, the Reconstruction of the former Confederacy, Sherman left no question about where he stood. When Southern states began passing "Black Codes," which were little more than thinly disguised updates of the old "Slave Codes," and designed to keep the former slaves "in their place," as their place was defined by Southern whites, Sherman seemed to have no reservations about such policy. If he did, he said nothing about it. While he did not wish to turn back the clock on the Thirteenth Amendment to the Constitution, he did not think that the newly freed African-Americans were qualified either to vote or to hold government office. He would leave Southern whites, as well as the freedmen, in the power of many of the same leaders who had established the Confederacy and brought on four years of war. No other men, in Sherman's estimate, neither common whites nor blacks, were qualified to control the Southern states. "The well disposed of the South must again be trusted," he told John; "we cannot help it." In Sherman's opinion, Southern whites would never accept black suffrage. He feared rioting and anarchy if it were forced upon them, which might well require massive intervention by the U.S. Army. The capabilities of the military would be overextended, considering the dramatic army downsizing following the defeat of the Confederacy, as well as being far too costly to be practical.[74]

Sherman's ideas were very close to those of President Johnson, who became locked in a struggle with Congress as he attempted to implement his minimal policy of Reconstruction. In 1867 Congress nullified Johnson's efforts and passed several acts establishing its own policy to deal with the former Confederacy. The South was divided into five military districts, each commanded by a major general. Southern states had to write new constitutions and establish new state governments, which would guarantee African-Americans (males) the right to vote and hold office. Each state had to ratify the Fourteenth Amendment, granting citizenship to blacks. If any state denied the franchise to blacks, its representation in the U.S. Congress and the electoral college would be proportionately reduced. Congress would decide when military rule would be lifted, and when a state was fit to be restored to the Union.

President Johnson was battling intensely with Congress, which was controlled by radical Republicans, many of whom were seeking to use Reconstruction for their party's political gain. Early in 1868 he attempted to enlist Sherman as an ally. Not only were Sherman's views of the Southern question close to his own; Johnson also considered the General trustworthy, and his military prestige was second only to Grant—indeed, it might even equal Grant's. Furthermore, Sherman's father-in-law was among those providing legal advice to the President (Thomas Ewing Sr. would also be involved in Johnson's defense when he was impeached). Already, more than once, Johnson had tried to entice Sherman to become secretary of war.

In February 1868, the President moved to create a Military Division of the Atlantic, composed of "the Department of the Lakes, the Department of the East, and the Department of Washington," to be commanded by Sherman, with headquarters at Washington, D.C. "I never felt so troubled in my life," Sherman told Grant when he learned of Johnson's intentions. He even thought, he said, about resigning from the army and asking Grenville Dodge to put him to work on the transcontinental railroad. Quickly realizing this was not a practical solution, he explained to Grant that "hard times and an expensive family have brought me back to starring the proposition square in the face." Sherman did not want to leave his western command and his headquarters in St. Louis. He certainly did not want to live in Washington. Nor did he want any part of Johnson's bitter brawl with Congress.[75]

He wrote a letter to the President, explaining his desire to remain where he was. He also wrote letters to John, Thomas Ewing Sr., Grant and others, making it clear—should the need for such clarity arise—that he had never sought to go to Washington. Because the nation's capital already headquartered a department, as well as the army itself, Sherman did not see how he could render military service there. Just being in Washington, he believed, would cause him to "be universally construed as a rival to the General-in-Chief [Grant], a position damaging to me in the highest degree." If he "could see my way clear to maintain my family," he would not hesitate to resign. Since this was not an option, he concluded: "I beg the privilege of taking post at New York, or any other point you may name within the new military division, other than Washington." When Johnson read the letter and realized how strongly Sherman opposed the new assignment, he backed off and told the General that he would be permitted to "retain your present command."[76]

IN THE SPRING of 1868, Ulysses S. Grant was nominated for the presidency by the Republican Party. Sherman had long refused to believe that Grant was interested in the office. John Sherman, who was more savvy about national politics than his brother, and read Grant easily, had told Cump as early as March 1866 that it was "evident that Grant has some political aspirations and can, if he wishes it, easily attain the Presidency." Sherman continued to insist that his friend had no intention of becoming the nation's chief executive. "Grant told me he would not accept a nomination for President," he wrote John in August 1867. A few weeks later, he assured John that Grant "writes me in the most unreserved confidence," and that he "never has said a word that looks like wanting the office of President." In that same letter to John, the General made a very significant comment, one that goes far in revealing his assessment of the military and politics: "I don't think Grant, Sheridan, Thomas, *or any real military man* [emphasis added] wants to be President." As a general in the U.S. Army, Sherman conceived of Grant, Sheridan, Thomas and of course himself as occupying a more worthy position as military men, and following a more honorable profession, than any politician who held any political office—even the presidency. But the close-mouthed Grant had probably never viewed the military in that vein, and in November 1868, he was elected as the eighteenth president of the United States.[77]

Chapter Twenty-Six

GENERAL-IN-CHIEF, I

When Grant ascended to the presidency in March 1869, Sherman succeeded him as general-in-chief of the army. Promoted to full general, he received a substantial pay increase, raising his annual salary to nearly $19,000. Yet he had been worried, and with good reason, that the high cost of living in Washington, coupled with the social obligations of the army's top general, would render the position financially intolerable. Sherman had been attempting, since soon after Grant was elected, to sell land in San Francisco and Leavenworth. The California property had been bought for Lizzie—with Ellen's money, which had been provided by her father. The Leavenworth holdings were also attained through Mr. Ewing. Ellen's letters to her father during the winter of 1869 clearly indicate that because of the money issue, the relationship between Ellen and Sherman had become severely strained.[1]

"Cump worried me dreadfully" about selling Lizzie's property, she wrote. "Weary of his complaints & sarcasm," although not in agreement with her husband, Ellen "was finally glad to sell for $2500," but she believed the land could have brought twice that much. Also, the religious issue continued to rankle. Ellen felt she was treated as "the subordinate of the General, who has consented to tolerate my religion provided I do not presume to express my devotion to it." She hoped that she might "have the consolation of spending much time" with her father. Ellen then declared, "I feel so totally estranged from Cump, and we are so out of sympathy with one another, & with each others friends, that life with them is a burden." She assured her father that "this is no feeling of impulse . . . but a settled conviction of mind and purpose."[2]

One of Sherman's major financial concerns in moving to Washington was where to live. Securing a suitable house loomed as his greatest expense. Fortunately, a number of wealthy New Yorkers and Bostonians, including Hamilton Fish, who would soon become Grant's secretary of state, raised $65,000 and offered to buy Grant's mansion, since he would be moving into the White House, and award it to Sherman. When Sherman learned about the project he was quite pleased, and told his brother that the fine house "would suit me to a T, and more especially would it suit Ellen and the family, who want a big house." While the gift home did resolve the immediate question of where to live, the cost of maintaining such an expensive house would quickly become yet another aggravation.[3]

Despite his dislike of the nation's capital, Sherman entered upon his new duties optimistically. He intended, with Grant's help, to resolve a long-standing problem in the administration of the army, one that he and Grant had discussed both during the war and after Grant's election. The heart of the issue was the prerogative of the secretary of war and the army's commanding general. Sherman, and apparently Grant too, planned to curtail what Sherman considered an abuse of power by the secretary of war, an abuse that was detrimental to the well-being of the army. Grant acted quickly following his inauguration, issuing General Orders No. 11, on March 5, requiring that all orders from the secretary of war to the army must be issued through the general-in-chief, and placing all the army departments and bureaus under his direct control. No longer would the secretary of war be able to go over the head of the army's general-in-chief. It meant that Sherman would not have to struggle with a politician for control of the U. S. Army.[4]

But Sherman's triumph, to his surprise and amazement, did not last for even a month. Grant's new secretary of war, John A. Rawlins, the President's former military chief of staff, with whom he was very close, convinced the President that the reforms gave Sherman too much power. He persuaded Grant to rescind his order. Sherman strongly challenged the President's change of policy, both in writing and in person; however, Grant expressed doubt that the reforms were legal, which he said troubled Rawlins greatly. The President also cited Rawlins's poor health (he was dying of tuberculosis), explaining that he did not want to worry the man during his last days. Sherman contended that the legal issue had already been taken into account, and while he sympathized with Rawlins, his health should not be a determining factor. But Grant stood firm. The conversation grew a bit testy, and when Sherman left, the relationship between the two had been taxed. Never again would Sherman feel close to Grant as he did during the war.[5]

Rawlins deteriorated rapidly, and he died in September 1869. The President consulted Sherman about a successor, and one of the men Sherman suggested was William W. Belknap, whom Grant then tapped for the position. Belknap had served as a division commander under Sherman during the war, and the General probably anticipated a good relationship with him. However, Sherman soon realized that Belknap was an aggressive power seeker, and much more of a problem than Rawlins had been. While John Rawlins usually sent orders to the army through Sherman, Belknap made a practice of bypassing the general-in-chief, as well as expanding his authority into areas previously considered the responsibility of the General, such as Indian affairs and West Point. "All the old abuses," wrote Sherman, "which had embittered the life of General Scott in the days of Secretaries of War [William L.] Marcy and [Jefferson] Davis, were renewed." Belknap was making a determined effort to take full control of the army. The situation was going from bad to worse—Colonel Audenried, for example, requested that Sherman not send him to Belknap again, because the secretary of war had "treated him with a rudeness and discourtesy he had never seen displayed by any officer to a soldier." Sherman appealed to Grant, but the President merely passed off the issue with some consoling but meaningless rhetoric.[6]

Another of Sherman's wartime subordinates arose against him in the winter of 1870. John Logan, who had become chairman of the House Military Affairs Committee, determined to have revenge on Sherman for not naming him to permanently command the Army of the Tennessee when General James McPherson was killed in the fighting for Atlanta. Black Jack Logan also nourished a deep-seated bias against West Point officers in general—all the more once Sherman had selected Oliver Howard, an academy graduate, to replace McPherson. Logan still did not know that General George Thomas had strongly urged Sherman not to appoint Logan, and possibly was decisive in influencing Sherman's decision.

The powerful Illinois congressman introduced a bill, which was soon passed, to cut the pay of the army's general-in-chief by approximately one-third, to reduce the number of officers in the army, as well as the salary of those who remained, and to eliminate the ranks of general and lieutenant general upon the death of Sherman and Phil Sheridan. Since taking command of the Division of the Missouri when Sherman became general-in-chief, Sheridan had held the rank of lieutenant general. His pay, like Sherman's, was to be slashed by about a third. When Logan's bill passed, it had been modified a bit, but still hit Sherman hard, especially financially. The General was enraged, hardly able to mention the bill without uttering an oath or two, all the more because he knew that Logan was not yet satisfied. Black Jack wanted more cuts in the size of the army, and he had a near vendetta attitude about West Point, the well-being of which always concerned Sherman deeply. Logan seemed to think that volunteers and state militia could deal with whatever military problems arose, and Sherman worried that Logan, a formidable foe, might even attempt a fatal blow against both the regular army and West Point.[7]

By the spring of 1871, Sherman had grown quite frustrated with his position as general-in-chief. To a great degree, Secretary of War Belknap had secured control of the army, and he consulted Sherman only spasmodically. Congress had drastically cut his pay, reduced the salary of all officers and further whittled down the size of the army. His influence with Grant seemed minimal, and "the elephant," as he remarked to Ord, of an overly expensive house, was weighing him down. Sherman wanted to return to St. Louis, remembering how a disgruntled Winfield Scott had moved his headquarters to New York City. Grant, however, made it clear that he wanted Sherman to remain in Washington. Thus, because he was strapped for money, Sherman was forced to live in one part of his house, and rent the other. As so often when the General was troubled, his mind turned to the great West.[8]

Reports seemed to indicate that violent intrusions upon white settlers by restless Indians might be on the rise, particularly in the Southwest. Sherman therefore had a reason, or at least an excuse, to get away from Washington and make an inspection tour of several army posts in west Texas and points northward. He decided to swing through Louisiana on the way to Texas and visit the Louisiana Military Academy, "whose professors and students," he told Ellen, "somehow regard me as still connected with them." He also stopped in New Orleans, where he was well received, as he had been at the military academy, and made a short speech. Its impact was remarkable. Basically, Sherman claimed that Northern reports of Southern outrages against blacks were exaggerations. He disliked the U.S. Army's being involved in Reconstruction and thought that Southern problems could best be resolved by Southerners. The speech was prominently reported with approval in Southern papers, which is hardly surprising, and some Southerners suggested that the General should run for president.[9]

Then it was on to Texas. By late April 1871, Sherman arrived in San Antonio and prepared for a trip, hundreds of miles long, northward through Native American country. Moving out on May 2, he was accompanied by Inspector General Randolph B. Marcy, a couple of staff members and a small escort of black soldiers from the Tenth Cavalry—buffalo soldiers, as the Indians called them, because of their color. Sherman's route generally followed a line of military installations, and for about 400 miles, although there was evidence of destruction carried out by raiding parties, he never saw an Indian.

Nevertheless, he would soon confront the most dangerous situation that he ever faced while in Indian territory. Unknown to Sherman, as he neared the northern boundary of Texas at the Red River, a band of Kiowas, along with some Comanches, was atop a hill watching his small group pass. A number of notable warriors, such as Satanta, Satank and

Big Tree, were among them. They chose not to attack, however, for Mamanti, the leader who had envisioned their raid, assured them that a greater prize would follow. As he had prophesied, a train of ten freight wagons appeared within a few hours. The Indians struck, killing seven teamsters. A few men escaped because the Indians fell to plundering the wagons. Hoping to find rifles and ammunition, but discovering little except corn, they took the mules and rode north to recross the Red River into Indian territory.

When Sherman learned of the attack, he ordered troops to the site, but the trail had grown cold. Five days later, he arrived at Fort Sill, some forty miles north of the Texas border, which was commanded by Benjamin Grierson, the cavalry commander who led the famous diversionary raid through Mississippi during the Vicksburg campaign. Shortly after Sherman reached Fort Sill, several Indian chiefs came in to draw their weekly rations, and the Indian agent Lawrie Tatum, whom the Indians called "Bald Head," inquired whether they knew anything about the ambush of the wagon train. Immediately Satanta claimed the honor of leading the raid. Actually, Mamanti was the leader, and why Satanta lied about it has been a subject of speculation ever since. Satanta also rebuked Tatum for the way the Indians were being treated, especially the fact that they had not received the arms and ammunition which they had requested. Tatum replied that he had no authority to issue weapons, but said that the great General Sherman was visiting Fort Sill, and the chiefs could ask him for arms and ammunition if they wished.

Upon learning that Satanta claimed he had led the raid, Sherman determined to meet with the Indians and arrest Satanta, along with Big Tree and Satank. On May 27, Sherman and Grierson, standing on the porch of Grierson's headquarters, received the chiefs. Wasting no time, Sherman denounced the Indians as murderers and stated that he was arresting the three named. At Sherman's signal, the shutters of the porch windows were opened, and about a dozen black troopers leveled their carbines at the Indians. Kicking Bird, another Kiowa chief, reportedly exclaimed at Sherman: "You have asked for these men to kill them. . . . You and I are going to die right here." About the same time, a number of black cavalry took positions along a fence facing the porch, with weapons ready for action.

The tense, dramatic situation quickly escalated. Another Kiowa, Lone Wolf, rode up, dismounted and strode toward the porch, carrying two repeating carbines. Reaching the porch steps, he handed a pistol to a chief, and one of the carbines to another, after which he sat down on the floor and stared at Sherman. Some remembered that Lone Wolf cocked his carbine, although Sherman said he did not see it. There was also a report that, in addition to the carbines, Lone Wolf gave a bow and arrows to yet another chief. A gunfight seemed ready to erupt at any second, with Sherman right in the middle of it. Exactly what occurred next is rather murky. According to one account, Benjamin Grierson suddenly seized Lone Wolf's carbine and ordered, through an interpreter, for the Indians to surrender, which they did. Another version credits Satanta, who was recognized as the most important of the chiefs, with throwing up his hands, and stopping the impending fight. However, precisely, the confrontation was resolved, a shoot-out was avoided, and Sherman had won a war of nerves.[10]

Satanta, Big Tree and Satank were clamped in irons and sent off to Texas for trial. Under cover of a blanket, Satank managed to wrench free from the manacles, ripping flesh from his hands as he did so. With a knife concealed in his clothing, he stabbed the nearest guard, threw him from the wagon and grabbed a carbine from another guard, only to be shot and killed in his effort to escape. Satank's body was left beside the road. Sherman thought that "hanging would have been better, but we can be content that he is now extinct." Satanta and Big Tree were tried for murder in Jacksboro, Texas, where the jury of ranchers and cowboys quickly found them guilty. They were sentenced to be hanged. But a national outcry proclaiming that the chiefs had not received a fair trial was so great—and the fear of the Kiowas going to war if they were executed so widespread—that Texas Governor E. J. Davis commuted their sentence to life in prison. After serving two years, and essentially becoming martyrs in the eyes of many humanitarians, the governor, under pressure from Washington, released them.[11]

Sherman bitterly denounced their release, warning that "no life from Kansas to the Rio Grande" would be safe. He even stated that when the two chiefs led another raid, which he declared was sure to happen, he hoped Governor Davis would be the first white they scalped—obviously, a thought better left unspoken. The governor kept his scalp, although Sherman was right about the raids soon beginning again. The Fort Sill confrontation and its aftermath proved to be a watershed in Sherman's toleration of Native Americans. His attitude toward them became more harsh, more vindictive, particularly toward the Kiowas and the Comanches. "If I ever come to Fort Sill [again]," he wrote, "and any of those Indians come about bragging of killing people in Texas, I won't bother their courts," he proclaimed. Instead, he promised to "have their graves dug at once." He made it very clear to Phil Sheridan, commanding the Division of the Missouri, who viewed Indians much as Sherman did and hardly needed any encouragement, that he wanted to implement a more aggressive policy in dealing with them. Any warriors discovered off the reservations were to be attacked, and forced back to their designated territory.[12]

WHEN SHERMAN GOT BACK to Washington, his relationship with Secretary of War Belknap was no better than when he left—not that he expected it to be. Sherman seized the chance to make a long desired tour of Europe. While preparing for the trip, which was expected to take well over half a year, his father-in-law died, on October 26, 1871. Two years earlier, the elder Ewing had fainted while addressing the Supreme Court, and he had struggled with failing health ever since. Because Thomas Ewing was only two months short of eighty-two, his death came as no great surprise. For many years Sherman had experienced ambiguous feelings about the foster father who then became his father-in-law. He admired Ewing's abilities and successes and acknowledged that he himself had benefited from his associations with the man. On the other hand, Ewing had tried to influence, and even determine, the course of Sherman's life. He sought also to keep Ellen close at hand, and she generally seemed quite willing to comply. Probably even more troubling to Sherman, he had long observed that his wife had more respect for and confidence in her father's judgments and opinions, about most matters, than she did her husband's.

Ironically, Mr. Ewing in death had an impact on Sherman that he never had in life. On his deathbed, Ewing accepted Catholicism. Although Ellen still said that "the brightness has gone out of everything," she could better accept her father's passing, believing that eternal salvation of his immortal soul had been secured. And more than ever, Ellen was emboldened in her efforts to persuade Cump to accept the faith. She hoped her father's example might influence her husband. She seemed never to understand the depth of Sherman's opposition to Catholicism. If the General believed in some kind of a higher power—which is debatable—he did not accept the God of Catholicism, or the God of any brand of Protestantism. Ellen's renewed campaign to convert him only irritated. The religious breach between husband and wife grew worse.[13]

In mid-November, Sherman sailed for Europe aboard the *Wabash*, a warship commanded by Rear Admiral James Alden, recently promoted to lead the U.S. Navy squadron operating in the Mediterranean Sea. Alden had invited Sherman to join him for the crossing, as far as Gibraltar. The General took up a forward position on the main deck, relishing the sensation of the vessel rising and falling as she moved out to sea. He was accompanied by one of his favorite aides, Colonel Joseph Audenried, and Lieutenant Fred Grant, the President's son, whom Grant requested Sherman take with him. Sherman thought the *Wabash* "a splendid vessel ... strong, safe and perfectly manned." He enjoyed the voyage. "I have not been sea sick of course," he wrote Ellen, commenting that "Audenried & Fred [had] been let off easy, [with] Neptune claiming but little of their time."[14]

While Sherman observed that "the ship sails well," he also noted that "her steam power is merely auxiliary and cannot be depended upon when the wind opposes." That fact was soon demonstrated as they approached Gibraltar, facing gale-force winds, which compelled them to head for the Spanish seaport of Cádiz instead, where they landed on

December 14. There Sherman began his tour, which lasted nearly ten months, traveling by train, steamboat and carriage through a dozen or more countries. Viewed everywhere as a renowned military figure, he would be received by royalty, army commanders and the wealthy. There was no need to request attention; Europeans, having followed the Civil War, knew his reputation and sought his company.[15]

Sherman was pleased to visit Cádiz, although he did not want to miss Gibraltar and arranged to spend a few days in the British colony, including Christmas. The United Kingdom had a fleet of six ironclads at anchor, and the commander conducted Sherman through his own ship, as well as another vessel, which the General thought was probably "the strongest ship now afloat." But Gibraltar proved to be an unpleasant visit physically. "I have been quite asthmatic with a good deal of cough," he informed Ellen on December 28, "and find the rooms cheerless & cold." Very few families, although coal from England was abundant, had "even fires in their sitting rooms, [and] none in bed rooms at all, though it is quite cold."[16]

Taking a steamboat to Málaga, Spain, he proceeded northward to visit Granada, Sevilla, Córdoba, Toledo and Madrid. Perturbed by an American girl who "rode in the car with me through the most interesting part of Spain," Sherman said that she "read a paper-back novel all the way." Realizing how much that young woman was missing, he told Ellen, who undoubtedly already knew the fact: "I never go to a place but I know all about it, its topography, geography and history." The last statement was no idle boast. Before leaving the United States, he had read a number of books pertaining to Europe, and throughout his journey, continued to learn all he could about every place he went. Evidently, judging from the length and detail of description that he wrote Ellen, Sherman was really fascinated by Córdoba; although, like Spain generally, he found the city quite cold. He remarked that he was "glad that he did not attempt to bring Minnie," because he knew "she would have actually suffered for a fire, which is something hardly comprehended . . . anywhere in Spain."[17]

By the time Sherman reached Madrid, he was convinced that historical figures of major significance were ignored throughout Spain.

He thought Mark Twain had it right: "You can see thousands of Saints sculptured and pictured, but no plain mortal who has done some act of historic merit, like Columbus." He declared to Ellen that "Cortes & Pizzaro [sic] are unknown in the land of their origin, while saints by the million are as cheap as dirt." Immediately he added, "I do not say this to hurt your feelings, but it is holy truth," and he believed that everybody would corroborate what he said.[18]

After passing through Saragossa and Barcelona, Sherman traveled along the French Riviera, and thence into Italy for an extended visit. He met Pope Pius IX, famous for proclaiming the "immaculate conception" of the Virgin Mary, as well as presiding over the Vatican Council of 1870, which affirmed the doctrine of papal infallibility whenever the pontiff speaks *ex cathedra* regarding faith or morals. If Sherman knew of these events, so momentous for faithful Catholics, he would hardly have been impressed. In Rome he watched the Pope as "plenty of Cardinals . . . kissed his hands and foot." When Pius was informed that "the illustrious General Sherman" was present, according to Sherman's account to Henry Turner, the Pope stopped, greeted him and Colonel Audenreid (Fred Grant was sick at the time), and invited them to accompany him as he welcomed the visitors of the morning. A number of American ladies were present, carrying rosaries and tokens, observed Sherman, "for this old man's blessing; and when the Pope was through, he turned and blessed us." Sherman took particular notice in Rome of the many nude statues and paintings, and wrote Ellen that "in stairway niches, on chandeliers, and over the mantles are figures, mostly female, as naked as Eve before the fall." He said that he found them "very beautiful," but was not about to "invest in any of them," because he knew, even though they were "sanctioned by the Pope himself," that Ellen surely "would consign them to the garret, or some worse place."[19]

While in Naples, Sherman dined one evening with "a Grand Dutchess Olga of Russia," who after dinner "brought in her pretty children." Sherman wrote Turner that he "picked up a pretty two-year-old boy, and kissed him as I would one of yours." From the stares he received, the General realized that such was not customary. "But the Grand Dutchess is a lady," he continued. She spoke English, read American books, "even Mark Twain, and really felt complimented at the Barbarian's notice of her fine chubby boy." Audenried, who kept valuable notes on the trip, told of going on an excursion to Pompeii, where a special excavation was conducted for Sherman to observe. Then they ascended Mt. Vesuvius, all of which made for a very tiring day. But Sherman usually held his own, or better. Audenried recorded that while in Egypt, when they climbed the Great Pyramid of Cheops, Sherman seemed to recover more quickly than either he or the much younger Grant.[20]

It was in Egypt that Sherman visited with the American officer Henry Stone, whom he found "installed as a sort of Adjutant General to the Egyptian army." In fact, he discovered an unusually large number of American military officers, seventeen in all, employed in Egypt, some from the North and some from the South. "All seemed equally glad to see me," Sherman told Turner. They passed some time reminiscing about "the terrible civil war," which had begun exactly ten years earlier.

Moving on to Constantinople, which he assessed as "probably the best sight [sic] for a great city in the world," he was particularly struck by its cosmopolitanism, possibly "the most heterogeneous people on the face of the globe." But while there, Sherman encountered, "much to my disgust," a newspaper correspondent, about whom he raged to Turner that if that man "is to travel with us," listening and reporting "our conversations ... to the world," he would simply "go through Russia like a rocket, and accept no invitations." Fortunately Sherman was spared such a fate, and very much enjoyed his time in Russia, where he was received by, among others, Tsar Alexander II.[21]

Indeed, Sherman was well received everywhere, with the single exception of Germany. The Grant administration had allowed the French to buy arms and ammunition worth millions of dollars while they were fighting the recent Franco-Prussian War. The victorious German emperor, still angered by the United States aid to France, showed no enthusiasm for the prospect of meeting Sherman. As soon as Sherman realized the situation, he left Berlin, heading for Austria, where he enjoyed a good visit in Vienna. Then it was on to Paris, where the General spent most of July, staying at the Grand Hotel, and having a wonderful time. Last on his agenda came the British Isles. He had received a message from Ellen, urging him to call on the Catholic archbishop when he reached England. Cump refused, contending that if he did so, without also visiting the Anglican authorities, it would be "whispered & printed that [he was] a Catholic." Sherman surely did not wish to be identified by the English press as a Catholic (which always irritated him wherever it occurred), and had no interest anyway in spending time with either Anglican or Catholic archbishops.[22]

By mid-September 1872, the General had returned to the United States. "Since I got back home," he wrote Turner, "I have had one of those severe attacks of asthma, that reminds me occasionally that I am mortal, but I think the newspapers exaggerate the severity." The situation at the War Department was unchanged, with the secretary of war continuing to act much as a general-in-chief. In November, General Grant was reelected to the presidency, overwhelmingly defeating Horace Greeley, the editor of the *New York Tribune*. Grant garnered 55.6 percent of the popular vote, the largest margin of victory since Andrew Jackson. Sherman had been disappointed in Grant as president, but he favored the General over Greeley, whom he told Ellen would have been "the worst President any country ever had."[23]

Sherman remained disgusted with Secretary Belknap's usurpation of power and, declaring that no part of the army was under his control, refused to make an annual report for 1873. Furthermore, he wrote in his memoirs, "I was gradually being impoverished." Real estate taxes on his Washington house had increased from about $400 annually to $1,500, in addition to "all sorts of special taxes." Also, the winter and spring of 1873 brought more Indian problems, resulting in the tragic fate of the Modocs, who lived along the California–Oregon border and had been friendly with the whites. A lengthy series of complex events reached a sad, decisive climax when a well-intentioned army officer, Brigadier General E. R. S. Canby, was killed by the Modoc chief Captain Jack.[24]

After Captain Jack had attempted several times to reach a satisfactory resolution of the Modoc differences with the whites, an aggressive group within the tribe mocked him for being a weak leader. Finally he agreed to their demands. If, upon asking General Canby "many times" more to grant the terms sought by the Modocs, the general did not agree, then Captain Jack would kill him. On April 11, in the midst of the negotiations, a frustrated Indian reportedly shouted, "We talk no more," whereupon Captain Jack drew his pistol and shot Canby in the head at virtually point-blank range. Another of the white negotiators was also killed.[25]

General Sherman had earlier advised Canby to deal with the Modocs so "that no other reservation for them will be necessary except graves among their chosen lava beds." Upon learning of Canby's death, he told General John Schofield, now commanding the Division of the Pacific, under whom Canby had served, that "any measure of severity to the savages will be sustained." Sherman named the aggressive Jefferson C. Davis to succeed Canby. Davis relentlessly pursued the Modoc warriors, his troops at last succeeding in surrounding and capturing Captain Jack and three other Modocs. They were given a trial, although a gallows was being constructed even as it proceeded. To no one's surprise, Captain Jack and three others were found guilty of murder and sentenced to be hanged, which was duly carried out. The surviving Modocs, about 150 men, women and children, were exiled to Indian Territory. In 1909, the U.S. government permitted them to return to a reservation in Oregon; by then, only approximately 50 Modocs remained.[26]

While Sherman had no doubt, he told a congressional investigating committee, "that the Indians, in the aggregate and in detail, have suffered great wrong at our hands," he rhetorically wondered how the continent could possibly be settled "without doing some harm to the Indians who stand in the way." He declared, "There has to be violence somewhere." Interestingly, when General Schofield published his memoirs in 1897, he decried the racial double standard: the Indians tried and executed "while those white men who, in no less fragrant disregard of the laws of civilization, brought on the war, were not called to any account for their crime." Schofield said that the natural law of the "survival of the fittest" would be cited by some "in explanation of all that has happened to the Indians"; but he did not consider it "a law of Christianity, nor of civilization, nor of wisdom," only the law of "greed and cruelty."[27]

BY THE SPRING of 1874, Sherman decided he could not stomach any more of the Washington situation. He determined to move his headquarters to St. Louis and formally requested the secretary of war to sanction the change. The expense of living in Washington was a great burden, and in St. Louis he would be well located to quickly proceed anywhere in the country that might require his presence. Secretary Belknap approved his stated reasons for the transfer, probably pleased to think that Sherman would be less inclined to interfere with his own power if in St. Louis. This time Grant also gave his assent, and that fall Sherman returned to his St. Louis house on Garrison Avenue. Shortly before leaving the capital, however, the General's daughter Minnie married Navy Lieutenant Thomas W. Fitch, in one of the most splendid weddings ever seen in Washington, and young Tom Sherman headed for New Haven, Connecticut, to begin studying at Yale. The mansion in the capital, whose maintenance had always been a burden, was sold.[28]

Sherman was very pleased to have Tom at Yale, and away from the Catholic academy associated with Georgetown University, which he had been attending. Yale's enviable academic reputation appealed to Sherman, but more important was the kind of men with whom Tom would be associated. In the General's judgment, the chief benefit of attending Yale would be the relationships formed with future leaders of the nation—a view presumably as relevant now as then. Tom Sherman was an energetic, hardworking person who took his college career quite seriously, and he was not particularly impressed by the Yale experience.

"The system of lectures," he said, was "very unsatisfactory," and he complained that the professors "do not encourage original thinking in their students." Becoming interested in studying law, he tried to start a debating society. The attempt failed, and Tom blamed the failure on the "miserable little secret societies" of the boys, which he declared wasted time and money, created jealousies and bickerings and largely prevented "anything open and manly" from finding favor—rather persuasive arguments. "I am very glad now," Tom wrote his father, "that I was not foolish enough to join one of those societies." No Skull & Bones man was he.[29]

With his interest in legal studies stirred, Tom consulted with Sherman about a future course of study. Tom seems to have been feeling his way, merely exploring the law and the possibilities of a legal career. Sherman assumed that his son was committing to the legal profession. Clearly the General was not happy with the manner in which the postwar army had developed, and he wanted to steer Tom away from either a military career or a religious vocation. For several years Sherman had favored the law for his son. Now he envisioned Tom returning to St. Louis, studying law at Washington University, and completing his preparations in the law office of Sherman's friend Colonel Henry Hitchcock. For a time after graduation from Yale, that is exactly what Tom did. But, totally unknown to the General, another consideration had long been weighing upon his son's mind—one that became, by 1878, irreversibly dominant.[30]

Tom had decided to become a priest. In mid-May he informed his parents about his intentions. Sherman was shocked. He reacted with bewilderment, sorrow and rage. Tom's decision, he wrote Minnie, "has embittered me more than I ought to write." While he said that he was trying "to check my feelings" against Tom personally, he found it impossible to do so "against the cause of his action, the Catholic Church." Furious toward the church, he heatedly told his daughter Minnie that now he was even suspicious of her; indeed, of "all Catholics."[31]

Time and again in the following weeks, Sherman excoriated the Catholic Church in the most bitter terms. Naturally he wrote to his close friend Henry Turner, who was a Catholic, and who must have been troubled by some of Sherman's invective remarks about the church. The General assured Turner that he would not turn against Tom (although at one point he did contemplate cutting him out of his will), "but I do against that Church which has poisoned his young mind . . . and weaned him from his father." Sherman said he had been "forced into the ranks

of those who regard the Catholic Church as one of our public enemies."
For several years he had been trying to groom his son to assume the role
of leader and financial provider for the family. Now all his designs were
destroyed. He looked upon Tom as having deserted his father and the
family. The financial security of the family would continue to rest solely
in the General's hands, and he was nearing retirement age. "I can hardly
stand it," he wrote Turner, "and can hardly venture to make any plans
or suggestions for the future." Tom was "the Keystone of my arch, and
his going away lets down the whole structure with a crash. I sometimes
think that Providence afflicts each of us in the most sensitive part."[32]

To another friend, Sherman said that he regarded Tom "as dead," and
declared his animosity toward the Catholic Church so strong that "the
bare sight of a Priest, or of any Catholic emblem," was like "the red flag
to an infuriated Bull." To his brother-in-law Charley Ewing he raged
that he had become "an enemy [of the Catholic Church] so bitter that
written words can convey no meaning." Undoubtedly, it grated hard on
Sherman that his own son not only accepted a religion which he himself
had rejected as foreign to all that he considered rational, but now had
chosen to dedicate his very life to that faith. Tom's decision left Sherman feeling isolated from both his wife, who of course supported Tom
strongly, and the rest of his children, all of whom were Catholic. He
wrote his daughter Elly that his "thoughts will go out more and more to
my Army comrades, because they now compose my family." He hoped
that somehow Tom, who had gone to England to prepare for the priesthood, just might change his mind, writing Turner in November, that
"as yet I see no signs of his changing his vocation, although as I understand, he has two years in which to take the final leap." There would be
no change.[33]

After Tom's decision to become a priest in the spring of 1878, Sherman and Ellen had little contact during the rest of the year. Their relationship was sorely troubled, probably worse than at any other time
of their marriage, with Cump regarding Ellen, in tandem with the
Catholic Church, as largely responsible for determining the direction
their son had taken. By this time, Sherman had moved his headquar-

ters back to Washington. Early in 1876, Secretary of War Belknap had resigned in disgrace when a congressional investigation revealed that he was receiving kickbacks from men chosen to operate Indian trading posts. When the new secretary of war, Alphonso Taft of Ohio, agreed to consult Sherman before taking action on army issues, the General returned to the nation's capital. However, the Washington papers soon got word of his family problems. The rumors were so persistent that Sherman issued a public denial of any marital strain over religion. Still, Ellen spent most of the fall of 1878 in Baltimore, where two of the children were in school, while Sherman worked in his Washington office, attended various meetings, and during the late summer, headed west for another military tour. Christmas 1878 found Ellen and the children, except for Tom, gathered in Baltimore, with the General alone in Washington. He was reunited with the family on New Years' Day, but soon left for another extended trip. Although he eventually renewed contact with Tom, both by letter and in person, Sherman could never really accept his son's choice of the priesthood, and he never forgave the Catholic Church.[34]

During the winter of 1879, Sherman traveled south, journeying through the former Confederacy, accompanied by a small group of officers and his daughter Lizzie. First retracing the Atlanta campaign and the march to Savannah, he told Turner, "If I were the devil incarnate, as many people thought me in 1865, I surely exposed myself to revenge or insult." People everywhere knew that Sherman was coming, and crowds of whites and blacks gathered at the depots, acting in a respectful manner, and "in not a single instance," wrote the General, "was a word uttered, within my hearing, that was rude, impolite, or offensive." He said that at every hotel his party was given the best rooms, the best tables, "and all classes came to me as I walked the streets or sat in my room, just as I wanted them to do." From Savannah, Sherman headed west to New Orleans, where he arrived in time for Mardi Gras, taking rooms on Dauphin Street near Canal Street, and receiving a command to "pay my personal and official respects to Rex," the King of Carnival.[35]

When King Rex disembarked from a steamboat at the foot of Canal,

Sherman was waiting at the place designated for their meeting, in company with former Confederate General John Bell Hood. Rex approached on horseback, in all his masked finery, recognized and saluted Sherman, and requested that the General attend his royal reception that evening. Sherman was pleased to do so, of course—he would be one of perhaps a hundred people who gathered at the Royal Banquet Hall. Everyone drank to Sherman's health, "and with evident heartiness," he declared to Turner. At the conclusion of Rex's welcoming speech, Sherman was made "a Duke of Louisiana" and awarded a decoration. He replied appropriately, and then John Bell Hood spoke, referring to "our former relations as opposing Generals," Sherman wrote, "but with compliments more than I expected." King Rex arranged that on the following day, when he reached the New Orleans Club, Sherman should meet him there, and they would drink champagne to each other's health. Sherman thought some ten thousand people were watching when they did so. The General certainly relished the prominent manner in which New Orleans had received him.[36]

After leaving the Crescent City, he next visited "my old school at Baton Rouge, saw the cadets drill and parade, made them an earnest speech, and had them cluster about me, and stayed with the professors until past midnight." From Baton Rouge he took a steamboat to Vicksburg, visited the lines where his troops had fought and then rode a train to Jackson, after which he headed north. Jefferson Davis, the former Confederate president, was traveling on the train out of Jackson. Informed that Davis was in the next car to him, Sherman wrote, "I did not feel like going out of my way to see Davis." He remained in his car, and Davis did the same. The General assessed the Southern trip as "in its whole extent most enjoyable, and the people high and low, received me with absolute cordiality and friendship."[37]

By this time, the last U.S. Army troops had been withdrawn from the South, which marked the end of Reconstruction. Sherman's journey across the Southern states did not alter his early formed, and strongly held view about the status of the former slaves. He told Turner that "the repression of the whites was carried too far, and too much support was given to the negroes." Declaring that "the freedom of the negro is sure," he said that blacks would only gain political influence to the degree that they could acquire "knowledge and property." Obviously Sherman did not see, or did not acknowledge, the factors already undermining any hope that African-Americans might achieve economic, political, and educational equality with whites—to say nothing of social equality. Such repressive measures as vagrancy laws, contract laws, the crop-lien system and literacy tests, as well as intimidation through harassment and violence, were denying many blacks their constitutional rights. At the worst, such measures were still enslaving African-Americans in the South.[38]

SHERMAN'S WORKING RELATIONSHIP with the several secretaries of war who came after William Belknap saw a marked and welcome improvement. But he still had to battle periodic attempts by Congress to cut the size of the army. If Sherman could have had his way, the regular army would have been about 100,000 strong. There was no chance of anything like that number winning congressional approval, as the General knew. Support for a total force of 25,000, especially after troops were withdrawn from the South, proved a continual challenge. Sherman did well to maintain the army at that level—which he knew was far less than he needed to adequately address the problems of the great western frontier. When George Armstrong Custer and 263 of his men died at the hands of the Sioux and Northern Cheyenne in the Battle of the Little Bighorn on June 25, 1876, Congress authorized an increase of 2,500 in the army's strength. After the passage of a little time, however, many congressmen would again favor a reduction of the army's numbers.[39]

As general-in-chief, Sherman hoped to use his position and influence to make some reforms in the army, particularly relating to military organization and the inevitable integration, in a democratic society, of military professionals with citizen-soldiers. In this connection, Sherman was greatly impressed by a highly talented young officer named Emory B. Upton, who had graduated from West Point in 1861. Upton experienced a spectacular Civil War career, rising to become a brevet major general at twenty-four. Disturbed by the thousands of lives that he saw wasted in frontal assaults, and especially perturbed by the generalship during the Wilderness campaign, Upton published a well-received book called *A New System of Infantry Tactics,* which offered a sophisticated, compelling and forward-looking analysis.

Sherman developed a close relationship with Upton, became sort of a patron and mentor of the bright officer and in 1875 placed him on a commission to propose army reforms. Soon after, he sent Upton and two other officers on a foreign study tour of various military forces and installations. While Sherman was especially interested in the Middle and Near East, primarily because he had found the geography and climate somewhat reminiscent of the American West, Upton centered his attention on Europe, was deeply impressed by the German military forces and came back convinced that the U.S. Army should be reorganized like the German army.[40]

But Sherman rejected the idea of adopting the German military system. As he analyzed the American situation, he saw no need for either compulsory military service or a huge army, because there was no country north or south of the United States that possessed the capability of challenging the nation; the idea of a European power crossing the ocean with sufficient forces to menace the United States was absurd. Obviously the army must continue dealing with the problems of Native Americans and white frontiersmen in the great West. But a new concern had also arisen. The 1870s, for the first time in American history, brought significant clashes between labor and capital. These surprised and alarmed a great many Americans, who had imagined that the United States was somehow immune from the class violence of Europe.

Terrorism involving the Molly Maguires in the eastern Pennsylvania coalfields, reached a peak in the mid-1870s. Named for an Irishman who led a violent movement against the British, the Molly Maguires, through intimidation and even killings, championed Irish-American workers who were perceived as being wronged by coal mine owners. Far more important, however, was the great railroad strike of 1877, and the resulting violence. Wage cuts caused the strike, which began on the Baltimore & Ohio line, but soon involved other railroads and spread across the country. From New York and Chicago to San Francisco, looting, rioting and burning destroyed millions of dollars in property and resulted in the death of more than a hundred people, with the worst violence occurring in Pittsburgh. A Pittsburgh newspaper feared the beginning "of a great civil war in this country between labor and capital." In some cities federal troops were brought in to restore order. Thus Sherman, who expected yet more labor violence, wanted to keep the army as strong as he possibly could. Militia, sympathizing with the strikers, might defect, but the army could be depended upon to follow orders, and Sherman's empathy lay with capital.[41]

The General concluded, and Upton supported him, that the nation's best military solution for the foreseeable future would be an expandable army—an updated and refined idea, traceable in a more simplified form back to John C. Calhoun's tenure as secretary of war. Sherman hoped that the regular army could be enlarged to some degree. Whether that happened or not, he wanted every army regiment organized with a capability of rapidly incorporating a large number of men in any time of emergency—be it war, labor violence or whatever. His goal would be a total force of 200,000, which he considered sufficient to meet any conceivable threat to the United States. The expandable army concept, which some scholars have concluded could not have worked, was rejected by Congress, and Sherman's hope of reform came to naught.[42]

He was successful, however, in spearheading significant educational advancements for army officers. Deemphasizing the engineering role of West Point, Sherman favored broadening the curriculum with more military-centered courses. Although he considered the study of history and literature advisable for a well-rounded education, he believed those subjects should be pursued during a cadet's free time. West Point's primary mission, as Sherman conceived it, was to prepare officers for war. That meant practical military studies must predominate. Furthermore, Sherman wanted West Point to serve as a preparatory institution, leading to more advanced and specialized military education. To that end, he backed a School of Application for Infantry and Cavalry at Fort Leavenworth, Kansas. It was the beginning of an army staff college dedicated to "the science and practice of war," later becoming the U.S. Army Command and General Staff College. It was one of Sherman's most important achievements while general-in-chief of the army. Sherman also founded, in 1878, the Military Service Institution, to bring together army officers "with a common interest in acquiring specialized knowledge."[43]

By the late 1870s, the first African-American had entered West Point, a development not to Sherman's liking. In the spring of 1880, Johnson C. Whitaker, a black cadet, claimed to have been attacked during the night by several white cadets. General John Schofield, then serving as superintendent of the academy, did not believe Whitaker's story. Schofield was convinced that the young black concocted an incident to avoid an examination for which he was not prepared (twice before he had been found deficient) and to seek revenge on white cadets who shunned him. Sherman supported Schofield strongly. "Even if Whitaker's story be true," Sherman wrote Henry Turner, "he is not the kind of man to fight battles or to command men." Sherman declared that Whitaker "should have resisted any three men, and made noise enough to attract attention ... —but he lay quiet feigning." What really convinced Sherman that the black cadet staged the whole thing was that, he told Turner, "His feet were tied gently, and his hands tied *in front*. He was not bruised a particle ... and the alleged maiming was simply farcial."[44]

The incident, however, created "great public excitement," in Schofield's words, and gained national attention. "The newspapers," said Sherman, "are like a pack of hounds—one barks and the others join in without knowing the cause." Whether deservedly or not, and Sherman thought not, West Point was subject to considerable criticism. President Rutherford B. Hayes, a brigadier general in the war, decided to intervene. He removed Schofield from the superintendency and replaced him with Oliver Howard. The President did not consult Sherman about the change. Sherman assured Henry Turner, also an academy man, that despite "the howl against West Point," the military academy "is in superb order, and the character of the young graduates compares most favorably with that of any previous period."[45]

MEANWHILE, SHERMAN'S RELATIONSHIP with Ellen remained quite rocky. Her general aversion to social occasions, well established long before Tom's priesthood decision entered the picture, became more pronounced as the years passed. She seldom accompanied Cump to the theater, which was probably his favorite entertainment, or to dinner parties, banquets and dances. In fact, Ellen wrote a letter to a Mr. Rulofson in 1877 that gained public notice, in which she castigated "the Evils of the Dance," and commended a book Rulofson had written against dancing. Dancing, of course, was a pleasure that Sherman had enjoyed since his teenage years. The General, a gregarious personality who relished an active social life and savored his fame, which was perhaps unsurpassed by any American, was never inclined to sit at home. Sometimes he escorted one of his daughters to the theater, or a banquet, or whatever occasion beckoned. At other times, and more frequently, his companion would be a female acquaintance, usually younger than he.[46]

In the early 1870s, Sherman had met Vinnie Ream, a sculptor and singer, then in her midtwenties. A talented artist, she was selected by a committee, of which Sherman was a member, to fashion a sculpted likeness of Admiral Farragut. Sherman and Vinnie developed a close relationship. When she married several years later, they still remained in contact from time to time.

Then in the spring of 1880, Colonel Joseph Audenried, Sherman's longtime aide and friend, suddenly died. Sherman was summoned to Audenried's bedside at 1:30 in the morning of June 3, and stayed with him until his death three hours later. The colonel left a widow who was in her thirties, and a young daughter who proved a challenge to manage. Sherman soon took it upon himself to look after Mary Audenried, and to some extent her daughter too—although not financially, for Mary came from a wealthy family which had provided generously for her. Sherman's relationship with Mary Audenried lasted through most of the 1880s. Of

Mary's association with the General, one historian stated unequivocally, "Within six months [of her husband's death] she took him to her
bed." (Mary Audenried had indicated to Sherman, in the early days of
her marriage, that she found him more attractive than her husband.)
Another historian wrote, in a more guarded assessment, that Sherman
"clearly ... enjoyed younger women, and there must have been some
flings...."[47]

Whatever the truth about sexual intimacy with other women, it
seems fair to say, that Sherman's relationships with Vinnie Ream, Mary
Audenried and perhaps others provided an emotional gratification that
was long missing from his relationship with Ellen.

Chapter Twenty-Seven

GENERAL-IN-CHIEF, II

Late in the morning of Wednesday, August 11, 1880, Sherman arrived in central Ohio. He traveled by rail with President Rutherford B. Hayes, a native Ohioan, and several other dignitaries, among them Major General William Hazen, Colonel Emory Upton and Lieutenant Johnny Clem, the celebrated "Drummer Boy of Shiloh." The occasion was a "grand reunion" of Federal Civil War veterans, and the President's train, anxiously anticipated by all, was hailed by a huge crowd as it steamed into the Columbus depot.[1]

Never in the state capital's history had there been a larger or more notable gathering. "The people are here and bent on having a reunion," exulted the *Ohio State Journal*. Estimates of the number of visitors thronging the streets of Columbus ranged between fifty and sixty thousand. "The streets were almost impassable," reported the paper, declaring also that "many of the veterans have grown old," and that thousands of the men were broken in health and disabled. Nevertheless, all seemed in good spirit and prepped for the celebration.[2]

The railcar in which President Hayes, Sherman and the others were traveling was uncoupled from the train, and transferred out to High Street, where the men stepped into carriages. There began a procession to the old Ohio State Fair Grounds (later Franklin Park), as people lined the streets, watching and applauding the President and his entourage. At the focal point of the festivities, a twenty-one-gun salute was fired, and a military band struck up a wartime medley, before President Hayes addressed the veterans.[3]

Unfortunately, although the weather was warm, the overcast day turned darker, and rain was falling by the time the President began speaking. The inclement weather discouraged many visitors, and also residents of the city, who stayed away from the midafternoon, open-air program. Regardless of the rain, perhaps ten thousand veterans were in attendance, according to the newspaper reports. President Hayes decided to cut his speech short, and allow the audience to find shelter from the bad weather. As Hayes concluded his brief remarks, the crowd applauded him warmly, but most of them were not inclined to leave, not just yet.

As the applause for the President died away, shouts of "Sherman!" "Sherman!" and "Speech!" "Speech!" sounded from the mass of veterans. "Let's hear from Uncle Billy!" some were yelling, recalling the name by which soldiers fondly acclaimed him during the war. More and more men took up the cry for Sherman to speak, and the crowd was soon clapping, as well as continuing to call out "Sherman!" "Sherman!" The General was not on the schedule to speak. But soon it became evident that the sea of Union veterans was not going to be satisfied until Sherman responded.

At last the General arose from his chair, strode to the speaker's lectern and was greeted by a roar of applause that the newspaper described as "tremendous and deafening." For a moment he gazed upon the crowd, waiting for the applause to subside. "Fellow soldiers," he began. "My speech is not written, nor has been even thought of by me. It delights my soul to see so many of the good old boys left yet. They are not afraid of rain; we have stood it many a time." Sherman noted that he had come to Columbus, not with the intention of speaking, but as a part of President Hayes's escort, planning "simply to look on and let the boys look at old Billy again." Declaring that "Uncle Billy loves . . . as his own flesh and blood . . . every soldier here today," the General proclaimed that "could I command the language, I would like to speak to you an hour."

It was at this point of his extemporaneous remarks that Sherman spoke the words for which he has been longest remembered. "The war now is away back in the past and you can tell what books can not," he stated. "When you talk you come down to the practical realities just as they happened. You all know this is not soldiering here. There is many a boy here today who looks on war as all glory, but boys it is all hell. You can bear this warning voice to generations yet to come. I look upon war with horror, but if it has to come, I am here." That remark was received with long applause, and vigorous hurrahs. Then the General concluded: "I wish to again congratulate you. Those who were at the rear in the war would have been gone from here covered with umbrellas before now. The country is now peaceful and long may it remain so. To you soldiers they owe the debt of gratitude."[4]

In a small group, or one on one, Sherman could be a fascinating conversationalist. Speaking before a crowd, the General could be electrifying. No American of his era, except for Abraham Lincoln, has been more widely quoted. But none of his often cited remarks—not "Atlanta is ours and fairly won," not "I beg to present you [the President], as a Christmas gift, the city of Savannah," not "War is cruelty and you can not refine it," not "I will not accept if nominated [for the Presidency], and will not serve if elected," nor any other—has equaled the pronouncement "War is all hell." Sherman had proclaimed the same sentiment before the Columbus remarks, and he would say it again in the future, but it was the Columbus declaration that came to be widely remembered.

SOME THREE WEEKS into August of 1880, Tom Sherman came back to the United States from England. The General and his son were reconciled, in the sense that they spent time together and engaged in polite conversation. "He seems in good health and condition," thought Sherman, and "looks as little like a Priest as any young gentleman." Tom was on his way "to some college near Baltimore," Sherman told Henry Turner, with plans to continue studying. He also wrote Turner that he had discussed "nothing" with Tom, "treated him kindly, and took him with me everywhere." Of course he continued to regret deeply Tom's decision to become a priest, and he always would. Another major family event had occurred a little earlier in the year, when Eleanor Sherman got married. Like Minnie, Elly too married a U.S. Navy man. In Sherman's approving assessment, her husband, Lieutenant Alexander M. Thackara, "is universally held as a first class officer."[5]

By late August, the General was preparing to depart, in company with President Hayes and others, on an extended trip to California. "I expect this trip to be my best and *last*," he told Turner. Possibly it may have been the best, but it would not be the last. Departing from Chicago by train in early September, the group headed west via the northern route, and quoting the General, traveled "in Palace Cars living like Princes." The President and his family had a car to themselves; so too did Secretary of War Alexander Ramsey and his guests; and of course Sherman and his party occupied still another, "all generously tendered," according to Sherman. Among those in the General's party were his daughter Rachel, who was now nineteen, and Mary Audenried. From Seattle, Washington, they journeyed south through Oregon and California, notably visiting San Francisco and Los Angeles. "I still believe in the Valley of the Mississippi," Sherman declared, "but this Coast has chances which can not be ignored." How right he was. One wonders what he might think today about California, with its almost forty million inhabitants. Continuing across the Southwest to Tucson, they next headed to Denver, and on through Kansas City, and St. Louis. Sherman arrived back in the nation's capital in November, in time to see the Potomac River frozen, for "the first time within the memory of the oldest inhabitant."[6]

November also saw the election of Republican James A. Garfield, another son of Ohio, as president of the United States, defeating the Democrat Winfield Scott Hancock, a West Point graduate who rose to the rank of major general in the Civil War and had been severely wounded at Gettysburg. Garfield, however, was the candidate Sherman preferred. A person of outstanding ability, Garfield had been born in a log cabin, grown up in a poverty-stricken family and worked hard to gain a college education. Admitted to the Ohio bar, he became president of Hiram College. He also took an active role in Republican politics and, developing a flair for oratory, was elected to the Ohio state senate shortly before the Civil War. During the war, although lacking any military experience, he learned quickly and proved to be a highly capable officer, distinguishing himself at Shiloh.

Promoted to major general of volunteers after the Battle of Chickamauga, Garfield was elected to Congress, eventually serving as Speaker of the House, and becoming one of the strongest supporters of the army, which obviously commended him to Sherman. Only a few months before the 1880 election, Sherman had presided at a banquet "given to General Garfield, not as a Politician, but as an army comrade." The discussion of politics was forbidden at the military affair, but Sherman afterward said that he considered Garfield "one of the strongest men of his age, in this or any country," and declared that the nation would be lucky to have such a man as its President.[7]

He visited with the president-elect soon after his triumph, and found Garfield "as cool and self possessed as ever." Sherman felt sure that he was going to make an outstanding chief executive. Buoyed with nationalistic optimism, Sherman declared to Turner, "I have no doubt we are destined to have a prolonged period of prosperity throughout the whole country, and I honestly believe all good men want the South to have a full share of this." In his closing sentence to Turner, he stated, "I think there is a better feeling toward the Army, than at any time since the War."[8]

Just as Sherman looked forward to working with President-elect Garfield, he was also pleased that the Hayes presidency was nearing its end. Declaring that he had been one of the outgoing president's "most steadfast friends," Sherman had recently become disappointed and irritated by "his behavior to Ord, to Schofield and many of our oldest, most faithful and approved officers—treating them as they should not have been treated, [which] has convinced me that he must be very weak . . . or that he is somewhat of a hypocrite, and it will take a good deal to convince me otherwise." Having supported the findings of the Schofield investigation into the alleged attack on the black cadet at West Point, Sherman resented the President's intervention and removal of Schofield from the superintendency of the military academy. He was equally incensed in the case of his friend Ord, whom Hayes forcibly retired in order to pro-mote Nelson A. Miles to brigadier general before leaving the presidency.

"There is such a thing as justice," Sherman wrote, "and we constantly flaunt it in the face of the world." Arguing that General Irvin McDow-ell should have been the one retired if anyone was going to be, Sherman noted that McDowell was older than Ord, "and as a soldier has been a failure, whereas Ord has been a success." Also McDowell was financially comfortable to retire, for he had "married a rich wife and Ord a poor one." Forcing out Ord and leaving McDowell was, in Sherman's opin-ion, "an act of palpable injustice." Cump was also angry that Stewart Van Vliet, another of his old friends, had been forced by Hayes to retire before he wanted to do so. Shortly before the inauguration of Garfield, Hayes paid a call on Sherman, which Sherman viewed as some sort of feeble effort to apologize. The general-in-chief was not impressed.[9]

The inauguration of James A. Garfield as the twentieth president of the United States went smoothly. Sherman thought the cabinet Garfield selected was a good one, and after visiting with the new president, he concluded that Garfield was "as much at home at the White House as if born there." Sherman was also pleased that his brother John had been returned to the U.S. Senate. Unfortunately the nation would never know how effective Garfield might have been as president, for tragically, a dis-gruntled, deranged office seeker named Charles Guiteau shot Garfield in the back on July 2. Guiteau proclaimed to the officers who immedi-ately arrested him, that "Arthur is now President of the United States." Actually Vice President Chester Alan Arthur was not yet president, for a suffering Garfield would linger near death for more than two months.[10]

On July 4, Sherman wrote Turner from the capital, "All things sink into insignificance in the face of the terrible events here in the past two days, the attempt at the assassination of the President." Informing Turner that Garfield "has a terrible wound in the back," he said that "the Doctors know as little as the rest of us. . . . I have seen him, spoken with him, and believe, because I want to believe, that he will survive—though I would not be surprised at any moment, to learn that his death is near." The General was encouraged some days later, by news which seemed to indicate that despite his awful wound, the President's mind was still sound. Sherman reported that Garfield had taken a pen, written his name and a short sentence in Latin, "Well damaged, but upper works all sound," and handed it to a doctor. In the latter part of August, however, the President's condition grew much worse. On Sunday, August 28, Sherman wrote that "All last week the President's life hung on a thread—on Friday all hope ceased." Everyone, including the doctors and the family, thought he was dying. Then he rallied, claimed to feel much better, and wanted to eat "some real food," to quote Sherman.[11]

But Sherman now feared, more than ever, that Garfield was not going to survive, and he was plagued by bad memories of California events in the 1850s. "It looks like a repetition of life to find myself again situated as in California at the time of the King-Casey affair," he confided to Turner. He was deeply worried about a lynch mob. "I know," he proclaimed, "that hundreds and thousands of good people in Church at this minute, think ... Hanging is too good for Guiteau." He said that if "the flag on the White House [were] to appear this bright Sunday, at half mast, I would expect to see thousands defile to the jail to demand the life of the murderer." Sherman depicted Guiteau as "a good-for-nothing fool," who thought he "had a hand in electing Garfield," and thus believed himself justified in killing the President when he did not get the "spoils of victory" which he sought. The general-in-chief declared that "a [lynch] mob in Washington would disgrace us all as a people," even if Guiteau's life "is not as valuable as that of a chicken." Sherman was determined to prevent a lynching.[12]

He considered the jail where Guiteau was being held to be "very strong," and after conferring with Secretary of State James G. Blaine and Secretary of War Robert T. Lincoln, he brought in additional forces to ensure order if Garfield died. "So we have 400 Regulars—100 Marines—and about 150 of the city's uniformed militia," he told Turner, "Enough for all possible contingencies." Should the President die and the lynch mob develop, Sherman intended to confront the irate mass, and make an appeal that the issue "is not Guiteau ... but ourselves, our honor, our name, our claim to a place among civilized people." Guiteau must be legally tried, which is the only course that "is right, [and] the other is wrong." The law must triumph "over the clamor of the mob or individual violence." On September 16, Sherman said of Garfield, "I still hope and believe that he will 'pull through,' as he himself said to me the night of the day in which he was shot."[13]

Fate decreed otherwise. Garfield had intended, before Guiteau shot him, to attend the eighteenth-anniversary commemoration of the great Battle of Chickamauga, September 19 and 20; and Sherman planned to be there with the President. Instead, Garfield died on the anniversary of that battle. The lynch mob Sherman feared did not develop—"I doubt if any other form of Government could have gone along so smoothly through such a crisis," wrote the General—and Guiteau was duly tried and convicted. An obviously demented man, Guiteau demanded that those who had benefited politically from his assassination of the President must contribute to his defense fund or he would "name names" (which he never did). He seemed to enjoy his trial, and all the publicity that the newspapers gave him, right up to the day he was hanged.[14]

ON THE NIGHT of November 14, 1881, Sherman arrived in Atlanta, Georgia, accompanied by, among others, his aide General Orlando Poe. Seventeen years earlier, on November 15, 1864, Sherman had ordered the destruction of Atlanta's railroad depot, machine shops and foundries as he set forth on the march to the sea. And it was Poe, then serving as the General's chief engineer, who carried out his order. An Atlanta evening paper, aware of the anniversary, claimed that Sherman had arrived at a time so sensitive for Atlanta's citizens, in order to "crow" over his destructive triumph. That was not the case at all, but it is a good example of how some Southerners viewed Sherman.[15]

Actually he was in Atlanta at the invitation of leading Southerners, and the occasion was an international cotton exposition that the city was hosting. Sherman, of course, had nothing to do with setting the date of the affair. Atlanta had recovered rapidly after the Civil War, succeeding in becoming the state capital in 1877, enticing various manufacturing enterprises to locate there, while claiming to be the center of a so-called New South and billing itself as the "New York of the South." By the time of the exposition, the South was producing more cotton than before the war, and cotton had become the principal export of the nation. Furthermore, the original idea of a cotton fair had been expanded to include a survey of all Southern industry.[16]

Sherman was invited to attend the exposition by Georgia's two U.S. senators, Joseph Brown, who had been governor during the war, and ex-Confederate general Benjamin H. Hill, who had called on the General at his Washington headquarters to issue a personal invitation. Sherman was pleased to be invited to such an important Southern event. Always keen to show that he held no grudge against former Confederates who now demonstrated their loyalty to and support of the United States, he promised to be present for the exhibition. Only those Southerners, in Sherman's opinion, who persisted in arguing that the Confederacy had been fully justified in warring against the United States—and he considered Jefferson Davis the foremost exponent of that point of view—were unworthy of resuming a respectable position in American society. Sherman's generally nonvindictive attitude toward Southerners had been strikingly illustrated during the *Virginius* affair of 1873, which saw several Americans charged with piracy and executed by Spanish authorities; war with Spain seemed a possibility. When Nathan Bedford Forrest, the famous Confederate cavalry commander whom Sherman had zealously tried to kill during the Civil War, applied to serve for the United States if the nation went to war against Spain, General Sherman heartily endorsed his application.[17]

While in Atlanta, Sherman stayed at the Kimball Hotel, which had been established by Hannibal I. Kimball, who migrated from Maine following the war, one of that infamous group regarded by Southerners as carpetbaggers. In some circles Kimball was "notorious for his adroit public thievery." Whatever his shortcomings, Kimball was a major supporter of the exposition, served as its president and accompanied Sherman to the fair on November 15, as did Senator Brown. The number in attendance that day was impressive, and the General thought—perhaps tongue in cheek?—that part of the attraction was "Sherman the Vandal." A meeting of Mexican War veterans was being held in one of the exhibition halls and Sherman was invited to attend, which he did. However, he declined to sit on the platform, instead taking his seat toward the front with the veterans. He judged the major oration, given by a former Confederate officer, to be "a little flowery," but overall "very good." When the program ended, the audience started calling "Sherman! Sherman!" The General insisted that he was only visiting, with no intention of speaking, but the crowd held firmly to their places, and a veteran appealed to him "as a Mexican War veteran to say a few words to my old comrades."[18]

Sherman considered this "a call no man could resist—so on the stage I went, and spoke for 15 minutes, earnestly and nationally," insisting that "we are and must continue to be a United People, with a Common Government." Whatever defects the nation might have, he thought them attributable to "a common human nature," and compared with other people, "there was reason to be . . . hopeful of the future." He spent two days in Atlanta, and wrote Turner that he felt "as much at home as in St. Louis, and concluded that as reasonable men we ought to be content." The nation had met "a terrible crisis" successfully, and whatever complications the future might hold, Sherman believed that they were likely to be "trifling in comparison to what we had to face in 1861."

On the return trip to Washington, he visited with friends in Chattanooga and Cincinnati. Altogether, the journey to Atlanta turned out satisfactorily and proved to be an enjoyable experience. His trip was too brief, and probably came too early, for the General to have fully sensed the growing "lost cause" mentality. In time this attitude would spread across most of the old Confederacy; it alleged that the South, rather than fighting for slavery, had heroically struggled against overwhelming numbers and resources, to defend hallowed principles of states' rights, constitutional government and an honorable agrarian way of life more virtuous than a Northern capitalistic society that, even though victorious, was essentially inferior.[19]

After twelve and a half years as general-in-chief, Sherman was now giving serious thought to retirement; in fact he had been contemplating it for quite some time. Not surprisingly, he planned to return to St. Louis, that city in which he had long felt comfortable. "Somehow, I always turn to St. Louis ... when in distress ... as a place of refuge," he wrote in August 1880, "and have always supposed that there I should end my career." Back in March 1873, the General had spoken to Henry Turner, who of course had long resided in St. Louis, about "the time of which we must dream occasionally, when you are a rich old fellow, and I a retired half pay officer living in St. Louis, waiting for the time for Bellefontaine [the cemetery] to reap another harvest." Convinced that he must return army headquarters to Washington in 1876, following two years that he had spent in St. Louis, Sherman told Turner, "I feel yet that some happy chance will enable me at some future time to settle finally in St. Louis." He promised in another letter to Turner: "If I live long enough, I will come back and spend my old days with you."[20]

Because of his longtime esteem for St. Louis, Sherman was troubled that the city was not, in his judgment, achieving its inherent potential; nor, for that matter, was the state of Missouri. "St. Louis, common to the Missouri, Mississippi, and Ohio Rivers," proclaimed the General in 1880, "is the natural center of population, when all of our territory is occupied ... [and] Missouri ought to be the best and most prosperous State in the Union." He declared that she should "have four millions of people before Kansas gets one million," but Kansas "has so advertised" that her population likely would surpass Missouri. Sherman chided Turner that "you all should *brag* more." St. Louis and Missouri ought to be trumpeted as "the Greatest City and the Greatest State in the world." And Missouri needed to put forth "her strongest efforts to utilize her iron, coal, lead, copper and zinc, and should advertise the land as it deserves." Sherman also believed that Missouri's national stature had been harmed by her classification as a Southern state, which, he persuasively argued, was inaccurate. "It is a wheat and corn State," he asserted, "with mines and metals inviting manufacturers. It is in no sense Southern for it has no cotton, sugar or tropical characters, and ought never to have been a slave state."[21]

Sherman's fears for St. Louis were confirmed by the 1880 census.

The news was worse than he expected. "I am astonished that St. Louis should have lost population ... in the past ten years." The publication of that fact, he predicted, would damage the city and the state. Sherman felt forced to admit that his earlier analysis of population growth, which seemed quite reasonable only a few years back, had been wrong. There was no denying the reality of Chicago's increasing predominance in comparison with St. Louis. With a swelling population and motivated by a public spirit, Chicago had proved "wide awake" to her opportunities. Strongly building on the railroads, "which ... played the deuce with Rivers," acknowledged the General, "and robbed them of their importance," Chicago was forging impressively ahead. Nevertheless, despite his disappointment, Sherman still prized and felt "bound to St. Louis for better or worse." He proclaimed: "I must cling to it to the end."[22]

In anticipation of a St. Louis retirement, Sherman expected to spend considerable time with Henry Turner, his "old and most dear friend." He warned Turner that he might be seeking his advice on financial matters. "Mrs. Sherman has absolute confidence in your business judgment," he wrote, "and a corresponding doubt of mine." He confessed that he had "failed to avail myself of opportunities ... which if taken advantage of would have made us rich." On the other hand, he quickly added: "I consider any man rich who owes nothing, and has income enough for necessary wants." That, he declared, "is our situation now."[23]

Henry Turner, however, was approximately a decade older than Sherman, and he was no longer in good health. In most of the letters that Sherman wrote to Turner in 1881, he attempted to play down his friend's age and physical issues. By the fall, though, if not before, Sherman knew that Turner's situation was serious. "I hope and pray, in my rough way," he wrote, "that you will regain much of your old vigor and be spared to us many a year. I was in hopes you would survive me and yet think you will." In late November, Turner's daughter served as an amanuensis, because of her father's "weakness and infirmity," and Sherman knew that the outlook was dire. On December 12, 1881, Sherman recalled "when ... [he and Turner] were first acquainted, [and] our limbs were strong and supple, and all our joys and sorrows lay ahead."

Looking back over forty years, he concluded: "I think you and I have done a reasonable share of work, and can afford gracefully to go down the hill together, hand in hand, trusting to Him, who made the sunshine and storm, to deal by us mercifully and justly." Four days later Turner died. His death left a major void in Sherman's life, one that no one else could possibly fill.[24]

IN JUNE 1882, Congress passed a law providing for the compulsory retirement of all army officers, regardless of rank, at the age of sixty-four. At the time the proposed law was being debated in Congress, several senators and congressmen consulted Sherman, offering to make an exception in his case, if he wanted to serve longer. Declaring that he neither expected nor desired to be treated any differently than other officers, Sherman explained his view that "no man could know or realize when his own mental and physical powers began to decline." The General thought it was a good law. He was to be retired at full salary, along with allowances, and he was quite pleased—"This is liberal and . . . all I or any one should ask," he told Ellen—for he had long believed his retirement pay would be less than, perhaps only half, of what he earned as general-in-chief. He did request, and would receive, the assistance of an army clerk to help him with his enormous correspondence, which was expected to continue (and it did) after he retired. Now he could retire with satisfactory financial provisions, rather than feeling compelled to stay on merely for the sake of enough money, and thereby holding back the advancement of lower-ranking officers. Phil Sheridan could advance to general-in-chief, which in turn would move up John Schofield, both of whom he considered friends whose well-being concerned him. Certainly Sherman was ready to retire, put behind him the Washington political scene, with its inevitable frustrations for the commanding general, and escape back to St. Louis.[25]

He would be sixty-four years old on February 8, 1884, a date that he considered "inconvenient to move, and not suited to other incidents." He suggested to Secretary of War Lincoln that he would prefer to turn over command of the army to General Sheridan on November 1, 1883, take his staff to St. Louis and there await the formal retirement on his sixty-fourth birthday. Lincoln presented the request to President Arthur, who readily agreed. With this arrangement, Sherman seemed well satisfied. "On the whole the time is most opportune," he told his brother John, "and I think I can leave my post with the general respect of my fellows." Declaring that "the country is now generally prosperous," he observed that the army was "in reasonably good condition, considering the fact that peace and politics are always more damaging than war."[26]

But before leaving the army, Sherman decided to make one more tour of the continent, arranging to do so during the summer of 1883. Beginning at Buffalo on June 21, he went out to the Pacific by a northern route, traveled through the Pacific coastal states and returned through the Southwest, finally concluding the journey at St. Louis on the last day of September. It was a fine trip, which came off without any serious incident, although he did not have the luxury of a palace car, as when he had traveled with President Hayes three years earlier. No doubt Sherman looked forward to being relieved of dealing with Native Americans. When Apaches, riding out of Mexico, had raided New Mexico and Arizona in March 1883, Sherman ordered Brigadier General George Crook to pursue and destroy them regardless of departmental lines or international boundaries. General Crook did obtain Mexican permission to move across the border and he succeeded, with the help of Apache scouts, in locating Geronimo's mountain sanctuary. Demonstrating courage, patience and understanding, Crook negotiated with Geronimo and other Indian leaders, arranging at last for the Apaches to return to their Arizona reservation. This did not end Apache troubles—neither for the Apaches nor the Americans—but when Apache warfare broke out again in 1885–1886, the problem was no longer Sherman's concern. In fact, for several years before Sherman's retirement, he had largely left Indian affairs to Phil Sheridan, who continued to command the vast Military Division of the Missouri until he succeeded Sherman as the army's general-in-chief.[27]

Retiring to St. Louis appealed to Sherman in various ways, not the least of which was that he again would be near Minnie, whose husband had left the navy and taken a position with the Harrison Wire Company in St. Louis. Minnie and Tom Fitch were living in a house that the General owned in the St. Louis suburb Cote Brilliante. Minnie had been overwhelmed in the summer of 1882, when two of her children, one not yet a year old, died within days of each other. Sympathizing deeply with her loss, and perhaps feeling closer to Minnie than any of his children since the death of Willie, Sherman welcomed the chance to see more of his eldest child.

Three of his children would be living with him in the Garrison Avenue house: Lizzie, who was in her early thirties; Rachel, who was twenty-three; and the youngest, Philemon Tecumseh, who was nearing college age, and whom all the family had come to call Cumpy. Sherman's daughters would continue to be a great help in taking Ellen's place at the many social functions that his wife preferred to avoid. As for Cumpy, the General could not help worrying that Ellen would somehow entice him into following his older brother's example, and "run off into the Church"— that church which, in the General's judgement, "committed a crime of such magnitude," by seducing Tom into the priesthood, "that the blood of a hundred martyrs can not wash it out."[28]

As soon as word spread that Sherman was retiring, a host of Republicans launched a campaign attempting to persuade the General to become their party's presidential candidate in the 1884 election. This was not the first time that Sherman's name had been prominently proposed for the presidency. Back in 1876, when the scandals of Grant's outgoing administration plagued the Republicans, and the Democrats put forth reformer Samuel J. Tilden as their candidate, some Republicans thought that Sherman—with his reputation as a scrupulously honest war hero—was the political savior who could carry the party to victory. Sherman was not at all interested, and he also knew that Ellen was adamantly opposed to his being a candidate. She argued that the newspaper abuse the family would have to endure "would be intolerable," and she firmly believed that her husband could not be elected anyway, because of his Catholic family.[29]

But once Sherman retired, the pressure on him to run for the presidency was greater than ever before. Several of the most prominent men in the Republican Party urged him to enter the race. Even James G. Blaine, who dearly wanted to be president, and did eventually receive the Republican nomination, wrote the General a letter marked "Strictly, Absolutely Confidential," in which he addressed the possibility of a convention deadlock between himself and President Arthur. In such a scenario, Blaine said it was inevitable that Sherman would be the man to whom the party would turn. In that case, declared Blaine, Sherman must accept the nomination, having no more right to decline than if he had "received an order as a lieutenant of the army." Former Missouri senator J. B. Henderson, who was Sherman's neighbor, contended that if a draft Sherman movement developed, as he believed very likely, then the General would have to accept, for no American citizen could disobey "the call of his country." Sherman responded that the Republican Convention in Chicago was not the country. When others, among them General Schofield and John Sherman, expressed the same sentiment as Henderson, Sherman simply reiterated his response.[30]

The major reason many Republican leaders wanted Sherman, in spite of the fact that Blaine had become the front-runner for the nomination, was that they doubted Blaine could be elected, and they believed Sherman would probably be a winner. "It is certain that if Blaine is not nominated in the early ballots," predicted John Sherman in a letter to the General dated May 4, 1884, "a movement will be made for your nomination, and if entered upon will go like wild fire." If such a thing happened, John advised his brother, "you ought to acquiesce. I believe it would be best for the country, honorable to you and your children, and far less irksome than you have thought."

But Sherman, difficult as it was for a lot of people to believe, really did not want to be the president. When letters and telegrams kept pouring in from Chicago to Sherman's home in St. Louis, urging him to accept the nomination if tendered, he wrote in pencil, cigar clamped between his teeth, and sent Henderson the famous statement: "I will not accept if nominated and will not serve if elected." The General was pleased, and doubtless quite relieved, when news came that the Republican Convention had finally nominated Blaine for president and John Logan as his running mate. Sherman had held firmly to his belief that politics was beneath a soldier.[31]

The thought of Sherman as president of the United States is intriguing. He would have had a good chance of receiving the Republican nomination if he had made a serious bid for it. Whether he could have been elected is more questionable. The 1884 race is often cited, with good reason, as the dirtiest presidential campaign in the nation's history. After bachelor Democrat Stephen Grover Cleveland was charged, at the instigation of Republicans, with fathering a child out of wedlock, the Democrats would surely have explored Sherman's relationships with women other than his wife—especially those who were much younger than he. Although the General was a war hero and a man of immense national popularity, when the presidency was the prize, the opposing party could be expected, at the very least, to engage in a strong campaign of innuendo. The Democrats did discover apparent evidence, and it was widely publicized, that Blaine and his wife had engaged in premarital sexual relations.

The Catholic factor would have hurt Sherman too, maybe even more than his relationships with the fair sex. Many Americans were bitterly anti-Catholic. That Sherman himself was not a Catholic, and in fact considered Catholicism utterly indefensible, probably would have been of little consequence, being trumped by his Catholic family, especially Ellen's widely known and pronounced (some would say fanatical) devotion to her faith. Sherman clearly would not have been a sure winner.

If elected, would the General have been a good chief executive? Unlike Grant, Sherman was not overly impressed or easily influenced by wealthy men, and given his abhorrence of ill-gotten gain, plus his keen awareness of what was occurring around him, a corrupt Sherman administration seems improbable. On the other hand, while general-in-chief, he had found working with Congress difficult and largely unrewarding. As a general, he was accustomed to making military decisions and having his orders obeyed at once. Also, because of a notable, long ingrained contempt for politicians, Sherman had little tact and patience when dealing with Congress. Unless his brother John, who was an astute politician, could have exerted a positive and powerful influence upon him, which certainly is questionable, there is little reason to think the General would have been a good president. That said, if Sherman had become the nation's chief executive, despite his temper and presumable dictatorial tendencies, he probably would have been no worse, and well might have been better, than a large number of the men who have occupied the Oval Office. Honesty, intelligence, popularity and a genuine concern for the best interests of the nation, as opposed to party loyalty, personal monetary gain and fame (which he already possessed), would all have been in his favor.

IF THE PAST is prologue to the future—and with lives that have spanned several decades it usually is—then Sherman's active retirement years should come as no surprise. As St. Louis's most prominent citizen, and one of the nation's most distinguished and widely respected personalities, Sherman was constantly in demand as a speaker and guest of honor at a host of events. The General possessed, as one historian wrote, "a charisma about him that the public ... found irresistible." The invitations he received were so numerous that, except for the distances involved, he literally could have been on a program nearly every night. Graciously declining an invitation to a celebration in Cincinnati soon after he retired, Sherman wrote: "I have *work* cut out for every day of September, indeed for every remaining day of the year 1884, and begin to realize that my old army comrades are not willing to concede that I am played out." He then asserted that they expected him "to dance and sing and be merry from New York to San Francisco all the time without a single day to have the privilege of enjoying the home which I have been ... years in building up at St. Louis."[32]

Always when attending reunions of veterans, even if not giving the main address, which he often did, it was assumed that Sherman would make some kind of a presentation, even if a brief one. West Point commencements and reunions were also high on the list of the General's preferred appearances. Banquet celebrations planned in his honor could hardly be turned down, at least not in most cases, although he did often request, notably, that "Marching Through Georgia" be omitted from the musical selections on such occasions. Sherman's favored piece was "The Battle Hymn of the Republic." Dedications of Civil War statues, which became frequent in the 1880s, meant still more invitations and speeches. He also supported several historical societies. There were funeral services too for a number of generals, and other officers. Of all Sherman's associations with veterans, none was as important to him as the Society of the Army of the Tennessee, for which he served as president from 1869 until his death.[33]

The General loved public speaking and he was extremely good at it. The lawyer and politician Chauncey M. Depew, who himself was a highly polished toastmaster, heard and analyzed Sherman's presentations upon many occasions and concluded that he was "the readiest and most original talker in the United States." Commenting at some length, Depew declared, "I don't believe that he ever made the slightest preparation." He thought that the General, while carrying on a conversation with those around him, somehow absorbed "the spirit of the occasion," and when he arose to speak, his sentiments, words and style always fit the occasion magnificently. Interestingly, Sherman did comment once to Henry Turner that when speaking to military people, from officers to academy cadets, he "rarely prepared." For some formal occasions, Sherman would write a speech, but once in front of his audience, he often did not stick to the manuscript. While the General relished speaking, he detested shaking hands. The story was told that at a reunion of the Grand Army of the Republic in Milwaukee, Sherman shoved his hands into his pockets when he saw the crowd approaching. "This is no place to shake hands," he declared, and telling them to come to his hotel, he then blurted, "I'll hire a man to shake hands for me."[34]

Both before he retired, and for some months afterward, Sherman engaged in preparing a revised edition of his memoirs, which had been published in May 1875. Presented by D. Appleton and Company, in two volumes, approximately 25,000 sets were sold at \$7 per set, for which Sherman received a total of \$25,000. The work was an instant best-seller, and well received by the general public. Just prior to the set's release, the General assured his brother John: "I have carefully eliminated everything calculated to raise controversy, except where sustained by documents embraced in the work itself, and then only with minor parties."[35]

Actually, the *Memoirs* triggered a great deal of controversy, especially among Civil War generals and newspapermen. While many praised both the substance and engaging style of the publication, others charged that Sherman's depiction of himself was extremely self-centered—a St. Louis reviewer sarcastically remarked that apparently "the suppression of the rebellion was the product of one man's supernatural genius"—as well as unjust to a number of generals whose contributions Sherman either downplayed or inordinately criticized. Such men as John McClernand, John Logan, Sooy Smith and George Morgan were quite angry about the way Sherman treated them, and many veterans of the Army of the Cumberland were offended by his comments about the fighting at Chattanooga. Some Ohio residents were upset that the General began the narrative in 1846, thus omitting anything about his early years in the Buckeye State.[36]

Of all the critics who spoke out when the first edition was published, the most severe was newspaper correspondent Henry Van Ness Boynton, who first published a series of scathing articles about the *Memoirs*, and then gathered them in book form under the title *Sherman's Historical Raid: The Memoirs in Light of the Record*. Boynton had commanded an Iowa regiment during the war, and thus was viewed in some circles as having a measure of military credibility. Carefully choosing his facts, and craftily shaping his narrative, Boynton presented Sherman in the worst possible light. If Sherman considered himself a great general, and he did, which his memoirs clearly indicate, Boynton described him as little more than an egotistical blunderer.

Sherman was enraged. He was sure that his enemies in the Grant administration, Secretary of War William Belknap and Orville E. Babcock, Grant's private secretary, had persuaded Boynton, whom they "paid partly out of Government money, to write me *down*." Boynton somehow had access to official military reports when preparing his articles, reports not yet published, and Sherman had no doubt Belknap was the man responsible for making those available to him. When Babcock was disgraced in 1875 by the Whiskey Ring tax frauds, and Belknap resigned the next year because of the Indian trading posts scandal, Sherman thought Boynton then "sung gently for a while." Several of Sherman's friends had also come to his defense, and launched counterattacks against Boynton. Nothing, however, was as satisfying to Sherman as when Grant, in 1876, told him that while "he would have omitted calling Logan and Blair politicians," he had read the memoirs with satisfaction, and essentially had no criticisms. Grant complimented Sherman on a task well performed.[37]

The Sherman-Boynton controversy heated up again in 1879–1880. Apparently Boynton was incensed when Sherman claimed, in a conversation that got back to Boynton, that "for a thousand dollars, he would slander his own mother." When Boynton questioned Sherman about the alleged statement in a letter, Sherman readily admitted that he had said just that. Boynton then wanted Sherman charged with "conduct unbecoming an officer and a gentleman." He requested President Hayes to have the General brought to trial. Nothing ever came of this, except for prolonging the bad blood between the two men. Perhaps Sherman may have been all the more motivated to publish the new edition of the *Memoirs*, which came out in 1885.[38]

Sherman added two chapters in the new edition, one at the beginning, entitled "From 1820 to the Mexican War," and the other at the end, in which he covered the period following the Civil War. He concluded the narrative at his retirement. The General also added an appendix, consisting mainly of documents supporting his arguments, as well as some maps and an index. In the preface to the new edition, Sherman said that he had made corrections wherever he had "found material error." The substance of the work remained basically unchanged from the first edition, with Sherman seeing no reason to modify his original analyses and conclusions. The minimal changes he did make were of a touching-up and moderating nature, as he toned down some of the more harsh adjectives that he had originally employed. The new edition, probably to his relief, did not generate anything like the heat that arose when the memoirs first appeared.[39]

On his retirement Sherman fully intended to spend the rest of his days in St. Louis, but his life did not work out that way. After the Harrison Wire Company failed, Tom Fitch and Minnie, along with their children, moved to Pennsylvania, where steel for wire was less expensive, and Fitch hoped to right his financial situation. The departure of Minnie and her family was a blow to Sherman. Elly and her husband were already living in Bryn Mawr. Then, when Cumpy went off to school at Yale, Ellen insisted on remaining close to her youngest child, in order, the General was convinced, to be sure that no one weaned him away from the Catholic Church. Ellen would "rather have him dead than a Protestant," Sherman declared. Despite his love for St. Louis, Sherman was aggravated by the city's raising the taxes on his house and assessing him for paving the street. In June 1886, although reluctant to the end to leave St. Louis, he moved to New York City, where Ellen could more readily spend time with her married daughters, and more easily keep an eye on Cumpy.[40]

Chapter Twenty-Eight

WE CAN ONLY BOW TO THE INEVITABLE

Sherman took up his New York residence at the famous old Fifth Avenue Hotel, located at the corner of Fifth Avenue and Twenty-third Street. He, Ellen, Rachel and Lizzie occupied three comfortable rooms on the second floor. Not surprisingly, Sherman was well received in New York, his popularity equaling, if not exceeding, the acclaim he had received in St. Louis. Soon he was attending the theater, appearing at dinner parties or participating in some other type of event three or four times a week. John Sherman was pleased by his brother's move to the east. "You must be aware," he wrote the General, "that the wonder has been that, having the whole country to choose as a home, you should settle upon St. Louis." John said that while he "could understand it, many others did not."[1]

The move to New York did not change Sherman's busy schedule of meeting with veterans all over the country. In early August 1886, he journeyed again to the West Coast, attending the Encampment of the Grand Army of the Republic in San Francisco, where he gave a featured speech, saying that the American desire to acquire California was the basic cause of the war with Mexico. On another memorable occasion in 1886, the General spoke at a banquet in honor of the dedication of the Statue of Liberty. Funerals also continued to demand his presence, and often his participation. Winfield Scott Hancock died in 1886, and at a Cincinnati meeting of the Loyal Legion of the United States, Sherman was pressured, on the spur of the moment, to reflect upon General Hancock. Speaking extemporaneously for about ten minutes, he had no chance to review and edit his remarks before they were in the hands of the press. The General was relieved when he afterward learned that Mrs. Hancock "was especially pleased" by what he had said. Without a doubt, highly accomplished though he was as a speaker, the pressure of funeral tributes was often a difficult experience for Sherman. In 1888, he declared to Ellen, "I am at the end of my rope; will attend my own funeral, but must be excused from others."[2]

Sherman's personality, as he aged, remained essentially unchanged. He was still outspoken and held many of the same beliefs and opinions as in his earlier years. When John Sherman, for example, made a trip to the Pacific over the Canadian Railroad in the summer of 1887, he wrote Cump, "If the population of Mexico and Canada were homogeneous with ours, the union of the three countries would make the whole the most powerful nation in the world. I am not so sure but this would be a good thing to do." The General shot back at once: "I am dead opposed to any more of Mexico. All the northern part is desert, like the worst parts of Texas, New Mexico, and Arizona. Further south the population is mixed Spanish and Indian, who never can be harmonized with our race. Eight millions of such people would endanger our institutions. We have already enough disturbing influences."[3]

While Sherman energetically pursued a variety of activities, both in New York and around the nation, Ellen spent a lot of time visiting with Minnie, Elly and the grandchildren. Typically she was away from New York for several weeks on such trips. She also tried to see Cumpy as frequently as possible. But her health, never really good, now deteriorated rapidly and she was often sick during 1888. When in New York, Ellen seldom went down to eat in the hotel dining room. In the summer, as she visited with Elly at her home, and then with Tom, who was at Woodstock, Sherman decided to buy a house in New York.

The General knew that his wife was tired of living in the hotel and thought that he might lift her spirits and also make a good investment with the purchase of a house. He wrote her that he had bought a spacious structure at 75 West Seventy-first Street, and was preparing it for her return. "I am charmed with the prospect of our home," Ellen replied. Eagerly she looked forward to arriving at the new place, "which I shall be slow to leave." She said that she almost felt "cured," just to know "that we . . . need never again endure hotel life." She seemed very pleased upon seeing the house, and celebrated her sixty-fourth birthday on October 4. However, she was far from well.[4]

Suffering heart attacks on November 7 and again on the twenty-fifth, according to her biographer, Ellen died on November 28—the day before Thanksgiving. A small service for family and friends was conducted at the house, and then they left for St. Louis aboard a private car provided by the Pennsylvania Railroad. There Ellen was buried in Calvary Cemetery, close to her beloved Willy and Charles Celestine. Inscribed on Willy's tombstone were the words "Our Little Sergeant; From the First Battalion, 13th U.S. Infantry. In his breast was no guile." Without a doubt, memories of Willy must have filled Sherman's mind again as he and the family committed Ellen to her grave. For some time after her death, Sherman experienced asthma attacks, some of which were severe. Probably the winter weather plagued him, and his asthma likely was made worse by the sorrow and stress of losing his longtime companion.[5]

Death continued to claim others among Sherman's friends, associates and relatives. Grant, who had suffered the humiliation of going broke in the early 1880s, had died in 1885, stricken with throat cancer, but somehow persevering to complete his memoirs a few days before his death. The memoirs became a best-seller, providing Grant's family an immense boon. In February 1886, his widow, Julia, received $200,000, the largest royalty check ever written in America to that date. Sherman had declined to speak at Grant's funeral, telling John Sherman that he feared he would "feel embarrassed in speaking of him, lest I say too much." While Sherman, for some years, had not been as close to Grant as during the war, he did speak very highly of the general upon several occasions in the years following his death. He was often at the funerals of other generals, among them Ambrose Burnside and Judson Kilpatrick. Sherman and Black Jack Logan, to some degree, had cleared the air of their differences, and the General was present in the U.S. Senate chamber for Logan's funeral on the last day of 1886.[6]

But of all the Union generals, the death of Phil Sheridan, which occurred only a few months before Ellen died, seemed to affect Sherman the most. Sheridan, who was more than a decade younger than Sherman, was buried in Arlington Cemetery, according to his wishes, high on a knoll looking eastward toward the capital. The day of the funeral was beautiful, and after the bugler sounded taps, the crowd slowly dispersed, leaving a single man standing at the grave side, weeping. That lone figure was General Sherman. "At last he turned," wrote Sheridan's biographer, "walking down the grassy knoll, past the white markers aligned in orderly ranks spreading out from the base, and away from the final encampment of General Sheridan." With Sheridan's death, Sherman was the only one of the top Union generals still alive. Afterward, he sometimes referred to himself as "the Last of the Mohicans."[7]

The support and presence of Sherman's daughters, Rachel and Lizzie, who continued to live with the General, helped him get through the trauma of Ellen's death. The companionship of friends was also uplifting for a man as socially inclined as Sherman. His birthday came early in the year of course, on February 8, and he enjoyed, he wrote, "a very pleasant birthday dinner party" at his home, in celebration of his sixty-ninth. He invited another set of friends for another dinner party a week after the birthday, and yet another set for the week following that. Sherman's daughters played a big role in arranging those festive events. By the time the celebrations of his birthday were over, the General was preparing to attend the inauguration of Benjamin Harrison as president of the United States.[8]

Harrison, who was a grandson of President William Henry Harrison, had been a brigadier general in the Civil War, and Sherman found himself inundated by men seeking an office in the new administration, who sought his influence with the country's in-coming chief executive. The assassination of President Garfield had led to the passage of a civil service reform act, attempting to eliminate the worst abuses of the "spoils system," but only a small percentage of public offices had been classified under the Civil Service Act when Harrison became the president. "Every acquaintance I have on earth," Sherman wrote his daughter Elly, "wants an office and says or writes they are 'Sure of Success' if only General Sherman will say a good word to General Harrison. Of course this I will not do, and from friends they pass into the camp of Enemies. . . . I would not be in Harrison's shoes for all the money in the Treasury."[9]

Sherman spent about a week in Washington, attending the inauguration ceremony, and enjoying visits with friends—that is, friends who were not trying to get some favor from him. Soon after his return to New York, the city became enthralled with preparations to celebrate the April centennial of George Washington's inauguration as the nation's first president. Sherman always enjoyed a big festive event, whether an opening night at the theater, a circus coming to town or a happening of historical significance, and he got right into the spirit of the occasion. He attended several of the special observances to celebrate the centennial and was present when President Harrison arrived by ship, coming ashore at the same place where Washington had landed in 1789. Sherman attended a series of dinners, too, complaining that each was so like the others that they grew monotonous. He told Elly that he "had seen everybody," many of them visiting in his home, among them Generals Dodge, Schofield and McCook, as well as former President and Mrs. Hayes. Sherman claimed there must have been two million people between Wall Street and Central Park, "well dressed and well behaved."[10]

Obviously, by late spring of 1889, General Sherman was back into the swing of activities that vied for his attention. In June, accompanied by Rachel, he again journeyed to West Point for the graduation ceremony, and planned to attend veteran reunions in August and September at Milwaukee and Cincinnati, respectively. He also arranged a trip to the Catskills with Lizzie. In July he made another railroad excursion to San Francisco, and notably missed Tom Sherman's ordination as a Jesuit priest on July 7, in Philadelphia. He did meet with his son in New York after he got back from the West Coast.[11]

The Cincinnati gathering of veterans in late September was the annual meeting of the Society of the Army of the Tennessee, and Sherman spent a week in Ohio's queen city on the river, enjoying the camaraderie with the men he had commanded when they were young. Clearly, however, such events had become very tiring, and he complained to Elly: "I want to throw off the burden of these Army meetings—they are very Exhausting & Expensive." A few months later, having declined to attend a Philadelphia meeting of the Loyal Legion of the United States, but anticipating trips to Boston for the Grand Army of the Republic Encampment in July 1890, which he characterized as a "must" attend affair, as well as Cincinnati again in September for the Society of the Army of the Tennessee, the General said, "They all promise not to tax me with speeches & hand shaking, but they can not keep their promises, because the Crowd . . . won't obey their officers." He declared to Elly that he was "resolved" to attend fewer of the veterans reunions; it had become too hard physically. A letter to brother John in late 1889 further confirms the many and constant calls for his presence. "I continue pretty much as always in universal demand," he wrote, "for soldiers' meetings, college commencements, and such like things—always with a promise that I will not be called on to speak, which is always broken."[12]

After the General had moved to New York, he and John saw each other more frequently, and so did not write nearly as many letters to each other as in the earlier years. Sherman certainly was proud of his younger brother's achievements, and in the above referenced letter of November 12, 1889, the General took the opportunity of praising the career of the senator. "To be a President for four years is not much of an honor," he declared, "but to have been senator continuously from 1861 to 1892 [when John's term would be up]—less the four years as Secretary of the Treasury—*is* an honor. Webster and Clay are better known to the world than Polk and Pierce."[13]

As Sherman drew nearer to his seventieth birthday and realized that his energy had been waning markedly, one of the burdens weighing upon him was the mortgage on the house he had bought shortly before Ellen's death. Probably spurred on by the memory of the dire financial straits in which his father had died, as well as thinking of Rachel and Lizzie, who made their home with him, Sherman desperately wanted to have the place paid for before his own death. "I still owe $14,000 on this house—and want to pay it off in 3 or 4 years," he wrote Elly in September 1889, remarking, "I hate debt worse than slavery." A year later, on September 26, 1890, he would record that he had made substantial progress, reducing the amount owed to $9,000. He thought that "in two more years I can close this out without selling anything at St. Louis."[14]

The General's seventieth birthday was an occasion of great celebration. While the New York winter may have been, as Sherman claimed, "enough to give anyone the blues if not the grippe," he refused to allow the inclement weather to hinder his festive plans. With the indispensable assistance of Rachel and Lizzie, he hosted dinner parties at his house on Saturday, February 8, and again on February 15. On the eighth he was showered by letters, telegrams, presents and flowers. And there was more, much more. On February 9, he acknowledged "the kind and gracious message," from Mary Audenreid, who had written him from Naples, as well as the bouquet of flowers received from the Honorable Charles F. Manderson and friends. Manderson, a lawyer who was a U.S. senator from Nebraska, had risen to the rank of colonel of volunteers in the Civil War. Sherman told Manderson that the bouquet "fell like the dew of Heaven on the head of your old Commander, and may revive his vital energy that he may yet dance at some of your funerals." Clearly in a spirited mood, and rather full of himself, Sherman then assured Manderson that his "hair is not silvered over, but yet remains the same old chestnut Sorrel it was in the days we played Soldier."[15]

Although ever more aware of an aging body, and in spite of his protests about engaging in too many tiring activities, Sherman cut back on his demanding way of life only minimally as 1890 progressed. On March 19, he hailed the approach, once again, of spring. "In two more days," he wrote, "the Sun will come north of the Equator, and winter will have to give up." With warmer weather, he felt more energized and continued to pursue a busy schedule throughout the summer and fall. In September, he again joined his comrades of the Society of the Army of the Tennessee. He was pleased, too, when he learned that Ellen's monument had been placed in Calvary Cemetery, and he was making provision for his own monument, "not to exceed in size or art" that of Ellen's, he assured his daughter. Sherman intended to make certain that his friends would not be called upon to contribute to the monument, as had occurred with some of the Civil War generals. On October 1, he spoke at a dinner, extemporaneously he remarked, in honor of the Count of Paris at the new Plaza Hotel. He did not get home until midnight, and on the next day was "caught in two hard rains," although he managed to keep "pretty dry." Still, he admitted to Elly, "I ought not to expose myself too much, as my cough is unusually severe."[16]

As the new year of 1891 dawned, Sherman's general health had deteriorated strikingly from a year earlier, and his asthma was worse. Nevertheless, he apparently kept up a grueling pace, especially considering his physical condition, and wrote John on February 3, "I am drifting along in the old rut in good strength, attending to about four dinners a week at public or private houses, and generally wind up for gossip at the Union League Club." Although he did attend a wedding with Rachel on February 5, the General was no longer attempting to host any of his friends and made no plans for celebrating his seventy-first birthday. In fact, he spent part of that day in bed, feeling miserable as the result of a cold he had contracted. Three days earlier, responding to a lady who invited him to attend the funeral of her son, he stated that while he sympathized with her loss, it was "simply impossible" for him to be present for the occasion, and then declared: "We can only bow to the inevitable."[17]

The day after his seventy-first birthday, Sherman was gradually growing worse; in all likelihood he had contracted pneumonia, which coupled with asthma, would prove too much for his weakened body to overcome. By February 11, his daughters were convinced that their father was dying. Late that evening they called in a Roman Catholic priest, who administered the rite of extreme unction to the General while he lay unconscious. Without question his daughters were acting from the purest of motives, desiring to save, as they believed, Sherman's immortal soul. But all through the years the General had denied, again and again, both publicly and privately, that he was a Catholic. He had refused to accept, despite his wife's frequent pleadings throughout their marriage, a religious dogma that he considered irrational. He had denounced the Catholic Church unequivocally.

The General died shortly before two o'clock on the afternoon of February 14. Sherman's desire was that his body be placed in the casket which he had selected and conveyed at once to St. Louis for burial. His passing was not to be that simple. A host of people wanted to honor one of America's greatest military men. Thus for two days the Sherman home was open to the public, the General's casket adorned with the American flag and his body arrayed in full uniform, as a vast number of people filed by his coffin. A Catholic funeral service was then held at Sherman's home, with Tom Sherman, who had just returned from England, presiding.

Five days after his death, an impressive funeral procession slowly made its way through the streets of New York. Thousands upon thousands of people lined the avenues, or gathered on balconies, rooftops and other vantage points, to silently, respectfully watch the General's casket, resting on a caisson drawn by four horses, as his body was borne, with military precision, to the tip of Manhattan. Ferried from there to a Pennsylvania Railroad train, Sherman's body was conveyed to St. Louis by a direct route. All along the way, crowds gathered beside the tracks in cities, towns and even, in some places, the countryside, to pay their respects as the heavily draped funeral car, its door open for people to see the coffin, passed by.

In St. Louis another service was held at a Catholic church, again led by Tom Sherman. Some of the General's military comrades, who knew him well, considered a Catholic service, as well as certain remarks made by Tom about his father's religious views, to be inappropriate. But what was done was done. The General was then interred in Calvary Cemetery, next to Ellen, Willy, and the little child he had never seen. While all the proceedings surrounding Sherman's death had not gone as he would have preferred, there were, in the end, two major events about which the General would have been quite pleased. A simple, ten-foot, self-designed, shaft monument, inscribed with the words "Faithful and Honorable," upon which Sherman had insisted, was soon put in place. And at last, permanently, the General was in St. Louis, residing close to the great Mississippi River.[18]

ACKNOWLEDGMENTS

Many people have assisted me with the preparation of this book, and I am grateful to them all. Some, for varying reasons, deserve specific recognition. Listed alphabetically, they are: John Earl Byrd; Jerry L. Gaw, Ph.D.; Sara J. Harwell; Timothy D. Johnson, Ph.D.; Thomas S. Johnston, M.D.; Carla J. McDonough, Ph.D.; Lizz McDonough; Nancy McDonough; Sharon McDonough, Ph.D.; James L. Moon Jr.; Wiley Sword; Ann Toplovich; and Caroline Wilson. A special category of appreciation is reserved for the people who have worked with me at W. W. Norton & Company. James L. Mairs, editor-at-large, offered wise advice and consistent encouragement over a period of several years. More recently, I am indebted to John A. Glusman, vice president and editor-in-chief, whose suggestions and editorial contributions have certainly made this a better book. Alexa Pugh, John's assistant, has been thoughtful and helpful in numerous ways. I appreciate the good work of all the staff at Norton for their part in the production of this biography.

Many libraries, archives and historical societies have rendered invaluable help. These include the Atlanta Historical Society; the California Historical Society, San Francisco; the Chickamauga–Chattanooga National Military Park Library; the Fairfield Heritage Association, Lancaster, Ohio; the P. K. Yonge Library of Florida History at the University of Florida, Gainesville; the Woodruff Library at Emory University, Atlanta; the Georgia Department of Archives and History, Atlanta;

the Georgia Historical Society, Savannah; the Henry E. Huntington Library, San Marino, California; the Illinois State Historical Library, Springfield; the Indiana Historical Society, Indianapolis; the Library of Congress; the Beaman Library at Lipscomb University, Nashville; the Missouri Historical Society, St. Louis; the Nashville Public Library; the National Archives; the Ohio History Connection, Columbus; the Shiloh National Military Park Library; the Tennessee Historical Society, Nashville; the Tennessee State Library and Archives, Nashville; the United States Military Academy Library, West Point; the University of Notre Dame Archives, Notre Dame, Indiana; and the Jean and Alexander Heard Library at Vanderbilt University, Nashville.

Because Sherman wrote prolifically, producing thirty to fifty letters on some days, many of which have survived, it is not surprising that numerous libraries and archives possess at least a few of his epistles. The great bulk of Sherman correspondence, however, and fortunately for scholars, is preserved in a few major depositories. They are: the Library of Congress, Washington, D.C.; the National Archives, also in Washington; the University of Notre Dame Archives, Notre Dame, Indiana; the Ohio History Connection, Columbus; and the Henry E. Huntington Library, San Marino, California.

These collections vary considerably in the areas that they cover. Approximately half of the Sherman papers in the Library of Congress concern his life after the Civil War, while the National Archives collection mainly involves the Civil War era. The Notre Dame holdings relate basically to the Sherman family and are particularly valuable for the extensive correspondence between Sherman and his wife. Sherman's letters to Ellen usually run from three to eight pages in length. Her letters to him are often also lengthy. Notable too are the many letters between Willian Tecumseh and his brother John. The Ohio History Connection has a wealth of Sherman letters and Sherman-related materials. I found the OHC especially helpful because of Sherman's sizable correspondence with several members of the Ewing family, as well as the letters between Sherman and his close friend Henry S. Turner, a correspondence extending over many years. The OHC also has copies of many Sherman materials that are in the Library of Congress, as well as copies of numerous Sherman family papers in the Notre Dame Archives. The Huntington Library holds important correspondence between Ellen Sherman and her mother, which proved to be very useful in understanding Ellen, as well as her parents.

While much less important than the above, I have benefited from a number of other manuscript collections, as well as the memoirs of key players in Sherman's life. Five edited books of selected Sherman correspondence and Sherman-related materials, have also been helpful.

One other primary source should be emphasized: *War of the Rebellion: A Compilation of the Official Records of the Union and Confederate Armies*. Many of these volumes are absolutely indispensable for any serious study of Sherman's Civil War service. I am particularly grateful to Timothy D. Johnson for making his copy of the 129 volumes of the *OR*, as it is generally known, available to me whenever, and for as long as, I needed them. Many secondary sources were also consulted, and I profited from some of them, but fundamentally, as I think is obvious from the source notes, this biography is grounded in primary sources.

NOTES

These shortened forms are used throughout the notes for frequently cited manuscript collections and selected books.

HHL — William Tecumseh Sherman Manuscripts, Henry E. Huntingon Library, San Marino, California

HLOS — M. A. DeWolfe Howe, ed., *Home Letters of General Sherman* (New York: Charles Scribner's Sons, 1909)

LC-CE — Charles Ewing Papers, Manuscripts Division, Library of Congress, Washington, D.C.

LC-TE — Thomas Ewing Papers, Manuscripts Division, Library of Congress, Washington, D.C.

LC-WTSP — William Tecumseh Sherman Papers, Manuscripts Division, Library of Congress, Washington, D.C.

Navy-OR — *Official Records of the Union and Confederate Navies in the War of the Rebellion* (Washington, D.C.: Government Printing Office, 1894–1927)

OHC-PBEP — Philemon B. Ewing Papers, Ohio History Connection, Columbus

OHC-WTSP — William Tecumseh Sherman Papers, Ohio History Connection, Columbus

OR — *War of the Rebellion: A Compilation of the Official Records of the Union and Confederate Armies*, 129 vols. (Washington D.C.: Government Printing Office, 1880–1901)

SCW — Brooks D. Simpson and Jean V. Berlin, eds., *Sherman's Civil War: Selected Correspondence of William T. Sherman, 1860–1865* (Chapel Hill: University of North Carolina Press, 1999)

Sword — Wiley Sword Collection

Thorndike — Rachel Sherman Thorndike, ed., *The Sherman Letters: Correspondence Between General and Senator Sherman from 1837 to 1891* (New York: Charles Scribner's Sons, 1894)

UND-SFP — William Tecumseh Sherman Family Papers, University of Notre Dame Archives, Notre Dame, Indiana

Other abbreviations used in the notes, especially regarding letter writers and recipients, are:

HBE   Hugh Boyle Ewing
PBE   Philemon Boyle Ewing
EES   Ellen Sherman, née Ewing
JS   John Sherman
WTS   William Tecumseh Sherman
HST   Henry S. Turner

PROLOGUE: DEATH STARED US ALL IN THE FACE

1   Lucius W. Barber, *Army Memoirs of Co. "D" 15th Illinois Volunteer Infantry* (Chicago: J.M.W. Jones Stationary and Printing Co., 1894), 56; B. F. Thomas, *14th Iowa Volunteer Infantry* (n.p.: privately printed, 1907), ch. v; Charles Hubert, *History of the 50th Regiment Illinois Volunteer Infantry* (Kansas City, Mo.: Western Veteran Publishing, 1894), 94; Wilbur F. Crummer, *With Grant at Fort Donelson, Shiloh, and Vicksburg* (Oak Park, Ill.: E.C. Crummer Co., 1915), 68; *OR*, 10 (pt. 1):582, 583.

2   John A. Cockerill, "A Boy at Shiloh," in *Under Both Flags*, ed. George M. Vickers (New York: Western M. Wilson, 1896), 370.

3   Thomas L. Livermore, *Numbers and Losses in the Civil War in America, 1861–1865* (Boston: Houghton Mifflin, 1900), 77–80. Total casualties at Shiloh are placed at 23,741 by Livermore, with the killed and wounded numbering 19,897, compared with 11,953 for the combined killed and wounded at the earlier battles of Manassas, Wilson's Creek, Fort Donelson and Pea Ridge.

4   James Lee McDonough, *Shiloh—In Hell before Night* (Knoxville: University of Tennessee Press, 1977), 25, 42, 45, 48, 50, 91, 124–25; O. Edward Cunningham, *Shiloh and the Western Campaign of 1862*, ed. Gary D. Joiner and Timothy B. Smith (New York: Savas Beatie, 2007), 221.

5   WTS to JS, April 22, 1862, in Thorndike, 143, 145; *OR*, 10 (pt. 2):50; McDonough, *Shiloh*, 52, 56, 73; Larry J. Daniel, *Shiloh: The Battle That Changed the Civil War* (New York: Simon and Schuster, 1997), 138.

6   William Tecumseh Sherman, *Memoirs of General W. T. Sherman*, 2 vols. (1885; repr., New York: Library of America, 1990), 1:249; McDonough, *Shiloh*, 54.

7   McDonough, *Shiloh*, 37–41, 45, 52; *OR*, 10 (pt. 2):46, 50–51; Steven E. Woodworth, *Sherman* (New York: Palgrave Macmillan, 2009), 49.

8   McDonough, *Shiloh*, 56.

9   *OR*, 10 (pt. 2):93, 94, and (pt. 1):89.

10 McDonough, *Shiloh*, 53; *Cincinnati Commercial*, December 11, 1861.

11 Alfred T. Andreas, "The 'Ifs and Buts' of Shiloh," in "Military Essays and Recollections," *Military Order of the Loyal Legions of the United States*, Illinois Commandery (Chicago: Dial Press, 1891), 1:123; McDonough, *Shiloh*, 92.

12 McDonough, *Shiloh*, 92; Sherman, *Memoirs*, 1:250, 256.

13 Lloyd Lewis, *Sherman: Fighting Prophet* (New York: Harcourt Brace, 1932), 223; John K. Duke, *History of the 53rd Ohio Volunteer Infantry* (Portsmouth, Ohio: Blade Printing Co., 1900), 43–45; *OR*, 10 (pt. 1):249; Sherman, *Memoirs*, 1:256–57.

14 McDonough, *Shiloh*, 124–25: WTS to EES, April 11, 1862, in *HLOS*, 222, 223; WTS to EES, April 24, 1862, in *SCW*, 209.

15   McDonough, *Shiloh*, 101; Cunningham, *Shiloh*, 174–76; Stacy D. Allen, "Shiloh! The Campaign and First Day's Battle," *Blue & Gray Magazine* (Winter 1997), 26.

16   John T. Taylor, "Reminiscences of Service as an Aide-de-Camp with General William Tecumseh Sherman," *War Talks in Kansas: A Series of Papers Read Before the Kansas Commandery of Military Order of the Loyal Legions of the United States* (Kansas City, Kans., 1908), 132; WTS to EES, April 11, 1862, in *HLOS*, 220.

17   McDonough, *Shiloh*, 114; Cockerill, "A Boy at Shiloh," 364.

18   Lewis, *Sherman*, 222.

19   Duke, *53rd Ohio*, 45–47.

20   WTS to JS, April 22, 1862, in Thorndike, 143; Allen, "Shiloh! First Day's Battle," 26–27; McDonough, *Shiloh*, 116.

21   McDonough, *Shiloh*, 116.

22   Ibid., 120; Allen, "Shiloh! First Day's Battle," 27; Cunningham, *Shiloh*, 219–23.

23   Sherman, *Memoirs*, 1:265–66; McDonough, *Shiloh*, 124–25; Allen, "Shiloh! First Day's Battle," 47; U. S. Grant, *Personal Memoirs*, 2 vols. (New York: Charles L. Webster & Co., 1885), 1:343.

24   Allen, "Shiloh! First Day's Battle," 47–49.

25   Ibid., 48–49; Cunningham, *Shiloh*, 221–37.

26   Allen, "Shiloh! First Day's Battle," 50.

27   Ibid.

28   Ibid., 50–51.

29   Wiley Sword, *Shiloh: Bloody April* (New York: William Morrow, 1974), 135; Daniel, *Shiloh*, 206.

30   McDonough, *Shiloh*, 128; Timothy B. Smith, *The Untold Story of Shiloh: The Battle and the Battlefield* (Knoxville: University of Tennessee Press, 2006), 29.

31   Smith, *Untold Story of Shiloh*, 29; Sherman, *Personal Memoirs*, 1:266; Grant, *Memoirs*, 1:367.

32   Grant, *Personal Memoirs*, 1:349; McDonough, *Shiloh*, 182–83; Stanley P. Hirshson, *The White Tecumseh: A Biography of General William T. Sherman* (New York: John Wiley & Sons, 1997), 120.

33   McDonough, *Shiloh*, 183.

34   Ibid., 196; *OR*, 10 (pt. 1):570; Sherman, *Memoirs*, 1:259–60.

35   Grant, *Personal Memoirs*, 1:343; *SCW*, 203, 204; Basil H. Liddell Hart, *Sherman: Soldier, Realist, American* (New York: Praeger, 1929), 133; Lewis, *Sherman*, 232.

36   WTS to EES, April 14, 1862, UND-SFP; WTS to Thomas Ewing Sr., April 27, 1862, and WTS to JS, May 12, 1862, *SCW*, 213, 217; William T. Sherman, *Report of the Proceedings of the Society of the Army of the Tennessee at the 14th Annual Meeting* (Cincinnati, 1881); John F. Marszalek, *Sherman: A Soldier's Passion for Order* (New York: Free Press, 1993), 182.

1. MY FATHER NAMED ME WILLIAM *TECUMSEH*

1   Lloyd Lewis, *Sherman: Fighting Prophet* (New York: Harcourt Brace, 1932), 10; Ronald N. Satz, *Tennessee's Indian Peoples: From White Contact to Removal, 1540–1840* (Knoxville: University of Tennessee Press, 1979), 34–38; Carl Waldman, *Atlas of the North American Indian*, 3rd ed. (New York: Checkmark Books, 2009), 150; Michael Johnson,

Encyclopedia of Native Tribes of North America (Edison, N.J.: Chartwell Books, 1999), 32; "Shawnees," in *The Tennessee Encyclopedia of History and Culture*, ed. Carroll Van West (Nashville: Tennessee Historical Society, 1998), 843–44.

2   Satz, *Tennessee's Indian Peoples*, 38; Waldman, *North American Indian*, 150.

3   Satz, *Tennessee's Indian Peoples*, 38, 39; Waldman, *North American Indian*, 151; George Brown Tindall with David E. Shi, *America: A Narrative History*, 3rd ed. (New York: W. W. Norton, 1992), 1:352, 353.

4   Waldman, *North American Indian*, 152, 153.

5   Lewis, *Sherman*, 22; Waldman, *North American Indian*, 153; Satz, *Tennessee's Indian Peoples*, 43; "Thames, Battle of," in *The Kentucky Encyclopedia*, ed. John E. Kleber, (Lexington: University of Kentucky Press, 1992), 877.

6   William Tecumseh Sherman, *Memoirs of General W. T. Sherman*, 2 vols. (1885; repr., New York: Library of America, 1990), 1:11.

7   Lewis, *Sherman*, 21; Waldman, *North American Indian*, 150, 152; Thomas A. Bailey and David M. Kennedy, *The American Pageant: A History of the Republic*, 8th ed. (Lexington, Mass.: D.C. Heath, 1987), 200.

8   Sherman, *Memoirs*, 1:11; Lewis, *Sherman*, 22; John F. Marszalek, *Sherman: A Soldier's Passion for Order* (New York: Free Press, 1993), 4.

9   WTS to JS, January 16, 1842, in Thorndike, 17–18.

10 WTS to HBE, March 10, 1844, OHC-WTSP.

11 WTS to EES, September 7, 1841, in *HLOS*, 14; Sherman, *Memoirs*, 1:24, 25; James M. Merrill, *William Tecumseh Sherman* (New York: Rand McNally, 1971), 47.

12 Lewis, *Sherman*, 596.

13 Ibid., 597; WTS to EES, August 22, 1868, UND-SFP; Stanley P. Hirshson, *The White Tecumseh: A Biography of General William T. Sherman* (New York: John Wiley & Sons, 1997), 338; Lee Kennett, *Sherman: A Soldier's Life* (2001; repr., New York: Perennial, 2002), 298.

14 Sherman, *Memoirs*, 1:9–10; Lewis, *Sherman*, 20–21; Marszalek, *Sherman*, 1–2.

15 Sherman, *Memoirs*, 1:10, 12; Lewis, *Sherman*, 20–21; Marszalek, *Sherman*, 4.

16 "The Thomas Ewing Family: Partial Genealogy," LC-TE; Lewis, *Sherman*, 18, 19, 26; Marszalek, *Sherman*, 8; Merrill, *Sherman*, 16–17.

17 Sherman, *Memoirs*, 1:11; Lewis, *Sherman*, 27, 18; Marszalek, *Sherman*, 5.

18 Lewis, *Sherman*, 24, 30–31; Sherman, *Memoirs*, 1:12–13.

19 Sherman, *Memoirs*, 1:13.

20 Ibid., 1:13–14; Thomas Ewing to EES, February 13, 1865, LC-TE.

21 Hirshson, *The White Tecumseh*, 6; Marszalek, *Sherman*, 9.

22 Lewis, *Sherman*, 24, 38.

23 Hirshson, *The White Tecumseh*, 5.

24 WTS to EES, September 17, 1844, in *HLOS*, 27; WTS to JS, July 14, 1841, LC-WTSP; Marszalek, *Sherman*, 8, 9, 15, 16; Lewis, *Sherman*, 41; Merrill, *Sherman*, 22, 26; WTS to JS, October 24, 1844, in Thorndike, 26.

25 Lewis, *Sherman*, 34; Sherman, *Memoirs*, 1:13.

26 Lewis, *Sherman*, 52, 621; Ellen Sherman, "Recollections for My Children," October 28, 1880, OHC-WTSP; Sherman, *Memoirs*, 1:11; Hirshson, *The White Tecumseh*, 7. It is interesting to note that Sherman's daughter, Rachel Sherman Thorndike, did not include the portion of Sherman's letter about not being a Catholic when she published

his December 29, 1875, communiqué to brother John, in *The Sherman Letters*, which she edited after her father died (see pp. 346–47).

27 WTS to EES, April 7, 1842, in Howe, *HLOS*, 20.

28 Lewis, *Sherman*, 621, 108; William Tecumseh Sherman to Charles Ewing, May 29, 1878, LC-CE.

29 Lewis, *Sherman*, 626, 650–51; Hirshson, *The White Tecumseh*, 387.

2. I WAS NOTIFIED TO PREPARE FOR WEST POINT

1 Lloyd Lewis, *Sherman: Fighting Prophet* (New York: Harcourt Brace, 1932), 39; John Marszalek, *Sherman: A Soldier's Passion for Order* (New York: Free Press, 1993), 14–15; William Tecumseh Sherman, *Memoirs of General W. T. Sherman*, 2 vols. (1885; repr., New York: Library of America, 1990), 1:13–14.

2 Stanley P. Hirshson, *The White Tecumseh: A Biography of General William T. Sherman* (New York: John Wiley & Sons, 1997), 2, 395.

3 Marszalek, *Sherman*, 12, 13.

4 James M. Merrill, *William Tecumseh Sherman* (New York: Rand McNally, 1971), 21.

5 Lewis, *Sherman*, 35.

6 Sherman, *Memoirs*, 1:11; Lewis, *Sherman*, 44.

7 Lewis, *Sherman*, 44–45; John Sherman, *Recollections of Forty Years in the House, Senate and Cabinet: An Autobiography*, 2 vols. (Chicago: Warner Co., 1895), 1:32–33.

8 Thomas Ewing to Lewis Cass, August 1, 1835, UND-SFP.

9 Sherman, *Memoirs*, 1:14.

10 Lewis, *Sherman*, 45; Marszalek, *Sherman*, 13.

11 Marszalek, *Sherman*, 13–14.

12 Stephen E. Ambrose, *Duty, Honor, Country: A History of West Point* (Baltimore: The Johns Hopkins University Press, 1966), 151; Marszalek, *Sherman*, 20.

13 Ambrose, *Duty, Honor, Country*, 151; Lewis, *Sherman*, 54.

14 Sherman, *Memoirs*, 1:14.

15 Ambrose, *Duty, Honor, Country*, 151–52.

16 Ibid., 152, 124.

17 WTS to Thomas Ewing, March 26, 1836, and Mary Sherman to Lewis Cass, Secretary of War, May 5, 1836, in Joseph H. Ewing, *Sherman at War* (Dayton, Ohio: Morningside House, 1992), 22; Sherman, *Memoirs*, 1:14–15.

18 Sherman, *Memoirs*, 1:15.

19 Ibid., 1:15–16.

20 Lewis, *Sherman*, 51.

21 Sherman, *Memoirs*, 1:16.

22 In the summer of 1990 I spent several weeks at the United States Military Academy on an ROTC fellowship. The description of West Point's geographic setting comes mainly from impressions and information gained at that time.

23 The description continues to draw upon my impressions of West Point and also draws upon Robert Cowley and Thomas Guinzburg, eds., *West Point: Two Centuries of Honor and Tradition* (New York: Warner Books, 2002), 19–20.

24 Ambrose, *Duty, Honor, Country*, 7–19, 44–61, 63.

25 Cowley and Guinzburg, eds., *West Point*, 30.

26 Ambrose, *Duty, Honor, Country*, 67, 154; Cowley and Guinzburg, eds., *West Point*, 34.

27 James M. Lynch and Ronald H. Bailey, *West Point: The First 200 Years* (Guilford, Conn.: Globe Pequot, 2002), 56.

28 Ibid., 57, 59.

29 Ibid., xv.

30 George W. Cullum, *Biographical Register of the Officers and Cadets of the United States Military Academy at West Point, New York, from Its Establishment, March 16, 1802, to the Army Re-organization of 1866–67*, 2 vols. (New York: D. Van Nostrand, 1868), 1:338.

3. IN THE SERVICE OF MY COUNTRY

1   WTS to HBE, January 25, 1844, OHC-WTSP (Sherman was describing for Hugh Boyle Ewing, who was considering attending West Point, what the academy had been like for him); William Tecumseh Sherman, *Memoirs of General W. T. Sherman*, 2 vols. (1885; repr., New York: Library of America, 1990), 1:16.

2   David S. Heidler and Jeanne T. Heidler, eds., *Encyclopedia of the American Civil War: A Political, Social, and Military History*. 5 vols. (Santa Barbara, Calif.: ABC-CLIO, 2000), 4:1807–8; Mark M. Boatner III, *The Civil War Dictionary* (New York: David McKay, 1959), 769; Sherman, *Memoirs*, 1:247.

3   WTS to HBE, January 25, 1844, OHC-WTSP.

4   Sherman, *Memoirs*, 1:16; WTS to HBE, January 25, 1844, OHC-WTSP.

5   Sherman, *Memoirs*, 1:16; Basil H. Liddell Hart, *Sherman: Soldier, Realist, American* (New York: Praeger, 1929), 9; Stanley P. Hirshson, *The White Tecumseh: A Biography of General William T. Sherman* (New York: John Wiley & Sons, 1997), 11.

6   James M. Lynch and Ronald H. Bailey, *West Point: The First 200 Years* (Guilford, Conn.: Globe Pequot, 2002), 42.

7   WTS to HBE, January 25, 1844, OHC-WTSP.

8   Lloyd Lewis, *Sherman: Fighting Prophet* (New York: Harcourt Brace, 1932), 55–56; Sherman, *Memoirs*, 1:16; John F. Marszalek, *Sherman: A Soldier's Passion for Order* (New York: Free Press, 1993), 22; WTS to PBE, September 30, 1837, OHC-PBEP.

9   Lewis, *Sherman*, 57.

10 WTS to Thomas Ewing, June 21, 1836, LC-TE; George W. Cullum, *Biographical Register of the Officers and Cadets of the United States Military Academy at West Point, New York, from Its Establishment, March 16, 1802, to the Army Re-organization of 1866–67*, 2 vols. (New York: D. Van Nostrand, 1868), 1:595, 598, 600; Lewis, *Sherman*, 62.

11 Sherman, *Memoirs*, 1:16; Ambrose, *Duty, Honor, Country*, 153.

12 Ambrose, *Duty, Honor, Country*, 148.

13 Sherman, *Memoirs*, 1:16–17; WTS to EES, August 21, 1839, in *HLOS*, 9; Marszalek, *Sherman*, 21; Lynch and Bailey, *West Point*, 53.

14 Sherman, *Memoirs*, 1:16; Ambrose, *Duty, Honor, Country*, 90–105.

15 Lewis, *Sherman*, 59; WTS to PBE, September 30, 1837, OHC-PBEP; WTS to EES, November 28, 1842, in *HLOS*, 24.

16 WTS to EES, November 28, 1842, in *HLOS*, 24.

17 WTS to PBE, October 13, 1838, OHC-PBEP; Hirshson, *The White Tecumseh*, 15, 17; Sherman, *Memoirs*, 1:16.

18   WTS to JS, January 14, 1840, in Thorndike, 10; WTS to PBE, October 13, 1838, OHC-PBEP; Liddell Hart, *Sherman*, 10.

19   WTS to EES, May 4, 1839, in *HLOS*, 7–9.

20   Lewis, *Sherman*, 61–62.

21   WTS to JS, March 7, 1840, in Thorndike, 11–13.

22   Sherman, *Memoirs*, 1:16; Hirshson, *The White Tecumseh*, 14.

23   Hirshson, *The White Tecumseh*, 13–14.

24   Robert Cowley and Thomas Guinzburg, eds., *West Point: Two Centuries of Honor and Tradition* (New York: Warner Books, 2002), 42; Ambrose, *Duty, Honor, Country*, 162–63.

25   Ambrose, *Duty, Honor, Country*, 163, 164; Marszalek, *Sherman*, 23.

26   Cullum, *Biographical Register of the USMA*, 1:592.

27   Ibid., 1:592, 597, 599, 602, 609, 619; Hirshson, *The White Tecumseh*, 12.

28   Cullum, *Biographical Register of the USMA*, 1:548–619; James Lee McDonough, *Stones River—Bloody Winter in Tennessee* (Knoxville: University of Tennessee Press, 1980), 79, 116.

29   WTS to PBE, July 11, 1837, OHC-PBEP; Marszalek, *Sherman*, 26.

30   WTS to EES, August 30, 1837, in *HLOS*, 4–5; Hirshson, *The White Tecumseh*, 14.

31   WTS to JS, December 6, 1837, in Thorndike, 3.

32   WTS to PBE, January 27, 1838, OHC-PBEP; Michael Fellman, *Citizen Sherman: A Life of William Tecumseh Sherman* (New York: Random House, 1995), 15.

33   WTS to JS, September 15, 1838, in Thorndike, 4, 5; Ellen Ewing's description of Cump's appearance is found in ibid., 3.

34   James M. Merrill, *William Tecumseh Sherman* (New York: Rand McNally, 1971), 34; Fellman, *Citizen Sherman*, 15.

35   Thomas A. Bailey and David M. Kennedy, *The American Pageant: A History of the Republic*, 8th ed. (Lexington, Mass.: D.C. Heath, 1987), 274.

36   WTS to EES, March 10, 1839, in *HLOS*, 6; WTS to JS, April 13, 1839, in Thorndike, 7–8; Liddell Hart, *Sherman*, 9.

37   Bailey and Kennedy, *American Pageant*, 274.

38   Liddell Hart, *Sherman*, 9; "Register of Delinquencies," 124, United States Military Academy Library, cited in Hirshson, *The White Tecumseh*, 14.

39   Liddell Hart, *Sherman*, 10.

40   Ibid.

41   Cullum, *Biographical Register of the USMA*, 1:592–619.

4. SAND AND SUN, SEMINOLES AND SPANIARDS

1   George Brown Tindall with David E. Shi, *America: A Narrative History*, 3rd ed. (New York: W. W. Norton, 1992), 1:427; Thomas A. Bailey and David M. Kennedy, *The American Pageant: A History of the Republic*, 8th ed. (Lexington, Mass.: D.C. Heath, 1987), 265.

2   PBE to Maria Ewing, June 21, 1840, UND-SFP; Tindall and Shi, *America*, 1:427–28.

3   Walter R. Borneman, *Polk: The Man Who Transformed the Presidency and America* (New York: Random House, 2008), 44.

4   Tindall and Shi, *America*, 1:429.

5   Lloyd Lewis, *Sherman: Fighting Prophet* (New York: Harcourt Brace, 1932), 67.

6   Ibid., 73; John F. Marszalek, *Sherman: A Soldier's Passion for Order* (New York: Free Press, 1993), 37; WTS to EES, September 7, 1841, in *HLOS*, 15.

7   WTS to JS, October 24, 1844, in Thorndike, 26.

8   William Tecumseh Sherman, *Memoirs of General W. T. Sherman*, 2 vols. (1885; repr., New York: Library of America, 1990), 1:17; Marszalek, *Sherman*, 30–31.

9   Sherman, *Memoirs*, 1:17; Stanley P. Hirshson, *The White Tecumseh: A Biography of General William T. Sherman* (New York: John Wiley & Sons, 1997), 17; James M. Merrill, *William Tecumseh Sherman* (New York: Rand McNally, 1971), 44.

10 Richard Delafield to Joseph G. Totten, September 22, 1840, and Totten to Delafield, September 26, 1840, UND-SFP.

11 Sherman, *Memoirs*, 1:17; WTS to Maria Ewing, October 2, 1840, UND-SFP.

12 Sherman, *Memoirs*, 1:17–18.

13 WTS to JS, March 30, 1841, in Thorndike, 13.

14 WTS to EES, September 7, 1841, in *HLOS*, 14.

15 WTS to JS, March 30, 1841, LC-WTSP; Russell F. Weigley, *History of the United States Army*, enlarged ed. (Bloomington: University of Indiana Press, 1984), 162.

16 Sherman, *Memoirs*, 1:25.

17 Weigley, *U.S. Army*, 161; Sherman, *Memoirs*, 1:19; Tindall and Shi, *America*, 1:375, 412. Russell F. Weigley, *The American Way of War: A History of U.S. Military Strategy and Policy* (Bloomington: University of Indiana Press, 1977), 67–68; Bailey and Kennedy, *American Pageant*, 257–58; Carl Waldman, *Atlas of the North American Indian*, 3rd ed. (New York: Checkmark Books, 2009), 157–59.

18 Sherman, *Memoirs*, 1:18–19.

19 WTS to PBE, October 24, 1840, OHC-PBEP; Basil H. Liddell Hart, *Sherman: Soldier, Realist, American* (New York: Praeger, 1929), 13; Merrill, *Sherman*, 50; Marszalek, *Sherman*, 38; WTS to EES, September 7, 1841, in *HLOS*, 16; Sherman, *Memoirs*, 1:19.

20 WTS to PBE, October 24, 1840, OHC-PBEP; Merrill, *Sherman*, 49.

21 Marszalek, *Sherman*, 35.

22 Sherman, *Memoirs*, 1:19–22.

23 Ibid., 1:19; WTS to PBE, March 19, 1841, OHC-PBEP.

24 Sherman, *Memoirs*, 1:23; WTS to PBE, June 2, 1841, OHC-PBEP.

25 Sherman, *Memoirs*, 1:22–25; Lewis, *Sherman*, 68.

26 WTS to JS, July 14, 1841, LC-WTSP.

27 WTS to EES, September 7, 1841, in *HLOS*, 14, 16.

28 Lewis, *Sherman*, 69.

29 WTS to JS, February 15, 1842, in Thorndike, 21.

30 Sherman, *Memoirs*, 1:26.

31 WTS to EES, January 13, 1842, in *HLOS*, 17–18; WTS to JS, February 15, 1842, in Thorndike, 21.

32 WTS to EES, January 13, 1842, in *HLOS*, 17–18; WTS to JS, February 15, 1842, in Thorndike, 21–22.

33 WTS to JS, February 15, 1842, in Thorndike, 22; WTS to EES, January 13, 1842, in *HLOS*, 18–19.

34 WTS to EES, April 7, 1842, in *HLOS*, 22.

5. MILITARY CAMARADERIE, SOUTHERN ARISTOCRACY, PROSPECTIVE MATRIMONY

1   WTS to EES, April 7, 1842, in *HLOS*, 19–20.

2   Ibid., 20.

3   Ibid.; William Tecumseh Sherman, *Memoirs of General W. T. Sherman*, 2 vols. (1885; repr., New York: Library of America, 1990), 1:27.

4   Sherman, *Memoirs*, 1:27; WTS to EES, April 7, 1842, in *HLOS*, 21–22.

5   WTS to EES, April 7, 1842, in *HLOS*, 22–23.

6   Sherman, *Memoirs*, 1:27.

7   Ibid., 1:33–34.

8   Ibid., 1:34; WTS to JS, May 23, 1843, LC-WTSP.

9   Sherman, *Memoirs*, 1:35; WTS to JS, May 23, 1843, LC-WTSP.

10 WTS to JS, May 23, 1843, LC-WTSP; WTS to HBE, March 10, 1844, OHC-WTSP.

11 WTS to JS, May 23, 1843, LC-WTSP.

12 John F. Marszalek, *Sherman: A Soldier's Passion for Order* (New York: Free Press, 1993), 43; WTS to JS, May 23, 1843, LC-WTSP.

13 Marszalek, *Sherman*, 48; James M. Merrill, *William Tecumseh Sherman* (New York: Rand McNally, 1971), 58; Stanley P. Hirshson, *The White Tecumseh: A Biography of General William T. Sherman* (New York: John Wiley & Sons, 1997), 22; WTS to EES, March 12, 1843, UND-SFP.

14 Sherman, *Memoirs*, 1:31; Marszalek, *Sherman*, 44.

15 WTS to EES, November 28, 1842, in HLOS, 24; Lloyd Lewis, *Sherman: Fighting Prophet* (New York: Harcourt Brace, 1932), 75.

16 WTS to JS, October 24, 1844, in Thorndike, 26; WTS to EES, June 14, 1844, UND-SFP.

17 WTS to JS, January 19, 1844, in Thorndike, 24; Marszalek, *Sherman*, 48, 49; WTS to EES, February 8 and September 17, 1844, UND-SFP. The February 8, 1844, letter to Ellen is both interesting and revealing, yet less than one-fifth of it was published in *HLOS* (pp. 24–25), a fact clearly demonstrating that a scholar should not rely solely upon an edited publication.

18 WTS to JS, January 19, 1844, in Thorndike, 24; Sherman, *Memoirs*, 1:28.

19 WTS to JS, January 19, 1844, in Thorndike, 24.

20 Sherman, *Memoirs*, 1:28; *Mark Twain*, a documentary by Ken Burns originally broadcast on PBS in 2009.

21 WTS to JS, January 19, 1844, in Thorndike, 24; Sherman, *Memoirs*, 1:28.

22 Sherman, *Memoirs*, 1:28, 29; WTS to JS, January 19, 1844, in Thorndike, 24, 25.

23 Sherman, *Memoirs*, 1:29; Marszalek, *Sherman*, 47.

24 WTS to JS, January 19, 1844, in Thorndike, 25.

25 Sherman, *Memoirs*, 1:29–30; WTS to EES, February 8, 1844, UND-SFP; WTS to PBE, February 20, 1844, OHC-PBEP; WTS to HBE, March 10, 1844, OHC-WTSP.

26 Sherman, *Memoirs*, 1:30.

27 Ibid.; Lee Kennett, *Sherman: A Soldier's Life* (New York: Perennial, 2002), 33.

28 WTS to EES, November 19, 1845, and January 31, 1846, UND-SFP.

29 Sherman, *Memoirs*, 1:31.

30 Ibid., 1:12.

6. AND THEN THERE WAS A WAR ON

1   WTS to EES, September 17, 1844, in *HLOS*, 25.

2   George Brown Tindall and David E. Shi, *America: A Narrative History*, 3rd ed. (New York: W. W. Norton, 1992), 1:539.

3   Bernard Mayo, *Henry Clay: Spokesman of the New West* (Boston: Houghton Mifflin, 1937), 367–68.

4   John Seigenthaler, *James K. Polk* (New York: Times Books, 2003), 71–72; Walter R. Borneman, *Polk: The Man Who Transformed the Presidency and America* (New York: Random House, 2008), 81–82, 122–23; Tindall and Shi, *America*, 1:538–39.

5   Borneman, *Polk*, 175–76.

6   Tindall and Shi, *America*, 1:539.

7   Ibid., 1:539, 541.

8   WTS to JS, August 29, 1845, and January 4, 1846, in Thorndike, 28, 29; WTS to EES, February 8, 1844, UND-SFP; William Tecumseh Sherman, *Memoirs of General W. T. Sherman*, 2 vols. (1885; repr., New York: Library of America, 1990), 1:34.

9   Tindall and Shi, *America*, 1:543–44; Borneman, *Polk*, 144–45.

10 WTS to EES, September 17, 1844, and June 9, 1845, in *HLOS*, 26, 29; Sherman, *Memoirs*, 1:32.

11 WTS to JS, April 4, 1845, and January 4, 1846, in Thorndike, 27, 29.

12 WTS to EES, June 14, 1844, UND-SFP.

13 Stanley P. Hirshson, *The White Tecumseh: A Biography of General William T. Sherman* (New York: John Wiley & Sons, 1997), 24–25.

14 James M. Merrill, *William Tecumseh Sherman* (New York: Rand McNally, 1971), 63 (quoting Sherman about the influence of West Point); Lee Kennett, *Sherman: A Soldier's Life* (New York: Perennial, 2002), 30, and 360n.

15 WTS to EES, June 9, 1845, in *HLOS*, 27–28.

16 WTS to EES, June 14, 1844, UND-SFP; WTS to HBE, March 10, 1844, OHC-WTSP.

17 WTS to EES, February 8, 1844, UND-SFP.

18 WTS to JS, January 4, 1846, in Thorndike, 29; WTS to EES, January 31, 1846, in *HLOS*, 32.

19 WTS to EES, January 31, 1846, in *HLOS*, 31; WTS to JS, January 4, 1846, in Thorndike, 30.

20 Sam W. Haynes, *James K. Polk and the Expansionist Impulse* (New York: Pearson Longman, 1997), 125; Seigenthaler, *Polk*, 132.

21 Borneman, *Polk*, 194–96; Thomas A. Bailey and David M. Kennedy, *The American Pageant: A History of the Republic*, 8th ed. (Lexington, Mass.: D.C. Heath, 1987), 281; Haynes, *Polk*, 122–23; Eugene Irving McCormac, *James K. Polk: A Political Biography* (Berkeley: University of California Press, 1922), 385.

22 Tindall and Shi, *America*, 1:544.

23 Ibid.; Haynes, *Polk*, 120.

24 Tindall and Shi, *America*, 1:538; Bailey and Kennedy, *American Pageant*, 280–81; Haynes, *Polk*, 126–32.

25 Haynes, *Polk*, 129–30; Bailey and Kennedy, *American Pageant*, 281.

26 Tindall and Shi, *America*, 1:544; Bailey and Kennedy, *American Pageant*, 281; Haynes, *Polk*, 143.

27 Bailey and Kennedy, *American Pageant*, 280.

28 Sherman, *Memoirs*, 1:35, 37; WTS to EES, June 11, 1846, UND-SFP; *HLOS*, 33–34.

29 WTS to EES, June 30, 1846, UND-SFP; Sherman, *Memoirs*, 1:37.

30 WTS to EES, June 30, 1846, UND-SFP.

31 WTS to EES, June 30, July 12 and August 3, 1846, UND-SFP.

32 WTS to EES, August 3, 1846, in *HLOS*, 38, 39.

33 WTS to EES, July 12, 1846, UND-SFP; Sherman, *Memoirs*, 1:37–38; WTS to EES, August 3, 1846, in *HLOS*, 40, 41, 44.

34 WTS to EES, August 3, 1846, in *HLOS*, 38, 40, 42.

35 Sherman, *Memoirs*, 1:38; WTS to EES, July 12 and August 3, 1846, in *HLOS*, 37, 43.

36 WTS to Thomas Ewing Sr., May 3, 1862, in *SCW*, 214.

37 WTS to EES, August 28, 1846, in *HLOS*, 44, 45; Sherman, *Memoirs*, 1:39.

38 WTS to EES, August 28, 1846, in *HLOS*, 46; Sherman, *Memoirs*, 1:39.

39 WTS to EES, September 12, 1846, in *HLOS*, 50.

40 WTS to EES, September 12 and 18, 1846, in *HLOS*, 50, 63; Sherman, *Memoirs*, 1:39.

41 WTS to EES, September 16 and 18, 1846, in *HLOS*, 52, 54, 57, 61–63; Sherman, *Memoirs*, 1:40.

42 Sherman, *Memoirs*, 1:40; WTS to EES, September 16, 1846, in *HLOS*, 60.

43 WTS to EES, September 16, 1846, in *HLOS*, 58.

44 Ibid., 61.

45 WTS to Elizabeth Sherman, November 10, 1846, in Thorndike, 31; WTS to EES, October 27, 1846, in *HLOS*, 64.

46 WTS to EES, October 27, 1846, in *HLOS*, 64, 65, 66; WTS to Elizabeth Sherman, November 10, 1846, in Thorndike, 31.

47 WTS to EES, November 6, 1846, in *HLOS*, 68.

48 WTS to Elizabeth Sherman, November 10, 1846, in Thorndike, 32.

49 Ibid.; WTS to EES, November 6, 1846, in *HLOS*, 67.

50 WTS to Elizabeth Sherman, November 10, 1846, in Thorndike, 34.

51 Ibid., 36; WTS to EES, November 24, 1846, in *HLOS*, 71–72.

7. DEPRIVED OF MILITARY GLORY

1 William Tecumseh Sherman, *Memoirs of General W. T. Sherman*, 2 vols. (1885; repr., New York: Library of America, 1990), 1:42, 43; WTS to EES, January 26, 1847, in *HLOS*, 81–82.

2 Sherman, *Memoirs*, 1:43.

3 Ibid., 1:43–44.

4 WTS to EES, April 25, 1847, in *HLOS*, 102.

5 WTS to EES, July 11, 1847, in *HLOS*, 107, 108; JS to WTS, May 2, 1847, in Thorndike, 38–39.

6 WTS to EES, November 10, 1847, and August 28, 1848, in *HLOS*, 109, 116.

7 WTS to EES, March 12, 1847, in *HLOS*, 94; Sherman, *Memoirs*, 1:46–48.

8 Sherman, *Memoirs*, 1:51, 52; WTS to EES, January 27, March 12, April 25, July 11, 1847, in *HLOS*, 85, 88, 101, 106, 108.

9 Sherman, *Memoirs*, 1:51, 52, 53.

10 Ibid., 1:52, 53.

11 WTS to EES, March 12, April 25, and May 1, 1847, in *HLOS*, 93, 99, 102.

12 WTS to EES, March 12, 1847, in *HLOS*, 90–91; Sherman, *Memoirs*, 1:45.

13 WTS to EES, March 12, 1847, in *HLOS*, 89–90.

14 WTS to EES, February 3, 1848, in *HLOS*, 110–11.

15 WTS to EES, March 12, 1847, in *HLOS*, 91–92.

16 WTS to EES, March 12, 1847, April 10 and August 28, 1848, in *HLOS*, 97, 114, 115, 117.

17 WTS to EES, April 10, 1848, in *HLOS*, 114.

18 WTS to EES, August 28, 1848, in *HLOS*, 116.

19 EES to WTS, January 19 and February 2, 1849, and WTS to EES, March 5, 1849, UND-SFP.

20 Basil H. Liddell Hart, *Sherman: Soldier, Realist, American* (New York: Praeger, 1929), 22.

21 WTS to EES, October 8, 1847, UND-SFP; Sherman, *Memoirs*, 1:54, 86–87.

22 Sherman, *Memoirs*, 1:87.

23 WTS to JS, April 18, 1848, in Thorndike, 39.

24 Ibid.

25 Sherman, *Memoirs*, 1:56, 61; WTS to EES, July 11, 1847, in *HLOS*, 106.

26 Sherman, *Memoirs*, 1:59–60.

27 Ibid., 1:61.

28 Ibid., 1:61–62.

29 WTS to JS, April 18, 1848, in Thorndike, 39; Sherman, *Memoirs*, 1:65.

30 Alan Brinkley, *American History: A Survey*, 10th ed. (New York: McGraw-Hill, 1999), 444; Irwin Unger, *These United States: The Questions of Our Past* (New York: Prentice Hall, 1999), 319; Sherman, *Memoirs*, 1:74–75.

31 Sherman, *Memoirs*, 1:64–65.

32 Ibid., 1:65.

33 Ibid., 1:70; Lee Kennett, *Sherman: A Soldier's Life* (New York: Perennial, 2002), 45–46.

34 Sherman, *Memoirs*, 1:70, 71, 73.

35 WTS to HST, August 25, 1848, in Thorndike, 44, 45.

36 Ibid., 46; WTS to JS, August 24, 1848, in Thorndike, 42. Sherman later wrote, "I prepared with great care the letter to the adjutant-general, which Colonel Mason modified in a few particulars; and as it was important to send not only the specimens which had been presented to us along our route of travel, I advised the colonel to ... send to Washington a large sample of the commercial gold in general use, and to pay for the same out of the money in his hands known as the 'civil fund,' arising from duties collected at the several ports in California. He consented to this." (Sherman, *Memoirs*, 1:81).

37 Walter R. Borneman, *Polk: The Man Who Transformed the Presidency and America* (New York: Random House, 2008), 308, 313; Allan R. Millett and Peter Maslowski, *For the Common Defense: A Military History of the United States of America*, rev. ed. (New York: Free Press, 1994), 157; David Herbert Donald, Jean Harvey Baker, and Michael F. Holt, *The Civil War and Reconstruction* (New York: W. W. Norton, 2001), 78; Thomas A. Bailey and David M. Kennedy, *The American Pageant: A History of the Republic*, 8th ed. (Lexington, Mass.: D.C. Heath, 1987), 285.

38 WTS to HST, August 25, 1848, in Thorndike, 46–47; WTS to EES, August 28, 1848, in *HLOS*, 117.

39 WTS to HST, August 25, 1848, in Thorndike, 47; Sherman, *Memoirs*, 1:80.

40 George Brown Tindall with David E. Shi, *America: A Narrative History*, 3rd ed. (New York: W. W. Norton, 1992), 1:596; Thomas Childers, "Europe and Western Civilization in the Modern Age," *Revolution in Central Europe* (a 1998 course from the Teaching Company, Chantilly, Va.) part 2, disc 3, lecture 14; Brinkley, *American History*, 444.

41 Brinkley, *American History*, 444; Tindall and Shi, *America*, 1:596; Sherman, *Memoirs*, 1:58.

42 Brinkley, *American History*, 444; WTS to HST, August 25, 1848, in Thorndike, 44–48.

43 Sherman, *Memoirs*, 1:82, 89–90, 101.

44 Brinkley, *American History*, 445, 446.

45 Sherman, *Memoirs*, 1:84–85.

46 Ibid., 1:87–89, 95; WTS to EES, March 5, 1849, UND-SFP.

47 Sherman, *Memoirs*, 1:92–94.

48 Ibid., 1:92–102; Kennett, *Sherman*, 48–49; WTS to HST, August 25, 1848, in Thorndike, 48.

49 Sherman, *Memoirs*, 1:103–4; Hirshson, *The White Tecumseh*, 32.

50 Sherman, *Memoirs*, 1:104.

8. CALIFORNIA AGAIN—A BRAND-NEW GAME

1 William Tecumseh Sherman, *Memoirs of General W. T. Sherman*, 2 vols. (1885; repr., New York: Library of America, 1990), 1:106; WTS to EES, March 29, 1850, UND-SFP.

2 Headquarters of the Army, February 28, 1850, Special Field Orders No. 17, granting a leave of absence of six months for W. T. Sherman, by command of Winfield Scott, UND-SFP; WTS to EES, March 27 and 29, 1850, UND-SFP.

3 Sherman, *Memoirs*, 1:106; EES to Maria Ewing, May 4, 1850, HHL.

4 WTS to EES, March 29, 1850, UND-SFP.

5 Sherman, *Memoirs*, 1:106; John F. Marszalek, *Sherman: A Soldier's Passion for Order* (New York: Free Press, 1993), 80; EES to Maria Ewing, May 8, 1850, HHL.

6 EES to Maria Ewing, May 9, 1850, HHL.

7 Ibid.

8 Maria Ewing to EES, May 9, 1850, HHL.

9 Maria Ewing to EES, June 21 and June 8, 1850, HHL.

10 George Brown Tindall with David E. Shi, *America: A Narrative History*, 3rd ed. (New York: W. W. Norton, 1992), 1:601.

11 Sherman, *Memoirs*, 1:106, 107.

12 Ibid., 1:107; WTS to JS, July 1850, in Thorndike, 48–49; James M. McPherson, *Battle Cry of Freedom: The Civil War Era* (New York: Oxford University Press, 1988), 68; William C. Davis, *Jefferson Davis: The Man and His Hour* (New York: HarperCollins, 1991), 196.

13 David M. Potter, *The Impending Crisis: 1848 to 1861* (New York: Harper and Row, 1976), 95; Tindall and Shi, *America*, 1:276. Also see the Constitution, article I, section 2, and the Thirteenth Amendment, section 1.

14 Tindall and Shi, *America*, 1:570–72; James G. Randall and David Donald, *The Civil War and Reconstruction*, 2nd ed. (Lexington, Mass.: D.C. Heath, 1969), 4–5.

15 The best single work on the period, for a combination of detailed information, excel-

lent analysis, and acceptable readability remains David Potter's *Impending Crisis*. See also Thomas A. Bailey and David M. Kennedy, *The American Pageant: A History of the Republic*, 8th ed. (Lexington, Mass.: D.C. Heath, 1987).

16   Tindall and Shi, *America*, 1:597.

17   Potter, *Impending Crisis*, 91, 95.

18   Ibid., 91, 92, 93; Bailey and Kennedy, *American Pageant*, 373.

19   Sherman, *Memoirs*, 1:100, 101, 104.

20   Sherman, *Memoirs*, 1:107; Potter, *Impending Crisis*, 97, 98, 100, 108.

21   Potter, *Impending Crisis*, 99, 100; Charles P. Roland, *An American Iliad: The Story of the Civil War* (New York: McGraw-Hill, 1991), 4, 5.

22   Sherman, *Memoirs*, 1:107; Roland, *American Iliad*, 8.

23   Sherman, *Memoirs*, 1:108, 109.

24   Potter, *Impending Crisis*, 108–13.

25   Ibid., 114; Roland, *American Iliad*, 8.

26   Roland, *American Iliad*, 8; Potter, *Impending Crisis*, 116, 117; Davis, *Jefferson Davis*, 203.

27   Marszalek, *Sherman*, 85; Sherman, *Memoirs*, 1:109.

28   WTS to HBE, January 5, 1851, OHC-WTSP; Sherman, *Memoirs*, 1:109, 110.

29   WTS to EES, October 8, 1850, UND-SFP; EES to Maria Ewing, May 22, 1850, HHL; WTS to EES, November 1, 1850, UND-SFP.

30   WTS to EES, October 23 and November 1, 1850, January 25, 1851, UND-SFP; WTS to JS, November 12, 1850, LC-WTSP; WTS to HBE, January 5, 1851, OHC-WTSP; WTS to JS, January 14, 1851, in Thorndike, 49.

31   Sherman, *Memoirs*, 1:110; WTS to HBE, June 15, 1852, OHC-WTSP; Marszalek, *Sherman*, 87.

32   WTS to HBE, April 30, 1856, OHC-WTSP; Maria Ewing to EES, June 12 and June 19, September 23, 1851, HHL.

33   WTS to HBE, June 15, 1852, OHC-WTSP; WTS to EES, May 30, 1852, UND-SFP.

34   Marszalek, *Sherman*, 88; WTS to EES, August 14, 1852, UND-SFP.

35   WTS to HBE, June 15, 1852, OHC-WTSP; Sherman, *Memoirs*, 1:110.

36   WTS to EES, September 30, 1852, UND-SFP.

37   Sherman, *Memoirs*, 1:112, 113; WTS to JS, November 17, 1852, LC-WTSP.

38   Sherman, *Memoirs*, 1:113; WTS to EES, November 4 and 16, December 2 and 14, 1852, UND-SFP.

39   Dwight L. Clarke, *William Tecumseh Sherman: Gold Rush Banker* (San Francisco: California Historical Society, 1969), 11, 12.

40   Ibid., 13, 15; Lee Kennett, *Sherman: A Soldier's Life* (2001; repr., New York: Perennial, 2002), 60.

41   Sherman, *Memoirs*, 1:114; Clarke, *Gold Rush Banker*, 10, 12, 13.

42   WTS to HBE, June 15, 1852, OHC-WTSP; Clarke, *Gold Rush Banker*, 12; Sherman, *Memoirs*, 1:114.

43   Maria Ewing to EES, February 27, 1853, HHL.

44   Clarke, *Gold Rush Banker*, 16; Sherman, *Memoirs*, 1:115–17.

45   Sherman, *Memoirs*, 1:121.

46   Ibid., 1:117.

47   Ibid., 1:118; Clarke, *Gold Rush Banker*, 17, and see also 363n32.

48   Sherman, *Memoirs*, 1:119, 120.

49   Ibid., 1:120.

50   Ibid., 1:121.

51   Clarke, *Gold Rush Banker*, 19; Sherman, *Memoirs*, 1:121, 122.

52   Marszalek, *Sherman*, 94, 95; Kennett, *Sherman*, 63; Sherman, *Memoirs*, 1:121.

53   Clarke, *Gold Rush Banker*, 18–19; WTS to JS, June 3, 1853, in Thorndike, 52, 53.

54   Clarke, *Gold Rush Banker*, 20; Sherman, *Memoirs*, 1:122.

55   Clarke, *Gold Rush Banker*, 20; Kennett, *Sherman*, 66; WTS to JS, June 3, 1853, LC-WTSP.

9. GOLDEN STATE BANKER

1   WTS to JS, July 14, 1841, and November 5, 1857, LC-WTSP; WTS to EES, July 29, 1857, in *HLOS*, 148.

2   WTS to HBE, December 15, 1854, in OHC-WTSP; Dwight L. Clarke, *William Tecumseh Sherman: Gold Rush Banker* (San Francisco: California Historical Society, 1969), 28; EES to Maria Ewing, December 8, 1853, HHL.

3   EES to Maria Ewing, February 19, 1854, HHL, tells of Thomas Ewing's "likeness" over the mantel in San Francisco. Many of the letters that Ellen Sherman wrote to her mother while in San Francisco are indisputable evidence documenting Cump's serious problems with asthma. See December 12, 23, 27, 29, 1853; January 3, 31, June 28, July 22, August 12, November 24, December 15, 1854; March 8, December 4, 17, 1855; January 14, 15, February 4, April 19, 1856, HHL. See also Clarke, *Gold Rush Banker*, vii.

4   Clarke, *Gold Rush Banker*, 5; John S. Littell, *The Commerce and Industries of the Pacific Coast of North America* (San Francisco: A. L. Bancroft, 1882), 126.

5   Clarke, *Gold Rush Banker*, viii, 7.

6   Ibid., 5, 7, 8.

7   Ibid., 8, 9, 13.

8   William Tecumseh Sherman, *Memoirs of General W. T. Sherman*, 2 vols. (1885; repr., New York: Library of America, 1990), 1:124, 125; Basil H. Liddell Hart, *Sherman: Soldier, Realist, American* (New York: Praeger, 1929), 38.

9   Clarke, *Gold Rush Banker*, 29, 30, 31, 32.

10   Ibid., 25, 34.

11   EES to Maria Ewing, November 19, 1853, and February 19, 1854, HHL.

12   Clarke, *Gold Rush Banker*, 23, 33; Sherman, *Memoirs*, 1:124.

13   Sherman, *Memoirs*, 1:125.

14   Ibid., 1:124, 125; Clarke, *Gold Rush Banker*, 24, 26, 33.

15   Clarke, *Gold Rush Banker*, 27, 40, 41, 49; Sherman, *Memoirs*, 1:125.

16   Clarke, *Gold Rush Banker*, 53; WTS to HST, August 31, 1854, OHC-WTSP.

17   EES to Maria Ewing, December 12, 23, 27, 1853, HHL.

18   EES to Maria Ewing, October 31, 1853, and October 7, 1854, HHL.

19   EES to Maria Ewing, October 31 and December 4 and 23, 1853, and March 19, 1854, HHL; Clarke, *Gold Rush Banker*, 33, 56.

20   Numerous letters from Ellen to her mother indicated that she considered the Ewing place in Lancaster to be "home"; see, for example, EES to Maria Ewing, July 10 and 22, December 15, 1854 (several other letters could be referenced).

21   Maria Ewing to EES, May 15, 1856, and EES to Maria Ewing, February 19, 1854, HHL.

22   George Brown Tindall and David E. Shi, *America: A Narrative History,* 3rd ed. (New York: W. W. Norton, 1992), 1:468–69; Thomas A. Bailey and David M. Kennedy, *The American Pageant: A History of the Republic,* 8th ed. (Lexington, Mass.: D.C. Heath, 1987), 319–20.

23   EES to Maria Ewing, October 29, 1854, HHL; Clarke, *Gold Rush Banker,* 57.

24   Douglas quoted in David H. Donald, Jean Harvey Baker, and Michael F. Holt, *The Civil War and Reconstruction* (New York: W. W. Norton, 2001), 90.

25   Irwin Unger, *These United States: The Questions of Our Past* (New York: Prentice Hall, 1999), 325; for Douglas quote, see Donald, Baker, and Holt, *Civil War and Reconstruction,* 88.

26   Tindall and Shi, *America,* 1:611, is the source of the voting figures.

27   Charles P. Roland, *An American Iliad: The Story of the Civil War* (New York: McGraw-Hill, 1991), 11; Tindall and Shi, *America,* 1:609–10.

28   David Donald, *Charles Sumner and the Coming of the Civil War* (New York: Alfred A. Knopf, 1960), 260–61.

29   Tindall and Shi, *America,* 1:611–12. David M. Potter, *The Impending Crisis: 1848 to 1861* (New York: Harper and Row, 1976), 145–76, presents a thorough and excellent account of the Kansas-Nebraska Act.

30   WTS to JS, November 30, 1854, in Thorndike, 53–54.

31   WTS to HST, June 15, 1854, OHC-WTSP.

32   EES to Maria Ewing, November 24, 1854, HHL.

33   EES to Maria Ewing, July 31, 1856, HHL; Clarke, *Gold Rush Banker,* 95.

34   EES to Maria Ewing, July 10 and 22, 1854, HHL; WTS to HBE, December 15, 1854, OHC-WTSP.

35   WTS to HST, December 23, 1854, OHC-WTSP; Clarke, *Gold Rush Banker,* 68, 73.

36   Sherman, *Memoirs,* 1:125; Clarke, *Gold Rush Banker,* 59, 60, 87, 95.

37   Sherman, *Memoirs,* 1:126; Clarke, *Gold Rush Banker,* 68, 139–40, 364–65.

38   Sherman, *Memoirs,* 1:127; Clarke, *Gold Rush Banker,* 69, 71.

39   Sherman, *Memoirs,* 1:127, 136; EES to Maria Ewing, February 15, 1855, HHL.

40   Sherman, *Memoirs,* 1:128, 129.

41   Ibid., 1:130.

42   Clarke, *Gold Rush Banker,* 118; Sherman, *Memoirs,* 1:130.

43   Clarke, *Gold Rush Banker,* 109, 110; Sherman, *Memoirs,* 1:133.

44   Sherman, *Memoirs,* 1:133.

45   Ibid., 1:134, 135; Clarke, *Gold Rush Banker,* 111, 380.

46   Sherman, *Memoirs,* 1:135; Clarke, *Gold Rush Banker,* 107, 111.

47   Sherman, *Memoirs,* 1:135; Clarke, *Gold Rush Banker,* 88, 107, 111, 116, 118.

48   EES to Maria Ewing, February 28, 1855, HHL; Clarke, *Gold Rush Banker,* 115.

49   EES to Maria Ewing, March 8, 1855, HHL; Clarke, *Gold Rush Banker,* 114.

50   EES to Maria Ewing, March 8, 1855, HHL.

51   Ibid.; Sherman, *Memoirs,* 1:136.

52   Sherman, *Memoirs,* 1:136–37.

53   Clarke, *Gold Rush Banker,* 99, 378, 391.

54   WTS to JS, March 20, 1856, OHC-WTSP; Clarke, *Gold Rush Banker,* 197.

55   WTS to HBE, June 29, 1855, OHC-WTSP.

56 WTS to HBE, December 15, 1854, June 29, 1855, and April 30, 1856, OHC-WTSP.
57 Clarke, *Gold Rush Banker*, 158; WTS to HBE, April 30, 1856, OHC-WTSP.
58 WTS to JS, August 19, 1856, OHC-WTSP; Clarke, *Gold Rush Banker*, 193, 203, 204, 209.
59 Sherman, *Memoirs*, 1:139; Clarke, *Gold Rush Banker*, 193, 207.
60 Sherman, *Memoirs*, 1:139; Clarke, *Gold Rush Banker*, 208, 209, 212, 213.
61 Clarke, *Gold Rush Banker*, 212, 216; Sherman, *Memoirs*, 1:143, 144; EES to Maria Ewing, June 16, 1856, HHL.
62 EES to Maria Ewing, June 16, 1856, and Maria Ewing to EES, June 30, 1856, HHL.
63 EES to Maria Ewing, May 20 and June 16, 1856, HHL.
64 EES to Maria Ewing, August 15, 1856, HHL.
65 Clarke, *Gold Rush Banker*, 220–21.
66 WTS to JS, July 7 and August 19, 1856, OHC-WTSP; Clarke, *Gold Rush Banker*, 223, 396, 397.
67 WTS to JS, July 7 and August 3, 1856, OHC-WTSP.
68 Potter, *Impending Crisis*, 209–24; Tindall and Shi, *America*, 1:612–15.
69 WTS to JS, August 19, 1856, OHC-WTSP.

10. I WAS FIT FOR THE ARMY BUT NOTHING ELSE

1 WTS to JS, August 3 and 19, 1856, OHC-WTSP.
2 WTS to JS, March 20, 1856, OHC-WTSP.
3 William Tecumseh Sherman, *Memoirs of General W. T. Sherman*, 2 vols. (1885; repr., New York: Library of America, 1990), 1:150; WTS to JS, August 19, 1856, OHC-WTSP.
4 Dwight L. Clarke, *William Tecumseh Sherman: Gold Rush Banker* (San Francisco: California Historical Society, 1969), 234; Sherman, *Memoirs*, 1:150.
5 Sherman, *Memoirs*, 1:151; EES to Maria Ewing, December 14, 1856, HHL.
6 EES to Maria Ewing, July 31, 1856, HHL.
7 Clarke, *Gold Rush Banker*, 278–79.
8 EES to Maria Ewing, April 5, 1857, HHL; Clarke, *Gold Rush Banker*, 230, 276.
9 Clarke, *Gold Rush Banker*, 292, 333; WTS to HTS, March 4, 1857, OHC-WTSP.
10 EES to Maria Ewing, April 5, 1857, HHL.
11 Clarke, *Gold Rush Banker*, 230, 276, 302, 312.
12 Sherman, *Memoirs*, 1:153–54; Kenneth M. Stampp, *America in 1857: A Nation on the Brink* (New York: Oxford University Press, 1990), 221–22.
13 Sherman, *Memoirs*, 1:154–55.
14 WTS to HTS, October 13, 1857, OHC-WTSP; Stampp, *America in 1857*, 224; George Brown Tindall with David E. Shi, *America: A Narrative History*, 3rd ed. (New York: W. W. Norton, 1992), 1:621; Alan Brinkley, *American History: A Survey*, 10th ed. (New York: McGraw-Hill, 1999), 457–58; Irwin Unger, *These United States: The Questions of Our Past* (New York: Prentice Hall, 1999), 218; Thomas A. Bailey and David M. Kennedy, *The American Pageant: A History of the Republic*, 8th ed. (Lexington, Mass.: D.C. Heath, 1987), 400–401.
15 Tindall and Shi, *America*, 1:621; Stampp, *America in 1857*, 229–30; Bailey and Kennedy, *American Pageant*, 401.
16 Sherman, *Memoirs*, 1:155; Clarke, *Gold Rush Banker*, 327.
17 Sherman, *Memoirs*, 1:155–56; Clarke, *Gold Rush Banker*, 328–29.

18 WTS to EES, August 24 and September 18, 1857, in *HLOS*, 149–50, 151; WTS to EES, October 6, 1857, UND-SFP.

19 Clarke, *Gold Rush Banker*, 324, 334; Sherman, *Memoirs*, 1:156; WTS to HST, August 10, 1857, and WTS to HBE, November 26, 1857, OHC-WTSP.

20 WTS to HBE, June 25 and November 26, 1857, OHC-WTSP.

21 WTS to EES, July 29, 1857, in *HLOS*, 149; WTS to EES, October 23, 1857, and EES to WTS, November 30, 1857, UND-SFP.

22 WTS to JS, December 1857, in Thorndike, 64; Clarke, *Gold Rush Banker*, 333.

23 Clarke, *Gold Rush Banker*, 318, 333–35, 339, 348; Sherman, *Memoirs*, 1:157–58.

24 WTS to EES, July 29, 1857, in *HLOS*, 148–49; John F. Marszalek, *Sherman: A Soldier's Passion for Order* (New York: Free Press, 1993), 112–13.

25 Sherman, *Memoirs*, 1:158; Clarke, *Gold Rush Banker*, 338, 339.

26 Sherman, *Memoirs*, 1:158; Howe, *HLOS*, 153.

27 Sherman, *Memoirs*, 1:158–59; Basil H. Liddell Hart, *Sherman: Soldier, Realist, American* (New York: Praeger, 1929), 48.

28 Sherman, *Memoirs*, 1:159; WTS to EES, September 25, 1858, in *HLOS*, 156.

29 EES to WTS, October 13, 1858, UND-SFP.

30 Ibid.; WTS to EES, October 12, 1858, UND-SFP.

31 EES to Maria Ewing, November 13, 1858, HHL.

32 EES to Maria Ewing, December 29, 1858, HHL.

33 WTS to HBE, January 20, 1859, OHC-WTSP.

34 Maria Ewing to EES, March 18, 1859, HHL; WTS to EES, April 15, 1859, in *HLOS*, 158–59.

35 Sherman, *Memoirs*, 1:160; WTS to JS, April 30, 1859, in Thorndike, 68–69.

36 Robert Ergang, *Europe Since Waterloo* (Boston: D.C. Heath, 1954), 142, 155–56.

37 WTS to JS, and JS to WTS, June 19, 1859, in Thorndike, 71, 72–75.

38 Sherman, *Memoirs*, 1:160.

39 Ibid.

40 Walter L. Fleming, ed., *General W. T. Sherman as College President: A Collection of Letters, Documents and Other Material, Chiefly from Private Sources* (Cleveland: Arthur H. Clark Co., 1912), 13, 14, 25; Sherman, *Memoirs*, 1:162–66.

41 WTS to G. Mason Graham, February 8 and 21, 1860, in Fleming, *Sherman as College President*, 153, 180.

42 WTS to G. Mason Graham, February 8, 1860, in ibid., 153–54.

11. IN A HELL OF A FIX

1 WTS to G. Mason Graham, August 20 and September 7, 1859, and George B. McClellan to WTS, October 23, 1859, in Walter L. Fleming, ed., *General W. T. Sherman as College President: A Collection of Letters, Documents, and Other material, Chiefly from Private Sources* (Cleveland: Arthur H. Clark Co., 1912), 33–34, 37–38, 40–42; William Tecumseh Sherman, *Memoirs of General W. T. Sherman*, 2 vols. (1885; repr., New York: Library of America, 1990), 1:163.

2 WTS to EES, December 12, 1859, in Fleming, *Sherman as College President*, 75–76.

3 WTS to JS, September 1859, in Fleming, *Sherman as College President*, 39; WTS to JS, October 1859, in Thorndike, 77.

4 Sherman, *Memoirs*, 2:1095.

5 Dwight L. Clarke, *William Tecumseh Sherman: Gold Rush Banker* (San Francisco: California Historical Society, 1969), 353.

6 George Brown Tindall with David E. Shi, *America: A Narrative History*, 3rd ed. (New York: W. W. Norton, 1992), 1:625–26; David H. Donald, Jean Harvey Baker, and Michael F. Holt, *The Civil War and Reconstruction* (New York: W. W. Norton, 2001), 114.

7 David M. Potter, *The Impending Crisis: 1848 to 1861* (New York: Harper and Row, 1976), 371, 372.

8 Thomas A. Bailey and David M. Kennedy, *The American Pageant: A History of the Republic*, 8th ed. (Lexington, Mass.: D.C. Heath, 1987), 404; Potter, *Impending Crisis*, 376; Tindall and Shi, *America*, 1:626.

9 Potter, *Impending Crisis*, 379.

10 Tindall and Shi, *America*, 1:626–27.

11 WTS to EES, December 12 and 16, 1859, and WTS to Thomas Ewing Jr., December 23, 1859, in Fleming, *Sherman as College President*, 77, 85, 89.

12 Tindall and Shi, *America*, 1:627; Bailey and Kennedy, *American Pageant*, 393.

13 Ibid.

14 WTS to EES, December 12, 1859, in *HLOS*, 167–68.

15 Ibid., 168; George W. Cullum, *Biographical Register of the Officers and Cadets of the United States Military Academy at West Point, New York, from Its Establishment, March 16, 1802, to the Army Re-organization of 1866–67*, 2 vols. (New York: D. Van Nostrand, 1868), 1:592; WTS to Thomas Ewing Jr., December 23, 1859, in Fleming, *Sherman as College President*, 88.

16 WTS to Thomas Ewing Jr., December 23, 1859, in Fleming, *Sherman as College President*, 88–89.

17 WTS to EES, December 12, 1859, in Fleming, *Sherman as College President*, 77; Tindall and Shi, *America*, 1:627.

18 Sherman, *Memoirs*, 1:164; article written by G. Mason Graham, in Fleming, *Sherman as College President*, 21; WTS to EES, November 12, 1859, and January 12 and 24, 1860, and WTS to Thomas Ewing Jr., May 11, 1860, in Fleming, *Sherman as College President*, 48–51, 117, 127, 213.

19 WTS to EES, January 12 and 24, 1860, in Fleming, *Sherman as College President*, 117–18, 127.

20 WTS to G. Mason Graham, January 13, 1860, WTS to Thomas Ewing Sr., January 29, 1860, WTS to EES, February 3 and June 28, 1860, and WTS to Thomas Ewing Jr., January 21, 1860, in Fleming, *Sherman as College President*, 120, 131, 140–41, 222, 125.

21 Sherman, *Memoirs*, 1:166; WTS to EES, February 17, 1860, and WTS to Thomas Ewing Jr., February 17, 1860, in Fleming, *Sherman as College President*, 169–70, 173.

22 WTS to Thomas Ewing Jr., January 21, 1860, in Fleming, *Sherman as College President*, 125; WTS to EES, February 21, 1860, UND-SFP.

23 WTS to HBE, April 15, 1860, OHC-WTSP.

24 WTS to G. Mason Graham, March 21, 1860, and WTS to EES, March 30, 1860, in Fleming, *Sherman as College President*, 192, 194.

25 WTS to Thomas Ewing Jr., January 21, 1860, in Fleming, *Sherman as College President*, 124–25.

26 WTS to JS, February, 1860, in Thorndike, 80.

27   Tindall and Shi, *America*, 1:627–28.

28   WTS to JS, May 8 and June 1860, in Thorndike, 83–84.

29   WTS to EES, July 10, 1860, in *HLOS*, 178–79.

30   Sherman, *Memoirs*, 1:168, 169.

31   Ibid., 1:169–70.

32   Ibid., 1:170; WTS to EES, November 10 and 23, 1860, in Fleming, *Sherman as College President*, 304, 205; Lloyd Lewis, *Sherman: Fighting Prophet* (New York: Harcourt Brace, 1932), 138.

33   Tindall and Shi, *America*, 1:631–32; Sherman, *Memoirs*, 1:171; WTS to EES, December 15, 1860, in Fleming, *Sherman as College President*, 315; WTS to EES, January 27, 1861, in *HLOS*, 193.

34   WTS to Minnie Sherman, December 15, 1860, and WTS to EES, January 1 and 8, 1861, in Fleming, *Sherman as College President*, 313–14, 325, 332.

35   Sherman, *Memoirs*, 1:172.

36   Ibid., 1:172, 173; WTS to G. Mason Graham, January 16 and 20, 1861, and WTS to JS, January 16, 1861, in *SCW*, 37, 44, 40.

37   Sherman, *Memoirs*, 1:180–82; Sherman Diary, February 22, 1861, UND-SFP.

38   Sherman, *Memoirs*, 1:184–86.

39   Ibid., 1:185–86.

12. NO MAN CAN FORESEE THE END

1   Lincoln's address can be found in David S. Heidler and Jeanne T. Heidler, eds., *Encyclopedia of the Civil War: A Political, Social, and Military History*, 5 vols. (Santa Barbara, Calif.: ABC-CLIO, 2000), 5:2376–77.

2   William Tecumseh Sherman, *Memoirs of General W. T. Sherman*, 2 vols. (1885; repr., New York: Library of America, 1990), 1:184.

3   WTS to Thomas Ewing Jr., June 3, 1861, LC-TE; WTS to Thomas Ewing Sr., May 17, 1861, in Joseph H. Ewing, *Sherman at War* (Dayton, Ohio: Morningside House, 1992), 27.

4   WTS to PBE, July 13, 1862, in Ewing, *Sherman at War*, 59; WTS to Thomas Ewing Sr., January 8, 1861, LC-TE.

5   J. David Hacker, "A Census-Based Count of the Civil War Dead," *Civil War History* (December 2011), 307–48. For further discussion of Civil War losses, see James M. McPherson, *Battle Cry of Freedom: The Civil War Era* (New York: Oxford University Press, 1988), 347, 485, 619, 854.

6   Stephens quoted in McPherson, *Battle Cry of Freedom*, 244.

7   Timothy D. Johnson, *A Gallant Little Army: The Mexico City Campaign* (Lawrence: University Press of Kansas, 2007), is an excellent study of Scott's campaign; Sherman, *Memoirs*, 1:196.

8   WTS to JS, April 25 and June 8, 1861, in Thorndike, 115, 123; WTS to JS, May 20, 1861, LC-WTSP.

9   WTS to Thomas Ewing Sr., May 31, 1861, and WTS to Thomas Ewing Jr., June 3, 1861, LC-TE; WTS to JS, May 20, 1861, LC-WTSP.

10   WTS to JS, April 12 and 14, May 24, 1861, in Thorndike, 110, 112, 122–23; WTS to Tom Ewing Jr., June 3, 1861, in *HLOS*, 198.

11   For more discussion of the evolution of warfare during the Civil War, the reader may

consult standard textbooks on the conflict, especially David Herbert Donald, Jean Harvey Baker, and Michael F. Holt, *The Civil War and Reconstruction* (New York: W. W. Norton, 2001), and James M. McPherson, *Ordeal by Fire: The Civil War and Reconstruction* (New York: Oxford University Press, 1992). In addition, Grady McWhiney and Perry D. Jamieson, *Attack and Die: Civil War Military Tactics and the Southern Heritage* (Tuscaloosa: University of Alabama Press, 1982), is helpful. Relative to the impact of the rifled musket, see Paddy Griffith, *Battle Tactics of the Civil War* (New Haven: Yale University Press, 1989), and Earl J. Hess, *The Rifle Musket in Civil War Combat: Reality and Myth* (Lawrence: University of Kansas Press, 2008).

12 WTS to EES, December 18 and 23, 1860, and January 5 and 27, 1861, WTS to Minnie Sherman, December 15, 1860, WTS to G. Mason Graham, January 5, 1861, and WTS to HBE, December 18, 1860, and January 12, 1861, all in *SCW*, 14, 18, 20, 22, 25, 26, 30, 31, 36, 47.

13 WTS to JS, December 9 and 18, 1860, January 16, 1861, and WTS to EES, February 1, 1861, in *SCW*, 16, 24, 41, 50.

14 JS to WTS, January 6, April 12 and 14, 1861, in Thorndike, 92, 110, 112; WTS to JS, January 16 and February 1, 1861, WTS to Charles Ewing, February 3, 1861, WTS to Tom Ewing Jr., February 3, 1861, WTS to EES, February 1, 1861, and EES to WTS, January 29, 1861, all in *SCW*, 41, 48, 49, 51, 52, 53, 55, 56; EES to WTS, January 4, 1861, UND-SFP; Sherman, *Memoirs*, 1:184; Lee Kennett, *Sherman: A Soldier's Life* (New York: Perennial, 2002), 114.

15 WTS to EES, January 20, 1861, UND-SFP; WTS to Minnie Sherman, December 15, 1860, and July 14, 1861, OHC-WTSP; Sherman, *Memoirs*, 2:966.

16 WTS to David Boyd, April 4, 1861, UND-SFP; WTS to JS, April 25, 1861, in Thorndike, 115.

17 WTS to EES, December 18, 1860, WTS to JS, December 18 and 29, 1860, March 21, 1861, and WTS to Charles Ewing, February 3, 1861, all in *SCW*, 22, 23, 28, 63, 52.

18 WTS to Thomas Ewing Sr., May 17, 1861, and WTS to Tom Ewing Jr., May 23, 1861, in *SCW*, 85, 91; WTS to JS, n.d., in Thorndike, 109; Basil H. Liddell Hart, *Sherman: Soldier, Realist, American* (New York: Praeger, 1929), 72.

19 Sherman, *Memoirs*, 1:186; WTS to JS, April 8, 1861, LC-WTSP; WTS to David Boyd, May 13, 1861, UND-SFP.

20 Maria Ewing to EES, April 14, 1861, HHL; WTS to JS, April 8, 1861, and Tom Ewing Jr., to WTS, May 6, 1861, LC-WTSP; Sherman, *Memoirs*, 1:188; JS to WTS, April 14 and May 30, 1861, in Thorndike, 112, 117.

21 WTS to JS, February 1, 1861, and WTS to Gov. Thomas O. Moore, January 18, 1861, LC-WTSP.

22 WTS to Tom Ewing Jr., February 3, 1861, LC-TE; WTS to David Boyd, April 4, 1861, UND-SFP.

23 S. A. Smith to WTS, April 24, 1861, in Walter L. Fleming, ed., *General W. T. Sherman as College President: A Collection of Letters, Documents and Other Material, Chiefly from Private Sources* (Cleveland: Arthur H. Clark Co., 1912), 378; Ewing, *Sherman at War*, 26.

24 Donald, Baker, and Holt, *Civil War and Reconstruction*, 176; McPherson, *Battle Cry of Freedom*, 290–91; McPherson, *Ordeal by Fire*, 158–59.

25 Sherman, *Memoirs*, 1:186–87.

26 Wiley Britton, *The Civil War on the Border* (New York: G. P. Putnam's Sons, 1899), 7; Jay Monaghan, *Civil War on the Western Border, 1854–1865* (Boston: Little, Brown, 1955), 131; McPherson, *Battle Cry of Freedom*, 291; Donald, Baker, and Holt, *Civil War and Reconstruction*, 176.

27 McPherson, *Battle Cry of Freedom*, 291; Donald, Baker, and Holt, *Civil War and Reconstruction*, 176; Sherman, *Memoirs*, 1:191.

28 Sherman, *Memoirs*, 1:191–92; WTS to Tom Ewing Jr., May 11, 1861, LC-TE.

29 Sherman, *Memoirs*, 1:192.

30 Ibid., 1:192–93; WTS to JS, June 20, 1861, in Thorndike, 124.

13. ACTION AT BULL RUN

1 WTS to JS, July 19, 1861, LC-WTSP.

2 A valuable account of First Bull Run is William C. Davis, *Battle at Bull Run: A History of the First Major Campaign of the Civil War* (New York: Doubleday, 1977). See also Bruce Catton, *The Coming Fury* (New York: Pocket, 1967), 449, as well as Catton's *This Hallowed Ground* (New York: Pocket, 1961), 56, 57. Helpful too is Shelby Foote, *The Civil War: A Narrative*, 3 vols. (New York: Random House, 1958–1974), 1:71–74.

3 Joseph B. Mitchell, *Decisive Battles of the Civil War* (New York: Fawcett, 1955), 27; Foote, *The Civil War*, 1:57–58; Ernest B. Furgurson, "The End of Illusions," *Smithsonian*, July–August, 2011, 56, 58; Davis, *Bull Run*, 15, 26, 64, 66.

4 Allan Nevins, *The War for the Union*, 4 vols. (New York: Scribner, 1959–1971), 1:211; Doris Kearns Goodwin, *Team of Rivals: The Political Genius of Abraham Lincoln* (New York: Simon and Schuster, 2005), 370; Richard N. Current, *The Lincoln Nobody Knows* (New York: Macmillan, 1958), 136; Benjamin P. Thomas, *Abraham Lincoln: A Biography* (New York: Alfred A Knopf, 1952), 270.

5 Current, *Lincoln Nobody Knows*, 137; Davis, *Bull Run*, 72; Catton, *Coming Fury*, 442.

6 Current, *Lincoln Nobody Knows*, 139; WTS to EES, July 19, 1861, UND-SFP; WTS to JS, July 19, 1861, LC-WTSP.

7 James M. McPherson, *Battle Cry of Freedom: The Civil War Era* (New York: Oxford University Press, 1988), 335–36; Foote, *The Civil War*, 1:71.

8 Davis, *Bull Run*, 72; William Tecumseh Sherman, *Memoirs of General W. T. Sherman*, 2 vols. (1885; repr., New York: Library of America, 1990), 1:197.

9 Davis, *Bull Run*, 72; Goodwin, *Team of Rivals*, 370; Nevins, *War for the Union*, 1:214; Sherman, *Memoirs*, 1:196.

10 Mitchell, *Decisive Battles*, 30; Catton, *Coming Fury*, 445–50; Foote, *The Civil War*, 1:71, 74; Francis F. Wilshin, "Manassas (Bull Run)," National Park Service Historical Handbook Series, no. 15 (Washington, D.C., 1957), 5, 6.

11 Catton, *Coming Fury*, 450; Catton, *Hallowed Ground*, 58.

12 Sherman, *Memoirs*, 1:199; Davis, *Bull Run*, 155–56.

13 Davis, *Bull Run*, 156; Wilshin, "Manassas," 9.

14 Davis, *Bull Run*, 155–56; Catton, *Coming Fury*, 453; Foote, *The Civil War*, 1:75.

15 Mitchell, *Decisive Battles*, 32.

16 Davis, *Bull Run*, 159–60; Catton, *Coming Fury*, 455.

17 Davis, *Bull Run*, 167–68; Foote, *The Civil War*, 1:75; Catton, *Coming Fury*, 455.

18 Basil H. Liddell Hart, *Sherman: Soldier, Realist, American* (New York: Praeger, 1929), 87; Mitchell, *Decisive Battles*, 33; Furgurson, "End of Illusions," 61.

19 WTS to EES, July 28, 1861, UND-SFP.

20 Wilshin, "Manassas," 10; Davis, *Bull Run*, 166, 171.

21 Davis, *Bull Run*, 175–77, 185; WTS to EES, July 28, 1861, UND-SFP.

22 WTS to EES, July 28, 1861, UND-SFP; Sherman, *Memoirs*, 1:200; Davis, *Bull Run*, 186.

23 Davis, *Bull Run*, 186, 188; Mitchell, *Decisive Battles*, 36; Liddell Hart, *Sherman*, 87.

24 Davis, *Bull Run*, 187; Goodwin, *Team of Rivals*, 371–72.

25 Liddell Hart, *Sherman*, 88.

26 Ibid.; Davis, *Bull Run*, 217–18; WTS to EES, July 28, 1861, UND-SFP; Sherman, *Memoirs*, 1:203. Sherman's letter to Ellen overstates the number of men wounded; possibly he reversed the five and the zero.

27 Davis, *Bull Run*, 224–25. For recent scholarly assessment of issues associated with the battle, see: "Historians' Forum: The First Battle of Bull Run," *Civil War History* 57, no. 2 (June 2011): 106–20.

28 Sherman, *Memoirs*, 1:205.

29 Catton, *Coming Fury*, 464–66; Mitchell, *Decisive Battles*, 37–38.

30 WTS to EES, July 28, 1861, UND-SFP.

31 WTS to EES, July 24 and August 3, 1861, UND-SFP.

32 Sherman, *Memoirs*, 1:205; WTS to JS, August 19, 1861, LC-WTSP; WTS to EES, July 28, August 3 and 20–27, 1861, UND-SFP.

33 Current, *Lincoln Nobody Knows*, 139; WTS to EES, August 3, 1861, UND-SFP.

34 WTS to EES, August 17 and 19, 1861, UND-SFP; WTS to JS, August 19, 1861, LC-WTSP; Sherman, *Memoirs*, 1:206.

35 Sherman, *Memoirs*, 1:207.

36 Ibid., 1:207, 208.

37 Ibid., 1:206, 208.

38 WTS to EES, August 3, 1861, UND-SFP.

39 WTS to EES, July 28, August 3, 12, and 17, 1861, UND-SFP.

40 WTS to EES, January 8, August 17 and 20–27, 1861, UND-SFP; WTS to JS, December 29, 1860, and September 9, 1861, LC-WTSP.

41 WTS to EES, August 3, 1861, UND-SFP.

42 WTS to Thomas Ewing Sr., September 15, 1861, LC-TE; WTS to EES, August 20–27, 1861, UND-SFP; WTS to JS, August 19, 1861, LC-WTSP.

43 Sherman, *Memoirs*, 1:210, 211; WTS to EES, August 19, 1861, UND-SFP.

44 Sherman, *Memoirs*, 1:210, 211; WTS to EES, August 20–27, 1861, UND-SFP.

14. "CRAZY" IN KENTUCKY

1 WTS to Salmon P. Chase, October 14, 1861, WTS to JS, October 5, 1861, WTS to David Boyd, May 13, 1861, all in *SCW*, 149, 144, 84.

2 Roy P. Basler, ed., *The Collected Works of Abraham Lincoln*, 8 vols. (New Brunswick, N.J.: Rutgers University Press, 1953), 4:532; James A. Rawley, *Turning Points of the Civil War* (Lincoln: University of Nebraska Press, 1966), 11; James M. McPherson, *Battle Cry of Freedom: The Civil War Era* (New York: Oxford University Press, 1988),

284. The land area figures are taken from a 2001 Rand McNally atlas. My calculation of free-state territory did not include the states of California and Oregon, which were essentially isolated on the West Coast and played no meaningful role in the military aspects of the Civil War.

3 WTS to JS, December 9, 1860, LC-WTSP; Rand McNally atlas.

4 Rawley, *Turning Points*, 14.

5 Bruce Catton, *Terrible Swift Sword* (Boston: Little, Brown, 1963), 34; Lee Kennett, *Sherman: A Soldier's Life* (New York: Perennial, 2002), 129.

6 Robert Selph Henry, *The Story of the Confederacy* (New York: Bobbs-Merrill, 1931), 70, 71.

7 William Tecumseh Sherman, *Memoirs of General W. T. Sherman*, 2 vols. (1885; repr., New York: Library of America, 1990), 1:211–12; WTS to EES, September 18, 1861, UND-SFP.

8 WTS to EES, September 18, 1861, UND-SFP.

9 Sherman, *Memoirs*, 1:214; *SCW*, 150.

10 WTS to EES, September 18, 1861, UND-SFP; Steven E. Woodworth, *Jefferson Davis and His Generals: The Failure of Confederate Command in the West* (Lawrence: University Press of Kansas, 1990), 39–41.

11 James Lee McDonough, *War in Kentucky: From Shiloh to Perryville* (Knoxville: University of Tennessee Press, 1994), 63–65.

12 Sherman, *Memoirs*, 1:214–15; Basil H. Liddell Hart, *Sherman: Soldier, Realist, American* (New York: Praeger, 1929), 100.

13 Sherman, *Memoirs*, 1:216; WTS to Thomas Ewing Sr., September 30, 1861, in *SCW*, 141; WTS to EES, October 6, 1861, UND-SFP; Liddell Hart, *Sherman*, 100; James Lee McDonough, "Tennessee and the Civil War," *Tennessee Historical Quarterly* 54, no. 3 (Fall 1995): 196; Charles P. Roland, *An American Iliad: The Story of the Civil War* (New York: McGraw-Hill, 1991), 58; Allan Nevins, *The War for the Union*, 4 vols. (New York: Scribner, 1959–1971), 2:20.

14 WTS to EES, October 6 and 12, 1861, UND-SFP; WTS to Thomas Ewing Sr., September 30, 1861, in *SCW*, 142.

15 WTS to JS, October 5, 1861, LC-WTSP; WTS to EES, October 6, 1861, UND-SFP.

16 Sherman, *Memoirs*, 1:216; *OR*, 4:296.

17 WTS to Abraham Lincoln, October 10, 1861, WTS to JS, October 26, 1861, and WTS to William Dennison Jr., November 6, 1861, all in *SCW*, 146, 153, 156.

18 John E. Kleber, ed., *The Kentucky Encyclopedia* (Lexington: University of Kentucky Press, 1992), 253; WTS to JS, November 21, 1861, LC-WTSP.

19 McDonough, "Tennessee and the Civil War," 196; Catton, *Terrible Swift Sword*, 59.

20 WTS to EES, October 12, 1861, UND-SFP; WTS to Salmon P. Chase, October 14, 1861, in *SCW*, 147, 149; Catton, *Terrible Swift Sword*, 59.

21 Sherman, *Memoirs*, 1:218.

22 Ibid., 1:218–19, 229.

23 Ibid., 1:219–20, 222, 231–32; *SCW*, 113, 148; WTS to Lorenzo Thomas, November 4, 1861, in *OR*, 4:333.

24 Sherman, *Memoirs*, 1:220–22, 229–32.

25 *New York Tribune*, October 30, 1861; Lloyd Lewis, *Sherman: Fighting Prophet* (New York: Harcourt Brace, 1932), 195.

26 WTS to Lorenzo Thomas, November 4 and 6, 1861, in *OR*, 4:333, 341.

27 Lewis, *Sherman*, 197; Kennett, *Sherman*, 139; Michael Fellman, *Citizen Sherman: A Life of William Tecumseh Sherman* (New York: Random House, 1995), 95; John Marszalek, *Sherman's Other War: The General and the Civil War Press* (Memphis: Memphis State University Press, 1981), 60–63;. WTS to William Dennison Jr., November 6, 1861, in *SCW*, 156–57.

28 EES to WTS, October 10, 1861, and WTS to EES, October 12, 1861, in *SCW*, 147, 148; WTS to JS, November 21, 1861, LC-WTSP.

29 WTS to JS, November 21, 1861, LC-WTSP.

30 WTS to JS, January 8, 1862, LC-WTSP.

31 Kennett, *Sherman*, 141; Fellman, *Citizen Sherman*, 97; John F. Marszalek, *Sherman: A Soldier's Passion for Order* (New York: Free Press, 1993), 167.

32 EES to JS, November 10, 1861, LC-WTSP; JS to WTS, November 17, 1861, UND-SFP; WTS to JS, November 21, 1861, LC-WTSP.

33 WTS to Thomas Ewing Sr., December 12, 1861, LC-WTSP; Liddell Hart, *Sherman*, 110, 111.

34 Liddell Hart, *Sherman*, 111; Lewis, *Sherman*, 200.

35 *Cincinnati Commercial*, December 11, 1861.

36 WTS to Thomas Ewing Sr., December 12, 1861, LC-WTSP; Lewis, *Sherman*, 203.

37 WTS to Henry Halleck, December 12, 1861, in *SCW*, 165; WTS to EES, January 1, 1862, UND-SFP; WTS to JS, January 4, 8, 9, 1862, LC-WTSP; WTS to Thomas Ewing Sr., December 24, 1861, LC-TE. Also see Simpson's and Berlin's introduction to chapter 4 of *SCW* (p. 166); JS to EES, December 14, 1861, UND-SFP; Stanley P. Hirshson, *The White Tecumseh: A Biography of General William T. Sherman* (New York: John Wiley & Sons, 1997), 103–6.

38 For various views of Sherman's mental state in the fall of 1861, see Fellman, *Citizen Sherman*, 99; Kennett, *Sherman*, 145–48; Lewis, *Sherman*, 201–7; Marszalek, *Sherman*, 164–69.

39 WTS to EES, January 1, 1862, UND-SFP.

40 WTS to EES, January 29, 1862, UND-SFP; WTS to JS, January 8, 1862, LC-WTSP.

41 WTS to JS, January 8, 1862, LC-WTSP.

42 Many sources attest to Sherman's health problems. Several letters of the General and Ellen inspired this paragraph on that topic. In addition to earlier discussion, see EES to JS, November 10, 1861, LC-WTSP; WTS to EES, October 12, 1861, and January 29, 1862, UND-SFP; WTS to JS, January 8, 1862, LC-WTSP.

43 WTS to JS, January 8, 1862, LC-WTSP.

44 Lewis, *Sherman*, 203–4.

45 WTS to JS, February 3, 1862, in Thorndike, 139; Sherman, *Memoirs*, 1:236; WTS to JS, December 24, 1861, LC-WTSP; WTS to EES, January 11, 1862, UND-SFP.

46 Lewis, *Sherman*, 207, 209–10; Fellman, *Citizen Sherman*, 102; Kennett, *Sherman*, 154; Marszalek, *Sherman*, 168; EES to WTS, January 8, 1862, and WTS to EES, January 11, 1862, UND-SFP.

47 Lewis, *Sherman*, 205–6. The description of Ellen's actions on behalf of her husband is in *SCW*, 188.

48 Lewis, *Sherman*, 205–9; EES to WTS, January 29, 1862, UND-SFP.

15. TRIUMPHANT IN TENNESSEE

1   William Tecumseh Sherman, *Memoirs of General W. T. Sherman*, 2 vols. (1885; repr., New York: Library of America, 1990), 1:238.

2   Ibid.

3   David S. Heidler and Jeanne T. Heidler, eds., *Encyclopedia of the American Civil War: A Political, Social, and Military History*. 5 vols. (Santa Barbara, Calif.: ABC-CLIO, 2000), 2:713, 863–72, and 4:1807–8.

4   *OR*, 7:73–74; U. S. Grant, *Personal Memoirs*, 2 vols. (New York: Charles L. Webster & Co., 1885), 1:286–87.

5   Grant, *Personal Memoirs*, 1:287.

6   *OR*, 8:509.

7   Ibid., 7:526, and 8:482, 503.

8   Ibid., 8:406, 411, 431, 475–76.

9   Ibid., 7:121, and 5:41.

10 Ibid., 7:571, 121.

11 Benjamin Franklin Cooling, *Forts Henry and Donelson: The Key to the Confederate Heartland* (Knoxville: University of Tennessee Press, 1987), 101–21, is the most detailed and scholarly history of the campaign.

12 Ibid., 103–6.

13 Stanley F. Horn, *The Army of Tennessee: A Military History* (New York: Bobbs-Merrill, 1941), 83. Grant's letter to his wife is quoted in Herman Hattaway and Archer Jones, *How the North Won: A Military History of the Civil War* (Chicago: University of Illinois Press, 1983), 156; see also 202n.

14 James Lee McDonough, "Tennessee and the Civil War," *Tennessee Historical Quarterly* 54, no. 3 (Fall 1995): 197–98; Charles P. Roland, *An American Iliad: The Story of the Civil War* (New York: McGraw-Hill, 1991), 58.

15 Cooling, *Forts Henry and Donelson*, 245; Robert Selph Henry, *The Story of the Confederacy* (New York: Bobbs-Merrill, 1931), 81; Basil H. Liddell Hart, *Sherman: Soldier, Realist, American* (New York: Praeger, 1929), 115; Benjamin Franklin Cooling, *To the Battles of Franklin and Nashville and Beyond* (Knoxville: University of Tennessee Press, 2011), 9. For detailed discussion of the 1862 Kentucky campaign, see James Lee McDonough, *War in Kentucky: From Shiloh to Perryville* (Knoxville: University of Tennessee Press, Tenn., 1994).

16 Sherman, *Memoirs*, 1:239; Liddell Hart, *Sherman*, 118; *OR*, 7:629; JS to WTS, February 15, 1862, in Thorndike, 140.

17 WTS to EES, February 17, 1862, WTS to JS, February 23, 1862, and WTS to Charley Ewing, February 27, 1862, all in *SCW*, 191, 193, 194.

18 Grant, *Personal Memoirs*, 1:315.

19 *OR*, 10 (pt. 2):28–29; Sherman, *Memoirs*, 1:245.

20 Bruce Catton, *Grant Moves South* (Boston: Little, Brown, 1960), 193; Grant, *Memoirs*, 1:325; Sherman, *Memoirs*, 1:245.

21 *OR*, 7:679–80, 682.

22 Larry J. Daniel, *Shiloh: The Battle That Changed the Civil War* (New York: Simon and Schuster, 1997), 75 and 336n51, gives a good summation of the number of transports carrying the Federal troops up the Tennessee. See also Stacy D. Allen, "Shiloh! The

Campaign and First Day's Battle," *Blue & Gray Magazine* (Winter 1997), 12; Edward Cunningham, *Shiloh and the Western Campaign of 1862*, eds. Gary D. Joiner and Timothy B. Smith (New York: Savas Beatie, 2007), 77, 78.

23   *OR*, 7:674, and 10 (pt. 1):22, and (pt. 2):6, 22; Sherman, *Memoirs*, 1:246–47; Allen, "Shiloh! First Day's Battle," 12.

24   Sherman, *Memoirs*, 1:247.

25   Ibid., 1:247–48; *OR*, 10 (pt. 1): 22–23, and (pt. 2): 34–36, 42, 43, 45; Allen, "Shiloh! First Day's Battle," 13.

26   James Lee McDonough, *Shiloh—In Hell before Night* (Knoxville: University of Tennessee Press, 1977), 44–45.

27   Sherman, *Memoirs*, 1:248.

28   *OR*, 10 (pt. 1):27; Timothy B. Smith, *Rethinking Shiloh: Myth and Memory* (Knoxville: University of Tennessee Press, 2013), 2.

29   *OR*, 10 (pt. 1):26–27, contains both of Sherman's communications dated March 17, 1862. See also Liddell Hart, *Sherman*, 121.

30   McDonough, *Shiloh*, 38–40.

31   Catton, *Grant Moves South*, 212–13; McDonough, *Shiloh*, 22.

32   Catton, *Grant Moves South*, 213; Lloyd Lewis, *Sherman: Fighting Prophet* (New York: Harcourt Brace, 1932), 213.

33   Allen, "Shiloh! First Day's Battle," 16; McDonough, *Shiloh*, 52.

34   Allen, "Shiloh! First Day's Battle," 18; McDonough, *Shiloh*, 52; *OR*, 10 (pt. 2):50.

35   WTS to EES, April 3, 1862, UND-SFP; WTS to Thomas Ewing Sr., April 4, 1862, in *SCW*, 198–200.

36   *OR*, 10 (pt. 2):91.

37   *OR*, 10 (pt. 2):93, 94, and (pt. 1): 89.

38   McDonough, *Shiloh*, 86–90.

39   WTS to EES, April 11, 1862, UND-SFP. For full coverage and analysis of the campaign and battle of Shiloh, see Allen, "Shiloh! First Day's Battle"; Stacy D. Allen, "Shiloh—The Second Day!" *Blue & Gray Magazine* (Spring 1998); Cunningham, *Shiloh*; Daniel, *Shiloh*; McDonough, *Shiloh*; Timothy B. Smith, *The Untold Story of Shiloh: The Battle and the Battlefield* (Knoxville: University of Tennessee Press, 2006); and Wiley Sword, *Shiloh: Bloody April* (New York: William Morrow, 1974).

40   *OR*, 10 (pt. 1):640.

41   Ibid.

42   Robert Selph Henry, *"First with the Most" Forrest* (New York: Bobbs-Merrill, 1944), 80–81; Robert Selph Henry, ed., *As They Saw Forrest* (Jackson, Tenn.: McCowat-Mercer Press, 1956), 39, 40; Stanley P. Hirshson, *The White Tecumseh: A Biography of General William T. Sherman* (New York: John Wiley & Sons, 1997), 123.

43   *OR*, 10 (pt. 1):113–14, 641; Allen, "The Second Day!" 47.

44   Thomas L. Livermore, *Numbers and Losses in the Civil War in America, 1861–1865* (Boston: Houghton Mifflin, 1900), 77–80; Lewis, *Sherman*, 232.

45   WTS to EES, April 14, 1862, UND-SFP; *OR*, 10 (pt. 1):644–46.

46   WTS to EES, April 14, 1862, UND-SFP.

47   Ibid.; EES to WTS, April 9, 1862, UND-SFP.

48   WTS to EES, April 14, 1862, UND-SFP.

49   WTS to William T. Sherman Jr., April 19, 1862, in *SCW*, 205–6.

50 Maria Ewing to EES, December 9, 1862, HHL.

51 *Cincinnati Gazette*, April 14, 1862; WTS to Thomas Ewing Sr., April 27 and May 3, 1862, in *SCW*, 212, 213.

52 *OR*, 10 (pt. 1):665; WTS to Thomas Ewing Sr., April 27, 1862, in *SCW*, 212; Allen, "The Second Day!" 49.

16. THIS IS NO COMMON WAR

1 Bruce Catton, *This Hallowed Ground* (New York: Pocket, 1961), 147; James Lee McDonough, *War in Kentucky: From Shiloh to Perryville* (Knoxville: University of Tennessee Press, 1994), 17, 18, 20.

2 Robert Selph Henry, *The Story of the Confederacy* (New York: Bobbs-Merrill, 1931), 130–31; Stacy D. Allen, "Shiloh—The Second Day!" *Blue & Gray Magazine* (Spring 1998), 55.

3 William Tecumseh Sherman, *Memoirs of General W. T. Sherman*, 2 vols. (1885; repr., New York: Library of America, 1990), 1:270–71.

4 Ibid., 1:275–76.

5 *OR*, 10 (pt. 1):665, 666.

6 Sherman, *Memoirs*, 1:272; James M. Merrill, *William Tecumseh Sherman* (New York: Rand McNally, 1971), 204; WTS to EES, May 26, 1862, UND-SFP.

7 WTS to EES, June 6, 1862, UND-SFP.

8 WTS to EES, May 26, 1862, UND-SFP.

9 Henry, *Story of the Confederacy*, 131; Sherman, *Memoirs*, 1:273; WTS to JS, May 31, 1862, LC-WTSP.

10 Henry, *Story of the Confederacy*, 131.

11 James M. McPherson, *Ordeal by Fire: The Civil War and Reconstruction* (New York: Oxford University Press, 1992), 231, called Farragut "the most remarkable naval commander of the war."

12 Sherman, *Memoirs*, 1:274, 275, 278.

13 WTS to JS, May 31, 1862, in Thorndike, 155; WTS to EES, June 10, 1862, UND-SFP; *OR*, 17 (pt. 2):100; Lloyd Lewis, *Sherman: Fighting Prophet* (New York: Harcourt Brace, 1932), 306.

14 For a discussion of Halleck's inauguration of the Chattanooga campaign, see McDonough, *War in Kentucky*, 37–42.

15 Sherman, *Memoirs*, 1:275, 278.

16 WTS to EES, June 27, 1862, UND-SFP; Sherman, *Memoirs*, 1:277.

17 WTS to B. Stanton, June 10, 1862, UND-SFP.

18 WTS to EES, June 10, 1862, and WTS to B. Stanton, June 10, 1862, UND-SFP.

19 WTS to S. S. L'Hommedieu, Esq., July 7, 1862, in *SCW*, 246–48.

20 EES to WTS, June 1, 1862, and WTS to EES, June 6 and 10, 1862, UND-SFP.

21 EES to WTS, June 20, 1862, UND-SFP; Merrill, *Sherman*, 202; WTS to PBE, July 14, 1862, in *SCW*, 230, 254.

22 For McClellan on Halleck, see James M. McPherson, *Battle Cry of Freedom: The Civil War Era* (New York: Oxford University Press, 1988), 525; WTS to General Halleck, July 16, 1862, and WTS to JS, August 13, 1862, in *SCW*, 255, 256, 273; Lewis, *Sherman*, 242.

23   WTS to Thomas Ewing Sr., June 7, 1862, WTS to PBE, July 13, 1862, and WTS to JS, August 13, 1862, all in *SCW*, 239, 253, 273; Merrill, *Sherman*, 204.

24   Sherman, *Memoirs*, 1:285.

25   Ibid.; WTS to EES, August 20, 1862, UND-SFP; Lewis, *Sherman*, 244.

26   *OR*, 17 (pt. 2):127.

27   Lewis, *Sherman*, 243–44; WTS to EES, December 14, 1862, UND-SFP.

28   WTS to EES, October 4, 1862, UND-SFP: WTS to Minnie Sherman, October 4, 1862, OHC-WTSP.

29   WTS to EES, August 10, September 22, December 14, 1862, UND-SFP.

30   *OR*, 3 (pt. 2):349, 402, and 17 (pt. 2):178; WTS to EES, August 20, 1862, UND-SFP.

31   *OR*, 17 (pt. 1):23. Back in 1861, General Halleck had assessed leading secessionists in Missouri thousands of dollars to compensate for destruction perpetrated by guerrillas: see Noel C. Fisher, "'Prepare Them for My Coming': General William T. Sherman, Total War, and Pacification in West Tennessee," *Tennessee Historical Quarterly* 51, no. 2 (Summer 1992): 80.

32   WTS to Thomas C. Hindman, October 17, 1862, and WTS to Mrs. Valeria Hurlbut, November 6, 1862, in *SCW*, 317, 321; *OR*, 17 (pt. 1):145; Lewis, *Sherman*, 252.

33   *OR*, 17 (pt. 1):144–45, and (pt. 2):235–36, 240, 261.

34   Ibid., 17 (pt. 2):280–81, 285; WTS to Edwin M. Stanton, December 16, 1862, in *SCW*, 347.

35   WTS to Miss P. A. Fraser, October 22, 1862, in *SCW*, 318.

36   WTS to JS, October 1, 1862, in Thorndike, 165; *OR*, 17 (pt. 2): 261; EES to WTS, August 30, 1862, UND-SFP.

37   WTS to "New York Gentlemen," September 17, 1862, in *SCW*, 296–97; Maria Ewing to EES, December 9, 1862, HHL.

38   Benjamin Franklin Cooling, *To the Battles of Franklin and Nashville and Beyond* (Knoxville: University of Tennessee Press, 2011), provides a recent, scholarly appraisal of partisan war in Tennessee and Kentucky.

39   WTS to Minnie Sherman, August 6, 1862, OHC-WTSP; WTS to John C. Pemberton, November 18, 1862, in *OR*, 17 (pt. 2):872–73.

40   David S. Heidler and Jeanne T. Heidler, eds., *Encyclopedia of the American Civil War: A Political, Social, and Military History*. 5 vols. (Santa Barbara, Calif.: ABC-CLIO, 2000), 1:477–79; *OR*, 17 (pt. 2):113, 158–60; Sherman, *Memoirs*, 1:285.

41   *OR*, 17 (pt. 2):113, 140, 158–59, 179, 201, 216.

42   WTS to JS, September 3 and October 1, 1862, LC-WTSP.

43   WTS to JS, September 22 and October 1, 1862, and WTS to Thomas Tasker Gantt, September 23, 1862, in *SCW*, 301, 311, 303.

44   Sherman, *Memoirs*, 1:285–86; *OR*, 3 (pt. 2):402, and 17 (pt. 2):140–41, 178–79.

45   WTS to EES, August 5, 1862, UND-SFP; WTS to EES, August 20, 1862, and WTS to W. H. H. Taylor, August 25, 1862, in *SCW*, 281–83, 287–88.

46   *OR*, 17 (pt. 2):150, 163, 186; WTS to EES, October 4, 1862, UND-SFP.

47   *OR*, 17 (pt. 2):150, 163, 170–71, 186; WTS to Lorenzo Thomas, August 11, 1862, in *OR*, 3 (pt. 2):350; WTS to JS, August 13, 1862, in *SCW*, 271, 272.

48   *OR*, 17 (pt. 2):117, 118, 128, 169, 187; WTS to PBE, November 2, 1862, in *SCW*, 319; Sherman, *Memoirs*, 1:307.

49   Lewis, *Sherman*, 251; WTS to Charles Ewing, July 8, 1862, in *SCW*, 248–49.

50   EES to WTS, April 13, 18, 26, 29, May 9, August 17, 1862, UND-SFP; WTS to Thomas Ewing Sr., June 7, 1862, and WTS to Charles Ewing, July 8, 1862, in *SCW*, 238–39, 248–50.

51   EES to WTS, August 1 and 17, 1862, and WTS to EES, September 25, October 1, December 14, 1862, UND-SFP; WTS to JS, August 26 and December 14, 1862, LC-WTSP.

52   WTS to PBE, July 13, 1862, WTS to EES, August 10, 1862, WTS to JS, August 13 and September 3, 1862, WTS to the Sherman children, December 8, 1862, and EES to JS, December 11, 1862, all in *SCW*, 251, 267, 273–74, 294, 340, 344; EES to Thomas Ewing Sr., November 5, 1862, UND-SFP. On the Gayoso House, see *The Tennessee Encyclopedia of History and Culture*, ed. Carroll Van West (Nashville: Tennessee Historical Society, 1998), 353.

53   WTS to EES, December 14, 1862, UND-SFP; WTS to JS, December 20, 1862, LC-WTSP; *Sherman, Memoirs*, 1:283–84; *OR*, 17 (pt. 2):273, 351–52, 856–57.

17. THE STRONGEST PLACE I EVER SAW

1   *OR*, 16 (pt. 2):14, 16, 63.

2   John Keegan, *The American Civil War: A Military History* (New York: Alfred A. Knopf, 2009), 207; James M. McPherson, *Battle Cry of Freedom: The Civil War Era* (New York: Oxford University Press, 1988), 421–22.

3   Kenneth P. Williams, *Lincoln Finds a General: A Military Study of the Civil War*, 5 vols. (New York: Macmillan, 1952), 4:26; James M. McPherson, *Ordeal by Fire: The Civil War and Reconstruction* (New York: Oxford University Press, 1992), 233–34, 254.

4   Bruce Catton, *This Hallowed Ground* (New York: Pocket, 1961), 259; Thomas L. Connelly, "Vicksburg: Strategic Point or Propaganda Device?" *Military Affairs* 34, no. 2 (April 1970): 49–53.

5   Lloyd Lewis, *Sherman: Fighting Prophet* (New York: Harcourt Brace, 1932), 254–55.

6   *OR*, 17 (pt. 2):244–45, 262, 285; Lewis, *Sherman*, 256.

7   *OR*, 17 (pt. 1):466–69.

8   Ibid., 17 (pt. 1):466–69, and (pt. 2):347.

9   William Tecumseh Sherman, *Memoirs of General W. T. Sherman*, 2 vols. (1885; repr., New York: Library of America, 1990), 1:302; *OR*, 17 (pt. 1):471.

10   Sherman, *Memoirs*, 1:304; *OR*, 17 (pt. 1):471, 472, 473.

11   Sherman, *Memoirs*, 1:304–8; *OR*, 17 (pt. 1):472–74.

12   James W. Denver to "My Dear Wife," November 29, 1862, James W. Denver Papers, Harrisburg Civil War Roundtable Collection, U.S. Army Military History Institute, Carlisle, Pennsylvania, cited in Steven E. Woodworth, *Sherman* (New York: Palgrave Macmillan, 2009), 62, 185.

13   WTS to JS, December 20, 1862, LC-WTSP; EES to WTS, December 23, 1862, UND-SFP.

14   *OR*, 17 (pt. 1):601; WTS to JS, December 14, 1862, LC-WTSP; David S. Heidler and Jeanne T. Heidler, eds., *Encyclopedia of the American Civil War: A Political, Social, and Military History*, 5 vols. (Santa Barbara, Calif.: ABC-CLIO, 2000), 3:1552.

15   WTS to JS, December 14, 1862, LC-WTSP; *OR*, 17 (pt. 1):605.

16   William Tecumseh Sherman, *Memoirs of General W. T. Sherman*, 2 vols. (1885; repr., New York: Library of America, 1990), 1:308, 312; Steven E. Woodworth, *Nothing But*

Victory: The Army of Tennessee, 1861–1865 (New York: Alfred A. Knopf, 2005), 262, 263; Michael B. Ballard, *Vicksburg: The Campaign That Opened the Mississippi* (Chapel Hill: University of North Carolina Press, 2004), 131.

17   U. S. Grant, *Personal Memoirs*, 2 vols. (New York: Charles L. Webster & Co.), 1:430–31; *OR*, 17 (pt. 1):474, 475.

18   Lewis, *Sherman*, 257–58; Williams, *Lincoln Finds a General*, 4:218, 219, 301, 524.

19   *OR*, 17 (pt. 1): 604, 605; Heidler and Heidler, *Encyclopedia of the American Civil War*, 1:431.

20   Sherman, *Memoirs*, 1:312; Williams, *Lincoln Finds a General*, 4:209.

21   Sherman, *Memoirs*, 1:312–13; WTS to JS, January 6, 1863, LC-WTSP.

22   *OR*, 17 (pt. 1):605; WTS to David Porter, December 28, 1862, HHL; William L. Shea and Terrence J. Winschel, *Vicksburg Is the Key: The Struggle for the Mississippi River* (Lincoln: University of Nebraska Press, 2003), 48; Sherman, *Memoirs*, 1:312–13, 318–19; WTS to EES, January 4, 1863, UND-SFP; Williams, *Lincoln Finds a General*, 4:544.

23   *OR*, 17 (pt. 1):606, 652; Sherman, *Memoirs*, 1:314; Shea and Winschel, *Vicksburg Is the Key*, 52.

24   *OR*, 17 (pt. 1):606–7; Sherman, *Memoirs*, 1:314–15.

25   Sherman, *Memoirs*, 1:315, 318; WTS to EES, January 4, 1863, UND-SFP; Clarence C. Buel and Robert U. Johnson, eds., *Battles and Leaders of the Civil War*, 4 vols. (1888; repr., New York: Castle Books, 1956), 3:468, 471. After Sherman's memoirs were published, George W. Morgan, in an article written for *Century Magazine* and later published in *Battles and Leaders*, claimed that Sherman had said before the assault that "we will lose 5000 men before we take Vicksburg, and may as well lose them here as anywhere else" (3:467).

26   Sherman, *Memoirs*, 1:316; *OR*, 17 (pt. 1):609, 610; WTS to EES, January 4, 1863, UND-SFP.

27   WTS to EES, January 4, 1863, UND-SFP; WTS to JS, January 6, 1863, LC-WTSP; Keegan, *The American Civil War*, 211.

28   Maria Ewing to EES, January 22, 1863, HHL.

29   WTS to JS, January 17, 1863, LC-WTSP.

30   Ibid.; WTS to EES, January 4 and 24, 1863, and EES to WTS, January 14, 1863, UND-SFP.

31   *OR*, 17 (pt. 2):528; Sherman, *Memoirs*, 1:316–19.

32   Sherman, *Memoirs*, 1:318–20.

33   Ibid.; Williams, *Lincoln Finds a General*, 4:292; *Navy-OR*, 23:602.

34   *OR*, 17 (pt. 1):755–56; Sherman, *Memoirs*, 1:320–21.

35   *OR*, 17 (pt. 1):719, 756, 784–85; Sherman, *Memoirs*, 1:321–23, 325.

36   *OR*, 17 (pt. 1):785; Sherman, *Memoirs*, 1:324.

37   WTS to EES, January 12, 16, 24, 1863, UND-SFP.

38   Sherman, *Memoirs*, 1:324–25; WTS to JS, January 17, 1863, LC-WTSP; WTS to EES, January 16, 1863, UND-SFP.

39   *OR*, 17 (pt. 1):700–710; Woodworth, *Nothing but Victory*, 280.

40   WTS to E. A. Hitchcock, January 25, 1863, in *SCW*, 369; WTS to JS, January 17 and 25, 1863, LC-WTSP; WTS to EES, January 12 and 24, 1863, UND-SFP; Sherman, *Memoirs*, 1:319–20.

41   *OR*, 17 (pt. 1):701, 603.

42 *OR*, 17 (pt. 2):553–54, 570–71, 586, 883; WTS to EES, January 4 and 12, 1863, UND-SFP.
43 WTS to Thomas Ewing Sr., January 16, 1863, in *SCW*, 354; WTS to JS, January 17, 1863, LC-WTSP; WTS to EES, January 16 and 28, February 6, 1863, UND-SFP.

18. THE RIVER OF OUR GREATNESS IS FREE

1   *OR*, 24 (pt. 1):11.
2   Ibid., 24 (pt. 1):9, 11.
3   Ibid., 24 (pt. 1):12, 13, 14.
4   Ibid., 17 (pt. 2):555.
5   WTS to EES, February 6, 1863, UND-SFP.
6   *OR*, 17 (pt. 2):572; WTS to Ethan A. Hitchcock, January 25, 1863, in *SCW*, 367.
7   *Chicago Tribune*, January 15, 1863, *New York Times*, January 19, 1863, and *Cincinnati Gazette*, January 31, 1863, all cited in John F. Marszalek, *Sherman's Other War: The General and the Civil War Press* (Memphis: Memphis State University Press, 1981), 120–22.
8   WTS to Thomas Ewing Sr., February 17, 1863, in *SCW*, 398.
9   Anna McAllister, *Ellen Ewing: Wife of General Sherman* (New York: Benziger Brothers, 1936), 246; Lloyd Lewis, *Sherman: Fighting Prophet* (New York: Harcourt Brace, 1932), 262.
10 JS to WTS, February 26, 1863, and WTS to JS, March 14, 1863, in *SCW*, 419, 421; EES to WTS, February 8, 11, 14, 1863, UND-SFP; McAllister, *Ellen Ewing*, 245–47.
11 WTS to Thomas Ewing Sr., April 27, 1862, in *SCW*, 212.
12 For information about the most important newspapers, see Marszalek, *Sherman's Other War*, 36–39.
13 WTS to Thomas Ewing Sr., January 16, 1863, in *SCW*, 355–56.
14 Ibid., 356; Stanley P. Hirshson, *The White Tecumseh: A Biography of General William T. Sherman* (New York: John Wiley & Sons, 1997), 131–32; Lee Kennett, *Sherman: A Soldier's Life* (New York: Perennial, 2002), 169–70.
15 *OR*, 17 (pt. 2):889; James M. McPherson, *Ordeal by Fire: The Civil War and Reconstruction* (New York: Oxford University Press, 1992), 294; Mark E. Neely Jr., *The Fate of Liberty: Abraham Lincoln and Civil Liberties* (New York: Oxford University Press, 1991), 35; Marszalek, *Sherman's Other War*, 129.
16 *OR*, 17 (pt. 2):580–81; *New York Herald*, January 18, 1863.
17 Ibid., 17 (pt. 2):890–91.
18 Ibid., 17 (pt. 2):894; Marszalek, *Sherman's Other War*, 142–43.
19 Ibid., 17 (pt. 2):894.
20 Ibid., 17 (pt. 2):895.
21 Marszalek, *Sherman's Other War*, 144–45.
22 EES to WTS, April 9, 1863, UND-SFP.
23 *OR*, 17 (pt. 2):895–97.
24 WTS to E. O. C. Ord, February 22, 1863, in *SCW*, 406.
25 Ibid.; WTS to JS, February 12, 1863, in *SCW*, 397.
26 WTS to JS, March 14, 1863, and WTS to E. O. C. Ord, February 22, 1863, in *SCW*, 420, 406; WTS to EES, February 22 and 26, 1863, UND-SFP.
27 McAllister, *Ellen Ewing*, 243; WTS to EES, February 22, 1863, UND-SFP.

28 WTS to EES, February 22, 1863, UND-SFP.

29 WTS to Benjamin H. Grierson, February 9, 1863, in *SCW*, 396.

30 WTS to JS, February 12, 1863, in *SCW*, 397.

31 Bruce Catton, *This Hallowed Ground* (New York: Pocket, 1861), 263.

32 *Navy-OR*, 24:474; William Tecumseh Sherman, *Memoirs of General W. T. Sherman*, 2 vols. (1885; repr., New York: Library of America, 1990), 1:329; WTS to EES, January 24, 1863, UND-SFP.

33 David D. Porter, *The Naval History of the Civil War* (Mineola, N.Y.: Dover, 1998), 303; *Navy-OR*, 24:474.

34 David D. Porter, *Incidents and Anecdotes of the Civil War* (New York: D. Appleton and Co., 1885), 145; *Navy-OR*, 24:474; Porter, *Naval History*, 304. Both dates and times differ somewhat in the various accounts of the expedition. I have accepted the dates given by an officer aboard the *Cincinnati*, who kept a daily journal published in *Navy-OR*, believing that his continual daily entries are more likely to be accurate about the date of events than someone, even Sherman or Porter, who later summarized the expedition.

35 *Navy-OR*, 24:474–75, 493; Porter, *Naval History*, 304.

36 Porter, *Incidents*, 145, 157; *Navy-OR*, 24:475, 493.

37 *Navy-OR*, 24:475; Porter, *Incidents*, 149–50.

38 Porter, *Naval History*, 305; *Navy-OR*, 24:494.

39 *Navy-OR*, 24:476–77; Porter, *Incidents*, 160–64; Porter, *Naval History*, 305.

40 Porter, *Incidents*, 162.

41 Ibid., 161; *OR*, 24 (pt. 1):436–37; Sherman, *Memoirs*, 1:332.

42 Sherman, *Memoirs*, 1:332; *OR*, 24 (pt. 1):433.

43 Sherman, *Memoirs*, 1:332.

44 *Navy-OR*, 24:488–89.

45 Sherman, *Memoirs*, 1:332–34; Porter, *Naval History*, 306.

46 Sherman, *Memoirs*, 1:333–34; Porter, *Naval History*, 306.

47 Porter, *Incidents*, 168–69; *Navy-OR*, 24:495.

48 *Navy-OR*, 24:479–80, 495.

49 Ibid., 24:496.

50 Ibid., 24:479.

51 *OR*, 24 (pt. 1):434, 436; WTS to EES, April 10, 1863, UND-SFP.

52 WTS to JS, April 10, 1863, in *SCW*, 450.

53 WTS to EES, April 17, 1863, UND-SFP.

54 WTS to JS, April 3, 1863, in *SCW*, 439.

55 Sherman, *Memoirs*, 1:339–43; WTS to JS, April 26, 1863, in *SCW*, 459.

56 WTS to EES, April 23, 1863, UND-SFP; Porter, *Naval History*, 310; Michael B. Ballard, *Vicksburg: The Campaign That Opened the Mississippi* (Chapel Hill: University of North Carolina Press, 2004), 199.

57 Porter, *Naval History*, 310, 311; William L. Shea and Terrence J. Winschel, *Vicksburg Is the Key: The Struggle for the Mississippi River* (Lincoln: University of Nebraska Press, 2003), 98–99.

58 Porter, *Naval History*, 311; Sherman, *Memoirs*, 1:343–44.

59 Ibid.; Porter, *Incidents*, 176.

60 Sherman, *Memoirs*, 1:344; Porter, *Naval History*, 312.

61   *OR*, 24 (pt. 3):158; Ballard, *Vicksburg*, 210.

62   *OR*, 24 (pt. 3):209, 762.

63   Ibid., 24 (pt. 3):240.

64   Ibid., 24 (pt. 3):242–43; Sherman, *Memoirs*, 1:345; Ballard, *Vicksburg*, 203, 213; Catton, *Hallowed Ground*, 285; Shea and Winschel, *Vicksburg Is the Key*, 94, 102–3.

65   Ballard, *Vicksburg*, 207–8; Shea and Winschel, *Vicksburg Is the Key*, 93–94; Catton, *Hallowed Ground*, 286; Shelby Foote, *The Civil War: A Narrative*, 3 vols. (New York: Random House, 1958–1974), 2:335, 341.

66   *OR*, 24 (pt. 3):211, and (pt. 1):80.

67   Ibid., 24 (pt. 1):80–81.

68   Ibid., 24 (pt. 1):84, 87.

69   U. S. Grant, *Personal Memoirs*, 2 vols. (New York: Charles L. Webster & Co., 1885), 1:474–76.

70   Ibid., 1:476–78.

71   Edwin C. Bearss, *Fields of Honor* (Washington, D.C.: National Geographic Society, 2006), 210–14; Grant, *Personal Memoirs*, 1:480.

72   WTS to EES, April 29, 1863, UND-SFP.

73   Ibid.; *OR*, 24 (pt. 3):274.

74   *OR*, 24 (pt. 1):33, 35, and (pt. 3):268–69, 285.

75   Ibid., 24 (pt. 3):285, and (pt. 1):755–56; Bearss, *Fields of Honor*, 214.

76   Grant, *Personal Memoirs*, 1:487–528; Sherman, *Memoirs*, 1:345–50. See also the official reports of Grant and Sherman in *OR*, 24 (pt. 1):48–54, 753–55. Additionally consulted were Ballard, *Vicksburg*, 226–318; Bearss, *Fields of Honor*, 210–33. For a full discussion of the battle of Champion's Hill, see Timothy B. Smith, *Champion's Hill: Decisive Battle for Vicksburg* (New York: Savas Beatie, 2004).

77   Grant, *Personal Memoirs*, 1:528.

78   The discussion of the May 19 and 22 attacks is based upon the accounts of Steven E. Woodworth, *Nothing but Victory: The Army of the Tennessee, 1861–1865* (New York: Alfred A. Knopf, 2005), 401–12; Shea and Winschel, *Vicksburg Is the Key*, 146–49; Sherman, *Memoirs*, 1:350–53.

79   Grant, *Personal Memoirs*, 1:531.

80   Sherman, *Memoirs*, 1:352–53; *OR*, 24 (pt. 1):86–87.

81   WTS to John Rawlins, June 17, 1863, in *SCW*, 486.

82   WTS to JS, June 27, 1863, in *SCW*, 495; *OR*, 24 (pt. 1):103. Consult Richard L. Kiper, *Major General John Alexander McClernand: Politician in Uniform* (Kent, Ohio: Kent State University Press, 1999), for a biographical study of the man.

83   Sherman, *Memoirs*, 1:353–54; WTS to EES, June 2 and 11, 1863, UND-SFP.

84   WTS to EES, June 27, 1863, UND-SFP.

85   Ibid.

86   Sherman, *Memoirs*, 1:354–56; Grant, *Personal Memoirs*, 1:555; *OR*, 24 (pt. 3): 461, 472.

87   WTS to EES, July 15, 1863, UND-SFP; *OR*, 24 (pt. 3):472.

19. WHY WAS I NOT KILLED AT VICKSBURG?

1   WTS to EES, July 5, 1863, UND-SFP; John F. Marszalek, *Sherman: A Soldier's Passion for Order* (New York: Free Press, 1993), 229; *OR*, 24 (pt. 2):533–34; William Tecumseh

Sherman, *Memoirs of General W. T. Sherman*, 2 vols. (1885; repr., New York: Library of America, 1990), 1:356.

2 Sherman, *Memoirs*, 1:356–57; WTS to JS, July 19, 1863, LC-WTSP; *OR*, 24 (pt. 3):531.

3 *OR*, 24 (pt. 3):531; WTS to JS, July 19, 1863, LC-WTSP; Lloyd Lewis, *Sherman: Fighting Prophet* (New York: Harcourt Brace, 1932), 295.

4 WTS to David Stuart, August 1, 1863, WTS to Edward O. C. Ord, August 3, 1863, and WTS to Thomas Ewing Sr., August 20, 1863, all in *SCW*, 512, 513, 523.

5 *OR*, 24 (pt. 3):473, 531.

6 Lewis, *Sherman*, 298.

7 Sherman, *Memoirs*, 1:370; WTS to PBE, July 28, 1863, in SCW, 508.

8 Sherman, *Memoirs*, 1:370; Anna McAllister, *Ellen Ewing: Wife of General Sherman* (New York: Benziger Brothers, 1936), 262; WTS to JS, July 28, 1863, in Thorndike, 209.

9 Henry W. Halleck to WTS, August 4, 1863, in Lee Kennett, *Sherman: A Soldier's Life* (New York: Perennial, 2002); Lewis, *Sherman*, 299; WTS to PBE, July 28, 1863, and WTS to Thomas Ewing Sr., August 13, 1863, in *SCW*, 508, 522.

10 WTS to PBE, July 28, 1863, and WTS to Thomas Ewing Sr., August 13, 1863, in *SCW*, 508, 521; McAllister, *Ellen Ewing*, 261–63.

11 WTS to EES, May 2, 1863, and WTS to William T. Sherman Jr., June 21, 1863, UND-SFP; McAllister, *Ellen Ewing*, 260.

12 McAllister, *Ellen Ewing*, 259; WTS to JS, September 9, 1863, LC-WTSP.

13 McAllister, *Ellen Ewing*, 264–65; WTS to JS, September 9, 1863, LC-WTSP; Sherman, *Memoirs*, 1:370–71.

14 WTS to JS, September 9, 1863, LC-WTSP; McAllister, *Ellen Ewing*, 264–65; Sherman, *Memoirs*, 1:371.

15 The summary of the battle of Chickamauga is based on James Lee McDonough *Chattanooga—A Death Grip on the Confederacy* (Knoxville: University of Tennessee Press, 1984), 3–19.

16 Sherman, *Memoirs*, 1:372–73.

17 McAllister, *Ellen Ewing*, 266–67; Sherman, *Memoirs*, 1:373–74.

18 Sherman, *Memoirs*, 1:374; John Y. Simon, ed., *The Papers of Ulysses S. Grant*, 31 vols. (Carbondale: Southern Illinois University Press, 1967–), 9:274–75; Lewis, *Sherman*, 309; *OR*, 30 (pt. 4):356–57; WTS to JS, October 24, 1863, LC-WTSP.

19 WTS to EES, October 6, 1863, UND-SFP.

20 WTS to EES, October 10, 1863, UND-SFP.

21 Sherman, *Memoirs*, 1:375; WTS to EES, October 14, 24, 28, 1863, and January 28, March 10, June 12, 26, 1864, UND-SFP; McAllister, *Ellen Ewing*, 267–72.

22 WTS to PBE, October 24, 1863, in *SCW*, 564.

23 *OR*, 30 (pt. 4):236.

24 Sherman, *Memoirs*, 1:376–78.

25 Marszalek, *Sherman*, 239; Sherman, *Memoirs*, 1:378; WTS to EES, October 14, 1863, UND-SFP.

26 Sherman, *Memoirs*, 1:378; *OR*, 30 (pt. 4):356; Lewis, *Sherman*, 312.

27 *OR*, 30 (pt. 4):236, 355, 404; McDonough, *Chattanooga*, 49.

28 Sherman, *Memoirs*, 1:383; Lewis, *Sherman*, 313.

29 Sherman, *Memoirs*, 1:383–84.

30 Ibid., 1:386; Lewis, *Sherman*, 314; WTS to EES, November 14, 1863, UND-SFP.

31   Sherman, *Memoirs*, 1:386; Marszalek, *Sherman*, 242.

32   McDonough, *Chattanooga*, 53.

33   Ibid., 55–58; Horace Porter, *Campaigning with Grant* (1897; repr., New York: Da Capo, 1986), 5.

34   McDonough, *Chattanooga*, 55–58, 76–88, 95–96; Porter, *Campaigning with Grant*, 8–9.

35   Grant, *Personal Memoirs*, 2:49, 58; McDonough, *Chattanooga*, 104.

36   *OR*, 31 (pt. 2):39, 64.

37   Ibid., 31 (pt. 2):41; Clarence C. Buel and Robert U. Johnson, eds., *Battles and Leaders of the Civil War*, 4 vols. (1888; repr., New York: Castle Books, 1956), 3:712; McDonough, *Chattanooga*, 118–19.

38   *OR*, 31 (pt. 2):572–73.

39   Henry H. Wright, *A History of the Sixth Iowa Infantry* (Iowa City: State Historical Society of Iowa, 1923), 235; *OR*, 31 (pt. 2):573.

40   McDonough, *Chattanooga*, 117–22.

41   Ibid., 122; Wiley Sword, *Mountains Touched with Fire: Chattanooga Besieged, 1863* (New York: St. Martin's, 1995), 237; *OR*, 31 (pt. 2):42, 573, 746–48; Steven E. Woodworth, *Six Armies in Tennessee: The Chickamauga and Chattanooga Campaigns* (Lincoln: University of Nebraska Press, 1998), 183.

42   McDonough, *Chattanooga*, 127–28.

43   *OR*, 31 (pt. 2):315; John Geary to Mary Geary, December 4, 1863, John W. Geary Letters, Chickamauga–Chattanooga National Military Park Library; McDonough, *Chattanooga*, 129–42.

44   McDonough, *Chattanooga*, 145; Lewis, *Sherman*, 320; *OR*, 31 (pt. 2):574; WTS to EES, July 15, 1863, UND-SFP.

45   *OR*, 31 (pt. 2):574, 631, 633, 636.

46   Ibid., 31 (pt. 2):574, 636.

47   McDonough, *Chattanooga*, 150–51.

48   *OR*, 31 (pt. 2):360–61, 369, 634, 655; McDonough, *Chattanooga*, 157; Norman D. Brown, ed., *One of Cleburne's Command: The Civil War Reminiscences and Diary of Captain Samuel T. Foster, Granbury's Texas Brigade, CSA* (Austin: University of Texas Press, 1980), 62.

49   *OR*, 31 (pt. 2):369, 634, 636–37, 644, 648, 649, 653, 737–38, 751; McDonough, *Chattanooga*, 154–56. This account benefits from a tour of the Sherman–Hardee/Cleburne battle area at the northern end of Missionary Ridge, led by James H. Ogden, historian/ranger with the National Park Service, Chickamauga–Chattanooga National Military Park, on Saturday, May 15, 2010.

50   Steven E. Woodworth, *Nothing but Victory: The Army of the Tennessee, 1861–1865* (New York: Alfred A. Knopf, 2005), 471.

51   Buel and Johnson, *Battles and Leaders*, 3:716–26; McDonough, *Chattanooga*, 164.

52   Buel and Johnson, *Battles and Leaders*, 3:716–26; McDonough, *Chattanooga*, 168–69, 174–76.

53   McDonough, *Chattanooga*, 176; Alexander W. Reynolds report, December 15, 1863, J. Patton Anderson Papers, in the P. K. Yonge Library of Florida History, University of Florida, Gainesville.

54   McDonough, *Chattanooga*, 161–80.

55   Buel and Johnson, *Battles and Leaders*, 3:725; McDonough, *Chattanooga*, 167.

56 *OR*, 31 (pt. 2):96; McDonough, *Chattanooga*, 167–68, 194.

57 For a detailed discussion of the fight for the center of Missionary Ridge, both the Union assault and the Confederate defense, see McDonough, *Chattanooga*, 161–205. I have walked the crest of the ridge all along the area where the Federals attacked, a distance of approximately two miles. I have also rapidly climbed the ridge (some years ago) at two markedly different places, in order to get some "feel" for the endeavor, both in terms of the time required to scale the height (without opposition obviously, and without carrying firearms) and the difficulties, as well as the advantages, presented by the terrain.

58 *OR*, 31 (pt. 2):34, 45.

59 McDonough, *Chattanooga*, 162; Sherman, *Memoirs*, 1:390; Grant, *Personal Memoirs*, 2:88.

60 Thomas L. Livermore, *Numbers and Losses in the Civil War in America, 1861–1865* (Boston: Houghton Mifflin, 1900), 106–8.

61 *OR*, 31 (pt. 2): 25, 45, 49–50.

62 Sherman, *Memoirs*, 1:393; WTS to EES, December 8, 1863, UND-SFP.

63 Sherman, *Memoirs*, 1:393–94.

64 Ibid., 1:394, 414, 417.

65 Grenville M. Dodge, *Personal Recollections of President Abraham Lincoln, General Ulysses Grant and General William T. Sherman* (n.p.: Monarch Printing Co., 1914), 138–42.

66 *OR*, 31 (pt. 3):497.

20. ONE HUNDRED THOUSAND STRONG

1 William Tecumseh Sherman, *Memoirs of General W. T. Sherman*, 2 vols. (1885; repr., New York: Library of America, 1990), 1:414, 417; WTS to EES, January 11, 1864, UND-SFP.

2 WTS to EES, January 5 and 11, 1864, UND-SFP; WTS to Minnie Sherman, January 6, 1864, OHC-WTSP; "Site of the Burnet House—Cincinnati, Ohio—American Waymarking.com," 1 and 2, as well as information from the historical marker placed on the site of the Burnet House in 2012.

3 Sherman, *Memoirs*, 1:417; WTS to EES, January 11 and 19, 1864, UND-SFP.

4 WTS to EES, January 11 and 19, 1864, UND-SFP; WTS to JS, January 28, 1864, LC-WTSP.

5 WTS to EES, January 28, 1864, UND-SFP; WTS to JS, January 28, 1864, LC-WTSP.

6 Basil H. Liddell Hart, *Sherman: Soldier, Realist, American* (New York: Praeger, 1929), 224; *OR*, 24 (pt. 3):472.

7 WTS to EES, January 11, 1864, UND-SFP.

8 *OR*, 24 (pt. 3):472; WTS to JS, April 3, 1863, in *SCW*, 437.

9 Sherman, *Memoirs*, 1:417–18; Steven E. Woodworth, *Nothing but Victory: The Army of the Tennessee, 1861–1865* (New York: Alfred A. Knopf, 2005), 480, placed Sherman's numbers at 27,000.

10 WTS to JS, January 28, 1864, LC-WTSP; WTS to EES, January 28, 1864, UND-SFP.

11 WTS to Minnie Sherman, January 28, 1864, OHC-WTSP.

12 *OR*, 32 (pt. 2):278–81.

13   WTS to JS, January 28, 1864, LC-WTSP.

14   Liddell Hart, *Sherman*, 225; WTS to EES, January 28, 1864, UND-SFP; Sherman, *Memoirs*, 1:419, 421; *OR*, 30 (pt. 4):236; Woodworth, *Nothing but Victory*, 481.

15   WTS to EES, February 7, 1864, UND-SFP; Woodworth, *Nothing but Victory*, 482–83.

16   WTS to EES, February 7 and March 10, 1864, UND-SFP.

17   Sherman, *Memoirs*, 1:420–21 (see also "Chronology," 2:1102); *OR*, 23 (pt. 2):175–76; Liddell Hart, *Sherman*, 226.

18   Sherman, *Memoirs*, 1:423; Woodworth, *Nothing but Victory*, 485.

19   WTS to EES, March 10, 1864, UND-SFP; Sherman, *Memoirs*, 1:418, 422–23.

20   *OR*, 32 (pt. 1):177; Sherman, *Memoirs*, 1:414–15, 421–22.

21   WTS to EES, March 10, 1864, UND-SFP.

22   Steven E. Woodworth, *This Great Struggle: America's Civil War* (Lanham, Md.: Rowman and Littlefield, 2011), 389; Gary W. Gallagher, "The War Was Won in the East," *Civil War Times* (February 2011), 21. A number of professional Civil War historians, while recognizing the dramatic appeal and profuse bloodletting of the Gettysburg clash, are convinced that the significance of the battle has been overrated, a point of view I have long held.

23   WTS to EES, March 12, 1864, UND-SFP.

24   Ibid.

25   James M. McPherson, *Ordeal by Fire: The Civil War and Reconstruction* (New York: Oxford University Press, 1992), 454–55, discusses the Southern view of blacks serving in the Union Army.

26   WTS to JS, April 22, 1864, LC-WTSP; WTS to Lorenzo Thomas, April 12, 1864, in *SCW*, 621.

27   Woodworth, *This Great Struggle*, 248.

28   Russell F. Weigley, *History of the United States Army*, enlarged ed. (Bloomington: University of Indiana Press, 1984), 211 (Weigley states that the U.S. government, by the time the war was over, had paid $585 million in total bounties, as much as the entire pay for the U.S. Army during the war); WTS to JS, April 5 and 11, 1864, and WTS to Minnie Sherman, May 1, 1864, in *SCW*, 613, 619, 633.

29   Sherman, *Memoirs*, 1:428–29.

30   WTS to JS, March 24 and April 5, 1864, in *SCW*, 610, 613.

31   Lloyd Lewis, *Sherman: Fighting Prophet* (New York: Harcourt Brace, 1932), 345; "Site of the Burnet House," 1 and 2, and historical marker.

32   Charles P. Roland, *An American Iliad: The Story of the Civil War* (New York: McGraw-Hill, 1991), 175; James M. McPherson, *Battle Cry of Freedom: The Civil War Era* (New York: Oxford University Press, 1988), 720–21.

33   Sherman, *Memoirs*, 2:490–92; *OR*, 32 (pt. 3):312–14.

34   David S. Heidler and Jeanne T. Heidler, eds., *Encyclopedia of the American Civil War: A Political, Social, and Military History*, 5 vols. (Santa Barbara, Calif.: ABC-CLIO, 2000), 1:174–76; Sherman, *Memoirs*, 2:489–92.

35   Sherman, *Memoirs*, 1:425, 2:492; WTS to EES, March 10, 1864, UND-SFP.

36   WTS to Thomas Ewing Sr., April 27, 1864, in *SCW*, 631.

37   Roland, *American Iliad*, 174–75; McPherson, *Battle Cry of Freedom*, 722–23; Sherman, *Memoirs*, 2:471; *OR*, 32 (pt. 3):491.

38   Roland, *American Iliad*, 176–80; *OR*, 46 (pt. 1):20.

39   WTS to EES, March 10, 1864, UND-SFP.

40   WTS to JS, March 24, 1864, in *SCW,* 609; Sherman, *Memoirs,* 2:465–66.

41   Sherman, *Memoirs,* 2:465–66, 468; *OR,* 38 (pt. 1):62.

42   Sherman, *Memoirs,* 2:468–69; *OR,* 32 (pt. 3):495.

43   James Lee McDonough, *War in Kentucky: From Shiloh to Perryville* (Knoxville: University of Tennessee Press, 1994), 43–44. My information about the railroads is taken from the *OR,* 16 (pt. 1): 248, 297, 391, 392, 608. I also have examined the tunnel near Cowan, as well as the area south of it. The length of the tunnel is taken from information available at the Cowan Railroad Museum. I viewed as well the curving tunnel, about a quarter of a mile long, located approximately halfway between Pulaski, Tennessee, and Athens, Alabama, on the Nashville & Decatur line. I have taken a look too at several vulnerable trestles, bridges and creek crossings south of Nashville, on all three railroads in question, as well as a number of places north of Nashville on the L & N road. The Federals certainly faced a major task in protecting those rails during the Atlanta campaign.

44   *OR,* 32 (pt. 3):471–72, 496–97.

45   Sherman, *Memoirs,* 2:467–69; John F. Marszalek, *Sherman: A Soldier's Passion for Order* (New York: Free Press, 1993), 261, and 545n3. See also Albert Castel, "Prevaricating Through Georgia: Sherman's *Memoirs* as a Source on the Atlanta Campaign," *Civil War History* 40, no. 1 (March 1994): 48–71. Accusing Sherman of "dubious or at least exaggerated statements . . . designed to create the impression of bold, innovative, yet pragmatic leadership," relative to logistic preparations for the campaign, Castel concluded that "the kindest thing that can be said about Sherman's account [in his memoirs] of how he allegedly obtained the additional rail transport needed to conduct the Atlanta campaign is that it is a 'tall story' designed to entertain readers" (51–52). Granted that Sherman's memoirs, like those of any general, must be read with caution; granted that Sherman in those memoirs casts himself in the best light possible; and granted that Castel is an accomplished and distinguished historian; nevertheless, Castel's assessment of Sherman, in my judgment, is overly critical. I agree with John Marszalek who, in an article in the same issue of *Civil War History* as Castel's, wrote that Castel "came to the task of this article all too ready to impute to Sherman conscious motives and aims that I am convinced Sherman never thought about or ever had." Stating that Sherman "pressured everyone in every way he knew to get the railroads organized behind him," Marszalek concluded, correctly I believe, that "without that pressure [Sherman] would have had available to him many fewer cars than he actually had, no matter what the technical aspects of the procurement were" (73–74).

46   Sherman, *Memoirs,* 2:467–69; WTS to JS, April 11, 1864, LC-WTSP; WTS to Charles A. Dana, April 21, 1864, in *SCW,* 619–20, 624.

47   Sherman, *Memoirs,* 2:467; *OR,* 38 (pt. 1):83.

48   Lewis, *Sherman,* 351; Wesley K. Clark, foreword to Steven E. Woodworth, *Sherman* (New York: Palgrave Macmillan, 2009), xiii.

49   WTS to Thomas Ewing Jr., April 18, 1864, in *SCW,* 622.

50   Ibid.; Lewis, *Sherman,* 355.

51   WTS to JS, April 22, 1864, LC-WTSP.

52   Ibid.

53   Sherman, *Memoirs,* 2:494.

54   *OR*, 38 (pt. 1):62–63; Jacob D. Cox, *Atlanta* (New York: Charles Scribner's Sons, 1882), 25.

55   WTS to EES, May 4, 1864, UND-SFP.

21. I KNEW MORE OF GEORGIA THAN THE REBELS DID

1   WTS to U. S. Grant, April 10, 1864, in *OR*, 32 (pt. 3):313; WTS to EES, May 22, 1864, UND-SFP.

2   William Tecumseh Sherman, *Memoirs of General W. T. Sherman*, 2 vols. (1885; repr., New York: Library of America, 1990), 2:496; Jacob D. Cox, *Atlanta* (New York: Charles Scribner's Sons, 1882), 29–31; Norman D. Brown, ed., *One of Cleburne's Command: The Civil War Reminiscences and Diary of Captain Samuel T. Foster, Granbury's Texas Brigade, CSA* (Austin: University of Texas Press, 1980), 72.

3   Cox, *Atlanta*, 29–31; Sherman, *Memoirs*, 2:496; Clarence C. Buel and Robert U. Johnson, eds., *Battles and Leaders of the Civil War*, 4 vols. (1888; repr., New York: Castle Books, 1956), 4:279, 296; Gilbert E. Govan and James W. Livingood, *A Different Valor: The Story of General Joseph E. Johnston, C.S.A.* (1956; repr., Westbury, Conn.: Greenwood Press, 1973), 261; *OR*, 38 (pt. 2):114.

4   Sherman, *Memoirs*, 2:488.

5   Ibid., 2:471–72, 488.

6   Cox, *Atlanta*, 31; Albert Castel, *Decision in the West: The Atlanta Campaign of 1864* (Lawrence: University Press of Kansas, 1992), 121; *OR*, 38 (pt. 1):59, 63. John M. Schofield, *Forty-Six Years in the Army* (New York: Century, 1897), 123.

7   Cox, *Atlanta*, 31–32; Sherman, *Memoirs*, 2:496; Schofield, *Forty-Six Years*, 123, 129; *OR*, 38 (pt. 1):59, 63.

8   *OR*, 38 (pt. 1):59, 63; Sherman, *Memoirs*, 2:496.

9   Richard M. McMurry, *John Bell Hood and the War for Southern Independence* (Lexington: University of Kentucky Press, 1982), 101; Thomas Lawrence Connelly, *Autumn of Glory: The Army of Tennessee, 1862–1865* (Baton Rouge: Louisiana State University Press, 1971), 336; Sherman, *Memoirs*, 2:496.

10   Sherman, *Memoirs*, 2:496–99; Lloyd Lewis, *Sherman: Fighting Prophet* (New York: Harcourt Brace, 1932), 357.

11   *OR*, 38 (pt. 1):63–64; Sherman, *Memoirs*, 2:499; Lewis, *Sherman*, 357.

12   Sherman, *Memoirs*, 2:500. For Sherman's official report of the action, see *OR*, 38 (pt. 1):63–64.

13   Steven E. Woodworth, *Sherman* (New York: Palgrave Macmillan, 2009), xii; Schofield, *Forty-Six Years*, 123–27.

14   Castel, *Decision in the West*, 181–82; Larry Daniel, *Days of Glory: The Army of the Cumberland, 1861–1865* (Baton Rouge: Louisiana State University Press, 2004), 395.

15   *OR*, 38 (pt. 3):483; Sherman, *Memoirs*, 2:409. Albert Castel's study of the Atlanta campaign is the most extensive and detailed work on the subject. The book has many pluses, and anyone who is seriously interested in the campaign should consider it imperative reading. However, I believe that Castel had difficulty treating Sherman objectively. Richard M. McMurry has also written a valuable book on the campaign: *Atlanta 1864: Last Chance for the Confederacy* (Lincoln: University of Nebraska Press, 2000). And

certainly Connelly's *Autumn of Glory* remains essential for any scholarly study of the campaign. Another book that should be consulted is Stephen Davis, *Atlanta Will Fall: Sherman, Joe Johnston, and the Yankee Heavy Battalions* (Wilmington, Del.: Scholarly Resources, 2001).

16　*OR*, 38 (pt. 1):64; Sherman, *Memoirs*, 2:500–503; Connelly, *Autumn of Glory*, 340–42.

17　Sherman, *Memoirs*, 2:503; Steven E. Woodworth, *Nothing but Victory: The Army of the Tennessee, 1861–1865* (New York: Alfred A. Knopf, 2005), 498; Connelly, *Autumn of Glory*, 342. Woodworth, *Sherman*, 112, described the shape of the Confederate position as like an arc. General Oliver O. Howard likened it to "a horse-shoe-shaped line" (Buel and Johnson, *Battles and Leaders*, 4:299), while Larry Daniel compared it to "a large shepherd's crook" (*Days of Glory*, 399).

18　Schofield, *Forty-Six Years*, 140–41.

19　*OR*, 38 (pt. 2):118; Andrew McCornack to his father, May 21, 1864, McCornack letters, Sword.

20　*OR*, 38 (pt. 1):64; Sherman, *Memoirs*, 2:503.

21　Eugene A. "Casey" McWayne to "Folks at Home," May 21, 1864, McWayne letters, Sword.

22　Andrew McCornack to parents and sisters, May 18 and 24, 1864, McCornack letters, Sword.

23　Woodworth, *Nothing but Victory*, 498–505.

24　McMurry, *Atlanta, 1864*, 73, 183.

25　Sherman, *Memoirs*, 2:504.

26　Cox, *Atlanta*, 56; *OR*, 38 (pt. 4):242.

27　Connelly, *Autumn of Glory*, 344–45; Steven E. Woodworth, *This Great Struggle: America's Civil War* (Lanham, Md.: Rowman and Littlefield, 2011), 276; Cox, *Atlanta*, 56; Shelby Foote, *The Civil War: A Narrative*, 3 vols. (New York: Random House, 1958–1975), 3:339.

28　Connelly, *Autumn of Glory*, 345–46; McMurry, *Atlanta, 1864*, 79–80; *OR*, 38 (pt. 4):242.

29　Castel, *Decision in the West*, 198; Connelly, *Autumn of Glory*, 345; McMurry, *Atlanta, 1864*, 80–81; *OR*, 38 (pt. 4):728 and (pt. 3):715.

30　McMurry, *Atlanta, 1864*, 81; Connelly, *Autumn of Glory*, 347; Castel, *Decision in the West*, 202.

31　*OR*, 38 (pt. 3):616; R. Lockwood Tower, ed., *A Carolinian Goes to War: The Civil War Narrative of Arthur Middleton Manigault, Brigadier General, C. S. A.* (Columbia: University of South Carolina Press, 1983), 187; Buel and Johnson, *Battles and Leaders*, 4:303, 305.

32　*OR*, 38 (pt. 4):299; WTS to EES, May 22, 1864, UND-SFP.

33　Connelly, *Autumn of Glory*, 352; *OR*, 38 (pt. 4):296; Davis, *Atlanta Will Fall*, 60; Jacob Dickason to brother, May 22, 1864, Sword.

34　Lewis, *Sherman*, 368; Sherman, *Memoirs*, 2:511.

35　*OR*, 38 (pt. 4):260–61. The distance figures are derived from the Georgia Official Highway and Transportation Map for 2009–2010.

36　*OR*, 38 (pt. 1):65 and (pt. 4):272, 288; Sherman, *Memoirs*, 2:512.

37　Davis, *Atlanta Will Fall*, 66; McMurry, *Atlanta, 1864*, 86, 88; Basil H. Liddell Hart, *Sherman: Soldier, Realist, American* (New York: Praeger, 1929), 259; Brown, *One of Cleburne's Command*, 80.

38   James Reston Jr., *Sherman's March and Vietnam* (New York: Macmillan, 1984), 25; Lewis, *Sherman*, 366.

39   Cox, *Atlanta*, 70; *OR*, 38 (pt. 1):143 and (pt. 2):123.

40   *OR*, 38 (pt. 2):123.

41   Daniel, *Days of Glory*, 401; Sherman, *Memoirs*, 2:513.

42   Cox, *Atlanta*, 72–73; Daniel, *Days of Glory*, 402; McMurry, *Atlanta, 1864*, 89; Castel, *Decision in the West*, 225; *OR*, 38 (pt. 2):60, 123; Sam Davis Elliott, *Soldier of Tennessee: General Alexander P. Stewart and the Civil War in the West* (Baton Rouge: Louisiana State University Press, 1999), 184; Lewis N. Wynne and Robert A. Taylor, eds., *This War So Horrible: The Civil War Diary of Hiram Smith Williams* (Tuscaloosa: University of Alabama Press, 1993), 81.

43   *OR*, 38 (pt. 2):48.

44   Ibid., 38 (pt. 2):14, 124, 125; Elliott, *Soldier of Tennessee*, 189; Hambleton Tapp and James C. Klotter, eds., *The Union, The Civil War, and John W. Tuttle: A Kentucky Captain's Account* (Frankfort: Kentucky Historical Society, 1980), 187.

45   *OR*, 38 (pt. 2):616, 818.

46   Ibid., 38 (pt. 1):66; Sherman, *Memoirs*, 2:513.

47   *OR*, 38 (pt. 1):193–94, 377, 423, 864–65, and (pt. 4):323, 327; Cox, *Atlanta*, 76.

48   Castel, *Decision in the West*, 230, tells about the buglers. See also *OR*, 38 (pt. 1):377, 865, 866, and (pt. 3):724.

49   *OR*, 38 (pt. 4):324; Cox, *Atlanta*, 77.

50   *OR*, 38 (pt. 1):865, 866, and (pt. 3):725, and (pt. 4):324; Daniel, *Days of Glory*, 403; Castel, *Decision in the West*, 235.

51   Brown, *One of Cleburne's Command*, 88; *OR*, 38 (pt. 3):616.

52   *OR*, 38 (pt. 1):195, 379, 423; Daniel, *Days of Glory*, 403.

53   Daniel, *Days of Glory*, 403; *OR*, 38 (pt. 4):326, 418.

54   Liddell Hart, *Sherman*, 260.

55   Castel, *Decision in the West*, 243; McMurry, *Atlanta, 1864*, 91; Tower, ed., *A Carolinian Goes to War*, 190. Manigault gives the march distance as eight or ten miles.

56   Nathaniel Cheairs Hughes Jr., *General William J. Hardee: Old Reliable* (Baton Rouge: Louisiana State University Press, 1965), 205; Castel, *Decision in the West*, 243–46; Foote, *The Civil War*, 3:350.

57   Robert G. Ardry to Dear Father, June 2, 1864, from the Ardry letters, Sword.

58   McCornack to Parents and Sisters, May 30, 1864, McCornack letters, Sword; Buel and Johnson, *Battles and Leaders*, 4:270; Castel, *Decision in the West*, 246.

59   Eugene A. "Casey" McWayne to Folks at Home, June 5, 1864, McWayne letters, Sword; Foote, *The Civil War*, 3:351; McMurry, *Atlanta, 1864*, 92–94; Cox, *Atlanta*, 80.

22. I WANT A BOLD PUSH FOR ATLANTA

1   Shelby Foote, *The Civil War: A Narrative*, 3 vols. (New York: Random House, 1958–1975), 3:290–99.

2   WTS to EES, May 20 and June 30, 1864, UND-SFP.

3   William Tecumseh Sherman, *Memoirs of General W. T. Sherman*, 2 vols. (1885; repr., New York: Library of America, 1990), 2:522–23; Basil H. Liddell Hart, *Sherman: Sol-*

dier, Realist, American (New York: Praeger, 1929), 261; WTS to EES, June 12, 1864, UND-SFP.

4   *OR*, 38 (pt. 4):474.

5   Ibid., 38 (pt. 4):480; Sherman, *Memoirs*, 2:523.

6   *OR*, 38 (pt. 4):480.

7   Thomas Lawrence Connelly, *Autumn of Glory: The Army of Tennessee, 1862–1865* (Baton Rouge: Louisiana State University Press, 1971), 373–80; Richard McMurry, *Atlanta, 1864: Last Chance for the Confederacy* (Lincoln: University of Nebraska Press, 2000), 97–99.

8   Andrew McCornack to Parents and Sisters, May 30 and June 8, 1864, McCornack letters, Sword.

9   Clarence C. Buel and Robert U. Johnson, eds., *Battles and Leaders of the Civil War*, 4 vols. (1888; repr., New York: Castle Books, 1956), 4:307; WTS to EES, June 12, 1864, UND-SFP; *OR*, 38 (pt. 4):507–8.

10 Andrew McCornack to Parents and Sisters, June 17, 1864, McCornack letters, Sword; WTS to EES, June 9 and 12, 1864, UND-SFP.

11 WTS to EES, June 12, 1864, UND-SFP.

12 WTS to EES, June 26, 1864, UND-SFP.

13 Buel and Johnson, *Battles and Leaders*, 4:309; Foote, *The Civil War*, 3:353, 355; Sherman, *Memoirs*, 2:523.

14 Steven E. Woodworth, *Sherman* (New York: Palgrave Macmillan, 2009), 116, 117.

15 Sherman, *Memoirs*, 2:524; *OR*, 38 (pt. 4):480.

16 Liddell Hart, *Sherman*, 264; Foote, *The Civil War*, 3:391.

17 Sherman, *Memoirs*, 2:527–28; James Lee McDonough, *Schofield: Union General in the Civil War and Reconstruction* (Tallahassee: Florida State University Press, 1972), 80–81; Liddell Hart, *Sherman*, 264; Foote, *The Civil War*, 3:392–93.

18 Noah G. Hill to Father, June 26, 1864, Sword.

19 *OR*, 38 (pt. 4):558; Sherman, *Memoirs*, 2:528–29.

20 Sherman, *Memoirs*, 2:529; John M. Schofield, *Forty-Six Years in the Army* (New York: Century, 1897), 134.

21 Sherman, *Memoirs*, 2:529–30.

22 N. A. Pinney, *History of the 104th Ohio Volunteer Infantry from 1862 to 1865* (Akron, Ohio: Werner and Lohmann, 1886), 45.

23 *OR*, 38 (pt. 4):492, 588.

24 Ibid., 38 (pt. 4):408, 466.

25 Ibid., 38 (pt. 4):507–8.

26 Ibid., 38 (pt. 4):572–73.

27 Ibid., 38 (pt. 1):68; Liddell Hart, *Sherman*, 265; Foote, *The Civil War*, 3:394.

28 *OR*, 38 (pt. 1):68; Foote, *The Civil War*, 3:395.

29 *OR*, 38 (pt. 1):68; Sherman, *Memoirs*, 2:530; McDonough, *Schofield*, 82–83; Schofield, *Forty-Six Years*, 142–44.

30 Larry J. Daniel, *Days of Glory: The Army of the Cumberland, 1861–1865* (Baton Rouge: Louisiana State University Press, 2004), 408–9; Foote, *The Civil War*, 3:397; Steven E. Woodworth, *Nothing but Victory: The Army of the Tennessee, 1861–1865* (New York: Alfred A. Knopf, 2005), 520–23.

31 *OR*, 38 (pt. 4):609, 610; Sherman, *Memoirs*, 2:531.

32   *OR*, 38 (pt. 1):69, and (pt. 4):611, 612; Liddell Hart, *Sherman*, 266.

33   *OR*, 38 (pt. 4):607; Woodworth, *Nothing but Victory*, 525.

34   *OR*, 38 (pt. 5):91.

35   Ibid., 38 (pt. 4):611; Buel and Johnson, *Battles and Leaders*, 4:310; Liddell Hart, *Sherman*, 266; William Farries to sister, June 29, 1864, and William Farries to brother, July 6, 1864, Farries letters, Sword.

36   WTS to EES, June 30, 1864, UND-SFP.

37   WTS to Minnie Sherman, June 30, 1864, in *SCW*, 661–62.

38   McDonough, *Schofield*, 84; Jacob D. Cox, *Atlanta* (New York: Charles Scribner's Sons, 1882), 122–31; Sherman, *Memoirs*, 2:531–32.

39   *OR*, 38 (pt. 5):3.

40   James P. Jones, *"Black Jack": John A. Logan and Southern Illinois in the Civil War Era* (Tallahassee: Florida State University Press, 1967), 209. Eugene A. "Casey" McWayne to Folks at Home, July 17, 1864, McWayne letters, Sword.

41   Sherman, *Memoirs*, 2:532–33.

42   Ibid., 2:535; Foote, *The Civil War*, 3:402.

43   Sherman, *Memoirs*, 2:535–36.

44   Ibid., 2:536; McDonough, *Schofield*, 85; Cox, *Atlanta*, 134.

45   *OR*, 38 (pt. 4):637; John F. Marszalek, *Sherman's Other War: The General and the Civil War Press* (Memphis: Memphis State University Press, 1981), 165–66.

46   *OR*, 38 (pt. 4):637, 642.

47   Marszalek, *Sherman's Other War*, 167, 180.

48   WTS to EES, June 12 and 30, July 9, 1864, UND-SFP; WTS to HBE, July 13, 1864, OHC-WTSP; WTS to PBE, July 13, 1864, in *SCW*, 666.

49   Sherman, *Memoirs*, 2:540.

50   Ibid., 2:536, 540; Connelly, *Autumn of Glory*, 392–93; Albert Castel, *Decision in the West: The Atlanta Campaign of 1864* (Lawrence: University Press of Kansas, 1992), 340.

51   *OR*, 38 (pt. 2):515; Sherman, *Memoirs*, 2:540; McDonough, *Schofield*, 86.

52   Cox, *Atlanta*, 140; Sherman, *Memoirs*, 2:541–42; *OR*, 38 (pt. 2):516. For a detailed account of the crossing, see McDonough, *Schofield*, 86–88.

53   Cox, *Atlanta*, 140; McDonough, *Schofield*, 87.

54   *OR*, 38 (pt. 5):68, 76, 92.

55   Ibid., 38 (pt. 5):68, 76, 92; Eugene A. "Casey" McWayne to Folks at Home, July 17, 1864, McWayne letters, Sword.

56   *OR*, 38 (pt. 2):761; McMurry, *Atlanta, 1864*, 117–18.

57   WTS to PBE, July 13, 1864, in *SCW*, 666–67; Foote, *The Civil War*, 3:406–7; William Farries to brother, July 15, 1864, Farries letters, Sword.

58   Castel, *Decision in the West*, 341–42; *OR*, 38 (pt. 5):881.

59   Connelly, *Autumn of Glory*, 396–97.

60   Ibid., 397–98.

61   *OR*, 38 (pt. 5):878, 881, 882.

62   Ibid., 38 (pt. 5):883.

63   *OR*, 38 (pt. 5):885; James Lee McDonough and Thomas L. Connelly, *Five Tragic Hours: The Battle of Franklin* (Knoxville: University of Tennessee Press, 1983), 3, 4.

64   Connelly, *Autumn of Glory*, 417; *OR*, 38 (pt. 5):879–80.

65 Connelly, *Autumn of Glory*, 417–21 (uses the term "liar" in speaking of Hood); Richard M. McMurry, *John Bell Hood and the War for Southern Independence* (Lexington: University of Kentucky Press, 1982), 118–23; Castel, *Decision in the West*, 352–58.

66 *OR*, 38 (pt. 5):66, 108.

67 Sherman, *Memoirs*, 2:540–42; *OR*, 38 (pt. 5):108; Castel, *Decision in the West*, 347–48.

68 *OR*, 38 (pt. 5):143–44, 149, 150.

69 Ibid., 38 (pt. 5):123, 150.

70 Ibid., 38 (pt. 5):128, 137, 141.

71 Sherman, *Memoirs*, 2:464, 466, 467.

72 *OR*, 38 (pt. 5):150–51.

73 Ibid., 38 (pt. 5):170; Jones, *"Black Jack,"* 210.

74 Sherman, *Memoirs*, 2:543–44; Schofield, *Forty-Six Years*, 231–32.

75 Foote, *The Civil War*, 3:472; Bruce Catton, *This Hallowed Ground* (New York: Pocket, 1961), 421; Connelly, *Autumn of Glory*, 439.

76 *OR*, 38 (pt. 3):630–31; J. B. Hood, *Advance and Retreat* (1880; repr., Secaucus, N.J.: Blue & Grey Press, 1985), 168, 169, 171; Nathaniel Cheairs Hughes Jr., *General William J. Hardee: Old Reliable* (Baton Rouge: Louisiana State University Press, 1965), 225; Cox, *Atlanta*, 151–59; Connelly, *Autumn of Glory*, 418, 423, 440–44; McMurry, *Atlanta, 1864*, 146–52; McMurry, *John Bell Hood*, 127–30; Daniel, *Days of Glory*, 412–14. Mark M. Boatner, *The Civil War Dictionary* (New York: David McKay, 1959), 626, was consulted for the casualty figures. Both Cox, *Atlanta*, and McMurry, in his biography of Hood, indicate that Confederate casualties may have been significantly higher. Woodworth, *This Great Struggle* (289), states that Confederate casualties totaled 4,796.

77 Woodworth, *Nothing but Victory*, 540–41; Castel, *Decision in the West*, 383–86; Jones, *"Black Jack,"* 213; *OR*, 38 (pt. 1):907, and (pt. 3):543, 746; Buel and Johnson, *Battles and Leaders*, 4:314; Irving A. Buck, *Cleburne and His Command*, ed. Thomas Robson Hays (1908; repr., Wilmington, N.C.: Broadfoot Publishing, 1987), 233.

78 Woodworth, *Nothing but Victory*, 542–43.

79 Jones, *"Black Jack,"* 213; Sherman, *Memoirs*, 2:549; Woodworth, *Nothing but Victory*, 543; Castel, *Decision in the West*, 386–87.

80 *OR*, 38 (pt. 3):631; Woodworth, *This Great Struggle*, 289.

81 Connelly, *Autumn of Glory*, 444–45; *OR*, 38 (pt. 3):631; Hood, *Advance and Retreat*, 173–77; McMurry, *Atlanta, 1864*, 153; Castel, *Decision in the West*, 389, 413.

82 Woodworth, *Nothing but Victory*, 543–46, 549; Castel, *Decision in the West*, 393; McMurry, *Atlanta, 1864*, 154.

83 Connelly, *Autumn of Glory*, 448; Woodworth, *Nothing but Victory*, 550; Castel, *Decision in the West*, 398.

84 Woodworth, *Nothing but Victory*, 550–52; Jones, *"Black Jack,"* 214; Sherman, *Memoirs*, 2:550.

85 *OR*, 38 (pt. 1):73, and (pt. 3):103; Sherman, *Memoirs*, 2:551; Jones, *"Black Jack,"* 116, 214–15.

86 *OR*, 38 (pt. 3):582–84.

87 Eugene A. "Casey" McWayne to "My Dear Mother and Sisters," August 1, 1864, McWayne letters, Sword.

88 *OR*, 38 (pt. 3):103, 262, 265.

89   Jones, *"Black Jack,"* 216; Castel, *Decision in the West*, 393; Sherman, *Memoirs*, 2:554; Schofield, *Forty-Six Years*, 147.

90   Schofield, *Forty-Six Years*, 147.

91   Woodworth, *Nothing but Victory*, 566; Jones, *"Black Jack,"* 216.

92   Boatner, *Civil War Dictionary*, 30; Castel, *Decision in the West*, 412 (which gives the Confederate loss as 5,500); *OR*, 38 (pt. 1):73, and (pt. 3):21; Cox, *Atlanta*, 176.

93   Sherman, *Memoirs*, 2:555; Foote, *The Civil War*, 3:482; Liddell Hart, *Sherman*, 284.

94   Schofield, *Forty-Six Years*, 147–48; Sherman, *Memoirs*, 2:553–54. Castel, *Decision in the West*, 413–14, claims Sherman "did not" order Thomas to make a lodgment in Atlanta. Castel does admit that Thomas and his soldiers were less than aggressive, and "more concerned . . . with being attacked than with making an attack."

95   Cox, *Atlanta*, 171; Castel, *Decision in the West*, 414. Cox states that Colonel John W. Sprague "was soon hard pressed in Decatur, but [brigade commander James W.] Reilly going to his assistance, [Confederate cavalry under Joseph] Wheeler was repulsed and the extreme flank . . . was made secure." Evidently Cox, who was Reilly's superior officer, considered the reinforcements ordered by Sherman both necessary and timely.

96   *OR*, 38 (pt. 1):73–74; Cox, *Atlanta*, 21.

97   Woodworth, *Nothing but Victory*, 569; Buel and Johnson, *Battles and Leaders*, 4:317; Catton, *Hallowed Ground*, 424.

98   WTS to Emily Hoffman, June 9, 1864, in *SCW*, 642.

99   WTS to Emily Hoffman, August 5, 1864, in *SCW*, 682–83; Catton, *This Hallowed Ground*, 424.

100 Sherman, *Memoirs*, 2:559; WTS to EES, July 29, 1864, UND-SFP.

101 *OR*, 38 (pt. 5):272–73; WTS to EES, August 2, 1864, UND-SFP; Jones, *"Black Jack,"* 222; WTS to John A. Logan, July 27, 1864, in *SCW*, 675.

102 WTS to EES, July 26, 1864, UND-SFP.

103 *OR*, 38 (pt. 1):77–78, and (pt. 3):104–5; Sherman, *Memoirs*, 2:561–64; Jones, *"Black Jack,"* 222–23.

104 Andrew McCornack to his parents and sisters, August 1, 1864, McCornack letters, Sword.

105 *OR*, 38 (pt. 1):77–78, and (pt. 3):104–5; Sherman, *Memoirs*, 2:561–64; Jones, *"Black Jack,"* 222–23.

106 Eugene A. "Casey" McWayne to "My Dear Mother and Sisters," August 1, 1864, and to "Dear Father," August 4, 1864, McWayne letters, Sword.

107 WTS to JS, July 31, 1864, in *SCW*, 679.

108 *OR*, 38 (pt. 1):78, and (pt. 3):86; Jones, *"Black Jack,"* 224, 225.

109 Schofield, *Forty-Six Years*, 155; *OR*, 38 (pt. 5):391–92, 408–9, 434, 447; McDonough, *Schofield*, 93.

110 *OR*, 38 (pt. 5):408–9, 434, 447, 452.

111 Eugene A. "Casey" McWayne to Dear Mother, August 8, 1864, McWayne letters, Sword.

112 *OR*, 38 (pt. 5):367, 390, 447.

113 Woodworth, *This Great Struggle*, 303; *OR*, 38 (pt. 1):80–82, and (pt. 5):482.

114 Buel and Johnson, *Battles and Leaders*, 4:321–22; Jones, *"Black Jack,"* 226; McDonough, *Schofield*, 95.

115 Liddell Hart, *Sherman*, 298; Buel and Johnson, *Battles and Leaders*, 4:322; McMurry, *Atlanta, 1864*, 165–66, 170–72; Sherman, *Memoirs*, 2:580; Andrew McCornack to Dear

Parents and Sisters, September 11, 1864, McCornack letters, Sword; Letter of Captain Samuel D. McConnell, September 23, 1864, Sword.

116 Cox, *Atlanta*, 207; Liddell Hart, *Sherman*, 302–3; McDonough, *Schofield*, 96–97.

117 *OR*, 38 (pt. 5):718, 719, 746; Liddell Hart, *Sherman*, 300–301; Sherman, *Memoirs*, 2:581.

118 Sherman, *Memoirs*, 2:582; *OR*, 38 (pt. 5):777.

23. IT'S A BIG GAME, BUT I *KNOW* I CAN DO IT

1 WTS to Thomas Ewing Sr., August 13, 1863, in *SCW*, 522; Lloyd Lewis, *Sherman: Fighting Prophet* (New York: Harcourt Brace, 1932), 509.

2 William Tecumseh Sherman, *Memoirs of General W. T. Sherman*, 2 vols. (1885; repr., New York: Library of America, 1990), 2:587, 589; *OR*, 38 (pt. 1):87; Lewis, *Sherman*, 409–10.

3 Basil H. Liddell Hart, *Sherman: Soldier, Realist, American* (New York: Praeger, 1929), 305; Richard E. Beringer, Herman Hattaway, Archer Jones, and William N. Still Jr., *Why the South Lost the Civil War* (Athens: University of Georgia Press, 1986), 326; Albert Castel, *Decision in the West: The Atlanta Campaign of 1864* (Lawrence: University Press of Kansas, 1992), 543–47.

4 JS to WTS, July 24, 1864, and WTS to JS, July 31, 1864, in *SCW*, 679, 680.

5 Stephen Davis, *What the Yankees Did to Us: Sherman's Bombardment and Wrecking of Atlanta* (Macon, Ga.: Mercer University Press, 2012), 377; Castel, *Decision in the West*, 543; Charles P. Roland, *An American Iliad: The Story of the Civil War* (New York: McGraw-Hill, 1991), 196.

6 WTS to Thomas Ewing Sr., August 11 and September 15, 1864, in *SCW*, 689, 712.

7 Maurice Matloff, ed., *American Military History* (Washington, D.C.: Government Printing Office, 1969), 7.

8 Sherman, *Memoirs*, 2:490.

9 Ibid., 2:491–92.

10 *OR*, 39 (pt. 2):355–56.

11 Ibid., 39 (pt. 2):412–13.

12 James Lee McDonough, *Nashville: The Western Confederacy's Final Gamble* (Knoxville: University of Tennessee Press, 2004), 8, 35, 36, 37.

13 *OR*, 39 (pt. 3):3, 135; Clarence C. Buel and Robert U. Johnson, eds., *Battles and Leaders of the Civil War*, 4 vols. (1888; repr., New York: Castle Books, 1956), 4:441; Sherman, *Memoirs*, 2:628.

14 *OR*, 39 (pt. 3):64, 162, 222.

15 Ibid., 39 (pt. 3):202, 203, 357, 395, 576, 594, 595.

16 Ibid., 39 (pt. 3):202, 395.

17 Ibid., 39 (pt. 3):358, 660.

18 Ibid., 39 (pt. 3):358, 359.

19 Basil H. Liddell Hart, *Strategy*, rev. ed. (New York: Frederick A. Praeger, 1968), 153.

20 *OR*, 39 (pt. 3):239, 594, 679.

21 Henry Hitchcock, *Marching with Sherman: Passages from the Letters and Campaign*

Diaries of Henry Hitchcock, ed. M. A. De Wolfe Howe (New Haven: Yale University Press, 1927), 21.

22   *OR*, 38 (pt. 5):794, and 39 (pt. 2):414.

23   *OR*, 39 (pt. 2):417, 418–19; Sherman, *Memoirs*, 2:592–603; John F. Marszalek, *Sherman: A Soldier's Passion for Order* (New York: Free Press, 1993), 289; WTS to Tom Sherman, November 10, 1864, OHC-WTSP.

24   Davis, *What the Yankees Did*, 257, 258, 427; Lee Kennett, *Marching Through Georgia: The Story of Soldiers and Civilians During Sherman's Campaign* (New York: HarperCollins, 1995), 125–26, 240; Castel, *Decision in the West*, 464, 488; Joseph T. Glatthaar, *The March to the Sea and Beyond: Sherman's Troops in the Savannah and Carolinas Campaigns* (New York: New York University Press, 1985), 136, 139; Sherman, *Memoirs*, 2:654; Burke Davis, *Sherman's March* (New York: Random House, 1980), 5, 29; Noah Andre Trudeau, *Southern Storm: Sherman's March to the Sea* (New York: HarperCollins, 2008), 68, 88.

25   *OR*, 39 (pt. 3):378; Sherman, *Memoirs*, 2:616.

26   Sherman, *Memoirs*, 2:646, 649.

27   *OR*, 39 (pt. 3):358; Sherman, *Memoirs*, 2:654, 656.

28   *OR*, 39 (pt.3):701.

29   Ibid., 39 (pt. 3):713–14.

30   Ibid., 39 (pt. 3):713.

31   Hitchcock, *Marching with Sherman*, 75, 76; Sherman, *Memoirs*, 2:659; John Bennett Walters, *Merchant of Terror: General Sherman and Total War* (New York: Bobbs-Merrill, 1973), 172.

32   Sherman, *Memoirs*, 2:659; Hitchcock, *Marching with Sherman*, 75.

33   Eugene A. "Casey" McWayne to mother and sisters, December 19, 1864, McWayne letters, Sword.

34   Stanley P. Hirshson, *The White Tecumseh: A Biography of General William T. Sherman* (New York: John Wiley & Sons, 1997), 257.

35   Hitchcock, *Marching with Sherman*, 75–76; Davis, *Sherman's March*, 30, 87; Glatthaar, *March to the Sea*, 71; Kennett, *Marching Through Georgia*, 301; Marszalek, *Sherman*, 302.

36   Sherman, *Memoirs*, 2:661–62; Hitchcock, *Marching with Sherman*, 83–85; Trudeau, *Southern Storm*, 118.

37   Anne J. Bailey, *The Chessboard of War: Sherman and Hood in the Autumn Campaigns of 1864* (Lincoln: University of Nebraska Press, 2000), 61–62; *OR*, 44:797–98; WTS to EES, January 15, 1865, UND-SFP; Victor Davis Hanson, *The Sound of Battle* (New York: Anchor, 2001), 170.

38   Hitchcock, *Marching with Sherman*, 85; George Ward Nichols, *The Story of the Great March from the Diary of a Staff Officer* (New York: Harper and Brothers, 1865), 56–58; Sherman, *Memoirs*, 2:663–65; Stanley Weintraub, *General Sherman's Christmas: Savannah, 1864* (New York: HarperCollins, 2009), 76; Davis, *Sherman's March*, 63.

39   Hitchcock, *Marching with Sherman*, 86; Weintraub, *Sherman's Christmas*, 80–81; Sherman, *Memoirs*, 2:666.

40   Nichols, *Story of the Great March*, 56; Weintraub, *Sherman's Christmas*, 87; Hitchcock, *Marching with Sherman*, 119, 122, 158.

41   Hitchcock, *Marching with Sherman*, 78.

42 Nichols, *Story of the Great March*, 84; Weintraub, *Sherman's Christmas*, 66, 85; Hitchcock, *Marching with Sherman*, 155.

43 Hitchcock, *Marching with Sherman*, 121–23.

44 Davis, *Sherman's March*, 46; Nichols, *Story of the Great March*, 101; Hitchcock, *Marching with Sherman*, 96, 127; Weintraub, *Sherman's Christmas*, 57; Walters, *Merchant of Terror*, 176, 177; Glatthaar, *March to the Sea*, 77, 78; Marszalek, *Sherman*, 305; Trudeau, *Southern Storm*, 325–26.

45 Jesse B. Connelly Diary, Indiana Historical Society, Indianapolis; James Lee McDonough, *War in Kentucky: From Shiloh to Perryville* (Knoxville: University of Tennessee Press, 1994), 193–96.

46 Bailey, *Chessboard of War*, 115–16; Weintraub, *Sherman's Christmas*, 127–29; Hirshson, *The White Tecumseh*, 260.

47 Sherman, *Memoirs*, 2:670; Hitchcock, *Marching with Sherman*, 161; Nichols, *Story of the Great March*, 86. Sherman gives the date as December 8 in his memoirs, but Hitchcock and Nichols, recording events during the march and riding with Sherman, both place the event as December 9.

48 Sherman, *Memoirs*, 2:670; Hitchcock, *Marching with Sherman*, 161–62; Nichols, *Story of the Great March*, 86.

49 Sherman, *Memoirs*, 2:671–72; Hitchcock, *Marching with Sherman*, 185–86.

50 Hitchcock, *Marching with Sherman*, 187; William B. Hazen, *A Narrative of Military Service* (Boston: Ticknor and Co., 1885), 333–34; WTS to EES, January 15, 1865, UND-SFP; Eugene A. "Casey" McWayne to "Dear Folks at Home," December 1864, McWayne letters, Sword.

51 Hitchcock, *Marching with Sherman*, 195–96, 198; *OR*, 44:702, 727, 783; Sherman, *Memoirs*, 2:711; Eugene A. "Casey" McWayne to "Dear Mother and Sisters," December 19, 1864, McWayne letters, Sword.

52 Weintraub, *Sherman's Christmas*, 167–68.

53 Sherman, *Memoirs*, 2:694–95; Hitchcock, *Marching with Sherman*, 199; WTS to EES, December 25, 1864, and January 2, 1865, UND-SFP; "Historical Reference Handbook for the Green-Meldrim House," edited by Jim Harden, and researched by Dr. Michael D. Morford. Thomas S. Johnston, M.D., kindly provided this last source for my research, and I am grateful to him. Peter W. Meldrim was the second owner, purchasing the house after the death of Charles Green.

54 "Handbook for the Green-Meldrim House."

55 Hitchcock, *Marching with Sherman*, 199; Weintraub, *Sherman's Christmas*, 176.

56 Hitchcock, *Marching with Sherman*, 201.

57 Sherman, *Memoirs*, 2:682.

58 *OR*, 44:6, 7, 726–28, 743.

59 Sherman, *Memoirs*, 2:700–701.

60 *OR*, 44:797–98.

61 Ibid., 44:798–800; Sherman, *Memoirs*, 2:697; Trudeau, *Southern Storm*, 243, 535; Davis, *Sherman's March* , 145, 210; Glatthaar, *March to the Sea*, 73; Kennett, *Marching Through Georgia*, 306, 307.

62 *OR*, 44:6–7, 841; WTS to EES, December 16, 1864, January 5 and 15, 1865, UND-SFP.

63 WTS to EES, December 25, 1864, and January 5, 1865, UND-SFP.

64 Hitchcock, *Marching with Sherman*, 202, 203; Nichols, *Story of the Great March*, 101; WTS to EES, December 25, 1864, UND-SFP.

65 Hitchcock, *Marching with Sherman*, 202, 203.

66 Sherman, *Memoirs*, 2:727–28.

67 *OR*, 47 (pt. 2):36–37.

68 WTS to Salmon P. Chase, January 11, 1865, in *SCW*, 794; Sherman, *Memoirs*, 2:729; Nichols, *Story of the Great March*, 103.

69 WTS to EES, January 15, 1865, UND-SFP.

70 *OR*, 47 (pt. 2):5–6; Sherman, *Memoirs*, 2:723.

71 Sherman, *Memoirs*, 2:725; *OR*, 47 (pt. 2):37–41.

72 *OR*, 47 (pt. 2):37–41; Sherman, *Memoirs*, 2:726–27; Nichols, *Story of the Great March*, 102.

73 *OR*, 47 (pt. 2):60–62; Hirshson, *The White Tecumseh*, 273; Sherman, *Memoirs*, 2:730–31.

24. TAKING THE WAR TO THE BRAGGART CAROLINIANS

1 WTS to EES, December 31, 1864, January 2 and 5, 1865, UND-SFP; WTS to Minnie Sherman, December 25, 1864, in *SCW*, 779.

2 EES to WTS, December 30, 1864, UND-SFP.

3 WTS to EES, January 15, 1865, UND-SFP.

4 Stanley P. Hirshson, *The White Tecumseh: A Biography of General William T. Sherman* (New York: John Wiley & Sons, 1997), 269–70; WTS to EES, March 10 and April 22, 1864, and WTS to PBE, January 29, 1865, in *SCW*, 608n4, 627n6, 814.

5 John Y. Simon, ed., *The Papers of Ulysses S. Grant*, 31 vols. (Carbondale: Southern Illinois University Press, 1967–), 13:148–49, 153–54.

6 WTS to JS, January 22, 1865, and WTS to PBE, January 29, 1865, in *SCW*, 809, 811–12; Simon, *Papers of Ulysses S. Grant*, 13:154.

7 WTS to JS, January 22, 1865, in *SCW*, 809; *OR*, 47 (pt. 2):102–4; Simon, *Papers of Ulysses S. Grant*, 13:350.

8 *OR*, 47 (pt. 2):102–4, 154–56.

9 Ibid., 44:702, and 47 (pt. 2):69; WTS to JS, December 31, 1864, in *SCW*, 786.

10 Manning F. Force, *General Sherman* (New York: D. Appleton and Co., 1899), 265–71; James P. Jones, *"Black Jack": John A. Logan and Southern Illinois in the Civil War Era* (Tallahassee: Florida State University Press, 1967), 244; Charles Royster, *The Destructive War: William Tecumseh Sherman, Stonewall Jackson, and the Americans* (New York: Alfred A. Knopf, 1991), 4.

11 Force, *General Sherman*, 269–70; Nathaniel Cheairs Hughes Jr., *General William J. Hardee: Old Reliable* (Baton Rouge: Louisiana State University Press, 1965), 276; Hirshson, *The White Tecumseh*, 277.

12 William Tecumseh Sherman, *Memoirs of General W. T. Sherman*, 2 vols. (1885; repr., New York: Library of America, 1990), 2:741, 752.

13 Ibid., 2:752; Richard Harwell and Philip N. Racine, eds., *The Fiery Trail: A Union Officer's Account of Sherman's Last Campaigns* (Knoxville: University of Tennessee Press, 1986), 90.

14 Harwell and Racine, *Fiery Trail*, 98.

15   Ibid., 92, 99, 101, 105.

16   Ibid., 92; Steven E. Woodworth, *Nothing but Victory: The Army of the Tennessee, 1861–1865* (New York: Alfred A. Knopf, 2005), 610.

17   Sherman, *Memoirs*, 2:754; Harwell and Racine, *Fiery Trail*, 106–8; George Ward Nichols, *The Story of the Great March from the Diary of a Staff Officer* (New York: Harper and Brothers, 1865), 150–51.

18   Force, *General Sherman*, 269–70; Sherman, *Memoirs*, 2:755.

19   Sherman, *Memoirs*, 2:755; Harwell and Racine, *Fiery Trail*, 119; Joseph T. Glatthaar, *The March to the Sea and Beyond: Sherman's Troops in the Savannah and Carolinas Campaigns* (New York: New York University Press, 1985), 142.

20   Glatthaar, *March to the Sea*, 142–43; Joseph B. Foraker, *Notes of a Busy Life* (Cincinnati: Stewart and Kidd Co., 1916), 53; Sherman, *Memoirs*, 2:734.

21   Nichols, *Story of the Great March*, 149; Harwell and Racine, *Fiery Trail*, 117.

22   Nichols, *Story of the Great March*, 149, 150.

23   Royster, *Destructive War*, 5–6. Nichols, *Story of the Great March*, 162.

24   Royster, *Destructive War*, 7.

25   Harwell and Racine, *Fiery Trail*, 103, 110, 122, 128, 129; Royster, *Destructive War*, 11, 12, 14, 16; Sherman, *Memoirs*, 2:761.

26   Harwell and Racine, *Fiery Trail*, 128; Nichols, *Story of the Great March*, 161, 162.

27   Sherman, *Memoirs*, 2:761, 762–64.

28   Ibid., 2:758, 761; Harwell and Racine, *Fiery Trail*, 128; Hirshson, *The White Tecumseh*, 282.

29   Sherman, *Memoirs*, 2:31, 761, 764–65.

30   Ibid., 2:765–66.

31   Ibid., 2:766; Book of Daniel 5:24–31 (Revised Standard Version); Glatthaar, *March to the Sea*, 143.

32   Force, *General Sherman*, 274; Harwell and Racine, *Fiery Trail*, 129; Royster, *Destructive War*, 20; Nichols, *Story the Great March*, 165; Sherman, *Memoirs*, 2:766–67.

33   Nichols, *Story of the Great March*, 165; Harwell and Racine, *Fiery Trail*, 129; Royster, *Destructive War*, 19.

34   Nichols, *Story of the Great March*, 165; Sherman, *Memoirs*, 2:767.

35   Royster, *Destructive War*, 19.

36   Harwell and Racine, *Fiery Trail*, 134; Royster, *Destructive War*, 30; *Louisville Courier-Journal*, July 8, 1875.

37   Sherman, *Memoirs*, 2:760, 768.

38   Ibid., 2:767; *New York Times*, June 9, 1881. For a full discussion of the issues, consult Marion B. Lucas, *Sherman and the Burning of Columbia* (College Station, Tex.: A & M University Press, 1976).

39   Harwell and Racine, *Fiery Trail*, 139.

40   Ibid., 143, 148, 149.

41   *OR*, 47 (pt. 2):533, 543–44, 554–55.

42   Ibid., 47 (pt. 2):546, 596–97.

43   WTS to EES, March 12, 1865, UND-SFP.

44   *OR*, 47 (pt. 2):154–56, 793–94; WTS to EES, December 31, 1864, UND-SFP.

45   *OR*, 47 (pt. 2):704, 717, 721.

46   Hirshson, *The White Tecumseh*, 290; Nichols, *Story of the Great March*, 249.

47 Sherman, *Memoirs*, 2:776–77; David S. Heidler and Jeanne T. Heidler, eds., *Encyclopedia of the American Civil War: A Political, Social, and Military History*, 5 vols. (Santa Barbara, Calif.: ABC-CLIO, 2000), 1:215, 216; *OR*, 47 (pt. 2):794–95.

48 Nichols, *Story of the Great March*, 252.

49 Hirshson, *The White Tecumseh*, 291; Nichols, *Story of the Great March*, 251; *OR*, 47 (pt. 1):909; Jacob Cox, *The March to the Sea; Franklin and Nashville* (New York: Charles Scribner's Sons, 1882), 147; James Lee McDonough, *Schofield: Union General in the Civil War and Reconstruction* (Tallahassee: Florida State University Press, 1972), 151.

50 Heidler and Heidler, *Encyclopedia of the Civil War*, 1:215–17; *OR*, 47 (pt. 2):949.

51 Heidler and Heidler, *Encyclopedia of the Civil War*, 1:215–17.

52 Sherman, *Memoirs*, 2:786; *OR*, 47 (pt. 2):919.

53 WTS to Thomas Ewing Sr., December 31, 1864, in *SCW*, 782.

54 Heidler and Heidler, *Encyclopedia of the Civil War*, 1:215–17.

55 Sherman, *Memoirs*, 2:788–89.

56 WTS to Minnie Sherman, March 24, 1865, in *SCW*, 834; WTS to EES, March 23, 1865, UND-SFP.

57 WTS to William M. McPherson, March 24, 1865, in *SCW*, 833.

58 WTS to Salmon P. Chase, January 11, 1865, and WTS to William M. McPherson, March 24, 1865, in *SCW*, 795, 833.

59 WTS to Thomas Turner, March 25, 1865, in *SCW*, 835–36.

60 *OR*, 47 (pt. 3):6.

61 Sherman, *Memoirs*, 2:810; Horace Porter, *Campaigning with Grant* (1897; repr., New York: Da Capo, 1986), 417–18.

62 Porter, *Campaigning with Grant*, 418–20; Sherman, *Memoirs*, 2:810.

63 Porter, *Campaigning with Grant*, 420–21.

64 Ibid., 422–23; Sherman, *Memoirs*, 2:811.

65 Sherman, *Memoirs*, 2:811; Porter, *Campaigning with Grant*, 413–14, 423; Doris Kearns Goodwin, *Team of Rivals: The Political Genius of Abraham Lincoln* (New York: Simon and Schuster, 2005), 711–12.

66 Porter, *Campaigning with Grant*, 423–24; Sherman, *Memoirs*, 2:811–12.

67 Sherman, *Memoirs*, 2:812, 813; Porter, *Campaigning with Grant*, 424; Goodwin, *Team of Rivals*, 713.

68 Porter, *Campaigning with Grant*, 424; Sherman, *Memoirs*, 2:812, 813.

69 WTS to EES, March 31 and April 5, 1865, UND-SFP.

70 Ibid.

71 WTS to Thomas Ewing, April 5, 1865, in *SCW*, 842.

72 *OR*, 47 (pt. 3):128–29; E. B. Long with Barbara Long, *The Civil War Day by Day: An Almanac, 1861–65* (New York: Doubleday, 1971), 675.

25. A SOLDIER OF RENOWN

1 William Tecumseh Sherman, *Memoirs of General W. T. Sherman*, 2 vols. (1885; repr., New York: Library of America, 1990), 2:836; *OR*, 47 (pt. 3):220–21.

2 Sherman, *Memoirs*, 2:837; *OR*, 47 (pt. 3):245.

3 Sherman, *Memoirs*, 2:837–38; Gilbert E. Govan and James W. Livingood, *A Different Valor: The Story of General Joseph E. Johnston, C.S.A.* (1956; repr., Westbury, Conn.:

Greenwood Press, 1973), 363–64; Joseph E. Johnston, *Narrative of Military Operations Directed During the Late War Between the States* (New York: D. Appleton, 1874), 402–4.

4   *OR*, 47 (pt. 3):238–39.

5   Sherman, *Memoirs*, 2:838–39; Henry Hitchcock, *Marching with Sherman: Passages from the Letters and Campaign Diaries of Henry Hitchcock*, ed. M. A. De Wolfe Howe (New Haven: Yale University Press, 1927), 309; Richard Harwell and Philip N. Racine, eds., *The Fiery Trail: A Union Officer's Account of Sherman's Last Campaigns* (Knoxville: University of Tennessee Press, 1986), 213.

6   Harwell and Racine, *Fiery Trail*, 213; James P. Jones, *"Black Jack": John A. Logan and Southern Illinois in the Civil War Era* (Tallahassee: Florida State University Press, 1967), 258.

7   Sherman, *Memoirs*, 2:839–40; Jones, *"Black Jack,"* 258.

8   Sherman, *Memoirs*, 2:840; Govan and Livingood, *A Different Valor*, 365.

9   *OR*, 47 (pt. 3):177, 221; Sherman, *Memoirs*, 2:840; Govan and Livingood, *A Different Valor*, 365.

10 Sherman, *Memoirs*, 2:840–41; Govan and Livingood, *A Different Valor*, 365.

11 Govan and Livingood, *A Different Valor*, 365–66.

12 Sherman, *Memoirs*, 2:814, 841; *OR*, 47 (pt. 3):243.

13 *OR*, 47 (pt. 3):243–44.

14 *OR*, 47 (pt. 3):263; Burke Davis, *Sherman's March* (New York: Random House, 1980), 270; Benjamin P. Thomas and Harold Hyman, *Stanton: The Life and Times of Lincoln's Secretary of War* (New York: Alfred A. Knopf, 1962), 401, 407.

15 *OR*, 47 (pt. 3):263, 334.

16 Ibid., 47 (pt. 1):37–38, and (pt. 3):277, 311–12, 454, 634.

17 Ibid., 47 (pt. 3):285–86, 334; Sherman, *Memoirs*, 2:860, 861–62.

18 Sherman, *Memoirs*, 2:851; Davis, *Sherman's March*, 272, 273; Brooks D. Simpson, *Let Us Have Peace: Ulysses S. Grant and the Politics of War and Reconstruction, 1861–1868* (Chapel Hill: University of North Carolina Press, 1991), 97.

19 *OR*, 47 (pt. 3):293, 301–2.

20 Ibid., 47 (pt. 3):311; Davis, *Sherman's March*, 275.

21 *OR*, 47 (pt. 3):263, 302.

22 John M. Gibson, *Those 163 Days: A Southern Account of Sherman's March from Atlanta to Raleigh* (New York: Coward-McCann, 1961), 286, 287; Davis, *Sherman's March*, 275.

23 *OR*, 47 (pt. 3):482; John M. Schofield, *Forty-Six Years in the Army* (New York: Century, 1897), 350–52; Davis, *Sherman's March*, 276; George Ward Nichols, *The Story of the Great March from the Diary of a Staff Officer* (New York: Harper and Brothers, 1865), 320.

24 Frederic Bancroft and William A. Dunning, eds., *The Reminiscences of Carl Schurz*, 3 vols. (New York: William S. Hein and Co., 1908), 3:116–17.

25 Tom Ewing quoted in Stanley P. Hirshson, *The White Tecumseh: A Biography of General William T. Sherman* (New York: John Wiley & Sons, 1997), 313.

26 *OR*, 47 (pt. 3):335; WTS to U. S. Grant, "private and confidential," May 10, 1865, in *SCW*, 894–95.

27 WTS to EES, May 8, 1865, UND-SFP; *OR*, 47 (pt. 3):478, 582.

28 Lloyd Lewis, *Sherman: Fighting Prophet* (New York: Harcourt Brace, 1932), 558–59.

29 *OR*, 47 (pt. 3):410–12.

30 Ibid., 47 (pt. 3):412.

31   WTS to EES, May 8 and 10, 1865, UND-SFP.

32   Lewis, *Sherman*, 564-65.

33   *OR*, 47 (pt. 3):435, 454-55; Davis, *Sherman's March*, 281; Anna McAllister, *Ellen Ewing: Wife of General Sherman* (New York: Benziger Brothers, 1936), 303-4; EES to WTS, May 17, 1865, UND-SFP.

34   *OR*, 47 (pt. 3):454-55.

35   WTS to James E. Yeatman, May 21, 1865, UND-SFP.

36   *OR*, 47 (pt. 3):531.

37   Hirshson, *The White Tecumseh*, 317; Sherman, *Memoirs*, 2:864.

38   Davis, *Sherman's March*, 287; Nichols, *Story of the Great March*, 354, 369.

39   Nichols, *Story of the Great March*, records the proceedings on 350-82; see particularly 354 and 365 for the quotations.

40   *OR*, 47 (pt. 3):532, 562; Jones, *"Black Jack,"* 261; Oliver O. Howard, *The Autobiography of Oliver Otis Howard*, 2 vols. (New York: Baker and Taylor, 1907), 2:210-11.

41   Sherman, *Memoirs*, 2:865; Lewis, *Sherman*, 572-73.

42   Sherman, *Memoirs*, 2:865; Jones, *"Black Jack,"* 262; Lewis, *Sherman*, 573-75; Bancroft and Dunning, *Reminiscences of Carl Schurz*, 3:137.

43   Sherman, *Memoirs*, 2:865-69; Lewis, *Sherman*, 575.

44   Sherman, *Memoirs*, 2:866; *OR*, 47 (pt. 3):586.

45   *OR*, 47 (pt. 3):576.

46   Ibid., 47 (pt. 3):582.

47   Ibid., 47 (pt. 3):582-83.

48   Ibid., 47 (pt. 3):586, and (pt. 1):44; Bancroft and Dunning, *Reminiscences of Carl Schurz*, 3:128.

49   Bancroft and Dunning, *Reminiscences of Carl Schurz*, 3:128-29; WTS to JS, August 3, 1865, in Thorndike, 252.

50   Lewis, *Sherman*, 583-84.

51   Ibid., 583, relates Scott's words to Sherman.

52   Sherman, *Memoirs*, 2:900; Lewis, *Sherman*, 584-86; McAllister, *Ellen Ewing*, 308-9; WTS to JS, December 22, 1865, in Thorndike, 260.

53   Sherman, *Memoirs*, 2:903.

54   Hirshson, *The White Tecumseh*, 323.

55   WTS to E. O. C. Ord, March 1, 1866, William T. Sherman MSS, Missouri Historical Society, St. Louis; Lewis, *Sherman*, 592.

56   Sherman, *Memoirs*, 2:901, 902; Robert G. Athearn, *William Tecumseh Sherman and the Settlement of the West* (Norman: University of Oklahoma Press, 1956), 13, 18, 19; Lewis, *Sherman*, 595, 599; Stephen E. Ambrose, *Nothing Like It in the World: The Men Who Built the Transcontinental Railroad 1863-1869* (New York: Simon and Schuster, 2000), 259.

57   Athearn, *Sherman*, 201, 202; WTS to E. O. C. Ord, May 28, 1867, Sherman MSS, Missouri Historical Society.

58   Athearn, *Sherman*, 66, 207-8; Russell F. Weigley, *History of the United States Army*, enlarged ed. (Bloomington: University of Indiana Press, 1984), 262, 267. See also Weigley's *The American Way of War: A History of United States Military Strategy and Policy* (Bloomington: University of Indiana Press, 1977), 157-59.

59   Sherman, *Memoirs*, 2:924-25; WTS to EES, September 19, 1867, UND-SFP.

60 Lee Kennett, *Sherman: A Soldier's Life* (New York: Perennial, 2002), 294; Athearn, *Sherman*, 205, 206; Lewis, *Sherman*, 596.

61 Athearn, *Sherman*, 202.

62 Ibid., 203–4; WTS to JS, June 11, 1868, in Thorndike, 318–19; Kennett, *Sherman*, 299.

63 Athearn, *Sherman*, 209; WTS to JS, September 23, 1868, in Thorndike, 321–22; WTS to EES, August 28, 1868, UND-SFP.

64 Sherman, *Memoirs*, 2:904–5; Lewis, *Sherman*, 588–89.

65 Sherman, *Memoirs*, 2:905–9; WTS to EES, October 26, 1866, UND-SFP.

66 WTS to EES, November 18, 1866, UND-SFP; WTS to JS, November 7, 1866, in Thorndike, 284–86.

67 Hirshson, *The White Tecumseh*, 329; Lewis, *Sherman*, 589; WTS to EES, November 18, 1866, UND-SFP.

68 McAllister, *Ellen Ewing*, 316–17.

69 Merrill, *Sherman*, 316; WTS to E. O. C. Ord, April 23, 1867, Sherman MSS, Missouri Historical Society.

70 Merrill, *Sherman*, 316–17.

71 WTS to JS, October 20, 1866, in Thorndike, 277; Athearn, *Sherman*, 212–17.

72 WTS to EES, May 10, 1867, UND-SFP; Lewis, *Sherman*, 595–96.

73 EES to Thomas Ewing Sr., March 5, 1868, UND-SFP.

74 Lewis, *Sherman*, 586–87; WTS to JS, n.d., September 21, November 4 and 29, 1865, and January 19, February 11, and n.d., 1866, in Thorndike, 254, 256, 257, 260, 261–62.

75 Sherman, *Memoirs*, 2:920, 921.

76 Ibid., 2:921, 922, 923.

77 JS to WTS, March 1866, and WTS to JS, August 3 and September 12, 1867, in Thorndike, 269, 292, 295.

26. GENERAL-IN-CHIEF, I

1 EES to Thomas Ewing Sr., January 19 and March 19, 1869, OHC-WTSP.

2 Ibid.

3 Lloyd Lewis, *Sherman: Fighting Prophet* (New York: Harcourt Brace, 1932), 604.

4 William Tecumseh Sherman, *Memoirs of General W. T. Sherman*, 2 vols. (1885; repr., New York: Library of America, 1990), 2:928, 931.

5 Ibid., 2:932–33; Lewis, *Sherman*, 601.

6 Sherman, *Memoirs*, 2:933–35.

7 James Pickett Jones, *John A. Logan: Stalwart Republican from Illinois* (Tallahassee: Florida State University Press, 1982), 28–29, 34–36, 39–41; Lewis, *Sherman*, 603; Stanley P. Hirshson, *The White Tecumseh: A Biography of General William T. Sherman* (New York: John Wiley & Sons, 1997), 343.

8 WTS to E. O. C. Ord, August 1, 1870, OHC-WTSP.

9 WTS to EES, April 21, 1871, UND-SFP; James M. Merrill, *William Tecumseh Sherman* (New York: Rand McNally, 1971), 338.

10 My account of the confrontation at Fort Sill is primarily based upon Dee Brown, *Bury My Heart at Wounded Knee: An Indian History of the American West* (New York: Holt, Rinehart and Winston, 1970), 244–46, 250–54. Also consulted were Paul Andrew

Hutton, *Phil Sheridan and His Army* (Lincoln: University of Nebraska Press, 1985), 234–36; Hirshson, *The White Tecumseh*, 346–47; John F. Marszalek, *Sherman: A Soldier's Passion for Order* (New York: Free Press, 1993), 394–95; Merrill, *Sherman*, 340; Robert G. Athearn, *William Tecumseh Sherman and the Settlement of the West* (Norman: University of Oklahoma Press, 1956), 290–96; Steven E. Woodworth, *Sherman* (New York: Palgrave Macmillan, 2009), 169–70.

11   Brown, *Bury My Heart*, 254–55; Hutton, *Phil Sheridan*, 236; Merrill, *Sherman*, 340.

12   Merrill, *Sherman*, 341; Marszalek, *Sherman*, 397; Athearn, *Sherman*, 296; Woodworth, *Sherman*, 170.

13   Lewis, *Sherman*, 609–11; Merrill, *Sherman*, 343.

14   Merrill, *Sherman*, 343–44; WTS to EES, December 4, 1871, OHC-WTSP.

15   WTS to EES, December 4 and 14, 1871, OHC-WTSP.

16   WTS to EES, December 28, 1871, OHC-WTSP.

17   Ibid.; WTS to EES, January 6, 1872, OHC-WTSP; Lewis, *Sherman*, 612.

18   WTS to EES, January 6, 1872, OHC-WTSP.

19   Williston Walker, *A History of the Christian Church*, 3d ed. (New York: Charles Scribner's Sons, 1970), 251, 523, 524; WTS to HST, March 1, 1872, OHC-WTSP; WTS to EES, February 18, 1872, UND-SFP.

20   WTS to HST, March 1, 1872, OHC-WTSP; Joseph Audenried, "Notes of Travel in Europe: General Sherman in Europe and the East," OHC-WTSP.

21   WTS to HST, April 16 and 25, 1872, OHC-WTSP.

22   Hirshson, *The White Tecumseh*, 350.

23   Sherman, *Memoirs*, 2:943; WTS to HST, November 5, 1872, OHC-WTSP; Lewis, *Sherman*, 613.

24   Merrill, *Sherman*, 349; Sherman, *Memoirs*, 2:943; Brown, *Bury My Heart*, 220–40; John M. Schofield, *Forty-Six Years in the Army* (New York: Century, 1897), 435.

25   Brown, *Bury My Heart*, 233–38.

26   Ibid., 230–31, 239–40.

27   Merrill, *Sherman*, 350; Schofield, *Forty-Six Years*, 437, 438.

28   Sherman, *Memoirs*, 2:943–44; Merrill, *Sherman*, 352–53; Lewis, *Sherman*, 615.

29   Joseph T. Durkin, S.J., *General Sherman's Son* (New York: Farrar, Straus and Cudahy, 1959), 36, 38, 40.

30   Ibid., 39.

31   Ibid., 52; WTS to Minnie Sherman Fitch, June 16, 1878, OHC-WTSP.

32   WTS to HST, May 27, June 28, July 24, 1878, OHC-WTSP; Merrill, *Sherman*, 372.

33   Hirshson, *The White Tecumseh*, 366–67; WTS to Elly Sherman, June 5, 1878, and WTS to HST, November 29, 1878, OHC-WTSP.

34   George Brown Tindall with David E. Shi, *America: A Narrative History*, 3rd ed. (New York: W. W. Norton, 1992), 2:726; Woodworth, *Sherman*, 171; Marszalek, *Sherman*, 413–14; WTS to HST, July 29, August 4 and 10, October 13, December 25, 1878, and March 9, 1879, OHC-WTSP.

35   WTS to HST, March 9, 1879, OHC-WTSP.

36   Ibid.

37   Ibid. The military academy, located at Alexandria when Sherman was connected with it, had been moved to Baton Rouge.

38   Ibid.

39   Kennett, *Sherman*, 311, 312; Sherman, *Memoirs*, 2:1113.

40   Russell F. Weigley, *The American Way of War: A History of U.S. Military Strategy and Policy* (Bloomington: University of Indiana Press, 1977), xx, 168; Allan R. Millett and Peter Maslowski, *For the Common Defense: A Military History of the United States of America*, rev. ed. (New York: Free Press, 1994), 272–73.

41   Tindall and Shi, *America*, 2:793–95; Kennett, *Sherman*, 312.

42   Millett and Maslowski, *For the Common Defense*, 274; Kennett, *Sherman*, 316.

43   Kennett, *Sherman*, 314; Millett and Maslowski, *For the Common Defense*, 271–72.

44   WTS to HST, May 2, 1880, OHC-WTSP; Schofield, *Forty-Six Years*, 445–46.

45   WTS to HST, May 2, 1880, OHC-WTSP; Schofield, *Forty-Six Years*, 445, 447.

46   Michael Fellman, *Citizen Sherman: A Life of William Tecumseh Sherman* (New York: Random House, 1995), 345; "The Evils of the Dance," EES to "Mr. Rulofson," December 2, 1877, OHC-WTSP.

47   EES to granddaughter Eleanor Fitch, June 3, 1880, OHC-WTSP; Fellman, *Citizen Sherman*, 359, 361; Marszalek, *Sherman*, 421.

27. GENERAL-IN-CHIEF, II

1   *Ohio State Journal*, August 12, 1880; *Columbus Evening Dispatch*, August 11, 1880.

2   *Ohio State Journal*, August 12, 1880; *Columbus Evening Dispatch*, August 13, 1880.

3   *Columbus Evening Dispatch*, August 11 and 12, 1880; *Ohio State Journal*, August 12, 1880.

4   *Columbus Evening Dispatch*, August 12, 1880; *Ohio State Journal*, August 12, 1880.

5   WTS to HST, May 16 and August 26, 1880, OHC-WTSP; William Tecumseh Sherman, *Memoirs of General W. T. Sherman*, 2 vols. (1885; repr., New York: Library of America, 1990), 2:1115.

6   WTS to HST, August 26, October 8, November 25, 1880, OHC-WTSP; Sherman, *Memoirs*, 2:1115; Michael Fellman, *Citizen Sherman: A Life of William Tecumseh Sherman* (New York: Random House, 1995), 359; John F. Marszalek, *Sherman: A Soldier's Passion for Order* (New York: Free Press, 1993), 419.

7   George Brown Tindall with David E. Shi, *America: A Narrative History*, 3rd ed. (New York: W. W. Norton, 1992), 2:869; WTS to HST, June 18, 1880, OHC-WTSP.

8   WTS to HST, November 25, 1880, OHC-WTSP.

9   WTS to HST, January 16 and 29, February 7, 1881, OHC-WTSP; Sherman, *Memoirs*, 2:1115–16.

10   WTS to HST, March 10, 1881, OHC-WTSP; Tindall and Shi, *America*, 2:869–70.

11   WTS to HST, July 4 and 30, August 28, 1881, OHC-WTSP.

12   WTS to HST, July 4 and August 28, 1881, OHC-WTSP.

13   WTS to HST, August 28 and September 16, 1881, OHC-WTSP.

14   Tindall and Shi, *America*, 2:870; WTS to HST, October 23 and November 24, 1881, OHC-WTSP; Thomas A. Bailey and David M. Kennedy, *The American Pageant: A History of the Republic*, 8th ed. (Lexington, Mass.: D. C. Heath, 1987), 493.

15   WTS to HST, November 24, 1881, OHC-WTSP.

16   William B. Hesseltine and David L. Smiley, *The South in American History*, 2nd ed. (Englewood Cliffs, N.J.: Prentice Hall, 1960), 395–96, 402, 412.

17   WTS to HST, November 24, 1881, OHC-WTSP; Howard Jones, *The Course of American*

        Diplomacy: From the Revolution to the Present, 2nd ed. (Chicago: Dorsey Press, 1988), 227; *New York Times*, November 28, 1873.

18   Hesseltine and Smiley, *The South*, 412; WTS to HST, November 24, 1881, OHC-WTSP.

19   WTS to HST, November 24, 1881, OHC-WTSP. On the Southern "lost cause" mentality, see John Latschar and Robert K. Sutton, eds., *The Civil War Remembered* (National Park Service, U. S. Department of the Interior, 2011), 158–60, 169, 171; Thomas L. Connelly, *The Marble Man: Robert E. Lee and His Image in American Society* (New York: Alfred A. Knopf, 1977), 91–98, 100–103; Richard E. Beringer, Herman Hattaway, Archer Jones, and William N. Still Jr., *Why the South Lost the Civil War* (Athens: University of Georgia Press, 1986), 405–8, 412–13; Gary W. Gallagher, *The Confederate War* (Cambridge, Mass.: Harvard University Press, 1997), 168–72.

20   WTS to HST, March 3, 1873, May 3 and 16, 1876, August 15, 1880, OHC-WTSP.

21   WTS to HST, October 22, 1879, June 23 and August 15, 1880, OHC-WTSP.

22   WTS to HST, March 3, 1879, June 23 and August 15, 1880, OHC-WTSP.

23   WTS to HST, August 21 and November 24, 1881, OHC-WTSP.

24   WTS to HST, November 5 and 24, December 12, 1881, OHC-WTSP.

25   Sherman, *Memoirs*, 2:948–49, 1116; WTS to EES, June 19 and 22, 1882, UND-SFP; JS to WTS, March 7, 1884, in Thorndike, 358–59 (see also p. 355).

26   Sherman, *Memoirs*, 2:949; WTS to JS, June 7, 1883, in Thorndike, 356–57.

27   Sherman, *Memoirs*, 2:949, 1116, 1117; WTS to JS, February 28, 1883, in Thorndike, 354; Angie Debo, *Geronimo: The Man, His Time, His Place* (Norman: University of Oklahoma Press, 1976), 172–92.

28   Marszalek, *Sherman*, 457, 484; Stanley P. Hirshson, *The White Tecumseh: A Biography of General William T. Sherman* (New York: John Wiley & Sons, 1997), 377; WTS to EES, September 16, 1883, UND-SFP.

29   EES to WTS, May 8, 1876, UND-SFP.

30   WTS to JS, June 7 and 15, 1884, in Thorndike, 361, 362; Hirshson, *The White Tecumseh*, 378.

31   JS to WTS, May 4, 1884, in Thorndike, 359; Lewis, *Sherman*, 631.

32   Marszalek, *Sherman*, 448; WTS to Lewis A. Leonard, September 4, 1884, Lewis A. Leonard Correspondence, Woodruff Library, Emory University, Atlanta.

33   Lloyd Lewis, *Sherman: Fighting Prophet* (New York: Harcourt Brace, 1932), 631–36.

34   Lewis, *Sherman*, 632; WTS to HST, June 18, 1880, OHC-WTSP.

35   Sherman, *Memoirs*, 2:1121.

36   Ibid. The *St. Louis Globe Democrat* is quoted in Lee Kennett, *Sherman: A Soldier's Life* (New York: Perennial, 2002), 319.

37   WTS to HST, February 1, 1880, OHC-WTSP; Kennett, *Sherman*, 317–21; Hirshson, *The White Tecumseh*, 356–58.

38   WTS to HST, February 1, 1880, OHC-WTSP.

39   Sherman, *Memoirs*, 2:5.

40   Hirshson, *The White Tecumseh*, 382.

28. WE CAN ONLY BOW TO THE INEVITABLE

1   JS to WTS, June 1886, in Thorndike, 373.

2   WTS to JS, February 23 and April 3, 1886, in Thorndike, 370; William Tecumseh

Sherman, *Memoirs of General W. T. Sherman*, 2 vols. (1885; repr., New York: Library of America, 1990), 2:1117, 1118; WTS to EES, September 16, 1888, UND-SFP.

3   JS to WTS, September 3, 1887, and WTS to JS, September 6, 1887, in Thorndike, 376–77.

4   Anna McAllister, *Ellen Ewing: Wife of General Sherman* (New York: Benziger Brothers, 1936), 365–67.

5   Ibid., 367–68; Sherman, *Memoirs*, 2:1118; Lloyd Lewis, *Sherman: Fighting Prophet* (New York: Harcourt Brace, 1932), 645.

6   William S. McFeely, *Grant: A Biography* (New York: W. W. Norton, 1982), 490–94, 500, 504–17; Lewis, *Sherman*, 639; James Pickett Jones, *John A. Logan: Stalwart Republican from Illinois* (Tallahassee: Florida State University Press, 1982), 223–24.

7   Paul Andrew Hutton, *Phil Sheridan and His Army* (Lincoln: University of Nebraska Press, 1985), 372–74; Lee Kennett, *Sherman: A Soldier's Life* (New York: Perennial, 2002), 335.

8   WTS to Elly Sherman Thackara, February 11, 1889, OHC-WTSP.

9   WTS to Elly Sherman Thackara, February 26, 1889, OHC-WTSP.

10 WTS to Elly Sherman Thackara, April 17 and May 3, 1889, OHC-WTSP.

11 WTS to Elly Sherman Thackara, May 20, June 25, August 4, September 6, 1889, OHC-WTSP; Joseph T. Durkin, S.J., *General Sherman's Son* (New York: Farrar, Straus and Cudahy, 1959), 109–10.

12 WTS to Elly Sherman Thackara, September 6, 1889, and March 19, 1890, OHC-WTSP; WTS to JS, November 12, 1889, in Thorndike, 379–80.

13 WTS to JS, November 12, 1889, in Thorndike, 379; see also p. 373.

14 WTS to Elly Sherman Thackara, September 6, 1889, and September 26, 1890, OHC-WTSP.

15 WTS to Elly Sherman Thackara, January 20, 1890, OHC-WTSP; WTS to Charles F. Manderson and others, February 9, 1890, HHL.

16 WTS to Elly Sherman Thackara, January 30, March 19, September 26, October 2, 1890, OHC-WTSP.

17 WTS to JS, February 3, 1891, in Thorndike, 381; WTS to Mrs. Kimble, February 5, 1891, Jean and Alexander Heard Library, Special Collections, Vanderbilt University, Nashville.

18 Stanley P. Hirshson, *The White Tecumseh: A Biography of General William T. Sherman* (New York: John Wiley & Sons, 1997), 386–88; Lewis, *Sherman*, 651–53; Kennett, *Sherman*, 336–37; John F. Marszalek, *Sherman: A Soldier's Passion for Order* (New York: Free Press, 1993), 492–99.

Index